THE FA AMATEUR CUP COMPLETE RESULTS

Qualifying Rounds and Rounds Proper 1893/94 to 1973/74

Fred Hawthorn

A *SoccerData* Publication
In association with 3-2 Books

Published in Great Britain by Tony Brown,
4 Adrian Close, Beeston, Nottingham NG9 6FL.
Telephone 0115 973 6086. E-mail soccer@innotts.co.uk
On the web at www.soccerdata.com

First published 2009

© Fred Hawthorn 2009
Database © Fred Hawthorn, Ron Price, Tony Brown 2009

All rights reserved. No part of this publication may be reproduced, stored in a retrieval system, or transmitted in any form, or by any means, electronic, mechanical, photocopying, recording, or otherwise without the prior permission in writing of the publisher, nor be otherwise circulated in any form or binding or cover other than in which it is published and without a similar condition being imposed on the subsequent publisher.

SoccerData publications from Tony Brown include seasonal 'match by match' books of Football League and FA Cup line-ups and "definitive" club histories of West Ham United, Bournemouth and Notts County amongst others. Please write for a catalogue.

ISBN 978-1-905891-15-3

Printed and bound by 4edge, Hockley, Essex
www.4edge.co.uk

ACKNOWLEDGEMENTS

I started this project fifteen years ago, since when which many people have played a part in bringing it to fruition. Firstly, I would like to thank FA Historian David Barber for allowing me unrestricted access to the FA Amateur Cup sub-committee minute books, which contained most of the draws, but no results from the qualifying rounds. A few draws could not be traced: a table in the appendices shows the details.

Secondly, I must thank John Powell for his tremendous efforts. John stopped his own research into Poole Town FC and athletics to assist in tracing hundreds of results, often the hard-to-find ones. Without his help this book would never have been finished.

Many others provided results for their club or area, including Mervyn Baker, Peter Barker, Jeremy Biggs, Mick Blakeman, the late Tony Booth, Lloyd Brown, Steve Carr, Martyn Davis, Barry Denyer, Steve Eeles, Robert Errington, Ian Fordyce, Nigel Gibb, Neil Harvey, David Kirkby, Steve Peart, Ronald Price (who also assisted with the brief history), Derek Seymour, Roger Sherlock, Steve Small and Alan Stewart.

Finally, but by no means last, my thanks to my publisher Tony Brown for creating the database to detail and analyze the results. His expertise in this area proved invaluable. Hopefully I have not omitted anyone, but if I have – sorry! Thanks to all of you.

I hope you find the book both interesting and useful. However, I am aware of the scope for errors in a work of this nature. Early qualifying rounds often went unreported, hence a few gaps. If you can provide any of the missing results, or correct any error, please contact me so that they can be incorporated into any future reprint.

Fred H Hawthorn
February 2009

PO Box 115
Upminster Essex
RM14 3AQ

Dedicated to my mother, Irene

A BRIEF HISTORY OF THE COMPETITION

At a meeting in August 1892, the Football Association (FA) considered and rejected an offer from Sheffield FC to donate a cup for a competition amongst its amateur member clubs. At its next meeting the FA resolved to introduce a competition along similar lines, with control vested in itself.

In February 1893, the rules were drawn up, based largely on those of the FA Challenge Cup competition. Entry was to be open to purely amateur clubs.
- The club drawn first would have the choice of venue.
- Extra time, at the discretion of the referee, would be played in the first tie.
- The dates for the rounds would be on the Saturday after the same round of the FA Cup.
- Clubs employing professionals were excluded.
- Players had to have been born or reside within six-mile radius of their club's designated ground or headquarters.

A proposal from the 'Provinces' to allow entry to all member clubs providing they could field a team of bona-fide amateurs, who were members of their respective clubs, failed. In the August, amateurs playing with professionals in the FA Challenge Cup were excluded.

The History of the Football Association, published in 1953, lists 81 entrant clubs to the first competition, compared to the 155 clubs who entered the FA Challenge Cup in 1893/94. However, the new competition failed to gain the interest or support of the general public. An editorial in *The Sportsman* doubted whether it should be continued; however, the FA Council accepted the Amateur Cup sub-committee's recommendation that the competition should be held again in 1894/95. The sub-committee was given the power to organize the second series in two or more divisions, to reduce travel. It was confirmed former professional players who had been reinstated as an amateur could take part.

In 1899 Royal Artillery Portsmouth were disqualified because the team went to Aldeburgh for a week's training at the club's expense.

In November 1902 E.L. Holland (Middlesex CFA) proposed an enquiry by a Commission, comprising of members of the Council and secretaries of amateur clubs, into the lack of support for the competition by clubs in the South of England. The report presented in May 1903 highlighted the long distances involved and the associated cost of travelling and hotel expenses and the inclusion of reinstated professionals. It also requested an increase in the representation of the Metropolitan Counties on the competition's sub-committee. The Commission made six recommendations and suggested the Referees Committee be asked to identify referees prepared to officiate in competition matches without charging a fee. The recommendations (of which the first three were implemented) were:
- A minimum admission price of three pence.
- Equal division of the gate after deduction of ground expenses <u>and</u> travelling expenses of the visiting team.
- Retention of the North and South Divisions with the sub-committee to group and regroup entrant clubs until the semi-final round.
- Exclusion of any professional reinstated as an amateur after 1902.
- The present compulsory additional half-hour in the case of a draw in the first tie is made optional.
- The six Metropolitan Counties is given three of the six South of England places on the sub-committee.

The competition was played in north and south sections up to the semi finals between 1903 and 1908; thereafter the competition went national after the Second Round. In terms of the number of entries the amateur split (which led to the creation of the AFA) had no effect.

In May 1913, it was agreed a player registered as a professional for five or more years, or a player who after the 1 May 1913 had received £2 or more per week, should not be eligible for reinstatement, thus paving the way to bring an end to the amateur split.

In 1921 a permit system was introduced which, if granted, allowed a former professional to play for an amateur club. Such clubs, provided their fielded a bona-fide amateur team could enter the competition. In the summer of 1922, the FA granted amateur status to former professional players who had never received more than ten shillings per match or per week, provided they applied prior to 1 October 1922.

Between the wars the competition was increasingly dominated by the 'senior amateur' clubs who recruited players by its benefactors providing employment opportunities. Of the 20 finals in this period, 14 were won by Isthmian League clubs, four by the Northern League clubs (all by Bishop Auckland), three by the Athenian League clubs and once by the 'Corinth of the North' – Northern Nomads.

This dominance was reinforced in 1950 when the FA introduced a pool to be shared equally between the 64 clubs playing in the competition proper, including the 40 clubs exempted to that stage. Clubs in the competition proper contributed 5% of their gates of ties from the First Round to the Fourth Round. The gates of the semi-finals and finals were allocated between the pool, the competing clubs, and the FA. The latter's share offset the costs of the coaching scheme, full and youth amateur internationals and representative matches.

In 1956 Bishop Auckland and Corinthian Casuals received £6,285 each as their share of the receipts from the Final tie and its replay; and a further £782 each (as did Kingstonian and Dulwich Hamlet) from the semi finals. A share of the pool was £84. The final had been played at Wembley Stadium since 1949 and in the 1950s five of these attracted a 100,000 sell out.

In 1963 entrants to the competition had to declare they only reimbursed their players' travel and hotel expenses actually incurred as the FA grew increasingly concerned at payments made outside the clubs' books. In 1966 the Chester Committee recommended the introduction of a new registration form for amateur players receiving expenses. Instead, the FA decided to end amateur status in favour of contract status players and non-contract status players. It was a further eight years before they were able to implement this proposal, bringing to an end the FA Amateur Cup after 71 competitions. Ten competitions were lost to the two World Wars.

EXEMPTION SCHEME

An exemption scheme had first operated for the FA Challenge Cup in 1888 to minimize 'mis-matches' between professional clubs and the smaller amateur clubs. The principle was incorporated into the FA Amateur Cup. For the first competition two clubs progressed from each qualifying division, thereafter only one club progressed. After the first season the four semi-finalists of the previous season were exempted to the First Round.

From 1936 the exemptions were based on clubs' performances in recent competitions having previously been selected by voting by FA Council members.

Over the years the exemption scheme was varied as under:

SEASONS	QUALIFYING DIVISIONS	EXEMPTION TO 4th QUALIFYING ROUND	EXEMPTION TO FIRST ROUND	TOTAL CLUBS IN FIRST ROUND
1893/94	8	-	16	32
1894-1896	8	-	24	32
1896-1899	12	-	20	32
1899-1903	10	-	22	32
1903-1907	12	-	20	32
1907-1936	24	-	40	64
1936-1974	24	24	40	64

The following clubs won through from the qualifying competition to the final. Of the ten clubs who did so, one, Royal Marine Light Infantry (Gosport) won the competition defeating South Bank at Bishop Auckland 2-1 in 1910.

    1895/96 Royal Artillery (Portsmouth)
    1897/98 Uxbridge
    1909/10 Royal Marine Light Infantry (Gosport)
    1922/23 Evesham Town
    1927/28 Cockfield
    1929/30 Bournemouth Gasworks Athletic
    1930/31 Hayes
    1937/38 Erith & Belvedere
    1951/52 Leyton
    1967/68 Chesham United

ROLL OF HONOUR

Clubs with final and semi-final appearances (excluding replays)

	Wins	Finals	SFs
Bishop Auckland	10	18	27
Clapton	5	6	9
Crook Town	5	5	7
Dulwich Hamlet	4	4	9
Stockton	3	8	9
Hendon	3	5	7
Leytonstone	3	3	9
Bromley	3	3	7
Leyton	2	6	6
Ilford	2	5	9
Enfield	2	4	7
Old Carthusians	2	3	3
Walthamstow Avenue	2	2	6
Middlesbrough	2	2	2
Pegasus	2	2	2
Barnet	1	3	9
South Bank	1	3	7
Wimbledon	1	3	4
Oxford City	1	3	3
Kingstonian	1	2	5
Wycombe Wanderers	1	2	5
Northern Nomads	1	2	4
Skelmersdale United	1	2	4
Willington	1	2	3
Casuals	1	2	2
London Caledonians	1	1	3
Old Malvernians	1	1	3
Walton & Hersham	1	1	3
Bishops Stortford	1	1	2
Wealdstone	1	1	2
Woking	1	1	2
North Shields	1	1	1
RMLI Gosport	1	1	1
Royal Engineers Depot Battn	1	1	1
Sheffield	1	1	1
West Hartlepool	1	1	1
Sutton United		2	4
Dagenham		2	2
Erith & Belvedere		2	2
Eston United		2	2
Harwich & Parkeston		2	2
Tufnell Park		1	4
Romford (2)		1	3
Southall		1	3
Barking Town		1	2
Bournemouth Gasworks Athletic		1	2
Cockfield		1	2
Corinthian Casuals		1	2
Ealing		1	2
Hayes		1	2
Hounslow Town		1	2
Lowestoft Town		1	2
Marine		1	2
Slough Town		1	2
West Auckland Town		1	2

	Finals	SFs
Chesham United	1	1
Evesham Town	1	1
King's Lynn	1	1
Royal Artillery (Portsmouth)	1	1
Swindon Victoria	1	1
Uxbridge	1	1
Whitby Town	1	1
St Albans City		4
Atherstone Town		2
Darlington		2
Hitchin Town		2
Leatherhead		2
Marlow		2
Whitley Bay		2
1st Royal Scots Guards		1
2nd Coldstream Guards		1
Alvechurch		1
Ashington		1
Barking		1
Blyth Spartans		1
Boldmere St Michaels		1
Briggs Sports		1
Cambridge Town		1
Cheshunt (1)		1
Chilton Colliery Recreation		1
Civil Service		1
Crook Colliery Welfare		1
Finchley		1
Grimsby All Saints		1
Highgate United (Birmingham)		1
Kings Own Lancs Regt Portsmouth		1
Leadgate Park		1
Loftus Albion		1
Maidenhead United		1
Metropolitan Police		1
New Crusaders		1
Norton Woodseats		1
RAMC Aldershot		1
Redhill		1
Royal Engineers (Aldershot)		1
Sherwood Foresters (Colchester)		1
Shrewsbury Town		1
Stanley United		1
Thornaby		1
Whitehall Printeries		1
Yorkshire Amateur		1

THE FINALS 1893/94 TO 1973/74

Year		Winner	Runner-up	Score		Attendance	Venue
1894		Old Carthusians	Casuals	2-1		3500	Athletic Gound, Richmond
1895		Middlesbrough	Old Carthusians	2-1		4000	Headingley, Leeds
1896		Bishop Auckland	Royal Artillery (Portsmouth)	1-0		3000	Filbert Street, Leicester
1897		Old Carthusians	Stockton	1-1		9000	Tufnell Park
	rep	Old Carthusians	Stockton	4-1		10000	Darlington
1898		Middlesbrough	Uxbridge	2-0		1500	The Crystal Palace
1899		Stockton	Harwich & Parkeston	1-0		7000	Linthorpe Rd, Middlesbrough
1900		Bishop Auckland	Lowestoft Town	5-1		1000	Filbert Street, Leicester
1901		Crook Town	King's Lynn	1-1		4000	Dovercourt, Harwich & Parkeston
	rep	Crook Town	King's Lynn	3-0		1500	Portman Road, Ipswich
1902		Old Malvernians	Bishop Auckland	5-1		1000	Headingley, Leeds
1903		Stockton	Oxford City	0-0		4000	Elm Park, Reading
	rep	Stockton	Oxford City	1-0		7000	Feethams, Darlington
1904		Sheffield	Ealing	3-1		6000	Valley Parade, Bradford
1905		West Hartlepool	Clapton	3-2		4000	Shepherds Bush
1906		Oxford City	Bishop Auckland	3-0		5000	Stockton
1907		Clapton	Stockton	2-1		6000	Stamford Bridge
1908		R. E. Depot Battn	Stockton	2-1		8000	Bishop Auckland
1909		Clapton	Eston United	6-0		5000	Ilford
1910		RMLI Gosport	South Bank	2-1		8000	Bishop Auckland
1911		Bromley	Bishop Auckland	1-0		3000	Herne Hill
1912		Stockton	Eston United	1-1		20000	Ayresome Park, Middlesbrough
	rep	Stockton	Eston United	1-0		12000	Ayresome Park, Middlesbrough
1913		South Bank	Oxford City	1-1		6000	Elm Park, Reading
	rep	South Bank	Oxford City	1-0		7000	Bishop Auckland
1914		Bishop Auckland	Northern Nomads	1-0		5000	Elland Road, Leeds
1915		Clapton	Bishop Auckland	1-0		6000	The Den, Millwall
1920		Dulwich Hamlet	Tufnell Park	1-0		12200	The Den, Millwall
1921		Bishop Auckland	Swindon Victoria	4-2		12864	Ayresome Park, Middlesbrough
1922		Bishop Auckland	South Bank	5-2		13300	Ayresome Park, Middlesbrough
1923		London Caledonians	Evesham Town	2-1		14132	The Crystal Palace
1924		Clapton	Erith & Belvedere	3-0		16492	The Den, Millwall
1925		Clapton	Southall	2-1		20000	The Den, Millwall
1926		Northern Nomads	Stockton	7-1		20000	Roker Park, Sunderland
1927		Barking Town	Leyton	1-3		20000	The Den, Millwall
1928		Leyton	Cockfield	3-2		20448	Ayresome Park, Middlesbrough
1929		Ilford	Leyton	3-1		21800	Highbury, Arsenal
1930		Ilford	Bournemouth Gasworks Ath.	5-1		22000	Upton Park, West Ham
1931		Wycombe Wanderers	Hayes	1-0		25000	Highbury, Arsenal
1932		Dulwich Hamlet	Marine	7-1		25000	Upton Park, West Ham
1933		Kingstonian	Stockton	1-1		25000	Dulwich Hamlet
	rep	Kingstonian	Stockton	4-1		25064	Darlington
1934		Dulwich Hamlet	Leyton	2-1		27000	Upton Park, West Ham
1935		Bishop Auckland	Wimbledon	0-0		32000	Ayresome Park, Middlesbrough
	rep	Bishop Auckland	Wimbledon	2-1		32000	Stamford Bridge
1936		Casuals	Ilford	1-1		33000	Selhurst Park
	rep	Casuals	Ilford	2-0		33000	Upton Park, West Ham
1937		Dulwich Hamlet	Leyton	2-0		33516	Upton Park, West Ham
1938		Bromley	Erith & Belvedere	1-0		35000	The Den, Millwall
1939		Bishop Auckland	Willington	3-0	e	20000	Roker Park, Sunderland
1946		Barnet	Bishop Auckland	3-2		53832	Stamford Bridge
1947		Leytonstone	Wimbledon	2-1		47000	Highbury, Arsenal
1948		Leytonstone	Barnet	1-0		59605	Stamford Bridge
1949		Bromley	Romford (2)	1-0		93000	Wembley
1950		Willington	Bishop Auckland	4-0		88000	Wembley
1951		Pegasus	Bishop Auckland	2-1		100000	Wembley
1952		Walthamstow Avenue	Leyton	2-1		100000	Wembley
1953		Pegasus	Harwich & Parkeston	6-0		100000	Wembley
1954		Crook Town	Bishop Auckland	2-2	e	100000	Wembley
	rep	Crook Town	Bishop Auckland	2-2		56008	St James' Park, Newcastle
	rep2	Crook Town	Bishop Auckland	1-0		36727	Ayresome Park, Middlesbrough
1955		Bishop Auckland	Hendon	2-0		100000	Wembley
1956		Bishop Auckland	Corinthian Casuals	1-1		80000	Wembley
	rep	Bishop Auckland	Corinthian Casuals	4-1		30000	Ayresome Park, Middlesbrough
1957		Bishop Auckland	Wycombe Wanderers	3-1		90000	Wembley
1958		Woking	Ilford	3-0		71000	Wembley
1959		Crook Town	Barnet	3-2		60000	Wembley
1960		Hendon	Kingstonian	2-1		30500	Wembley
1961		Walthamstow Avenue	West Auckland Town	2-1		33000	Wembley
1962		Crook Town	Hounslow Town	1-1		37000	Wembley
	rep	Crook Town	Hounslow Town	4-0		38000	Ayresome Park, Middlesbrough
1963		Wimbledon	Sutton United	4-2		41000	Wembley
1964		Crook Town	Enfield	2-1		43000	Wembley
1965		Hendon	Whitby Town	3-1		43000	Wembley
1966		Wealdstone	Hendon	3-1		45000	Wembley
1967		Enfield	Skelmersdale United	0-0		45000	Wembley
	rep	Enfield	Skelmersdale United	3-0		45000	Maine Road, Manchester
1968		Leytonstone	Chesham United	1-0		45000	Wembley
1969		North Shields	Sutton United	2-1		45000	Wembley
1970		Enfield	Dagenham	5-1		47500	Wembley
1971		Skelmersdale United	Dagenham	4-1		52000	Wembley
1972		Hendon	Enfield	2-0		55388	Wembley
1973		Walton & Hersham	Slough Town	1-0		60000	Wembley
1974		Bishops Stortford	Ilford	4-1		75000	Wembley

HOW TO USE THE BOOK

The book contains every FA Amateur Cup result including all the qualifying rounds. You can treat it as a reference book and go straight to the season you are interested in. Use the bold headings at the top of each page to find the season, noting that some pages contain more than one. Alternatively, you can use the index of clubs first, so that you know which seasons to look at in the results pages for a particular club.

Please note that there was no competition for seasons 1915/16 to 1918/19 and 1940/41 to 1944/45 because of the two World Wars. The draw was made for the competition of 1939/40 started but no games had been played when the season was cancelled.

The result listings include the group number (if it was a qualifying round game) and markers such as "e" to indicate extra time. The group number will help you find a particular club in the qualifying rounds.

As an example of the use of the club index, say you want to follow the exploits of Gedling Colliery. You will find from the index that they appeared 40 times between seasons 1923/24 and 1958/59. Now, imagine the letter "S" superimposed on the map of England and Wales. The start of the "S", in the North East, has the low numbered groups in the qualifying rounds. The tail of the "S", in the South West, has the high numbers. If you know Gedling were a Nottinghamshire club, then try a group in the middle of the range. Start with the preliminary round; if they are not there, try the extra preliminary round or the first qualifying round. Although the number of groups has changed over the years, and clubs can appear in different groups from season to season, you will find they are a handy method of following particular clubs.

The task of finding a particular club in the qualifying rounds is complicated by the fact that they may have had an exemption to a later round. The list of dates of rounds in appendix two will show you the number of rounds played each season. This will help you see the rounds when exempt clubs might have entered.

THE SEASON BY SEASON RESULTS

Key to the listings

The home club is listed first, unless the game was played on a neutral ground. It is possible that a few games are listed the wrong way round - the convention in newspapers used to be to list the winning club first, so without a copy of the draw it is often difficult to establish who was at home. Also, clubs originally drawn at home had the right (with the FA's permission) to play the game on the opponent's ground.

Club names are generally those in use at the time. A list in appendix one shows the clubs that changed their names. However, if different clubs have the same name, a number in brackets has been used to distinguish between them. The index of club appearances should also help to clarify which club is which.

The first column shows the group number if it is a qualifying round game, and a replay indicator "r". You will also find "r2, r3" and so on for second and subsequent replays.

In the score column, the entry "wo/s" shows that the first named club "walked over" because the second club scratched. If both clubs scratched the entry is "sc/sc". Also, "wo/d" is used occasionally, to show that a game did not take place because the second named club had been disqualified prior to the game. A number of results have not been found; these are shown as "n/a" for "not available". In some circumstances one or both of the clubs playing in the tie is also unknown. The Soccerdata web site will provide a list of missing results and those found after publication of this book.

The following markers appear after the score:

"e" indicates that the game went to extra time. This information is often not recorded in match reports of the time and the indicator is only set when it is known for certain that extra time was played.

"N" indicates that the game was played on a neutral ground. However, this marker is generally not used when a club has lost the use of its ground temporarily and is playing elsewhere. In later years particularly, some club's home grounds were not up to FA standards, so arrangements were made to play all their home cup-ties on a neutral ground.

"v" indicates a void game, usually as a result of a protest by the losing club. The game will have been replayed.

"D" indicates that the home club was disqualified, usually as a result of a protest by the other club.

"d" indicates the away club was disqualified.

"r" indicates a club was given byes through to a later round because of another clubs withdrawal.

"a" indicates that the game was abandoned in extra time and was later replayed. Games abandoned before ninety minutes are not included, but note that in these circumstances the subsequent game is often described as "a replay" in match reports of the time.

1893/94 to 1895/96

1893/94

Qualifying Round One

9	Dover v Sheppey United	1-4
	Sittingbourne v Royal Engineers Training Battn	1-2
10	Erith v Cray Wanderers	0-2
	New Brompton v Maidstone	7-0
12	Norwich Thorpe v Clapton	wo/s
14	Old Foresters v Swifts	2-1
15	Freemantle (Southampton) v Windsor & Eton	5-0
	Maidenhead v Old Weymouthians	2-1
	Reading v Chesham	4-0

Qualifying Round Two

1	Berwick Rangers v Darlington St Hildas	wo/s
	Leadgate Park v Leadgate Exiles	0-1
2	Darlington St Augustines v Willington Athletic	2-3e
	Kendal v Ashington	2-4
3	Saltburn Swifts v South Bank	4-6
	South Bank Blue Star v North Skelton Rovers	4-0
4	Loftus v Scarborough	4-2
	Whitby v Scarborough Rangers	wo/s
8	Rushden v Hunts County	12-1
9	Ashford United v Folkestone	0-6
	Royal Engineers Training Battn v Sheppey United	1-4
10	Cray Wanderers v Royal Ordnance Factory	0-3
	New Brompton v Royal Fusiliers	2-0
11	Clapham Rovers v Crouch End	2-0
	Tottenham Hotspur v Vampires	3-1
12	Ilford v Ipswich Town	1-0
	Norwich Thorpe v West Herts	2-6
13	Old Harrovians v Old St Marks	2-3
	Surbiton Hill v Old Etonians	0-5
14	Old Foresters v Old St Stephens	0-1
	Old Wykehamists v Old Cranleighans	6-1
15	Maidenhead v Freemantle (Southampton)	3-1
	Reading v Chesham Generals	2-1
16	Bedminster v Home Park (Plymouth)	0-3
	Bristol St George v Warmley	1-0

Qualifying Round Three

1	Berwick Rangers v Leadgate Exiles	1-2
2	Willington Athletic v Ashington	4-0
3	South Bank v South Bank Blue Star	2-0
4	Whitby v Loftus	2-0
5	Warrington St Elphins - Bye	
6	Rhos - Bye	
7	Beeston v Lincoln Lindum	8-0
8	Wellingborough Town v Rushden	1-4
9	Folkestone v Sheppey United	1-1
10	New Brompton v Royal Ordnance Factory	1-2
11	Clapham Rovers v Tottenham Hotspur	wo/s
12	Ilford v West Herts	2-0
13	Old St Marks v Old Etonians	2-5
14	Old Wykehamists v Old St Stephens	3-4
15	Reading v Maidenhead	3-3
16	Home Park (Plymouth) v Bristol St George	2-1
9r	Sheppey United v Folkestone	2-1 v
15r	Maidenhead v Reading	0-4 v
9r2	Sheppey United v Folkestone	4-1
15r2	Maidenhead v Reading	3-4e

Round One

Bishop Auckland v Clapham Rovers	wo/s
Casuals v Sheffield	3-1
Chatham v Willington Athletic	1-0
Chirk v South Bank	3-1
Ilford v Whitby	2-1
Marlow v Darlington	1-0
Middlesbrough v Leadgate Exiles	8-0
Old Brightonians v Old Westminsters	wo/s
Old Carthusians v Crusaders	4-2
Old St Stephens v Warrington St Elphins	wo/s
Reading v Royal Ordnance Factory	3-2
Rhos v Rushden	2-4
Sheppey United v Old Etonians	1-3
Sherwood Foresters (Colchester) v Swindon Town	2-1
Shrewsbury Town v Beeston	5-2
Stockton v Home Park (Plymouth)	5-0

Round Two

Bishop Auckland v Ilford	4-2
Chatham v Casuals	0-2
Chirk v Old Brightonians	4-3
Marlow v Rushden	2-0
Old Etonians v Middlesbrough	4-2e
Old St Stephens v Shrewsbury Town	2-2
Reading v Old Carthusians	1-4
Sherwood Foresters (Colchester) v Stockton	1-4 d
r Shrewsbury Town v Old St Stephens	4-0

Round Three

Bishop Auckland v Shrewsbury Town	3-1
Casuals v Chirk	wo/s
Old Carthusians v Marlow	4-1
Old Etonians v Sherwood Foresters (Colchester)	2-5

Semi Finals

Casuals v Sherwood Foresters (Colchester)	1-0 N
Old Carthusians v Bishop Auckland	5-1 N

Final

Old Carthusians v Casuals	2-1 N

1894/95

Qualifying Round One

1	Darlington St Augustines v Leadgate Exiles	5-4
4	Chesham v St Albans	2-4
	Windsor & Eton v Slough	1-1e
5	Tottenham Hotspur v Old Harrovians	7-0
7	Sittingbourne v Hastings Athletic	3-1
8	Hereford Thistle v Bournemouth	2-0
4r	Slough v Windsor & Eton	3-1

Qualifying Round Two

1	Howden Rangers v Berwick Rangers	3-1
	Leadgate Park v Willington Athletic	2-0
	Loftus v Darlington St Augustines	5-2
	Saltburn Swifts v Whitby	2-1
4	Newbury v Chesham Generals	4-1
	Slough v Oxford City	3-3
	St Albans v Maidenhead	0-2
	West Herts v Wycombe Wanderers	5-1
5	Crouch End v Old St Marks	3-3a
	London Welsh v 3rd Grenadier Guards	4-2
	Romford (1) v Woodville	1-1
	Tottenham Hotspur v City Ramblers	6-1
6	1st Highland Light Infantry v Clapham Rovers	wo/s
	Old Cranleighans v Old Wilsonians	7-1
	Surbiton Hill v Polytechnic	2-1
	Vampires v Ealing	2-5
7	Evergreen (Tunbridge Wells) v Ashford United	1-7
	Faversham v 2nd Royal Scots Fusiliers	1-2
	Folkestone v Royal Engineers Training Battn	2-4
	Maidstone v Sittingbourne	0-5
8	Bristol South End v Hereford Thistle	2-4
	Bristol St George v Clifton	3-3e
	Old Weymouthians v Bedminster	3-2
	Warmley v Kings Own Lancs Regt Portsmouth	0-3
4r	Oxford City v Slough	8-0
5r	Old St Marks v Crouch End	0-5
r	Woodville v Romford (1)	1-3
8r	Clifton v Bristol St George	3-2

Qualifying Round Three

1	Howden Rangers v Leadgate Park	2-0
	Saltburn Swifts v Loftus	10-1
2	Aston Old Edwardians v Liverpool Ramblers	wo/s
	Beeston v Leicester YMCA	8-0
3	Norwich CEYMS v Ipswich Town	1-3
4	Newbury v Oxford City	2-2
	West Herts v Maidenhead	1-1a
5	London Welsh v Crouch End	3-1
	Romford (1) v Tottenham Hotspur	0-8
6	1st Highland Light Infantry v Old Cranleighans	n/a
	Ealing v Surbiton Hill	3-3
7	2nd Royal Scots Fusiliers v R Engineers Training Bn	1-3
	Sittingbourne v Ashford United	1-0
8	Clifton v Kings Own Lancs Regt Portsmouth	1-1
	Hereford Thistle v Old Weymouthians	1-2
4r	Maidenhead v West Herts	4-2
r	Oxford City v Newbury	3-0
6r	Surbiton Hill v Ealing	0-3
8r	Clifton v Kings Own Lancs Regt Portsmouth	1-2

Qualifying Round Four

1	Saltburn Swifts v Howden Rangers	3-1
2	Beeston v Aston Old Edwardians	4-1
3	Ipswich Town v Peterborough	7-1
4	Maidenhead v Oxford City	5-0
5	Tottenham Hotspur v London Welsh	1-1
6	Ealing v 1st Highland Light Infantry	wo/s
7	Sittingbourne v Royal Engineers Training Battn	2-0
8	Kings Own Lancs Regt P'mth v Old Weymouthians	3-0
5r	London Welsh v Tottenham Hotspur	3-3
5r2	Tottenham Hotspur v London Welsh	4-2 N

Round One

Bishop Auckland v Middlesbrough	2-3
Clapton v Kings Own Lancs Regt Portsmouth	0-4
Cliftonville v Buxton	2-0
Crewe Alexandra v Sheffield	7-0
Crusaders v Chatham	wo/s
Darlington v Saltburn Swifts	3-2
Ealing v Marlow	3-4
Ipswich Town v 2nd Scots Guards	0-0
Leek v Shrewsbury Town	3-3
Maidenhead v Old Brightonians	2-4e
Old Carthusians v Swindon Town	wo/s
Old Etonians v Sittingbourne	wo/s
Old Westminsters v Sheppey United	wo/s
Reading v Casuals	3-1
Stockton v South Bank	1-3
Tottenham Hotspur v Beeston	2-0
r Ipswich Town v 2nd Scots Guards	2-1
r Shrewsbury Town v Leek	2-0

Round Two

Crewe Alexandra v Shrewsbury Town	2-0
Darlington v Middlesbrough	1-1
Ipswich Town v Old Etonians	1-1
Marlow v Kings Own Lancs Regt Portsmouth	2-4
Old Brightonians v Crusaders	wo/s
Old Westminsters v Reading	2-8
South Bank v Cliftonville	wo/s
Tottenham Hotspur v Old Carthusians	0-5
r Middlesbrough v Darlington	1-1e
r Old Etonians v Ipswich Town	7-3
r2 Middlesbrough v Darlington	2-0

Round Three

Kings Own Lancs Regt Portsmouth v Old Etonians	wo/s
Old Brightonians v Middlesbrough	0-8 N
Old Carthusians v Crewe Alexandra	1-0
South Bank v Reading	5-2

Semi Finals

Middlesbrough v Kings Own Lancs Regt Portsmouth	4-0 N
Old Carthusians v South Bank	1-1 N
r Old Carthusians v South Bank	3-2eN

Final

Middlesbrough v Old Carthusians	2-1 N

1895/96

Qualifying Round One

4	Bedminster v Bristol St George	0-3
	Bournemouth v Gloucester	n/a
	Clifton v Bournemouth Wanderers	3-1
	Old Weymouthians v Weymouth	n/a
5	Newbury v Watford St Marys	5-0
	Reading Ams v 2nd East Lancs Regt (Aldershot)	2-4
6	Clapham Rovers v 2nd Coldstream Guards	2-3
	Crouch End v City Ramblers	2-2
	Crusaders v Old St Marks	2-2
	Old Wilsonians v Old Cranleighans	3-1
8	Romford (1) v Colchester	1-1a
6r	City Ramblers v Crouch End	wo/s
r	Old St Marks v Crusaders	1-3
8r	Colchester v Romford (1)	1-0

Qualifying Round Two

1	Berwick Rangers v Tow Law	2-5
	Birtley v Leadgate Park	2-1
	Howden-le-Wear v Leadgate Exiles	3-0
	Jarrow v Willington Athletic	1-2
2	Loftus v Darlington St Augustines	4-2
	West Hartlepool NER v Saltburn Swifts	2-1
3	Aston Old Edwardians v Northwich Victoria	wo/s
4	Bournemouth v Trowbridge Town	3-4e
	Old Weymouthians v Bristol South End	3-1
	Plymouth v Bristol St George	1-5
	Royal Artillery (Portsmouth) v Clifton	10-0
5	Ealing v 2nd East Lancs Regt (Aldershot)	1-2
	Slough v 2nd Royal Scots Fusiliers	1-2
	Windsor & Eton v Chesham Generals	1-2e
	Wycombe Wanderers v Newbury	1-0
6	Casuals v 2nd Coldstream Guards	3-0
	City Ramblers v Old Westminsters	2-4
	Crusaders v Old Wilsonians	4-0
	Queen's Park Rangers v Surbiton Hill	2-1
8	Braintree v Cheshunt (1)	2-2
	Colchester v Barking Woodville	0-2
	Peterborough v Chelmsford	1-3
	St Albans v Harwich & Parkeston	1-0
8r	Cheshunt (1) v Braintree	3-0

Qualifying Round Three

1	Howden-le-Wear v Willington Athletic	0-3
	Tow Law v Birtley	6-0
2	Loftus v Hull Albany	6-0
	West Hartlepool NER v Hunslet	6-4 v
3	Cheshire Magpies v Aston Old Edwardians	0-6
	Derby Amateurs v Sheffield	4-5
4	Old Weymouthians v Trowbridge Town	5-1
	Royal Artillery (Portsmouth) v Bristol St George	wo/s
5	Chesham Generals v 2nd East Lancs Regt (A'rshot)	2-3
	Wycombe Wanderers v 2nd Royal Scots Fusiliers	9-0
6	Crusaders v Old Westminsters	1-7
	Queen's Park Rangers v Casuals	1-5
7	2nd Royal Scots Fusiliers v Eastbourne Swifts	1-0
	Faversham v Sittingbourne	2-5

10

1895/96 to 1897/98

8 Barking Woodville v Chelmsford	5-4 v	
Cheshunt (1) v St Albans	wo/s	
2r Hunslet v West Hartlepool NER	8-1	
8r Chelmsford v Barking Woodville	0-1	

Qualifying Round Four

1 Willington Athletic v Tow Law	3-1
2 Hunslet v Loftus	5-4
3 Aston Old Edwardians v Sheffield	1-5
4 Royal Artillery (Portsmouth) v Old Weymouthians	5-1
5 2nd East Lancs Regt (Aldershot) v Wycombe Wan.	2-3
6 Old Westminsters v Casuals	1-2
7 2nd Royal Scots Fusiliers v Sittingbourne	4-0
8 Cheshunt (1) v Barking Woodville	2-3

Round One

Barking Woodville v 2nd Royal Scots Fusiliers	1-3
Casuals v Hunslet	2-4e
Chesham Generals v Tottenham Hotspur	wo/s
Darlington v Whitby	2-0
Eastbourne v Old Brightonians	2-5
Hunslet v Buxton	3-1
Ipswich Town v Old Harrovians	6-2
Maidenhead v London Welsh	0-0a
Marlow v Wycombe Wanderers	3-2
Middlesbrough v Willington Athletic	6-2
Old Carthusians v Oxford City	wo/s
Old Etonians v Leek	wo/s
Royal Artillery (Portsmouth) v 3rd Grenadier Guards	1-1
Sheffield v Bishop Auckland	3-4
Stockton v South Bank	4-3
West Herts v Wolverton LNWR Works	4-3
r 3rd Grenadier Guards v Royal Artillery (Portsmouth)	2-2e
r London Welsh v Maidenhead	4-3 D
r2 Royal Artillery (Portsmouth) v 3rd Grenadier Guards	1-0 N

Round Two

2nd Royal Scots Fusiliers v Stockton	1-4
Bishop Auckland v Ipswich Town	3-1
Hunslet v Old Etonians	3-2
Maidenhead v West Herts	1-0
Marlow v Chesham Generals	1-0
Middlesbrough v Royal Artillery (Portsmouth)	1-2
Old Carthusians v Darlington	1-1e
Shrewsbury Town v Old Brightonians	6-2
r Darlington v Old Carthusians	4-3

Round Three

Bishop Auckland v Stockton	2-1
Darlington v Hunslet	6-0
Maidenhead v Royal Artillery (Portsmouth)	0-5
Marlow v Shrewsbury Town	1-2

Semi Finals

Bishop Auckland v Darlington	3-2 N
Royal Artillery (Portsmouth) v Shrewsbury Town	2-0 N

Final

Bishop Auckland v Royal Artillery (Portsmouth)	1-0 N

1896/97

Qualifying Round One

4 Bradford v Derby Amateurs	9-0
11 Henley v 2nd Gordon Highlanders	0-7
Reading Amateurs v Windsor & Eton	1-2
12 Southbroom (Devizes) v Bournemouth	5-2
Yeovil Casuals v Clifton	5-1

Qualifying Round Two

1 Rutherford College v Wallsend Park Villa	2-4
Sunderland Nomads v Wolsingham	wo/s
2 Howden-le-Wear v Leadgate Exiles	2-1
Shildon United v Crook Town	3-0
West Hartlepool NER v Leadgate Park	1-2
3 Redcar Crusaders v Thornaby Utopians	2-9
Saltburn Swifts v Loftus	3-1
4 Derby Constitutional v Hunslet	0-1
Huddersfield v Cannock	wo/s
Peterborough v Old Wulfrunians	wo/s
Sheffield v Bradford	1-2
6 Leytonstone v Braintree	1-1
7 Clapham Rovers v Old Harrovians	6-0
Old St Marks v Old Wilsonians	1-3
Old Wykehamists v Old Cranleighans	2-1
8 1st Scots Guards v 2nd Coldstream Guards	3-1
Civil Service v 1st Coldstream Guards	1-1
Queen's Park Rangers v Hammersmith Athletic	3-1
Wandsworth v Stanley (Fulham)	0-3 v
9 Cheshunt (1) v St Albans	wo/s
Watford St Marys v Dunstable Town (1)	5-2
West Herts v Bradfield Waifs (Norbury Park)	3-1

10 Eastbourne Swifts v Sittingbourne	wo/s
Faversham v Royal Engineers Training Battn	wo/s
11 2nd East Lancs Regt (Aldershot) v Old Swindon	3-0
2nd Grenadier Guards v Chesham Generals	2-1
Newbury v Slough	5-1
Windsor & Eton v 2nd Gordon Highlanders	2-6
12 Bedminster v Bristol South End	3-3
Bristol St George v Old Plymouthians	4-4
Trowbridge Town v Southbroom (Devizes)	2-1
Yeovil Casuals v Weymouth	2-1
6r Braintree v Leytonstone	1-2
8r 1st Coldstream Guards v Civil Service	3-2
r Wandsworth v Stanley (Fulham)	wo/s
12r Bristol South End v Bedminster	2-1
r Old Plymouthians v Bristol St George	0-2

Qualifying Round Three

1 Brandon Rovers v Sunderland Nomads	1-1
Shankhouse v Wallsend Park Villa	3-1
2 Howden-le-Wear v Kelloe United	4-0
Shildon United v Leadgate Park	1-2
3 Darlington St Augustines v Thornaby	1-2
Saltburn Swifts v Thornaby Utopians	2-3
4 Bradford v Hunslet	0-2
Peterborough v Huddersfield	2-0
5 Colchester v Kirkley	0-5
Norwich CEYMS v Harwich & Parkeston	0-3
6 Leytonstone v Romford (1)	4-2
Upton Park v Chelmsford	2-0
7 Clapham Rovers v Old Wilsonians	0-5
Old Wykehamists v Crouch End	2-8
8 1st Coldstream Guards v Wandsworth	1-1
1st Scots Guards v Queen's Park Rangers	1-1
9 Cheshunt (1) v West Herts	5-2
Watford St Marys v Enfield	3-2
10 Eastbourne Swifts v Faversham	1-2
Lewisham St Marys v Mid Kent	4-0
11 2nd East Lancs Reg (A'shot) v 2nd Grenadier Gds	3-0
Newbury v 2nd Gordon Highlanders	4-2
12 Bristol South End v Trowbridge Town	3-0
Bristol St George v Yeovil Casuals	8-0
1r Sunderland Nomads v Brandon Rovers	3-3e
8r Queen's Park Rangers v 1st Scots Guards	3-0
r Wandsworth v 1st Coldstream Guards	2-1
1r2 Brandon Rovers v Sunderland Nomads	2-4

Qualifying Round Four

1 Shankhouse v Sunderland Nomads	4-0
2 Leadgate Park v Howden-le-Wear	2-0
3 Thornaby Utopians v Thornaby	3-1
4 Hunslet v Peterborough	8-1
5 Harwich & Parkeston v Kirkley	0-2
6 Upton Park v Leytonstone	0-4
7 Old Wilsonians v Crouch End	3-2
8 Wandsworth v Queen's Park Rangers	3-3
9 Watford St Marys v Cheshunt (1)	1-2
10 Faversham v Lewisham St Marys	7-0
11 2nd East Lancs Regt (Aldershot) v Newbury	4-2
12 Bristol St George v Bristol South End	0-2
8r Queen's Park Rangers v Wandsworth	0-2

Round One

2nd East Lancs Regt (A'shot) v 3rd Grenadier Gds	3-1
Bishop Auckland v Tow Law	1-0
Bristol South End v Old Carthusians	0-10
Cheshunt (1) v Old Brightonians	1-3
Darlington v Thornaby Utopians	3-2
Ipswich Town v Ealing	1-3
Kirkley v Old Weymouthians	5-1
Leadgate Park v Whitby	1-0
Leytonstone v Faversham	4-3
Maidenhead v Old Westminsters	0-2
Old Etonians v Royal Artillery (Portsmouth)	2-3
Old Wilsonians v Hunslet	0-6
Shankhouse v Middlesbrough	3-1
Stockton v South Bank	4-0 v
Wandsworth v Marlow	1-6
Wycombe Wanderers v Casuals	3-5
r Stockton v South Bank	2-0

Round Two

Bishop Auckland v Hunslet	4-0
Casuals v Royal Artillery (Portsmouth)	3-2
Darlington v Stockton	4-6
Leadgate Park v Shankhouse	3-1
Leytonstone v Marlow	2-6
Old Brightonians v Kirkley	0-2
Old Carthusians v Ealing	2-1
Old Westminsters v 2nd East Lancs Regt (Aldershot)	4-1

Round Three

Leadgate Park v Bishop Auckland	2-0
Marlow v Kirkley	1-1
Old Carthusians v Old Westminsters	3-1
Stockton v Casuals	4-0
r Kirkley v Marlow	1-0 D

Semi Finals

Old Carthusians v Marlow	0-0 N
Stockton v Leadgate Park	2-0 N
r Old Carthusians v Marlow	2-1 N

Final

Old Carthusians v Stockton	1-1 N
r Old Carthusians v Stockton	4-1 N

1897/98

Qualifying Round One

6 Barking Woodville v Romford (1)	3-1
Braintree v London Hospital	0-3
South West Ham (1) v Olympian	5-3
7 London Welsh v Old Wykehamists	wo/s
Novocastrian v Clapham Rovers	1-1
Old Cranleighans v Hampstead	4-2
Old Malvernians v Old Brightonians	9-0
8 Fulham v Eversleigh (Balham)	3-0
Hammersmith Athletic v 1st Scots Guards	1-2
Metropolitan Railway v Civil Service	2-0
Southall v Hounslow	6-2
Uxbridge v Stanley (Fulham)	3-2
Wandsworth v Brentford	wo/s
11 Aylesbury United v Swindon Amateurs	2-1
Burnham v Oxford City	2-1
12 Clifton v Chippenham Town	1-0
Old Weymouthians v Barton Hill (Bristol)	wo/s
Street v Southbroom (Devizes)	3-0
Weymouth v Bournemouth	1-0
7r Clapham Rovers v Novocastrian	0-5

Qualifying Round Two

1 Mickley v Shankhouse	wo/s
2 Leadgate Exiles v Kelloe St Helens	4-1
Stanley United v Shildon United	3-1
3 Darlington St Augustines v South Bank	0-1
Rise Carr Rangers v Loftus	3-1
Thornaby v West Hartlepool NER	5-1
5 Great Yarmouth v Norwich CEYMS	1-2
Norwich VA v Harwich & Parkeston	1-3
Wisbech v King's Lynn	3-5
6 Barking Woodville v Upton Park	4-1
Grays United v Enfield	7-0
Ilford v South West Ham (1)	4-3
Leytonstone v London Hospital	3-2
7 Barnet (1) v London Welsh	3-3
Novocastrian v Old Cranleighans	5-0
Old Malvernians v Bradfield Waifs (Norbury Park)	3-2
Old St Marks v Old Felstedians	2-1
8 1st Coldstream Guards v Metropolitan Railway	4-2
2nd Grenadier Guards v 1st Scots Guards	2-1
Southall v Fulham	1-0
Uxbridge v Wandsworth	2-0
10 Eastbourne Swifts v 2nd Royal Scots Fusiliers	0-2
Faversham v Mid Kent	13-1
Southwick v Eastbourne	1-0
11 2nd Gordon Highlanders v Burnham	wo/s
Aylesbury United v Slough	3-1
Chesham Generals v Newbury	wo/s
Reading Amateurs v Oxford Cygnets	1-2
12 Bedminster v Yeovil Casuals	1-0
Clifton v Street	2-4
Melksham v Bedminster St Pauls	4-1
Weymouth v Old Weymouthians	1-1
7r London Welsh v Barnet (1)	4-2
12r Old Weymouthians v Weymouth	2-0

Qualifying Round Three

1 Rutherford College v Berwick Rangers	7-3
Workington v Mickley	0-2
2 Crook Town v Stanley United	4-1
Leadgate Exiles v Howden-le-Wear	8-0
3 South Bank v Scarborough	6-0
Thornaby v Rise Carr Rangers	3-1
4 Grimsby All Saints v Hull	4-2
5 Harwich & Parkeston v Sudbury	2-2
Norwich CEYMS v King's Lynn	1-2
6 Grays United v Ilford	2-2
Leytonstone v Barking Woodville	3-1
7 Old Malvernians v London Welsh	5-1
Old St Marks v Novocastrian	1-4
8 1st Coldstream Guards v Southall	1-1
Uxbridge v 2nd Grenadier Guards	6-0
9 Apsley v Dunstable Town (1)	2-2
10 Southwick v 2nd Royal Scots Fusiliers	0-1
Tunbridge Wells v Faversham	1-2
11 2nd Gordon Highlanders v Oxford Cygnets	5-0
Aylesbury United v Chesham Generals	1-5
12 Bedminster v Old Weymouthians	3-1
Street v Melksham	8-0
5r Sudbury v Harwich & Parkeston	3-1
6r Ilford v Grays United	2-3
8r Southall v 1st Coldstream Guards	1-0
9r Dunstable Town (1) v Apsley	3-1

11

1897/98 to 1899/1900

Qualifying Round Four

1 Rutherford College v Mickley	1-1e
2 Crook Town v Leadgate Exiles	5-2
3 South Bank v Thornaby	0-2
4 Grimsby All Saints v Sheffield	2-3
5 King's Lynn v Sudbury	4-0
6 Grays United v Leytonstone	5-0
7 Novocastrian v Old Malvernians	0-7
8 Southall v Uxbridge	1-0 v
9 Cheshunt (1) v Dunstable Town (1)	5-0
10 2nd Royal Scots Fusiliers v Faversham	1-3
11 Chesham Generals v 2nd Gordon Highlanders	3-1e
12 Bedminster v Street	1-4
1r Mickley v Rutherford College	1-3
8r Uxbridge v Southall	4-1

Round One

2nd Coldstream Guards v Street	3-0
Chesham Generals v 3rd Grenadier Guards	4-1
Cheshunt (1) v Marlow	1-2
Darlington v Hunslet	4-1
Ipswich Town v Uxbridge	1-2
Kirkley v Casuals	1-1e
Maidenhead v Ealing	3-1
Middlesbrough v Leadgate Park	4-0
Old Etonians v Grays United	wo/s
Old Malvernians v King's Lynn	3-0
Old Westminsters v Wycombe Wanderers	0-5
Sheffield v Crook Town	2-1
Stockton v Rutherford College	3-1
Thornaby v Bishop Auckland	2-0
Thornaby Utopians v Tow Law	1-0
Weybridge v Faversham	5-0
r Casuals v Kirkley	6-1

Round Two

Casuals v Old Etonians	0-0e
Chesham Generals v Marlow	4-2
Darlington v Stockton	1-0
Maidenhead v Old Malvernians	2-3e
Middlesbrough v Thornaby Utopians	1-1e
Sheffield v Thornaby	1-3
Uxbridge v Weybridge	1-0
Wycombe Wanderers v 2nd Coldstream Guards	3-1
r Middlesbrough v Thornaby Utopians	3-2
r Old Etonians v Casuals	1-3

Round Three

Casuals v Middlesbrough	0-1
Old Malvernians v Chesham Generals	4-2
Thornaby v Darlington	3-1
Uxbridge v Wycombe Wanderers	1-1e
r Wycombe Wanderers v Uxbridge	2-4

Semi Finals

Middlesbrough v Thornaby	2-1 N
Uxbridge v Old Malvernians	1-0 N

Final

Middlesbrough v Uxbridge	2-0 N

1898/99

Qualifying Round One

7 Old Brightonians v Metropolitan Railway	1-2
Old Weymouthians v Old Felstedians	6-0
West Hampstead v Hampstead	4-0
8 Ealing v Wandsworth	2-1
Fulham v 2nd Coldstream Guards	4-2
Hammersmith Athletic v Civil Service	2-1
Hounslow v London Welsh	2-4
11 Aylesbury United v Windsor & Eton	11-0

Qualifying Round Two

2 Hobson Wanderers (Durham) v Leadgate Park	1-2
Howden-le-Wear v Annfield Plain Celtic	1-2
Shildon United v Stanley United	2-2
Willington Rovers v Rutherford College	1-1
3 Darlington St Augustines v Loftus	9-0
Grangetown Athletic v Brotton	1-2
4 Boston Victoria v Grimsby All Saints	0-3
Liverpool Casuals v Lincoln Lindum	8-2
Sheffield v Hunslet	2-4
5 Beccles Caxton v Norwich CEYMS	3-1
Bury St Edmunds v Harwich & Parkeston	0-0e
Great Yarmouth v Ipswich Town	1-0
Lowestoft Town v King's Lynn	0-1
6 Harrow Athletic v Romford (1)	12-0
Leytonstone v Upton Park	5-0
Olympic v London Hospital	1-2
7 Old Etonians v Old Weymouthians	2-3
Surbiton Hill v Old St Marks	9-3
West Hampstead v Metropolitan Railway	0-1
Weybridge v Bradfield Waifs (Norbury Park)	4-1
8 3rd Grenadier Guards v Fulham	1-8
Ealing v 3rd Coldstream Guards	10-1
London Welsh v Hammersmith Athletic	1-4
Richmond Association v 1st Coldstream Guards	2-1
10 1st Royal Scots Fusiliers v Horsham	7-1
11 Aylesbury United v Burnham	4-1
Oxford Cygnets v Slough	0-3
Reading Amateurs v Newbury	3-2
Thame v Oxford City	0-2
12 Bournemouth v Chippenham Town	wo/s
2r Rutherford College v Willington Rovers	5-0
r Stanley United v Shildon United	0-1
5r Harwich & Parkeston v Bury St Edmunds	3-0

Qualifying Round Three

2 Leadgate Park v Annfield Plain Celtic	3-1
Rutherford College v Shildon United	wo/s
3 Darlington St Augustines v Brotton	1-3
Whitby v Scarborough	3-0
4 Beverley Church Institute v Grimsby All Saints	1-4
Hunslet v Liverpool Casuals	1-0
5 Great Yarmouth v King's Lynn	2-0
Harwich & Parkeston v Beccles Caxton	3-1
6 Harrow Athletic v London Hospital	2-1
Leytonstone v Olympian	5-1
7 Metropolitan Railway v Weybridge	4-2
Old Weymouthians v Surbiton Hill	3-0
8 Hammersmith Athletic v Fulham	1-0
Richmond Association v Ealing	0-0
9 Dunstable Town (1) v Apsley	3-1
Ware v Cheshunt (1)	0-1
10 1st Royal Scots Fusiliers v Southwick	wo/s
Eastbourne v Eastbourne Swifts	1-1
11 Aylesbury United v Oxford City	4-2
Reading Amateurs v Slough	1-1a
12 Devizes Town v Street	3-2
Royal Engineers v Bournemouth	wo/s
8r Ealing v Richmond Association	1-2
10r Eastbourne v Eastbourne Swifts	2-0
11r Slough v Reading Amateurs	1-1a
11r2 Reading Amateurs v Slough	1-0 N

Qualifying Round Four

1 Mickley v Workington	wo/s
2 Rutherford College v Leadgate Park	2-1
3 Whitby v Brotton	2-1
4 Grimsby All Saints v Hunslet	2-1
5 Great Yarmouth v Harwich & Parkeston	0-1
6 Leytonstone v Harrow Athletic	2-0
7 Metropolitan Railway v Old Weymouthians	0-4
8 Richmond Association v Hammersmith Athletic	4-0
9 Cheshunt (1) v Dunstable Town (1)	4-0
10 1st Royal Scots Fusiliers v Eastbourne	1-5
11 Aylesbury United v Reading Amateurs	3-2e
12 Devizes Town v Royal Engineers	2-1

Round One

Bishop Auckland v Darlington	0-3
Chesham Generals v Marlow	3-3
Cheshunt (1) v Weymouth	wo/s
Devizes Town v Aylesbury United	1-1e
Maidenhead v Leytonstone	4-3
Middlesbrough v Thornaby Utopians	0-1
Old Malvernians v Eastbourne	5-1
Old Weymouthians v Grimsby All Saints	1-4 N
Richmond Association v Casuals	1-2
Royal Artillery (Portsmouth) v Kirkley	4-0
South Bank v Rutherford College	5-1
Stockton v Tow Law	4-2
Thornaby v Mickley	0-1
Uxbridge v Harwich & Parkeston	1-1e
Whitby v Crook Town	9-0
Wycombe Wanderers v Brentford	2-3
r Aylesbury United v Devizes Town	1-0
r Harwich & Parkeston v Uxbridge	1-0
r Marlow v Chesham Generals	1-1e
r2 Chesham Generals v Marlow	1-8 N

Round Two

Aylesbury United v Old Malvernians	2-3
Casuals v Cheshunt (1)	4-0 v
Darlington v South Bank	4-1
Grimsby All Saints v Brentford	wo/s
Harwich & Parkeston v Maidenhead	3-0
Mickley v Whitby	1-3
Royal Artillery (Portsmouth) v Marlow	2-0
Thornaby Utopians v Stockton	0-3
r Cheshunt (1) v Casuals	2-0

Round Three

Grimsby All Saints v Darlington	1-0
Harwich & Parkeston v Royal Artillery (Portsmouth)	1-3 d
Old Malvernians v Cheshunt (1)	3-1
Stockton v Whitby	6-2

Semi Finals

Harwich & Parkeston v Grimsby All Saints	2-1 N
Stockton v Old Malvernians	2-0 N

Final

Stockton v Harwich & Parkeston	1-0 N

1899/1900

Preliminary Round

8 Hoddesdon v Cheshunt (1)	0-1
Leighton Cee Springs v Old Danes	5-0
Old St Marks v Muswell Hill	3-1

Qualifying Round One

2 Grangetown Athletic v Leadgate Park	7-1
Stockton St Johns v West Hartlepool	0-2
Willington Rovers v Hobson Wanderers (Durham)	2-1
7 3rd Kent VA v Clapham Rovers	2-4
Bradfield Waifs (Norbury Park) v Eversleigh (Balham)	7-4
Civil Service v West Croydon	1-2
Kingston-on-Thames v Guildford	1-2
Lee v 1st Royal Scots Fusiliers	wo/s
Norwood & Selhurst v 1st Scots Guards	2-1
Wandsworth v Royal Engineers United	wo/s
West Norwood v Black Watch	wo/s
8 Cheshunt (1) v Crouch End Vampires	3-0
Dunstable Thursday v Upton Park	6-1
Hammersmith Athletic v Old Weymouthians	0-2
Leighton Cee Springs v London Welsh	2-3
Old St Marks v West Hampstead	1-6
Olympian v Hitchin	1-4
Olympic v Hampstead	n/a
Romford (1) v Ware	1-3
9 Apsley v Maidenhead Norfolkians	1-2
Berkhamsted Sunnyside v Chesham Generals	1-1
Chesham Generals v Berkhamsted Sunnyside	4-2
Harrow Athletic v Oxford City	0-2
Henley v Maidenhead	1-3
Oxford Cygnets v Burnham	wo/s
Reading Amateurs v Reading Biscuit Factory	8-0
Uxbridge v Aylesbury United	2-0
Wycombe Wanderers v Slough	3-1

Qualifying Round Two

2 Crook Town v Howden-le-Wear	2-1
Stanley United v 1st Yorkshire Regiment	wo/s
Willington Rovers v West Hartlepool	2-2
4 King's Lynn v Lincoln Lindum	6-1
5 Colchester Town v Ipswich Town	2-1
7 Bradfield Waifs (Norbury Park) v Guildford	1-1
Clapham Rovers v Wandsworth	0-3
West Croydon v Lee	9-1
West Norwood v Norwood & Selhurst	4-1
8 Cheshunt (1) v Dunstable Thursday	8-3
Old Weymouthians v West Hampstead	1-0
Olympic v London Welsh	8-3
Ware v Hitchin	0-0
9 Maidenhead v Wycombe Wanderers	0-6
Maidenhead Norfolkians v Reading Amateurs	1-5
Oxford City v Chesham Generals	1-0
Oxford Cygnets v Uxbridge	wo/s
10 Devizes Town v Yeovil Casuals	3-3
Street v Bristol Amateurs	4-1
Weymouth v Bradford-on-Avon	wo/s
2r West Hartlepool v Willington Rovers	3-2
7r Guildford v Bradfield Waifs (Norbury Park)	wo/s
8r Hitchin v Ware	3-2
10r Devizes Town v Yeovil Casuals	wo/s

Qualifying Round Three

1 Mickley v Scarborough	1-0
Rutherford College v Prudhoe	2-3
2 Stanley United v Grangetown Athletic	2-0
West Hartlepool v Crook Town	1-1
4 King's Lynn v Boston	5-1
Whitwick White Star v Wisbech	wo/s
5 Bury St Edmunds v Colchester Town	0-4
Norwich CEYMS v Halesworth	4-2
6 Eastbourne v Eastbourne Swifts	3-0
Worthing v Horsham	1-1
7 Guildford v West Norwood	2-5
West Croydon v Wandsworth	2-0
8 Cheshunt (1) v Olympic	2-1
Hitchin v Old Weymouthians	1-3
9 Oxford Cygnets v Reading Amateurs	1-2
Wycombe Wanderers v Oxford City	2-0
10 Devizes Town v 1st Highland Light Infantry	wo/s
Weymouth v Street	3-0
2r Crook Town v West Hartlepool	wo/s
6r Horsham v Worthing	1-0

Qualifying Round Four

1 Mickley v Prudhoe	4-1
2 Stanley United v Crook Town	1-1
3 Liverpool Casuals v 1st South Lancs Regiment	wo/s
4 King's Lynn v Whitwick White Star	3-2
5 Colchester Town v Norwich CEYMS	wo/s
6 Eastbourne v Horsham	0-1
7 West Croydon v West Norwood	3-0
8 Cheshunt (1) v Old Weymouthians	3-1

12

1899/1900 to 1901/02

9 Wycombe Wanderers v Reading Amateurs	3-0
10 Weymouth v Devizes Town	1-0
2r Crook Town v Stanley United	1-0

Round One

Bishop Auckland v Darlington St Augustines	6-0
Colchester Town v Ealing	3-2
Grimsby All Saints v Sheffield	5-1
Harwich & Parkeston v West Croydon	0-0
Horsham v Cheshunt (1)	4-7
Hunslet v Thornaby	4-0
King's Lynn v Thornaby Utopians	3-0
Kirkley v Leytonstone	2-4
Liverpool Casuals v Mickley	wo/s
Lowestoft Town v Richmond Association	6-1
Old Etonians v Weymouth	8-0
Old Malvernians v Weybridge	7-2
South Bank v Crook Town	0-2
Stockton v Tow Law	2-0
Whitby v Darlington	1-5
Wycombe Wanderers v Marlow	1-1
r Marlow v Wycombe Wanderers	1-0
r West Croydon v Harwich & Parkeston	wo/s

Round Two

Colchester Town v Old Malvernians	3-3
Grimsby All Saints v Hunslet	3-2
King's Lynn v Crook Town	wo/s
Leytonstone v Old Etonians	2-0
Liverpool Casuals v Darlington	2-4
Lowestoft Town v Cheshunt (1)	9-0
Marlow v West Croydon	3-0
Stockton v Bishop Auckland	2-4
r Old Malvernians v Colchester Town	9-2

Round Three

Bishop Auckland v King's Lynn	4-1
Darlington v Grimsby All Saints	6-2
Lowestoft Town v Leytonstone	9-0
Marlow v Old Malvernians	3-1

Semi Finals

Bishop Auckland v Darlington	2-2 N
Lowestoft Town v Marlow	1-0 N
r Bishop Auckland v Darlington	2-0 N

Final

Bishop Auckland v Lowestoft Town	5-1 N

1900/01

Qualifying Round One

5 Bury St Edmunds v Colchester Town	0-2
7 Civil Service v Redhill	3-2
Norwood & Selhurst v West Croydon	1-2
Surbiton Hill v Kingston-on-Thames	wo/s
Tunbridge Wells v 1st Coldstream Guards	wo/s
Weybridge v Lee	6-1
8 Bowes Park v Hampstead	0-2
Cheshunt (1) v Leighton Cee Springs	4-0
Old St Marks v West Ham Garfield	wo/s
Olympic v Upton Park	1-2
9 Reading Amateurs v Aylesbury United	2-2
9r Aylesbury United v Reading Amateurs	wo/s

Qualifying Round Two

2 Grangetown Athletic v West Auckland	wo/s
Stanley United v Howden-le-Wear	0-1
Thornaby Utopians v Leadgate Park	2-1
5 Colchester Town v Halesworth	4-0
Leiston v Kirkley	2-3
Norwich CEYMS v Lynn Swifts	7-1
6 Eastbourne Swifts v St Leonards	0-2
7 Chatham Amateurs v West Croydon	4-2
Civil Service v Weybridge	4-0
Eversleigh (Balham) v 3rd Kent VA	1-3
Surbiton Hill v Tunbridge Wells	4-1
8 Crouch End Vampires v Old St Marks	1-1
Hitchin v Hampstead	1-1
Upton Park v Cheshunt (1)	2-5
Willesden Town v Ware	3-2
9 Aylesbury United v Maidenhead Norfolkians	0-3
Harrow Athletic v Oxford City	2-0
Henley v Slough	0-1
Maidenhead v Apsley	2-3
10 Bedminster St Francis v Street	wo/s
Trowbridge Town v Yeovil Casuals	0-2
8r Crouch End Vampires v Old St Marks	3-0
r Hampstead v Hitchin	wo/s

Qualifying Round Three

2 Howden-le-Wear v Grangetown Athletic	5-2
Thornaby Utopians v Willington Rovers	3-0
3 Scarborough v West Hartlepool	3-0
4 Lincoln Lindum v Whitwick White Cross	2-6
5 Kirkley v Great Yarmouth Town	1-1
Norwich CEYMS v Colchester Town	2-2
6 Horsham v St Leonards	6-2
Worthing v Eastbourne	1-4
7 3rd Kent VA v Civil Service	0-2
Surbiton Hill v Chatham Amateurs	6-1
8 Crouch End Vampires v Cheshunt (1)	3-0
Willesden Town v Hampstead	0-3
9 Harrow Athletic v Maidenhead Norfolkians	3-0
Slough v Apsley	3-2
10 Chippenham Town v Bedminster St Francis	2-4
Yeovil Casuals v Weymouth	3-2
5r Colchester Town v Norwich CEYMS	1-0
r Great Yarmouth Town v Kirkley	2-1

Qualifying Round Four

1 Mickley - Bye	
2 Howden-le-Wear v Thornaby Utopians	1-3
3 Scarborough v Skinningrove Ironworks	0-0 d
4 Loughborough Corinthians v Whitwick White Cross	2-0
5 Great Yarmouth Town v Colchester Town	2-0
6 Horsham v Eastbourne	1-5
7 Surbiton Hill v Civil Service	3-0
8 Hampstead v Crouch End Vampires	0-2
9 Harrow Athletic v Slough	0-1
10 Bedminster St Francis v Yeovil Casuals	7-1

Round One

Bedminster St Francis v Eastbourne	3-2
Bishop Auckland v Loughborough Corinthians	3-1
Crook Town v Stockton	2-1
Crouch End Vampires v Old Malvernians	3-5
Darlington v Stockton St Johns	2-0
Darlington St Augustines v South Bank	2-0
Hunslet v Tow Law	6-1
Ipswich Town v Old Etonians	2-6
King's Lynn v Lowestoft Town	2-1
Marlow v Harwich & Parkeston	1-2
Scarborough v Grimsby All Saints	1-3
Sheffield v Mickley	0-2
Slough v Ealing	0-2
Surbiton Hill v Great Yarmouth Town	4-1
Thornaby Utopians - Bye	
Wycombe Wanderers v Richmond Association	4-0

Round Two

Bishop Auckland v Darlington St Augustines	2-1
Crook Town v Mickley	5-0
Darlington v Grimsby All Saints	1-0
Ealing v Wycombe Wanderers	5-2
King's Lynn v Bedminster St Francis	4-2
Old Etonians v Harwich & Parkeston	1-4e
Old Malvernians v Surbiton Hill	4-3
Thornaby Utopians v Hunslet	2-0

Round Three

Darlington v Crook Town	0-2
Hunslet v Bishop Auckland	0-3
King's Lynn v Harwich & Parkeston	3-1
Old Malvernians v Ealing	0-3

Semi Finals

Crook Town v Bishop Auckland	2-0 N
King's Lynn v Ealing	1-0 N

Final

Crook Town v King's Lynn	1-1 N
r Crook Town v King's Lynn	3-0 N

1901/02

Preliminary Round

8 Carter's Engineering Works v Willesden Town	wo/s
Olympic v Upton Park	n/a

Qualifying Round One

5 Beccles Caxton v Colchester Town	2-0e
Lynn Swifts v Leiston	wo/s
6 Horsham v Worthing	6-0
St Leonards v Eastbourne Old Town	3-1
Tunbridge Wells v Hastings & St Leonards	0-1
7 Norwood & Selhurst v Chatham Amateurs	2-1
Wandsworth v West Croydon	2-0
8 Carter's Engineering Wks v Berkhamsted Sunnyside	5-1
Cheshunt (1) v Old St Marks	9-0
Crouch End Vampires v Vulcan (Acton)	4-2
Leighton Cee Springs v Hampstead	1-3
Luton Amateur (Chatham) v Bowes Park	5-1
Southall v Upton Park	1-0
Ware v Richmond Association	0-5
Woodford v West Ham Garfield	3-0
9 Aylesbury United v Windsor & Eton	12-1
Chesham Town v Henley	wo/s
Maidenhead Norfolkians v Maidenhead	1-2
Oxford City v Stantonbury St James	3-0
Reading Amateurs v Harrow Athletic	7-2
Wycombe Wanderers v Chesham Generals	3-1
10 Street v Chippenham Town	1-2
Whiteheads (Weymouth) v Bedminster St Francis	3-1

Qualifying Round Two

2 Darlington St Hildas v Whitby	4-0
Skinningrove Ironworks v Grangetown Athletic	1-0
5 Great Yarmouth Town v Lynn North End	5-1
Harwich & Parkeston v Lynn Swifts	1-0
Kirkley v Beccles Caxton	3-1
Norwich CEYMS v Chelmsford	6-0
6 Hastings & St Leonards v Shoreham	2-3
Horsham v Eastbourne Swifts	1-1
Newhaven Cement Works v Eastbourne	2-1
St Leonards v Hove	2-3
7 3rd Kent VA v Lee	3-2
Norwood & Selhurst v Royal Engineers	1-2
Redhill v Eversleigh (Balham)	5-4
Wandsworth v New Brompton Amateurs	1-2
8 Carter's Engineering Works v Woodford	2-4
Hampstead v Cheshunt (1)	0-2
Luton Amateur (Chatham) v Crouch End Vampires	1-1
Southall v Richmond Association	1-0
9 Apsley v Aylesbury United	0-5
Chesham Town v Maidenhead	3-0
Reading Amateurs v Oxford City	1-2
Slough v Wycombe Wanderers	0-2
10 Chippenham Town v Bridgwater	3-0
Weymouth v Cotham Amateurs	4-1
Whiteheads (Weymouth) v Bristol St George	1-0
Yeovil Casuals v Avalon Rovers	7-0
6r Horsham v Eastbourne Swifts	3-0
8r Crouch End Vampires v Luton Amateur (Chatham)	1-1
8r2 Crouch End Vampires v Luton Amateur (Chatham)	2-0

Qualifying Round Three

1 Rutherford College v Mickley	1-1
Stanley United v Leadgate Park	2-1
2 Darlington St Hildas v York St Clements	6-1
Skinningrove Ironworks v Rowntrees	4-1
3 Melling v Winsford United	wo/s
Old Xaverians v Bury Athenaeum	0-0a
4 Derby Hills Ivanhoe v Loughborough Corinthians	3-0
5 Harwich & Parkeston v Norwich CEYMS	1-1e
Kirkley v Great Yarmouth Town	4-0
6 Hove v Horsham	0-3
Newhaven Cement Works v Shoreham	0-0a
7 3rd Kent VA v Redhill	1-3
New Brompton Amateurs v Royal Engineers	1-0
8 Cheshunt (1) v Woodford	3-4
Crouch End Vampires v Southall	2-3
9 Aylesbury United v Oxford City	1-4
Wycombe Wanderers v Chesham Town	5-0
10 Whiteheads (Weymouth) v Weymouth	3-1
Yeovil Casuals v Chippenham Town	4-1
1r Mickley v Rutherford College	1-2
3r Bury Athenaeum v Old Xaverians	4-0
5r Norwich CEYMS v Harwich & Parkeston	2-0
6r Shoreham v Newhaven Cement Works	4-1

Qualifying Round Four

1 Stanley United v Rutherford College	3-0
2 Darlington St Hildas v Skinningrove Ironworks	2-1
3 Bury Athenaeum v Melling	wo/s
4 Derby Hills Ivanhoe v Huddersfield	wo/s
5 Norwich CEYMS v Kirkley	0-2
6 Shoreham v Horsham	4-1
7 Redhill v New Brompton Amateurs	3-3
8 Woodford v Southall	3-3
9 Oxford City v Wycombe Wanderers	2-1
10 Yeovil Casuals v Whiteheads (Weymouth)	0-1
7r New Brompton Amateurs v Redhill	6-1
8r Southall v Woodford	4-1

Round One

Bishop Auckland v Hunslet	5-1e
Bury Athenaeum v Scarborough	5-1
Civil Service v Ilford	1-2e
Crook Town v Derby Hills Ivanhoe	0-3
Darlington St Augustines v West Hartlepool	2-0
Darlington St Hildas v Darlington	3-1
King's Lynn v Kirkley	2-0

1901/02 to 1903/04

Marlow v Oxford City	3-4e
New Brompton Amateurs v Old Etonians	4-3
Old Malvernians v Southall	5-1
Sheffield v Stanley United	7-3
Shoreham v Ealing	1-3
South Bank v Tow Law	4-1
Stockton v Stockton St Johns	0-1
Surbiton Hill v Ipswich Town	1-1e
Whiteheads (Weymouth) v Lowestoft Town	3-1
r Ipswich Town v Surbiton Hill	3-0

Round Two

Bishop Auckland v Stockton St Johns	5-2
Bury Athenaeum v Derby Hills Ivanhoe	1-3
Darlington St Hildas v Sheffield	3-1
Ealing v Ipswich Town	1-2
Ilford v Oxford City	1-0
New Brompton Amateurs v Whiteheads (Weymouth)	0-1
Old Malvernians v King's Lynn	3-0
South Bank v Darlington St Augustines	4-3

Round Three

Derby Hills Ivanhoe v Bishop Auckland	1-4
Ilford v Whiteheads (Weymouth)	1-1
Old Malvernians v Ipswich Town	10-0
South Bank v Darlington St Hildas	4-2
r Whiteheads (Weymouth) v Ilford	3-6e

Semi Finals

Bishop Auckland v South Bank	5-2 N
Old Malvernians v Ilford	6-4 N

Final

Old Malvernians v Bishop Auckland	5-1 N

1902/03

Qualifying Round One

5 Lowestoft Town v Ipswich Town	5-0
Norwich CEYMS v Great Yarmouth Town	3-1
Norwich City v King's Lynn	5-0
6 Eastbourne v Eastbourne Old Town	2-2
Lewes v Hove	1-2
Tunbridge Wells v Hastings & St Leonards	5-3
Worthing v Shoreham	3-3
8 Crouch End Vampires v Apsley	9-0
Hampstead v Civil Service	0-8
Leighton Cee Springs v Bowes Park	2-0
Luton Clarence v Olympic	wo/s
Muswell Hill v West Ham Garfield	0-3
Norsemen v Berkhamsted Sunnyside	wo/s
Vulcan (Acton) v Upton Park	0-3
Ware v Luton Amateur (Chatham)	3-2
9 Aylesbury United v Chesham Town	5-3
Henley v Wallingford	1-4
10 Glastonbury v Cotham Amateurs	0-0
Street v Devizes Town	2-5
6r Eastbourne Old Town v Eastbourne	0-3
r Shoreham v Worthing	1-1a
10r Cotham Amateurs v Glastonbury	1-3
6r2 Shoreham v Worthing	2-1 N

Qualifying Round Two

2 West Hartlepool v Whitby	wo/s
York St Clements v Grangetown Athletic	2-12
3 Blackpool Amateurs v Northern Nomads	wo/s
Burnley Belvedere v Liverpool Casuals	6-2
Old Xaverians v Rhyl Athletic	wo/s
4 Loughborough Corinthians v Kimberley St Johns	1-2
Notts Magdala v Irthlingborough	2-1
Notts Magdala Amateurs v Coalville Town	2-6
5 Colchester Crown v Norwich CEYMS	3-1
Halesworth v Chelmsford	3-6
Harwich & Parkeston v Beccles Caxton	wo/s
Lowestoft Town v Norwich City	4-2
6 Eastbourne v Littlehampton	0-1
Newhaven Cement Works v St Leonards	3-1
Shoreham v Hove	4-3
Tunbridge Wells v Horsham	2-2e
7 Eversleigh (Balham) v Lee	3-0
Old St Marks v Croydon Wanderers	10-2
West Croydon v Redhill	0-6
8 Civil Service v Leighton Cee Springs	1-0
Crouch End Vampires v Upton Park	2-3
Norsemen v Luton Clarence	2-1
Ware v West Ham Garfield	1-0
9 Chesham Generals v Burnham	9-2
Slough v Maidenhead	4-0
Wallingford v Aylesbury United	2-4
Wycombe Wanderers v Maidenhead Norfolkians	0-2
10 Freemantle (South'pton) v Whiteheads (Weymouth)	0-6
Paulton Rovers v Devizes Town	1-0
Poole v Glastonbury	4-2
Staple Hill v Weymouth	1-6
6r Horsham v Tunbridge Wells	1-1e
6r2 Tunbridge Wells v Horsham	3-0 N

Qualifying Round Three

2 Stanley United v Grangetown Athletic	3-1
West Hartlepool v Skinningrove Ironworks	4-2
3 Burnley Belvedere v Old Xaverians	1-2
Liverpool Leek v Blackpool Amateurs	n/a
4 Kimberley St Johns v Coalville Town	wo/s
Lawrence's Athletic v Notts Magdala	4-0
5 Colchester Crown v Chelmsford	0-0
Lowestoft Town v Harwich & Parkeston	6-1
6 Littlehampton v Newhaven Cement Works	0-0
Shoreham v Tunbridge Wells	2-2a
7 Army Service Corps (Woolwich) v Old St Marks	3-1
Redhill v Eversleigh (Balham)	6-4
8 Norsemen v Civil Service	0-3
Upton Park v Ware	wo/s
9 Chesham Generals v Aylesbury United	0-0
Slough v Maidenhead Norfolkians	3-1
10 Poole v Paulton Rovers	2-1
Weymouth v Whiteheads (Weymouth)	1-1
5r Chelmsford v Colchester Crown	8-0
6r Newhaven Cement Works v Littlehampton	2-2a
r Tunbridge Wells v Shoreham	1-1
9r Aylesbury United v Chesham Generals	1-3
10r Whiteheads (Weymouth) v Weymouth	3-3
6r2 Newhaven Cement Works v Littlehampton	1-2 N
r2 Tunbridge Wells v Shoreham	1-1ed
10r2 Weymouth v Whiteheads (Weymouth)	4-1

Qualifying Round Four

1 Rutherford College v Leadgate Park	1-3
2 West Hartlepool v Stanley United	4-0
3 Liverpool Leek v Old Xaverians	3-5
4 Kimberley St Johns v Lawrence's Athletic	6-2
5 Lowestoft Town v Chelmsford	3-1
6 Tunbridge Wells v Littlehampton	9-1
7 Army Service Corps (Woolwich) v Redhill	4-4a
8 Civil Service v Upton Park	3-2
9 Slough v Chesham Generals	1-2
10 Poole v Weymouth	4-2
7r Redhill v Army Service Corps (Woolwich)	2-2a
7r2 Redhill v Army Service Corps (Woolwich)	1-3 N

Round One

Army Service Corps (Woolwich) v Civil Service	2-2
Bedminster St Francis v Cheshunt (1)	1-4
Bishop Auckland v Darlington	3-0
Darlington St Augustines v Stockton	1-4
Derby Hills Ivanhoe v Leadgate Park	1-0
Ealing v Kirkley	1-0
Ilford v New Brompton Amateurs	1-0
Kimberley St Johns v Darlington St Hildas	0-2
Lowestoft Town v Poole	2-0
Old Xaverians v South Bank	2-3
Oxford City v Woodford	3-0
Sheffield v Scarborough	3-0
Southall v Chesham Generals	5-1
Tow Law v Crook Town	0-1
Tunbridge Wells v Marlow	2-1
West Hartlepool v Stockton St Johns	1-0
r Civil Service v Army Service Corps (Woolwich)	2-0

Round Two

Bishop Auckland v South Bank	6-1
Cheshunt (1) v Lowestoft Town	2-3
Civil Service v Southall	8-1
Darlington St Hildas v Stockton	1-2
Ealing v Tunbridge Wells	4-3e
Ilford v Oxford City	0-1e
Sheffield v Crook Town	0-1
West Hartlepool v Derby Hills Ivanhoe	2-1

Round Three

Bishop Auckland v Crook Town	7-0
Civil Service v Oxford City	1-1e
Ealing v Lowestoft Town	1-5
West Hartlepool v Stockton	0-4
r Oxford City v Civil Service	3-1

Semi Finals

Oxford City v Lowestoft Town	1-1 N
Stockton v Bishop Auckland	3-1 N
r Oxford City v Lowestoft Town	4-0 N

Final

Stockton v Oxford City	0-0 N
r Stockton v Oxford City	1-0 N

1903/04

Qualifying Round One

7 Beccles Caxton v Ipswich Town	3-3
Colchester Town v Kirkley	3-7
Harwich & Parkeston v Colchester Crown	3-1
Peterborough Town v Norwich CEYMS	0-2
8 2nd Royal Fusiliers v Reading Amateurs	0-2
Chesham Generals v Luton Amateur (Chatham)	2-0
Chesham Town v Apsley	5-1
Slough v Marlow	11-2
Uxbridge v Maidenhead	2-3
9 3rd Kent VA v Grays United	wo/s
Croydon Wanderers v Croydon	1-6
Godalming v Woking	1-3
Maidstone Church Institute v Woolwich Polytechnic	4-0
New Brompton Amateurs v Swanscombe	2-1
Royal Engineers Service v Northfleet United	1-1
Townley Park v West Norwood	2-2
10 Bognor v Worthing	1-0
Horsham v Newhaven Cement Works	1-0
Lewes v Eastbourne Old Town	0-2
Littlehampton v Brighton Amateurs	1-2
St Leonards v Hastings & St Leonards	4-0
Worthing v Bognor	5-2ev
11 Crouch End Vampires v Willesden Town	3-1
Eversleigh (Balham) v West Brixton	1-1
Shepherds Bush (1) v War Office	1-2
South Weald v Bowes Park	3-2
Ware v Wanstead	1-3
West Hampstead v Hampstead	8-3
Woodford v Upton Park	1-3
12 Devizes Town v Glastonbury	2-0
Longfleet St Marys v Bournemouth Wanderers	5-0
Oldland v Bedminster St Francis	wo/s
Warmley Amateurs v Brislington	0-1
Wells City v Street	1-0
7r Ipswich Town v Beccles Caxton	2-3
9r Northfleet United v Royal Engineers Service Battn	3-3
r West Norwood v Townley Park	1-1
11r Eversleigh (Balham) v West Brixton	5-0
9r2 Northfleet United v Royal Engineers Service Battn	0-5
r2 West Norwood v Townley Park	1-3

Qualifying Round Two

1 Eldon Albion v Shildon Athletic	0-1
Leadgate Park v Stanley United	0-0
Rutherford College v West Auckland	4-1
5 Blackburn Crosshill v Liverpool Ramblers	1-4
Burnley Belvedere v Northern Nomads	wo/s
Hesketh Park v Old Xaverians	1-3
6 Derby Hills Ivanhoe v Notts Magdala Amateurs	2-1
Lawrence's Athletic v Notts Magdala	3-1
Long Eaton Villa v Forest Amateurs	1-0
Loughborough Corinthians v Bridgford Athletic	3-3
7 Kirkley v Chelmsford	wo/s
Leiston v Beccles Caxton	1-0
Norwich CEYMS v Great Yarmouth Town	2-1
Norwich City v Harwich & Parkeston	5-1
8 Chesham Generals v Maidenhead Norfolkians	1-2
Maidenhead v Chesham Town	7-1
Reading Amateurs v Wycombe Wanderers	1-2
Slough v Leighton Cee Springs	5-1
9 3rd Kent VA v Maidstone Church Institute	1-2
Croydon v Redhill	2-1
Royal Engineers Service Bn v New Brompton Ams	2-2
Townley Park v Woking	4-0
10 Bognor v St Leonards	2-1
Eastbourne v Horsham	2-2
Shoreham v Eastbourne Old Town	3-2
Tunbridge Wells v Brighton Amateurs	3-0
11 Lee v South Weald	2-1
Wanstead v Eversleigh (Balham)	5-1
War Office v Crouch End Vampires	2-0
West Hampstead v Upton Park	4-1
12 Brislington v Paulton Rovers	0-4
Devizes Town v Oldland	3-0
Staple Hill v Wells City	wo/s
Weymouth v Longfleet St Marys	1-3
1r Stanley United v Leadgate Park	2-1
6r Bridgford Athletic v Loughborough Corinthians	0-2
9r New Brompton Ams v Royal Engineers Service Bn	2-4
10r Horsham v Eastbourne	3-3
10r2 Eastbourne v Horsham	8-2 N

Qualifying Round Three

1 Rutherford College v Stanley United	1-0
Shildon Athletic v Tow Law	2-1
2 Stockton St Johns v Skinningrove United	n/a
Whitby v Saltburn	0-0a
4 Ripon United v Rowntrees	4-2
York City St Clements v Heckmondwike	wo/s
5 Liverpool Casuals v Old Xaverians	n/a
Liverpool Ramblers v Burnley Belvedere	3-2
6 Lawrence's Athletic v Long Eaton Villa	6-1
Loughborough Corinthians v Derby Hills Ivanhoe	3-1
7 Kirkley v Norwich CEYMS	2-2
Leiston v Norwich City	1-5
8 Maidenhead Norfolkians v Wycombe Wanderers	2-1
Slough v Maidenhead	4-1

1903/04 to 1904/05

9 Maidstone Church Institute v R Engineers Service Bn	1-1
Townley Park v Croydon	1-2
10 Bognor v Shoreham	2-4
Eastbourne v Tunbridge Wells	1-2
11 War Office v Lee	0-1
West Hampstead v Wanstead	4-2
12 Devizes Town v Staple Hill	wo/s
Paulton Rovers v Longfleet St Marys	2-2
2r Saltburn v Whitby	2-0
7r Norwich CEYMS v Kirkley	3-3e
9r R Engineers Service Bn v Maidstone Church Institute	2-2
12r Longfleet St Marys v Paulton Rovers	2-3
7r2 Kirkley v Norwich CEYMS	1-1e
9r2 R Engineers Service Bn v Maidstone Church Institute	3-2
7r3 Kirkley v Norwich CEYMS	2-1 N

Qualifying Round Four

1 Rutherford College v Shildon Athletic	3-2
2 Saltburn v Skinningrove United	3-1
3 Hessle v Rotherham Amateurs	3-2
4 Ripon United v York City St Clements	1-1
5 Liverpool Casuals v Liverpool Ramblers	4-2
6 Loughborough Corinthians v Lawrence's Athletic	5-2
7 Kirkley v Norwich City	0-2
8 Slough v Maidenhead Norfolkians	1-1
9 Croydon v Royal Engineers Service Battn	4-2
10 Tunbridge Wells v Shoreham	12-1
11 West Hampstead v Lee	3-0
12 Paulton Rovers v Devizes Town	1-0a
4r York City St Clements v Ripon United	9-1
8r Maidenhead Norfolkians v Slough	6-1
12r Paulton Rovers v Devizes Town	wo/s

Round One

Cheshunt (1) v Civil Service	2-1e
Darlington v West Hartlepool	4-2
Darlington St Augustines v Rutherford College	1-1
Ealing v Southall	4-0
Grangetown Athletic v Crook Town	1-0
Ilford v King's Lynn	5-1e
Loughborough Corinthians v Liverpool Casuals	8-1
Maidenhead Norfolkians v Tunbridge Wells	2-2
Norwich City v Lowestoft Town	3-0
Paulton Rovers v Oxford City	2-2
Poole v Whiteheads (Weymouth)	0-2
Sheffield v Hessle	5-3
South Bank v Bishop Auckland	0-2
Stockton v Saltburn	3-1
West Hampstead v Croydon	6-0
York City St Clements v Scarborough	0-2
r Oxford City v Paulton Rovers	2-0e
r Rutherford College v Darlington St Augustines	1-2e
r Tunbridge Wells v Maidenhead Norfolkians	2-1e

Round Two

Cheshunt (1) v Oxford City	1-1
Darlington v Bishop Auckland	1-4
Darlington St Augustines v Scarborough	3-1
Loughborough Corinthians v Sheffield	1-4
Norwich City v Ilford	4-0
Stockton v Grangetown Athletic	5-2
Tunbridge Wells v Ealing	3-3
West Hampstead v Whiteheads (Weymouth)	2-4
r Ealing v Tunbridge Wells	4-0
r Oxford City v Cheshunt (1)	4-5

Round Three

Bishop Auckland v Stockton	4-1
Ealing v Norwich City	0-0
Sheffield v Darlington St Augustines	7-0
Whiteheads (Weymouth) v Cheshunt (1)	2-2
r Cheshunt (1) v Whiteheads (Weymouth)	4-0
r Norwich City v Ealing	1-2

Semi Finals

Ealing v Cheshunt (1)	2-0 N
Sheffield v Bishop Auckland	5-2 N

Final

Sheffield v Ealing	3-1 N

1904/05

Preliminary Round

7 Felstead (Silvertown) v Southend Athletic	0-3
Kirkley v Cromer	5-1
Lowestoft Town v Leiston	6-0
Norwich CEYMS v Beccles Caxton	6-0
South Weald v Wanstead	3-2
Upton Park v Woodford	0-7
8 Reading Amateurs v Maidenhead Norfolkians	2-4
Windsor & Eton v Marlow	4-0
9 3rd Kent RGA Volunteers v Oaklands (Woolwich)	0-2
Alleyn v Clapham	4-0
Bromley v Woolwich Polytechnic	3-2
Croydon Wanderers v Croydon	1-3
Dulwich Hamlet v West Norwood	1-2
Eversleigh (Balham) v West Brixton	2-3
Godalming v Woking	0-1
Lee v Middlesex Wanderers	12-0
Northfleet United v New Brompton Amateurs	3-4
Nunhead v Lewisham Montrose	7-0
Redhill v Guildford	4-0
Royal Engineers v Guards Depot (Caterham)	4-1
11 Kensington Town v Hanwell	0-0
11r Hanwell v Kensington Town	4-2

Qualifying Round One

6 Handsworth Oakhill v Long Eaton Villa	7-1
7 Chelmsford v Colchester Crown	1-2
Great Yarmouth Town v Lowestoft Town	0-2
Harwich & Parkeston v Bury Alexandra	8-3
Norwich CEYMS v Kirkley	2-2
Romford (1) v Woodford	1-1
Southend Athletic v South Weald	2-2
8 Chesham Generals v Biggleswade & District	5-1
Chesham Town v Apsley	6-0
Maidenhead v Slough	2-1
Uxbridge v Maidenhead Norfolkians	1-6
Windsor & Eton v 2nd Grenadier Guards	2-2
Wycombe Wanderers v Henley	11-0
9 Alleyn v Croydon	0-0
Dartford v New Brompton Amateurs	1-4
Lee v Bromley	1-3
Nunhead v Oaklands (Woolwich)	4-0
Redhill v Reigate Priory	1-1
Royal Engineers v Woking	1-3
R Engineers Service Bn v Maidstone Church Institute	4-0
West Norwood v West Brixton	4-0
10 Eastbourne Old Town v Hastings & St Leonards	3-1
Horsham v Bognor	6-0
Newhaven v Eastbourne	1-0
Shoreham v Worthing Rovers	7-0
St Leonards v Brighton Amateurs	0-0
Steyning v Hove	3-4
Tunbridge Wells v Hastings Rock-a-Nore	4-1
Worthing v Littlehampton	1-1
11 City of Westminster v Richmond Association	2-1
Crouch End Vampires v Finchley	2-5
Enfield v Hoddesdon	8-0
Great Western Railway Athletic v Hampstead	5-3
Hanwell v War Office	9-0
Olympic v Olympian	6-1
Ware v Bowes Park	5-3
West Hampstead v Grove Park	6-0
12 Bournemouth v Bournemouth Wanderers	2-3
Oldland v Devizes Town	1-3
Paulton Rovers v Warmley Amateurs	3-1
Ryde v Longfleet St Marys	wo/s
Weymouth v Salisbury City	0-0
Whiteheads (Weymouth) v Poole	8-0
7r Kirkley v Norwich CEYMS	3-0
r South Weald v Southend Athletic	0-1
r Woodford v Romford (1)	4-0
8r 2nd Grenadier Guards v Windsor & Eton	2-1
9r Croydon v Alleyn	3-1
r Reigate Priory v Redhill	3-2
10r Brighton Amateurs v St Leonards	0-4
r Littlehampton v Worthing	3-2
12r Salisbury City v Weymouth	0-1

Qualifying Round Two

1 Leadgate Park v Shildon Athletic	4-0
Seaham White Star v Crook Town	2-0 v
Stanley United v Tow Law	5-3
West Auckland v Eldon Albion	1-2
2 Saltburn v Whitby	5-0
Scarborough v Redcar Crusaders	2-1
3 Goole Amateurs v Hessle	1-1
Hull Albany v Hull Central HG Old Boys	2-3
6 Derby Nomads v Notts Magdala	n/a
Handsworth Oakhill v Bridgford Athletic	8-1
Long Eaton Victoria v Notts Magdala Amateurs	2-2
Notts Jardines v Loughborough Corinthians	3-2
7 Colchester Crown v Harwich & Parkeston	2-2
King's Lynn v Peterborough Town	4-2
Lowestoft Town v Kirkley	3-3
Woodford v Southend Athletic	1-2
8 Chesham Generals v Leighton Cee Springs	6-1
Luton Amateur (Chatham) v Chesham Town	1-3
Maidenhead v Maidenhead Norfolkians	1-3
Wycombe Wanderers v 2nd Grenadier Guards	3-0
9 Bromley v Nunhead	6-1
Croydon v West Norwood	3-0
New Brompton Ams v Royal Engineers Service Bn	1-3
Woking v Reigate Priory	0-1
10 Littlehampton v Hove	1-2
Newhaven v St Leonards	1-0
Shoreham v Horsham	5-2
Tunbridge Wells v Eastbourne Old Town	3-2
11 City of Westminster v West Hampstead	1-4
Hanwell v Great Western Railway Athletic	4-2
Olympic v Enfield	2-3
Ware v Finchley	0-1
12 Bournemouth Wanderers v Ryde	wo/s
Brislington v Welton Rovers	3-1
Paulton Rovers v Devizes Town	6-1
Weymouth v Whiteheads (Weymouth)	0-3
1r Crook Town v Seaham White Star	1-4
3r Goole Amateurs v Hessle	2-3
6r Notts Magdala v Derby Nomads	n/a
r Notts Magdala Amateurs v Long Eaton Victoria	1-3
7r Harwich & Parkeston v Colchester Crown	7-0
r Kirkley v Lowestoft Town	1-1
7r2 Kirkley v Lowestoft Town	4-1 N

Qualifying Round Three

1 Leadgate Park v Stanley United	3-2
Seaham White Star v Eldon Albion	1-1
2 Scarborough v Skinningrove United	0-0
West Hartlepool v Saltburn	5-1
3 Hessle v Hull Central HG Old Boys	0-1
Sheffield Grasshoppers v Rotherham Amateurs	2-1
4 Romanby (Northallerton) v Knaresborough	3-3
5 Hesketh Park v Blackburn Crosshill	2-1
6 Long Eaton Victoria v Notts Magdala	2-2
Notts Jardines v Handsworth Oakhill	1-1
7 Harwich & Parkeston v Southend Athletic	1-4
Kirkley v King's Lynn	3-1
8 Chesham Generals v Chesham Town	1-2
Wycombe Wanderers v Maidenhead Norfolkians	2-4
9 Croydon v Bromley	1-1
Royal Engineers Service v Reigate Priory	4-2
10 Shoreham v Hove	2-1
Tunbridge Wells v Newhaven	3-2
11 Enfield v Finchley	3-0
Hanwell v West Hampstead	5-2
12 Bournemouth Wanderers v Whiteheads (Weymouth)	3-4
Brislington v Paulton Rovers	2-0 v
1r Eldon Albion v Seaham White Star	0-2
2r Skinningrove United v Scarborough	1-0
4r Knaresborough v Romanby (Northallerton)	2-2
6r Handsworth Oakhill v Notts Jardines	1-3
r Notts Magdala v Long Eaton Victoria	3-0
9r Bromley v Croydon	4-3
12r Paulton Rovers v Brislington	4-2
4r2 Knaresborough v Romanby (Northallerton)	2-1 N

Qualifying Round Four

1 Leadgate Park v Seaham White Star	2-2
2 Skinningrove United v West Hartlepool	1-3
3 Sheffield Grasshoppers v Hull Central HG Old Boys	7-1
4 Ripon United v Knaresborough	2-1
5 Hesketh Park v Northern Nomads	1-4
6 Notts Jardines v Notts Magdala	2-1
7 Southend Athletic v Kirkley	2-1
8 Chesham Town v Maidenhead Norfolkians	3-1
9 Royal Engineers Service v Bromley	4-1
10 Tunbridge Wells v Shoreham	5-1
11 Hanwell v Enfield	3-0
12 Whiteheads (Weymouth) v Paulton Rovers	2-1
1r Seaham White Star v Leadgate Park	1-2

Round One

Bishop Auckland v Leadgate Park	1-0
Cheshunt (1) v Southend Athletic	2-2
Civil Service v Chesham Town	3-0
Clapton v Ipswich Town	9-0
Darlington v Stockton	3-0
Darlington St Augustines v Rutherford College	wo/s
Derby Hills Ivanhoe v Notts Jardines	1-3
Hanwell v Ealing	1-6
Ilford v Norwich City	wo/s
Northern Nomads v Old Xaverians	4-1 v
Oxford City v Whiteheads (Weymouth)	2-1
Royal Engineers Service v Townley Park	3-3
Sheffield Grasshoppers v Sheffield	2-1
Shepherds Bush (1) v Tunbridge Wells	5-1
South Bank v Ripon United	12-0
West Hartlepool v Grangetown Athletic	2-1
r Old Xaverians v Northern Nomads	wo/s
r Southend Athletic v Cheshunt (1)	6-0
r Townley Park v Royal Engineers Service Battn	0-2

Round Two

Bishop Auckland v Sheffield Grasshoppers	5-1
Civil Service v Ilford	1-3
Darlington v South Bank	6-2
Darlington St Augustines v Old Xaverians	6-1
Ealing v Oxford City	1-1
Notts Jardines v West Hartlepool	1-4 N
Shepherds Bush (1) v Royal Engineers Service Bn	0-1
Southend Athletic v Clapton	0-1
r Oxford City v Ealing	1-0

Round Three

Bishop Auckland v Darlington	1-0
Clapton v Oxford City	3-0
Darlington St Augustines v West Hartlepool	0-1
Ilford v Royal Engineers Service Battn	5-1

1904/05 to 1906/07

Semi Finals

Clapton v Ilford	2-1 N
West Hartlepool v Bishop Auckland	2-1 N

Final

West Hartlepool v Clapton	3-2 N

1905/06

Preliminary Round

7	Barking v East Ham	5-3
	Beccles Caxton v Bury Alexandra	4-1
	Bury St Edmunds v Kirkley	1-1
	Colchester Town v Seven Kings	0-3
	Harwich & Parkeston v Colchester Crown	wo/s
	King's Lynn v Cromer	5-1
	Norwich CEYMS v Peterborough Town	3-0
	South Weald v Southend Athletic	1-1
	Upton Park v Leytonstone	0-1
	Wanstead v Woodford	3-1
8	Reading Amateurs v Maidenhead	4-1
	Windsor & Eton v Maidenhead Norfolkians	3-3
9	Bromley v Maidstone Church Institute	1-3
	Clapham v Guards Depot (Caterham)	n/a
	Croydon v 3rd Kent RGA Volunteers	0-1
	Dartford v New Brompton Amateurs	2-3
	Eversleigh (Balham) v Wimbledon	2-4
	Godalming v Woking	2-1
	Guildford v Redhill	0-3
	New Crusaders v Parthians (Clapham)	5-0
	Oaklands (Woolwich) v Nunhead	0-2
	Plumstead St Johns Institute v Lee	3-0
	Reigate Priory v Dorking	0-0
	Rochester Argyll v Royal Engineers Service Battn	n/a
	Royal Engineers v 1st Grenadier Guards	7-0
	West Norwood v Alleyn	5-1
	Woolwich Polytechnic v Croydon Wanderers	4-1
11	2nd Coldstream Guards v Richmond Association	2-4
	Bowes Park v Olympian	6-0
	Clove v Crouch End Vampires	0-6
	Highgate v Barnet Alston Athletic	0-6
	Olympic v 2nd Grenadier Guards	n/a
	West Hampstead v Hampstead	1-1
12	Bournemouth Wanderers v Whiteheads (Weymouth)	0-7
	Brislington St Annes v Devizes Town	3-1
	Paulton Rovers v Warmley Amateurs	6-0
	Poole v Longfleet St Marys	0-5
	Radstock Town v Glastonbury	7-1
	Weymouth v Bournemouth	4-2
7r	Kirkley v Bury St Edmunds	6-0
r	South Weald v Southend Athletic	1-0
8r	Maidenhead Norfolkians v Windsor & Eton	2-1
9r	Dorking v Reigate Priory	1-3
11r	Hampstead v West Hampstead	2-1

Qualifying Round One

6	Loughborough Corinthians v Burton Casuals	4-0
	Notts Jardines v Bridgford Athletic	3-2
7	Chelmsford v Romford (1)	2-3
	Harwich & Parkeston v Seven Kings	2-0
	Leiston v Kirkley	1-2
	Lowestoft Town v Beccles Caxton	5-1
	Norwich CEYMS v Great Yarmouth Town	1-0
	Peterborough GN Loco v King's Lynn	1-1
	South Weald v Leytonstone	2-1
	Wanstead v Barking	3-4
8	Apsley v Leighton Cee Springs	wo/s
	Aylesbury United v Chesham Generals	1-0
	Chesham Town v Wycombe Wanderers	2-0
	Dunstable Rangers v Luton Trinity	12-0
	Hanwell v Uxbridge	1-4
	Marlow v Maidenhead Norfolkians	0-5
	Reading Amateurs v Slough	3-0
	Staines v Goldsmith's Institute	1-2
9	3rd Kent RGA Volunteers v Woolwich Polytechnic	2-2
	Godalming v Redhill	2-3
	Guards Depot (Caterham) v Wimbledon	2-2
	Maidstone Church Institute v R Engineers Service Bn	2-2
	New Brompton Amateurs v Luton Amateur (Chatham)	2-0
	Nunhead v Plumstead St Johns Institute	1-2
	Royal Engineers v Reigate Priory	7-1
	West Norwood v New Crusaders	3-7
10	Brighton Amateurs v Hove	1-3
	Eastbourne v Hastings Rock-a-Nore	3-0
	Rye v Newhaven	3-1
	Shoreham v Bognor	4-1
	Tunbridge Wells v St Leonards	7-1
	Worthing v Horsham	2-1
11	2nd Grenadier Guards v Richmond Association	5-0
	Barnet Alston Athletic v Crouch End Vampires	2-2
	Enfield v Page Green Old Boys	3-1
	Finchley v Bowes Park	1-3
	Hampstead v Great Western Railway Athletic	4-1
	Hoddesdon v Ware	0-2
	Marcians v Grove Park	6-0
	Shepherds Bush (1) v City of Westminster	7-0

12	Basingstoke v Gosport United	0-4
	Branksome Gasworks Athletic v Longfleet St Marys	0-4
	Cheltenham Town - Bye	
	Radstock Town v Brislington St Annes	4-1
	Taunton Castle v Paulton Rovers	1-5
	Whiteheads (Weymouth) v Weymouth	4-0
	Winchester v Ryde	0-2
7r	King's Lynn v Peterborough GN Loco	4-3
9r	R Engineers Service Bn v Maidstone Church Institute	4-1
r	Wimbledon v Guards Depot (Caterham)	1-3
r	Woolwich Polytechnic v 3rd Kent RGA Volunteers	2-2
11r	Crouch End Vampires v Barnet Alston Athletic	8-2
9r2	Woolwich Polytechnic v 3rd Kent RGA Volunteers	1-0

Qualifying Round Two

1	Crook Town v Spennymoor United	2-0
	Eldon Albion v Leadgate Park	2-0
	Shildon Athletic v Rutherford College	3-3
	West Auckland v Stanley United	2-2
2	Saltburn v Skinningrove United	0-0
6	Loughborough Corinthians v Buxton	0-1
	Notts Jardines v Notts Magdala Amateurs	2-0
	Notts Magdala v Derby Hills Ivanhoe	8-1
	Sneinton v Handsworth Oakhill	2-1
7	Barking v South Weald	2-2
	Lowestoft Town v Kirkley	3-2
	Norwich CEYMS v King's Lynn	1-3
	Romford (1) v Harwich & Parkeston	6-0
8	Apsley v Dunstable Rangers	3-2
	Aylesbury United v Chesham Town	3-2
	Goldsmith's Institute v Uxbridge	1-7
	Reading Amateurs v Maidenhead Norfolkians	3-2
9	Guards Depot (Caterham) v New Crusaders	2-11
	New Brompton Ams v Royal Engineers Service Bn	2-4
	Royal Engineers v Redhill	4-1
	Woolwich Polytechnic v Plumstead St Johns Institute	3-3
10	Eastbourne Old Town v Eastbourne	0-1
	Littlehampton v Worthing	2-2
	Shoreham v Hove	3-0
	Tunbridge Wells v Rye	4-2 r
11	Bowes Park v Crouch End Vampires	1-0
	Hampstead v 2nd Grenadier Guards	0-2
	Shepherds Bush (1) v Marcians	5-0
	Ware v Enfield	3-1
12	Cheltenham Town - Bye	
	Gosport United v Ryde	5-1
	Paulton Rovers v Radstock Town	4-3
	Whiteheads (Weymouth) v Longfleet St Marys	1-3
1r	Shildon Athletic v Rutherford College	3-1
r	Stanley United v West Auckland	2-3
2r	Skinningrove United v Saltburn	n/a
7r	South Weald v Barking	2-1
9r	Plumstead St Johns Institute v Woolwich Polytechnic	5-2
10r	Worthing v Littlehampton	2-2
10r2	Littlehampton v Worthing	2-1 N

Qualifying Round Three

1	Crook Town v Shildon Athletic	4-4
	Eldon Albion v West Auckland	2-1
2	Scarborough v Whitby	3-2
	Skinningrove United v Redcar Crusaders	wo/s
3	Northallerton v Romanby (Northallerton)	2-0
4	Hessle v Goole Town	0-8
	Sheffield Grasshoppers v Brunswick Institute	2-1
5	Blackburn Crosshill v Hesketh Park	4-1
	Liverpool Balmoral v Cavendish Amateurs (Barrow)	wo/s
6	Buxton v Notts Magdala	1-1
	Notts Jardines v Sneinton	3-2
7	Lowestoft Town v King's Lynn	0-2
	Romford (1) v South Weald	2-1
8	Apsley v Aylesbury United	5-1
	Uxbridge v Reading Amateurs	1-1
9	New Crusaders v Plumstead St Johns Institute	6-0
	Royal Engineers Service v Royal Engineers	1-0
10	Eastbourne - Bye	
	Shoreham v Littlehampton	3-1
11	2nd Grenadier Guards v Ware	6-0
	Shepherds Bush (1) v Bowes Park	5-0
12	Longfleet St Marys v Gosport United	1-8
	Paulton Rovers v Cheltenham Town	6-0
1r	Shildon Athletic v Crook Town	2-1
6r	Notts Magdala v Buxton	1-6
8r	Reading Amateurs v Uxbridge	4-4
8r2	Uxbridge v Reading Amateurs	1-0 N

Qualifying Round Four

1	Shildon Athletic v Eldon Albion	3-1
2	Scarborough v Skinningrove United	3-0
3	Northallerton v Goole Town	0-2
4	Sheffield Grasshoppers v Goole Town	2-1
5	Blackburn Crosshill v Liverpool Balmoral	wo/s
6	Notts Jardines v Buxton	1-1
7	King's Lynn v Romford (1)	1-1
8	Apsley v Uxbridge	0-5
9	New Crusaders v Royal Engineers Service Battn	2-0
10	Eastbourne v Shoreham	5-0
11	Shepherds Bush (1) v 2nd Grenadier Guards	0-2
12	Gosport United v Paulton Rovers	9-0
6r	Notts Jardines v Buxton	wo/s
7r	Romford (1) v King's Lynn	3-1

Round One

2nd Grenadier Guards v Eastbourne	1-1
Bishop Auckland v Darlington St Augustines	5-3
Blackburn Crosshill v Sheffield Grasshoppers	5-1
Clapton v Civil Service	3-0
Darlington v South Bank	0-0
Ealing v Gosport United	2-1
Grangetown Athletic v West Hartlepool	1-1
Ilford v Cheshunt (1)	1-3
New Crusaders v Townley Park	6-2
Northern Nomads v Notts Jardines	2-1
Oxford City v Dulwich Hamlet	4-0
Romford (1) v Ipswich Town	4-2
Scarborough v Old Xaverians	2-1
Sheffield v Bingley	7-1
Stockton v Shildon Athletic	5-1
Uxbridge v Tunbridge Wells	4-2
r Eastbourne v 2nd Grenadier Guards	1-0
r South Bank v Darlington	2-1
r West Hartlepool v Grangetown Athletic	0-2

Round Two

Bishop Auckland v Northern Nomads	3-1
Blackburn Crosshill v Grangetown Athletic	3-3
Cheshunt (1) v Clapton	1-1
Ealing v New Crusaders	1-5
Romford (1) v Eastbourne	6-3
Scarborough v South Bank	2-4
Sheffield v Stockton	0-6
Uxbridge v Oxford City	1-1
r Clapton v Cheshunt (1)	0-1
r Grangetown Athletic v Blackburn Crosshill	4-0
r Oxford City v Uxbridge	5-1

Round Three

Grangetown Athletic v Stockton	1-5
Oxford City v Cheshunt (1)	4-1
Romford (1) v New Crusaders	0-0
South Bank v Bishop Auckland	2-2
r Bishop Auckland v South Bank	2-1
r New Crusaders v Romford (1)	1-1
r2 New Crusaders v Romford (1)	4-1 N

Semi Finals

Bishop Auckland v Stockton	0-0 N
Oxford City v New Crusaders	4-2 N
r Bishop Auckland v Stockton	1-0eN

Final

Oxford City v Bishop Auckland	3-0 N

1906/07

Extra Preliminary Round

7	Halesworth v Leiston	0-0
	Leigh Ramblers v Upton Park	wo/s
	Southend Athletic v Limehouse Town	4-0
9	Eversleigh (Balham) v Hatcham Athletic	1-4
	Farncombe v Royal Engineers	1-4
	Holborn v Norwood Association	1-9
	Metrogas v Townley Park	5-1
	Summerstown v West Norwood	wo/s
	Weybridge v Reigate Priory	2-2
	Woking v Kingston-on-Thames	1-1
12	2nd Royal Warwicks Regiment v Bridport	wo/s
	Boscombe v Longfleet St Marys	1-3
	Bournemouth v Bournemouth Wanderers	1-0
	Devizes Town v Bath City	5-1
	RGA Weymouth v Portland PO & Portland United	3-2
	Whiteheads (Weymouth) v Poole	7-1
7r	Leiston v Halesworth	2-1
9r	Kingston-on-Thames v Woking	0-0a
r	Reigate Priory v Weybridge	4-3
9r2	Kingston-on-Thames v Woking	3-2 N

Preliminary Round

6	North Staffordshire Casuals v Old Wulfrunians	1-3
7	4th Kings Royal Rifles - Bye	
	Chelmsford v Harwich & Parkeston	0-3
	Colchester Crown - Bye	
	Colchester Town - Bye	
	Cromer - Bye	
	Custom House v East Ham	n/a
	Great Yarmouth Town v Peterborough Town	4-1
	Ipswich Town v Beccles Caxton	4-2
	Kirkley v Bury Alexandra	7-0
	Leiston v Bury St Edmunds	2-1
	Leytonstone v Southend Athletic	2-0
	Lowestoft Town v Cambridge St Marys	2-1
	Norwich CEYMS - Bye	
	Peterborough GN Loco v King's Lynn	0-2
	South Weald v Leigh Ramblers	3-0
	Woodford v Barking	1-2

16

1906/07 to 1907/08

8	Luton Clarence v Leighton Cee Springs	4-1
	Maidenhead v Maidenhead Norfolkians	2-1
	Stony Stratford Town v Apsley	0-1
	Windsor & Eton v Marlow	1-0
9	3rd Kent RGA Volunteers v Croydon	1-4
	Bromley v Margate	3-1
	Clapham v Parthians (Clapham)	1-4
	Dartford v Royal Engineers Depot Battn	1-1
	Lee v Croydon Wanderers	wo/s
	Margate St Johns Guild v Ramsgate St Georges	3-2
	Metrogas v Guards Depot (Caterham)	2-2
	Nunhead - Bye	
	Old Tiffinian v Godalming	2-2
	Ramsgate Town v Margate Holy Trinity	2-1
	Redhill v Kingston-on-Thames	3-2
	Reigate Priory v Guildford	2-0
	Royal Engineers v Dorking	1-2
	Summerstown v Hatcham Athletic	2-1
	Wimbledon v Norwood Association	1-1
	Woolwich Polytechnic v Plumstead St Johns Institute	3-5
11	Bowes Park v Page Green Old Boys	3-2
	Enfield v Crouch End Vampires	2-2
	Finchley v Clove	3-1
	Hampstead v Richmond Association	n/a
	Highgate v Casuals	1-2
	Ware v Barnet Alston Athletic	2-2
12	2nd Lincolnshire Regiment v Basingstoke	4-0
	2nd Royal Warwicks Regiment v RGA Weymouth	3-1
	Alton - Bye	
	Bournemouth v Radipole	3-1
	Bristol St Philips - Bye	
	Cheltenham Town v Warmley Amateurs	5-1
	Chippenham Town v Wells City	1-1
	Frome Town v Haydon Street Workmen	3-2
	Gosport United - Bye	
	Longfleet St Marys v Branksome Gasworks Athletic	1-1
	Paulton Rovers - Bye	
	Radstock Town v Devizes Town	5-0
	Ryde - Bye	
	Swindon Amateurs v Wantage Town	n/a
	Welton Rovers - Bye	
	Whiteheads (Weymouth) v Weymouth	10-0
9r	Dartford v Royal Engineers Depot Battn	2-0
r	Godalming v Old Tiffinian	4-2
r	Metrogas v Guards Depot (Caterham)	1-2
r	Norwood Association v Wimbledon	1-2
11r	Barnet Alston Athletic v Ware	5-1
r	Crouch End Vampires v Enfield	1-3
12r	Branksome Gasworks Athletic v Longfleet St Marys	1-1e
r	Wells City v Chippenham Town	5-4e
12r2	Branksome Gasworks Athletic v Longfleet St Marys	1-2

Qualifying Round One

1	Leadgate Park v Crook Town	0-5
	Stanley United v Rutherford College	4-1
	West Auckland v Eldon Albion	3-1
5	New Brighton Tower Amateurs v Fleetwood Ams	2-1
	Old Xaverians v Liverpool Balmoral	1-1
6	Bridgford Athletic v Mansfield Amateurs	1-0
	Burton Casuals v Handsworth Oakhill	0-7
	Notts Magdala v Notts Magdala Amateurs	0-0
	Old Wulfrunians v Birmingham University Assoc.	1-1
	Stamford Town v Spalding Town	wo/s
7	4th Kings Royal Rifles v Colchester Crown	6-0
	Barking v South Weald	2-2
	Custom House v Leytonstone	2-2
	Harwich & Parkeston v Colchester Town	3-0
	Ipswich Town v Kirkley	9-0
	King's Lynn v Great Yarmouth Town	3-1
	Lowestoft Town v Leiston	3-0
	Norwich CEYMS v Cromer	1-2
8	Apsley v Dunstable Rangers	0-3
	Aylesbury United v Wycombe Wanderers	2-3
	Chesham Town v Chesham Generals	3-3
	Hanwell v Hounslow	1-6
	Reading Amateurs v Windsor & Eton	3-1
	Slough v Maidenhead	3-2
	Staines v Uxbridge	1-3
	Wolverton Town v Luton Clarence	1-0 v
9	Bromley v Dartford	4-1
	Croydon v Plumstead St Johns Institute	3-0
	Godalming v Reigate Priory	2-1
	Margate St Johns Guild v Ramsgate Town	3-3
	Nunhead v Lee	3-3
	Parthians (Clapham) v Summerstown	0-1
	Redhill v Dorking	2-2
	Wimbledon v Guards Depot (Caterham)	1-2
10	Eastbourne v Newhaven	9-2
	Hastings Amateurs v Tunbridge Wells	4-0
	Helmston (Brighton) v Hove	3-1
	Hove Park v Horsham	7-1
	Littlehampton v Bognor	6-0
	Worthing v Shoreham	3-1
11	1st Scots Guards v Richmond Association	2-3
	Casuals v St Albans Abbey	3-3
	Enfield v Bowes Park	3-1
	Finchley v London Caledonians	2-3
	Hoddesdon v Barnet Alston Athletic	0-3
	Olympic v Great Western Railway Athletic	1-1
	Shepherds Bush (1) v Marcians	3-0
	Sutton Court v Marlborough (Acton)	6-0
12	2nd Royal Warwicks Rgmt v Whiteheads (Weymouth)	1-0
	Alton v 2nd Lincolnshire Regiment	0-7
	Bournemouth v Longfleet St Marys	2-1
	Bristol St Philips v Cheltenham Town	2-1
	Frome Town v Swindon Amateurs	2-0
	Gosport United v Ryde	2-2
	Paulton Rovers v Welton Rovers	3-1
	Radstock Town v Wells City	4-2
5r	Liverpool Balmoral v Old Xaverians	1-4
6r	Birmingham University Assoc. v Old Wulfrunians	0-5
r	Notts Magdala Amateurs v Notts Magdala	1-3e
7r	Leytonstone v Custom House	4-2
r	South Weald v Barking	1-1a
8r	Chesham Generals v Chesham Town	1-2
r	Luton Clarence v Wolverton Town	6-0
9r	Dorking v Redhill	3-3
r	Lee v Nunhead	1-4
r	Ramsgate Town v Margate St Johns Guild	2-1
11r	Great Western Railway Athletic v Olympic	5-3
r	St Albans Abbey v Casuals	wo/s
12r	Ryde v Gosport United	4-0
7r2	Barking v South Weald	4-1 N
9r2	Redhill v Dorking	4-1 N

Qualifying Round Two

1	Croft v Shildon Athletic	0-2
	Darlington St Augustines v Spennymoor United	0-2
	Riley Bros v Crook Town	1-5
	Stanley United v West Auckland	0-0
2	Saltburn v Whitby	4-0
4	Bradford Airedale v York NER United	5-3
5	Buxton - Bye	
	Fairfield (Buxton) - Bye	
	New Brighton Tower Amateurs v Manchester Univ.	4-2
	Old Xaverians v Hesketh Park	n/a
6	Loughborough Corinthians - Bye	
	Notts Magdala v Bridgford Athletic	1-1
	Old Wulfrunians v Handsworth Oakhill	wo/s
	Stamford Town v Grantham West End Albion	6-2
7	Harwich & Parkeston v 4th Kings Royal Rifles	1-3
	Ipswich Town v Lowestoft Town	6-0
	King's Lynn v Cromer	4-0
	Leytonstone v Barking	2-1
8	Dunstable Rangers v Luton Clarence	3-5
	Slough v Reading Amateurs	1-4
	Uxbridge v Hounslow	2-0
	Wycombe Wanderers v Chesham Town	4-2
9	Bromley v Ramsgate Town	9-2
	Croydon v Nunhead	wo/s
	Godalming v Redhill	1-1
	Guards Depot (Caterham) v Summerstown	1-5
10	Eastbourne v Hastings Amateurs	8-0
	Hastings Rock-a-Nore v Brighton Amateurs	4-0
	Littlehampton v Helmston (Brighton)	1-4
	Worthing v Hove Park	5-3
11	Enfield v Barnet Alston Athletic	2-2
	London Caledonians v St Albans Abbey	1-1
	Richmond Association v Great Western Railway Ath.	2-2
	Shepherds Bush (1) v Sutton Court	4-1
12	2nd Lincolnshire Regiment v Ryde	2-0
	2nd Royal Warwicks Regiment v Bournemouth	wo/s
	Bristol St Philips v Paulton Rovers	1-4
	Frome Town v Radstock Town	0-4
1r	West Auckland v Stanley United	0-0
6r	Bridgford Athletic v Notts Magdala	2-1
9r	Redhill v Godalming	6-0
11r	Barnet Alston Athletic v Enfield	2-1
r	Great Western Railway Ath. v Richmond Association	1-1
r	St Albans Abbey v London Caledonians	0-1
1r2	Stanley United v West Auckland	3-2e
11r2	Richmond Association v Great Western Railway Ath.	3-1 N

Qualifying Round Three

1	Crook Town v Shildon Athletic	6-3
	Stanley United v Spennymoor United	4-4
2	Saltburn v Scarborough	2-0
	Skinningrove United v Redcar Crusaders	4-0
4	Bradford Airedale v Sheffield Grasshoppers	1-3
	Rotherham Amateurs v Brunswick Institute	5-0
5	Fairfield (Buxton) v Buxton	1-2
	New Brighton Tower Amateurs v Old Xaverians	2-1
6	Bridgford Athletic v Old Wulfrunians	1-1
	Loughborough Corinthians v Stamford Town	7-1
7	King's Lynn v Ipswich Town	4-0
	Leytonstone v 4th Kings Royal Rifles	5-1
8	Reading Amateurs v Uxbridge	5-1
	Wycombe Wanderers v Luton Clarence	5-0
9	Bromley v Croydon	5-0
	Redhill v Summerstown	4-0
10	Eastbourne v Hastings Rock-a-Nore	8-1
	Worthing v Helmston (Brighton)	1-2
11	Richmond Association v Barnet Alston Athletic	1-2
	Shepherds Bush (1) v London Caledonians	0-1
12	2nd Lincolnshire Rgmt v 2nd Royal Warwicks Rgmt	5-1
	Radstock Town v Paulton Rovers	2-2
1r	Spennymoor United v Stanley United	1-2
6r	Old Wulfrunians v Bridgford Athletic	1-4
12r	Paulton Rovers v Radstock Town	4-0

Qualifying Round Four

1	Crook Town v Stanley United	0-2
2	Skinningrove United v Saltburn	0-2
3	Romanby (Northallerton) - Bye	
4	Sheffield Grasshoppers v Rotherham Amateurs	0-2
5	New Brighton Tower Amateurs v Buxton	1-0
6	Bridgford Athletic v Loughborough Corinthians	1-3
7	King's Lynn v Leytonstone	3-0
8	Wycombe Wanderers v Reading Amateurs	1-0e
9	Bromley v Redhill	2-2
10	Eastbourne v Helmston (Brighton)	7-1
11	Barnet Alston Athletic v London Caledonians	0-0a
12	Paulton Rovers v 2nd Lincolnshire Regiment	0-1
9r	Redhill v Bromley	0-0a
11r	Barnet Alston Athletic v London Caledonians	wo/s
9r2	Redhill v Bromley	3-1 N

Round One

	2nd Lincolnshire Regiment v Wanstead	5-0
	Barnet Alston Athletic v Cheshunt (1)	4-0
	Bishop Auckland v Loughborough Corinthians	4-1
	Civil Service v Ealing	3-2
	Eastbourne v Clapton	1-2
	Ilford v New Crusaders	1-1
	King's Lynn v Dulwich Hamlet	1-3
	New Brighton Tower Amateurs v Northern Nomads	1-2
	Redhill v Oxford City	1-4
	Romanby (Northallerton) v Rotherham Amateurs	0-5
	Saltburn v Grangetown Athletic	1-0 D
	Sheffield v Darlington	4-2
	Stanley United v Notts Jardines	1-1
	Stockton v Blackburn Crosshill	8-1
	West Hartlepool v South Bank	1-1
	Wycombe Wanderers v 2nd Grenadier Guards	3-5
r	New Crusaders v Ilford	4-1
r	Notts Jardines v Stanley United	2-3
r	South Bank v West Hartlepool	3-1

Round Two

	2nd Lincolnshire Regiment v Barnet Alston Athletic	3-2
	Bishop Auckland v Grangetown Athletic	5-2
	Clapton v 2nd Grenadier Guards	1-0
	Dulwich Hamlet v Civil Service	0-5
	New Crusaders v Oxford City	0-1
	Northern Nomads v South Bank	0-0
	Sheffield v Rotherham Amateurs	1-2
	Stockton v Stanley United	2-0
r	South Bank v Northern Nomads	4-1

Round Three

	Civil Service v 2nd Lincolnshire Regiment	3-1 N
	Clapton v Oxford City	1-0
	South Bank v Bishop Auckland	1-1
	Stockton v Rotherham Amateurs	1-1
r	Bishop Auckland v South Bank	0-2
r	Rotherham Amateurs v Stockton	0-1

Semi Finals

	Clapton v Civil Service	1-0 N
	Stockton v South Bank	1-0 N

Final

	Clapton v Stockton	2-1 N

1907/08

Qualifying Round One

11	Leigh Ramblers v Custom House	0-4
	South East Ham v Newportonians	0-1
12	1st Scots Guards v Page Green Old Boys	4-1
	Sutton Court v Waltham Glendale	4-2
13	Great Western Railway Athletic v Hanwell	2-4
	Slough v Uxbridge	2-3
	Staines v Hounslow	4-1
	Windsor & Eton v 1st Grenadier Guards	4-2
19	Farncombe v Southfields	1-6
20	Burgess Hill v Helmston (Brighton)	1-3
	Shoreham v Newhaven	9-2
	Southwick v Littlehampton	2-0
	Worthing v Horsham	8-2
21	Basingstoke v RFA Farnborough	2-4
	North Hants Ironworks v Farnham	1-0
	Royal Engineers (Aldershot) v 1st Cheshire Rgmt	2-3
22	Boscombe v Branksome Gasworks Athletic	2-2
	Bournemouth Wanderers v Longfleet St Marys	3-0
	Portland PO & Portland U v Whiteheads (Weymouth)	0-2
23	Bath City v Wells City	4-1
	Frome Town v Camerton	1-0
22r	Branksome Gasworks Athletic v Boscombe	0-2

1907/08 to 1908/09

Qualifying Round Two

1	Eston United v Redcar Crusaders	6-0
	Guisborough Red Rose v Charlton Rovers	0-0
	North Skelton v Brotton	wo/s
	Skinningrove United v Saltburn	2-3
2	Eldon Albion v Croft	1-0
	Leadgate Park v Darlington Trinity	1-1
	Rutherford College v Darlington St Augustines	1-5
	Spennymoor United v Stockton OB	8-1
3	Beverley Town v Scarborough	3-7
	Northallerton v Kellbank Rangers	1-1
	Rotherham Amateurs v Holy Guild (Sheffield)	1-4
	Sheffield Grasshoppers v Leeds Amateurs	4-5
4	Haslington v Liverpool Balmoral	n/a
	Tottington v Manchester University	n/a
5	Mansfield Amateurs v Basford United	3-4
	Notts Jardines v Bridgford Athletic	3-0
7	Atherstone Town v North Stafford Nomads	10-3
	Leicester Nomads v Uppingham	9-2
	Long Eaton Waverley v Loughborough Corinthians	3-1
	Old Wulfrunians v Aston Old Edwardians	8-1
8	Cambridge St Marys v Chatteris Engineering Works	0-1
	St Ives Town v St Neots	4-1
	Stamford Town v Grantham West End Albion	2-1
9	Kirkley v Great Yarmouth Town	3-0
	Leiston v Beccles Caxton	3-2
	Norwich CEYMS v Cromer	1-2
	Orwell Works v Haverhill Rovers	5-1
10	Chelmsford v Chelmsford Swifts	2-0
	Colchester Town v 4th Kings Royal Rifles	3-4
11	East Ham v Wanstead	1-5
	Limehouse Town v Barking	0-3
	Manor Park Albion v Newportonians	2-1
	Woodford v Custom House	0-3
12	Clove v Tufnell Park	3-2
	Enfield v 1st Scots Guards	1-3
	Sutton Court v Finchley	1-6
	West Hampstead v Ware	1-0
13	Hanwell v Uxbridge	3-0
	Luton Clarence v Watford Victoria Works	1-0
	St Albans Abbey - Bye	
	Staines v Windsor & Eton	1-1
15	Maidstone Church Institute v 1st Royal Scots Guards	2-2
	Ramsgate Town v Margate Holy Trinity	7-2
16	Deptford Invicta v Plumstead St Johns Institute	2-0
	Rochester v Crayford	3-2
17	Chesham Generals v Thame	3-4
18	Dorking v Redhill	5-1
	Leatherhead v Norwood Association	2-2
19	Polytechnic v Clapham	1-0
	Summerstown v Southfields	2-1
	Walton-on-Thames v Wimbledon	3-2
	Woking v Kingston-on-Thames	0-0
20	Hailsham v Hastings Rock-a-Nore	2-3
	Shoreham v Helmston (Brighton)	5-1
	Southwick v Worthing	2-4
	Tunbridge Wells v Eastbourne St Marys	4-4
21	2nd Lincolnshire Regiment v 1st Cheshire Regiment	n/a
	Gosport United v Cowes	3-2
	North Hants Ironworks v RFA Farnborough	0-0
	Ryde v United Services Officers	4-2
22	Bournemouth v Bournemouth Wanderers	6-0
	Poole v Boscombe	0-2
	RGA Weymouth v Radipole	0-3
	Whiteheads (Weymouth) v Weymouth	5-0
23	Frome Town v Welton Rovers	4-3
	Haydon Street Workmen v Chippenham Town	1-3
	Shepton Mallet Town v Bath City	1-2
	Wantage Town - Bye	
24	Bristol St Philips v Clevedon	2-2
1r	Charlton Rovers v Guisborough Red Rose	2-1
2r	Darlington Trinity v Leadgate Park	2-2
3r	Kellbank Rangers v Northallerton	1-0
13r	Windsor & Eton v Staines	4-2
15r	1st Royal Scots Guards v Maidstone Church Institute	3-0
18r	Leatherhead v Norwood Association	1-1e
19r	Kingston-on-Thames v Woking	2-1
20r	Tunbridge Wells v Eastbourne St Marys	4-0
21r	RFA Farnborough v North Hants Ironworks	5-1
24r	Clevedon v Bristol St Philips	1-1
2r2	Darlington Trinity v Leadgate Park	wo/s
18r2	Leatherhead v Norwood Association	0-2
24r2	Bristol St Philips v Clevedon	0-0 N
24r3	Clevedon v Bristol St Philips	5-3

Qualifying Round Three

1	Charlton Rovers v North Skelton	3-2
	Saltburn v Eston United	3-2
2	Darlington St Augustines v Darlington Trinity	5-0
	Spennymoor United v Eldon Albion	4-2
3	Kellbank Rangers v Holy Guild (Sheffield)	3-2
	Scarborough v Leeds Amateurs	16-1
4	Manchester University v unknown	n/a
	Old Xaverians v New Brighton Tower Amateurs	2-4
5	Basford United v Sneinton	0-0
	Notts Magdala Amateurs v Notts Jardines	2-4
7	Leicester Nomads v Long Eaton Waverley	0-1
	Old Wulfrunians v Atherstone Town	1-2
8	St Ives Town v Chatteris Engineering Works	0-4
	Stamford Albion v Stamford Town	1-1
9	Cromer v Kirkley	0-5
	Orwell Works v Leiston	6-0
10	Colchester Crown v Chelmsford	4-2
	Harwich & Parkeston v 4th Kings Royal Rifles	3-9
11	Custom House v Barking	0-0
	Wanstead v Manor Park Albion	2-9
12	Finchley v Clove	2-0
	West Hampstead v 1st Scots Guards	0-1
13	Luton Clarence v St Albans Abbey	wo/s
	Windsor & Eton v Hanwell	2-1
14	Maidenhead v Caversham Rovers	3-2
	Reading Grovelands v Abingdon	3-2
15	Margate v Ramsgate Town	1-6
	Margate St Johns Guild v 1st Royal Scots Guards	0-2
16	Cray Wanderers v Dartford	4-5
	Deptford Invicta v Rochester	3-0
17	Chesham Town v Stony Stratford Town	9-0
	Thame v Aylesbury United	1-2
18	Balham v Bohemians	5-1
	Norwood Association v Dorking	0-2
19	Summerstown v Kingston-on-Thames	1-1
	Walton-on-Thames v Polytechnic	3-2
20	Tunbridge Wells v Hastings Rock-a-Nore	1-3
	Worthing v Shoreham	4-1
21	2nd Lincolnshire Regiment v RFA Farnborough	0-0
	Ryde v Gosport United	5-2
22	Bournemouth v Boscombe	5-1
	Whiteheads (Weymouth) v Radipole	1-0
23	Bath City v Frome Town	0-4
	Wantage Town v Chippenham Town	wo/s
24	Clevedon v Gloucester City	5-1
	Paulton Rovers v Warmley Amateurs	5-1
5r	Sneinton v Basford United	2-1
8r	Stamford Town v Stamford Albion	3-1
11r	Barking v Custom House	0-2
19r	Kingston-on-Thames v Summerstown	1-4
21r	RFA Farnborough v 2nd Lincolnshire Regiment	0-2

Qualifying Round Four

1	Charlton Rovers v Saltburn	2-2
2	Darlington St Augustines v Spennymoor United	0-1
3	Scarborough v Kellbank Rangers	4-1
4	Manchester University v New Brighton Tower Ams	4-1
5	Sneinton v Notts Jardines	2-1
6	Fairfield (Buxton) v Buxton	1-6
7	Atherstone Town v Long Eaton Waverley	7-0
8	Stamford Town v Chatteris Engineering Works	2-2
9	Orwell Works v Kirkley	0-6
10	Colchester Crown v 4th Kings Royal Rifles	0-7
11	Custom House v Manor Park Albion	3-0
12	1st Scots Guards v Finchley	6-0
13	Windsor & Eton v Luton Clarence	2-1
14	Reading Grovelands v Maidenhead	3-3
15	Ramsgate Town v 1st Royal Scots Guards	0-1
16	Dartford v Deptford Invicta	2-4
17	Chesham Town v Aylesbury United	9-4
18	Balham v Dorking	4-4
19	Summerstown v Walton-on-Thames	2-1
20	Worthing v Hastings Rock-a-Nore	4-2
21	Ryde v 2nd Lincolnshire Regiment	1-2
22	Bournemouth v Whiteheads (Weymouth)	2-3
23	Wantage Town v Frome Town	wo/s
24	Paulton Rovers v Clevedon	4-2
1r	Saltburn v Charlton Rovers	7-1
8r	Chatteris Engineering Works v Stamford Town	2-3
14r	Maidenhead v Reading Grovelands	2-2
18r	Dorking v Balham	3-1
14r2	Reading Grovelands v Maidenhead	1-0

Round One

	2nd Grenadier Guards v Guildford	2-2
	2nd Lincolnshire Regiment v Dorking	0-3
	Apsley v 1st Royal Scots Guards	1-1
	Atherstone Town v Notts Magdala	4-1
	Bromley v West Norwood	2-2
	Clapton v 4th Kings Royal Rifles	4-1
	Custom House v South Weald	1-0
	Darlington v West Auckland	0-2
	Dulwich Hamlet v 1st Scots Guards	0-0
	Guards Depot (Caterham) v Deptford Invicta	0-2
	Ilford v Romford (1)	3-2
	King's Lynn v Kirkley	3-0
	Leytonstone v Upton Park	5-1
	London Caledonians v Nunhead	0-3
	Lowestoft Town v Stamford Town	0-0
	Manchester University v Northern Nomads	1-2
	Marlow v Maidenhead Norfolkians	1-4
	Radstock Town v Whiteheads (Weymouth)	4-1
	Reading Amateurs v Wycombe Wanderers	0-0
	Reading Grovelands v Oxford City	2-4
	Royal Engineers Depot Battn v Barnet Alston Athletic	0-0
	Saltburn v Grangetown Athletic	1-1
	Scarborough v Spennymoor United	0-1
	Sheffield v Blackburn Crosshill	0-0
	Shepherds Bush (1) v Chesham Town	2-0
	Sneinton v Buxton	2-1
	South Bank v Crook Town	2-1
	Stockton v Stanley United	1-1
	Wantage Town v Paulton Rovers	1-2
	West Hartlepool v Bishop Auckland	0-3
	Windsor & Eton v Summerstown	2-0
	Worthing v Godalming	5-0
r	1st Royal Scots Guards v Apsley	3-0
r	1st Scots Guards v Dulwich Hamlet	2-2
r	Barnet Alston Athletic v Royal Engineers Depot Battn	2-4
r	Blackburn Crosshill v Sheffield	1-0
r	Grangetown Athletic v Saltburn	2-0
r	Guildford v 2nd Grenadier Guards	0-2
r	Stamford Town v Lowestoft Town	3-0
r	Stanley United v Stockton	0-1
r	West Norwood v Bromley	0-2
r	Wycombe Wanderers v Reading Amateurs	5-3
r2	Dulwich Hamlet v 1st Scots Guards	3-4

Round Two

	1st Royal Scots Guards v Bromley	2-0
	2nd Grenadier Guards v Shepherds Bush (1)	2-2
	Atherstone Town v Sneinton	3-0
	Custom House v King's Lynn	4-1
	Deptford Invicta v Nunhead	2-1
	Dorking v Worthing	1-4
	Grangetown Athletic v West Auckland	0-2
	Ilford v Stamford Town	8-0
	Leytonstone v Clapton	1-1
	Maidenhead Norfolkians v Wycombe Wanderers	6-0
	Oxford City v Windsor & Eton	5-0
	Paulton Rovers v Radstock Town	4-1
	Royal Engineers Depot Battn v 1st Scots Guards	4-0
	South Bank v Northern Nomads	1-1
	Spennymoor United v Bishop Auckland	1-1
	Stockton v Blackburn Crosshill	8-0
r	Bishop Auckland v Spennymoor United	3-1
r	Clapton v Leytonstone	2-0
r	Northern Nomads v South Bank	4-2
r	Shepherds Bush (1) v 2nd Grenadier Guards	1-0

Round Three

	Bishop Auckland v West Auckland	3-1
	Clapton v 1st Royal Scots Guards	2-3
	Maidenhead Norfolkians v Ilford	2-6
	Oxford City v Deptford Invicta	6-2
	Paulton Amateurs v Atherstone Town	2-2
	Royal Engineers Depot Battn v Shepherds Bush (1)	3-0
	Stockton v Northern Nomads	3-1
	Worthing v Custom House	6-0
r	Atherstone Town v Paulton Rovers	1-0

Round Four

	Atherstone Town v Oxford City	2-1
	Ilford v 1st Royal Scots Guards	1-1
	Royal Engineers Depot Battn v Worthing	1-1
	Stockton v Bishop Auckland	5-3
r	1st Royal Scots Guards v Alford	1-0
r	Worthing v Royal Engineers Depot Battn	0-1

Semi Finals

	Royal Engineers Depot Bn v 1st Royal Scots Guards	2-0 N
	Stockton v Atherstone Town	3-0 N

Final

	Royal Engineers Depot Battn v Stockton	2-1 N

1908/09

Preliminary Round

3	Hathersage v Nether Edge Amateurs	3-2

Qualifying Round One

2	Redcar Crusaders v Eston United	1-2
3	Hathersage v Sheffield Grasshoppers	1-2
	Knaresborough v Kellbank Rangers	9-2
	Potternewton St Martins v Leeds Amateurs	2-3
	Rotherham Amateurs v Woodseat Reform	wo/s
	York City v Withernsea	2-1
	York St Pauls v Hull Kingston Amateurs	3-0
10	Barking v Woodford	7-0
	North Woolwich v Shoeburyness Garrison	3-2
13	Southall v Sutton Court	1-1
	Staines v Yiewsley	1-1
	Uxbridge v City of Westminster	7-1
	Windsor & Eton v Hounslow	0-0
18	Redhill v Croydon	4-0
19	Summerstown v Clapham	4-2
	Wimbledon v Kingston-on-Thames	0-3
21	Basingstoke v 2nd Scottish Rifles	0-2
	Royal Engineers (Aldershot) v North Hants Ironworks	7-0
	Ryde v RMLI Gosport	2-0
22	Longfleet St Marys v Boscombe	3-1
	Poole v Branksome Gasworks Athletic	6-1
	Portland PO & Portland U v Tavistock Battery RFA	2-0
24	Bradford-on-Avon v Camerton	1-0
13r	Hounslow v Windsor & Eton	0-1
r	Sutton Court v Southall	1-3e
r	Yiewsley v Staines	5-0

1908/09 to 1909/10

Qualifying Round Two

1 Cockfield v Langley Park	1-1
Esh Winning Rangers v Darlington Trinity	5-0
Sedgefield Town v Croft	n/a
West Hartlepool Expansion v Rutherford College	5-3
2 Eston United v Thornaby St Patricks	2-1
Grangetown Athletic v Saltburn	3-1
Skinningrove United v Charlton Rovers	3-0
Whitby Shamrock v Marske Parish Church	2-1
3 Knaresborough v Rotherham Amateurs	4-1
Leeds Amateurs v Sheffield Grasshoppers	2-4
Scarborough v Beverley Town	1-1
York St Pauls v York City	1-3
4 Blackburn Crosshill v Tottington	1-1
Liverpool Balmoral v Old Xaverians	1-1
5 Basford United v Netherfield Rangers	0-1
Notts Jardines v South Nottingham	2-4
6 Old Wulfrunians v Loughborough Corinthians	0-0
7 Stamford Albion v St Neots	1-0 v
8 Carrow Works v Norwich CEYMS	0-3
Great Yarmouth Town v Gorleston	3-1
Leiston v Beccles Caxton	5-1
Lowestoft Town v Cromer	1-0
9 Chelmsford v Colchester Crown	6-2
Colchester Town v Harwich & Parkeston	1-1
10 Custom House v Wanstead	0-2
East Ham v Barking	2-3
Grays Athletic v North Woolwich	3-1
Limehouse Town v South East Ham	wo/s
11 Waltham Glendale v Hoddesdon	1-3
Ware v Enfield	4-0
12 1st Scots Guards v St Albans City	8-1
Finchley v Apsley	1-1
Tufnell Park v 3rd Grenadier Guards	6-1
West Hampstead v 2nd Coldstream Guards	4-2
13 Slough v Hanwell	2-2
Southall v 1st Grenadier Guards	4-3
Uxbridge v Yiewsley	2-0
Windsor & Eton v Great Western Railway Athletic	6-0
14 Abingdon v Maidenhead Norfolkians	2-4
Marlow v Maidenhead	5-2
Reading Grovelands v Caversham Rovers	1-1
Wycombe Wanderers v Thame	9-1
16 Charlton Albion v Plumstead St Johns	3-2
Foots Cray v Woolwich Polytechnic	2-1
Rochester v Wolseley (Crayford)	wo/s
17 Luton Celtic v Leighton Town	1-2
18 Dorking v Norwood Association	6-0
Godalming v Guildford	3-1
Leatherhead v East Grinstead	2-1
Redhill v Guards Depot (Caterham)	3-0
19 Chertsey v Metrogas Athletic	2-4
Farncombe v Kingston-on-Thames	0-3
Old Kingstonians v Polytechnic	6-1
Summerstown v Walton-on-Thames	4-1
20 Littlehampton v Horsham	2-0
Rye v Hastings Rock-a-Nore	1-0
Shoreham v Bognor	10-1
Southwick v Hailsham	7-1
21 2nd Scottish Rifles v RAMC Aldershot	1-0
Cowes v 87th Royal Irish Fusiliers	3-1
RFA Farnborough v Ryde	4-2
Royal Engineers (Aldershot) v Farnham	2-0
22 Bournemouth Wanderers v Weymouth	3-1
Longfleet St Marys v Bournemouth	0-3
Poole v Portland PO & Portland United	5-1
Radipole v RGA Weymouth	1-2
23 Wantage Town v Haydon Street Workmen	3-0
24 Bradford-on-Avon v Paulton Rovers	1-1
Street v Bath City	0-1
Wells City v Clevedon	1-4
Welton Rovers v Frome Town	4-0
1r Langley Park v Cockfield	3-0
3r Scarborough v Beverley Town	4-0
4r Old Xaverians v Liverpool Balmoral	n/a
r Tottington v Blackburn Crosshill	n/a
6r Loughborough Corinthians v Old Wulfrunians	3-1
7r St Neots v Stamford Albion	2-3
9r Harwich & Parkeston v Colchester Town	1-3
12r Apsley v Finchley	3-1
13r Slough v Hanwell	2-3
14r Caversham Rovers v Reading Grovelands	6-3
24r Paulton Rovers v Bradford-on-Avon	4-2

Qualifying Round Three

1 Croft v Langley Park	3-2
West Hartlepool Expansion v Esh Winning Rangers	3-2
2 Eston United v Whitby Shamrock	2-0
Grangetown Athletic v Skinningrove United	3-0
3 Scarborough v York City	2-2
Sheffield Grasshoppers v Knaresborough	0-2
4 Manchester University v Liverpool Balmoral	4-1
Tottington v New Brighton Tower Amateurs	1-2
5 Notts Olympic v South Nottingham	0-3
Southwell Town v Netherfield Rangers	2-7
6 Bournville Athletic v Hoobrook Olympic	4-1
Loughborough Corinthians v Asbury Richmond	
7 Chesterton Laurels v Stamford Town	0-4
Stamford Albion v Chatteris Engineering Works	1-4
8 Great Yarmouth Town v Norwich CEYMS	1-0
Lowestoft Town v Leiston	6-0
9 Orwell Works v Chelmsford	1-2
South Weald v Colchester Town	2-1
10 Barking v Grays Athletic	wo/s
Limehouse Town v Wanstead	2-3
11 Clove v Hoddesdon	6-2
Ware v Page Green Old Boys	wo/s
12 1st Scots Guards v Tufnell Park	0-2
Apsley v West Hampstead	2-2a
13 Uxbridge v Southall	2-2
Windsor & Eton v Hanwell	0-2
14 Marlow v Caversham Rovers	0-1
Wycombe Wanderers v Maidenhead Norfolkians	4-3
15 Margate v 1st Leicestershire Regiment	2-5
Ramsgate Town v Maidstone Athletic	0-2
16 Foots Cray v Gravesend Amateurs	wo/s
Rochester v Charlton Albion	7-2
17 Aylesbury United v Chesham Generals	1-2
Leighton Town v Luton Clarence	3-7
18 Dorking v Leatherhead	1-0
Redhill v Godalming	3-1
19 Old Kingstonians v Kingston-on-Thames	4-5
Summerstown v Metrogas Athletic	2-4
20 Littlehampton v Shoreham	1-0
Rye v Southwick	2-4
21 2nd Scottish Rifles v Cowes	wo/s
RFA Farnborough v Royal Engineers (Aldershot)	1-1
22 Bournemouth Wanderers v Bournemouth	2-1
Poole v RGA Weymouth	4-1
23 Gloucester City v Wantage Town	wo/s
Hereford City v Swindon Amateurs	6-1
24 Clevedon v Bath City	wo/s
Paulton Rovers v Welton Rovers	0-2
3r York City v Scarborough	1-4
12r West Hampstead v Apsley	1-4
13r Southall v Uxbridge	0-1
21r Royal Engineers (Aldershot) v RFA Farnborough	0-4

Qualifying Round Four

1 Croft v West Hartlepool Expansion	3-5
2 Eston United v Grangetown Athletic	2-2
3 Knaresborough v Scarborough	1-2
4 New Brighton Tower Ams v Manchester University	3-1
5 South Nottingham v Netherfield Rangers	5-2
6 Bournville Athletic v Loughborough Corinthians	5-2
7 Chatteris Engineering Works v Stamford Town	3-1
8 Lowestoft Town v Great Yarmouth Town	1-1
9 Chelmsford v South Weald	4-2
10 Wanstead v Barking	1-3
11 Clove v Ware	1-2
12 Apsley v Tufnell Park	1-1
13 Uxbridge v Hanwell	2-2
14 Wycombe Wanderers v Caversham Rovers	3-4
15 1st Leicestershire Regiment v Maidstone Athletic	2-0
16 Foots Cray v Rochester	1-0
17 Luton Clarence v Chesham Generals	4-2
18 Redhill v Dorking	5-1
19 Metrogas Athletic v Kingston-on-Thames	3-2
20 Littlehampton v Southwick	1-5
21 2nd Scottish Rifles v RFA Farnborough	1-0
22 Poole v Bournemouth Wanderers	2-0
23 Gloucester City v Hereford City	2-4
24 Welton Rovers v Clevedon	1-1
2r Grangetown Athletic v Eston United	0-1
8r Great Yarmouth Town v Lowestoft Town	4-0
12r Tufnell Park v Apsley	4-1
13r Hanwell v Uxbridge	2-3
24r Clevedon v Welton Rovers	1-1e
24r2 Welton Rovers v Clevedon	3-3e
24r3 Clevedon v Welton Rovers	2-1

Round One

1st Leicestershire Regiment v Woking	2-1
4th Kings Royal Rifles v Ware	9-4
Barking v Cavendish	4-1
Bournville Athletic v Atherstone Town	1-5
Clapton v Newportonians	4-0
Crook Town v West Auckland	0-2
Darlington St Augustines v Bishop Auckland	4-2
Deptford Invicta v Bromley	2-2
Dulwich Hamlet v Foots Cray	4-0
Great Yarmouth Town v Chatteris Engineering Works	2-1
Hereford City v Clevedon	1-2
Ilford v Romford (1)	4-4
King's Lynn v Kirkley	2-0
Leytonstone v Barnet Alston Athletic	4-0
London Caledonians v Tufnell Park	1-2
Luton Clarence v Chesham Town	2-4
Metrogas Athletic v Nunhead	0-7
New Brighton Tower Amateurs v Preston Winckley	1-3
Northern Nomads v Sheffield	3-1
Oxford City v Uxbridge	4-1
Poole v 2nd Scottish Rifles	0-2
Reading Amateurs v Caversham Rovers	1-4
Redhill v Shepherds Bush (1)	0-1
Royal Engineers Depot Battn v West Norwood	1-0
South Bank v West Hartlepool Expansion	4-1
South Nottingham v Sneinton	3-0
Stanley United v Leadgate Park	4-2
Stockton v Eston United	1-2
Upton Park v 2nd Grenadier Guards	2-1
West Hartlepool v Scarborough	8-2
Whiteheads (Weymouth) v Radstock Town	4-0
Worthing v Southwick	3-1
r Bromley v Deptford Invicta	4-1
r Romford (1) v Ilford	0-1

Round Two

2nd Scottish Rifles v Shepherds Bush (1)	2-1
4th Kings Royal Rifles v Ilford	1-1
Barking v Upton Park	3-0
Chesham Town v Caversham Rovers	5-1
Clevedon v Whiteheads (Weymouth)	3-0
Darlington St Augustines v Northern Nomads	2-0 v
Dulwich Hamlet v 1st Leicestershire Regiment	3-1
Eston United v Preston Winckley	3-0
Great Yarmouth Town v Clapton	0-1
King's Lynn v Leytonstone	2-2
Nunhead v Worthing	2-0
Royal Engineers Depot Battn v Bromley	0-0
South Nottingham v Atherstone Town	n/a
Tufnell Park v Oxford City	3-2
West Auckland v Stanley United	4-0 v
West Hartlepool v South Bank	1-4
r Atherstone Town v South Nottingham	2-0
r Bromley v Royal Engineers Depot Battn	2-0
r Ilford v 4th Kings Royal Rifles	5-2
r Leytonstone v King's Lynn	2-1
r Northern Nomads v Darlington St Augustines	2-2
r Stanley United v West Auckland	0-2
r2 Darlington St Augustines v Northern Nomads	1-2 N

Round Three

2nd Scottish Rifles v Atherstone Town	2-2
Bromley v Ilford	4-2
Clapton v Tufnell Park	5-1
Clevedon v Barking	1-2
Dulwich Hamlet v Chesham Town	2-0
Eston United v West Auckland	4-2
Leytonstone v Nunhead	2-1
South Bank v Northern Nomads	1-0
r Atherstone Town v 2nd Scottish Rifles	3-1

Round Four

Atherstone Town v Barking	6-1
Dulwich Hamlet v Bromley	3-0
Leytonstone v Clapton	1-8
South Bank v Eston United	1-2

Semi Finals

Clapton v Atherstone Town	3-0 N
Eston United v Dulwich Hamlet	2-1 N

Final

Clapton v Eston United	6-0 N

1909/10

Qualifying Round One

1 Dorman Long & Co. United v Skinningrove United	2-0
Grangetown Athletic v Stockton Victoria	5-2
Redcar Victoria v Thornaby St Patricks	0-4
Saltburn v Whitby Shamrock	2-0
2 Esh Winning Rangers v Walker Church Institute	4-1
Leadgate Park v Leadgate Villa	7-0
Sedgefield Town v Stanley United	0-4
Tow Law Town v Willington Temperance	1-1
3 Bridlington Athletic v Grimsby Rovers Amateurs	1-4
Driffield Town v Filey United	3-5
Hull Day Street OB v Hull Kingston Amateurs	wo/s
9 Gorleston v Great Yarmouth Town	1-3
12 Hertford Town v St Albans City	2-5
Ware v Enfield	4-8
13 Gramophone v Polytechnic	1-2
Hanwell v Hounslow	wo/s
Ravenscourt Amateurs v City of Westminster	1-3
Southall v 1st Grenadier Guards	8-2
Staines v 3rd Grenadier Guards	4-5
Sutton Court v Yiewsley	5-0
Uxbridge v Fulham Amateurs	2-0
Windsor & Eton v 2nd Coldstream Guards	1-2
14 Henley v Abingdon	1-2
Slough v Maidenhead	3-4
Thame v Reading Amateurs	3-3
16 Catford Southend v Charlton Albion	1-0
19 Guildford v Tooting Graveney	1-3
Hersham United v Farnham	2-5
Wimbledon v Summerstown	3-2
Woking v Farncombe	4-0
20 Mount Pleasant (Tunbridge Wells) v Shoreham	1-6
21 16th Co. RGA v RMLI Gosport	3-4
1st Scots Guards v 87th Royal Irish Fusiliers	2-2
Cowes v Royal Engineers (Aldershot)	1-3
22 Boscombe v Pokesdown	5-2
Branksome Gasworks Athletic v RGA Weymouth	1-2
Weymouth v Longfleet St Marys	0-1

1909/10 to 1910/11

24	Frome Town v Devizes Town	1-1
	Wells City v Paulton Rovers	0-4
2r	Willington Temperance v Tow Law Town	4-2
13r	2nd Coldstream Guards v Windsor & Eton	2-1
14r	Thame v Reading Amateurs	2-2
21r	87th Royal Irish Fusiliers v 1st Scots Guards	2-1
24r	Devizes Town v Frome Town	2-1
14r2	Thame v Reading Amateurs	3-2

Qualifying Round Two

1	Cambridge House v Saltburn	1-1
	Grangetown Athletic v West Hartlepool Expansion	2-2
	Lazenby Institute v Dorman Long & Co. United	1-1
	Thornaby St Patricks v Charlton Rovers	n/a
2	Esh Winning Rangers v Rutherford College	6-1
	Leadgate Park v Langley Park	5-2
	Rise Carr Primitive Methodists v Rise Carr Rangers	1-0
	Willington Temperance v Stanley United	2-2a
3	Filey United v Grimsby Rovers Amateurs	1-1
	Heworth Parish Church v Kellbank Rangers	3-0
	Hull Day Street OB v Withernsea	3-0
	York St Pauls v York City	1-7
4	Rotherham Ams v Sheffield Commercial Travellers	2-1
	Sheffield Grasshoppers v Leeds St Martins	3-1
5	Manchester University v Blackburn Crosshill	n/a
	Tottington v Hesketh Park	n/a
8	Chatteris Engineering Works v St Neots	wo/s
	Hitchin v Leagrave United	2-1
	Luton Celtic v Luton Clarence	0-3
9	Fakenham v Cromer	4-2
	Kirkley v Great Yarmouth Town	2-2
	Lowestoft Town v Leiston	2-0
	Norwich CEYMS v Beccles Caxton	wo/s
10	Chelmsford v Colchester Crown	5-0
	South Weald v Harwich & Parkeston	4-0
11	Custom House v Woodford	5-2
	North Woolwich v East Ham	3-1
	Upton Park v Grays Athletic	5-2
	Wanstead v Romford United	2-5
12	Enfield v Finchley	3-4
	Hoddesdon v Waltham Glendale	0-6
	St Albans City v Tufnell Park	1-4
	Wood Green Town v West Hampstead	4-1
13	2nd Coldstream Guards v Sutton Court	2-3
	3rd Grenadier Guards v Hanwell	3-4
	Polytechnic v Southall	1-7
	Uxbridge v City of Westminster	4-1
14	Maidenhead Norfolkians v Caversham Rovers	2-2
	Marlow v Maidenhead	3-3
	Reading Grovelands v Wokingham Athletic	2-2
	Thame v Abingdon	1-0
16	1st Duke of Cornwall LI v Army Ordnance Corps	1-3
	Catford Southend v Metrogas Athletic	0-1
	Chatham Institute v Plumstead St Johns	1-2
	Woolwich Polytechnic v Beckenham Rovers	1-1
17	Leavesden Asylum v Aylesbury United	2-2
18	Leatherhead v Guards Depot (Caterham)	4-8
	Redhill v East Grinstead	4-0
19	Farnham v Godalming	5-1
	Tooting Graveney v Walton-on-Thames	4-0
	Wimbledon v Old Kingstonians	1-1
	Woking v Clapham	3-1
20	Horsham v Seaford	2-1
	Littlehampton v Rye	wo/s
	Southwick v Shoreham	1-2
	Worthing v Helmston (Brighton)	3-2
21	2nd Scottish Rifles v Ryde	wo/s
	87th Royal Irish Fusiliers v Basingstoke	7-6
	RAMC Aldershot v Royal Engineers (Aldershot)	1-0
	RMLI Gosport v 37th Co. RGA	4-0
22	Boscombe v Longfleet St Marys	2-2
	Bournemouth v Whiteheads (Weymouth)	wo/s
	Poole Wednesday v RGA Weymouth	3-0
	Portland v Bournemouth Wanderers	4-3
23	Stroud v Gloucester City	2-5
	Swindon Amateurs v Wantage Town	wo/s
24	Camerton v RGA Plymouth	1-1
	Devizes Town v Street	4-3
	Trowbridge Town v Clevedon	0-2
	Welton Rovers v Paulton Rovers	3-3
1r	Dorman Long & Co. United v Lazenby Institute	5-0
r	Saltburn v Cambridge House	2-2
r	West Hartlepool Expansion v Grangetown Athletic	3-1
2r	Stanley United v Willington Temperance	0-0e
3r	Grimsby Rovers Amateurs v Filey United	7-0
9r	Great Yarmouth Town v Kirkley	1-1
14r	Caversham Rovers v Maidenhead Norfolkians	2-2a
r	Maidenhead v Marlow	1-0
r	Wokingham Athletic v Reading Grovelands	5-2
16r	Beckenham Rovers v Woolwich Polytechnic	n/a
17r	Aylesbury United v Leavesden Asylum	2-2
19r	Old Kingstonians v Wimbledon	4-1
22r	Longfleet St Marys v Boscombe	4-2
24r	Paulton Rovers v Welton Rovers	1-1a
r	RGA Plymouth v Camerton	1-0
1r2	Saltburn v Cambridge House	2-1
2r2	Stanley United v Willington Temperance	0-1
9r2	Kirkley v Great Yarmouth Town	wo/s
14r2	Caversham Rovers v Maidenhead Norfolkians	7-1 N
17r2	Aylesbury United v Leavesden Asylum	1-1
24r2	Welton Rovers v Paulton Rovers	3-0
17r3	Aylesbury United v Leavesden Asylum	1-2

Qualifying Round Three

1	Dorman Long & Co. United v Thornaby St Patricks	2-0
	West Hartlepool Expansion v Saltburn	2-1
2	Esh Winning Rgs v Rise Carr Primitive Methodists	3-1
	Leadgate Park v Willington Temperance	3-2
3	Grimsby Rovers Amateurs v Heworth Parish Church	12-1
	York City v Hull Day Street OB	1-5
4	Rotherham Amateurs v Barnsley Corinthians	3-0
	Sheffield Grasshoppers v Nether Edge Amateurs	1-0
5	Liverpool Balmoral v Tottington	2-1
	New Brighton Tower Amateurs v Blackburn Crosshill	2-2
6	Mapperley v Bulwell Town	1-1
	Notts Rangers v Basford United	0-3
7	Old Wulfrunians v Atherstone Town	2-2
8	Chatteris Engineering Works v Luton Clarence	0-7
	Hitchin v Welwyn	2-0
9	Fakenham v Lowestoft Town	1-0
	Kirkley v Norwich CEYMS	2-4
10	Chelmsford v Orwell Works	8-1
	South Weald v Colchester Town	4-1
11	North Woolwich v Custom House	3-3
	Romford United v Upton Park	5-3
12	Finchley v Wood Green Town	3-6
	Waltham Glendale v Tufnell Park	1-5
13	Hanwell v Sutton Court	2-2
	Uxbridge v Southall	0-0
14	Thame v Caversham Rovers	1-3
	Wokingham Athletic v Maidenhead	1-1
15	Margate v Ramsgate Town	2-4
16	Metrogas Athletic v Plumstead St Johns	2-2
	Woolwich Polytechnic v Army Ordnance Corps	n/a
17	Apsley v Chesham Generals	5-3
	Leighton Town v Leavesden Asylum	2-1
18	Croydon v Redhill	2-2
	Dorking v Guards Depot (Caterham)	3-0
19	Farnham v Woking	0-2
	Tooting Graveney v Old Kingstonians	1-3
20	Shoreham v Littlehampton	12-3
	Worthing v Horsham	5-1
21	2nd Scottish Rifles v 87th Royal Irish Fusiliers	n/a
	RAMC Aldershot v RMLI Gosport	1-2
22	Bournemouth v Poole Wednesday	9-0
	Portland v Longfleet St Marys	3-1
23	Gloucester City v Swindon Amateurs	3-2
	Hereford City v Swindon Social Union	3-0
24	Clevedon v Devizes Town	3-0
	RGA Plymouth v Welton Rovers	2-2
5r	Blackburn Crosshill v New Brighton Tower Amateurs	0-1
6r	Bulwell Town v Mapperley	0-2
7r	Atherstone Town v Old Wulfrunians	2-1
11r	Custom House v North Woolwich	1-0
13r	Hanwell v Sutton Court	2-4
r	Southall v Uxbridge	0-1
14r	Maidenhead v Wokingham Athletic	1-0
16r	Plumstead St Johns v Metrogas Athletic	2-4
18r	Redhill v Croydon	2-0
24r	Welton Rovers v RGA Plymouth	2-1

Qualifying Round Four

1	West Hartlepool Expansion v Dorman Long & Co U	3-2 v
2	Leadgate Park v Esh Winning Rangers	1-0
3	Hull Day Street OB v Grimsby Rovers Amateurs	4-1
4	Sheffield Grasshoppers v Rotherham Amateurs	0-5
5	New Brighton Tower Amateurs v Liverpool Balmoral	3-2
6	Mapperley v Basford United	0-2
7	Asbury Richmond v Atherstone Town	1-7
8	Luton Clarence v Hitchin	6-3
9	Norwich CEYMS v Fakenham	3-1
10	South Weald v Chelmsford	1-0
11	Custom House v Romford United	1-0
12	Tufnell Park v Wood Green Town	0-0
13	Sutton Court v Uxbridge	0-4
14	Caversham Rovers v Maidenhead	3-1
15	Ramsgate Town v 1st Leicestershire Regiment	1-0
16	Metrogas Athletic v Woolwich Polytechnic	0-1
17	Leighton Town v Apsley	1-9
18	Dorking v Redhill	1-9
19	Woking v Old Kingstonians	5-1
20	Worthing v Shoreham	2-1
21	RMLI Gosport v 2nd Scottish Rifles	2-0
22	Bournemouth v Portland	6-1
23	Gloucester City v Hereford City	1-4
24	Clevedon v Welton Rovers	0-1
1r	West Hartlepool Expansion v Dorman Long & Co U	4-0
12r	Wood Green Town v Tufnell Park	1-1
12r2	Tufnell Park v Wood Green Town	1-0

Round One

Apsley v Luton Clarence	0-2
Atherstone Town v Sneinton	1-1
Bournemouth v Poole	3-0
Bromley v South Weald	2-0
Chesham Town v Oxford City	2-3
Clapton v London Caledonians	3-0
Custom House v 2nd Grenadier Guards	2-0
Hereford City v Welton Rovers	2-1
Hull Day Street OB v Notts Jardines	2-3
Ilford v Clove	3-0
Kingston-on-Thames v West Norwood	1-0
Leadgate Park v Darlington St Augustines	3-0
Leytonstone v Dulwich Hamlet	3-0
Newportonians v Barking	2-5
Northern Nomads v Rotherham Amateurs	5-0
Norwich CEYMS v King's Lynn	4-1
Nunhead v Woking	5-4
Ramsgate Town v Deptford Invicta	3-3
Redhill v Loughborough Corinthians	wo/s
Royal Engineers Depot Bn v Woolwich Polytechnic	2-2
Scarborough v New Brighton Tower Amateurs	1-0
Sheffield v Preston Winckley	2-5
Shepherds Bush (1) v Shoeburyness Garrison	2-2
South Bank v Bishop Auckland	2-0
South Nottingham v Basford United	4-0
Stockton v Crook Town	4-1
Tufnell Park v Romford (1)	2-1 v
Uxbridge v Barnet Alston Athletic	0-2
West Hartlepool v Eston United	3-2
West Hartlepool Expansion v West Auckland	2-1
Woolwich Polytechnic v Royal Engineers Depot Bn	1-5
Worthing v RMLI Gosport	0-4
Wycombe Wanderers v Caversham Rovers	5-0
r Deptford Invicta v Ramsgate Town	4-1
r Shepherds Bush (1) v Shoeburyness Garrison	2-2
r Sneinton v Atherstone Town	3-0
r Tufnell Park v Romford (1)	1-0
r Woolwich Polytechnic v Royal Engineers Depot Bn	1-5
r2 Shepherds Bush (1) v Shoeburyness Garrison	2-0

Round Two

Barking v Shepherds Bush (1)	3-0
Bournemouth v RMLI Gosport	1-3
Clapton v Ilford	1-2 v
Custom House v Nunhead	2-1
Deptford Invicta v Royal Engineers Depot Battn	1-0
Hereford City v South Nottingham	4-2
Kingston-on-Thames v Redhill	0-3
Leytonstone v Norwich CEYMS	2-0
Northern Nomads v Scarborough	0-0
Oxford City v Bromley	0-2
Sneinton v Notts Jardines	2-2
South Bank v Leadgate Park	3-0
Stockton v Preston Winckley	3-4
Tufnell Park v Barnet Alston Athletic	1-0
West Hartlepool Expansion v West Hartlepool	1-1
Wycombe Wanderers v Luton Clarence	2-0
r Clapton v Ilford	2-1
r Notts Jardines v Sneinton	3-2
r Scarborough v Northern Nomads	2-0
r West Hartlepool v West Hartlepool Expansion	1-2

Round Three

Barking v Notts Jardines	7-2
Bromley v RMLI Gosport	1-2
Deptford Invicta v Clapton	1-3
Redhill v Custom House	1-1
Scarborough v Preston Winckley	1-0 D
South Bank v West Hartlepool Expansion	2-1
Tufnell Park v Hereford City	3-1
Wycombe Wanderers v Leytonstone	3-2
r Custom House v Redhill	1-0

Round Four

Barking v Tufnell Park	1-5
Clapton v Wycombe Wanderers	4-1
Custom House v RMLI Gosport	0-2
Preston Winckley v South Bank	0-2

Semi Finals

RMLI Gosport v Tufnell Park	4-0 N
South Bank v Clapton	2-1 N

Final

RMLI Gosport v South Bank	2-1 N

1910/11

Qualifying Round One

1	Charlton Rovers v Middlesbrough OB	n/a
	Dorman Long & Co. United v Grangetown Athletic	0-3
	Lazenby Institute v Stockton St Marys	1-1
	Norton v Thornaby St Patricks	3-3
	Skelton Celtic v Whitby Shamrock	n/a
2	Esh Winning Rangers v Walker Church Institute	2-1
	Langley Park v Leadgate Park	2-0
	Tow Law Town v Rutherford College	0-0
3	Heworth Parish Church v York St Pauls	n/a
	Hull Day Street OB v 5th Northumberland Fusiliers	1-2
	York City v Nether Edge Amateurs	6-1
10	1st Scots Guards v 3rd Grenadier Guards	n/a
	Grays Athletic v East Ham	3-2
	North Woolwich v 1st Grenadier Guards	2-0
	Romford United v Upton Park	wo/s
	Wanstead v Shoeburyness Garrison	2-2

1910/11 to 1911/12

12	Hanwell v Uxbridge	2-2
	Kilburn v Gramophone	8-1
	Maidenhead Norfolkians v Ravenscourt Amateurs	3-2
	Marlow v City of Westminster	1-1
	Slough v Fulham Amateurs	3-2
	Southall v Maidenhead	6-0
	Sutton Court v Polytechnic	6-2
	Windsor & Eton v Staines	5-0
15	Orpington v Plumstead St Johns	5-1
19	Horsham v Hove	1-2
	Southwick v Mount Pleasant (Tunbridge Wells)	10-0
22	Dorchester Town v Boscombe	1-4
	Portland v RGA Weymouth	2-0
24	Devizes Town v Camerton	1-1
	Peasedown St Johns v Shepton Mallet Town	wo/s
1r	Stockton St Marys v Lazenby Institute	5-2e
r	Thornaby St Patricks v Norton	2-1
2r	Rutherford College v Tow Law Town	1-4
10r	Shoeburyness Garrison v Wanstead	5-2
12r	City of Westminster v Marlow	3-0
r	Uxbridge v Hanwell	3-2
24r	Camerton v Devizes Town	3-0

Qualifying Round Two

1	Charlton Rovers v Thornaby St Patricks	1-3
	Grangetown Athletic v Eston United	2-3
	Skelton Celtic v Skinningrove United	1-4
	Stockton St Marys v Saltburn	3-1
2	Craghead United v Esh Winning Rangers	2-1
	Iverston Villa v Tow Law Town	1-1
	Rise Carr Primitive Methodists v Langley Park	2-2
	Willington Temp. v Walker Church Lads Brigade	3-0
3	Heworth Parish Ch. v 5th Northumberland Fusiliers	2-6
	Sheffield Commercial Travellers v Hornsea	3-5
	Sheffield Grasshoppers v Withernsea	n/a
	York City v Hull St Georges	6-3
4	Liverpool Balmoral v New Brighton Tower Amateurs	0-3
	Old Xaverians v Hesketh Park	4-0
	Sandbach Ramblers v Manchester University	n/a
	Southport YMCA v Marlborough OB	5-1
5	GER Loco v Notts Rangers	2-3
	Grantham v Loughborough Corinthians	1-2
	Horncastle United v Netherfield Rangers	2-1
	Mapperley v Basford United	0-3
8	Cromer v Lowestoft Town	4-1
	Leiston v Carrow	0-1
	Norwich CEYMS v Kirkley	2-0
9	Colchester Crown v Orwell Works	1-1
	Harwich & Parkeston v Colchester Town	2-0
10	Custom House v North Woolwich	0-1
	Grays Athletic v Romford United	6-3
	Newportonians v 1st Scots Guards	n/a
	Shoeburyness Garrison v Romford (1)	5-2
11	Clove v Ware	6-2
	Enfield v West Hampstead	4-0
	Waltham Glendale v Finchley	2-3
12	Maidenhead Norfolkians v City of Westminster	2-4
	Southall v Sutton Court	3-2
	Uxbridge v Kilburn	1-3
	Windsor & Eton v Slough	3-1
13	Abingdon v Thame	1-1
	Banbury Central v Reading Amateurs	2-3
	Henley v Caversham Rovers	1-2
	Reading Grovelands v Wokingham Athletic	2-0
15	Army Ordnance Corps v RMLI Chatham	n/a
	Army Service Corps (Woolwich) v Woolwich Poly	2-0
	Cray Wanderers v Orpington	1-1
	Deptford Invicta v RN Depot	1-4
17	East Grinstead v Dorking	4-2
	Redhill v Sutton United	1-0
	Tooting Graveney v Summerstown	3-3
18	Farncombe v Old Kingstonians	0-9
	Godalming v Kingston-on-Thames	1-2
	Hersham United v Cranleigh	8-0
	Walton-on-Thames v Guildford	1-2
19	Hailsham v Hove	1-4
	Southwick v Shoreham	2-0
	St Leonards Amateurs v Seaford	5-0
	Worthing v Steyning	5-1
20	2nd Grenadier Guards v 4th Middlesex Regiment	3-0
	Army Service Corps (A'shot) v R Engineers (A'shot)	2-3
21	East Cowes Victoria v Ryde	2-1
	Gosport United v RGA Inner Defence	0-3
	Southsea St Simons v 1st Kings Royal Rifles	2-4
22	Branksome Gasworks Athletic v Bournemouth	2-0
	Longfleet St Marys v Boscombe	1-6
	Pokesdown v Poole	2-4
	Portland v Bournemouth Wanderers	1-2
24	Camerton v Trowbridge Town	2-0
	Lysaght's Excelsior v Street	2-1
	Melksham Town v Clevedon	1-3
	Paulton Rovers v Peasedown St Johns	4-0
2r	Langley Park v Rise Carr Primitive Methodists	5-1
r	Tow Law Town v Iverston Villa	4-0
9r	Orwell Works v Colchester Crown	3-0
13r	Thame v Abingdon	4-0
15r	Orpington v Cray Wanderers	8-2
17r	Summerstown v Tooting Graveney	7-1

Qualifying Round Three

1	Eston United v Thornaby St Patricks	2-1
	Skinningrove United v Stockton St Marys	2-0
2	Langley Park v Tow Law Town	3-1
	Willington Temperance v Craghead United	2-1
3	Hornsea v Sheffield Grasshoppers	0-0
	York City v 5th Northumberland Fusiliers	3-0
4	New Brighton Tower Amateurs v Southport YMCA	2-2
	Sandbach Ramblers v Old Xaverians	4-2
5	Horncastle United v Notts Rangers	0-1
	Loughborough Corinthians v Basford United	6-0
7	Cambridge United v Luton Crusaders	5-3
	Leagrave United v Luton Clarence	0-4
8	Carrow v Great Yarmouth Town	0-4
	Cromer v Norwich CEYMS	3-3
9	Orwell Works v 2nd Scottish Rifles	2-4
	South Weald v Harwich & Parkeston	4-1
10	1st Scots Guards v North Woolwich	n/a
	Shoeburyness Garrison v Grays Athletic	0-0
11	Clove v Wood Green Town	1-3
	Enfield v Finchley	2-1
12	City of Westminster v Kilburn	1-7
	Windsor & Eton v Southall	0-2
13	Reading Amateurs v Caversham Rovers	1-3
	Thame v Reading Grovelands	4-2
14	Margate v Folkestone Gas	1-2
	Ramsgate Town v 1st North Staffs Regiment	0-5
15	Army Ordnance Crps v Army Service Crps (W'wich)	2-1
	RN Depot v Orpington	wo/s
16	Aylesbury United v Chesham Generals	3-1
	Leighton Town v Apsley	0-2
17	East Grinstead v Redhill	0-3
	Summerstown v Croydon	8-2
18	Hersham United v Old Kingstonians	1-3
	Kingston-on-Thames v Guildford	3-1
19	Southwick v Worthing	7-0
	St Leonards Amateurs v Hove	1-1
20	Farnham v Royal Engineers (Aldershot)	0-7
	RAMC Aldershot v 2nd Grenadier Guards	1-0
21	1st Kings Royal Rifles v RGA Inner Defence	2-1
	East Cowes Victoria v Chichester	9-2
22	Bournemouth Wanderers v Poole	3-1
	Branksome Gasworks Athletic v Boscombe	2-1
23	Swindon Victoria v Bradford-on-Avon	4-2
	Wantage Town v Swindon Amateurs	n/a
24	Clevedon v Paulton Rovers	3-2
	Lysaght's Excelsior v Camerton	2-2
3r	Sheffield Grasshoppers v Hornsea	0-2
4r	Southport YMCA v New Brighton Tower Amateurs	0-4
8r	Norwich CEYMS v Cromer	4-2
10r	Grays Athletic v Shoeburyness Garrison	0-3
19r	St Leonards Amateurs v Hove	2-0
24r	Camerton v Lysaght's Excelsior	4-3

Qualifying Round Four

1	Eston United v Skinningrove United	2-2
2	Langley Park v Willington Temperance	1-0
3	York City v Hornsea	6-1
4	Sandbach Ramblers v New Brighton Tower Ams	3-2
5	Loughborough Corinthians v Notts Rangers	3-3
6	Old Wulfrunians v Salopian Amateurs	5-2
7	Luton Clarence v Cambridge United	7-1
8	Norwich CEYMS v Great Yarmouth Town	1-0
9	South Weald v 2nd Scottish Rifles	7-1
10	Shoeburyness Garrison v North Woolwich	6-2
11	Enfield v Wood Green Town	6-1
12	Southall v Kilburn	1-0
13	Caversham Rovers v Thame	6-0
14	1st North Staffs Regiment v Folkestone Gas	5-0
15	RN Depot v Army Ordnance Corps	1-3
16	Aylesbury United v Apsley	3-2
17	Redhill v Summerstown	3-1
18	Kingston-on-Thames v Old Kingstonians	0-3
19	St Leonards Amateurs v Southwick	1-1
20	Royal Engineers (Aldershot) v RAMC Aldershot	5-0
21	1st Kings Royal Rifles v East Cowes Victoria	4-0
22	Branksome Gasworks Ath. v Bournemouth Wan.	9-2
23	Swindon Amateurs v Swindon Victoria	0-3
24	Clevedon v Camerton	1-0
1r	Skinningrove United v Eston United	2-3
5r	Notts Rangers v Loughborough Corinthians	1-2
19r	Southwick v St Leonards Amateurs	wo/s

Round One

	1st Kings Royal Rifles v Aylesbury United	10-1
	Barking v South Weald	4-3
	Barnet Alston Athletic v King's Lynn	5-1
	Bromley v Catford Southend	1-0
	Chelmsford v South Nottingham	2-2
	Chesham Town v Shepherds Bush (1)	1-3
	Clapton v 2nd Coldstream Guards	0-1
	Darlington St Augustines v Bishop Auckland	0-2
	Hereford City v Royal Engineers (Aldershot)	2-2a
	Ilford v Leytonstone	2-1
	Loughborough Corinthians v London Caledonians	2-0
	Luton Clarence v Enfield	3-2
	Northern Nomads v Eston United	0-0
	Notts Jardines v Atherstone Town	4-0
	Old Kingstonians v Branksome Gasworks Athletic	1-1a
	Oxford City v Royal Engineers Depot Battn	wo/s
	Preston Winckley v Stanley United	0-4
	RMLI Gosport v Dulwich Hamlet	0-2
	Redhill v Caversham Rovers	3-1
	Sandbach Ramblers v Sheffield	4-0
	Scarborough v Langley Park	3-2
	Sneinton v Norwich CEYMS	2-1
	South Bank v Rotherham Amateurs	1-1
	Southall v Nunhead	1-2
	Southwick v 1st North Staffs Regiment	1-3
	St Albans City v Army Ordnance Corps	2-0
	Stockton v West Auckland	0-0
	Tufnell Park v Shoeburyness Garrison	5-2
	West Norwood v Old Wulfrunians	2-1
	Woking v Clevedon	4-3
	Wycombe Wanderers v Swindon Victoria	1-1
	York City v Crook Town	1-2
r	Branksome Gasworks Athletic v Old Kingstonians	3-2
r	Eston United v Northern Nomads	wo/s
r	Royal Engineers (Aldershot) v Hereford City	3-0
r	South Bank v Rotherham Amateurs	0-1
r	South Nottingham v Chelmsford	2-1
r	West Auckland v Stockton	2-1
r	Wycombe Wanderers v Swindon Victoria	2-1

Round Two

	1st North Staffs Regiment v South Nottingham	7-1
	2nd Coldstream Guards v R Engineers (Aldershot)	3-1
	Barking v Oxford City	4-1
	Barnet Alston Athletic v Nunhead	1-0
	Branksome Gasworks Ath v Loughboro' Corinthians	wo/s
	Bromley v Tufnell Park	4-1
	Ilford v St Albans City	2-0
	Luton Clarence v Shepherds Bush (1)	2-1
	Notts Jardines v 1st Kings Royal Rifles	1-1
	Redhill v Dulwich Hamlet	1-0
	Rotherham Amateurs v Bishop Auckland	2-1 v
	Sandbach Ramblers v Crook Town	3-1
	Sneinton v West Norwood	3-0
	Stanley United v Scarborough	2-0
	West Auckland v Eston United	2-1
	Wycombe Wanderers v Woking	4-3
r	1st Kings Royal Rifles v Notts Jardines	2-1
r	Bishop Auckland v Rotherham Amateurs	4-1

Round Three

	2nd Coldstream Guards v Redhill	2-0
	Barking v Luton Clarence	4-3
	Barnet Alston Athletic v 1st North Staffs Regiment	5-2
	Branksome Gasworks Athletic v Ilford	0-2
	Bromley v Sneinton	6-2
	Sandbach Ramblers v Stanley United	2-1 v
	West Auckland v Bishop Auckland	1-4
	Wycombe Wanderers v 1st Kings Royal Rifles	4-2
r	Sandbach Ramblers v Stanley United	wo/s

Round Four

	Barking v Ilford	1-2
	Barnet Alston Athletic v Bromley	0-1
	Bishop Auckland v Sandbach Ramblers	6-0
	Wycombe Wanderers v 2nd Coldstream Guards	2-3

Semi Finals

	Bishop Auckland v Ilford	6-0 N
	Bromley v 2nd Coldstream Guards	0-0 N
r	Bromley v 2nd Coldstream Guards	3-0 N

Final

	Bromley v Bishop Auckland	1-0 N

1911/12

Qualifying Round One

1	Guisborough Erimus v Grangetown Athletic	1-2
	Lazenby Institute v Saltburn	n/a
	Rise Carr v Stockton St Marys	1-2
	Thornaby St Patricks v Dorman Long & Co. United	1-1
2	Craghead United v Iverston Villa	13-0
	Esh Winning Rangers v Langley Park	1-2
	Hebburn Old Boys v Walker Church Institute	2-0
	Tow Law Town v Leadgate Park	0-0
	Walker Wellbeck v Rutherford College	1-4
3	Cottingham v Sheffield Grasshoppers	1-0
	Hull St Georges v Hull Day Street OB	2-1
	Scunthorpe & Lindsey United v Nether Edge Ams	0-1
7	Cromer v Lowestoft Town	5-1
10	Finchley v Barnet (2)	6-3
11	3rd Grenadier Guards v Fulham Amateurs	n/a
	Fulham St Andrews v Sutton Court	2-2
	Kilburn v West London OB	5-0
	Staines v Hanwell	1-0
12	Windsor & Eton v 2nd Grenadier Guards	2-2
14	Army Service Corps (Woolwich) v Cray Wanderers	wo/s
17	Farncombe v Hersham United	3-4
18	Horsham v St Leonards Amateurs	1-1
	Littlehampton v Vernon Athletic	3-3
	Southwick v Shoreham	1-3

1911/12 to 1912/13

21	Bournemouth Wanderers v Bournemouth	3-2
	Carter's Potteries Ath. v Boscombe	2-7
1r	Dorman Long & Co. United v Thornaby St Patricks	2-1
2r	Leadgate Park v Tow Law Town	1-2
11r	Fulham St Andrews v Sutton Court	1-6
12r	2nd Grenadier Guards v Windsor & Eton	2-0
18r	Littlehampton v Vernon Athletic	0-1
r	St Leonards Amateurs v Horsham	6-0

Qualifying Round Two

1	Ashmore Benson Pease & Co. v Norton	6-2
	Middlesbrough OB v Grangetown Athletic	n/a
	Saltburn v Dorman Long & Co. United	5-2
	Stockton St Marys v Skinningrove & Carlin How U	4-1
2	Craghead United v Tow Law Town	2-0
	Hebburn Old Boys v Walker St Christophers	n/a
	Langley Park v Willington	2-2
	Pandon Temperance v Rutherford College	0-1
3	Cottingham v 2nd Northumberland Fusiliers	2-4
	Hull St Georges v Leeds United	wo/s
	Nether Edge Amateurs v Sutton-on-Hull	5-2
	York St Pauls v Hallam	n/a
4	Liverpool Balmoral v Manchester University	2-0
	Old Xaverians v Broughton	1-3
	Sandbach Ramblers v Northern Nomads	n/a
5	Basford United v Horncastle United	6-0
	Mapperley v Loughborough Corinthians	2-4
	Notts Rangers v Netherfield Rangers	1-4
7	Carrow v Kirkley	2-0
	Cromer v King's Lynn	5-3
	Great Yarmouth Town v Leiston	4-2
	Norwich CEYMS v Wisbech St Augustines	9-0
8	Chelmsford v Harwich & Parkeston	3-1
	Paxman's Athletic v Hoffmann Athletic (Chelmsford)	1-3
9	East Ham v Shoeburyness Garrison	1-2
	Grays Athletic v Walthamstow Grange	0-2
	Romford Town v Newportonians	8-1
10	Enfield v Tufnell Spartan	4-1
	Hertford Town v Luton Amateur	6-3
	Ware v Luton Crusaders	1-2
	Wood Green Town v Finchley	0-2
11	Polytechnic v Kilburn	1-3
	Ravenscourt Amateurs v Sutton Court	1-2
	Southall v Staines	5-0
	Uxbridge v 3rd Grenadier Guards	2-3
12	Abingdon v Slough	1-1
	Maidenhead v Reading Grovelands	5-0
	Maidenhead Norfolkians v Caversham Rovers	1-0
	Marlow v 2nd Grenadier Guards	0-2
14	Bronze Athletic v Army Service Corps (Woolwich)	3-1
	Deptford Invicta v Army Ordnance Corps	1-1
	Faversham v Royal Naval Depot (Chatham)	1-2
	Gillingham Old Collegians v Whitstable	3-7
15	Aylesbury United v Chesham Generals	4-1
16	Croydon v Dorking	7-1
	Guards Depot (Caterham) v Summerstown	2-2
	Sutton United v East Grinstead	3-0
	Tooting v Redhill	0-4
17	Cranleigh v Kingston-on-Thames	1-2
	Farnham v Walton-on-Thames	2-3
	Godalming v Surrey Wanderers	0-2
	Hersham United v Guildford	1-2
18	Hove Belmont v Seaford	8-1
	Lewes v Vernon Athletic	4-1
	St Leonards Amateurs v Worthing	1-1
	Tunbridge Wells v Shoreham	5-2
20	1st Heavy Brigade RGA v Ryde	1-0
	Chichester v Southsea St Simons	3-3a
	Gosport United v RM Artillery	3-1
21	Dorchester Town v Pokesdown	2-3
	Poole v Boscombe	2-6
	Portland v Bournemouth Wanderers	1-2
	RGA Weymouth v Longfleet St Marys	2-0
22	Devizes Town v Melksham Town	1-3
	Swindon Victoria v Trowbridge Town	0-3
23	Welton Rovers v Clevedon	5-0
2r	Willington v Langley Park	3-1
12r	Slough v Abingdon	1-0
14r	Army Ordnance Corps v Deptford Invicta	n/a
16r	Summerstown v Guards Depot (Caterham)	n/a
18r	Worthing v St Leonards Amateurs	2-0
20r	Chichester v Southsea St Simons	3-1

Qualifying Round Three

1	Ashmore Benson Pease & Co. v Saltburn	1-0
	Grangetown Athletic v Stockton St Marys	1-0
2	Craghead United v Hebburn Old Boys	7-0
	Willington v Rutherford College	3-2
3	2nd Northumberland Fusiliers v Hull St Georges	3-1
	Nether Edge Amateurs v York St Pauls	5-1
4	Liverpool Balmoral v Marlborough OB	1-0
	Northern Nomads v Broughton	2-0
5	Loughborough Corinthians v Basford United	0-1
	Netherfield Rangers v Leicester Nomads	3-0
6	Arden v Banbury Central	2-1
7	Carrow v Cromer	1-8
	Great Yarmouth Town v Norwich CEYMS	2-0
8	Hoffmann Athletic (Chelmsford) v Colchester Town	0-1
	South Weald v Chelmsford	4-3
9	1st Grenadier Guards v Shoeburyness Garrison	1-3
	Romford Town v Walthamstow Grange	0-1
10	Enfield v Hertford Town	6-0
	Luton Crusaders v Finchley	1-2
11	Kilburn v Sutton Court	1-3
	Southall v 3rd Grenadier Guards	3-2
12	Maidenhead Norfolkians v 2nd Grenadier Guards	1-4
	Slough v Maidenhead	4-0
13	Folkestone Gas v Margate	1-1
	Ramsgate Town v 2nd Kings Royal Rifles	1-2
14	Bronze Athletic v Whitstable	5-0
	RN Depot (Chatham) v Army Ordnance Corps	0-0
15	Apsley v Chesham Town	5-3
	Aylesbury United v Leavesden Asylum	1-1
16	Guards Depot (Caterham) v Croydon	5-0
	Sutton United v Redhill	0-3
17	Guildford v Surrey Wanderers	4-1
	Kingston-on-Thames v Walton-on-Thames	1-1
18	Hove Belmont v Lewes	1-1
	Tunbridge Wells v Worthing	6-1
19	Royal Engineers (Aldershot) v Basingstoke	6-1
20	1st Heavy Brigade RGA v 2nd Wilts Rgmt (Gosport)	1-1
	Gosport United v Chichester	5-1
21	Boscombe v Bournemouth Wanderers	2-3
	RGA Weymouth v Pokesdown	0-4
22	Swindon Amateurs v Melksham Town	4-3
	Trowbridge Town v Wantage Town	wo/s
23	2nd Lancs Fusiliers v Welton Rovers	wo/s
	Sherwood F'sters (Ply'th) v 1st Duke of Cornwall LI	4-1
24	Hereford City v Cardiff Corinthians	3-6
13r	Margate v Folkestone Gas	3-2
14r	Army Ordnance Corps v RN Depot	n/a
15r	Leavesden Asylum v Aylesbury United	4-0
17r	Walton-on-Thames v Kingston-on-Thames	3-1
18r	Lewes v Hove Belmont	3-2
20r	2nd Wilts Rgmt (Gosport) v 1st Heavy Brigade RGA	1-0

Qualifying Round Four

1	Grangetown Athletic v Ashmore Benson Pease &Co	3-2
2	Willington v Craghead United	1-0
3	2nd Northumberland Fusiliers v Nether Edge Ams	4-1
4	Northern Nomads v Liverpool Balmoral	4-2
5	Basford United v Netherfield Rangers	2-1
6	Arden v Old Wulfrunians	3-0
7	Great Yarmouth Town v Cromer	5-1
8	Colchester Town v South Weald	5-2
9	Walthamstow Grange v Shoeburyness Garrison	0-0
10	Finchley v Enfield	1-0
11	Southall v Sutton Court	3-2
12	Slough v 2nd Grenadier Guards	1-3
13	2nd Kings Royal Rifles v Margate	1-0
14	Royal Naval Depot (Chatham) v Bronze Athletic	3-1
15	Apsley v Leavesden Asylum	4-1
16	Redhill v Guards Depot (Caterham)	1-1
17	Walton-on-Thames v Guildford	4-3
18	Lewes v Tunbridge Wells	1-1
19	RAMC Aldershot v Royal Engineers (Aldershot)	1-1
20	2nd Wiltshire Regiment (Gosport) v Gosport United	1-0
21	Bournemouth Wanderers v Pokesdown	2-5
22	Trowbridge Town v Swindon Amateurs	4-1
23	Sherwood Foresters (Ply'th) v 2nd Lancs Fusiliers	1-0
24	Cardiff Corinthians v Lysaght's Excelsior	2-0
9r	Shoeburyness Garrison v Walthamstow Grange	0-1
16r	Guards Depot (Caterham) v Redhill	1-1
18r	Tunbridge Wells v Lewes	3-1
19r	Royal Engineers (Aldershot) v RAMC Aldershot	1-0
16r2	Redhill v Guards Depot (Caterham)	1-0

Round One

	1st Kings Royal Rifles v RMLI Gosport	5-1
	Apsley v Southall	1-2
	Arden v South Nottingham	5-3
	Barking v Custom House	2-2
	Barnet Alston Athletic v London Caledonians	0-3
	Basford United v Notts Jardines	1-0
	Branksome Gasworks Ath v 2nd Wiltshire Regiment	4-3
	Colchester Town v Walthamstow Grange	2-3
	Crook Town v South Bank	1-0
	Darlington St Augustines v Eston United	2-5
	Dulwich Hamlet v 2nd Kings Royal Rifles	4-0
	Ilford v Great Yarmouth Town	5-3
	Leytonstone v Clapton	1-2
	Luton Clarence v Tufnell Park	1-1a
	Nunhead v Catford Southend	3-1
	Redhill v Old Kingstonians	3-0
	Rotherham Ams v 2nd Northumberland Fusiliers	2-0
	RN Depot (Chatham) v 2nd Coldstream Guards	1-0
	Scarborough v Northern Nomads	6-1
	Shepherds Bush (1) v Wycombe Wanderers	2-0
	Sherwood Foresters (Plym'th) v R Engrs (Aldershot)	2-2
	Sneinton v Oxford City	0-2
	Southport YMCA v Sheffield	4-0
	St Albans City v 2nd Grenadier Guards	0-2
	Stanley United v Bishop Auckland	1-2
	Stockton v Grangetown Athletic	1-0
	Trowbridge Town v Cardiff Corinthians	1-2
	Tunbridge Wells v Walton-on-Thames	2-0
	Waltham v Finchley	1-0
	West Norwood v Bromley	1-4
	Willington v West Auckland	2-0
	Woking v Pokesdown	5-0
r	Custom House v Barking	2-3
r	R Engrs (Aldershot) v Sherwood Foresters (Ply'mth)	3-1
r	Tufnell Park v Luton Clarence	2-0

Round Two

	2nd Grenadier Guards v Oxford City	0-4
	Basford United v Arden	2-1
	Cardiff Corinthians v Branksome Gasworks Athletic	0-0
	Clapton v Barking	1-2
	Crook Town v Southport YMCA	4-0
	Dulwich Hamlet v Tunbridge Wells	2-0
	Eston United v Scarborough	7-0
	Ilford v Waltham	3-1
	Nunhead v Shepherds Bush (1)	2-1
	Redhill v Woking	1-2
	Rotherham Amateurs v Willington	2-1
	Royal Engineers (Aldershot) v 1st Kings Royal Rifles	2-1
	Royal Naval Depot (Chatham) v Bromley	1-6
	Southall v London Caledonians	0-0
	Stockton v Bishop Auckland	3-1
	Walthamstow Grange v Tufnell Park	0-1
r	Branksome Gasworks Athletic v Cardiff Corinthians	5-2
r	London Caledonians v Southall	1-1 N
r2	Southall v London Caledonians	1-0 N

Round Three

	Barking v Oxford City	2-0
	Basford United v Tufnell Park	0-1
	Branksome Gasworks Athletic v Redhill	1-0
	Crook Town v Royal Engineers (Aldershot)	1-2
	Ilford v Rotherham Amateurs	1-0
	Southall v Bromley	0-2
	Stockton v Nunhead	1-1
	Woking v Eston United	2-4
r	Nunhead v Stockton	1-2

Round Four

	Eston United v Barking	5-2
	Ilford v Royal Engineers (Aldershot)	2-2
	Stockton v Bromley	1-0
	Tufnell Park v Dulwich Hamlet	2-0
r	Royal Engineers (Aldershot) v Ilford	3-2

Semi Finals

	Eston United v Tufnell Park	1-0 N
	Stockton v Royal Engineers (Aldershot)	1-0 N

Final

	Stockton v Eston United	1-1 N
r	Stockton v Eston United	1-0 N

1912/13

Qualifying Round One

1	Ashmore Benson Pease & Co. v Barnard Castle	7-0
	Dorman Long & Co. United v Guisborough United	4-1
	Great Ayton Rovers v Shildon Wanderers	4-1
	Tow Law Town v Saltburn	2-0
	West Auckland v Grangetown St Marys	0-1
	West Hartlepool St Josephs v Thornaby St Patricks	3-0
2	Brooms (Leadgate) v Walker Church Institute	2-4
	Consett Swifts v Rutherford College	0-0
	Craghead United v Pandon Temperance	1-0
	Dipton United v Leadgate Park	1-0
	Esh Winning Rangers v Sacriston United	3-0
	Herrington Swifts v Iverston Villa	2-0
	Hobson Wan. (Durham) v Newcastle Bohemians	1-1
	Langley Park v Edmondsley Heroes	wo/s
3	Hull OB v York St Pauls	3-1
	Nether Edge Amateurs v Sutton-on-Hull	6-0
7	Cromer v Cambridge United	wo/s
	Huntingdon Town v Lowestoft Town	1-1
	Kirkley v Morton's Athletic	0-1
8	2nd Durham LI v Hoffmann Athletic (Chelmsford)	5-1
9	Newportonians v Grays Athletic	0-6
10	Finchley v Luton Amateur	3-1
	Hampstead Town v Luton Albion	2-4
	Page Green Old Boys v Waltham	2-5
	Tufnell Spartan v Ware	4-1
11	Kilburn v Staines	3-1
12	Slough v Windsor & Eton	1-0
14	Army Ordnance Depot (Plumstead) v RN Depot	2-2
16	Dorking v Beddington Corner	3-2
	Guards Depot (Caterham) v Tooting	0-0
18	Eastbourne St Marys v Horsham	2-2
	Littlehampton v Hove Belmont	1-2
	Tunbridge Wells v St Leonards Amateurs	0-0
21	Bournemouth Wanderers v 1st Royal Welsh Fusiliers	0-3
	Dorchester Town v Boscombe	0-6
	Longfleet St Marys v Poole	1-6
	Portland v Christchurch	1-7
2r	Leadgate Park v Dipton United	3-0
r	Newcastle Bohemians v Hobson Wan (Durham)	0-4
r	Rutherford College v Consett Swifts	0-1
7r	Lowestoft Town v Huntingdon Town	1-0
14r	RN Depot v Army Ordnance Depot (Plumstead)	n/a
16r	Tooting v Guards Depot (Caterham)	0-2
18r	Horsham v Eastbourne St Marys	1-4
r	St Leonards Amateurs v Tunbridge Wells	2-2e
18r2	Tunbridge Wells v St Leonards Amateurs	3-1 N

1912/13 to 1913/14

Qualifying Round Two

1 Ashmore Benson Pease & Co. v Grangetown Ath. 3-0
Dorman Long & Co. United v Great Ayton Rovers 1-4
Grangetown St Marys v Brotton 3-1
West Hartlepool St Josephs v Tow Law Town 3-1
2 Consett Swifts v Herrington Swifts 0-1
Esh Winning Rangers v Craghead United 0-0
Langley Park v Walker Church Institute 1-3
Leadgate Park v Hobson Wanderers (Durham) 0-0
3 2nd Northumberland Fusiliers v Hathersage 2-0
Hull OB v Sheffield Grasshoppers 3-2
Nether Edge Amateurs v Sheffield 3-2
Withernsea v Cottingham 1-2
4 Old Xaverians v Orrell 1-3
5 Notts Rangers v Spilsby United wo/s
South Nottingham v Netherfield Rangers 1-4
6 Erdington v Old Wulfrunians 1-2
Walsall Phoenix v Arden 1-1
7 King's Lynn v Great Yarmouth Town 3-1
Lowestoft Town v Norwich CEYMS 2-4
Morton's Athletic v Carrow 2-1
Wisbech St Augustines v Cromer 0-1
8 Bury St Edmunds v Chelmsford 1-1
Leiston v Sudbury Town wo/s
Paxman's Athletic v Harwich & Parkeston 0-0
Stowmarket v 2nd Durham Light Infantry 0-4
9 Romford Town v Grays Athletic 1-2
Shoeburyness Garrison v East Ham 2-0
Walthamstow Grange v Southend Amateurs 6-1
Woodford Albion v 2nd Grenadier Guards 2-7
10 Enfield v Hertford Town 4-2
Luton Albion v Tufnell Spartan 2-1
Luton Crusaders v Finchley 2-0
Waltham v Wood Green Town 2-3
11 Fulham Amateurs v Liberty n/a
Fulham St Andrews v Polytechnic 1-0
Sutton Court v West London OB 4-2
Uxbridge v Kilburn 2-3
12 Abingdon v Thame 5-2
Marlow v Maidenhead Norfolkians 0-0
Slough v Maidenhead 1-2
Wycombe Wanderers v Reading Grovelands 5-0
13 Folkestone Gas v Margate 3-1
14 2nd Royal Dublin Fusiliers v Army Service Corps 1-1
Army Ordnance Corps v Bronze Athletic 2-3
Braby's v RN Depot 1-0
Chatham Amateurs v Deptford Invicta 1-0
15 Chesham Generals v Apsley 3-1
Watford Orient v Leavesden Asylum 1-3
16 2nd Scots Guards v East Grinstead 4-2
Dorking v Croydon 1-0
South Tooting v Redhill 0-1
Sutton United v Guards Depot (Caterham) 3-3
17 Cranleigh v Surrey Wanderers 3-1
Guildford v Old Kingstonians 1-1
Kingston-on-Thames v Godalming United 5-1
Walton-on-Thames v Farnham 5-0
18 Eastbourne St Marys v Lewes 4-3
Hove Belmont v Southwick 2-3
Tunbridge Wells v Vernon Athletic 3-0
Worthing v Brighton West End (Newcastle) wo/s
19 1st Grenadier Guards v RAMC Aldershot 1-0
3rd Grenadier Guards v 4th Royal Fusiliers 1-1
Southampton Cambridge v 1st Loyal N Lancs Rgmt 2-2
20 1st Heavy Brigade RGA v Chichester 7-3
Portsmouth Amateurs v Southsea St Simons 1-4
21 Boscombe v RGA Weymouth 0-1
Carter's Potteries Ath. v Christchurch 0-6
Pokesdown v Bournemouth 2-11
Poole v 1st Royal Welsh Fusiliers 1-1
22 Swindon Victoria v Swindon St Pauls Athletic 3-1
Trowbridge Town v Devizes Town 4-1
2r Craghead United v Esh Winning Rangers 2-1
r Leadgate Park v Hobson Wanderers (Durham) 1-0
6r Arden v Walsall Phoenix 9-0
8r Chelmsford v Bury St Edmunds 5-1
r Harwich & Parkeston v Paxman's Athletic 9-0
12r Maidenhead Norfolkians v Marlow 2-0
14r Army Service Corps v 2nd Royal Dublin Fusiliers wo/s
16r Guards Depot (Caterham) v Sutton United 5-0
17r Old Kingstonians v Guildford 10-0
19r 1st Loyal N Lancs Regt v Southampton Cambridge 2-0
r 4th Royal Fusiliers v 3rd Grenadier Guards 3-1
21r 1st Royal Welsh Fusiliers v Poole 2-0

Qualifying Round Three

1 Grangetown St Marys v Ashmore Benson Pease&Co 2-0
West Hartlepool St Josephs v Great Ayton Rovers 2-1
2 Leadgate Park v Craghead United 2-2
Walker Church Institute v Herrington Swifts 2-0
3 Cottingham v Nether Edge Amateurs 2-1
Hull OB v 2nd Northumberland Fusiliers 3-5
4 Broughton v Marlborough OB 2-1
Orrell v Liverpool Balmoral 0-0
5 Mapperley v Notts Rangers 3-2
Netherfield Rangers v Leicester Nomads 5-2
6 Banbury Central v Wolverhampton Old Church 3-3
Old Wulfrunians v Arden 4-2
7 Cromer v Morton's Athletic 4-1
King's Lynn v Norwich CEYMS 1-0
8 2nd Durham Light Infantry v Harwich & Parkeston 0-0
Leiston v Chelmsford 1-3
9 2nd Grenadier Guards v Shoeburyness Garrison 0-1
Grays Athletic v Walthamstow Grange 1-1
10 Enfield v Wood Green Town 2-0
Luton Crusaders v Luton Albion 3-2
11 Kilburn v Sutton Court 2-2
Liberty v Fulham St Andrews 3-3
12 Maidenhead Norfolkians v Maidenhead 1-0
Wycombe Wanderers v Abingdon 2-6
13 2nd Lancs Fusiliers v Whitstable 3-0
Ramsgate Town v Folkestone Gas 1-1
14 Army Service Corps (Woolwich) v Braby's 1-1
Chatham Amateurs v Bronze Athletic 2-3
15 Aylesbury United v Leavesden Asylum 1-4
Chesham Generals v Chesham Town 1-1
16 2nd Scots Guards v Dorking 1-4
Redhill v Guards Depot (Caterham) 4-2
17 Cranleigh v Walton-on-Thames 1-0 v
Kingston-on-Thames v Old Kingstonians 1-4
18 Tunbridge Wells v Southwick 1-1
Worthing v Eastbourne St Marys 4-1
19 1st Loyal North Lancs Regt v 1st Grenadier Guards 2-0
Camberley & Yorktown v 4th Royal Fusiliers 2-0
20 1st Heavy Brigade RGA v RMLI Gosport 2-3
Southsea St Simons v Gosport United 0-1
21 Bournemouth v Christchurch 1-0
RGA Weymouth v 1st Royal Welsh Fusiliers 0-6
22 Swindon Victoria v Warminster Town wo/s
Trowbridge Town v Wantage Town 5-0
24 Cardiff Corinthians v Hereford City 2-2
Lysaght's Excelsior v Caerleon Athletic 3-1
2r Craghead United v Leadgate Park 0-1
4r Liverpool Balmoral v Orrell 2-6
6r Wolverhampton Old Church v Banbury Central 2-3
8r Harwich & Parkeston v 2nd Durham Light Infantry 0-1
9r Walthamstow Grange v Grays Athletic 0-1
11r Fulham St Andrews v Liberty 4-1
r Kilburn v Sutton Court 4-0
13r Folkestone Gas v Ramsgate Town 3-2
14r Braby's v Army Service Corps (Woolwich) n/a
15r Chesham Town v Chesham Generals 0-2
17r Walton-on-Thames v Cranleigh 4-2
18r Southwick v Tunbridge Wells 3-1
24r Hereford City v Cardiff Corinthians 0-3

Qualifying Round Four

1 Grangetown St Marys v West Hartlepool St Josephs 4-3
2 Leadgate Park v Walker Church Institute 3-0
3 2nd Northumberland Fusiliers v Cottingham 4-1
4 Broughton v Orrell 2-1
5 Netherfield Rangers v Mapperley 3-1
6 Banbury Central v Old Wulfrunians 1-6
7 King's Lynn v Cromer 2-2
8 Chelmsford v 2nd Durham Light Infantry 1-4
9 Shoeburyness Garrison v Grays Athletic 1-1
10 Enfield v Luton Crusaders 4-0
11 Fulham St Andrews v Kilburn 1-2
12 Maidenhead Norfolkians v Abingdon 4-1
13 Folkestone Gas v 2nd Lancs Fusiliers 0-3
14 Bronze Athletic v Army Service Corps (Woolwich) 0-1
15 Chesham Generals v Leavesden Asylum 3-2
16 Redhill v Dorking 3-1
17 Old Kingstonians v Walton-on-Thames 3-1
18 Southwick v Worthing 1-3
19 1st Loyal North Lancs Regt v Camberley & Yorktown 1-1
20 Gosport United v RMLI Gosport 1-5
21 Bournemouth v 1st Royal Welsh Fusiliers 2-1
22 Trowbridge Town v Swindon Victoria 3-1
23 4th Middlesex Regiment v Clevedon 5-2
24 Lysaght's Excelsior v Cardiff Corinthians 0-3
7r Cromer v King's Lynn 1-0
9r Grays Athletic v Shoeburyness Garrison 5-1
19r Camberley & Yorktown v 1st Loyal North Lancs Regt 2-2
19r2 1st Loyal North Lancs Regt v Camberley & Yorktown 4-0

Round One

1st Kings Royal Rifles v Branksome Gasworks Ath. 3-0
1st Loyal North Lancs Regt v RMLI Gosport 1-1
2nd Coldstream Guards v London Caledonians 1-2
2nd Lancs Fusiliers v Redhill 3-2
2nd Northumberland Fusiliers v Leadgate Park 3-3
4th Middlesex Rgmt v Sherwood Foresters (Ply'mth) 1-6
Barking v Cromer 1-1a
Barnet & Alston v Maidenhead Norfolkians 3-0
Bishop Auckland v Stanley United 2-1
Bournemouth v Royal Engineers (Aldershot) 1-2
Catford Southend v Summerstown 2-0
Clapton v 2nd Durham Light Infantry 6-2
Darlington St Augustines v Stockton 2-3
Dulwich Hamlet v Woking 5-0
Enfield v Luton Clarence 3-2
Grangetown St Marys v Crook Town 1-2
Ilford v Custom House 1-4
Kilburn v Southall 0-5
Leytonstone v Grays Athletic 0-1
Notts Jardines v Basford United 0-1
Nunhead v Army Service Corps (Woolwich) 2-0
Old Kingstonians v Bromley 0-0
Old Wulfrunians v Netherfield Rangers 2-4
Rotherham Amateurs v Broughton 3-1
Shepherds Bush (1) v St Albans City 0-2
Sneinton v Oxford City 1-8
South Bank v Eston United 3-2
Southport YMCA v Northern Nomads 1-7
Trowbridge Town v Cardiff Corinthians 2-3
Tufnell Park v Chesham Generals n/a
West Norwood v Worthing 3-3
Willington v Scarborough 4-2
r Bromley v Old Kingstonians 2-0
r Chesham Generals v Tufnell Park 3-1
r Cromer v Barking 0-2
r Leadgate Park v 2nd Northumberland Fusiliers 0-1
r RMLI Gosport v 1st Loyal North Lancs Regt 3-1
r Worthing v West Norwood 3-0

Round Two

1st Kings Royal Rifles v RMLI Gosport 1-0
2nd Northumberland Fusiliers v Northern Nomads 3-2
Barking v Custom House 2-1
Barnet & Alston v Southall 5-3
Bishop Auckland v Stockton 2-3
Catford Southend v 2nd Lancs Fusiliers 2-2
Crook Town v South Bank 0-0
Dulwich Hamlet v Bromley 0-1
Grays Athletic v Clapton 0-3
London Caledonians v Enfield 1-0
Netherfield Rangers v Basford United 2-1
Nunhead v Worthing 5-0
Oxford City v Royal Engineers (Aldershot) 5-1
Sherwood Foresters (Plymouth) v Cardiff Corinthians 9-1
St Albans City v Chesham Generals 1-0
Willington v Rotherham Amateurs 1-5
r 2nd Lancs Fusiliers v Catford Southend 2-5
r South Bank v Crook Town 2-0

Round Three

2nd Northumberland Fusiliers v Catford Southend 1-1a
Bromley v Netherfield Rangers 5-2
Clapton v Barnet & Alston 3-0
London Caledonians v Nunhead 1-1
Oxford City v 1st Kings Royal Rifles 4-1
Rotherham Amateurs v South Bank 0-0
Sherwood Foresters (Plymouth) v Barking 4-0
Stockton v St Albans City 1-1
r Catford Southend v 2nd Northumberland Fusiliers 2-1
r Nunhead v London Caledonians 2-1
r South Bank v Rotherham Amateurs 2-0
r St Albans City v Stockton 3-2

Round Four

Bromley v St Albans City 4-1
Clapton v Nunhead 4-1
Oxford City v Sherwood Foresters (Plymouth) 3-1
South Bank v Catford Southend 0-0
r Catford Southend v South Bank 0-3

Semi Finals

Oxford City v Clapton 2-0 N
South Bank v Bromley 2-1 N

Final

South Bank v Oxford City 1-1 N
r South Bank v Oxford City 1-0 N

1913/14

Preliminary Round

1 Saltburn v Redcar 1-7
Scarborough v Grangetown Athletic 2-1
West Hartlepool St Josephs v Eston United 2-0

Qualifying Round One

1 Brotton v Skelton Celtic 2-3
Dorman Long & Co. United v Grangetown St Marys 1-2
Lingdale Mines v West Hartlepool Expansion 3-4
Loftus Albion v Darlington East End 2-1
North Skelton Swifts v Great Ayton Rovers 3-1
Redcar v Stillington St Johns 2-0
Scarborough v Tow Law Town 4-0
West Hartlepool St Josephs v Middlesbro' Cargo Ath 5-1
2 Dipton United v Stanley United 3-4e
Langley Park v Brooms (Leadgate) 0-0e
Leadgate Park v Newcastle Bohemians 4-2
3 Barnsley OG v Hathersage 0-6
Chilton Street OB v Beresford Athletic 0-1
Nether Edge Amateurs v York St Pauls 8-0
Rose Amateurs v Headingley wo/s
Withernsea v Sheffield 2-3
7 Cambridge United v King's Lynn 3-0
Great Yarmouth Town v Morton's Athletic 1-0
Norwich CEYMS v Kirkley 2-0
Wisbech St Augustines v Huntingdon United 3-1
8 Hoffmann Athletic (Chelmsford) v Stowmarket 5-0
9 2nd Grenadier Guards v Leyton 0-1
East Ham v Woodford Albion 2-1
Newportonians v Woodford Crusaders 0-2
Romford Town v Walthamstow Grange 2-0

1913/14

10 Finchley v Enfield	0-1
Hampstead Town v Wood Green Town	2-0
Harpenden Town v Luton Reliance	4-4
Hertford Town v Luton Albion	0-3
Luton Crusaders v Luton Trinity	0-5
Ware v Tufnell Spartan	0-4
11 3rd Coldstream Guards v City of Westminster	n/a
12 Maidenhead Norfolkians v Marlow	0-0
Wycombe Wanderers v Newbury Town	5-2
16 Croydon v Wimbledon	1-1
South Tooting v Redhill	0-1e
Sutton United v Metrogas	0-1
Tooting v Beddington Corner	7-1
18 Eastbourne St Marys v Horsham	1-1
Hastings & St Leonards v Hove	1-2e
Worthing v Littlehampton	6-0
20 Chichester v Portsmouth Amateurs	0-4
21 Dorchester Town v 1st Royal Welsh Fusiliers	1-3
Pokesdown v Bournemouth Wanderers	2-3
Poole v Longfleet St Marys	7-2
2r Brooms (Leadgate) v Langley Park	2-2e
10r Harpenden Town v Luton Reliance	2-1
12r Marlow v Maidenhead Norfolkians	3-2
16r Wimbledon v Croydon	1-3
18r Horsham v Eastbourne St Marys	1-5
2r2 Brooms (Leadgate) v Langley Park	2-1e

Qualifying Round Two

1 Loftus Albion v West Hartlepool St Josephs	1-1
North Skelton Swifts v Grangetown St Marys	0-1
Redcar v West Hartlepool Expansion	1-0
Skelton Celtic v Scarborough	3-2
2 Brighton West End (Newcastle) v Stanley United	2-3
Craghead United v Consett Swifts	4-0
Leadgate Park v Pandon Temperance	3-0
Rutherford College v Brooms (Leadgate)	3-4
3 Cottingham v Nether Edge Amateurs	2-1
Hull OB v Hathersage	2-3
Rose Amateurs v Beresford Athletic	0-0
Sheffield Grasshoppers v Sheffield	1-1
4 Liverpool Balmoral v Heaton Chapel	2-0
Manchester University v Brooklands	n/a
5 Sneinton v Notts Rangers	2-0
6 Cannock Amateurs v Banbury Central	3-0
Durham Light Infantry v Wolverhampton Old Church	2-0
7 Cambridge United v Wisbech St Augustines	6-1
Gorleston v Great Yarmouth Town	2-2
Lowestoft Town v Cromer	4-1
Norwich CEYMS v Carrow	2-0
8 Bury St Edmunds v Clacton Town	1-1
Hoffmann Athletic (Chlm'ford) v Harwich & Parkeston	5-1
Leiston v Colchester Town	3-5
Paxman's Athletic v Chelmsford	1-6
9 East Ham v 1st Grenadier Guards	0-6
Grays Athletic v Leyton	3-1
Romford Town v Shoeburyness Garrison	1-0
Southend Amateurs v Woodford Crusaders	1-1
10 Enfield v Tufnell Spartan	1-1
Hampstead Town v Luton Trinity	3-0
Harpenden Town v Page Green Old Boys	0-1 v
Luton Amateur v Luton Albion	3-2
11 2nd Scots Guards v 3rd Grenadier Guards	3-2
Polytechnic v 3rd Coldstream Guards	1-4
Wealdstone v Sutton Court	5-1
West London OB v Uxbridge	6-0
12 Abingdon v Wycombe Wanderers	0-6
Henley v Maidenhead	2-6
Slough v Reading Grovelands	3-2
Windsor & Eton v Marlow	3-1
14 Army Ordnance Corps v RN Depot	0-8
Army Service Corps (Woolwich) v Deptford Invicta	3-1
Chatham Amateurs v Snodland Town	3-1
New Crusaders v Bronze Athletic	5-1
15 Aylesbury United v Wolverton Town	3-2
Leavesden Asylum v Apsley	4-1
16 Croydon v Guards Depot (Caterham)	0-2
Dorking v Summerstown	0-4
Redhill v Metrogas	2-4
Tooting v East Grinstead	6-1
17 Godalming United v Hersham United	1-2
Guildford v Ash United	3-2
Walton-on-Thames v Kingston-on-Thames	1-2
18 Brighton St Margarets Athletic v Vernon Athletic	0-2
Eastbourne St Marys v Hove Belmont	2-0
Tunbridge Wells v Hove	3-0
Worthing v Southwick	2-3
20 1st Heavy Brigade RGA v RMA Portsmouth	5-5
Gosport United v HMS Excellent	0-1
RGA Portsmouth v Portsmouth Amateurs	0-4
Southsea St Simons v RMLI Gosport	1-3
21 1st Royal Welsh Fusiliers v Bournemouth	1-0
Carter's Potteries Ath. v Christchurch	1-6
Poole v Bournemouth Wanderers	4-1 v
RGA Weymouth v Wareham Town	4-1
22 Chippenham Town v Devizes Town	5-0
Trowbridge Town v Wantage Town	6-0
Warminster Town v Frome Town	2-2a

1r West Hartlepool St Josephs v Loftus Albion	n/a
3r Beresford Athletic v Rose Amateurs	n/a
r Sheffield v Sheffield Grasshoppers	5-2
7r Great Yarmouth Town v Gorleston	2-0
8r Clacton Town v Bury St Edmunds	3-0
9r Woodford Crusaders v Southend Amateurs	3-2
10r Enfield v Tufnell Spartan	2-1
r Harpenden Town v Page Green Old Boys	2-0
20r RMA Portsmouth v 1st Heavy Brigade RGA	4-2
21r Bournemouth Wanderers v Poole	4-1
22r Frome Town v Warminster Town	0-4

Qualifying Round Three

1 Redcar v Grangetown St Marys	1-1
West Hartlepool St Josephs v Skelton Celtic	5-1
2 Craghead United v Leadgate Park	3-1
Stanley United v Brooms (Leadgate)	1-0
3 Hathersage v Cottingham	4-0
Sheffield v Beresford Athletic	1-1
4 Liverpool Balmoral v Ogden's Athletic	0-2
Marlborough OB v Manchester University	3-1
5 Mapperley v Players Athletic	1-1
Sneinton v South Nottingham	2-1
6 Cannock Amateurs v Headingley	2-7
Erdington v Durham Light Infantry	3-3
7 Great Yarmouth Town v Cambridge United	2-0
Norwich CEYMS v Lowestoft Town	2-4
8 Clacton Town v Colchester Town	0-3
Hoffmann Athletic (Chelmsford) v Chelmsford	3-2
9 Grays Athletic v 1st Grenadier Guards	5-3
Woodford Crusaders v Romford Town	2-4
10 Hampstead Town v Luton Amateur	4-2
Harpenden Town v Enfield	0-2
11 2nd Scots Guards v West London OB	1-0
3rd Coldstream Guards v Wealdstone	4-0
12 Slough v Maidenhead	4-1
Wycombe Wanderers v Windsor & Eton	2-5
13 Margate v Ramsgate Town	0-3
14 Army Service Corps (Woolwich) v Chatham Ams	2-1
RN Depot v New Crusaders	4-2
15 Aylesbury United v Chesham Town	3-1
Leavesden Asylum v Watford Orient	1-0
16 Metrogas v Guards Depot (Caterham)	2-1
Summerstown v Tooting	1-0
17 Farnham v Hersham United	1-7
Kingston-on-Thames v Guildford	2-0
18 Southwick v Eastbourne St Marys	3-0
Tunbridge Wells v Vernon Athletic	1-0
19 1st Loyal North Lancs Regt v Rifle Depot	3-1
Camberley & Yorktown v RAMC Aldershot	0-7
20 Portsmouth Amateurs v RMA Portsmouth	2-1
RMLI Gosport v HMS Excellent	3-2
21 1st Royal Welsh Fusiliers v Christchurch	4-1
Bournemouth Wanderers v RGA Weymouth	2-3
22 Trowbridge Town v Swindon Victoria	4-0
Warminster Town v Chippenham Town	1-1a
1r Grangetown St Marys v Redcar	2-1
3r Beresford Athletic v Sheffield	3-4e
5r Players Athletic v Mapperley	7-0
6r Durham Light Infantry v Erdington	1-2
22r Chippenham Town v Warminster Town	3-1

Qualifying Round Four

1 West Hartlepool St Josephs v Grangetown St Marys	3-1
2 Craghead United v Stanley United	1-1
3 Hathersage v Sheffield	5-2
4 Ogden's Athletic v Marlborough OB	2-0
5 Sneinton v Players Athletic	2-1
6 Erdington v Headingley	2-4
7 Lowestoft Town v Great Yarmouth Town	0-5
8 Hoffmann Athletic (Chelmsford) v Colchester Town	1-2
9 Romford Town v Grays Athletic	0-0
10 Enfield v Hampstead Town	4-1
11 3rd Coldstream Guards v 2nd Scots Guards	1-0
12 Windsor & Eton v Slough	0-1
13 Whitstable v Ramsgate Town	0-1
14 RN Depot v Army Service Corps (Woolwich)	2-3
15 Aylesbury United v Leavesden Asylum	2-1
16 Metrogas v Summerstown	4-0
17 Kingston-on-Thames v Hersham United	1-2
18 Tunbridge Wells v Southwick	2-1
19 RAMC Aldershot v 1st Loyal North Lancs Regt	7-0
20 Portsmouth Amateurs v RMLI Gosport	4-1
21 1st Royal Welsh Fusiliers v RGA Weymouth	3-0
22 Chippenham Town v Trowbridge Town	0-0
23 4th Middlesex Regiment - Bye	
24 Hereford City v Cardiff Corinthians	1-1
2r Craghead United v Stanley United	2-1
9r Grays Athletic v Romford Town	3-2
22r Trowbridge Town v Chippenham Town	3-0
24r Cardiff Corinthians v Hereford City	1-0

Round One

1st Kings Royal Rifles v Woking	2-1
1st Royal Welsh Fusiliers v Cardiff Corinthians	3-3
2nd Coldstream Guards v Aylesbury United	5-0
3rd Coldstream Guards v Army Service Corps	1-6
4th Middlesex Regiment v Trowbridge Town	7-4
Barnet & Alston v Slough	5-0
Basford United v Sneinton	3-1
Bishop Auckland v Craghead United	4-1
Bromley v Catford Southend	1-0
Broughton v Old Xaverians	6-1
Clapton v Great Yarmouth Town	2-1
Colchester Town v Barking	4-2
Crook Town v Willington	1-0
Darlington St Augustines v South Bank	0-1
Enfield v Shepherds Bush (1)	1-1a
Esh Winning Rangers v West Hartlepool St Josephs	1-1a
Grays Athletic v Custom House	0-0a
Headingley v Old Wulfrunians	3-2
Leytonstone v Ilford	2-1
London Caledonians v Chesham Generals	5-0
Metrogas v Hersham United	4-3
Nunhead v Ramsgate Town	7-1
Ogden's Athletic v Northern Nomads	1-1
Old Kingstonians v Dulwich Hamlet	0-1
Oxford City v Netherfield Rangers	3-1
RAMC Aldershot v Portsmouth Amateurs	4-1
Rotherham Amateurs v Hathersage	1-1
R Engineers (Aldershot) v Branksome Gasworks Ath	1-1a
Southall v St Albans City	4-0
Stockton v Sherwood Foresters (Plymouth)	4-3
Tufnell Park v Luton Clarence	4-2
Tunbridge Wells v West Norwood	0-0 v
r Branksome Gasworks Ath v R Engineers (Aldershot)	2-1
r Cardiff Corinthians v 1st Royal Welsh Fusiliers	2-1
r Custom House v Grays Athletic	1-1a
r Hathersage v Rotherham Amateurs	4-0
r Northern Nomads v Ogden's Athletic	4-1
r Shepherds Bush (1) v Enfield	0-0
r Tunbridge Wells v West Norwood	4-0
r West Hartlepool St Josephs v Esh Winning Rangers	1-0
r2 Enfield v Shepherds Bush (1)	
r2 Grays Athletic v Custom House	2-1

Round Two

2nd Coldstream Guards v Barnet & Alston	1-2
Bishop Auckland v Hathersage	4-4a
Branksome Gasworks Athletic v Oxford City	0-1
Cardiff Corinthians v 4th Middlesex Regiment	4-2
Clapton v Grays Athletic	5-1
Colchester Town v Leytonstone	1-2
Crook Town v South Bank	5-1
Dulwich Hamlet v Army Service Corps (Woolwich)	2-0
Headingley v Basford United	5-3
Metrogas v Tunbridge Wells	5-1
Northern Nomads v Broughton	1-0
Nunhead v Bromley	0-0
RAMC Aldershot v 1st Kings Royal Rifles	2-0
Southall v Enfield	4-1
Tufnell Park v London Caledonians	3-1
West Hartlepool St Josephs v Stockton	1-2
r Bishop Auckland v Hathersage	2-1
r Bromley v Nunhead	3-1

Round Three

Barnet & Alston v Cardiff Corinthians	3-1
Bishop Auckland v Leytonstone	5-1
Clapton v Crook Town	3-2
Dulwich Hamlet v Southall	4-1
Northern Nomads v Metrogas	3-1
RAMC Aldershot v Bromley	2-2
Stockton v Oxford City	1-0
Tufnell Park v Headingley	5-0
r RAMC Aldershot v Bromley	6-1

Round Four

Barnet & Alston v RAMC Aldershot	1-3
Clapton v Bishop Auckland	1-2
Dulwich Hamlet v Tufnell Park	0-0
Northern Nomads v Stockton	2-0
r Tufnell Park v Dulwich Hamlet	3-1

Semi Finals

Bishop Auckland v RAMC Aldershot	0-0 N
Northern Nomads v Tufnell Park	2-0 N
r Bishop Auckland v RAMC Aldershot	3-1 N

Final

Bishop Auckland v Northern Nomads	1-0 N

1914/15

1914/15

Qualifying Round One

1	Brotton v Lingdale Mines	2-0
	Cargo Fleet Ironworks v Belmont Athletic Athletic	n/a
2	Dorman Long & Co. United v Grangetown Athletic	n/a
	Grangetown St Marys v Eston United	1-1
3	West Auckland v Harrogate	wo/s
4	North Skelton Swifts v Stillington St Johns	6-1
	Skelton Celtic v Loftus Albion	3-1
5	Pandon Temp v Brighton West End (Newcastle)	n/a
	Rutherford College v Newcastle Derby PMG	1-2
6	Consett Swifts v Brooms (Leadgate)	0-1
	Dipton United v Langley Park	0-2
8	Hallam v Lowther United (York)	6-1
	West Hull Albion v Sheffield University	1-2
9	Harrowby v Liverpool Balmoral	n/a
11	King's Lynn v Huntingdon Town	1-0
	Lynn St Nicholas v Wisbech St Augustines	wo/s
12	Norwich CEYMS v Carrow	1-2
13	Newportonians v Hoffmann Athletic (Chelmsford)	3-2
	Woodford Crusaders v Romford Town	3-1
14	Grays Athletic v Custom House	9-0
16	Hampstead Town v Finchley	n/a
	Page Green Old Boys v Hampstead Town	4-2
17	Luton Amateur v Luton Trinity	n/a
	Luton Reliance v Luton Albion	1-9
18	Charlton Athletic v Burberry	wo/s
	City of Westminster v Woolwich Polytechnic	3-1
20	Croydon v Wimbledon	1-0
	Tooting v South Tooting	3-1
21	Guildford v Walton-on-Thames	7-1
22	Hove v Eastbourne St Marys	wo/s
23	Portsmouth Amateurs v Gosport United	3-1
2r	Eston United v Grangetown St Marys	n/a

Qualifying Round Two

1	Belmont Athletic Athletic v Brotton	3-3e
2	Grangetown Athletic v Grangetown St Marys	2-4
3	Darlington East End v West Auckland	0-7
4	North Skelton Swifts v Skelton Celtic	n/a
5	Newcastle Derby PMG v Pandon Temperance	0-3
6	Langley Park v Brooms (Leadgate)	0-0a
7	Stanley United v Cockfield	2-1
8	Sheffield University v Hallam	0-6
9	Harrowby v Old Xaverians	wo/s
10	Mapperley v Wolverhampton Old Church	wo/s
11	King's Lynn v Lynn St Nicholas	3-1
12	Lowestoft Town v Carrow	4-0
13	Newportonians v Woodford Crusaders	1-3
14	Grays Athletic v Barking	6-0
15	Harpenden Town v Apsley	2-0
16	Finchley v Page Green Old Boys	0-1
17	Luton Albion v Luton Amateur	1-1
18	Charlton Athletic v City of Westminster	6-1
19	Strood v Cray Wanderers	wo/s
20	Tooting v Croydon	1-0
21	Guildford v Redhill	4-1
22	Hove v Horsham	wo/s
23	Longfleet St Marys v Portsmouth Amateurs	0-6
24	Swindon Victoria v Warminster Town	9-0
1r	Belmont Athletic Athletic v Brotton	wo/s
4r	North Skelton Swifts v Skelton Celtic	wo/s
6r	Langley Park v Brooms (Leadgate)	1-3
17r	Luton Amateur v Luton Albion	0-2

Round One

Barnet & Alston v Harpenden Town	3-1
Basford United v Mapperley	4-0
Belmont Athletic Athletic v Grangetown St Marys	1-0
Bishop Auckland v West Auckland	3-0
Bromley v Summerstown	5-1
Brooms (Leadgate) v Darlington St Augustines	6-0
Catford Southend v West Norwood	2-2a
Chelmsford v Ilford	1-6
Clapton v Leytonstone	2-1
Crook Town v Willington	2-1
Grays Athletic v Charlton Athletic	4-1
Great Yarmouth Town v King's Lynn	3-1
Guildford v Metrogas	wo/s
Hallam v Rotherham Amateurs	4-2
Hathersage - Bye	
Leadgate Park v Esh Winning Rangers	4-1
London Caledonians v Tufnell Park	wo/s
Lowestoft Town v Cambridge Town	wo/s
Luton Albion v Luton Clarence	4-2
Netherfield Rangers v Sneinton	8-0
Northern Nomads v Harrowby	0-0a
Nunhead v Old Kingstonians	wo/s
Oxford City v Slough	10-0
Page Green Old Boys v Enfield	wo/s
Portsmouth Amateurs v Hove	3-0
Royal Engineers (Aldershot) v Shepherds Bush (1)	2-4
South Bank v Scarborough	1-0
Southall v Swindon Victoria	3-2
Stanley United v Pandon Temperance	4-1
Stockton v North Skelton Swifts	4-0
Tooting v Strood	wo/s
Walthamstow Grange v Woodford Crusaders	3-2
r Catford Southend v West Norwood	2-0
r Harrowby v Northern Nomads	7-1

Round Two

Barnet & Alston v Ilford	1-2
Bishop Auckland v Belmont Athletic Athletic	4-1
Clapton v Southall	5-1
Grays Athletic v London Caledonians	1-3
Harrowby v Hallam	2-1
Hathersage v Basford United	5-1
Lowestoft Town v Great Yarmouth Town	2-0
Luton Albion v Nunhead	1-4
Oxford City v Netherfield Rangers	3-2
Page Green Old Boys v Shepherds Bush (1)	2-0
Portsmouth Amateurs v Guildford	3-2
South Bank v Crook Town	4-6
Stanley United v Leadgate Park	6-0
Stockton v Brooms (Leadgate)	4-1
Tooting v Bromley	0-1
Walthamstow Grange v Catford Southend	6-2

Round Three

Bishop Auckland v Stanley United	3-2
Clapton v Bromley	2-1
Hathersage v Harrowby	1-1
Ilford v Portsmouth Amateurs	8-0
London Caledonians v Oxford City	2-0
Page Green Old Boys v Lowestoft Town	2-1
Stockton v Crook Town	2-4
Walthamstow Grange v Nunhead	1-2
r Harrowby v Hathersage	4-0

Round Four

Ilford v Harrowby	1-0
London Caledonians v Crook Town	6-1
Nunhead v Bishop Auckland	3-6
Page Green Old Boys v Clapton	0-0
r Clapton v Page Green Old Boys	3-1

Semi Finals

Bishop Auckland v Ilford	2-0 N
Clapton v London Caledonians	0-0 N
r Clapton v London Caledonians	1-0 N

Final

Clapton v Bishop Auckland	1-0 N

1914/15 to 1918/19

No competition due to WWI

1919/20 to 1920/21

1919/20

Qualifying Round One

14	2nd Coldstream Guards v Burberry	0-5
	Aquarius v Croydon	wo/s
	Wimbledon v Kingstonian	6-1
15	Chesham United v Uxbridge Town	8-0
	Chiswick Town v Tufnell Spartan	2-0
	Hampstead Town v Sutton Court	3-1
	Yiewsley v Handley Page	1-4 d

Qualifying Round Two

7	Sheffield v Yorkshire Amateur	0-7
9	Leicester Belvoir v Boots Athletic	0-2
	Wolverhampton Town v Old Wulfrunians	2-2
10	Cambridge Town v Huntingdon Town	6-0
	King's Lynn v Boston Town	wo/s
11	Cromer v Great Yarmouth Town	1-4
	Gorleston v Lowestoft Town	4-1
	Morton's Athletic v Norwich CEYMS	3-3
	Orwell Works v Leiston Works Athletic	0-0e
12	Chelmsford v Colchester Town	5-1
	GER Romford v Newportonians	5-1
	Temple Mills v Hoffmann Athletic (Chelmsford)	1-2
	Woodford Crusaders v Leyton	3-2
13	Barking Town v Green & Silley Weir Athletic	2-0
	Blackwall & TIW v Jurgens	wo/s
	Woolwich Polytechnic v Custom House	0-4
14	Guards Depot (Caterham) v Metrogas	0-7
	Sutton United v Aquarius	3-4
	Tooting Town v Burberry	4-1
	Wimbledon v Adam Grimaldi	10-0
15	Chesham United v Wealdstone	4-2
	Hampstead Town v Botwell Mission	4-3
	Napier v Page Green Old Boys	3-3
	Yiewsley v Chiswick Town	2-0
16	Arlesey Town v Waterlows Amateur	0-2
	Luton Amateur v St Albans City	0-3
17	Dorking v Camberley & Yorktown	1-4
	Redhill v Guildford	0-1
	Walton-on-Thames v Thorneycroft Athletic	1-0
	Woking v RAE Farnborough	1-5
18	Marlow v Newbury Town	1-3
	Slough v Maidenhead United	3-2
	Windsor & Eton v Reading United	2-1 v
19	Cheshunt (1) v Hertford Town	5-2
20	Eastbourne v Vernon Athletic	4-3
	Southwick v Brighton & Hove Amateurs	1-2
21	Bournemouth v Bournemouth Tramways	1-4
	Gosport Athletic v Portsmouth Amateurs	1-2
	RMA Portsmouth v RMLI Gosport	1-3
22	Calne Town v Chippenham Town	1-0
	Clandown v Devizes Town	4-0
9r	Old Wulfrunians v Wolverhampton Town	n/a
11r	Leiston Works Athletic v Orwell Works	3-2e
r	Norwich CEYMS v Morton's Athletic	2-0
15r	Napier v Page Green Old Boys	1-0
18r	Reading United v Windsor & Eton	8-1

Qualifying Round Three

1	Guisborough Belmont Athletic v Skelton Celtic	3-1
	Lingdale Institute v Brotton	2-2
2	Grangetown St Marys v Eston United	2-3
	Redcar v South Bank East End	7-3
3	Cockfield v Darlington Railway Athletic	3-3
	Middleton Athletic v Rise Carr	0-4
4	Brighton West End (Newcastle) v Rutherford College	2-1
	Pandon Temperance v Newcastle Bohemians	0-3
5	Craghead Heroes v Langley Park	0-2
6	Stillington St Johns v West Hartlepool Expansion	0-4
7	Hallam v Rothwell OB	2-0
	Yorkshire Amateur v Hull OB	5-0
9	Boots Athletic v Newark Athletic	7-0
	Siddeley Deasy v Old Wulfrunians	3-2
10	Cambridge Town v King's Lynn DS&S Federation	4-0
	King's Lynn v Lynn St Nicholas	2-0
11	Gorleston v Norwich CEYMS	2-1
	Leiston Works Athletic v Great Yarmouth Town	3-0
12	Chelmsford v Woodford Crusaders	3-2
	GER Romford v Hoffmann Athletic (Chelmsford)	4-0
13	Blackwall & TIW v Ordnance (Woolwich)	1-2
	Custom House v Barking Town	1-1
14	Tooting Town v Aquarius	6-0
	Wimbledon v Metrogas	2-2
15	Hampstead Town v Napier	4-1
	Yiewsley v Chesham United	1-5
16	Vauxhall Motors v Luton Comrades	wo/s
	Waterlows Amateur v St Albans City	1-3
17	RAE Farnborough v Guildford	2-5
	Walton-on-Thames v Camberley & Yorktown	0-0a
18	Newbury Town v Henley on Thames	7-1
	Slough v Reading United	5-3
19	Islington Town v Cheshunt (1)	1-5 N
	Leavesden Mental Hospital v Enfield	2-2 v
20	Brighton & Hove Amateurs v Eastbourne	0-2
21	Poole & St Marys v Bournemouth Tramways	1-6
	Portsmouth Amateurs v RMLI Gosport	0-0
22	Calne Town v Clandown	1-1
	Paulton Rovers v Swindon Victoria	0-1
1r	Brotton v Lingdale Institute	4-3
3r	Darlington Railway Athletic v Cockfield	2-3
13r	Barking Town v Custom House	0-0e
14r	Metrogas v Wimbledon	1-2
17r	Walton-on-Thames v Camberley & Yorktown	0-2
19r	Leavesden Mental Hospital v Enfield	4-1
21r	RMLI Gosport v Portsmouth Amateurs	2-0
22r	Clandown v Calne Town	7-0
13r2	Custom House v Barking Town	0-3 N

Qualifying Round Four

1	Brotton v Guisborough Belmont Athletic	3-3a
2	Redcar v Eston United	2-1
3	Cockfield v Rise Carr	1-0
4	Brighton West End(N'wcstle) v N'wcstle Bohemians	4-2
5	Langley Park v St Helens United	1-0
6	W Hartlepool St Josephs v W Hartlepool Expansion	1-1
7	Hallam v Yorkshire Amateur	3-1
8	Old Xaverians v Liverpool Balmoral	7-2
9	Siddeley Deasy v Boots Athletic	1-7
10	King's Lynn v Cambridge Town	3-0
11	Gorleston v Leiston Works Athletic	2-2
12	GER Romford v Chelmsford	1-1
13	Barking Town v Ordnance (Woolwich)	3-5
14	Tooting Town v Wimbledon	2-1a
15	Hampstead Town v Chesham United	1-2
16	St Albans City v Vauxhall Motors	0-2 d
17	Camberley & Yorktown v Guildford	0-3
18	Newbury Town v Slough	3-5
19	Leavesden Mental Hospital v Cheshunt (1)	1-0a
21	Bournemouth Tramways v RMLI Gosport	1-2
22	Swindon Victoria v Clandown	0-1
23	Sunningend Works v Cheltenham Town	0-1
24	Cardiff Corinthians v Cardiff Harlequins	2-0
1r	Guisborough Belmont Athletic v Brotton	3-0
6r	W Hartlepool Expansion v W Hartlepool St Josephs	1-3
11r	Leiston Works Athletic v Gorleston	2-1
12r	Chelmsford v GER Romford	0-2
14r	Wimbledon v Tooting Town	6-2
19r	Leavesden Mental Hospital v Cheshunt (1)	3-1

Round One

Barnet v Leavesden Mental Hospital	2-3
Basford United v Boots Athletic	1-2
Bournemouth Gasworks Athletic v Worthing	2-1
Brighton West End (Newcastle) v Bishop Auckland	0-3
Cardiff Corinthians v RAMC Aldershot	2-1
Catford Southend v Bromley	1-3
Charlton Athletic v Oxford City	1-2
Cheltenham Town v Clandown	0-2
Chesham United v Aylesbury United	2-0
Crook Town v Willington	1-0
Dulwich Hamlet v Wimbledon	9-2
Esh Winning v West Hartlepool St Josephs	0-3
Grays Athletic v London Caledonians	2-3
Guildford v RMLI Gosport	3-4
Guisborough Belmont Athletic v Stanley United	1-2
Harrowby v Old Xaverians	4-0
Ilford v Walthamstow Grange	3-1
Langley Park v South Bank	2-1
Leiston Works Athletic v King's Lynn	2-1
Leytonstone v Clapton	3-0
Luton Clarence v St Albans City	4-3
Northern Nomads v Hallam	5-2
Nunhead v Summerstown	4-1
Ordnance (Woolwich) v Eastbourne	3-3
RN Depot v West Norwood	3-2
Redcar v Stockton	2-1
Rotherham Amateurs v Hathersage	1-2
Scarborough v Cockfield	3-2
Shoeburyness Garrison v GER Romford	0-1
Sneinton v Netherfield Rangers	6-1
Southall v Slough	4-2
Tufnell Park v Wycombe Wanderers	6-2
r Eastbourne v Ordnance (Woolwich)	3-2

Round Two

Bishop Auckland v West Hartlepool St Josephs	2-0
Bournemouth Gasworks Athletic v Clandown	5-0
Bromley v Chesham United	5-0
Cardiff Corinthians v Dulwich Hamlet	1-2
Crook Town v Stanley United	0-1
Eastbourne v Sneinton	0-1
Langley Park v Scarborough	2-1
Leavesden Mental Hospital v Southall	2-1
Leiston Works Athletic v Nunhead	0-2
London Caledonians v Luton Clarence	1-0
Northern Nomads v Harrowby	2-1
Oxford City v Boots Athletic	1-0
RMLI Gosport v Ilford	1-2
RN Depot v Leytonstone	1-3
Redcar v Hathersage	2-0
Tufnell Park v GER Romford	0-1a
r GER Romford v Tufnell Park	2-3

Round Three

Bournemouth Gasworks Athletic v Oxford City	0-1
Dulwich Hamlet v Bishop Auckland	5-1
Ilford v Northern Nomads	2-2
Langley Park v Leavesden Mental Hospital	3-1
Nunhead v Bromley	0-2
Sneinton v Leytonstone	1-8
Stanley United v Redcar	5-0
Tufnell Park v London Caledonians	1-1
r Northern Nomads v Ilford	2-1

Round Four

Bromley v Langley Park	3-1
Oxford City v Dulwich Hamlet	1-2
Stanley United v Leytonstone	2-1
Tufnell Park v Northern Nomads	2-1

Semi Finals

Dulwich Hamlet v Bromley	2-1 N
Tufnell Park v Stanley United	1-0 N

Final

Dulwich Hamlet v Tufnell Park	1-0 N

1920/21

Qualifying Round One

5	West Hartlepool Grays v W Hartlepool St Josephs	2-1
8	Lidgett Park v Yorkshire Amateur	2-9
	Nether Edge Amateurs v Hallam	1-1e
	Old Xaverians v Liverpool Balmoral	4-1
9	CSD (Hereford) v Badsey Rangers	1-6
	Headingley v Birmingham University	n/a
	Hereford St Martins v Hereford Thistle	0-1
	Netherfield Rangers v Nottinghamshire	5-3
	Silhill v West Bromwich Baptists	3-0
	Walsall Phoenix v Old Wulfrunians	2-3
	Wolverhampton Amateurs v Erdington	3-3
11	Sheringham v Terrington	11-0
12	Gorleston v Lowestoft Town	2-0
	Great Yarmouth Town v Norwich Federation	0-0e
	Harwich & Parkeston v Parkeston GER	4-1
	Ipswich Works v Ipswich Town	0-3
	Morton's Athletic v Beccles Town	2-2 d
	North Walsham Town v Norwich CEYMS	0-2
	Stowmarket v Orwell Works	2-1
13	Blackwall & TIW v Sterling Athletic	4-7
	Chelmsford v Leyton	3-1
	Clacton Town v Green & Silley Weir Athletic	0-2
	Colchester Town v Southend Corinthians	2-4
	Grays Athletic v GER Romford	5-1
	Hoffmann Athletic (Chelmsford) v Limehouse Town	1-2
	Newportonians v Temple Mills	n/a
14	Metrogas v Woolwich Polytechnic	3-0
15	Earlsfield Town v Civil Service	1-1
	Kingstonian v Tooting Town	5-0
	West Norwood v Summerstown	0-1
16	Botwell Mission v Polytechnic	8-2
	Chiswick Town v Sutton Court	2-1
	Harrow Weald v Wealdstone	1-1e
	Hyde & Kingsbury v Yiewsley	4-1
	Uxbridge Town v Hampstead Town	4-3
	Watford OB v Depot Middx Regt	3-1
19	Abingdon Town v Chesham United	1-3
	Banbury Early Closers v Reading United	1-6
	Henley Comrades v Henley on Thames	1-1
	Marlow v Slough Trading Co	2-2
21	Chichester v Littlehampton	3-2
	RE Eastbourne v Signal Service TC	1-4
	Rock-a-Nore v Brighton & Hove Amateurs	2-3
	Southwick v Vernon Athletic	0-3
	Worthing v Eastbourne	2-3
22	Blandford v Osborne Athletic	2-1
	Bournemouth v East Cowes Victoria	0-0
	Bournemouth Tramways v Deanery Southampton	6-0
	Poole v Ryde Sports	3-0
	Portland United v Portsmouth Amateurs	1-0
	RMA Portsmouth v Southsea Rovers	wo/s
23	Chippenham Rovers v Spencer Moulton	0-2
	Chippenham Town v Warminster Town	6-4
	Devizes Town v Swindon Corinthians	1-0e
	Glastonbury v Clutton Wanderers	4-2
	Holt v Pewsey Vale	1-2
	Minehead v Paulton Rovers	0-2
	Shepton Mallet Town v Peasedown Athletic	1-5
	Swindon Victoria v Calne Town	9-0
8r	Hallam v Nether Edge Amateurs	0-0a
12r	Norwich Federation v Great Yarmouth Town	0-1
15r	Civil Service v Earlsfield Town	3-1
16r	Wealdstone v Harrow Weald	2-1e
19r	Henley on Thames v Henley Comrades	2-2e
r	Slough Trading Co v Marlow	2-1
22r	Bournemouth v East Cowes Victoria	6-0
8r2	Hallam v Nether Edge Amateurs	3-2
19r2	Henley on Thames v Henley Comrades	4-0

1920/21 to 1921/22

Qualifying Round Two

1	Carlin How United v Lingdale Institute	4-4
2	Cargo Fleet Ironworks v Liverton Mines	5-0
	Skelton Celtic v North Skelton Swifts	7-0
	South Skelton v South Bank East End	3-3
	Stockton Enterprise Rangers v Middleton Athletic	7-2
5	Heaton Stannington v Stillington St Johns	4-2
	Newcastle Bohemians v Haverton Hill	0-4
	W Hartlepool Expansion v Brighton West End (Newc)	2-1
	West Hartlepool Grays v Pandon Temperance	1-3
6	Cottingham v Hull OB	1-1e
	Hessle v Withernsea	2-0
	Hornsea Town v Sutton	3-1
	Marfleet v Nunburnholme Liberal	3-0
7	Acomb Working Men v Selby Olympic	6-1
	Bridlington v York YMCA	wo/s
	Lowther United (York) v Filey	7-0
8	Hallam v Sheffield	4-3
	Malin Bridge OB v Rotherham Amateurs	4-0
	Old Xaverians v Calverley	2-2
	Rawdon v Yorkshire Amateur	3-4
9	Badsey Rangers v Netherfield Rangers	5-1
	Basford United v Headingley	6-0
	Erdington v Silhill	n/a
	Hereford Thistle v Old Wulfrunians	1-0e
10	RAF Cranwell v Horncastle Town	3-3e
11	Cambridge Town v Cromer	4-0
	King's Lynn v Lynn St Nicholas	2-0
	Lynn Swifts v Huntingdon Town	1-2e
	Wisbech Town v Sheringham	1-2
12	Bury St Edmunds v Norwich CEYMS	3-3e
	Gorleston v Ipswich Town	5-2
	Great Yarmouth Town v Morton's Athletic	1-0
	Stowmarket v Harwich & Parkeston	1-4
13	Green & Silley Weir Athletic v Sterling Athletic	3-2e
	Limehouse Town v Grays Athletic	0-3
	Shoeburyness Garrison v Chelmsford	2-0
	Southend Corinthians v Temple Mills	5-0
14	Belvedere v Catford Southend	0-3
	Metrogas v 1st Royal Warwickshire Regm	4-1
	Ordnance (Woolwich) v 2nd Connaught Rangers	3-3e
	Royal Engineers Depot Battn v Bexleyheath Labour	2-0
15	Aquarius v Civil Service	2-6
	Burberry v Sutton United	0-3
	Kingstonian v Leyland Motors	5-3
	Summerstown v Pearl Assurance	15-0
16	Botwell Mission v West London OB	2-0
	Hyde & Kingsbury v Watford OB	5-2e
	Uxbridge Town v Chiswick Town	2-1
	Wealdstone v Willesden Town	3-0
17	Frickers Athletic v Vauxhall Motors	1-2
	Northampton Nomads v Luton Amateur	2-1
18	Dorking v Camberley & Yorktown	1-4
	Hersham United v RAE Farnborough	5-1 D
	Redhill v Walton-on-Thames	3-2
	Woking v Guildford	0-1
19	Aylesbury United v Chesham United	0-2
	Newbury Town v Reading United	0-2
	Slough v Windsor & Eton	3-4e
	Slough Trading Co v Henley on Thames	2-1e
20	Enfield v Wood Green	3-2
	Gnome Athletic v Cheshunt (1)	4-1
	Hertford Town v Islington Town	wo/s
	Waterlows Walthamstow v Walthamstow Grange	1-3
21	Brighton & Hove Amateurs v Newhaven	1-3
	Chichester v Shoreham	1-4
	Eastbourne v Vernon Athletic	2-1
	Signal Service TC v Lewes	4-2
22	Gosport Athletic v Bournemouth Tramways	2-1
	Poole v Blandford	4-1
	RMA Portsmouth v Portland United	2-1
	Stamshaw OB v Bournemouth	3-2
23	Chippenham Town v Glastonbury	4-0
	Peasedown Athletic v Paulton Rovers	3-0
	Pewsey Vale v Devizes Town	2-4
	Spencer Moulton v Swindon Victoria	2-3
1r	Lingdale Institute v Carlin How United	n/a
2r	South Bank East End v South Skelton	n/a
6r	Hull OB v Cottingham	4-1
8r	Calverley v Old Xaverians	n/a
10r	Horncastle Town v RAF Cranwell	1-1e
12r	Norwich CEYMS v Bury St Edmunds	2-1
14r	2nd Connaught Rangers v Ordnance (Woolwich)	2-3
10r2	RAF Cranwell v Horncastle Town	6-0

Qualifying Round Three

1	Guisborough Belmont Athletic v Carlin How United	2-1
	Loftus Albion v Brotton	n/a
2	Cargo Fleet Ironworks v Skelton Celtic	4-3
	South Bank East End v Stockton Enterprise Rangers	2-0
3	Cockfield v Esh Winning	0-0e
	Rise Carr v Darlington Railway Athletic	2-2
4	Coundon United v Tow Law Town	2-0
	West Auckland Town v Langley Park	0-1
5	Haverton Hill v Pandon Temperance	4-0
	West Hartlepool Expansion v Heaton Stannington	3-1
6	Hessle v Hornsea Town	n/a
	Hull OB v Marfleet	2-1
7	Bridlington v Lowther United (York)	2-1
	Scarborough v Acomb Working Men	2-0
8	Calverley v Hallam	5-2
	Yorkshire Amateur v Malin Bridge OB	2-1
9	Badsey Rangers v Erdington	8-0
	Basford United v Hereford Thistle	2-0
10	RAF Cranwell v Boston Town	wo/s
	Skegness United v Horncastle Athletic	1-6
11	King's Lynn v Cambridge Town	3-0
	Sheringham v Huntingdon Town	4-0
12	Harwich & Parkeston v Great Yarmouth Town	4-2
	Norwich CEYMS v Gorleston	1-2
13	Grays Athletic v Shoeburyness Garrison	4-3
	Green & Silley Weir Athletic v Southend Corinthians	2-2
14	Metrogas v Catford Southend	5-1
	Ordnance (Woolwich) v Royal Engineers Depot Battn	3-0
15	Kingstonian v Sutton United	1-0
	Summerstown v Civil Service	4-1
16	Botwell Mission v Uxbridge Town	2-6
	Wealdstone v Hyde & Kingsbury	3-1e
17	Rushden Town v Northampton Nomads	6-3
	Vauxhall Motors v Waterlows Dunstable	4-0
18	Camberley & Yorktown v Guildford	2-1
	RAE Farnborough v Redhill	1-2
19	Chesham United v Windsor & Eton	3-1
	Slough Trading Co v Reading United	1-2
20	Hertford Town v Enfield	1-3
	Walthamstow Grange v Gnome Athletic	0-1 d
21	Newhaven v Signal Service TC	3-7
	Shoreham v Eastbourne	0-2
22	Gosport Athletic v Poole	7-0
	RMA Portsmouth v Stamshaw OB	0-1
23	Devizes Town v Peasedown Athletic	1-2
	Swindon Victoria v Chippenham Town	3-1
24	Cardiff Albion v Pembroke Dock Town	wo/s
	Swansea Amateurs v Cardiff Harlequins	6-1
3r	Darlington Railway Athletic v Rise Carr	n/a
r	Esh Winning v Cockfield	5-0
13r	Southend Corinthians v Green & Silley Weir Athletic	1-0e

Qualifying Round Four

1	Guisborough Belmont Athletic v Loftus Albion	0-0
2	Cargo Fleet Ironworks v South Bank East End	3-1
3	Rise Carr v Esh Winning	1-1
4	Coundon United v Langley Park	1-1
5	West Hartlepool Expansion v Haverton Hill	4-2
6	Hornsea Town v Hull OB	1-0
7	Bridlington v Scarborough	1-3
8	Calverley v Yorkshire Amateur	4-0
9	Basford United v Badsey Rangers	2-4
10	Horncastle Athletic v RAF Cranwell	0-2
11	King's Lynn v Sheringham	3-0
12	Gorleston v Harwich & Parkeston	1-0
13	Southend Corinthians v Grays Athletic	0-2
14	Ordnance (Woolwich) v Metrogas	1-2
15	Summerstown v Kingstonian	1-2
16	Wealdstone v Uxbridge Town	4-3
17	Vauxhall Motors v Rushden Town	2-5
18	Redhill v Camberley & Yorktown	5-2
19	Reading United v Chesham United	1-2
20	Enfield v Walthamstow Grange	2-2
21	Eastbourne v Signal Service TC	4-4
22	Gosport Athletic v Stamshaw OB	4-0
23	Peasedown Athletic v Swindon Victoria	1-1
24	Swansea Amateurs v Cardiff Albion	wo/s
1r	Loftus Albion v Guisborough Belmont Athletic	3-2
3r	Esh Winning v Rise Carr	2-1
4r	Langley Park v Coundon United	4-1
20r	Walthamstow Grange v Enfield	2-3
21r	Signal Service TC v Eastbourne	2-1
23r	Swindon Victoria v Peasedown Athletic	3-1

Round One

	Barking Town v Gorleston	5-1
	Barnet v Clapton	4-0
	Bromley v Redhill	5-0
	Cardiff Corinthians v Swansea Amateurs	4-2
	Cargo Fleet Ironworks v Eston United	2-2
	Crook Town v Stockton	3-0
	Enfield v Luton Clarence	2-6
	Esh Winning v Langley Park	1-0
	Gosport Athletic v RMLI Gosport	2-3
	Grays Athletic v Custom House	3-5
	Hathersage v Calverley	1-1
	King's Lynn v Leiston Works Athletic	4-2
	Leavesden Mental Hospital v Chesham United	2-3
	Loftus Albion v Redcar	5-1
	London Caledonians v Leytonstone	2-1a
	Maidenhead United v Kingstonian	1-2
	Metrogas v Southall	4-1
	Northern Nomads v Harrowby	4-1
	Nunhead v RN Depot	6-2
	Oxford City v Badsey Rangers	5-0
	RAMC Aldershot v Bournemouth Gasworks Athletic	2-0
	Rushden Town v Boots Athletic	4-2 v
	Scarborough v Hornsea Town	3-1
	Sneinton v RAF Cranwell	1-0
	South Bank v Grangetown St Marys	1-0
	St Albans City v Ilford	0-4
	Stanley United v Bishop Auckland	0-3
	Swindon Victoria v Clandown	8-0
	Wealdstone v Tufnell Park	0-0
	Willington v West Hartlepool Expansion	4-0
	Wimbledon v Dulwich Hamlet	2-1
	Wycombe Wanderers v Signal Service TC	3-2
r	Boots Athletic v Rushden Town	2-0
r	Calverley v Hathersage	3-2
r	Eston United v Cargo Fleet Ironworks	3-1
r	Leytonstone v London Caledonians	3-1
r	Tufnell Park v Wealdstone	2-1

Round Two

	Bromley v Sneinton	5-1
	Cardiff Corinthians v Barking Town	3-1
	Chesham United v Tufnell Park	0-2
	Esh Winning v Eston United	3-2
	King's Lynn v Boots Athletic	3-1
	Kingstonian v Custom House	3-2
	Loftus Albion v Scarborough	3-1
	Luton Clarence v RAMC Aldershot	4-3
	Metrogas v Nunhead	2-0
	Northern Nomads v Calverley	3-1
	Oxford City v Leytonstone	1-2
	RMLI Gosport v Swindon Victoria	0-1
	South Bank v Bishop Auckland	1-2
	Willington v Crook Town	2-0
	Wimbledon v Ilford	3-2
	Wycombe Wanderers v Barnet	4-3

Round Three

	Kingstonian v Bishop Auckland	0-2
	Loftus Albion v King's Lynn	6-0
	Luton Clarence v Esh Winning	0-1
	Metrogas v Leytonstone	1-1
	Swindon Victoria v Bromley	1-0
	Tufnell Park v Wycombe Wanderers	1-2
	Willington v Northern Nomads	1-0
	Wimbledon v Cardiff Corinthians	1-0
r	Leytonstone v Metrogas	3-2

Round Four

	Esh Winning v Bishop Auckland	4-5
	Leytonstone v Wimbledon	1-0
	Loftus Albion v Wycombe Wanderers	2-0
	Willington v Swindon Victoria	1-2

Semi Finals

	Bishop Auckland v Loftus Albion	2-1 N
	Swindon Victoria v Leytonstone	3-1 N

Final

	Bishop Auckland v Swindon Victoria	4-2 N

1921/22

Preliminary Round

6	Manchester Insurance v Bolton SS OB	1-0
	Old Boltonians v Old Chorltonians	1-3
9	Birmingham YMCA v Rowley	n/a
	Hereford CSD v Kepax	0-2
	Hereford St Martins v Hereford Thistle	0-1
	Kings Heath v Bilston Amateurs	2-2
	Manders Sports v Dawley Amateurs	0-3
	Moor Green v Headingley	1-1
	Revenue v Birmingham University	3-8
	Smethwick Old Church v Handsworth GS OB	4-6
12	Beccles Town v Norwich Priory Athletic	1-0
	Brantham Athletic v Ipswich Works	2-0
	Norwich Athletic v Lowestoft Town	3-4e
	Sheringham v Norwich B.L.	3-0
	Walton United v Leiston Works Athletic	1-3
16	Hounslow v Staines Lagonda	1-1e
	RAF Uxbridge v Arlington	9-0
19	Maidenhead United v Windsor & Eton	1-2e
	Slough Trading Co v Reading B.W.I.	2-1
21	Horsham v Hastings & St Leonards	2-2e
22	Blandford v Poole	3-1
	Bournemouth Tramways v Exeter Argyle	5-0
	Fareham v Ryde Sports	wo/s
	Glastonbury v Ferndale Road Working Mens	5-2
	Gosport Athletic v RN Depot Portsmouth	0-2
	Portland United v Dorchester Town	5-1
	Portsea Island Gas Co v RE Southampton	0-1
	Portsmouth Caledonians v RMLI Gosport	0-3
	RGA Gosport v Stanhope Rovers	3-0
	Salisbury Corinthians v Bournemouth	4-5
	Shaftesbury v Christchurch	5-3
	Southampton Post Office v Osborne Athletic	wo/s
	Westham v Wareham	5-2
23	Clandown v Peasedown St Johns Athletic	1-0
	Devizes Town v Trowbridge Town	0-2
	Frome Town v Shepton Mallet Town	7-0
	Melksham & Avon United v Westbury United	1-2
	Pewsey Vale v Holt	1-0
	Spencer Moulton v Clutton Wanderers	2-0
	Street v Radstock Town	0-2
	Swindon Casuals v Minehead	wo/s
	Timsbury Athletic v Purton Workmen	2-1
	Wells City v Bristol St Georges Sports	2-4

1921/22

9r	Bilston Amateurs v Kings Heath	0-6
r	Headingley v Moor Green	1-2
16r	Staines Lagonda v Hounslow	2-0
21r	Hastings & St Leonards v Horsham	5-0

Qualifying Round One

1	Lingdale Institute v Scarborough	1-4
	North Skelton Swifts v Whitby Whitehall Swifts	0-1
3	Coundon United v Rise Carr	3-2e
4	W Hartlepool Expansion v Brighton West End (Newc)	wo/s
5	Burton Lane Club & Institute v Lidgett Park	4-1
	Harrogate Amateurs v Armley	1-3
	Leeds Malvern v Leeds Harehills	1-0
	Monk Bridge Sports v Guiseley	1-2
	Richmond Hill Athletic v Yeadon Celtic	1-2
6	Hollinwood v Manchester YMCA	3-2
	Liverpool Balmoral v Harrowby	0-4
	Liverpool University v Whalley Range	4-1
	Manchester Insurance v Old Chorltonians	n/a
	Marine v Bury Amateurs	6-1
	Orrell v Heaton Chapel Amateurs	5-1
	Stand v Smithills Amateurs	n/a
	Whiston Parish v Old Xaverians	2-1 D
7	Dronfield Woodhouse v Chesterfield Corinthians	4-2
	Hathersage v Osborn's Sports	5-1
	Nether Edge Amateurs v Hallam	1-2
	Norfolk Amateurs v Rotherham Amateurs	2-1
8	South Nottingham v Nottingham Magdala Amateurs	0-4
9	Badsey Rangers v Silhill	10-0
	Birmingham University v Dawley Amateurs	n/a
	Erdington v Old Wulfrunians	1-3
	Evesham Town v Rowley	1-1e
	Hereford Thistle v Handsworth GS OB	2-1
	Kepax v Arden	3-0
	Kings Heath v Moor Green	0-2
	Wolverhampton Amateurs v Walsall Phoenix	1-2
10	Grimsby Haycroft Rovers v Spalding United	2-1
	Hull OB v Hessle	n/a
	Skegness United v Horncastle Town	wo/s
12	Great Yarmouth Town v Lowestoft Town	0-1
	Harwich & Parkeston v Colchester Town	4-0
	Ipswich Town v Clacton Town	3-1
	North Walsham Town v Morton's Athletic	0-0e
	Norwich CEYMS v Gorleston	2-0
	Orwell Works v Brantham Athletic	4-0
	Sheringham v Beccles Town	0-0e
	Stowmarket v Leiston Works Athletic	2-1
13	Chelmsford v Grays Athletic	2-2
	Gnome Athletic v Dick & Co's Sports	13-1
	Temple Mills v Leyton	3-0
	Walthamstow Avenue v GER Romford	2-3
	Walthamstow Grange v Sterling Athletic	3-2
14	Bostall Heath v Catford Southend	2-0
	Dover United v Woolwich Polytechnic	1-0
	RA Woolwich v 2nd Connaught Rangers	8-1
	Royal Engineers Depot Battn v Orpington	1-3
15	Kingstonian v Croydon	2-2e
	Summerstown v Aquarius	3-2e
16	Chiswick Town v Wealdstone	0-1
	Hyde & Kingsbury v Depot Middx Regt	2-1
	Polytechnic v Southall	1-1
	RAF Uxbridge v Hampstead Town	2-3
	Staines Lagonda v Harrow Weald	5-0
	Sutton Court v Uxbridge Town	2-3
	Willesden Town v 1st Grenadier Guards	0-2
	Yiewsley v Hanwell Athletic	7-2
18	Aldershot Town v Aldershot Excelsior	0-3
	Camberley & Yorktown v Guildford	1-3
	Dorking v Woking	3-6e
	Farnham United Breweries v Hersham United	4-1
	RAE Farnborough v Royal Engineers (Aldershot)	0-3e
	Redhill v Aldershot Institute Albion	2-2e
19	Abingdon Town v Banbury Harriers	0-1
	Aylesbury United v Slough Trading Co	2-1
	Chipping Norton v Cowley	1-3
	Henley Comrades v Reading Amateurs	1-4
	Marlow v Chesham United	0-2
	Newbury Town v Wantage Town	3-4
	Stones Athletic v Morris Motors	2-0
	Windsor & Eton v Henley Town	6-1
20	Leavesden Mental Hospital v Hertford Town	3-1
	Watford OB v Finchley	3-2
21	Arundel v Shoreham	2-3e
	Bognor Town v Newhaven	3-6
	Brighton & Hove Ams v Eastbourne RE Old Coms	0-1
	East Grinstead v Vernon Athletic	1-11
	Eastbourne v Worthing	2-4
	Hastings & St Leonards v Southwick	3-1
	Lewes v Chichester	4-2
	Littlehampton v Wick	2-3
22	Blandford v Bournemouth Tramways	2-2e
	Bournemouth v Portsmouth Amateurs	3-2
	Fareham v RN Depot Portsmouth	1-5
	Portland United v RMA Portsmouth	0-2
	RGA Gosport v RMLI Gosport	2-2
	Southampton Post Office v RE Southampton	1-0
	Southsea Rovers v Shaftesbury	3-2
	Westham v Stamshaw OB	6-1
23	Bristol St Georges Sports v Warminster Town	1-0
	Calne & Harris United v Swindon Casuals	5-2
	Glastonbury v Chippenham Town	2-3
	Pewsey Vale v Spencer Moulton	0-3
	Radstock Town v Clandown	1-0
	Timsbury Athletic v Chippenham Rovers	3-0
	Trowbridge Town v Frome Town	4-1
	Westbury United v Swindon Corinthians	1-2
9r	Evesham Town v Rowley	3-2
12r	Beccles Town v Sheringham	2-1e
r	Morton's Athletic v North Walsham Town	7-0
13r	Grays Athletic v Chelmsford	2-1
15r	Croydon v Kingstonian	0-4
16r	Southall v Polytechnic	wo/s
18r	Aldershot Institute Albion v Redhill	0-1
22r	Bournemouth Tramways v Blandford	4-1
r	RMLI Gosport v RGA Gosport	3-1

Qualifying Round Two

1	Grosmont v Lazenby Institute	0-5
	Scarborough v Guisborough Belmont Athletic	1-0
	Skelton Celtic v Malton Town	3-1
	Whitby Whitehall Swifts v Staithes United	3-3
2	Haverton Hill v Grangetown St Marys	n/a
	Norton United v Marske United	4-0
	Smiths Dock v Redcar	n/a
	South Bank East End v Cargo Fleet Ironworks	n/a
3	Cockfield v Leasingthorne Eden Rovers	1-0
	Consett Ironworks v Stillington St Johns	wo/s
	Coundon United v Eldon Albion	4-2
	Ferryhill Athletic v Tow Law Town	3-0
4	Heaton Stannington v Walker Park	2-0
	Percy Main Amateurs v Newcastle Bohemians	4-1
	West Hartlepool Expansion v Pandon Temperance	2-1
	West Hartlepool St Josephs v Twizell United	1-1
5	Acomb Working Men v Guiseley	5-1
	Burton Lane Club & Institute v Yeadon Celtic	3-2
	Leeds Malvern v Rawdon	4-0
	Yorkshire Amateur v Armley	0-0
6	Harrowby v Hollinwood	3-0
	Marine v Orrell	2-1
	Old Chorltonians v Liverpool University	2-0
	Smithills Amateurs v Old Xaverians	2-1
7	Gleadless v Dronfield Woodhouse	3-2
	Hallam v Malin Bridge OB	3-1
	Hathersage v Fulwood	2-1
	Sheffield v Norfolk Amateurs	4-1
8	Basford United v Woodthorpe	2-5
	Newark Athletic v Netherfield Rangers	8-1
	Nottingham Magdala Amateurs v Eastwood Town	3-2e
	Nottinghamshire v Clifton Colliery	2-5
9	Evesham Town v Walsall Phoenix	5-0
	Hereford Thistle v Kepax	2-1
	Moor Green v Birmingham University	1-3
	Old Wulfrunians v Badsey Rangers	0-2
10	Grimsby Haycroft Rovers v Hornsea Town	6-2
	Horncastle Athletic v Hull Young Peoples Institute	3-1
	Hull Dairycoates v Skegness United	4-0
	RAF Cranwell v Hull OB	1-0
11	Cambridge Town v Wisbech Town	5-0
	Huntingdon Town v St Ives Town	2-1
	Thetford Recreation v Lynn Swifts	6-1
12	Beccles Town v Orwell Works	3-0
	Harwich & Parkeston v Morton's Athletic	1-2
	Lowestoft Town v Stowmarket	5-2
	Norwich CEYMS v Ipswich Town	0-3
13	Clapton v Temple Mills	4-2
	GER Romford v Walthamstow Grange	1-2
	Grays Athletic v Blackwall & TIW	6-1
	Newportonians v Gnome Athletic	0-5
14	Orpington v Dover United	2-1
	RMLI Chatham v Belvedere	4-2
	RN Depot v RA Woolwich	4-1
	Woolwich v Bostall Heath	3-2e
15	Burberry v Leyland Motors	2-1
	Kingstonian v West Norwood	2-1
	Summerstown v Tooting Town	1-2
	Sutton United v Earlsfield Town	1-1
16	Hampstead Town v Hyde & Kingsbury	6-2
	Southall v Wealdstone	1-0
	Uxbridge Town v 1st Grenadier Guards	0-2
	Yiewsley v Staines Lagonda	0-2
17	Frickers Athletic v Arlesey Town	3-1
	Luton Amateur v Rushden Town	2-3
	Northampton Nomads v RAF Henlow	3-3e
	Waterlows Dunstable v Hitchin Blue Cross	0-2
18	Aldershot Excelsior v Farnham United Breweries	1-2
	Guildford v Woking	2-1
	Walton-on-Thames v Redhill	2-3
	Wellington Works v Royal Engineers (Aldershot)	2-3
19	Banbury Harriers v Wantage Town	wo/s
	Chesham United v Reading Amateurs	2-1
	Stones Athletic v Cowley	1-2
	Windsor & Eton v Aylesbury United	2-1e
20	Cheshunt (1) v Wood Green	0-1
	Edmonton (1) v Hemel Hempstead Town	1-0
	Watford OB v Leavesden Mental Hospital	2-0
	Welwyn v Berkhamsted Town	2-0
21	Eastbourne RE Old Comrades v Worthing	2-1
	Hastings & St Leonards v Lewes	3-0
	Newhaven v Wick	4-0
	Shoreham v Vernon Athletic	0-3
22	Bournemouth v RMLI Gosport	4-1
	RN Depot Portsmouth v RMA Portsmouth	3-4
	Southsea Rovers v Bournemouth Tramways	2-3
	Westham v Southampton Post Office	1-2
23	Bristol St Georges Sports v Trowbridge Town	2-6
	Radstock Town v Swindon Corinthians	3-0
	Spencer Moulton v Chippenham Town	2-1
	Timsbury Athletic v Calne & Harris United	4-0
24	Cardiff Amateurs v Swansea Amateurs	1-2
	Cardiff CS v Cardiff Bohemians	1-2
	Oakdale v Lovells Athletic	wo/s
1r	Staithes United v Whitby Whitehall Swifts	9-1
4r	Twizell United v West Hartlepool St Josephs	1-0
5r	Armley v Yorkshire Amateur	6-2
15r	Earlsfield Town v Sutton United	0-2
17r	RAF Henlow v Northampton Nomads	1-5

Qualifying Round Three

1	Lazenby Institute v Scarborough	5-0
	Staithes United v Skelton Celtic	n/a
2	Norton United v Redcar	3-2
	South Bank East End v unknown	n/a
3	Cockfield v Ferryhill Athletic	1-0
	Coundon United v Consett Ironworks	3-1
4	Percy Main Amateurs v Heaton Stannington	1-0
	West Hartlepool Expansion v Twizell United	2-1
5	Armley v Burton Lane Club & Institute	3-0
	Leeds Malvern v Acomb Working Men	4-1
6	Harrowby v Old Chorltonians	3-1
	Marine v Smithills Amateurs	6-2
7	Gleadless v Sheffield	2-1
	Hathersage v Hallam	1-0
8	Clifton Colliery v Nottingham Magdala Amateurs	6-2
	Woodthorpe v Newark Athletic	2-2e
9	Badsey Rangers v Birmingham University	0-0
	Evesham Town v Hereford Thistle	1-0
10	Grimsby Haycroft Rovers v RAF Cranwell	3-0
	Horncastle Athletic v Hull Dairycoates	3-2
11	Bury St Edmunds v Cambridge Town	3-5
	Thetford Recreation v Huntingdon Town	4-0
12	Ipswich Town v Lowestoft Town	7-0
	Morton's Athletic v Beccles Town	3-2
13	Clapton v Grays Athletic	3-2
	Walthamstow Grange v Gnome Athletic	1-3
14	Orpington v RMLI Chatham	2-1
	Woolwich v RN Depot	3-2
15	Kingstonian v Tooting Town	5-1 D
	Sutton United v Burberry	4-2a
16	Hampstead Town v Staines Lagonda	3-0
	Southall v 1st Grenadier Guards	1-0
17	Frickers Athletic v Rushden Town	1-0
	Hitchin Blue Cross v Northampton Nomads	1-3
18	Redhill v Guildford	5-1a
	Royal Engineers (Aldershot) v Farnham U Breweries	1-2
19	Banbury Harriers v Cowley	1-3
	Windsor & Eton v Chesham United	2-0
20	Edmonton (1) v Welwyn	1-0
	Wood Green v Watford OB	5-1
21	Eastbourne RE Old Comrades v Newhaven	4-0
	Hastings & St Leonards v Vernon Athletic	2-1
22	Bournemouth Tramways v RMA Portsmouth	1-1
	Southampton Post Office v Bournemouth	2-3
23	Timsbury Athletic v Spencer Moulton	2-1
	Trowbridge Town v Radstock Town	0-1
24	Oakdale v Cardiff Camerons	0-1
	Swansea Amateurs v Cardiff Bohemians	n/a
8r	Newark Athletic v Woodthorpe	1-3
9r	Birmingham University v Badsey Rangers	0-3
15r	Burberry v Sutton United	0-2
18r	Guildford v Redhill	8-0
22r	RMA Portsmouth v Bournemouth Tramways	1-1e
22r2	RMA Portsmouth v Bournemouth Tramways	2-0

Qualifying Round Four

1	Lazenby Institute v Staithes United	4-0
2	South Bank East End v Norton United	5-1
3	Cockfield v Coundon United	4-2
4	Percy Main Amateurs v West Hartlepool Expansion	3-0
5	Armley v Leeds Malvern	1-1
6	Harrowby v Marine	2-4
7	Hathersage v Gleadless	6-0
8	Clifton Colliery v Woodthorpe	6-3
9	Evesham Town v Badsey Rangers	3-3
10	Grimsby Haycroft Rovers v Horncastle Athletic	3-0
11	Cambridge Town v Thetford Recreation	2-0a
12	Ipswich Town v Morton's Athletic	1-0
13	Clapton v Gnome Athletic	2-0
14	Orpington v Woolwich	3-4
15	Sutton United v Tooting Town	1-1
16	Southall v Hampstead Town	1-2
17	Frickers Athletic v Northampton Nomads	1-1
18	Farnham United Breweries v Guildford	4-2
19	Cowley v Windsor & Eton	0-2
20	Wood Green v Edmonton (1)	1-2
21	Hastings & St Leonards v Eastbourne RE Old Coms	2-1
22	Bournemouth v RMA Portsmouth	0-2
23	Timsbury Athletic v Radstock Town	1-0
24	Cardiff Camerons v Swansea Amateurs	0-4
5r	Leeds Malvern v Armley	4-1
9r	Badsey Rangers v Evesham Town	0-0e
11r	Cambridge Town v Thetford Recreation	4-0

1921/22 to 1922/23

15r	Tooting Town v Sutton United	1-2a
17r	Northampton Nomads v Frickers Athletic	4-0
9r2	Evesham Town v Badsey Rangers	0-1 v
15r2	Tooting Town v Sutton United	0-2
9r3	Evesham Town v Badsey Rangers	4-2

Round One

	Barking Town v Barnet	3-1
	Bishop Auckland v Langley Park	4-0
	Botwell Mission v Slough	1-1
	Bournemouth Gas'rks Ath v Royal Corps of Signals	2-1
	Bromley v Clapton	2-1
	Calverley v Marine	1-2
	Cambridge Town v Leytonstone	1-1
	Cockfield v Willington	4-1
	Custom House v Oxford City	0-0
	Edmonton (1) v Nunhead	2-4
	Esh Winning v Crook Town	5-0
	Eston United v Stockton	1-1
	Evesham Town v Clifton Colliery	1-2
	Hampstead Town v Civil Service	2-0
	Hathersage v Grimsby Haycroft Rovers	3-1
	Ilford v London Caledonians	3-2
	King's Lynn v Ipswich Town	3-3
	Leeds Malvern v Darlington Railway Athletic	2-2
	Luton Clarence v Northampton Nomads	3-3
	Metrogas v Wimbledon	2-1
	Percy Main Amateurs v Stanley United	1-2
	RAMC Aldershot v Hastings & St Leonards	2-2
	RMA Portsmouth v Farnham United Breweries	1-1
	Sneinton v Boots Athletic	1-3
	South Bank v Loftus Albion	3-0
	South Bank East End v Lazenby Institute	2-0
	St Albans City v Sutton United	3-2
	Swansea Amateurs v Cardiff Corinthians	0-1
	Swindon Victoria v Timsbury Athletic	2-0
	Tufnell Park v Windsor & Eton	1-3
	Woolwich v Dulwich Hamlet	0-2
	Wycombe Wanderers v Enfield	7-2
r	Darlington Railway Athletic v Leeds Malvern	2-3
r	Farnham United Breweries v RMA Portsmouth	0-2
r	Hastings & St Leonards v RAMC Aldershot	0-2
r	Ipswich Town v King's Lynn	3-0
r	Leytonstone v Cambridge Town	3-1
r	Northampton Nomads v Luton Clarence	4-1
r	Oxford City v Custom House	2-0
r	Slough v Botwell Mission	1-4
r	Stockton v Eston United	2-0

Round Two

	Barking Town v Ipswich Town	5-0
	Boots Athletic v Hathersage	5-1
	Botwell Mission v Windsor & Eton	0-3
	Bromley v Wycombe Wanderers	6-0
	Cardiff Corinthians v Hampstead Town	5-0
	Clifton Colliery v Stanley United	2-1 N
	Cockfield v South Bank	1-5
	Dulwich Hamlet v Leytonstone	4-3
	Esh Winning v Bishop Auckland	0-2
	Ilford v RAMC Aldershot	3-1
	Leeds Malvern v South Bank East End	4-3 N
	Metrogas v Bournemouth Gasworks Athletic	2-0
	Northampton Nomads v Nunhead	5-0
	St Albans City v Oxford City	3-2
	Stockton v Marine	4-0
	Swindon Victoria v RMA Portsmouth	1-2

Round Three

	Barking Town v Bromley	2-1
	Bishop Auckland v Cardiff Corinthians	2-1
	Boots Athletic v Stockton	0-1
	Ilford v Windsor & Eton	0-1
	Metrogas v Clifton Colliery	2-1
	Northampton Nomads v South Bank	3-4
	RMA Portsmouth v Leeds Malvern	1-1
	St Albans City v Dulwich Hamlet	2-2
r	Dulwich Hamlet v St Albans City	3-1
r	Leeds Malvern v RMA Portsmouth	1-2 N

Round Four

	Barking Town v Stockton	5-2
	Dulwich Hamlet v Windsor & Eton	4-0
	RMA Portsmouth v Bishop Auckland	0-1
	South Bank v Metrogas	2-0

Semi Finals

	Bishop Auckland v Dulwich Hamlet	1-1 N
	South Bank v Barking Town	4-1 N
r	Bishop Auckland v Dulwich Hamlet	3-0 N

Final

	Bishop Auckland v South Bank	5-2 N

1922/23

Preliminary Round

5	Bingley Town v Yorkshire Amateur	2-1
	Birstall Parish Church v Silsden	1-3
	Cleckheaton v Starbeck Athletic	9-1
	East End Park v Apperley Bridge	1-3
	Ings House v Scholes Athletic	0-4
	Liversedge v Guiseley	2-0
	Monk Bridge Sports v Boothtown	1-1
9	Birmingham University v Smethwick Old Church	1-2
	Hereford Thistle v Hereford St Martins	2-1e
	RAOC Hereford v Evesham Town	0-4
	West Bromwich Amateurs v Bilston Amateurs	1-2
	Wolverhampton Amateurs v Rubery St Chads	3-2
12	Carrow Works v Norwich CEYMS	2-1
	Clacton Town v Paxman's Athletic	3-1
	Great Yarmouth Town v Lowestoft Town	0-1
	Leiston Works Athletic v Sudbury Town	4-0
21	Eastbourne RE Old Comrades v Arundel	5-1
	Southwick v Vernon Athletic	4-2
24	Chippenham Rovers v Ferndale Road WM	5-0
	Chippenham Town v Devizes Town	2-2e
	Clutton Wanderers v Coleford Athletic	2-2
	Glastonbury v Wells City	1-1
	Melksham & Avon United v Westbury United	6-1
	Peasedown St Johns Athletic v Ilfracombe Town	7-2
	Purton Workmen v Calne & Harris United	0-1
	Radstock Town v Frome Town	3-0
	Spencer Moulton v Warminster Town	2-0
	Street v Timsbury Athletic	1-2e
	Swindon Victoria v Pewsey Vale	8-0
5r	Boothtown v Monk Bridge Sports	4-1
24r	Coleford Athletic v Clutton Wanderers	4-1
r	Devizes Town v Chippenham Town	2-5
r	Wells City v Glastonbury	2-0

Qualifying Round One

1	Carlin How Athletic v Brotton	1-0
	Lazenby Institute v Guisborough Belmont Athletic	6-0
	Skelton Celtic & South Skelton U v N Skelton Swifts	0-2
	Staithes United v Loftus Albion	2-3
2	Blairs v Normanby Magnesite	1-2e
	Feversham Street v Cargo Fleet Ironworks	n/a
	Grangetown St Marys v Eston United	1-4
	Haverton Hill v Furness Athletic	n/a
	Marske v Redcar	0-9
	Marske United v Tarmac	n/a
	Middlesbrough Athletic v South Bank East End	n/a
	Norton United v New Skelton Vulcan	3-1
3	Ferryhill Athletic v Eldon Albion	4-0
	Trimdon Grange v Darlington Railway Athletic	1-3
5	Apperley Bridge v Silsden	6-1
	Bingley Town v Liversedge	1-4
	Cleckheaton v Wibsey	0-4
	Garforth v Bowling Albion	0-1
	Harrogate Amateurs v Thornton United	1-2
	Morley St Andrews v Leeds Harehills	1-3
	Rawdon v Greenfield Athletic	4-2
	Scholes Athletic v Boothtown	0-1
6	Liverpool University v Orrell	3-5
7	Norfolk Amateurs v Hathersage	5-1
	Rotherham Amateurs v Alvaston & Boulton	6-1
8	South Nottingham v Basford United	1-3
9	Arden v Headingley	n/a
	Coombs Wood v Erdington Celtic	2-2
	Hereford Thistle v Old Wulfrunians	2-1
	Kepax v Evesham Town	0-2
	Kington Town v Badsey Rangers	1-2
	Moor Green v Bilston Amateurs	4-1
	Smethwick Old Church v Erdington	1-1
	Wolverhampton Ams v Wolverhampton Gas Co	5-0
11	Bury St Edmunds v King's Lynn Swifts	1-0
	Huntingdon Town v Thetford Recreation	4-2
	Newmarket Town v St Neots & District	3-4
	Wisbech Town v King's Lynn	2-4e
12	Carrow Works v Stowmarket	0-2
	Colchester Town v Orwell Works	2-2
	Cromer v Norwich B.L.	4-1
	Gorleston v North Walsham Town	6-1
	Harwich & Parkeston v Leiston Works Athletic	2-1
	Lowestoft Town v Morton's Athletic	1-0
	Parkeston GER v Clacton Town	0-3
	Sheringham v Norwich Priory Athletic	0-1
13	Custom House v Chelmsford	4-0
14	Artillery College Sports v R Engineers Depot Battn	2-1
	Catford Southend v RN Depot	1-2
	Orpington v Erith & Belvedere	0-9
	Woolwich v Cray Wanderers	4-3
15	Burberry v Gwynne's Athletic	4-3
	Liversey United v Dorking	1-4
	Merton Town v Leyland Motors	1-2
	Redhill v Casuals	2-4
	Sutton United v Carshalton Athletic	1-1e
	West Norwood v Tooting Town	1-4
	Wimbledon v Aquarius	4-3e
16	Egham v Botwell Mission	2-1
	Hounslow v Staines Lagonda	3-2
	Old Latymerians v Deerfield Athletic	6-3
	Old Lyonians v L&NW Railway	1-2
	Uxbridge Town v Southall	2-4
	Wealdstone v Polytechnic	2-0
	Yiewsley v Harrow Weald	0-2
17	Berkhamsted Town v Wolverton Town	3-2
	Luton Amateur v Luton Clarence	0-0e
18	Camberley & Yorktown v Wellington Works	wo/s
	Farnham United Breweries v Hersham United	4-3
	Guildford v Aldershot Traction Company	7-1
	Royal Engineers (Aldershot) v RAE Farnborough	4-1
19	Cowley v Bicester Town	3-0
	Henley Town v Reading B.W.I.	2-3
	Maidenhead United v Henley Comrades	2-3
	Marlow v Wantage Town	6-2
	Newbury Town v Reading Amateurs	3-0
	Oxford Gasworks Athletic v Banbury Harriers	5-2
	St Frideswides v Headington United	2-2e
	Stones Athletic v Abingdon Town	3-1
20	Barnet v Hitchin Athletic	6-0
	Edmonton (1) v Baldock Town	6-1
	Finchley v Welwyn	1-3
	Hitchin Blue Cross v Railway Clearing House	1-1e
21	Bognor Town v Hove	1-2
	Broadwater v Littlehampton	1-0
	Horsham v Rock-a-Nore	3-2
	Newhaven v Chichester	3-4e
	Royal Corps of Signals v Lewes	4-3
	Shoreham v Eastbourne RE Old Comrades	2-1
	Southwick v Worthing	2-1
	Wick v Hastings & St Leonards	1-3
22	HMS Excellent v Portsmouth Amateurs	5-0
	Portsea Island Gas Co v Shanklin	2-0
	Portsmouth Corinthians v RE Southampton	1-2
	RMLI Gosport v Newport I of W	5-0
	Ryde Sports v RN Depot Portsmouth	1-3
23	Bournemouth Tramways v Shaftesbury	5-0
	Dorchester Town v Blandford	5-2
	Poole v Portland United	0-1
24	Calne & Harris United v Trowbridge Town	1-4
	Chippenham Town v Swindon Corinthians	2-1
	Clandown v Peasedown St Johns Athletic	2-0
	Holt v Swindon Victoria	1-9
	Melksham & Avon United v Spencer Melksham	3-2
	Radstock Town v Coleford Athletic	2-0
	Spencer Moulton v Chippenham Rovers	5-0
	Timsbury Athletic v Wells City	2-3e
9r	Arden v Headingley	2-1
r	Coombs Wood v Erdington Celtic	2-3
r	Erdington v Smethwick Old Church	0-3
12r	Colchester Town v Orwell Works	3-1
15r	Carshalton Athletic v Sutton United	4-0
17r	Luton Clarence v Luton Amateur	2-1e
19r	Headington United v St Frideswides	4-0
20r	Railway Clearing House v Hitchin Blue Cross	2-2e
20r2	Hitchin Blue Cross v Railway Clearing House	3-2 N

Qualifying Round Two

1	Lazenby Institute v Carlin How Athletic	n/a
	Loftus Albion v Malton Town	wo/s
	Scarborough v Grosmont	3-1
	Whitby Whitehall Swifts v North Skelton Swifts	3-0
2	Eston United v Marske United	4-2
	Feversham Street v Redcar	3-1
	Normanby Magnesite v South Bank East End	2-1
	Norton United v Haverton Hill	10-2
3	Chilton Colliery Recreation v Coundon United	2-1
	Darlington Railway Athletic v Stanley United	3-1
	Ferryhill Athletic v Consett Ironworks	4-0
	West Auckland Town v Rise Carr	3-0
4	Pandon Temperance v Newcastle Bohemians	2-2
	Percy Main Amateurs v Walker Park	6-0
	West Hartlepool St Josephs v Heaton Stannington	n/a
5	Apperley Bridge v Bingley Town	6-1
	Boothtown v Wibsey	0-1
	Bowling Albion v Thornton United	2-0
	Leeds Harehills v Rawdon	4-2
6	Earle v Liverpool Tramways	2-3
	Hoylake Trinity v Harrowby	2-2e
	Orrell v Old Xaverians	3-2
	Whalley Range v Old Chorltonians	3-2
7	Chesterfield Corinthians v Norfolk Amateurs	0-1
	Rotherham Amateurs v Fulwood	5-1
	Sheffield v Stockbridge & District	5-1
	Youlgrave v Sheffield Panthers	5-1
8	Basford United v Nottingham Magdala Amateurs	4-1
	Nottinghamshire v Netherfield Rangers	5-3e
	Players Athletic v Sneinton	1-0e
	Woodthorpe v Mapperley Park	0-1
9	Badsey Rangers v Moor Green	1-0
	Erdington Celtic v Evesham Town	0-4
	Hereford Thistle v Wolverhampton Amateurs	3-2
	Smethwick Old Church v Arden	0-0
10	Grimsby Rovers v Brunswick Institute	3-0
	Hornsea Town v Hull OB	4-3
	RAF Cranwell v Horncastle Athletic	wo/s
	Spalding United v Skegness United	3-2
11	Bury St Edmunds v King's Lynn	0-1
	Cambridge Town v Ely City	7-2
	Lynn St Nicholas v Huntingdon Town	1-2
	St Ives Town v St Neots & District	2-1

1922/23 to 1923/24

12	Colchester Town v Lowestoft Town	1-2
	Cromer v Norwich Priory Athletic	3-1
	Gorleston v Clacton Town	2-0
	Harwich & Parkeston v Stowmarket	4-1
13	Gnome Athletic v Custom House	1-2
	Leyton v Sterling Athletic	3-2
	Temple Mills v GER Romford	2-1
	Walthamstow Avenue v Walthamstow Grange	4-3
14	Artillery College Sports v Bexleyheath Town	4-1
	Bostall Heath v Erith & Belvedere	1-2
	Dover United v RN Depot	4-3
	Woolwich v Woolwich Polytechnic	0-2
15	Carshalton Athletic v Burberry	2-3
	Kingstonian v Casuals	1-1e
	Tooting Town v Leyland Motors	2-3
	Wimbledon v Dorking	7-0
16	Hanwell Athletic v Southall	0-1
	L&NW Railway v Harrow Weald	6-5e
	Old Latymerians v Hounslow	3-2
	Wealdstone v Egham	6-0
17	Apsley v Waterlows Dunstable	wo/s
	Aylesbury United v Frickers Athletic	3-0
	Berkhamsted Town v Luton Clarence	2-1
	Leavesden Mental Hospital v Leighton United	5-1
18	Camberley & Yorktown v 1st Grenadier Guards	wo/s
	Farnham United Breweries v Aldershot Institute Alb.	4-0
	Guildford v Woking	1-2
	Royal Engineers (Aldershot) v Walton-on-Thames	5-3
19	Henley Comrades v Cowley	2-3
	Marlow v Stones Athletic	1-1e
	Newbury Town v Headington United	6-1
	Oxford Gasworks Athletic v Reading B.W.I.	0-3
20	Barnet v Hertford Town	2-0
	Cheshunt (1) v Hitchin Blue Cross	10-1
	Enfield v Wood Green	2-0
	Welwyn v Edmonton (1)	1-2
21	Chichester v Broadwater	1-1
	Hastings & St Leonards v Hove	3-3e
	Royal Corps of Signals v Horsham	4-2
	Southwick v Shoreham	2-1e
22	Gosport v HMS Excellent	0-1
	Portsea Island Gas Co v Stamshaw OB	0-0
	RE Southampton v Osborne Athletic	3-2e
	RN Depot Portsmouth v RMLI Gosport	1-4
23	Bournemouth Tramways v Dorchester Town	11-1
	Portland United v Wimborne	2-0
	Salisbury Corinthians v Bournemouth	4-0
	Westham v Christchurch	4-1
24	Melksham Town & Avon United v Chippenham Town	2-1
	Radstock Town v Spencer Moulton	4-3
	Trowbridge Town v Clandown	1-0
	Wells City v Swindon Victoria	1-3
6r	Harrowby v Hoylake Trinity	2-2
9r	Arden v Smethwick Old Church	6-0
15r	Casuals v Kingstonian	2-2
19r	Stones Athletic v Marlow	1-0
21r	Broadwater v Chichester	1-2
r	Hastings & St Leonards v Hove	4-1
22r	Stamshaw OB v Portsea Island Gas Co	0-1
6r2	Hoylake Trinity v Harrowby	2-1
15r2	Kingstonian v Casuals	1-4

Qualifying Round Three

1	Lazenby Institute v Loftus Albion	1-1
	Whitby Whitehall Swifts v Scarborough	4-2
2	Feversham Street v Eston United	1-3
	Norton United v Normanby Magnesite	0-1
3	Chilton Colliery Recreation v Darlington Railway Ath	2-4e
	Ferryhill Athletic v West Auckland Town	2-2e
4	Heaton Stannington v Pandon Temperance	1-0
	Leslies v Percy Main Amateurs	1-3
5	Leeds Harehills v Apperley Bridge	4-4
	Wibsey v Bowling Albion	5-2
6	Hoylake Trinity v Orrell	2-0
	Liverpool Tramways v Whalley Range	3-2
7	Norfolk Amateurs v Youlgrave	3-1
	Sheffield v Rotherham Amateurs	2-0
8	Basford United v Nottinghamshire	1-5
	Players Athletic v Mapperley Park	11-0
9	Badsey Rangers v Arden	4-1
	Evesham Town v Hereford Thistle	4-0
10	Hornsea Town v Grimsby Rovers	0-5
	Spalding United v RAF Cranwell	1-0
11	Cambridge Town v St Ives Town	5-0
	King's Lynn v Huntingdon Town	6-1
12	Cromer v Harwich & Parkeston	1-2
	Gorleston v Lowestoft Town	1-0
13	Custom House v Walthamstow Avenue	2-0
	Leyton v Temple Mills	5-1 v
14	Artillery College Sports v Erith & Belvedere	1-1
	Woolwich Polytechnic v Dover United	1-3
15	Leyland Motors v Casuals	1-5
	Wimbledon v Burberry	4-3
16	Old Latymerians v L&NW Railway	2-0
	Wealdstone v Southall	1-1a
17	Apsley v Berkhamsted Town	1-2e
	Leavesden Mental Hospital v Aylesbury United	1-0
18	Camberley & Yorktown v R Engineers (Aldershot)	0-1
	Farnham United Breweries v Woking	1-3
19	Cowley v Newbury Town	1-0
	Reading B.W.I. v Stones Athletic	7-1
20	Edmonton (1) v Cheshunt (1)	1-3
	Enfield v Barnet	1-2
21	Hastings & St Leonards v Chichester	4-0
	Southwick v Royal Corps of Signals	0-1
22	Portsea Island Gas Co v HMS Excellent	0-5
	RE Southampton v RMLI Gosport	1-4
23	Bournemouth Tramways v Salisbury Corinthians	4-1
	Portland United v Westham	3-0
24	Swindon Victoria v Melksham Town & Avon United	3-0
	Trowbridge Town v Radstock Town	3-1
1r	Loftus Albion v Lazenby Institute	2-0
3r	West Auckland Town v Ferryhill Athletic	2-1
5r	Apperley Bridge v Leeds Harehills	1-0
13r	Leyton v Temple Mills	6-1
14r	Erith & Belvedere v Artillery College Sports	1-0
16r	Southall v Wealdstone	6-0

Qualifying Round Four

1	Loftus Albion v Whitby Whitehall Swifts	6-0
2	Eston United v Normanby Magnesite	1-1
3	West Auckland Town v Darlington Railway Athletic	2-1
4	Heaton Stannington v Percy Main Amateurs	1-0
5	Apperley Bridge v Wibsey	2-0
6	Hoylake Trinity v Liverpool Tramways	1-0
7	Norfolk Amateurs v Sheffield	4-0
8	Players Athletic v Nottinghamshire	7-0
9	Badsey Rangers v Evesham Town	1-2
10	Grimsby Rovers v Spalding United	4-4
11	Cambridge Town v King's Lynn	0-1
12	Gorleston v Harwich & Parkeston	2-0
13	Custom House v Leyton	3-3
14	Erith & Belvedere v Dover United	3-3
15	Wimbledon v Casuals	1-1
16	Old Latymerians v Southall	2-9
17	Berkhamsted Town v Leavesden Mental Hospital	1-2
18	Woking v Royal Engineers (Aldershot)	1-0
19	Cowley v Reading B.W.I.	3-0
20	Barnet v Cheshunt (1)	3-1
21	Hastings & St Leonards v Royal Corps of Signals	4-2
22	HMS Excellent v RMLI Gosport	3-1
23	Bournemouth Tramways v Portland United	3-0
24	Trowbridge Town v Swindon Victoria	1-1
2r	Normanby Magnesite v Eston United	1-2
10r	Spalding United v Grimsby Rovers	4-2
13r	Leyton v Custom House	1-3
14r	Dover United v Erith & Belvedere	1-2
15r	Wimbledon v Casuals	6-2
24r	Swindon Victoria v Trowbridge Town	2-0e

Round One

	Apperley Bridge v Marine	5-1
	Barking Town v Chesham United	4-2
	Barnet v Nunhead	1-2
	Bourn'mth Gasworks Ath v Hastings & St Leonards	1-0
	Civil Service v Cowley	0-0
	Clifton Colliery v Spalding United	0-0
	Crook Town v Langley Park	5-2
	Custom House v Ilford	0-2
	Dulwich Hamlet v Leavesden Mental Hospital	0-2
	Eastbourne v Bournemouth Tramways	0-0
	Eston United v Leeds Malvern	4-1
	Evesham Town v Norfolk Amateurs	2-1
	Grays Athletic v Hampstead Town	3-1
	HMS Excellent v RAMC Aldershot	1-2
	Heaton Stannington v Stockton	0-3
	Hoylake Trinity v Calverley	3-1
	Ipswich Town v Clapton	0-1
	Loftus Albion v West Auckland Town	1-4
	London Caledonians v Slough	10-2
	Oxford City v Gorleston	5-2
	Players Athletic v Boots Athletic	1-1
	South Bank v Bishop Auckland	1-1
	Southall v Windsor & Eton	4-0
	St Albans City v RAF Uxbridge	8-0
	Summerstown v Bromley	2-1
	Swindon Victoria v RMA Portsmouth	wo/s
	Tow Law Town v Cockfield	1-2
	Tufnell Park v Leytonstone	0-5
	Willington v Esh Winning	0-1
	Wimbledon v Northampton Nomads	0-2
	Woking v Erith & Belvedere	1-1
	Wycombe Wanderers v King's Lynn	6-4
r	Bishop Auckland v South Bank	4-0
r	Boots Athletic v Players Athletic	2-1
r	Bournemouth Tramways v Eastbourne	0-1
r	Cowley v Civil Service	0-1
r	Erith & Belvedere v Woking	1-1
r	Spalding United v Clifton Colliery	0-2
r2	Erith & Belvedere v Woking	6-1

Round Two

	Barking Town v Civil Service	2-1
	Boots Athletic v Crook Town	0-1
	Bournemouth Gasworks Athletic v Clapton	0-1
	Clifton Colliery v Cockfield	0-2
	Erith & Belvedere v Swindon Victoria	1-0
	Esh Winning v Apperley Bridge	2-0
	Eston United v Hoylake Trinity	6-0
	Evesham Town v West Auckland Town	5-1
	Ilford v Oxford City	1-1
	Leavesden Mental Hospital v Grays Athletic	1-0
	Northampton Nomads v Leytonstone	5-1
	Nunhead v Southall	0-2
	RAMC Aldershot v London Caledonians	1-1
	Stockton v Bishop Auckland	2-0
	Summerstown v Eastbourne	2-1
	Wycombe Wanderers v St Albans City	1-2
r	London Caledonians v RAMC Aldershot	2-0
r	Oxford City v Ilford	0-1

Round Three

	Erith & Belvedere v Clapton	4-3
	Esh Winning v Cockfield	0-1
	Eston United v Stockton	2-1
	Evesham Town v Crook Town	1-0
	Northampton Nomads v Leavesden Mental Hospital	2-1
	Southall v Ilford	1-1
	St Albans City v Barking Town	4-1
	Summerstown v London Caledonians	0-2
r	Ilford v Southall	7-2

Round Four

	Cockfield v Erith & Belvedere	4-0
	Evesham Town v Eston United	2-1
	Ilford v London Caledonians	0-1
	Northampton Nomads v St Albans City	0-1

Semi Finals

	Evesham Town v Cockfield	4-2 N
	London Caledonians v St Albans City	2-0 N

Final

	London Caledonians v Evesham Town	2-1 N

1923/24

Preliminary Round

5	East End Park v Leeds Harehills	1-2
	Low Moor v Liversedge	0-2
11	Beccles Town v Carrow Works	5-0
	Bury St Edmunds v King's Lynn Swifts	0-1
	Ely GE United v Lynn St Nicholas	1-0
	Godmanchester Town v King's Lynn	4-5
	Great Yarmouth Town v Norwich City Wanderers	1-0e
	Kirkley v Cromer	6-0
	Newmarket Town v St Ives Town	4-0
12	Shoeburyness Garrison v Chelmsford	1-3
	Sterling Athletic v Walthamstow Town	0-2
18	Cowley v St Frideswides	1-0
	Headington United v Witney Town	2-1
	Windsor & Eton v Slough	3-7
19	Arlesey Town v Barnet	0-4
	Bishops Stortford v Railway Clearing House	6-0
	Edmonton (1) v Boreham Wood	5-1
	RAF Henlow v Welwyn	1-2
	Ware v Cheshunt (1)	3-1
20	East Grinstead v Hove	0-1
	Felpham v Eastbourne RE Old Comrades	0-5
	Horsham v Wick	2-1
	Littlehampton v Hastings & St Leonards	0-2
	Newhaven v Southwick	3-0
24	Radstock Town v Newton Town	3-1

Qualifying Round One

1	Loftus Albion v Scarborough	2-3
2	Furness Athletic v Stockton Newtown	n/a
	Normanby Magnesite v Feversham United	3-2
	Stockton Malleable Institute v Cargo Fleet Ironworks	1-1
3	Eldon Albion v Stanley United	1-3
	Wooley Legion v Sunnybrow Olympic	2-0
5	Bingley Town v Liversedge	2-3
	Calverley v Silsden	4-3
	Rawdon v Bowling Albion	1-0
	Siddal v Cleckheaton	2-6
	Starbeck Athletic v Leeds Harehills	1-7
	Thornton United v Garforth	n/a
	Whitehall Printeries v Leeds Malvern	3-0
	Wibsey v Yorkshire Amateur	7-0
6	Birkenhead Amateurs v Harrowby	1-2
	Earle v Whalley Range	0-1
	Hoylake Trinity v Old Xaverians	4-3e
7	Attercliffe United v Bolsover Colliery	wo/s
8	Stapleford Brookhill v Gedling Colliery	3-1
9	Badsey Rangers v RAOC Hereford	4-3
	Birmingham University v Wolverhampton Amateurs	3-0
	Glendale Athletic v Boldmere St Michaels	n/a
	Golden Cross v Rowley Associates	3-1
	Hereford Thistle v Hereford City	3-1
	Kington Town v Hereford St Martins	1-3
	Sutton Town v Rubery St Chads	4-2
	Walsall Phoenix v Handsworth GS OB	n/a
11	Ely City v King's Lynn Swifts	3-1
	Great Yarmouth Town v Gorleston	1-4
	King's Lynn v Wisbech Town	4-0
	Lowestoft Town v Sheringham	2-0
	Morton's Athletic v Cambridge Town	0-3
	Newmarket Town v Ely GE United	3-1
	Norwich CEYMS v Beccles Town	3-2
	Norwich Priory Athletic v Kirkley	7-1

1923/24

12	1st Welsh Guards v Custom House	0-2
	Chelmsford v Walthamstow Grange	2-2
	GER Romford v Walthamstow Town	1-1e
	Harwich & Parkeston v Clacton Town	2-0
	Leiston Works Athletic v Stowmarket	n/a
	Orwell Works v Colchester Town	0-3
	Paxman's Athletic v Parkeston Railway	2-1
	Walthamstow Avenue v Leyton	0-2
13	Bexleyheath Town v Artillery College Sports	8-2
	Woolwich Polytechnic v Bostall Heath	0-4
14	Dorking v Aquarius	4-3
	Gwynne's Athletic v Merton Town	1-1
	Leyland Motors v Sutton United	2-2a
	Mitcham Wanderers v Metrogas	wo/s
	Redhill v Old Carthusians	4-0
	Tooting Town v Carshalton Athletic	4-2
15	Hampstead Town v Hounslow	6-4
	Harrow Weald v Hanwell Athletic	3-0
	Old Latymerians v Ashford (Middx)	3-3
	Old Lyonians v RAF Uxbridge	2-3
	Staines Lagonda v Savoy Hotel	2-1
	Uxbridge Town v Polytechnic	0-1
	Wealdstone v 12th London Regt Rangers	22-0
16	Leighton United v Aylesbury United	1-5
	Northampton Wanderers v Frickers Athletic	0-3
17	Farnham United Breweries v Hersham United	4-0
	Guildford v Camberley & Yorktown	1-0
	RAMC Aldershot v RAE Farnborough	0-1
	R Engineers (Aldershot) v Aldershot Institute Albion	3-4
	Walton-on-Thames v Aldershot Traction Company	1-4
	Weybridge v Egham	0-4
	Woking v RASC Aldershot	2-1a
18	Abingdon Town v Cowley	1-5
	Banbury Harriers v Abingdon Pavlova	1-4
	Henley Town v Newbury Town	2-0
	Marlow v Reading B.W.I.	0-4
	Morris Motors v Headington United	2-0
	Reading Biscuit Factory v Henley Comrades	2-1
	Slough v Maidenhead United	7-2
	Stones Athletic v Thame United	3-2a
19	Edmonton (1) v Barnet	1-3
	Enfield v Baldock Town	6-0
	Finchley v Ware	4-1
	Hertford Town v Stevenage Town	1-2
	Hitchin Athletic v Latymer OB	2-1
	Hitchin Blue Cross v Hoddesdon Town	7-1
	Welwyn v Bishops Stortford	3-1
	Wood Green v Bush Hill Park	5-2
20	Arundel v Hove	1-7
	Chichester v Eastbourne	4-1
	Eastbourne RE Old Comrades v Lewes	4-0
	Hastings & St Leonards v Rock-a-Nore	2-1
	Newhaven v Midhurst	3-3
	Shoreham v Bognor Town	2-2
	Vernon Athletic v Horsham	5-0
	Worthing v Allen West	2-1
21	2nd Argyll & Sutherland Highlanders v Burfield Park	4-0
	Gosport v Newport I of W	1-2
	Gosport Athletic v Gosport Albion Sports	2-1
	Osborne Athletic v Ryde Sports	3-5
	Portsea Island Gas Co v RN Depot Portsmouth	1-3
	RMLI Gosport v HMS Excellent	1-0
	Southampton CS v Shanklin	3-2
22	Blandford v Warminster Town	2-4
	Blandford Institute v Frome Town	4-3
	Bournemouth v Shaftesbury	3-0
	Christchurch v Salisbury Corinthians	0-3
	Portland United v Dorchester Town	6-0
	Westbury United v Bournemouth Tramways	3-8
	Westham v Wimborne	2-2
23	Brimscombe v Ferndale Road Working Mens	6-1
	Bristol St Georges Sports v Hanham Athletic	3-0
	Calne & Harris United v Cheltenham Town	1-0
	Chippenham Town v Leckhampton Sports	7-1
	Sneyd Park v Chippenham Rovers	4-5e
	Spencer Moulton v Clevedon	4-1
	Weston-super-Mare v Dursley Town	5-1
24	Clutton Wanderers v Clandown	2-1
	Coleford Athletic v Wells City	0-1
	Devizes Town v Gorsehill Workmen	2-2
	Glastonbury v Spencer Melksham	1-1e
	Heavitree United v Ilfracombe Town	1-1
	Pewsey Vale v Melksham Town & Avon United	3-2
	Radstock Town v Street	6-0
	Trowbridge Town v Peasedown St Johns Athletic	2-2e
2r	Cargo Fleet Ironworks v Stockton Malleable Institute	n/a
5r	Garforth v Thornton United	1-0
12r	Walthamstow Grange v Chelmsford	4-1e
r	Walthamstow Town v GER Romford	4-2
14r	Merton Town v Gwynne's Athletic	1-2
r	Sutton United v Leyland Motors	0-1a
15r	Ashford (Middx) v Old Latymerians	1-2
17r	Woking v RASC Aldershot	1-3
18r	Thame United v Stones Athletic	5-1
20r	Bognor Town v Shoreham	3-1
r	Midhurst v Newhaven	5-6e
22r	Wimborne v Westham	3-0
24r	Gorsehill Workmen v Devizes Town	4-3e
r	Ilfracombe Town v Heavitree United	0-1
r	Peasedown St Johns Athletic v Trowbridge Town	2-3
r	Spencer Melksham v Glastonbury	3-1
14r2	Sutton United v Leyland Motors	1-3 N

Qualifying Round Two

1	Carlin How Athletic v Scarborough Penguins	4-0
	Guisborough Belmont Athletic v Scarborough	2-1
	Lingdale Institute v Whitby Whitehall Swifts	3-1
	Whitby v Grosmont	3-1
2	Furness Athletic v Grangetown St Marys	4-3
	Haverton Hill v Cargo Fleet Ironworks	3-2e
	Normanby Magnesite v Stillington St Johns	1-0
	Stockton v South Bank East End	3-0
3	Chilton Colliery Recreation v Wooley Legion	8-0
	Ferryhill Athletic v Darlington Railway Athletic	5-2
	Stanley United v Coundon United	5-0
	West Auckland Town v Sunnyside United	2-0
4	Heaton Stannington v St Peters Albion	1-3
	Walker Park v Percy Main Amateurs	2-3
5	Cleckheaton v Wibsey	4-2
	Garforth v Whitehall Printeries	3-1
	Leeds Harehills v Calverley	2-0
	Rawdon v Liversedge	3-1
6	Harrowby v Old Chorltonians	n/a
	Liverpool Tramways v Hoylake Trinity	2-3
	Northern Nomads v Whalley Range	6-1
	Orrell v Collegiate OB	4-2
7	Attercliffe United v Youlgrave	1-0
	Hallam v Handsworth	7-0
	Norfolk Amateurs v Rotherham Amateurs	4-4e
	Sheffield Panthers v Sheffield	0-2
8	Basford United v Sneinton	4-1
	Players Athletic v Nottingham Magdala Amateurs	7-1
	Stapleford Brookhill v Lenton	0-1
	Woodthorpe v South Nottingham	1-0e
9	Badsey Rangers v Walsall Phoenix	6-1
	Birmingham University v Glendale Athletic	3-2
	Golden Cross v Hereford St Martins	6-3
	Sutton Town v Hereford Thistle	4-0
10	RAF Cranwell v Skegness United	wo/s
11	Ely City v Norwich Priory Athletic	1-5
	Gorleston v Cambridge Town	4-2
	Lowestoft Town v Norwich CEYMS	3-1
	Newmarket Town v King's Lynn	2-0
12	Colchester Town v Paxman's Athletic	5-1
	Harwich & Parkeston v Leiston Works Athletic	4-3
	Walthamstow Grange v Leyton	0-4
	Walthamstow Town v Custom House	1-1e
13	Dover United v Bostall Heath	3-6
	Old Charlton v Lamorbey	1-2
	RMLI Chatham v Cray Wanderers	4-0
	Royal Engineers Depot Battn v Bexleyheath Town	2-1
14	Gwynne's Athletic v Brighton Railway Athletic	3-2
	Leyland Motors v Tooting Town	2-1
	Mitcham Wanderers v Dorking	3-1
	Redhill v Kingstonian	4-3
15	Hampstead Town v Harrow Weald	2-2
	Old Latymerians v Polytechnic	1-3
	Staines Lagonda v Yiewsley	4-0
	Wealdstone v RAF Uxbridge	6-0
16	Aylesbury United v Luton Clarence	3-1
	Berkhamsted Town v Apsley	0-3
	Frickers Athletic v Luton Amateur	2-0
	Harpole Stars v Equitation School	0-1
17	Aldershot Institute Albion v Godalming	6-3
	Egham v RASC Aldershot	4-1
	Farnham United Breweries v Guildford	2-1
	RAE Farnborough v Aldershot Traction Company	2-0
18	Abingdon Pavlova v Cowley	5-1
	Reading B.W.I. v Reading Biscuit Factory	7-0
	Slough v Henley Town	4-1
	Thame United v Morris Motors	2-3
19	Enfield v Barnet	0-4
	Finchley v Hitchin Blue Cross	1-4e
	Hitchin Athletic v Welwyn	3-4
	Wood Green v Stevenage Town	5-1
20	Hastings & St Leonards v Bognor Town	2-2
	Newhaven v Hove	5-2
	Vernon Athletic v Eastbourne RE Old Comrades	1-4
	Worthing v Chichester	4-2
21	2nd Argyll & Sutherland Highlanders v Ryde Sports	5-0
	Newport I of W v RN Depot Portsmouth	2-4
	Portsmouth Amateurs v Gosport Athletic	0-3
	RMLI Gosport v Southampton CS	1-0
22	Bournemouth v Blandford Institute	1-0
	Portland United v Salisbury Corinthians	5-1
	Warminster Town v Poole	wo/s
	Wimborne v Bournemouth Tramways	1-4
23	Brimscombe v Weston-super-Mare	2-5
	Bristol St Georges Sports v Calne & Harris United	3-2
	Chippenham Rovers v Spencer Moulton	2-1
	Swindon Victoria v Chippenham Town	0-0e
24	Heavitree United v Clutton Wanderers	2-1e
	Pewsey Vale v Trowbridge Town	2-1
	Radstock Town v Gorsehill Workmen	2-1
	Spencer Melksham v Wells City	2-5
7r	Rotherham Amateurs v Norfolk Amateurs	3-2
12r	Custom House v Walthamstow Town	3-2
15r	Harrow Weald v Hampstead Town	2-5
20r	Bognor Town v Hastings & St Leonards	2-0
23r	Chippenham Town v Swindon Victoria	2-1

Qualifying Round Three

1	Carlin How Athletic v Whitby	2-2
	Guisborough Belmont Athletic v Lingdale Institute	2-0
2	Haverton Hill v Furness Athletic	2-2
	Normanby Magnesite v Stockton	2-2
3	Chilton Colliery Recreation v Stanley United	3-1
	West Auckland Town v Ferryhill Athletic	1-0
4	South Hetton Royal Rovers v Consett Ironworks	wo/s
	St Peters Albion v Percy Main Amateurs	n/a
5	Leeds Harehills v Cleckheaton	4-1
	Rawdon v Garforth	3-0
6	Harrowby v Northern Nomads	3-3
	Hoylake Trinity v Orrell	4-0
7	Rotherham Amateurs v Attercliffe United	0-1
	Sheffield v Hallam	1-4
8	Basford United v Players Athletic	1-4
	Lenton v Woodthorpe	2-1
9	Badsey Rangers v Golden Cross	1-0
	Sutton Town v Birmingham University	3-0
10	Grimsby Rovers v Hull Young Peoples Institute	2-1
	RAF Cranwell v Hull OB	3-2
11	Gorleston v Norwich Priory Athletic	3-1
	Lowestoft Town v Newmarket Town	1-1a
12	Colchester Town v Custom House	1-2
	Harwich & Parkeston v Leyton	2-4
13	Bostall Heath v Royal Engineers Depot Battn	5-2
	Lamorbey v RMLI Chatham	1-2
14	Mitcham Wanderers v Gwynne's Athletic	2-0
	Redhill v Leyland Motors	4-3
15	Hampstead Town v Polytechnic	7-2
	Staines Lagonda v Wealdstone	2-0
16	Aylesbury United v Frickers Athletic	3-1
	Equitation School v Apsley	1-2
17	Aldershot Institute Albion v RAE Farnborough	5-0
	Egham v Farnham United Breweries	1-2
18	Abingdon Pavlova v Reading B.W.I.	3-1
	Slough v Morris Motors	5-1
19	Barnet v Hitchin Blue Cross	4-2
	Welwyn v Wood Green	2-2
20	Newhaven v Bognor Town	4-0
	Worthing v Eastbourne RE Old Comrades	5-2
21	Gosport Athletic v 2nd Argyll & Sutherland Highl'drs	3-3
	RMLI Gosport v RN Depot Portsmouth	2-1
22	Bournemouth v Portland United	3-1
	Warminster Town v Bournemouth Tramways	1-2
23	Chippenham Rovers v Bristol St Georges Sports	1-3
	Weston-super-Mare v Chippenham Town	2-2
24	Radstock Town v Heavitree United	4-0
	Wells City v Pewsey Vale	2-1
1r	Whitby v Carlin How Athletic	1-2
2r	Furness Athletic v Haverton Hill	2-1
r	Stockton v Normanby Magnesite	2-0
6r	Northern Nomads v Harrowby	2-1
11r	Newmarket Town v Lowestoft Town	1-1a
19r	Wood Green v Welwyn	5-0
21r	2nd Argyll & Sutherland Highlanders v Gosport Ath.	1-2
23r	Chippenham Town v Weston-super-Mare	2-4
11r2	Newmarket Town v Lowestoft Town	3-0

Qualifying Round Four

1	Guisborough Belmont Athletic v Carlin How Athletic	2-0
2	Stockton v Furness Athletic	6-1
3	Chilton Colliery Recreation v West Auckland Town	3-1
4	St Peters Albion v South Hetton Royal Rovers	3-2
5	Leeds Harehills v Rawdon	0-0
6	Hoylake Trinity v Northern Nomads	2-9
7	Attercliffe United v Hallam	5-0
8	Players Athletic v Lenton	6-0
9	Sutton Town v Badsey Rangers	1-2
10	Grimsby Rovers v RAF Cranwell	2-1 v
11	Newmarket Town v Gorleston	4-5e
12	Custom House v Leyton	2-1
13	Bostall Heath v RMLI Chatham	1-2
14	Mitcham Wanderers v Redhill	0-3
15	Staines Lagonda v Hampstead Town	2-0
16	Apsley v Aylesbury United	1-2
17	Farnham United Breweries v Aldershot Institute Alb.	7-1
18	Abingdon Pavlova v Slough	2-6
19	Barnet v Wood Green	1-0
20	Newhaven v Worthing	3-5
21	RMLI Gosport v Gosport Athletic	1-0
22	Bournemouth Tramways v Bournemouth	1-1
23	Bristol St Georges Sports v Weston-super-Mare	0-0
24	Wells City v Radstock Town	1-0
5r	Rawdon v Leeds Harehills	3-0
10r	RAF Cranwell v Grimsby Rovers	3-1
22r	Bournemouth v Bournemouth Tramways	2-1
23r	Weston-super-Mare v Bristol St Georges Sports	0-1

Round One

Attercliffe United v Northern Nomads	2-1
Aylesbury United v Leavesden Mental Hospital	2-2a
Barnet v Chesham United	4-1
Bishop Auckland v Willington	1-0
Boots Athletic v Evesham Town	2-1
Botwell Mission v RN Depot	3-1
Bristol St Georges Sports v B'mouth Gasworks Ath.	1-0
Bromley v Nunhead	1-1
Chilton Colliery Rec. v Guisborough Belmont Ath.	5-0

1923/24 to 1924/25

Clapton v Ipswich Town	4-0
Clifton Colliery v Players Athletic	0-2
Cockfield v South Bank	1-0
Custom House v Barking Town	1-2
Dulwich Hamlet v Farnham United Breweries	4-1
Erith & Belvedere v Slough	5-3
Esh Winning v St Peters Albion	3-1
Eston United v Langley Park	3-1
Grays Athletic v Ilford	0-2
Leytonstone v Gorleston	1-0
London Caledonians v Civil Service	1-0
Marine v Rawdon	2-1
Northampton Nomads v Oxford City	4-2
RAF Cranwell v Badsey Rangers	2-1
Redhill v Summerstown	1-1a
Southall v Casuals	3-1
St Albans City v Wycombe Wanderers	1-1
Staines Lagonda v Wimbledon	1-0
Stockton v Apperley Bridge	1-1
Tow Law Town v Crook Town	5-3
Tufnell Park v RMLI Chatham	0-2
Wells City v Bournemouth	1-3
Worthing v RMLI Gosport	1-2
r Apperley Bridge v Stockton	0-5
r Leavesden Mental Hospital v Aylesbury United	1-2
r Nunhead v Bromley	3-1
r Summerstown v Redhill	1-0
r Wycombe Wanderers v St Albans City	2-1

Round Two

Attercliffe United v Stockton	1-0
Aylesbury United v Northampton Nomads	1-1a
Barking Town v London Caledonians	1-2
Boots Athletic v Players Athletic	2-1
Botwell Mission v Bristol St Georges Sports	6-1
Bournemouth v Barnet	3-1
Chilton Colliery Recreation v Tow Law Town	3-0
Clapton v Southall	3-0
Esh Winning v RAF Cranwell	1-1
Eston United v Bishop Auckland	0-1
Leytonstone v Dulwich Hamlet	1-4
Marine v Cockfield	3-0
Nunhead v RMLI Gosport	0-0a
RMLI Chatham v Erith & Belvedere	2-2
Summerstown v Staines Lagonda	1-1a
Wycombe Wanderers v Ilford	1-0
r Erith & Belvedere v RMLI Chatham	4-1
r Northampton Nomads v Aylesbury United	10-1
r Nunhead v RMLI Gosport	1-1
r RAF Cranwell v Esh Winning	1-2
r Staines Lagonda v Summerstown	2-1
r2 RMLI Gosport v Nunhead	1-1
r3 RMLI Gosport v Nunhead	2-1 N

Round Three

Attercliffe United v Dulwich Hamlet	1-2
Boots Athletic v Northampton Nomads	3-5
Bournemouth v Botwell Mission	0-1
Chilton Colliery Recreation v Bishop Auckland	2-0
Clapton v RMLI Gosport	6-1
Erith & Belvedere v Esh Winning	1-0
London Caledonians v Marine	5-0
Staines Lagonda v Wycombe Wanderers	1-2

Round Four

Botwell Mission v Erith & Belvedere	0-3
Dulwich Hamlet v Chilton Colliery Recreation	1-1
Northampton Nomads v Clapton	2-4
Wycombe Wanderers v London Caledonians	0-3
r Chilton Colliery Recreation v Dulwich Hamlet	3-0

Semi Finals

Clapton v Chilton Colliery Recreation	3-0 N
Erith & Belvedere v London Caledonians	1-1 N
r Erith & Belvedere v London Caledonians	0-0 N
r2 Erith & Belvedere v London Caledonians	3-1 N

Final

Clapton v Erith & Belvedere	3-0 N

1924/25

Preliminary Round

5	Whitehall Printeries v Selby Olympic	4-1
11	Beccles Town v Great Yarmouth Town	0-2
	Carrow Works v Norwich City Wanderers	3-2e
	Cromer v 5th Co BB OB	5-0
	Kirkley v Gorleston	2-1
	Newmarket Town v Godmanchester Town	2-0
	Norwich CEYMS v Lowestoft Town	2-3e
	St Ives Town v Bury Town	1-2
	Thetford Recreation v Ely City	3-1
12	2nd Royal Scots v Leiston Works Athletic	5-0
	Brentwood Mental Hospital v Barking Town	2-4
	Custom House v Leytonstone	0-1
	GER Romford v Walthamstow Grange	2-1
	Parkeston Railway v Orwell Works	3-1
18	Abingdon Town v Headington United	2-1
	Cowley v Banbury Harriers	2-0
	Henley Town v Caversham St Andrews	4-0
	Windsor & Eton v Slough	0-6
19	Bishops Stortford v Wood Green	1-0
20	Broadwater v Midhurst	3-2
	Chichester v Portslade	3-0
	East Grinstead v Bognor Town	1-5
	Littlehampton v Lewes	2-3
	Rock-a-Nore v Felpham	5-0
	Shoreham v Worthing	0-3
	Southwick v Allen West	5-1
	Wick v Royal Corps of Signals	0-5
23	Bradford Town v Sharpness	4-0
	Bristol St George v Swindon Casuals	3-1e
	Calne & Harris United v Swindon Victoria	1-4
	Chippenham Rovers v Kingswood	2-2
	Dursley Town v Cheltenham Town	1-0
	Gorsehill Workmen v Swindon Corinthians	n/a
	Sneyd Park v Frome Town	2-4
23r	Kingswood v Chippenham Rovers	2-0

Qualifying Round One

2	Normanby Magnesite v Grangetown St Marys	n/a
	Skelton Celtic & S Skelton U v Guisboro' Belmont	0-3
5	Apperley Bridge v Silsden	2-0
	Cleckheaton v Starbeck Athletic	11-1
	Leeds City v Rothwell Athletic	2-1
	Liversedge v Yorkshire Amateur	3-2
	Low Moor v Whitehall Printeries	1-4
	Otley v Siddal	2-1e
	Rawdon v Guiseley	4-3
	Wibsey v Calverley	3-2
6	Earle v Old Chorltonians	2-1
	Harrowby v Alderley Edge Athletic	4-1
	Northern Nomads v Whalley Range	2-0
	Old Xaverians v Furness Withy	2-6
	Orrell Athletic v Birkenhead Amateurs	3-0
7	Fulwood v Handsworth	3-6
9	Bournville Athletic v Badsey Rangers	5-0
	Golden Cross v Kepax	4-2e
	Headingley v Kington Town	5-1
	Hereford City v Birmingham YMCA	8-2
	Moor Green v Hereford Thistle	2-0
	Rowley Associates v Glendale Athletic	n/a
	Walsall Phoenix v Wolverhampton Amateurs	1-2
	West Bromwich Amateurs v Humber Recreation	0-2e
11	Cambridge Town v Bury Town	2-1
	Great Yarmouth Town v Norwich Priory Athletic	2-1
	Halesworth Town v Cromer	2-4
	King's Lynn v Norwich YMCA	3-0
	Kirkley v Lowestoft Town	1-2
	Sheringham v Carrow Works	1-3
	Thetford Recreation v Newmarket Town	1-2
	Wisbech Town v Lynn St Nicholas	4-2
12	2nd Royal Scots v Ipswich Works	3-0
	Chelmsford v Millwall United	5-4 D
	Clacton Town v Stowmarket	2-1
	Colchester Town v Harwich & Parkeston	3-1
	Hoffmann Athletic (Chelmsford) v Barking Town	1-5
	Ipswich Town v Parkeston Railway	1-3
	Leytonstone v Walthamstow Avenue	3-2a
	Walthamstow Town v GER Romford	1-6
13	Bostall Heath v Royal Engineers Depot Battn	2-0
	RN Depot v Lamorbey	3-2
14	Dorking v Leyland Motors	0-3
	Merton Town v Mitcham Wanderers	0-3
	Metropolitan Police v Carshalton Athletic	2-4
	Redhill v Tooting Town	4-1
	Southern Railway (1) v Sutton United	1-3
15	Old Latymerians v Hanwell Town	2-3
	Old Lyonians v Harrow Weald	1-0
	Polytechnic v Yiewsley	2-3
	Savoy Hotel v RAF Uxbridge	7-2
	Wealdstone v Ashford (Middx)	5-0
16	Aylesbury United v Luton Frickers	1-0
	Leavesden Mental Hospital v Luton Amateur	1-1a
	Luton Clarence v Berkhamsted Town	1-2a
	Stead & Simpson v Rushden OB BC	1-3
	Watford Corinthians v Leighton United	2-4
	Watford OB v Apsley	3-2e
	Wolverton Town v Daventry	6-2
17	1st Middx Regt v Wellington Works	0-2
	Addlestone United v Egham	0-2
	Aldershot Albion v Walton-on-Thames	3-2
	Aldershot Traction Co v Camberley & Yorktown	8-1
	Farnham United Breweries v Godalming	12-0
	RAMC Aldershot v Guildford	12-4
	Weybridge v RASC Aldershot	2-5
	Woking v Royal Engineers (Aldershot)	2-1
18	Abingdon Pavlova v Witney Town	4-3
	Bicester Town v St Fridewsides	0-2
	Cowley v Abingdon Town	3-2
	Henley Comrades v Henley Town	3-0
	Maidenhead United v Slough	1-4
	Marlow v Chesham United	0-3
	Reading B.W.I. v Newbury Town	3-4a
	Stones Athletic v Morris Motors	2-1
19	Baldock Town v Arlesey Town	2-1
	Bishops Stortford v Bush Hill Park	5-0
	Finchley v Cheshunt (1)	2-0
	Hoddesdon Town v Hertford Town	3-5
	Latymer OB v Edmonton (1)	2-3
	Railway Clearing House v Hitchin Blue Cross	2-5
	Ware v Enfield	0-1
	Welwyn v Stevenage Town	1-0
20	Bognor Town v Hove	3-1
	Eastbourne Old Comrades v Horsham Trinity	3-2e
	Horsham v Southwick	2-1
	Lewes v Broadwater	3-2
	Newhaven v Arundel	6-0
	Rock-a-Nore v Hastings & St Leonards	0-3
	Royal Corps of Signals v Vernon Athletic	7-0
	Worthing v Chichester	3-0
21	Burfield Park v HMS Excellent	0-5
	Fareham v RN Depot Portsmouth	4-0
	Portsea Island Gas Co v 2nd Argyll & Sutherland H.	3-1
	RE Southampton v Gosport Athletic	0-1
	Southampton CS v Gosport	5-0
22	Bournemouth Tramways v Wimborne	4-1
	Salisbury Corinthians v Dorchester Town	3-0
	Swanage v Blandford	1-4e
23	Bradford Town v Swindon Corinthians	1-6
	Butlers v Swindon Victoria	1-1e
	Clevedon v Bromham	7-0
	Dursley Town v Frome Town	1-0
	Spencer Moulton v Westbury United	4-1
	Trowbridge Town v Kingswood	4-2
	Warminster Town v Bristol St George	2-3e
	Weston-super-Mare v Chippenham Town	2-0
24	Devizes Town v Wells City	1-3
	Melksham Town & Avon United v Glastonbury	6-3
	Minehead v Ilfracombe Town	w/o/s
	Pewsey Vale v Radstock Town	1-3
	Spencer Melksham v Clutton Wanderers	0-2
	Street v Clandown	0-1
	Welton Rovers v Peasedown St Johns Athletic	2-0
12r	Walthamstow Avenue v Leytonstone	1-8
16r	Berkhamsted Town v Luton Clarence	2-5
r	Luton Amateur v Leavesden Mental Hospital	1-0
18r	Newbury Town v Reading B.W.I.	3-2
23r	Swindon Victoria v Butlers	n/a

Qualifying Round Two

1	Carlin How Athletic v Whitby Town	4-1
	Grosmont v Scarborough Penguins	2-2
	Loftus Albion v Scarborough	3-2
	Whitby Whitehall Swifts v Lingdale Institute	6-2
2	Guisborough Belmont Ath v South Bank East End	1-0
	South Bank Gasworks v Normanby Magnesite	n/a
	Stockton Malleable Institute v Haverton Hill	n/a
	Stockton Shamrock v Feversham United	6-4
3	Coundon United v Sunnybrow Olympic	2-1
	Crook Town v Stanley United	6-3e
	Darlington Railway Athletic v Eldon Albion	4-2
	Esh Winning v Willington	1-1e
5	Cleckheaton v Apperley Bridge	2-0
	Leeds City v Otley	8-1
	Whitehall Printeries v Rawdon	1-0
	Wibsey v Liversedge	2-1
6	Blundellsands v Collegiate OB	7-2
	Earle v Orrell Athletic	1-3
	Harrowby v Furness Withy	0-5
	Northern Nomads v Orrell	5-0
7	Handsworth v Sheffield Municipal Officers	2-3
	Ravens Amateurs (Sheffield) v Youlgrave	1-5
	Rotherham Amateurs v Sheffield Panthers	3-0
	Sheffield v Hallam	0-1
8	Gedling Colliery v Ransome & Marles	4-2
	Lenton v Basford United	3-2
	Nottingham Magdala Amateurs v South Nottingham	2-3a
	Sneinton v Clifton Colliery	2-2
9	Bournville Athletic v Humber Recreation	0-2
	Headingley v Golden Cross	3-3
	Hereford City v Moor Green	2-1
	Wolverhampton Amateurs v Rowley Associates	0-1a
10	Hull OB v unknown	n/a
11	Carrow Works v Cambridge Town	0-4
	Cromer v Newmarket Town	4-1
	King's Lynn v Great Yarmouth Town	3-2
	Wisbech Town v Lowestoft Town	3-2
12	Barking Town v Leytonstone	2-2a
	Clacton Town v GER Romford	0-2
	Colchester Town v Millwall United	4-2
	Parkeston Railway v 2nd Royal Scots	2-3

32

1924/25 to 1925/26

13 Artillery College Sports v Cray Wanderers	7-2
Bostall Heath v Woolwich Polytechnic	4-2e
Dover United v Bexleyheath Town	2-0
RM Chatham v RN Depot	0-0
14 Carshalton Athletic v Sutton United	1-4
Epsom Town v West Norwood	3-0
Leyland Motors v Redhill	0-4
Mitcham Wanderers v Aquarius	1-0
15 Hampstead Town v Yiewsley	9-0
Hanwell Town v Old Lyonians	4-2
Savoy Hotel v Hounslow	0-3
Wealdstone v Uxbridge Town	1-3
16 Aylesbury United v Luton Amateur	3-0
Luton Clarence v Wellingborough Nomads	6-4
Rushden OB BC v Watford OB	0-4
Wolverton Town v Leighton United	2-2
17 Aldershot Traction Company v Wellington Works	3-2
Egham v RASC Aldershot	3-3e
Farnham United Breweries v Woking	3-1
RAMC Aldershot v Aldershot Albion	3-1
18 Chesham United v St Frideswides	7-2
Henley Comrades v Abingdon Pavlova	0-5
Slough v Cowley	8-1
Stones Athletic v Newbury Town	3-4
19 Baldock Town v Edmonton (1)	0-3
Bishops Stortford v Finchley	1-5
Enfield v Hitchin Blue Cross	3-0
Welwyn v Hertford Town	1-5
20 Eastbourne Old Comrades v Worthing	2-3e
Hastings & St Leonards v Newhaven	2-1
Horsham v Bognor Town	3-2
Royal Corps of Signals v Lewes	3-0
21 Gosport Albion Sports v Fareham	6-2
HMS Excellent v Gosport Athletic	0-0
Ryde Sports v Portsea Island Gas Co	2-7
Southampton CS v Osborne Athletic	4-0
22 Blandford v Gillingham Town	12-0
Castle Hill v Bournemouth Gasworks Athletic	2-3
Salisbury Corinthians v Portland United	4-2
Shaftesbury v Bournemouth Tramways	2-3e
23 Clevedon v Bristol St George	2-0
Dursley Town v Swindon Corinthians	2-4
Spencer Moulton v Trowbridge Town	0-0e
Swindon Victoria v Weston-super-Mare	2-1
24 Clandown v Clutton Wanderers	4-3
Coleford Athletic v Minehead	3-2
Radstock Town v Wells City	0-3
Welton Rovers v Melksham Town & Avon United	5-2
1r Scarborough Penguins v Grosmont	2-1
3r Willington v Esh Winning	2-2e
8r Clifton Colliery v Sneinton	3-2e
r South Nottingham v Nottingham Magdala Amateurs	1-4
9r Golden Cross v Headingley	1-3
r Wolverhampton Amateurs v Rowley Associates	1-4
12r Leytonstone v Barking Town	2-1
13r RN Depot v RM Chatham	1-3
16r Leighton United v Wolverton Town	1-3 d
17r RASC Aldershot v Egham	2-1
21r Gosport Athletic v HMS Excellent	3-2
23r Trowbridge Town v Spencer Moulton	5-1
3r2 Willington v Esh Winning	2-2 N
3r3 Willington v Esh Winning	2-3 N

Qualifying Round Three

1 Carlin How Athletic v Whitby Whitehall Swifts	5-0
Loftus Albion v Scarborough Penguins	6-2
2 Normanby Magnesite v Stockton Malleable Institute	2-3
Stockton Shamrock v Guisborough Belmont Athletic	3-2
3 Coundon United v Darlington Railway Athletic	2-1
Crook Town v Esh Winning	3-0
4 Langley Park v Heaton Stannington	3-1
Walker Park v Percy Main Amateurs	0-1
5 Cleckheaton v Leeds City	4-3
Wibsey v Whitehall Printeries	1-2
6 Northern Nomads v Blundellsands	2-1
Orrell Athletic v Furness Withy	4-3
7 Hallam v Rotherham Amateurs	3-1
Sheffield Municipal Officers v Youlgrave	3-3a
8 Clifton Colliery v Nottingham Magdala Amateurs	2-1
Lenton v Gedling Colliery	1-1
9 Headingley v Rowley Associates	2-3
Hereford City v Humber Recreation	1-2
10 Hull Young Peoples Inst. v Hull Technical College	8-0
Red Cross v Spalding United	n/a
11 King's Lynn v Cromer	0-4
Wisbech Town v Cambridge Town	2-3
12 GER Romford v 2nd Royal Scots	2-0
Leytonstone v Colchester Town	4-2
13 Artillery College Sports v Dover United	2-2
Bostall Heath v RM Chatham	3-1
14 Epsom Town v Redhill	0-5
Mitcham Wanderers v Sutton United	3-0
15 Hampstead Town v Uxbridge Town	5-1
Hounslow v Hanwell Town	4-2
16 Aylesbury United v Leighton United	3-4
Luton Clarence v Watford OB	2-1
17 Aldershot Traction Co v Farnham United Breweries	3-1
RASC Aldershot v RAMC Aldershot	2-1
18 Abingdon Pavlova v Newbury Town	1-3
Chesham United v Slough	2-0
19 Enfield v Edmonton (1)	3-0
Finchley v Hertford Town	1-3

20 Hastings & St Leonards v Horsham	9-2
Royal Corps of Signals v Worthing	5-1
21 Gosport Albion Sports v Gosport Athletic	1-1
Southampton CS v Portsea Island Gas Co	0-3
22 Blandford v Bournemouth Gasworks Athletic	1-1
Bournemouth Tramways v Salisbury Corinthians	1-0
23 Swindon Corinthians v Clevedon	0-0
Trowbridge Town v Swindon Victoria	1-0
24 Clandown v Wells City	1-1
Welton Rovers v Coleford Athletic	5-0
7r Youlgrave v Sheffield Municipal Officers	5-1
8r Gedling Colliery v Lenton	1-2
13r Bostall Heath v RM Chatham	3-1
r Dover United v Artillery College Sports	2-3
21r Gosport Athletic v Gosport Albion Sports	2-0
22r Bournemouth Gasworks Athletic v Blandford	1-1e
23r Clevedon v Swindon Corinthians	3-1
24r Wells City v Clandown	5-1
22r2 Bournemouth Gasworks Athletic v Blandford	2-1

Qualifying Round Four

1 Loftus Albion v Carlin How Athletic	1-0
2 Stockton Malleable Institute v Stockton Shamrock	1-2
3 Crook Town v Coundon United	3-0
4 Langley Park v Percy Main Amateurs	3-1
5 Whitehall Printeries v Cleckheaton	4-1
6 Orrell Athletic v Northern Nomads	2-3
7 Youlgrave v Hallam	1-2
8 Clifton Colliery v Lenton	0-0
9 Humber Recreation v Rowley Associates	3-2
10 Red Cross v Hull Young Peoples Institute	3-3
11 Cambridge Town v Cromer	2-2
12 Leytonstone v GER Romford	3-3
13 Bostall Heath v Artillery College Sports	5-1
14 Mitcham Wanderers v Redhill	4-2
15 Hounslow v Hampstead Town	0-4
16 Leighton United v Luton Clarence	2-2
17 RASC Aldershot v Aldershot Traction Company	1-2
18 Chesham United v Newbury Town	4-1
19 Hertford Town v Enfield	2-4
20 Hastings & St Leonards v Royal Corps of Signals	1-0
21 Gosport Athletic v Portsea Island Gas Co	1-1
22 B'nemouth Gasworks Ath v Bournemouth Tramways	3-0
23 Clevedon v Trowbridge Town	4-1
24 Welton Rovers v Wells City	7-0
8r Lenton v Clifton Colliery	2-1
10r Hull Young Peoples Institute v Red Cross	5-1
11r Cromer v Cambridge Town	1-3
12r GER Romford v Leytonstone	1-2
16r Luton Clarence v Leighton United	1-1a
21r Portsea Island Gas Co v Gosport Albion Sports	3-0
16r2 Leighton United v Luton Clarence	4-3

Round One

Aldershot Traction Company v Wycombe Wan.	3-1
Bishop Auckland v South Bank	2-1
Botwell Mission v Barnet	0-2
Bournemouth v RM Portsmouth	3-5
B'nemouth Gasworks Ath v Hastings & St Leonards	1-1
Bromley v St Albans City	0-5
Cambridge Town v Northampton Nomads	2-0
Chilton Colliery Recreation v Stockton Shamrock	2-1
Civil Service v Tufnell Park	0-2
Clapton v London Caledonians	2-0
Clevedon v Welton Rovers	2-1
Crook Town v Stockton	1-1
Dulwich Hamlet v Enfield	1-1
Eastbourne v Portsea Island Gas Co	1-1
Grays Athletic v Southall	0-4
Hallam v Whitehall Printeries	0-0
Hampstead Town v Casuals	2-0
Hull Young Peoples Institute v Attercliffe United	0-2
Humber Recreation v Evesham Town	2-5
Ilford v Chesham United	1-0
Kingstonian v Leyton	0-1
Langley Park v Cockfield	2-1
Lenton v Boots Athletic	0-2
Leytonstone v Oxford City	1-2
Loftus Albion v Ferryhill Athletic	2-3
Marine v Northern Nomads	0-3
Mitcham Wanderers v Erith & Belvedere	3-1
Nunhead v Summerstown	3-1
Players Athletic v RAF Cranwell	5-1
Staines Lagonda v Leighton United	4-2
Tow Law Town v Eston United	7-1
Wimbledon v Bostall Heath	0-3
r Enfield v Dulwich Hamlet	0-4
r Hastings & St Leonards v B'emouth Gasworks Ath.	4-0
r Portsea Island Gas Co v Eastbourne	1-0
r Stockton v Crook Town	4-0
r Whitehall Printeries v Hallam	0-1 N

Round Two

Barnet v Staines Lagonda	2-0
Bishop Auckland v Tow Law Town	3-2
Boots Athletic v Players Athletic	3-6
Cambridge Town v Clevedon	3-1
Chilton Colliery Recreation v Stockton	2-1
Clapton v Mitcham Wanderers	3-1
Dulwich Hamlet v Aldershot Traction Company	3-1
Hallam v Attercliffe United	0-0
Hampstead Town v Bostall Heath	1-3
Hastings & St Leonards v St Albans City	1-7
Ilford v Southall	0-1
Langley Park v Ferryhill Athletic	3-2
Northern Nomads v Evesham Town	3-1
Nunhead v RM Portsmouth	2-0
Oxford City v Leyton	4-2
Tufnell Park v Portsea Island Gas Co	8-0
r Attercliffe United v Hallam	1-3

Round Three

Bostall Heath v St Albans City	0-1
Cambridge Town v Clapton	1-3
Chilton Colliery Recreation v Langley Park	3-0
Hallam v Bishop Auckland	2-1
Nunhead v Dulwich Hamlet	1-1
Oxford City v Barnet	2-5
Players Athletic v Northern Nomads	2-3
Tufnell Park v Southall	1-4
r Dulwich Hamlet v Nunhead	2-1

Round Four

Barnet v St Albans City	1-2
Chilton Colliery Recreation v Northern Nomads	0-2
Clapton v Hallam	1-0
Southall v Dulwich Hamlet	1-0

Semi Finals

Clapton v Northern Nomads	2-1 N
Southall v St Albans City	1-1 N
r Southall v St Albans City	1-0 N

Final

Clapton v Southall	2-1 N

1925/26

Preliminary Round

11 Beccles Town v Carrow Works	2-1
Cromer v Sheringham	1-0
Godmanchester Town v St Neots & District	2-5
Gorleston v Halesworth Town	13-1
King's Lynn WM v Ely City	3-5
Kirkley v Norwich YMCA	4-1
Lynn United v Thetford Recreation	0-1
March GE United v King's Lynn	0-4
Norwich Priory Athletic v Great Yarmouth Town	1-5
Wisbech Town v Bury Town	6-1
12 Brentwood & Warley v Chelmsford	3-0
Brentwood Mental Hospital v Coryton	3-0
Clacton Town v Orwell Works	6-4
Hays Wharf v Grays Athletic	0-2
Hoffmann Athletic (Chelmsford) v GER Romford	3-4
Ipswich Town v 2nd Leicestershire Regt	wo/s
Ipswich Works v Leiston Works Athletic	3-2
Millwall United v Walthamstow Avenue	3-1
Stowmarket v Colchester Town	3-2
Walton United v Brantham Athletic	3-3
17 Aldershot Albion v RASC Aldershot	1-0
Camberley & Yorktown v R Engineers (Aldershot)	10-1
Thorneycroft Athletic v Godalming	5-1
18 Banbury Harriers v Bicester Town	2-5
Morris Motors v Cowley	6-2
Reading B.W.I. v Slough	1-8
Stones Athletic v Oxford City	0-10
20 East Grinstead v Hastings & St Leonards	1-2
Hove v Vernon Athletic	1-0 N
Lewes v Worthing	4-5
Rock-a-Nore v Vale Orton United	0-1
Southwick v Shoreham	3-2
Wick v Newhaven	0-1
23 Chalford v Swindon Victoria	3-1
Dursley Town v Cadbury's Athletic	1-3
24 Bromham v Westbury United	0-4
Chippenham Rovers v Spencer Melksham	1-2
Coleford Athletic v Radstock Town	1-2e
Pewsey Vale v Devizes Town	3-1
Street v Wells City	0-1
Trowbridge Town v Spencer Moulton	5-0
Warminster Town v Melksham Town & Avon United	2-5
12r Brantham Athletic v Walton United	6-4

1925/26

Qualifying Round One

3	Cockfield v 6th Durham Light Infantry	2-1
	Darlington Railway Athletic v West Auckland Town	1-6
	Esh Winning v Butter Knowle WM	3-2
	Sunnybrow Olympic v Thornley Albion	0-4
5	Apperley Bridge v Cleckheaton	5-5e
	Guiseley v Low Moor	6-0
	Liversedge v Luddendenfoot	11-1
	Otley v Rawdon	0-5
	Rothwell Athletic v Silsden	9-0
	Scholes Athletic v Ilkley	12-0
	Whitehall Printeries v Siddal	3-0
	Yorkshire Amateur v Cleator Moor Celtic	1-0
6	Blundellsands v Orrell Athletic	3-3
	Collegiate OB v Harrowby	3-4e
	Earle v West Kirby	0-1
	Old Chorltonians v Marine	1-4
	Orrell v Formby	6-3
	Whalley Range v Birkenhead Amateurs	4-0
7	Norfolk Amateurs v Chesterfield Corinthians	11-0
	Norton Woodseats v Sheffield University	6-4e
8	Arnold Town v South Nottingham	1-2
	Cammell Laird v Stapleford Brookhill	0-1
	Hucknall Byron v Lenton	1-3
9	Badsey Rangers v Kington Town	3-1
	Bournville Athletic v Birmingham YMCA	3-1
	Glendale Athletic v Humber Recreation	3-5
	Kepax v Hereford City	1-3
	Old Wulfrunians v Braunston United	0-1
	Oldbury Town Recreation v Wolverhampton Ams	3-1
	Peel Corner v Barnt Green United	2-3
	Rugeley Villa v Moor Green	5-2
11	Beccles Town v Gorleston	4-0
	Great Yarmouth Town v Cromer	5-2
	Kirkley v Lowestoft Town	2-1
	Lynn St Nicholas v Wisbech Town	2-9
	Norwich City Wanderers v Norwich CEYMS	5-4
	St Ives Town v Newmarket Town	5-1
	St Neots & District v King's Lynn	2-5
	Thetford Recreation v Ely City	1-1e
12	Brentwood Mental Hospital v Custom House	1-0
	Crittall Athletic v Harwich & Parkeston	1-5
	Grays Athletic v Brentwood & Warley	6-1
	Ipswich Town v Ipswich Works	5-0
	Millwall United v Walthamstow Grange	6-2
	Parkeston Railway v Brantham Athletic	2-1
	Shoeburyness Garrison v GER Romford	1-2
	Stowmarket v Clacton Town	5-2
13	1st Queens Royal Regt v Dover Marine Station	3-4
	Artillery College Sports v Woolwich Polytechnic	4-1
	Bexleyheath Town v Beckenham	7-1
	Bromley v Sidcup	4-1
	Erith & Belvedere v Woolwich	1-0
	RM Chatham v Royal Engineers Depot Battn	3-1
	Siemen's Sports v Cray Wanderers	1-5
14	Aquarius v Reigate Priory	7-0
	Epsom Town v Sutton United	0-1
	Summerstown v Mitcham Wanderers	2-1 v
	Tooting Town v Wimbledon	3-2
	West Norwood v Carshalton Athletic	4-2
15	Ashford (Middx) v Hendon Town	0-4
	Hanwell Town v Polytechnic	2-1
	Hounslow v RAF Uxbridge	6-1
	Staines Town v Wealdstone	3-2
	Sutton Court v Old Lyonians	1-2
16	Boxmoor v Leavesden Mental Hospital	2-4
	Leagrave & District v Luton Clarence	wo/s
	Leighton United v Daventry	3-1
	Watford OB v Aylesbury United	5-0
	Wellingborough Nomads v Walgrave Amber	3-5
17	10th Royal Hussars v Camberley & Yorktown	6-0
	2nd Rifle Brigade v Egham	3-0
	Addlestone v Weybridge	0-1
	Aldershot Albion v 1st Middx Regt	2-4
	Guildford v Farnham United Breweries	2-5
	Thorneycroft Athletic v Walton-on-Thames	8-1
	Wellington Works v RAMC Aldershot	0-3
	Woking v Aldershot Traction Company	2-2e
18	Abingdon Town v Windsor & Eton	0-7
	Bicester Town v Maidenhead United	1-3
	Henley Comrades v St Frideswides	2-4
	Morris Motors v Caversham St Andrews	4-2
	Newbury Town v Abingdon Pavlova	2-0
	Oxford City v Headington United	6-0
	Slough v Marlow	6-2
	Witney Town v Henley Town	3-0
19	Bishops Stortford v Thorley Works	4-7
	Bush Hill Park v Hoddesdon Town	6-1
	Finchley v Cheshunt (1)	0-1
	Hertford Town v Arlesey Town	10-3
	Letchworth Town v Baldock Town	5-1
	Welwyn v Hitchin Blue Cross	1-3
	Wood Green v Enfield	3-1
20	Chichester v Southwick	3-6
	Eastbourne Old Comrades v Bognor Town	4-1
	Hastings & St Leonards v Vale Orton United	5-1
	Horsham v Allen West	4-1
	Horsham Trinity v Hove	2-7
	Newhaven v Littlehampton	6-3
	Pulborough v Broadwater	2-1
	Worthing v Portslade	2-0
21	East Cowes v Osborne Athletic	5-3
	Emsworth v HMS Excellent	1-2
	Gosport Albion Sports v Ryde Sports	3-1
	RM Portsmouth v RAOC Portsmouth	5-1
	RN Depot Portsmouth v Portsea Island Gas Co	3-2
23	Brimscombe v Cadbury's Athletic	3-5
	Cheltenham Town v Swindon Corinthians	0-4
	Clevedon v Sneyd Park	3-2
	Hanham Athletic v Bristol St George	2-1
	Sharpness v Chalford	5-3
	Swindon Casuals v Leckhampton	3-2
	Union Jack v Kingswood	1-2
	Weston-super-Mare v Staple Hill Athletic	4-2
24	Calne & Harris United v Pewsey Vale	7-1
	Chippenham Town v Spencer Melksham	3-0
	Frome Town v Glastonbury	2-1
	Melksham Town & Avon United v Bradford Town	8-0
	Peasedown St Johns Athletic v Clandown	0-4
	Radstock Town v Clutton Wanderers	1-0
	Trowbridge Town v Westbury United	1-3
	Welton Rovers v Wells City	4-3
5r	Cleckheaton v Apperley Bridge	2-1e
6r	Orrell Athletic v Blundellsands	2-8
11r	Ely City v Thetford Recreation	2-5
14r	Mitcham Wanderers v Summerstown	n/a
17r	Aldershot Traction Company v Woking	2-3

Qualifying Round Two

1	Carlin How Athletic v Guisborough Belmont Athletic	4-1
	Scarborough v Scarborough Penguins	2-1
	Whitby Town v Lingdale Institute	6-5e
	Whitby Whitehall Swifts v Loftus Albion	2-0
2	Grangetown St Marys v Feversham United	1-1
	Normanby Magnesite v South Bank East End	7-3
	Stockton Malleable Institute v Eston United	4-2
	Stockton Shamrock v Stockton Tilery	4-0
3	Cockfield v Thornley Albion	2-1
	Esh Winning v Coundon United	7-1
	West Auckland Town v Stanley United	2-1
	Willington v Eldon Albion	10-3
5	Cleckheaton v Liversedge	2-4
	Guiseley v Rawdon	2-2
	Rothwell Athletic v Whitehall Printeries	1-6
	Scholes Athletic v Yorkshire Amateur	2-1
6	Blundellsands v Orrell	2-6
	Furness Withy v Old Xaverians	5-2
	Marine v Harrowby	5-1
	West Kirby v Whalley Range	3-1
7	Norton Woodseats v Norfolk Amateurs	3-0
	Sheffield v Rotherham Amateurs	7-3
	Sheffield Municipal Officers v Fulwood	5-2
	Youlgrave v Ravens Amateurs (Sheffield)	3-1
8	Clifton Colliery v Stapleford Brookhill	1-3
	Gedling Colliery v South Nottingham	4-1
	Lenton v Nottingham Magdala Amateurs	3-0
	Sneinton v Basford United	2-4
9	Bournville Athletic v Hereford City	6-1
	Humber Recreation v Braunston United	4-2
	Oldbury Town Recreation v Barnt Green United	8-3
	Rugeley Villa v Badsey Rangers	5-2
10	Hull OB v Old Cravonians	2-1
	RAF Cranwell v Grimsby Albion	4-2e
11	Kirkley v Beccles Town	4-3a
	Norwich City Wanderers v King's Lynn	4-3
	Thetford Recreation v St Ives Town	2-0
	Wisbech Town v Great Yarmouth Town	1-8
12	Brentwood Mental Hospital v Millwall United	5-3
	GER Romford v Grays Athletic	3-3a
	Harwich & Parkeston v Ipswich Town	1-2
	Stowmarket v Parkeston Railway	6-1
13	Bexleyheath Town v Erith & Belvedere	1-5
	Bromley v Dover Marine Station	8-1
	RM Chatham v Artillery College Sports	3-2
	RN Depot v Cray Wanderers	6-1
14	Dorking v Tooting Town	0-2
	Leyland Motors v Mitcham Wanderers	0-2
	Metropolitan Police v West Norwood	2-4
	Sutton United v Aquarius	4-2
15	Hanwell Town v Savoy Hotel	3-1
	Old Lyonians v Hounslow	5-3
	Staines Town v Hendon Town	5-1
	Yiewsley v Harrow Weald	1-0
16	Berkhamsted Town v Watford OB	4-3
	Leavesden Mental Hospital v Apsley	0-2
	Leighton United v Leagrave & District	2-5
	Luton Amateur v Walgrave Amber	2-5
17	1st Middx Regt v Weybridge	4-3
	2nd Rifle Brigade v Woking	6-1
	Farnham United Breweries v RAMC Aldershot	3-1
	Thorneycroft Athletic v 10th Royal Hussars	6-4
18	Newbury Town v Maidenhead United	6-5
	Oxford City v Morris Motors	4-3
	Slough v Windsor & Eton	2-3
	Witney Town v St Frideswides	4-3
19	Cheshunt (1) v Thorley Works	9-2
	Hitchin Blue Cross v Hertford Town	1-3
	Letchworth Town v Bush Hill Park	8-0
	Wood Green v Edmonton (1)	3-1
20	Horsham v Eastbourne Old Comrades	3-2
	Newhaven v Southwick	1-2
	Pulborough v Hastings & St Leonards	1-4
	Worthing v Hove	1-2
21	2nd Argyll & Sutherland H. v RN Depot Portsmouth	4-2
	Gosport Athletic v Fareham	6-1
	HMS Excellent v East Cowes	9-0
	RM Portsmouth v Gosport Albion Sports	5-2
22	Bournemouth Tramways v B'nemouth Gasworks Ath.	2-0
	Portland United v Gillingham Town	7-1
	Salisbury Corinthians v RE Southampton	0-1
	Wimborne v Blandford	1-3
23	Cadbury's Athletic v Kingswood	0-1
	Hanham Athletic v Clevedon	2-1
	Sharpness v Weston-super-Mare	3-1
	Swindon Corinthians v Swindon Casuals	2-1
24	Chippenham Town v Clandown	3-1
	Frome Town v Westbury United	2-3
	Melksham Town & Avon United v Calne & Harris U	6-2
	Radstock Town v Welton Rovers	2-2e
2r	Feversham United v Grangetown St Marys	n/a
5r	Rawdon v Guiseley	4-1
11r	Beccles Town v Kirkley	2-0
12r	GER Romford v Grays Athletic	4-2
24r	Welton Rovers v Radstock Town	7-4

Qualifying Round Three

1	Carlin How Athletic v Whitby Whitehall Swifts	3-0
	Scarborough v Whitby Town	10-0
2	Feversham United v Stockton Malleable Institute	4-1
	Stockton Shamrock v Normanby Magnesite	2-1
3	Cockfield v Esh Winning	3-1
	Willington v West Auckland Town	2-2
4	New York United v Jesmond Villa	4-2
	Percy Main Amateurs v Newcastle Bohemians	4-2
5	Rawdon v Liversedge	1-4
	Scholes Athletic v Whitehall Printeries	1-3
6	Furness Withy v Orrell	5-4e
	Marine v West Kirby	4-1
7	Sheffield v Youlgrave	2-3
	Sheffield Municipal Officers v Norton Woodseats	4-5
8	Gedling Colliery v Basford United	1-2
	Lenton v Stapleford Brookhill	7-2
9	Bournville Athletic v Rugeley Villa	5-1
	Oldbury Town Recreation v Humber Recreation	1-3
10	Hull Young Peoples Institute v Hull OB	5-2
	Ruston & Hornsby v RAF Cranwell	0-4
11	Norwich City Wanderers v Beccles Town	1-3
	Thetford Recreation v Great Yarmouth Town	1-3
12	Ipswich Town v Brentwood Mental Hospital	1-4
	Stowmarket v GER Romford	0-4
13	Erith & Belvedere v Bromley	2-0
	RM Chatham v RN Depot	2-2
14	Mitcham Wanderers v West Norwood	0-1
	Sutton United v Tooting Town	2-2
15	Staines Town v Old Lyonians	3-2
	Yiewsley v Hanwell Town	0-4
16	Apsley v Walgrave Amber	4-2
	Berkhamsted Town v Leagrave & District	1-7
17	Farnham United Breweries v 1st Middx Regt	1-3
	Thorneycroft Athletic v 2nd Rifle Brigade	2-5
18	Windsor & Eton v Oxford City	0-2
	Witney Town v Newbury Town	2-2
19	Letchworth Town v Hertford Town	0-2
	Wood Green v Cheshunt (1)	1-2
20	Horsham v Southwick	1-4
	Hove v Hastings & St Leonards	5-0
21	2nd Argyll & Sutherland H. v RM Portsmouth	3-0
	HMS Excellent v Gosport Athletic	0-0
22	Portland United v Blandford	7-2
	RE Southampton v Bournemouth Tramways	0-1
23	Hanham Athletic v Swindon Corinthians	1-1
	Kingswood v Sharpness	3-1
24	Melksham Town & Avon United v Chippenham Town	1-3
	Westbury United v Welton Rovers	1-2
3r	West Auckland Town v Willington	3-1
13r	RN Depot v RM Chatham	1-2
14r	Tooting Town v Sutton United	0-1
18r	Newbury Town v Witney Town	2-0
21r	Gosport Athletic v HMS Excellent	1-3
23r	Swindon Corinthians v Hanham Athletic	2-4

Qualifying Round Four

1	Scarborough v Carlin How Athletic	9-4
2	Feversham United v Stockton Shamrock	2-7
3	West Auckland Town v Cockfield	0-2
4	Percy Main Amateurs v New York United	3-2
5	Whitehall Printeries v Liversedge	1-0
6	Marine v Furness Withy	1-3
7	Youlgrave v Norton Woodseats	3-0 v
8	Basford United v Lenton	2-1
9	Humber Recreation v Bournville Athletic	1-0
10	RAF Cranwell v Hull Young Peoples Institute	2-2
11	Beccles Town v Great Yarmouth Town	2-3
12	GER Romford v Brentwood Mental Hospital	3-1
13	RM Chatham v Erith & Belvedere	0-2
14	West Norwood v Sutton United	1-0
15	Hanwell Town v Staines Town	1-0
16	Apsley v Leagrave & District	3-4
17	1st Middx Regt v 2nd Rifle Brigade	3-0
18	Oxford City v Newbury Town	2-2
19	Hertford Town v Cheshunt (1)	1-2
20	Southwick v Hove	2-4
21	HMS Excellent v 2nd Argyll & Sutherland Highl'ndrs	4-2
22	Portland United v Bournemouth Tramways	1-0

1925/26 to 1926/27

23 Hanham Athletic v Kingswood	0-2
24 Chippenham Town v Welton Rovers	1-1
7r Norton Woodseats v Youlgrave	4-1
10r Hull Young Peoples Institute v RAF Cranwell	0-6
18r Newbury Town v Oxford City	2-3
24r Welton Rovers v Chippenham Town	5-1

Round One

1st Middx Regt v London Caledonians	1-4
Barking Town v Leyton	0-4
Barnet v Hampstead Town	3-5
Basford United v Attercliffe United	5-2
Bishop Auckland v Stockton	2-2
Bostall Heath v Nunhead	1-5
Botwell Mission v Kingstonian	1-2
Bournemouth v Portland United	1-2
Cambridge Town v Great Yarmouth Town	3-2
Casuals v Oxford City	6-4 v
Chesham United v Redhill	1-2
Cheshunt (1) v HMS Excellent	3-2
Chilton Colliery Recreation v Cockfield	2-0
Civil Service v Southall	2-2
Erith & Belvedere v Eastbourne	5-1
Ferryhill Athletic v Langley Park	4-1
GER Romford v Northampton Nomads	3-1
Hallam v Players Athletic	9-4
Hanwell Town v Uxbridge Town	1-3
Humber Recreation v Whitehall Printeries	2-4
Kingswood v Welton Rovers	1-2
Leytonstone v Leagrave & District	1-1
Northern Nomads v Furness Withy	2-0
Norton Woodseats v Boots Athletic	3-1
Percy Main Amateurs v Crook Town	1-4
RAF Cranwell v Evesham Town	0-2
Scarborough v South Bank	7-2
St Albans City v Clapton	3-1
Tow Law Town v Stockton Shamrock	2-2
Tufnell Park v Ilford	1-6
West Norwood v Dulwich Hamlet	0-5
Wycombe Wanderers v Hove	10-2
r Leagrave & District v Leytonstone	1-6
r Oxford City v Casuals	1-0 v
r Southall v Civil Service	4-1
r Stockton v Bishop Auckland	5-1
r Stockton Shamrock v Tow Law Town	2-3
r2 Oxford City v Casuals	1-0 N

Round Two

Crook Town v Chilton Colliery Recreation	3-1
Ferryhill Athletic v Tow Law Town	2-1
GER Romford v London Caledonians	1-1
Hallam v Basford United	5-1
Hampstead Town v Wycombe Wanderers	1-0
Kingstonian v Redhill	1-4
Leytonstone v Cambridge Town	3-0
Northern Nomads v Whitehall Printeries	5-2
Norton Woodseats v Evesham Town	3-1
Nunhead v Erith & Belvedere	3-2
Oxford City v Dulwich Hamlet	5-1
Portland United v Lenton	1-1
Scarborough v Stockton	1-3
Southall v Welton Rovers	3-1
St Albans City v Cheshunt (1)	3-1
Uxbridge Town v Ilford	3-3
r Ilford v Uxbridge Town	10-2
r Leyton v Portland United	4-1
r London Caledonians v GER Romford	3-1

Round Three

Ferryhill Athletic v Hampstead Town	4-0
Northern Nomads v Hallam	5-1
Norton Woodseats v Crook Town	1-1
Nunhead v Leytonstone	5-1
Oxford City v Leyton	2-3
Redhill v Ilford	4-1
Southall v St Albans City	1-1
Stockton v London Caledonians	2-1
r Crook Town v Norton Woodseats	4-2
r St Albans City v Southall	3-2

Round Four

Crook Town v Northern Nomads	1-3
Redhill v Leyton	3-2
St Albans City v Ferryhill Athletic	4-1
Stockton v Nunhead	2-1

Semi Finals

Northern Nomads v Redhill	7-1 N
Stockton v St Albans City	2-1 N

Final

Northern Nomads v Stockton	7-1 N

1926/27

Preliminary Round

11 Beccles Town v Sheringham	4-0
Diss Town v Carrow Works	1-3
Ely City v Lowestoft Town	0-4
Godmanchester Town v King's Lynn WM	4-1
Gorleston v March Town	12-2
King's Lynn v Lynn United	4-1e
Kirkley v Cromer	3-2
March GE United v Norwich City Wanderers	4-3
St Ives Town v Great Yarmouth Town	1-8
St Neots & District v Wisbech Town	5-4
12 Clacton Town v Hays Wharf	2-0
Colchester Town v Crittall Athletic	2-0
Grays Athletic v Hoffmann Athletic (Chelmsford)	8-1
Harwich & Parkeston v Tate Institute	3-1
Ipswich Town v Millwall United	4-4e
Leiston Works Athletic v 2nd Leicestershire Regt	0-6
Stowmarket v Orwell Works	5-2
Walton United v Custom House	3-4
17 Weybridge v Aldershot Albion	5-0
18 Bicester Town v Abingdon Pavlova	4-0
Henley Town v Caversham St Andrews	3-5
20 Allen West v East Grinstead	1-2e
Hollington United v Worthing	3-3e
Rock-a-Nore v Littlehampton	1-5
Shoreham v Broadwater	3-0
23 Cheltenham Town v Chalford	1-2
Clevedon v Swindon Casuals	4-0
Dursley Town v Sneyd Park	2-5
Keynsham v Bristol St George	1-4
Swindon Corinthians v Weston-super-Mare	0-1
Tewkesbury Town v Hanham Athletic	5-2
Union Jack v Cadbury's Athletic	1-2
24 Bradford Town v Chippenham Rovers	2-1e
Chippenham Town v Trowbridge Town	3-1
Glastonbury v Street	3-4
Radstock Town v Frome Town	1-0
Wells City v Bromham	4-1
Westbury United v Welton Rovers	0-1
12r Millwall United v Ipswich Town	1-0
20r Worthing v Hollington United	3-0

Qualifying Round One

3 Butter Knowle WM v Etherley Welfare	0-3a
Darlington Railway Athletic v Thornley Albion	0-1
Sunnybrow Olympic v West Auckland Town	0-1
Witton Park Institute v Coundon United	0-1
5 Apperley Bridge v Rothwell Athletic	4-2
6 Alderley Edge United v Marine	3-6
Blundellsands v Furness Withy	1-6
Formby v Hoylake United	5-0
Harrowby v Birkenhead Amateurs	2-3
Old Xaverians v Ulverston Town	wo/s
Port Sunlight Amateurs v Orrell Athletic	2-0
Thorndale v West Kirby	wo/s
Whalley Range v Earle	3-5
7 Attercliffe United v Rotherham Amateurs	2-6e
Attercliffe Victory v Norfolk Amateurs	3-3
Eckington Works v Warmsworth	3-4
Youlgrave v Clowne Liberal	4-3
9 Birmingham Tramways v Walsall Phoenix	1-0
Coventry Magnet v Golden Cross	1-4
Exhall Colliery v Oldbury Town	4-5
Kington Town v Malvern Holy Trinity	3-1
Moor Green v Wolseley Athletic	1-3
Western Road House v Humber Recreation	2-1
Wolverhampton Amateurs v Old Wulfrunians	2-2e
11 Abbey United v Norwich YMCA	2-3
Beccles Town v Newmarket Town	2-1
Carrow Works v Lowestoft Town	1-2e
Great Yarmouth Town v Norwich CEYMS	5-1
Kirkley v Godmanchester Town	10-1
Lynn St Nicholas v King's Lynn	2-10
March GE United v St Neots & District	7-2
Norwich Priory Athletic v Gorleston	0-5
12 2nd Leicestershire Regt v Brentwood & Warley	4-1
Chelmsford v Ipswich Works	5-1
Clacton Town v Brentwood Mental Hospital	1-2
Colchester Town v Custom House	4-3
Harwich & Parkeston v Stowmarket	1-4
Millwall United v Walthamstow Avenue	1-2
Parkeston Railway v Grays Athletic	1-5
Walthamstow Grange v Brantham Athletic	5-4
13 Beckenham v Sidcup	4-2
Catford Southend v Bostall Heath	0-4
Erith & Belvedere v Foots Cray	2-1
Lamorbey v RN Depot	1-0
RM Chatham v Bexleyheath Town	1-0
Swanley Athletic v Royal Engineers Depot Battn	2-1
Woolwich Polytechnic v Cray Wanderers	2-4
14 Carshalton Athletic v Sutton United	1-3
Epsom Town v Aquarius	2-0
Leyland Motors v Mitcham Wanderers	4-2e
Reigate Priory v Tooting Town	0-6
West Norwood v Metropolitan Police	1-0

15 Ashford (Middx) v Hanwell Town	1-4
Civil Service v Wealdstone	1-2e
Hounslow v Polytechnic	2-3
Savoy Hotel v Hendon Town	3-5
Sutton Court v Yiewsley	6-1
16 Apsley v Wellingborough Nomads	4-1
Aylesbury United v Luton Amateur	6-1
Leighton United v Leavesden Mental Hospital	4-1
Walgrave Amber v Berkhamsted Town	2-1
Watford OB v Daventry Town	5-4
17 2nd Rifle Brigade v 10th Royal Hussars	4-1
Addlestone v Wellington Works	5-1
Camberley & Yorktown v RE Civilian Staff	1-2e
Farnham United Breweries v Aldershot Traction Co	4-1
Guildford v Egham	1-2
RAMC Aldershot v Walton-on-Thames	2-0
RASC Aldershot v Weybridge	7-0
Woking v Godalming	5-2
18 Bicester Town v Banbury Harriers	4-0
Headington United v Abingdon Town	3-1
Maidenhead United v Reading B.W.I.	5-3
Marlow v Cowley	0-3e
Morris Motors v Newbury Town	2-3
Slough v Caversham St Andrews	5-2
Stones Athletic v Witney Town	3-5
Windsor & Eton v St Frideswides	wo/s
19 Cheshunt (1) v Stevenage Town	6-1
Edmonton (1) v Baldock Town	1-0
Enfield v Arlesey Town	9-0
Hoddesdon Town v Hertford Town	1-4
Letchworth Town v Finchley	2-4
Thorley Works v Bishops Stortford	2-3
Ware v Hitchin Blue Cross	3-4
Welwyn Garden City v Wood Green	1-1
20 Chichester v Portslade	6-2
East Grinstead v Felpham	3-0
Eastbourne Old Comrades v Horsham Trinity	10-0
Horsham v Pulborough	3-0
Hove v Shoreham	5-2
Southwick v Bognor Town	10-1
Vernon Athletic v Worthing	0-6
Wick v Littlehampton	2-4
21 2nd Argyll & Sutherland Highlanders v Fareham	3-1
Newport I of W v Gosport Athletic	3-1
Portsmouth Gas Co v East Cowes	0-2
RAOC Hilsea v Gosport Albion Sports	0-0
RN Depot Portsmouth v Osborne Athletic	wo/s
Sandown v HMS Excellent	1-3
22 Bournemouth v Shaftesbury	3-1
Wimborne v Swanage	1-4
23 Clevedon v Chalford	4-2
Kingswood v Gloucester City	3-1
Sharpness v St Philips Athletic	2-1
Sneyd Park v Cadbury's Athletic	4-1
Staple Hill Athletic v Brimscombe	3-1
Sunningend v Swindon Victoria	1-4
Tewkesbury Town v Bristol St George	0-4
Weston-super-Mare v Garrard Athletic	2-3
24 Chippenham Town v Melksham Town	5-4
Clutton Wanderers v Radstock Town	0-0e
Devizes Town v Calne & Harris United	2-6
Paulton Rovers v Warminster Town	0-1
Spencer Moulton v Bradford Town	1-0
Street v Coleford Athletic	2-5
Wells City v Pewsey Vale	6-1
Welton Rovers v Clandown	3-2
3r Butter Knowle WM v Etherley Welfare	2-3
7r Norfolk Amateurs v Attercliffe Victory	3-2
9r Old Wulfrunians v Wolverhampton Amateurs	0-1
19r Wood Green v Welwyn Garden City	5-1
21r Gosport Albion Sports v RAOC Hilsea	4-3
24r Radstock Town v Clutton Wanderers	1-2

Qualifying Round Two

1 Carlin How Athletic v Lingdale Institute	6-1
2 Feversham United v Stockton Tilery	2-4
Grangetown St Marys v Eston United	3-2
South Bank East End v Normanby Magnesite	1-2
Stockton Malleable Institute v South Bank St Peters	n/a
3 6th Durham Light Infantry v Cockfield	4-0
Stanley United v Etherley Welfare	3-1
Tow Law Town v Thornley Albion	4-0
West Auckland Town v Coundon United	4-3e
4 Walker Park v Heaton Stannington	5-2
5 Cleckheaton v Yorkshire Amateur	6-1
Guiseley v Luddendenfoot	7-0
Otley v Rawdon	3-2
Whitehall Printeries v Apperley Bridge	2-0
6 Earle v Furness Withy	2-1
Formby v Old Xaverians	4-1
Marine v Birkenhead Amateurs	4-0
Thorndale v Port Sunlight Amateurs	1-0
7 Chesterfield Corinthians v Warmsworth	1-5
Norfolk Amateurs v Sheffield	5-2
Ravens Amateurs (Sheffield) v Rotherham Amateurs	2-6
Youlgrave v Sheffield Municipal Officers	3-0
8 Arnold Town v Basford United	1-4
Lenton v Clifton Colliery	2-1
Sneinton v South Nottingham	4-2
Sutton Junction v Hucknall Byron	3-1

1926/27 to 1927/28

9	Birmingham Tramways v Rugeley Villa	4-3
	Oldbury Town v Kington Town	2-1
	Western Road House v Golden Cross	n/a
	Wolseley Athletic v Wolverhampton Amateurs	3-0
11	Beccles Town v Kirkley	6-2
	King's Lynn v Great Yarmouth Town	2-5
	Lowestoft Town v Gorleston	0-1
	Norwich YMCA v March GE United	6-1
12	Brentwood Mental Hosp. v 2nd Leicestershire Regt	4-0
	Chelmsford v Colchester Town	7-1
	Stowmarket v Walthamstow Avenue	1-5
	Walthamstow Grange v Grays Athletic	2-3
13	Beckenham v Woolwich	1-0
	Bostall Heath v Erith & Belvedere	1-2
	RM Chatham v Cray Wanderers	2-2
	Swanley Athletic v Lamorbey	1-2
14	Leyland Motors v Epsom Town	2-5
	Summerstown v Sutton United	3-2
	West Norwood v Tooting Town	2-1
	Wimbledon v Dorking	5-0
15	Hendon Town v Sutton Court	4-1
	Old Lyonians v Hanwell Town	9-0
	RAF Uxbridge v Staines Town	4-4e
	Wealdstone v Polytechnic	2-1
16	Apsley v Leagrave & District	4-2
	Aylesbury United v Watford OB	5-0
	Leighton United v Northampton Nomads	0-3
	Walgrave Amber v Vauxhall Motors	5-1
17	Addlestone v 2nd Rifle Brigade	5-2
	Egham v RAMC Aldershot	0-2
	Farnham United Breweries v RASC Aldershot	2-3
	Woking v RE Civilian Staff	4-1
18	Maidenhead United v Cowley	3-1
	Newbury Town v Headington United	7-0
	Slough v Bicester Town	1-0
	Witney Town v Windsor & Eton	3-2
19	Cheshunt (1) v Hertford Town	4-1
	Edmonton (1) v Hitchin Blue Cross	4-2
	Enfield v Bishops Stortford	5-1
	Wood Green v Finchley	2-2
20	Chichester v East Grinstead	3-1
	Eastbourne Old Comrades v Littlehampton	4-3
	Horsham v Worthing	1-2e
	Southwick v Hove	3-4
21	East Cowes v 2nd Argyll & Sutherland Highlanders	1-2
	Harland & Wolff v Gosport Albion Sports	0-1
	RM Portsmouth v Newport I of W	3-0
	RN Depot Portsmouth v HMS Excellent	1-2
22	Blandford v Bournemouth Gasworks Athletic	2-1
	Bournemouth Tramways v Gillingham Town	4-1
	Castle Hill v Swanage	2-1
	Dorchester Town v Bournemouth	0-4
23	Clevedon v Bristol St George	4-2
	Sneyd Park v Garrard Athletic	1-4
	Staple Hill Athletic v Kingswood	3-4
	Swindon Victoria v Sharpness	4-1
24	Spencer Moulton v Calne & Harris United	5-2
	Warminster Town v Coleford Athletic	3-2
	Wells City v Chippenham Town	2-1
	Welton Rovers v Clutton Wanderers	6-1
13r	Cray Wanderers v RM Chatham	4-1
15r	Staines Town v RAF Uxbridge	1-2
19r	Finchley v Wood Green	3-0

Qualifying Round Three

1	Guisborough Belmont Athletic v Carlin How Athletic	n/a
	Loftus Albion v Whitby United	3-2
2	Grangetown St Marys v Normanby Magnesite	2-0
	Stockton Malleable Institute v Stockton Tilery	5-2
3	6th Durham Light Infantry v Stanley United	2-1
	Tow Law Town v West Auckland Town	6-2
4	Langley Park v Walker Park	2-0
	Percy Main Amateurs v Jesmond Villa	6-3
5	Guiseley v Whitehall Printeries	2-1
	Otley v Cleckheaton	3-5
6	Earle v Formby	4-2
	Thorndale v Marine	2-5
7	Norfolk Amateurs v Warmsworth	2-2
	Rotherham Amateurs v Youlgrave	5-3
8	Lenton v Basford United	7-0
	Sutton Junction v Sneinton	3-3
9	Birmingham Tramways v Oldbury Town	3-1
	Golden Cross v Wolseley Athletic	4-0
10	RAF Cranwell v Spalding United	5-0
11	Beccles Town v Norwich YMCA	0-1a
	Great Yarmouth Town v Gorleston	3-0
12	Chelmsford v Brentwood Mental Hospital	1-2
	Grays Athletic v Walthamstow Avenue	1-0a
13	Cray Wanderers v Lamorbey	4-0
	Erith & Belvedere v Beckenham	1-0
14	Epsom Town v West Norwood	2-1
	Wimbledon v Summerstown	3-2
15	Old Lyonians v Hendon Town	3-4
	Wealdstone v RAF Uxbridge	9-3
16	Aylesbury United v Walgrave Amber	5-1
	Northampton Nomads v Apsley	4-3
17	Addlestone v Woking	1-5
	RASC Aldershot v RAMC Aldershot	3-0
18	Newbury Town v Witney Town	0-0
	Slough v Maidenhead United	2-5
19	Cheshunt (1) v Enfield	4-4
	Edmonton (1) v Finchley	1-1a
20	Hove v Chichester	8-2
	Worthing v Eastbourne Old Comrades	0-1a
21	Gosport Albion Sports v HMS Excellent	0-1
	RM Portsmouth v 2nd Argyll & Sutherland Highl'ndrs	2-0
22	Bournemouth Tramways v Bournemouth	0-3
	Castle Hill v Blandford	3-5
23	Garrard Athletic v Clevedon	2-1
	Kingswood v Swindon Victoria	3-1
24	Spencer Moulton v Welton Rovers	3-4
	Wells City v Warminster Town	3-1
7r	Warmsworth v Norfolk Amateurs	4-2
8r	Sutton Junction v Sneinton	3-2
11r	Beccles Town v Norwich YMCA	0-1
12r	Grays Athletic v Walthamstow Avenue	2-6
18r	Witney Town v Newbury Town	1-4
19r	Enfield v Cheshunt (1)	9-2
r	Finchley v Edmonton (1)	4-1
20r	Worthing v Eastbourne Old Comrades	2-2e
20r2	Eastbourne Old Comrades v Worthing	5-3

Qualifying Round Four

1	Guisborough Belmont Athletic v Loftus Albion	1-2
2	Stockton Malleable Institute v Grangetown St Marys	0-0
3	6th Durham Light Infantry v Tow Law Town	4-2
4	Langley Park v Percy Main Amateurs	1-2
5	Cleckheaton v Guiseley	2-3
6	Marine v Earle	6-1
7	Rotherham Amateurs v Warmsworth	2-1
8	Sutton Junction v Lenton	1-1
9	Birmingham Tramways v Golden Cross	5-1
10	Hull OB v RAF Cranwell	2-1
11	Great Yarmouth Town v Norwich YMCA	2-0
12	Brentwood Mental Hospital v Walthamstow Avenue	2-3
13	Cray Wanderers v Erith & Belvedere	4-0
14	Epsom Town v Wimbledon	1-3
15	Hendon Town v Wealdstone	1-4
16	Aylesbury United v Northampton Nomads	2-3
17	Woking v RASC Aldershot	7-0
18	Maidenhead United v Newbury Town	4-5 d
19	Finchley v Enfield	2-2
20	Eastbourne Old Comrades v Hove	4-2
21	RM Portsmouth v HMS Excellent	2-2
22	Blandford v Bournemouth	1-1
23	Kingswood v Garrard Athletic	4-0
24	Welton Rovers v Wells City	6-2
2r	Grangetown St Marys v Stockton Malleable Institute	2-5
8r	Lenton v Sutton Junction	2-3
19r	Enfield v Finchley	3-4
21r	HMS Excellent v RM Portsmouth	2-1
22r	Bournemouth v Blandford	0-2

Round One

	Barking Town v Kingstonian	6-1
	Barnet v Eastbourne Old Comrades	3-0
	Boots Athletic v Birmingham Tramways	1-2
	Botwell Mission v Chesham United	4-3
	Bournville Athletic v 6th Durham Light Infantry	1-2
	Bromley v Cray Wanderers	3-1
	Chilton Colliery Recreation v Bishop Auckland	1-1
	Crook Town v Players Athletic	3-1
	Ferryhill Athletic v Sutton Junction	6-2
	Finchley v Leyton	0-3
	GER Romford v Portland United	1-3
	Great Yarmouth Town v Nunhead	0-1
	Guiseley v Loftus Albion	4-2
	HMS Excellent v Southall	2-3
	Hallam v Esh Winning	1-1
	Hampstead Town v Casuals	3-3
	Leytonstone v Dulwich Hamlet	1-3
	London Caledonians v Cambridge Town	4-1
	Northern Nomads v Percy Main Amateurs	4-0
	Oxford City v Blandford	6-0
	Redhill v Northampton Nomads	4-1
	Rotherham Amateurs v Stockton Malleable Institute	0-0
	South Bank v Norton Woodseats	1-0
	Stockton v Hull OB	7-0
	Tufnell Park v Clapton	4-2
	Uxbridge Town v Kingswood	0-1
	Wealdstone v Maidenhead United	1-2
	Welton Rovers v Eastbourne	4-0
	Willington v Marine	5-3
	Wimbledon v Ilford	1-1
	Woking v St Albans City	1-4
	Wycombe Wanderers v Walthamstow Avenue	3-2
r	Bishop Auckland v Chilton Colliery Recreation	0-0
r	Casuals v Hampstead Town	3-2
r	Esh Winning v Hallam	2-1
r	Ilford v Wimbledon	4-0
r	Stockton Malleable Institute v Rotherham Amateurs	2-0
r2	Chilton Colliery Recreation v Bishop Auckland	1-0

Round Two

	Crook Town v Willington	3-0
	Dulwich Hamlet v Botwell Mission	6-1
	Esh Winning v Northern Nomads	1-3
	Guiseley v Chilton Colliery Recreation	1-6
	Leyton v Oxford City	8-0
	Maidenhead United v Bromley	3-2
	Nunhead v Tufnell Park	2-2
	Portland United v Casuals	2-3
	Redhill v Barking Town	1-2
	South Bank v 6th Durham Light Infantry	1-1
	Southall v Ilford	3-2
	St Albans City v Barnet	6-1
	Stockton v Birmingham Tramways	4-0
	Stockton Malleable Institute v Ferryhill Athletic	2-7
	Welton Rovers v Kingswood	2-1
	Wycombe Wanderers v London Caledonians	3-2
r	6th Durham Light Infantry v South Bank	1-6 N
r	Tufnell Park v Nunhead	0-3

Round Three

	Barking Town v Maidenhead United	3-1
	Leyton v Northern Nomads	2-1
	Nunhead v Ferryhill Athletic	6-2
	Southall v Casuals	4-2
	St Albans City v Crook Town	0-2
	Stockton v Dulwich Hamlet	1-1
	Welton Rovers v South Bank	3-3
	Wycombe Wanderers v Chilton Colliery Recreation	3-1
r	Dulwich Hamlet v Stockton	7-2
r	South Bank v Welton Rovers	6-2

Round Four

	Barking Town v Wycombe Wanderers	3-2
	Nunhead v Leyton	1-2
	South Bank v Dulwich Hamlet	2-1
	Southall v Crook Town	4-0

Semi Finals

	Barking Town v South Bank	2-1 N
	Leyton v Southall	2-2 N
r	Leyton v Southall	2-1 N

Final

	Leyton v Barking Town	3-1 N

1927/28

Preliminary Round

11	Bury Town v Cromer	2-4
	Chatteris Town v Lynn United	1-0
	Great Yarmouth Town v Norwich CEYMS	2-1
	Lowestoft Town v Beccles Town	7-1
	Newmarket Town v Wisbech Town	3-4
	Norwich City Wanderers v Diss Town	1-2
	Thetford Town v St Ives Town	5-1
12	2nd Rifle Brigade v Custom House	1-5
	Brantham Athletic v Brentwood Mental Hospital	3-1
	Chelmsford v Millwall United	5-4
	Colchester Town v Brentwood & Warley	4-3e
	Crittall Athletic v Ipswich St John	10-0
	Grays Athletic v Orwell Works	9-1
	Great Yarmouth Town v Gorleston	4-2
	Leiston Works Athletic v Walton United	1-4
	Stowmarket v Ipswich Works	4-3
	Walthamstow Avenue v Tilbury	3-2
	Walthamstow Grange v Clacton Town	3-2
	Woodbridge Town v Shoeburyness Garrison	5-2
18	Henley Town v Windsor & Eton	0-10
20	Hollington United v Hastings & St Leonards	2-0
	Horsham v Eastbourne Old Comrades	4-7
	Southwick v Haywards Heath	5-2
	Vernon Athletic v Arundel	wo/s
23	Cadbury's Athletic v Hanham Athletic	1-7
	Garrard Athletic v Tewkesbury Town	7-1
	Kingswood v Bristol St George	5-2
	Sharpness v Bedminster Down	3-2
	St Annes Oldland v Brimscombe	1-1
	Stonehouse v Swindon Victoria	5-1
	Swindon Corinthians v Listers	7-1
23r	Brimscombe v St Annes Oldland	4-2

Qualifying Round One

3	Sunnybrow Olympic v Evenwood Town	0-2
	West Auckland Town v Leasingthorne CW	8-0
	W Hartlepool Perseverance v Wingate Alb Coms	1-4
5	Farsley Celtic v Boothtown	5-0
6	Earle v Marine	2-9
8	Gedling Colliery v Ransome & Marles	1-3
9	Walsall LMS Engineering v Brereton Social	5-2
	Walsall Phoenix v Hereford City	wo/s
10	Old Cravonians v Reckitts	n/a
11	Chatteris Town v Norwich YMCA	1-9
	Cromer v Sheringham	1-4
	Ely City v Great Yarmouth Town	4-5
	King's Lynn v Diss Town	6-1
	Kirkley v Lowestoft Town	2-3
	March Town v Lynn St Nicholas	1-4
	Norwich Priory Athletic v Gorleston	5-3a
	Wisbech Town v Thetford Town	6-0
12	Colchester Town v Tate Institute	1-3
	Crittall Athletic v Walthamstow Grange	5-4
	Custom House v Woodbridge Town	3-1
	Grays Athletic v Chelmsford	4-2
	Harwich & Parkeston v GER Romford	0-2
	Ipswich Town v Parkeston Railway	2-0
	Stowmarket v Brantham Athletic	6-4
	Walthamstow Avenue v Walton United	6-0

1927/28

13 Bexleyheath Town v Royal Engineers Depot Battn 3-1
Cray Wanderers v Sidcup 5-1
Erith & Belvedere v RM Chatham 0-2
Lamorbey v Woolwich 5-1
Woolwich Polytechnic v Bostall Heath 2-6
14 Leyland Motors v Dorking 4-4e
Mitcham Wanderers v Aquarius 2-2
Summerstown v Metropolitan Police 0-2
Sutton United v West Norwood 3-1
15 Polytechnic v Hendon Town 1-4
Staines Town v Old Latymerians 7-2
Wealdstone v Uxbridge Town 4-3
16 Berkhamsted Town v Kingsthorpe Church Institute 4-0
Leavesden Mental Hospital v Watford OB 4-3
Leighton United v Leagrave & District 2-3
17 Addlestone v Walton-on-Thames 2-1
Farnham United Breweries v Camberley & Yorktown 3-1
RASC Aldershot v Aldershot Albion wo/s
Vickers v Guildford 2-0
Wellington Works v Egham 2-5
18 Abingdon Town v Witney Town 2-3
Bicester Town v Banbury Harriers 10-0
Marlow v Cowley 2-8
Newbury Town v Abingdon Pavlova 1-2
Oxford City v Morris Motors 2-0
Slough v Caversham St Andrews 3-2
Stones Athletic v Reading B.W.I. 4-4
Windsor & Eton v Headington United 6-1
19 Arlesey Town v Stevenage Town 2-3
Cheshunt (1) v Haywards Sports 4-1
Edmonton (1) v Hitchin Blue Cross 7-4
Enfield v Waltham Comrades 5-1
Finchley v Baldock Town 4-1
Welwyn Garden City v Ware 4-2
Wood Green v Letchworth Town 0-4
20 Broadwater v Rock-a-Nore 9-0
Eastbourne Old Comrades v Bognor Town 4-4e
Hollington United v Wick 10-1
Lewes v Hove 7-4
Newhaven v Worthing 1-4
Pulborough v East Grinstead 3-4
Southwick v Horsham Trinity 9-0
Vernon Athletic v Littlehampton 2-6
21 Gosport Albion Sports v Osborne Athletic 3-1
HMS Victory v Newport I of W wo/s
Lymington v RM Portsmouth 4-5e
RAOC Hilsea v East Cowes wo/s
23 Brimscombe v Kingswood 3-1 v
Chalford v Sharpness 3-2e
Cheltenham Town v Keynsham 4-3
Garrard Athletic v Swindon Casuals 3-7
Hanham Athletic v Clevedon 2-1
Sneyd Park v Gloucester City 2-4e
St Philips Athletic v Swindon Victoria 5-2
Swindon Corinthians v Weston-super-Mare 4-2
24 Calne & Harris United v Coleford Athletic 3-4e
Chippenham Rovers v Westbury United 3-0
Chippenham Town v Street 6-4e
Frome Town v Clandown 4-0
Glastonbury v Devizes Town 5-2
Melksham Town v Trowbridge Town 2-1
Radstock Town v Wells City 5-1
Spencer Moulton v Bromham 7-2
11r Gorleston v Norwich Priory Athletic 6-2
14r Dorking v Leyland Motors 4-3
r Mitcham Wanderers v Aquarius 1-2
18r Reading B.W.I. v Stones Athletic 4-1
20r Bognor Town v Eastbourne Old Comrades 2-3
23r Kingswood v Brimscombe 5-0

Qualifying Round Two

2 Eston United v Normanby Magnesite 3-2
Grangetown St Marys v Darlington Railway Athletic 7-2
Stockton Malleable Institute v South Bank East End 4-1
Stockton Shamrock v Stockton Tilery 5-3
3 6th Durham Light Infantry v Howden Rangers 4-3
Cockfield v Stanley United 6-2
West Auckland Town v Witton Park Institute 3-1
Wingate Albion Comrades v Evenwood Town 4-4
4 Esh Winning v Howden BL 3-1
Percy Main Amateurs v Walker Park 4-1
5 Apperley Bridge v Yorkshire Amateur 1-6
Fulford United v Whitehall Printeries 0-4
Guiseley v Farsley Celtic 6-2
Luddendenfoot v Horsforth 1-5
6 Formby v Old Xaverians 4-0
Harrowby v Thorndale 3-1
Marine v Birkenhead Amateurs 4-0
Whalley Range v Furness Withy 2-5
7 Pilkington Recreation v Anston Reading Room 7-2
Rawmarsh Athletic v Rotherham Amateurs 1-0
Sheffield Municipal Officers v Attercliffe United 3-3
Warmsworth v Sheffield 8-2
8 Clifton Colliery v Arnold Town 3-1
Leicestershire Nomads v Sneinton 2-3
Ransome & Marles v Lenton 4-0
Sutton Junction v South Nottingham 5-3
9 Birmingham Tramways v Moor Green 4-2
Malvern Holy Trinity v Wolseley Athletic 4-2
Rugeley Villa v Walsall LMS Engineering 1-1
Walsall Phoenix v Wolverhampton Amateurs 3-3
10 Filey Town v Hull OB 3-2
Grimsby Rovers v Driffield North End 8-0
Reckitts v Hull Young Peoples Institute 3-1
Spalding United v RAF Cranwell 0-0
11 Gorleston v King's Lynn 9-5
Lowestoft Town v Norwich YMCA 4-4e
Sheringham v Lynn St Nicholas 4-0
Wisbech Town v Great Yarmouth Town 2-2e
12 Crittall Athletic v Walthamstow Avenue 2-1
Custom House v GER Romford 3-3
Grays Athletic v Tate Institute 5-0
Stowmarket v Ipswich Town 0-2
13 Bexleyheath Town v Beckenham 4-3
Bostall Heath v RM Chatham 3-4e
Lamorbey v Foots Cray 1-3
RN Depot v Cray Wanderers 6-0
14 Aquarius v Metropolitan Police 1-4
Dorking v Carshalton Athletic 5-4e
Epsom Town v Reigate Priory 7-1
Sutton United v Tooting Town 5-2
15 Hendon Town v Wealdstone 4-6
Old Lyonians v Civil Service 3-5e
RAF Uxbridge v Botwell Mission 4-3
Staines Town v Hounslow 5-2
16 Apsley v Berkhamsted Town 6-0
Aylesbury United v Northampton Nomads 0-6
Leavesden Mental Hospital v Leagrave & District 3-3
Walgrave Amber v Luton Amateur 2-1
17 Addlestone v Aldershot Traction Company 3-4
Farnham United Breweries v RAMC Aldershot 2-3
Godalming v Egham 2-4
Vickers v RASC Aldershot 3-6
18 Cowley v Bicester Town 4-0
Slough v Abingdon Pavlova 2-1
Windsor & Eton v Oxford City 3-4
Witney Town v Reading B.W.I. 6-0
19 Bishops Stortford v Letchworth Town 4-2
Cheshunt (1) v Welwyn Garden City 3-2
Enfield v Stevenage Town 18-0
Finchley v Edmonton (1) 5-1a
20 Broadwater v Hollington United 1-3
Littlehampton v East Grinstead 5-5e
Southwick v Eastbourne Old Comrades 5-2
Worthing v Lewes 4-2
21 Fareham v HMS Victory 3-2
Gosport Albion Sports v Portsmouth Gas Co 2-4
HMS Excellent v Gosport Athletic 6-0
RM Portsmouth v RAOC Hilsea 4-2
22 Bournemouth v 5th Royal Tank Corps 1-2
Bournemouth Gasworks Athletic v Blandford 7-0
Dorchester Town v Bournemouth Tramways 0-3
Salisbury Corinthians v Castle Hill 3-1
23 Chalford v Hanham Athletic 0-6
Cheltenham Town v Swindon Casuals 6-0
Gloucester City v St Philips Athletic 1-2
Swindon Corinthians v Kingswood 3-0
24 Chippenham Town v Melksham Town 4-3
Frome Town v Coleford Athletic 0-1
Glastonbury v Chippenham Rovers 2-4
Radstock Town v Spencer Moulton 1-2
3r Evenwood Town v Wingate Albion Comrades 6-0
7r Attercliffe United v Sheffield Municipal Officers 6-1
9r Walsall LMS Engineering v Rugeley Villa 0-5
r Wolverhampton Amateurs v Walsall Phoenix 2-1e
10r RAF Cranwell v Spalding United 2-5
11r Great Yarmouth Town v Wisbech Town 4-0
r Lowestoft Town v Norwich YMCA 1-2
12r GER Romford v Custom House 4-2
16r Leagrave & District v Leavesden Mental Hospital 4-2
19r Edmonton (1) v Finchley 2-3
20r East Grinstead v Littlehampton 5-2

Qualifying Round Three

1 Guisborough Belmont Athletic v Loftus Albion n/a
Whitby United v Lingdale Institute 9-0
2 Stockton Malleable Institute v Eston United 3-5
Stockton Shamrock v Grangetown St Marys 3-0
3 Cockfield v 6th Durham Light Infantry 2-2
West Auckland Town v Evenwood Town 0-4
4 Esh Winning v Heaton Stannington 3-1
Langley Park v Percy Main Amateurs 5-2
5 Horsforth v Guiseley 1-8
Whitehall Printeries v Yorkshire Amateur 3-2
6 Formby v Harrowby 1-1
Furness Withy v Marine 0-4
7 Rawmarsh Athletic v Pilkington Recreation 4-0
Warmsworth v Attercliffe United 7-3
8 Ransome & Marles v Clifton Colliery 5-2
Sneinton v Sutton Junction 1-2
9 Birmingham Tramways v Rugeley Villa 9-1
Wolverhampton Amateurs v Malvern Holy Trinity 3-3
10 Filey Town v Reckitts 4-0
Spalding United v Grimsby Rovers 1-5
11 Great Yarmouth Town v Norwich YMCA 2-1
Sheringham v Gorleston 2-2
12 Grays Athletic v GER Romford 3-0
Ipswich Town v Crittall Athletic 2-3
13 Foots Cray v Bexleyheath Town 2-3
RN Depot v RM Chatham 4-1
14 Dorking v Sutton United 1-7
Epsom Town v Metropolitan Police 0-3
15 Civil Service v Wealdstone 3-2
RAF Uxbridge v Staines Town 3-2
16 Apsley v Leagrave & District 4-5
Northampton Nomads v Walgrave Amber 6-1
17 Aldershot Traction Company v Egham 2-1
RASC Aldershot v RAMC Aldershot 4-1
18 Oxford City v Witney Town 9-3
Slough v Cowley 1-3
19 Bishops Stortford v Enfield 2-4
Cheshunt (1) v Finchley 2-2
20 East Grinstead v Hollington United 4-1
Worthing v Southwick 3-3e
21 Fareham v RM Portsmouth 2-3
HMS Excellent v Portsmouth Gas Co 7-0
22 Bournemouth Tramways v B'nemouth Gasworks Ath 1-1
Salisbury Corinthians v 5th Royal Tank Corps 2-2e
23 Hanham Athletic v Cheltenham Town 2-1
Swindon Corinthians v St Philips Athletic 4-4
24 Chippenham Town v Spencer Moulton 3-2
Coleford Athletic v Chippenham Rovers 5-1
1r Loftus Albion v Guisborough Belmont Athletic 2-1
3r 6th Durham Light Infantry v Cockfield 2-2
6r Harrowby v Formby 1-1a
9r Malvern Holy Trinity v Wolverhampton Amateurs 1-3
11r Gorleston v Sheringham 7-1
19r Finchley v Cheshunt (1) 3-2
20r Southwick v Worthing 2-0
22r 5th Royal Tank Corps v Salisbury Corinthians 4-1
r Bournemouth Gasworks Ath v B'nemouth Tramways 3-2
23r St Philips Athletic v Swindon Corinthians 1-0
3r2 6th Durham Light Infantry v Cockfield 0-2
6r2 Harrowby v Formby 2-3 N

Qualifying Round Four

1 Whitby United v Loftus Albion 2-0
2 Stockton Shamrock v Eston United 4-4
3 Evenwood Town v Cockfield 2-2
4 Esh Winning v Langley Park 5-2
5 Guiseley v Whitehall Printeries 0-0
6 Marine v Formby 2-2
7 Rawmarsh Athletic v Warmsworth 3-1
8 Sutton Junction v Ransome & Marles 7-2
9 Birmingham Tramways v Wolverhampton Amateurs 3-2
10 Filey Town v Grimsby Rovers 2-1
11 Great Yarmouth Town v Gorleston 4-2
12 Crittall Athletic v Grays Athletic 2-4
13 RN Depot v Bexleyheath Town 2-2
14 Metropolitan Police v Sutton United 0-1
15 Civil Service v RAF Uxbridge 2-0
16 Leagrave & District v Northampton Nomads 1-4
17 Aldershot Traction Company v RASC Aldershot 2-3
18 Oxford City v Cowley 1-1
19 Enfield v Finchley 2-2
20 East Grinstead v Southwick 2-7
21 HMS Excellent v RM Portsmouth 0-0
22 5th Royal Tank Corps v Bournemouth Gasworks Ath 2-1
23 Hanham Athletic v St Philips Athletic 2-0
24 Coleford Athletic v Chippenham Town 2-4
2r Eston United v Stockton Shamrock 0-3
3r Cockfield v Evenwood Town 3-2
5r Whitehall Printeries v Guiseley 4-1
6r Formby v Marine 0-4
13r Bexleyheath Town v RN Depot 1-5
18r Cowley v Oxford City 0-0
19r Finchley v Enfield 2-3
21r RM Portsmouth v HMS Excellent 1-1e
18r2 Oxford City v Cowley 7-1
21r2 RM Portsmouth v HMS Excellent 1-0

Round One

Barking Town v Northampton Nomads 9-1
Barnet v Chesham United 4-2
Bournville Athletic v Hallam 2-6
Cambridge Town v RASC Aldershot 3-1
Chilton Colliery Recreation v Boots Athletic 6-0
Chippenham Town v Dulwich Hamlet 2-3
Civil Service v Ilford 1-5
Clapton v Sutton United 1-2
Crook Town v Bishop Auckland 2-1 D
Enfield v London Caledonians 1-5
Ferryhill Athletic v Esh Winning 0-5
Great Yarmouth Town v St Albans City 2-2
Hampstead Town v RN Depot 1-2
Hanham Athletic v Portland United 1-3
Kingstonian v Redhill 3-5
Leyton v Bromley 4-4
Maidenhead United v Leytonstone 2-0a
Marine v Northern Nomads 2-0
Norton Woodseats v Cockfield 1-1
Nunhead v 5th Royal Tank Corps 5-3
Players Athletic v Filey Town 7-0
RM Portsmouth v Grays Athletic 3-4
Rawmarsh Athletic v Stockton 1-1
Stockton Shamrock v Sutton Junction 2-1
Tow Law Town v South Bank 4-2
Tufnell Park v Eastbourne 4-3
Welton Rovers v Southall 3-4
Whitby United v Birmingham Tramways 1-1
Whitehall Printeries v Willington 2-3
Wimbledon v Oxford City 3-1
Woking v Casuals 2-2
Wycombe Wanderers v Southwick 4-2

1927/28 to 1928/29

r	Birmingham Tramways v Whitby United	2-6
r	Bromley v Leyton	1-4
r	Casuals v Woking	1-5
r	Cockfield v Norton Woodseats	1-0
r	Maidenhead United v Leytonstone	1-3
r	St Albans City v Great Yarmouth Town	6-0
r	Stockton v Rawmarsh Athletic	7-0

Round Two

	Barnet v Dulwich Hamlet	2-1
	Bishop Auckland v Tow Law Town	2-0
	Cambridge Town v Wycombe Wanderers	1-1
	Cockfield v Stockton Shamrock	3-0
	Hallam v Marine	2-1
	Leyton v Redhill	5-1
	Nunhead v Sutton United	3-2
	Players Athletic v Whitby United	2-1
	Portland United v Barking Town	1-3
	Southall v Grays Athletic	1-0
	St Albans City v Ilford	3-2
	Stockton v Chilton Colliery Recreation	3-1
	Tufnell Park v Leytonstone	1-3
	Willington v Esh Winning	6-0
	Wimbledon v RN Depot	4-2
	Woking v London Caledonians	0-1
r	Wycombe Wanderers v Cambridge Town	0-3

Round Three

	Barking Town v London Caledonians	0-0
	Barnet v Hallam	3-1
	Bishop Auckland v Southall	2-1
	Cambridge Town v Stockton	2-1
	Nunhead v Leyton	1-2
	St Albans City v Cockfield	0-1
	Willington v Players Athletic	5-1
	Wimbledon v Leytonstone	0-3
r	London Caledonians v Barking Town	0-1

Round Four

	Barking Town v Cambridge Town	2-3
	Bishop Auckland v Cockfield	0-0
	Leyton v Leytonstone	3-0
	Willington v Barnet	2-1
r	Cockfield v Bishop Auckland	2-1

Semi Finals

	Cockfield v Willington	2-2 N
	Leyton v Cambridge Town	5-2 N
r	Cockfield v Willington	2-1 N

Final

	Leyton v Cockfield	3-2 N

1928/29

Preliminary Round

11	Abbey United v Soham Rangers	1-0
	Beccles Town v Thetford Town	0-1
	Chatteris Town v March Town	3-1
	Diss Town v Carrow Works	1-3
	Ely City v St Ives Town	1-2
	Lynn St Nicholas v Huntingdon Town	1-5
	Norwich CEYMS v Great Yarmouth Town	4-3
	Norwich YMCA v Bury Town	4-3
	Sheringham v Kirkley	1-3
	Wisbech Town v Lynn United	4-0
12	2nd Rifle Brigade v Stowmarket	2-4
	Brantham Athletic v Severalls Athletic	0-3
	Brentwood & Warley v Custom House	5-3
	Brentwood Mental Hospital v GER Romford	1-3
	Grays Athletic v Tate Institute	4-1
	Harwich & Parkeston v Woodbridge Town	5-0
	Ipswich Town v Felixstowe Town	3-2
	Leiston Works Athletic v Parkeston Railway	3-1
	Millwall United v Walthamstow Grange	2-0
	Orwell Works v Colchester Town	0-3
	Shoeburyness Garrison v Chelmsford	1-2
18	Thame United v Thatcham	9-5
19	Hertford Town v Old Johnians	2-4
	Hitchin Town v Hoddesdon Town	5-0
	Waltham Town v Alexandra Park	0-1e
20	Bexhill v Worthing	0-0
	East Grinstead v Crawley	5-1
	Hastings & St Leonards v Hollington United	7-0
24	Bromham v Frome Town	1-6
	Chippenham Town v Spencer Moulton	2-0
	Clutton Wanderers v Street	3-5
	Devizes Town v Calne & Harris United	2-5
	Warminster Town v Swindon Corinthians	3-6
	Wells City v Paulton Rovers	2-1
	Welton Rovers v Coleford Athletic	2-0
20r	Worthing v Bexhill	3-0

Qualifying Round One

3	6th Durham Light Infantry v Bishop Auckland	0-2
	Burnhope Institute v Leasingthorne CW	0-1
	Evenwood Town v Willington	2-1
	Sunnybrow Olympic v Chilton Colliery Recreation	2-2e
	Witton Park Institute v Cockfield	3-1
7	Edlington Welfare v Hathersage	2-1
	Treeton Reading Room v Anston Reading Room	4-1
11	Abbey United v Thetford Town	2-1
	Carrow Works v Norwich CEYMS	1-2
	Chatteris Town v Newmarket Town	1-0
	Gorleston v Wisbech Town	9-2
	Huntingdon Town v King's Lynn	1-3
	Kirkley v Norwich Priory Athletic	4-0
	Lowestoft Town v St Ives Town	4-2e
	Norwich YMCA v Cromer	5-4e
12	Brentwood & Warley v Clacton Town	1-3e
	Crittall Athletic v Severalls Athletic	0-2
	GER Romford v Stowmarket	10-1
	Grays Athletic v Chelmsford	0-1
	Harwich & Parkeston v Millwall United	2-0
	Ipswich Town v Walton United	1-2
	Leiston Works Athletic v Colchester Town	0-3
	Walthamstow Avenue v Tilbury	1-3
13	Beckenham v Bexleyheath Town	1-4
	Bostall Heath v Callender Athletic	1-3
	Erith & Belvedere v Swanley Athletic	2-0
	Maidstone United v Foots Cray	4-0
	Woolwich Polytechnic v Lamorbey	wo/s
14	Epsom Town v Aquarius	4-3
	Leyland Motors v Carshalton Athletic	0-3
	Reigate Priory v Sutton United	0-2
	Tooting Town v Dorking	1-0 v
	Wallington v Beddington Corner	1-0
15	Botwell Mission v Hendon Town	3-0
	Hounslow v Wealdstone	2-2e
	Old Lyonians v Civil Service	1-2
	Polytechnic v Old Isleworthians	5-3
16	Apsley v Leighton United	1-0
	Aylesbury United v Northampton Nomads	2-0
	Berkhamsted Town v Daventry Town	5-0
	Kingsthorpe Church Institute v Mount Pleasant	7-1
	Leagrave & District v Watford OB	1-3
	Leavesden Mental Hospital v Langford	6-0
	Luton Amateur v Kempston Rovers	5-5e
17	1st Royal Warwickshire Regm v Wellington Works	3-4
	Addlestone v 1st Kings Own Scots Borderers	0-6
	Aldershot Traction Company v Walton-on-Thames	6-0
	Camberley & Yorktown v 2nd Kings Royal Rifles	2-3
	Egham v Thorneycroft Athletic	4-2
	Guildford v RAMC Aldershot	1-3
	Weybridge v RASC Aldershot	1-6
18	Bicester Town v Stones Athletic	3-2
	Caversham St Andrews v Headington United	4-1
	Henley Town v Banbury Harriers	3-1
	Maidenhead United v Abingdon Town	13-0
	Marlow v Morris Motors	1-0
	Thame United v Newbury Town	0-4
	Windsor & Eton v Cowley	3-1
	Witney Town v Slough	0-4
19	Alexandra Park v Stevenage Town	4-5
	Baldock Town v Finchley	3-2 d
	Bishops Stortford v Wood Green	2-1
	Cheshunt (1) v Tufnell Park	1-1
	Hitchin Town v Enfield	1-3
	Letchworth Town v Ware	3-1
	Waltham Comrades v Old Johnians	0-2
	Welwyn Garden City v Haywards Sports	0-5
20	Bognor Town v Hove	2-3
	East Grinstead v Littlehampton	3-2
	Eastbourne Old Comrades v Rock-a-Nore	5-0
	Hastings & St Leonards v Broadwater	9-0
	Haywards Heath v Worthing	5-5e
	Lewes v Pulborough	10-2
	Newhaven v Vernon Athletic	6-2
	Wick v Horsham	1-1e
21	Osborne Athletic v HMS Excellent	0-7
	Ryde Sports v HMS Victory	4-2
22	Swanage v Blandford	4-1
23	Brimscombe v Bristol St George	1-6
	Chalford v Gloucester City	2-3
	Clevedon v St Philips Marsh Adult School	2-1
	Listers v Stonehouse	1-0
	Mount Hill Enterprise v Kingswood	2-1
	Sneyd Park v Keynsham	2-1
	St Philips Athletic v Hanham Athletic	3-2 D
	Weston-super-Mare v Minehead	2-3
24	Clandown v Wells City	2-1
	Garrard Athletic v Frome Town	6-2
	Glastonbury v Trowbridge Town	1-4
	Melksham Town v Swindon Victoria	1-6
	Radstock Town v Chippenham Town	1-1e
	Street v Swindon Casuals	7-1
	Swindon Corinthians v Westbury United	7-1
	Welton Rovers v Calne & Harris United	2-0
3r	Chilton Colliery Recreation v Sunnybrow Olympic	5-2
14r	Dorking v Tooting Town	4-1
15r	Wealdstone v Hounslow	3-2
16r	Kempston Rovers v Luton Amateur	3-2e
19r	Tufnell Park v Cheshunt (1)	8-1
20r	Horsham v Wick	8-2
r	Worthing v Haywards Heath	6-0
24r	Chippenham Town v Radstock Town	4-4e
24r2	Chippenham Town v Radstock Town	0-1

Qualifying Round Two

3	Bishop Auckland v Leasingthorne CW	4-2
	Evenwood Town v Witton Park Institute	1-0
	Ferryhill Athletic v Chilton Colliery Recreation	5-5e
	West Auckland Town v Stanley United	0-0e
4	Percy Main Amateurs v Esh Winning	3-0
5	Boothtown v Farsley Celtic	0-1
	Guiseley v Luddendenfoot	3-1
	Manningham Mills v Sowerby United	5-1
	Yorkshire Amateur v Horsforth	13-0
6	Earle v Old Xaverians	6-4e
	Harrowby v Blundellsands	1-3
7	Pilkington Recreation v Edlington Welfare	5-1
	Rawmarsh Athletic v Rotherham Amateurs	2-0
	Sheffield Municipal Officers v Handsworth U Sports	3-2
	Treeton Reading Room v Sheffield	3-0
9	Malvern Holy Trinity v Badsey Rangers	6-1
	Old Wulfrunians v Moor Green	3-5
10	Cleethorpes Town v Filey Town	1-2
	Grimsby Rovers v Grimsby Haycroft Rovers	6-2
	Hull Young Peoples Institute v Reckitts	6-4e
	Old Cravonians v Normanby Park Steels	7-5
11	Gorleston v Chatteris Town	11-1
	King's Lynn v Abbey United	2-1
	Kirkley v Norwich CEYMS	1-2
	Norwich YMCA v Lowestoft Town	0-3
12	Chelmsford v Harwich & Parkeston	0-3
	Colchester Town v Severalls Athletic	3-2
	GER Romford v Walton United	3-0
	Tilbury v Clacton Town	3-2
13	Callender Athletic v Maidstone United	2-3
	Erith & Belvedere v Cray Wanderers	0-1
	RM Chatham v Bexleyheath Town	2-3
	Sidcup v Woolwich Polytechnic	3-1
14	Carshalton Athletic v West Norwood	4-2e
	Dorking v Mitcham Wanderers	3-0
	Metropolitan Police v Wallington	8-2
	Sutton United v Epsom Town	3-2
15	Civil Service v Polytechnic	7-1
	Old Latymerians v Uxbridge Town	0-5
	Staines Town v RAF Uxbridge	1-1e
	Wealdstone v Botwell Mission	5-3
16	Berkhamsted Town v Aylesbury United	0-3
	Kempston Rovers v Walgrave Amber	6-1
	Kingsthorpe Church Institute v Apsley	6-1
	Watford OB v Leavesden Mental Hospital	3-4e
17	1st Kings Own Scots Borderers v RASC Aldershot	3-5e
	Egham v Aldershot Traction Company	0-1
	Godalming v Wellington Works	2-5
	RAMC Aldershot v 2nd Kings Royal Rifles	2-2
18	Maidenhead United v Henley Town	10-1
	Newbury Town v Bicester Town	1-5
	Slough v Caversham St Andrews	8-1
	Windsor & Eton v Marlow	5-4
19	Baldock Town v Letchworth Town	6-1
	Enfield v Stevenage Town	6-0
	Haywards Sports v Bishops Stortford	2-1
	Tufnell Park v Old Johnians	4-2
20	East Grinstead v Worthing	2-4
	Eastbourne Old Comrades v Hove	4-1
	Hastings & St Leonards v Horsham	4-1
	Lewes v Newhaven	4-0
21	Fareham v RM Portsmouth	3-3
	Gosport v HMS Excellent	2-6
	Portsmouth Gas Co v RAOC Hilsea	2-5
	Ryde Sports v Lymington	7-3
22	5th Royal Tank Corps v Bournemouth Tramways	9-4
	Bournemouth v Dorchester Town	2-1
	Bournemouth Gasworks Ath v Salisbury Corinthians	9-0
	Swanage v Castle Hill	1-3
23	Clevedon v Minehead	1-4
	Hanham Athletic v Gloucester City	4-2
	Mount Hill Enterprise v Listers	4-2
	Sneyd Park v Bristol St George	5-2
24	Clandown v Swindon Corinthians	3-2
	Radstock Town v Street	4-1
	Swindon Victoria v Welton Rovers	2-4
	Trowbridge Town v Garrard Athletic	3-2
3r	Chilton Colliery Recreation v Ferryhill Athletic	3-2
r	Stanley United v West Auckland Town	4-3
15r	RAF Uxbridge v Staines Town	4-2
17r	2nd Kings Royal Rifles v RAMC Aldershot	2-1
21r	RM Portsmouth v Fareham	1-6

Qualifying Round Three

1	Whitby Albion Rangers v Lingdale Institute	2-4
	Whitby United v Loftus Albion	9-1
2	Normanby Magnesite v Stockton Tilery	4-1
	West Hartlepool Perseverance v Eston United	3-0
3	Evenwood Town v Bishop Auckland	2-1
	Stanley United v Chilton Colliery Recreation	2-0
4	Langley Park v Heaton Stannington	3-2
	Percy Main Amateurs v Howden BL	n/a
5	Farsley Celtic v Manningham Mills	0-4
	Guiseley v Yorkshire Amateur	2-5
6	Earle v Whalley Range	n/a
	Thorndale v Blundellsands	1-3
7	Pilkington Recreation v Sheffield Municipal Officers	6-2
	Rawmarsh Athletic v Treeton Reading Room	3-0
8	RAF Grantham v Basford United	3-2
	South Nottingham v Sneinton	1-5
9	Ledbury Town v Moor Green	1-6
	Malvern Holy Trinity v Wolverhampton Amateurs	2-2

1928/29 to 1929/30

10 Filey Town v Old Cravonians	4-0
Grimsby Rovers v Hull Young Peoples Institute	8-1
11 King's Lynn v Gorleston	2-2
Norwich CEYMS v Lowestoft Town	3-3
12 Colchester Town v Harwich & Parkeston	6-2
Tilbury v GER Romford	5-2
13 Bexleyheath Town v Sidcup	2-1
Cray Wanderers v Maidstone United	4-1
14 Carshalton Athletic v Dorking	7-3
Sutton United v Metropolitan Police	4-0
15 Civil Service v Uxbridge Town	3-4
Wealdstone v RAF Uxbridge	4-1
16 Aylesbury United v Leavesden Mental Hospital	4-0
Kempston Rovers v Kingsthorpe Church Institute	4-2
17 Aldershot Traction Company v RASC Aldershot	9-1
Wellington Works v 2nd Kings Royal Rifles	2-2
18 Maidenhead United v Slough	3-1
Windsor & Eton v Bicester Town	8-0
19 Enfield v Baldock Town	2-2
Tufnell Park v Haywards Sports	4-2
20 Eastbourne Old Comrades v Hastings & St Leonards	2-2e
Lewes v Worthing	1-3
21 Fareham v Ryde Sports	2-1
RAOC Hilsea v HMS Excellent	0-2
22 5th Royal Tank Corps v Bournemouth Gasworks Ath	3-6
Bournemouth v Castle Hill	2-1
23 Minehead v Hanham Athletic	1-3
Mount Hill Enterprise v Sneyd Park	2-1
24 Radstock Town v Clandown	2-0
Trowbridge Town v Welton Rovers	1-2
9r Wolverhampton Amateurs v Malvern Holy Trinity	1-3
11r Gorleston v King's Lynn	2-0
r Lowestoft Town v Norwich CEYMS	5-1
17r 2nd Kings Royal Rifles v Wellington Works	3-2
19r Baldock Town v Enfield	4-3
20r Hastings & St Leonards v Eastbourne Old Coms	3-1

Qualifying Round Four

1 Whitby United v Lingdale Institute	7-0
2 W Hartlepool Perseverance v Normanby Magnesite	6-3
3 Evenwood Town v Stanley United	4-2
4 Percy Main Amateurs v Langley Park	5-0
5 Manningham Mills v Yorkshire Amateur	2-2
6 Blundellsands v Earle	5-3
7 Pilkington Recreation v Rawmarsh Athletic	2-0
8 Sneinton v RAF Grantham	8-2
9 Moor Green v Malvern Holy Trinity	3-1
10 Grimsby Rovers v Filey Town	1-6
11 Gorleston v Lowestoft Town	0-0
12 Colchester Town v Tilbury	4-0
13 Cray Wanderers v Bexleyheath Town	1-4
14 Sutton United v Carshalton Athletic	7-3
15 Uxbridge Town v Wealdstone	3-4
16 Kempston Rovers v Aylesbury United	0-4
17 Aldershot Traction Co v 2nd Kings Royal Rifles	4-1
18 Windsor & Eton v Maidenhead United	2-3
19 Tufnell Park v Baldock Town	8-1
20 Worthing v Hastings & St Leonards	1-2
21 HMS Excellent v Fareham	3-0
22 Bournemouth Gasworks Athletic v Bournemouth	2-1
23 Hanham Athletic v Mount Hill Enterprise	5-1
24 Radstock Town v Welton Rovers	1-1
5r Yorkshire Amateur v Manningham Mills	8-0
11r Lowestoft Town v Gorleston	1-2
24r Welton Rovers v Radstock Town	4-1e

Round One

Aldershot Traction Company v Portland United	2-1
Barking Town v Woking	6-1
Birmingham Tramways v Players Athletic	1-1
Bournemouth Gasworks Athletic v Tufnell Park	3-0
Bromley v Wimbledon	2-1
Cambridge Town v Oxford City	2-2
Chesham United v St Albans City	1-0
Clapton v Nunhead	2-0
Colchester Town v Barnet	1-7
Eastbourne v Dulwich Hamlet	1-7
Evenwood Town v Pilkington Recreation	4-1 D
Filey Town v West Hartlepool Perseverance	3-5
Gorleston v Southall	1-1
Hanham Athletic v Leytonstone	1-1
Kingstonian v Leyton	0-1
London Caledonians v Hastings & St Leonards	1-0
Maidenhead United v Hampstead Town	2-4
Marine v Moor Green	5-0
Norton Woodseats v Whitehall Printeries	2-3
Percy Main Amateurs v Boots Athletic	7-0
RN Depot v Bexleyheath Town	4-1
Sneinton v Bournville Athletic	2-0
South Bank v Northern Nomads	6-6
Southwick v Casuals	2-2
Stockton v Hull OB	8-0
Sutton United v HMS Excellent	3-0
Tow Law Town v Blundellsands	6-1
Wealdstone v Ilford	3-3
Welton Rovers v Redhill	3-0
Whitby United v Hallam	1-1
Wycombe Wanderers v Aylesbury United	3-1
Yorkshire Amateur v Stockton Shamrock	4-0
r Casuals v Southwick	2-3
r Hallam v Whitby United	4-3
r Ilford v Wealdstone	8-0
r Leytonstone v Hanham Athletic	6-3
r Northern Nomads v South Bank	2-2
r Oxford City v Cambridge Town	4-2
r Players Athletic v Birmingham Tramways	5-0
r Southall v Gorleston	1-1
r2 Gorleston v Southall	2-2 N
r2 South Bank v Northern Nomads	0-3 N
r3 Gorleston v Southall	2-1 N

Round Two

Aldershot Traction Company v Barking Town	4-1
Barnet v Welton Rovers	2-3
Clapton v RN Depot	5-4
Dulwich Hamlet v Bromley	4-2
Gorleston v Ilford	0-3
Hallam v Sneinton	6-4
London Caledonians v Leyton	0-1
Northern Nomads v Percy Main Amateurs	5-0
Oxford City v Leytonstone	0-3
Southwick v Chesham United	2-1
Stockton v West Hartlepool Perseverance	4-1
Sutton United v Hampstead Town	4-3
Tow Law Town v Players Athletic	4-1
Whitehall Printeries v Marine	4-1
Wycombe Wanderers v Bournemouth Gasworks Ath	5-2
Yorkshire Amateur v Pilkington Recreation	3-0

Round Three

Dulwich Hamlet v Wycombe Wanderers	7-1
Hallam v Welton Rovers	0-3
Leyton v Yorkshire Amateur	4-0
Northern Nomads v Ilford	2-4
Southwick v Clapton	1-2
Stockton v Tow Law Town	3-1
Sutton United v Leytonstone	6-3
Whitehall Printeries v Aldershot Traction Company	3-5

Round Four

Clapton v Welton Rovers	5-1
Dulwich Hamlet v Aldershot Traction Company	7-0
Ilford v Stockton	4-2
Leyton v Sutton United	0-1 d

Semi Finals

Ilford v Dulwich Hamlet	4-1 N
Leyton v Clapton	2-1 N

Final

Ilford v Leyton	3-1 N

1929/30

Preliminary Round

12 Boulton & Paul v Sheringham	3-7
Norwich Civil Service v Norwich CEYMS	1-2
13 2nd Rifle Brigade v Harwich & Parkeston	0-2
Brantham Athletic v Felixstowe Town	4-0
Brentwood Mental Hospital v Walthamstow Avenue	0-6
Custom House v Rovers (Poplar)	2-0
GER Romford v Dagenham Town	0-2
Grays Athletic v Romford (2)	7-0
Parkeston Railway v Severalls Athletic	2-4
Walthamstow Grange v Tate Institute	3-2
19 Abingdon Town v Bicester Town	2-1
Henley Town v Cowley	3-4
21 Bexhill v Rock-a-Nore	9-2
Crawley v Broadwater	3-2
Eastbourne Old Comrades v Sidley United	3-0
Haywards Heath v East Grinstead	1-3
Littlehampton v Wick	1-2
24 Bromham v Chippenham Town	2-8
Chippenham Rovers v Trowbridge Town	2-2e
Devizes Town v Swindon Victoria	1-2
Frome Town v Petters Westland Works	1-5
Melksham Town v Warminster Town	4-2
Paulton Rovers v Coleford Athletic	1-4
Radstock Town v St Cuthberts Works	6-0
24r Trowbridge Town v Chippenham Rovers	3-1

Qualifying Round One

11 Bury Town v Newmarket Town	3-0
Ely City v Huntingdon Town	wo/s
St Ives Town v Soham Rangers	2-2e
Thetford Town v Chatteris Town	2-4
12 Beccles Town v Ipswich Town	2-7
Carrow Works v Diss Town	0-4
Great Yarmouth Town v Norwich YMCA	7-2
Kirkley & Waveney v Norwich Priory Athletic	4-0
Leiston Works Athletic v Sheringham	5-0
Orwell Works v Lowestoft Town	0-6
Stowmarket v Cromer	3-4
Woodbridge Town v Norwich CEYMS	1-6
13 Brantham Athletic v Clacton Town	3-4aD
Brentwood & Warley v Crittall Athletic	4-2
Chelmsford v Custom House	5-2
Colchester Town v Grays Athletic	3-4
Harwich & Parkeston v Shoeburyness Garrison	0-1
Tilbury v Severalls Athletic	5-1
Walthamstow Avenue v Walthamstow Grange	1-0
Walton United v Dagenham Town	2-3
14 Bexleyheath Town v RM Chatham	2-6
Erith & Belvedere v Woolwich Polytechnic	1-0
RN Depot v Beckenham	6-2
UGBM Sports v Foots Cray	1-3
15 Aquarius v Reigate Priory	6-3
Carshalton Athletic v Beddington Corner	6-0
Dorking v Sutton United	2-4
Leyland Motors v Whyteleafe Albion	2-13
Metropolitan Police v Tooting Town	4-0
Mitcham Wanderers v Redhill	0-1
Wallington v West Norwood	2-4
16 Napier v Hounslow	0-1
Old Latymerians v Polytechnic	10-0
Standard Telephones v Old Isleworthians	2-3
Uxbridge Town v Old Lyonians	2-4
Wealdstone v RAF Uxbridge	3-0
17 Apsley v Leighton United	4-3
Berkhamsted Town v Luton Amateur	6-1
Kingsthorpe Church Institute v Daventry Town	5-1
Leagrave & District v Kempston Rovers	1-0
Mount Pleasant v Wolverton Town	2-3
Northampton Nomads v Walgrave Amber	2-1
Watford OB v Leavesden Mental Hospital	8-1
18 1st Kings Own Scots Borderers v Thorneycroft Ath	wo/s
Egham v 1st Kings Own Yorkshire LI	0-0e
Guildford v Godalming	3-4
Hersham v Woking	1-5
RAMC Aldershot v Camberley & Yorktown	4-1
RASC Aldershot v Wellington Works	wo/s
Walton-on-Thames v Addlestone	4-1
19 Banbury Harriers v Morris Motors	2-3
Cowley v Abingdon Town	2-1
Maidenhead United v Thatcham	6-2
Marlow v Newbury Town	3-3e
Oxford City v Headington United	3-0
Slough v Caversham St Andrews	12-2
Stones Athletic v Thame United	2-3
Windsor & Eton v Witney Town	8-1
20 Baldock Town v Ware	1-2
Bishops Stortford v Welwyn Garden City	2-4
Enfield v Hoddesdon Town	7-0
Finchley v Wood Green	7-0
Hertford v Cheshunt (1)	3-1
Hitchin Town v Letchworth Town	0-3
Old Johnians v Haywards Sports	1-4
Stevenage Town v Waltham Comrades	1-5
21 Bognor Town v Newhaven	5-2
Crawley v Horsham	0-6
Eastbourne v Bexhill	4-2
Eastbourne Old Comrades v East Grinstead	3-2
Lewes v Hollington United	7-0
Pulborough v Hove	2-6
Vernon Athletic v Wick	5-4eN
Worthing v Hastings & St Leonards	1-2
22 5th Royal Tank Corps v Portsmouth Gas Co	4-0
Bournemouth Gasworks Athletic v Blandford	6-0
Dorchester Town v Bournemouth Tramways	3-2
Fareham v Bournemouth	3-2
Gosport v RAOC Portsmouth	6-1
RE Southampton v Castle Hill	4-3
RM Portsmouth v Osborne Athletic	6-3
Salisbury Corinthians v HMS Victory	3-0
23 Chalford v Hanham Athletic	1-2
Cheltenham Town v Stonehouse	4-0
Gloucester City v Bristol St George	4-3
Keynsham v Mount Hill Enterprise	4-0
Kingswood v St Philips Athletic	6-0
Sneyd Park v Fry & Sons	5-0
St Philips Marsh Adult School v Listers	5-2
Weston-super-Mare v Minehead	2-2
24 Calne & Harris United v Radstock Town	0-3
Chippenham Town v Trowbridge Town	3-1
Spencer Moulton v Petters Westland Works	4-2
Street v Glastonbury	0-3
Swindon Casuals v Swindon Victoria	0-2
Swindon Corinthians v Garrard Athletic	1-3
Wells City v Melksham Town	2-0
Westbury United v Coleford Athletic	3-3
11r Soham Rangers v St Ives Town	0-4
18r Egham v 1st Kings Own Yorkshire LI	1-0
19r Newbury Town v Marlow	6-4
23r Minehead v Weston-super-Mare	4-1
24r Coleford Athletic v Westbury United	5-0

Qualifying Round Two

3 Cockfield v Chilton Colliery Recreation	3-2e
Stanley United v Crook	3-3e
West Auckland Town v Bishop Auckland	4-3
Willington v Ferryhill Athletic	3-2
5 Farsley Celtic v Manningham Mills	8-1
Knaresborough Town v Luddendenfoot	10-1
Methley Perseverance v Guiseley	6-1
6 Earle v South Salford Amateurs	4-2
Marine v Harrowby	3-0
Old Xaverians v Formby	3-0

39

1929/30 to 1930/31

1929/30 (continued)

7 Handsworth United Sports v Rawmarsh Welfare	1-2
Sheffield University v Hathersage	5-3
10 Filey Town v Hull OB	5-2
11 Chatteris Town v Bury Town	8-3
Ely City v March Town	0-1e
St Ives Town v Abbey United	4-1
Wisbech Town v King's Lynn	2-6
12 Ipswich Town v Diss Town	4-2
Kirkley & Waveney v Great Yarmouth Town	4-2a
Lowestoft Town v Leiston Works Athletic	3-0
Norwich CEYMS v Cromer	5-7
13 Chelmsford v Tilbury	3-4
Clacton Town v Walthamstow Avenue	0-7
Dagenham Town v Brentwood & Warley	2-2e
Shoeburyness Garrison v Grays Athletic	0-5
14 Bostall Heath v RM Chatham	4-0
Callender Athletic v Foots Cray	0-2
Erith & Belvedere v Maidstone United	2-4
RN Depot v Cray Wanderers	6-0
15 Aquarius v Whyteleafe Albion	3-2
Carshalton Athletic v Metropolitan Police	0-2
Epsom Town v Redhill	1-3
Sutton United v West Norwood	4-1
16 Hounslow v Old Isleworthians	8-1
Old Lyonians v Hayes	0-7
Wealdstone v Old Latymerians	8-1
17 Apsley v Kingsthorpe Church Institute	7-1
Aylesbury United v Berkhamsted Town	2-3
Leagrave & District v Watford OB	6-1
Northampton Nomads v Wolverton Town	0-1
18 Egham v 1st Kings Own Scots Borderers	2-2e
RAMC Aldershot v Weybridge	3-1
RASC Aldershot v Woking	3-5e
Walton-on-Thames v Godalming	2-0
19 Cowley v Maidenhead United	0-1
Newbury Town v Morris Motors	4-0
Slough v Oxford City	7-2
Thame United v Windsor & Eton	1-5
20 Enfield v Haywards Sports	4-0
Finchley v Waltham Comrades	6-1
Hertford Town v Letchworth Town	2-4
Ware v Welwyn Garden City	5-2
21 Eastbourne v Vernon Athletic	7-2
Hastings & St Leonards v Hove	4-4e
Horsham v Bognor Town	4-2
Lewes v Eastbourne Old Comrades	2-3
22 5th Royal Tank Corps v Gosport	3-1
Bournemouth Gasworks Athletic v RE Southampton	2-0
Dorchester Town v RM Portsmouth	2-2
Fareham v Salisbury Corinthians	3-2
23 Cheltenham Town v Hanham Athletic	4-3
Gloucester City v St Philips Marsh Adult School	2-0
Keynsham v Sneyd Park	3-2
Minehead v Kingswood	3-4
24 Chippenham Town v Swindon Victoria	4-2
Coleford Athletic v Glastonbury	6-1
Radstock Town v Wells City	2-1e
Spencer Moulton v Garrard Athletic	2-5
3r Crook v Stanley United	1-1e
12r Great Yarmouth Town v Kirkley & Waveney	2-1
13r Brentwood & Warley v Dagenham Town	0-3
18r 1st Kings Own Scots Borderers v Egham	4-1
21r Hastings & St Leonards v Hove	5-1
22r RM Portsmouth v Dorchester Town	3-0
3r2 Crook v Stanley United	1-3

Qualifying Round Three

1 Loftus Albion v Whitby United	2-2
Whitby Albion Rangers v Lingdale Institute	3-2
2 Egglescliffe & District v Normanby Magnesite	4-1
3 Stanley United v Cockfield	1-0
West Auckland Town v Willington	2-1
4 Burnhope Institute v Newcastle Bohemians	2-1
Esh Winning v Langley Park	2-2
5 Farsley Celtic v Horsforth	1-3
Methley Perseverance v Knaresborough Town	6-1
6 Earle v Ellesmere Port Town	wo/s
Marine v Old Xaverians	7-1
7 Nether Edge Amateurs v Sheffield University	4-2
Rawmarsh Welfare v Sheffield	4-0
8 Basford United v Sutton Junction	5-4
RAF Grantham v Nottingham Magdala Amateurs	4-1
9 Moor Green v Wolverhampton Amateurs	2-1
10 Cleethorpes Town v Hull Young Peoples Institute	7-1
Filey Town v Humber United	2-3
11 King's Lynn v Chatteris Town	4-1
St Ives Town v March Town	2-1
12 Great Yarmouth Town v Ipswich Town	0-2
Lowestoft Town v Cromer	2-0
13 Dagenham Town v Tilbury	1-3 v
Walthamstow Avenue v Grays Athletic	1-2
14 Bostall Heath v Foots Cray	2-1
Maidstone United v RN Depot	3-7
15 Aquarius v Metropolitan Police	1-3
Redhill v Sutton United	4-0
16 Hounslow v Hayes	2-1
Staines Town v Wealdstone	1-4
17 Apsley v Berkhamsted Town	1-1
Wolverton Town v Leagrave & District	1-2
18 1st Kings Own Scots Borderers v Walton-on-Thames	8-2
Woking v RAMC Aldershot	3-2
19 Newbury Town v Maidenhead United	1-3
Windsor & Eton v Slough	0-3
20 Enfield v Letchworth Town	2-0
Finchley v Ware	9-0
21 Eastbourne v Eastbourne Old Comrades	1-0
Horsham v Hastings & St Leonards	3-1
22 Bournemouth Gasworks Athletic v RM Portsmouth	3-2
Fareham v 5th Royal Tank Corps	2-1e
23 Keynsham v Gloucester City	2-0
Kingswood v Cheltenham Town	4-1
24 Coleford Athletic v Garrard Athletic	3-0
Radstock Town v Chippenham Town	3-1
1r Whitby United v Loftus Albion	3-1
4r Langley Park v Esh Winning	0-1
13r Dagenham Town v Tilbury	0-0e
17r Berkhamsted Town v Apsley	2-1
13r2 Dagenham Town v Tilbury	3-1 N

Qualifying Round Four

1 Whitby United v Whitby Albion Rangers	3-2
2 W Hartlepool Perseverance v Egglescliffe & District	2-3
3 Stanley United v West Auckland Town	2-1
4 Burnhope Institute v Esh Winning	1-1
5 Horsforth v Methley Perseverance	2-0
6 Marine v Earle	6-1
7 Rawmarsh Welfare v Nether Edge Amateurs	2-1
8 RAF Grantham v Basford United	2-1
9 Malvern Holy Trinity v Moor Green	4-1
10 Cleethorpes Town v Humber United	3-1
11 St Ives Town v King's Lynn	1-1
12 Lowestoft Town v Ipswich Town	3-1
13 Grays Athletic v Dagenham Town	4-0
14 Bostall Heath v RN Depot	2-2
15 Metropolitan Police v Redhill	2-1
16 Hounslow v Wealdstone	4-1
17 Leagrave & District v Berkhamsted Town	0-0
18 1st Kings Own Scots Borderers v Woking	2-3
19 Slough v Maidenhead United	2-2
20 Finchley v Enfield	2-3
21 Horsham v Eastbourne	1-8
22 Bournemouth Gasworks Athletic v Fareham	2-0
23 Keynsham v Kingswood	0-0
24 Coleford Athletic v Radstock Town	3-2
4r Esh Winning v Burnhope Institute	4-0
11r King's Lynn v St Ives Town	3-0
14r RN Depot v Bostall Heath	4-1
17r Berkhamsted Town v Leagrave & District	3-1
19r Maidenhead United v Slough	2-1e
23r Kingswood v Keynsham	5-1

Round One

Barking Town v Maidenhead United	5-1
Bournemouth Gasworks Athletic v Wycombe Wan.	2-1
Chesham United v King's Lynn	3-2
Clapton v Barnet	0-4
Dulwich Hamlet v Casuals	4-0
Enfield v St Albans City	2-0
Esh Winning v Birmingham Tramways	4-0
Gorleston v Portland United	4-0
Grays Athletic v Lowestoft Town	8-1
Hampstead Town v Woking	3-2
Ilford v Eastbourne	13-1
Kingstonian v Hounslow	1-0
Leyton v Coleford Athletic	7-0
Leytonstone v London Caledonians	0-6
Malvern Holy Trinity v Hallam	3-3
Metropolitan Police v Bromley	2-1
Nunhead v Berkhamsted Town	10-0
Percy Main Amateurs v Cleethorpes Town	2-2
Pilkington Recreation v Marine	2-2
Players Athletic v Evenwood Town	2-2
Rawmarsh Welfare v Egglescliffe & District	2-1
Sneinton v Horsforth	2-3
South Bank v Yorkshire Amateur	0-2
Southall v HMS Excellent	0-0
Southwick v Cambridge Town	0-2
Stanley United v Norton Woodseats	1-0
Stockton v Whitehall Printeries	4-1
Tow Law Town v RAF Grantham	4-2
Tufnell Park v RN Depot	3-1
Welton Rovers v Kingswood	4-1
Whitby United v Northern Nomads	2-4
Wimbledon v Aldershot Traction Company	4-3
r Cleethorpes Town v Percy Main Amateurs	3-4
r Evenwood Town v Players Athletic	5-0
r HMS Excellent v Southall	3-2a
r Hallam v Malvern Holy Trinity	6-4
r Marine v Pilkington Recreation	7-1
r2 HMS Excellent v Southall	3-1 N

Round Two

Barnet v HMS Excellent	2-1
Bournemouth Gasworks Athletic v Welton Rovers	4-0
Cambridge Town v Wimbledon	0-2
Dulwich Hamlet v Tufnell Park	4-3
Enfield v Metropolitan Police	0-2
Esh Winning v Stockton	3-3
Evenwood Town v Horsforth	3-1
Gorleston v Leyton	0-1
Hampstead Town v Barking Town	1-4
Kingstonian v Grays Athletic	4-1
London Caledonians v Ilford	1-3
Northern Nomads v Hallam	3-1
Nunhead v Chesham United	1-3
Percy Main Amateurs v Rawmarsh Welfare	3-0
Tow Law Town v Marine	2-1
Yorkshire Amateur v Stanley United	3-0
r Stockton v Esh Winning	4-0

Round Three

Bournemouth Gasworks Athletic v Barnet	3-1
Dulwich Hamlet v Chesham United	2-0
Ilford v Evenwood Town	3-0
Kingstonian v Leyton	0-1
Percy Main Amateurs v Yorkshire Amateur	1-1
Stockton v Barking Town	4-1
Tow Law Town v Northern Nomads	0-3
Wimbledon v Metropolitan Police	2-1
r Yorkshire Amateur v Percy Main Amateurs	0-1

Round Four

Bournemouth Gasworks Ath v Percy Main Amateurs	2-0
Ilford v Dulwich Hamlet	2-1
Leyton v Wimbledon	0-1
Northern Nomads v Stockton	1-0

Semi Finals

Bournemouth Gasworks Athletic v Wimbledon	2-0 N
Ilford v Northern Nomads	0-0 N
r Ilford v Northern Nomads	4-2 N

Final

Ilford v Bournemouth Gasworks Athletic	5-1 N

1930/31

Preliminary Round

12 Norwich St Barnabas v Stoke Institute	5-2
13 4th Divisional Signals Regiment v Severalls Ath.	3-1
Brentwood Mental Hospital v Leytonstone	3-1
Crittall Athletic v 2nd Black Watch	11-4
Felixstowe Town v Clacton Town	2-2e
GER Loughton v Romford (2)	3-4
Harwich & Parkeston v Walton United	1-1
RA Shoeburyness v Chelmsford	0-4
Tilbury v Jurgens	4-2
Walthamstow Grange v Rovers (Poplar)	4-1
17 Leavesden Mental Hospital v Arlesey Town	2-1
Luton Amateur v Waterlows Dunstable	n/a
RAF Henlow v Wootton Blue Cross	8-1
Watford Spartans v Apsley	2-5
21 East Grinstead v Rock-a-Nore	9-1
Eastbourne v Hove	5-1
Littlehampton v Broadwater	5-1
24 Calne & Harris United v Frome Town	4-1
Chippenham Town v Glastonbury	1-2
Clandown v St Cuthberts Works	6-3
Melksham Town v Swindon Corinthians	0-1
Paulton Rovers v Wells City	0-2
Purton v Trowbridge Town	2-3
Watchet v Street	0-2
Westbury United v Minehead	3-0
13r Clacton Town v Felixstowe Town	7-2
r Walton United v Harwich & Parkeston	1-4

Qualifying Round One

3 Cockfield v Chilton Colliery Recreation	1-2
Stanley United v Ferryhill Athletic	2-3e
Sunnybrow Olympic v Tow Law Town	3-1
11 Bury Town v Chatteris Town	0-5
Ely City v Wisbech Town	0-3
March Town v Warboys Town	2-4
12 Cromer v Leiston Works Athletic	6-3
Diss Town v Orwell Works	1-2
Great Yarmouth Town v Norwich Civil Service	6-1
Ipswich Town v Boulton & Paul	3-0
Kirkley & Waveney v Woodbridge Town	6-3
Lowestoft Town v Beccles Town	10-0
Norwich CEYMS v Sheringham	3-1
Stowmarket v Norwich St Barnabas	4-1
13 4th Divisional Signals Regiment v Clacton Town	3-1
Brentwood Mental Hospital v Grays Athletic	1-3
Chelmsford v Brentwood & Warley	1-0 v
Colchester Town v Crittall Athletic	1-5
Dagenham Town v Romford (2)	1-2
Harwich & Parkeston v Parkeston Railway	2-3
Tilbury v Custom House	3-0
Walthamstow Grange v Brantham Athletic	4-6
14 Beckenham v UGBM Sports	2-0
Callender Athletic v Woolwich Polytechnic	2-3
Cray Wanderers v RM Chatham	2-5
Foots Cray v Erith & Belvedere	2-1
Maidstone United v Bostall Heath	5-2
RN Depot v Catford Wanderers	4-2
Standard Telephones v 1st Sherwood Foresters	3-4

40

1930/31

15	Beddington Corner v Leyland Motors	4-0
	Carshalton Athletic v Tooting Town	3-2
	Dorking v Redhill	3-2e
	Epsom Town v West Norwood	3-2
	Mitcham Wanderers v Reigate Priory	7-0
	Sutton United v Wallington	4-2
16	Civil Service v Old Latymerians	5-0
	Hendon Town v Hayes	2-7
	Old Lyonians v Polytechnic	3-2
	RAF Uxbridge v Standard Telephones	wo/s
	Staines Town v Lyons	2-1
	Uxbridge Town v Hounslow	1-4
17	Aylesbury United v Leighton United	6-1
	Berkhamsted Town v Walgrave Amber	8-2
	Chesham United v Leagrave & District	6-1
	Daventry Town v Waterlows Dunstable	2-1
	Kempston Rovers v Mount Pleasant	2-1
	Kingsthorpe Church Institute v Wolverton Town	2-4
	Leavesden Mental Hospital v Apsley	3-1
	RAF Henlow v Northampton Nomads	0-1
18	Abingdon Town v Slough	2-3
	Cowley v Maidenhead United	0-3
	Littlemore v Henley Town	2-2e
	Marlow v Banbury Harriers	9-0
	Oxford City v Bicester Town	3-1
	Suttons v Morris Motors	0-6
	Thame United v Newbury Town	3-4
	Windsor & Eton v Witney Town	4-1e
19	Baldock Town v Letchworth Town	2-2
	Cheshunt (1) v Hoddesdon Town	4-1
	Haywards Sports v Welwyn Garden City	9-1
	Hertford Town v Bishops Stortford	2-4
	Hitchin Town v Wood Green Town	2-0
	Old Johnians v Ware	1-4
	Tufnell Park v Waltham Comrades	8-0
20	2nd Beds & Herts Regiment v Wellington Works	4-2
	Aldershot Traction Company v Walton-on-Thames	0-3
	Camberley & Yorktown v Addlestone	4-3
	Courage & Co's Sports v Guildford	3-4
	Egham v 1st Border Regt	2-1
	Godalming v 1st Kings Own Yorkshire LI	1-1
	Hersham v RAMC Aldershot	0-7
21	Bexhill v Eastbourne Comrades	1-7
	Bognor Regis v Wick	8-2
	Eastbourne v East Grinstead	6-3
	Haywards Heath v Vernon Athletic	8-1
	Horsham v Hollington United	6-3
	Littlehampton v Pulborough	4-2
	Newhaven v Crawley	10-0
	Worthing v Hastings & St Leonards	4-2
22	Blandford v Bournemouth Tramways	2-5
	Bournemouth v Dorchester Town	3-5
	Castle Hill v 2nd Kings Royal Rifles	4-6e
	Fareham v RM Portsmouth	2-0
	Osborne Athletic v Ryde Sports	3-7
	Poole Town v Gosport	2-1
	Portsmouth Gas Co v HMS Victory	3-0
23	Cheltenham Town v Hanham Athletic	2-4
	Keynsham v Chalford	7-2
	Mount Hill Enterprise v Kingswood	1-1
	Sneyd Park v St Philips Athletic	3-4
	Weston-super-Mare v Fry & Sons	4-2
24	Calne & Harris United v Trowbridge Town	1-2
	Chippenham Rovers v Warminster Town	1-7
	Clandown v Glastonbury	2-1
	Coleford Athletic v Garrard Athletic	9-1
	Devizes Town v Westbury United	3-3e
	Radstock Town v Wells City	3-1
	Swindon Corinthians v Street	2-2
	Swindon Victoria v Spencer Moulton	4-2
13r	Brentwood & Warley v Chelmsford	3-1
18r	Henley Town v Littlemore	8-1
19r	Letchworth Town v Baldock Town	3-2e
20r	1st Kings Own Yorkshire v Godalming	1-2
23r	Kingswood v Mount Hill Enterprise	0-3
24r	Street v Swindon Corinthians	5-7
r	Westbury United v Devizes Town	3-1

Qualifying Round Two

3	Chilton Colliery Recreation v Eden CW	5-3
	Crookhall CW v Leasingthorne CW	1-0
	Trimdon Grange Colliery v Ferryhill Athletic	4-2
	West Auckland Town v Sunnybrow Olympic	2-1
5	Manningham Mills v Farsley Celtic	3-2
	Whitehall Printeries v Luddendenfoot	2-0
7	Pilkington Recreation v Sheffield Municipal Officers	6-3
8	Matlock Town v Nottingham Magdala Amateurs	8-0
	Players Athletic v Celanese Amateurs	6-2
	Stapleford Brookhill v Sutton Junction	1-2
9	Boldmere St Michaels v Moor Green	4-3
	Wolverhampton Amateurs v Birmingham Tramways	1-3
11	Newmarket Town v Chatteris Town	5-3
	Thetford Town v St Ives Town	3-1
	Warboys Town v King's Lynn	3-3e
	Wisbech Town v Soham Rangers	7-2
12	Great Yarmouth Town v Cromer	7-2
	Ipswich Town v Stowmarket	4-2e
	Lowestoft Town v Orwell Works	6-1
	Norwich CEYMS v Kirkley & Waveney	1-3
13	4th Divisional Signals Regiment v Grays Athletic	5-2
	Brantham Athletic v Tilbury	2-4
	Parkeston Railway v Brentwood & Warley	1-3
	Romford (2) v Crittall Athletic	3-2
14	Beckenham v Foots Cray	4-2
	Maidstone United v Bexleyheath & Welling	3-2
	RM Chatham v 1st Sherwood Foresters	wo/s
	Woolwich Polytechnic v RN Depot	2-2
15	Carshalton Athletic v Epsom Town	1-6
	Dorking v Sutton United	4-2e
	Mitcham Wanderers v Beddington Corner	4-1
	Whyteleafe Albion v Aquarius	4-2
16	Hounslow v Hayes	1-4
	Old Lyonians v Civil Service	1-1e
	Staines Town v Southall	0-2
	Wealdstone v RAF Uxbridge	12-0
17	Berkhamsted Town v Aylesbury United	4-5
	Chesham United v Kempston Rovers	10-0
	Leavesden Mental Hospital v Daventry Town	1-0
	Wolverton Town v Northampton Nomads	1-1
18	Maidenhead United v Oxford City	5-1
	Marlow v Newbury Town	5-1
	Morris Motors v Windsor & Eton	6-3
	Slough v Henley Town	4-3
19	Hitchin Town v Finchley	5-1
	Letchworth Town v Cheshunt (1)	7-2
	Tufnell Park v Haywards Sports	4-3
	Ware v Bishops Stortford	3-6
20	Camberley & Yorktown v Guildford	2-2
	Egham v RASC Aldershot	3-0
	Godalming v 2nd Beds & Herts Regiment	5-2
	Walton-on-Thames v RAMC Aldershot	2-2e
21	Eastbourne v Newhaven	5-1
	Haywards Heath v Eastbourne Comrades	4-1
	Horsham v Bognor Regis	6-0
	Worthing v Littlehampton	5-1
22	2nd Kings Royal Rifles v Dorchester Town	3-0
	Bournemouth Tramways v Poole Town	3-1
	RAOC Hilsea v Fareham	4-2e
	Ryde Sports v Portsmouth Gas Co	4-0
23	Cadbury Heath YMCA v Keynsham	3-1
	Gloucester City v Weston-super-Mare	0-0e
	Hanham Athletic v Mount Hill Enterprise	3-1
	Listers v St Philips Athletic	1-3
24	Clandown v Coleford Athletic	4-2
	Radstock Town v Westbury United	3-1
	Swindon Corinthians v Swindon Victoria	2-2
	Warminster Town v Trowbridge Town	2-4
11r	King's Lynn v Warboys Town	3-6e
14r	RN Depot v Woolwich Polytechnic	3-2
16r	Civil Service v Old Lyonians	1-2
17r	Northampton Nomads v Wolverton Town	9-0
20r	Guildford v Camberley & Yorktown	5-2
r	RAMC Aldershot v Walton-on-Thames	2-2
23r	Weston-super-Mare v Gloucester City	1-0
24r	Swindon Victoria v Swindon Corinthians	2-0
20r2	Walton-on-Thames v RAMC Aldershot	2-0

Qualifying Round Three

2	Egglescliffe & District v Normanby Magnesite	2-3
3	Chilton Colliery Recreation v Crookhall CW	1-0e
	Trimdon Grange Colliery v West Auckland Town	1-0
4	Newcastle West End Amateurs v Esh Winning	6-1
5	Guiseley v Manningham Mills	1-3
	Leeds University v Whitehall Printeries	0-3
6	Earle v South Salford Amateurs	2-2
	Old Xaverians v Harrowby	1-3
7	Handsworth United Sports v Sheffield	3-2
	Pilkington Recreation v Norton Woodseats	2-2
8	Players Athletic v Sutton Junction	4-1
	Ransome & Marles v Matlock Town	2-1
9	Birmingham Gas Officials v Boldmere St Michaels	4-3
	Birmingham Tramways v Malvern Holy Trinity	1-3
10	Hull Young Peoples Institute v Humber United	2-4
	RAF Grantham v Hull OB	11-0
11	Thetford Town v Newmarket Town	2-6
	Wisbech Town v Warboys Town	7-0
12	Ipswich Town v Great Yarmouth Town	2-2
	Kirkley & Waveney v Lowestoft Town	0-1
13	Romford (2) v Brentwood & Warley	2-1
	Tilbury v 4th Divisional Signals Regiment	3-2
14	Maidstone United v Beckenham	2-1
	RM Chatham v RN Depot	4-1
15	Dorking v Whyteleafe Albion	0-1
	Mitcham Wanderers v Epsom Town	1-1
16	Old Lyonians v Hayes	1-6
	Southall v Wealdstone	2-3
17	Aylesbury United v Northampton Nomads	4-3
	Leavesden Mental Hospital v Chesham United	3-1
18	Marlow v Maidenhead United	1-1
	Slough v Morris Motors	3-0
19	Hitchin Town v Bishops Stortford	2-0
	Letchworth Town v Tufnell Park	1-5
20	Guildford v Egham	3-4
	Walton-on-Thames v Godalming	3-2
21	Haywards Heath v Eastbourne	2-3
	Horsham v Worthing	1-5
22	2nd Kings Royal Rifles v Bournemouth Tramways	4-1
	RAOC Hilsea v Ryde Sports	0-2
23	Cadbury Heath YMCA v Hanham Athletic	1-2
	Weston-super-Mare v St Philips Athletic	1-3
24	Clandown v Swindon Victoria	3-3
	Radstock Town v Trowbridge Town	1-2
6r	South Salford Amateurs v Earle	3-1
7r	Norton Woodseats v Pilkington Recreation	3-3e
12r	Great Yarmouth Town v Ipswich Town	3-2
15r	Epsom Town v Mitcham Wanderers	5-1
18r	Maidenhead United v Marlow	2-0
24r	Swindon Victoria v Clandown	3-0
7r2	Norton Woodseats v Pilkington Recreation	2-1 N

Qualifying Round Four

1	Whitby Albion Rangers v Lingdale Institute	5-1
2	Normanby Magnesite v W Hartlepool Perseverance	4-2
3	Chilton Colliery Rec. v Trimdon Grange Colliery	3-1
4	Newcastle West End Amateurs v Burnhope Institute	5-0
5	Manningham Mills v Whitehall Printeries	2-1
6	Harrowby v South Salford Amateurs	1-1
7	Handsworth United Sports v Norton Woodseats	3-3
8	Players Athletic v Ransome & Marles	2-1
9	Birmingham Gas Officials v Malvern Holy Trinity	4-2
10	Humber United v RAF Grantham	6-2
11	Wisbech Town v Newmarket Town	9-1
12	Great Yarmouth Town v Lowestoft Town	2-3
13	Romford (2) v Tilbury	1-0
14	RM Chatham v Maidstone United	1-0
15	Whyteleafe Albion v Epsom Town	1-2
16	Wealdstone v Hayes	2-4
17	Leavesden Mental Hospital v Aylesbury United	8-3
18	Slough v Maidenhead United	3-5
19	Tufnell Park v Hitchin Town	1-1
20	Egham v Walton-on-Thames	6-1
21	Eastbourne v Worthing	1-3
22	2nd Kings Royal Rifles v Ryde Sports	4-4
23	St Philips Athletic v Hanham Athletic	1-1
24	Trowbridge Town v Swindon Victoria	4-0
6r	South Salford Amateurs v Harrowby	5-3
7r	Norton Woodseats v Handsworth United Sports	4-2
19r	Hitchin Town v Tufnell Park	3-0
22r	Ryde Sports v 2nd Kings Royal Rifles	4-2
23r	Hanham Athletic v St Philips Athletic	1-2e

Round One

	Barking Town v Bromley	5-1
	Barnet v Bournemouth Gasworks Athletic	9-3
	Birmingham Gas Officials v South Salford Amateurs	2-1
	Bishop Auckland v Evenwood Town	1-1
	Clapton v HMS Excellent	1-1
	Egham v Romford (2)	0-3
	Epsom Town v Ilford	2-5
	Hampstead Town v Welton Rovers	2-6
	Hitchin Town v Leyton	0-3
	Humber United v Rawmarsh Welfare	1-1
	Kingstonian v Enfield	3-1
	London Caledonians v Wycombe Wanderers	1-4
	Lowestoft Town v St Philips Athletic	1-0
	Manningham Mills v Percy Main Amateurs	2-1
	Marine v Whitby United	7-2
	Newcastle West End Ams v Chilton Colliery Rec.	2-3
	Northern Nomads v Yorkshire Amateur	3-2
	Norton Woodseats v Normanby Magnesite	3-1
	Nunhead v Leavesden Mental Hospital	4-0
	Players Athletic v South Bank	1-0
	Portland United v Dulwich Hamlet	4-2
	RM Chatham v Casuals	3-4
	Ryde Sports v Maidenhead United	5-5
	Sneinton v Hallam	2-0
	Southwick v Walthamstow Avenue	1-2
	St Albans City v Wimbledon	1-5
	Stockton v Horsforth	6-2
	Trowbridge Town v Gorleston	2-0
	Whitby Albion Rangers v Willington	4-4
	Wisbech Town v Hayes	1-6
	Woking v Cambridge Town	3-1
	Worthing v Metropolitan Police	0-3
r	Bishop Auckland v Evenwood Town	5-1
r	HMS Excellent v Clapton	1-2
r	Maidenhead United v Ryde Sports	6-1
r	Rawmarsh Welfare v Humber United	1-0
r	Willington v Whitby Albion Rangers	6-1

Round Two

	Barking Town v Wimbledon	0-1
	Barnet v Clapton	1-3
	Bishop Auckland v Marine	2-1
	Casuals v Ilford	2-4
	Lowestoft Town v Welton Rovers	1-2
	Maidenhead United v Portland United	3-3
	Manningham Mills v Northern Nomads	1-2e
	Nunhead v Metropolitan Police	0-2
	Players Athletic v Willington	2-3
	Rawmarsh Welfare v Chilton Colliery Recreation	3-0
	Romford (2) v Kingstonian	5-1
	Sneinton v Birmingham Gas Officials	2-1
	Stockton v Norton Woodseats	7-2
	Trowbridge Town v Hayes	1-2
	Woking v Leyton	4-0
	Wycombe Wanderers v Walthamstow Avenue	6-1
r	Portland United v Maidenhead United	0-0
r	Welton Rovers v Lowestoft Town	2-1
r2	Maidenhead United v Portland United	2-2 N
r3	Portland United v Maidenhead United	4-1 N

1930/31 to 1931/32

Round Three

	Bishop Auckland v Ilford	6-2
	Clapton v Rawmarsh Welfare	2-1
	Metropolitan Police v Welton Rovers	3-1e
	Northern Nomads v Willington	3-1
	Stockton v Sneinton	7-2
	Wimbledon v Hayes	2-3e
	Woking v Portland United	2-1
	Wycombe Wanderers v Romford (2)	6-2

Round Four

	Bishop Auckland v Stockton	5-3
	Clapton v Woking	0-1
	Metropolitan Police v Wycombe Wanderers	1-1e
	Northern Nomads v Hayes	1-2
r	Wycombe Wanderers v Metropolitan Police	2-1

Semi Finals

	Hayes v Bishop Auckland	1-0 N
	Wycombe Wanderers v Woking	3-0 N

Final

	Wycombe Wanderers v Hayes	1-0 N

1931/32

Preliminary Round

12	Long Melford v Norwich YMCA	5-1
	Norwich St Barnabas v Beccles Town	3-1
13	Brentwood & Warley v Clacton Town	7-3
	Colchester Town v Felixstowe Town	7-3
	Crittall Athletic v 2nd Black Watch	2-1
	Dagenham Town v RAF Felixstowe	6-2
	Harwich & Parkeston v Tate Institute	1-0
	Parkeston Railway v Custom House	4-2
	RA Shoeburyness v 4th Divisional Signals Regiment	2-3
14	Aylesford Paper Mills v UGBM Sports	3-1
	Bostall Heath v Gravesend Territorials	8-1
	Dover United v RM Deal	3-1
	Sittingbourne v Swanley Athletic	2-3
	Woolwich Boro Council Ath v Bexleyheath & Welling	3-7
	Woolwich Polytechnic v Erith & Belvedere	1-3
18	Osberton Radiator v Headington United	5-4
	Stones Athletic v Gradwells Sports	1-4
21	Eastbourne Comrades v East Grinstead	1-2
	Hastings & St Leonards v Hollington United	12-1
24	Devizes Town v Calne & Harris United	3-1
	Frome Town v Chippenham Town	2-2
	Garrard Athletic v Trowbridge Town	0-3
	Radstock Town v Clandown	2-0
24r	Chippenham Town v Frome Town	6-3

Qualifying Round One

8	Coventry Strollers v Headingley	2-1
	Red Hill Amateurs v Courtaulds	4-3
	Warwick Town v Badsey Rangers	2-7
10	Bletchley Town v Wolverton Town	3-2
	Northampton Nomads v Brackley Town	10-0
11	Ely City v Histon Institute	3-4
	Huntingdon Town v March Town	6-2
	Newmarket Town v King's Lynn	1-2
	St Ives Town v Abbey United	5-0
	Thetford Town v Soham Rangers	6-2
	Wisbech Town v Warboys Town	6-1
12	Cromer v Orwell Works	4-5e
	Diss Town v Norwich St Barnabas	2-0e
	Great Yarmouth Town v Stowmarket	7-4
	Ipswich Town v Long Melford	6-2
	Leiston Works Athletic v Kirkley & Waveney	0-1
	Lowestoft Town v Boulton & Paul	2-1
	Norwich CEYMS v Sheringham	4-3
	Woodbridge Town v Norwich Civil Service	3-2
13	Brentwood & Warley v Harwich & Parkeston	3-4
	Chelmsford v Severalls Athletic	7-0
	Colchester Town v Walton United	7-2
	Crittall Athletic v Jurgens	8-2
	Dagenham Town v Leytonstone	3-0
	Grays Athletic v 4th Divisional Signals Regiment	3-2
	Parkeston Railway v GER Loughton	wo/s
	Tilbury v Brantham Athletic	3-4
14	Beckenham v RM Chatham	1-2
	Bromley v Standard Telephones	3-2
	Callender Athletic v Foots Cray	6-2
	Cray Wanderers v Aylesford Paper Mills	1-0
	Erith & Belvedere v Bexleyheath & Welling	4-3
	Maidstone United v Dover United	1-2
	RN Depot v Catford Wanderers	1-0
	Swanley Athletic v Bostall Heath	0-2
15	Beddington Corner v Mitcham Wanderers	2-10
	Dorking v Reigate Priory	5-3
	Merton v Aquarius	4-0
	Metropolitan Police v Epsom Town	1-1e
	Redhill v RNVR Mitcham	12-1
	Sutton United v Leyland Motors	2-0
	Tooting Town v West Norwood	2-1
16	Old Latymerians v Civil Service	0-1
	Park Royal v Southall	0-4
	Uxbridge Town v 1st Kings Dragoon Guards	wo/s
17	Berkhamsted Town v Vauxhall Motors	2-1
	Luton Amateur v Apsley	1-4
	RAF Henlow v Leavesden Mental Hospital	1-1e
18	Abingdon Town v Morris Motors	3-2
	Banbury Harriers v Oxford City	1-4
	Cowley v Windsor & Eton	1-6
	Gradwells Sports v Thame United	5-0
	Marlow v Osberton Radiator	5-2
	Newbury Town v Littlemore	3-0
	Slough v Henley Town	8-1
	Witney Town v Bicester Town	4-2
19	Enfield v Old Johnians	2-0
	Finchley v Bishops Stortford	2-1
	Hertford Town v Waltham Comrades	7-3
	Hitchin Town v Welwyn Garden City	7-0
	Letchworth Town v Hoddesdon Town	3-1
	Shredded Wheat v Stevenage Town	4-2
	Ware v Baldock Town	3-0
	Wood Green Town v Tufnell Park	4-5
20	2nd Beds & Herts Rgmt v Camberley & Yorktown	0-5
	Egham v Aldershot Traction Company	2-3
	Wellington Works v 1st Border Regt	2-4
21	Bexhill v East Grinstead	2-0
	Bognor Regis v Pulborough	5-1
	Eastbourne v Rock-a-Nore	8-1
	Hastings & St Leonards v Newhaven	3-2
	Haywards Heath v Wick	8-0
	Horsham v Vernon Athletic	6-2
	Littlehampton v Hove	3-0
	Worthing v Broadwater	3-0
22	Blandford v Bournemouth Transport	4-3
	Bournemouth v 2nd Kings Royal Rifles	1-2
	Bournemouth Gasworks Athletic v RAOC Hilsea	2-1
	Dorchester Town v RM Portsmouth	1-7
	Poole Town v Gosport	4-1
	Portsmouth Gas Co v Osborne Athletic	2-1
	Ryde Sports v HMS Victory	2-0
	South Hants Nomads v Fareham	0-4
23	Cadbury Heath YMCA v Clevedon	2-2
	Chalford v St Philips Marsh Adult School	4-1
	Hanham Athletic v Fry & Sons	4-1
	Keynsham v Wesley Rangers	3-1
	Kingswood v Warmley Amateurs	5-2
	Listers v Gloucester City	4-2
	Warmley v Cheltenham Town	1-6
	Weston-super-Mare v Mount Hill Enterprise	3-2
24	Chippenham Rovers v Swindon Corinthians	2-6
	Coleford Athletic v Glastonbury	4-3
	Devizes Town v Purton	5-3
	Melksham Town v Spencer Moulton	4-6
	Minehead v Wells City	1-3
	Radstock Town v Paulton Rovers	3-2
	Trowbridge Town v Swindon Victoria	4-1
	Westbury United v Chippenham Town	3-2
15r	Epsom Town v Metropolitan Police	2-1
17r	Leavesden Mental Hospital v RAF Henlow	2-3
23r	Clevedon v Cadbury Heath YMCA	7-0

Qualifying Round Two

1	Normanby Magnesite v South Bank East End	5-1
2	1st Durham Light Infantry v Thornley CW	3-0
	Crookhall CW v Ferryhill Athletic	3-3e
	Stanley United v Chilton Colliery Recreation	5-1
	Trimdon Grange Colliery v Leasingthorne CW	2-0
3	Esh Winning v Barnard Castle Athletic	2-0
	Stanhope v Burnhope Institute	2-1
	Tow Law Town v Newcastle West End Amateurs	3-0
	West Auckland Town v Cockfield	3-2e
4	Harrogate v Horsforth	3-4e
	Meltham Mills v Guiseley	6-2
	Whitehall Printeries v Farsley Celtic	3-1
5	Ellesmere Port Town v Harrowby	2-6
	Old Xaverians v Preston GS OB	3-3e
8	Boldmere St Michaels v Wolverhampton Amateurs	2-2
	Coventry Strollers v Moor Green	0-3
	Malvern Holy Trinity v Badsey Rangers	4-3
	Red Hill Amateurs v Birmingham Gas Officials	4-1
10	Daventry Town v Bletchley Town	1-2
	Kingsthorpe Church Institute v Kempston Rovers	wo/s
	Leighton United v Northampton Nomads	2-2
	Walgrave Amber v Mount Pleasant	5-1
11	Bury Town v Histon Institute	3-0
	Chatteris Town v Huntingdon Town	2-5
	Thetford Town v St Ives Town	1-2
	Wisbech Town v King's Lynn	0-1
12	Great Yarmouth Town v Woodbridge Town	12-1
	Ipswich Town v Diss Town	3-2a
	Norwich CEYMS v Lowestoft Town	3-4e
	Orwell Works v Kirkley & Waveney	1-0
13	Brantham Athletic v Dagenham Town	0-5
	Chelmsford v Harwich & Parkeston	2-3e
	Colchester Town v Parkeston Railway	6-0
	Grays Athletic v Crittall Athletic	4-2
14	Bostall Heath v Bromley	4-2
	Erith & Belvedere v Callender Athletic	3-2
	RM Chatham v Dover United	3-0
	RN Depot v Cray Wanderers	4-2
15	Dorking v Merton	1-5
	Epsom Town v Tooting Town	3-1
	Redhill v Mitcham Wanderers	2-1
	Sutton United v Carshalton Athletic	3-1
16	Hounslow Town v Uxbridge Town	4-3
	Old Lyonians v Hendon Town	0-3
	Southall v Lyons	2-0
	Staines Town v Civil Service	2-3
17	Apsley v Berkhamsted Town	3-1
	Arlesey Town v Watford Spartans	1-5
	Aylesbury United v Chesham United	1-3
	RAF Henlow v Waterlows Dunstable	0-4
18	Abingdon Town v Slough	2-13
	Marlow v Witney Town	5-1
	Newbury Town v Gradwells Sports	2-3
	Windsor & Eton v Oxford City	1-0
19	Enfield v Tufnell Park	1-0e
	Finchley v Ware	4-0
	Hertford Town v Hitchin Town	3-6
	Letchworth Town v Shredded Wheat	7-1
20	Camberley & Yorktown v Aldershot Traction Co	1-4e
	Courage & Co's Sports v Hersham	2-3
	Godalming v Guildford	2-4
	RAMC Aldershot v 1st Border Regt	2-1
21	Bognor Regis v Worthing	0-1
	Eastbourne v Haywards Heath	3-4
	Hastings & St Leonards v Horsham	3-2e
	Littlehampton v Bexhill	2-3
22	Blandford v Ryde Sports	0-7
	Bournemouth Gasworks Athletic v RM Portsmouth	4-0
	Fareham v Portsmouth Gas Co	2-0
	Poole Town v 2nd Kings Royal Rifles	3-0
23	Cheltenham Town v Weston-super-Mare	1-0
	Clevedon v Listers	9-2
	Hanham Athletic v Chalford	1-0
	Keynsham v Kingswood	2-2e
24	Devizes Town v Coleford Athletic	2-1
	Radstock Town v Wells City	2-2
	Swindon Corinthians v Spencer Moulton	2-0
	Westbury United v Trowbridge Town	1-3
2r	Ferryhill Athletic v Crookhall CW	2-1
5r	Preston GS OB v Old Xaverians	3-1
8r	Wolverhampton Amateurs v Boldmere St Michaels	2-1
10r	Northampton Nomads v Leighton United	6-0
12r	Ipswich Town v Diss Town	4-2
23r	Kingswood v Keynsham	2-4
24r	Wells City v Radstock Town	2-1

Qualifying Round Three

1	Portrack Shamrocks v Normanby Magnesite	1-2e
	Whitby Albion Rgrs v W Hartlepool Perseverance	5-3
2	1st Durham Light Infantry v Stanley United	2-1
	Ferryhill Athletic v Trimdon Grange Colliery	1-2
3	Stanhope v Esh Winning	2-0
	West Auckland Town v Tow Law Town	0-1
4	Meltham Mills v Luddendenfoot	6-2
	Whitehall Printeries v Horsforth	8-1
5	Harrowby v Cadby Hall	2-3
	South Salford Amateurs v Preston GS OB	7-1
6	Handsworth United Sports v Sheffield	2-2
	Norton Woodseats v Sheffield Municipal Officers	8-1
7	Stapleford Brookhill v Nottingham Magdala Ams	3-1
8	Malvern Holy Trinity v Moor Green	1-3e
	Wolverhampton Amateurs v Red Hill Amateurs	2-3
9	Hull Young Peoples Institute v RAF Grantham	3-8
	Humber United v Pilkington Recreation	2-0
10	Northampton Nomads v Bletchley Town	8-2
	Walgrave Amber v Kingsthorpe Church Institute	4-4e
11	Huntingdon Town v Bury Town	2-3
	St Ives Town v King's Lynn	3-1
12	Great Yarmouth Town v Lowestoft Town	2-3
	Ipswich Town v Orwell Works	6-3
13	Dagenham Town v Colchester Town	2-2e
	Grays Athletic v Harwich & Parkeston	1-0
14	Bostall Heath v RM Chatham	2-0
	Erith & Belvedere v RN Depot	3-1
15	Epsom Town v Merton	2-0
	Redhill v Sutton United	6-2
16	Civil Service v Hendon Town	3-1
	Hounslow Town v Southall	1-4
17	Apsley v Chesham United	1-3
	Waterlows Dunstable v Watford Spartans	1-0
18	Marlow v Gradwells Sports	5-2e
	Windsor & Eton v Slough	2-6
19	Enfield v Finchley	3-0
	Hitchin Town v Letchworth Town	5-2
20	Aldershot Traction Company v Guildford	2-5
	Hersham v RAMC Aldershot	1-2
21	Bexhill v Worthing	2-4
	Haywards Heath v Hastings & St Leonards	3-2e
22	Bournemouth Gasworks Athletic v Fareham	6-1
	Ryde Sports v Poole Town	7-1
23	Clevedon v Cheltenham Town	1-3
	Hanham Athletic v Keynsham	4-1 D
24	Devizes Town v Swindon Corinthians	6-2
	Trowbridge Town v Wells City	3-1
6r	Sheffield v Handsworth United Sports	5-2
10r	Kingsthorpe Church Institute v Walgrave Amber	5-0
13r	Colchester Town v Dagenham Town	6-1

Qualifying Round Four

1	Whitby Albion Rangers v Normanby Magnesite	5-0
2	Trimdon Grange Colliery v 1st Durham Light Infantry	2-3
3	Tow Law Town v Stanhope	1-2
4	Meltham Mills v Whitehall Printeries	3-1 D
5	Cadby Hall v South Salford Amateurs	0-3
6	Norton Woodseats v Sheffield	6-0

1931/32 to 1932/33

7 Stapleford Brookhill v Excelsior Foundry 2-2
8 Moor Green v Red Hill Amateurs 1-1
9 RAF Grantham v Humber United 2-0
10 Kingsthorpe Church Institute v Northampton Nomads 0-3
11 St Ives Town v Bury Town 1-1
12 Ipswich Town v Lowestoft Town 2-0
13 Colchester Town v Grays Athletic 4-1
14 Erith & Belvedere v Bostall Heath 2-2 d
15 Redhill v Epsom Town 1-2
16 Civil Service v Southall 2-4
17 Chesham United v Waterlows Dunstable 2-1
18 Slough v Marlow 3-3
19 Hitchin Town v Enfield 5-1
20 Guildford v RAMC Aldershot 1-3
21 Haywards Heath v Worthing 4-4
22 Bournemouth Gasworks Athletic v Ryde Sports 3-1
23 Keynsham v Cheltenham Town 5-1
24 Trowbridge Town v Devizes Town 9-1
7r Excelsior Foundry v Stapleford Brookhill 1-0
8r Red Hill Amateurs v Moor Green 1-4
11r Bury Town v St Ives Town 3-3
18r Marlow v Slough 2-5
21r Worthing v Haywards Heath 4-3
11r2 St Ives Town v Bury Town 3-2

Round One

1st Durham Light Infantry v Bishop Auckland 1-2
Barking Town v Wycombe Wanderers 2-3
Barnet v Hayes 1-4
Cambridge Town v St Ives Town 7-4
Chesham United v Bournemouth Gasworks Athletic 1-4
Clapton v Welton Rovers 0-1
Erith & Belvedere v Colchester Town 4-1
Excelsior Foundry v Rawmarsh Welfare 1-6
Gorleston v Dulwich Hamlet 1-2
HMS Excellent v Portland United 0-5
Hitchin Town v Nunhead 4-2
Ilford v Trowbridge Town 5-0
Ipswich Town v Epsom Town 2-4
Keynsham v Hampstead Town 2-7
Kingstonian v Wealdstone 6-1
Leyton v Southwick 3-0
London Caledonians v Wimbledon 1-3
Maidenhead United v Woking 4-0
Manningham Mills v Northern Nomads 2-1
Marine v Northampton Nomads 4-2
Moor Green v Evenwood Town 1-3
Players Athletic v South Salford Amateurs 4-1
RAF Grantham v Stanhope 2-2
South Bank v Sneinton 6-0
Southall v Romford (2) 1-3
St Albans City v Slough 2-1
Stockton v Norton Woodseats 4-3
Walthamstow Avenue v Casuals 4-2
Whitby United v Whitby Albion Rangers 3-1
Willington v Whitehall Printeries 0-1
Worthing v RAMC Aldershot 2-1
Yorkshire Amateur v Percy Main Amateurs 4-1
r Stanhope v RAF Grantham 4-3

Round Two

Bournemouth Gasworks Athletic v Hayes 2-1
Dulwich Hamlet v Cambridge Town 7-1
Erith & Belvedere v Maidenhead United 2-4
Hampstead Town v Portland United 0-0
Hitchin Town v Walthamstow Avenue 2-1
Manningham Mills v Stockton 1-2
Players Athletic v Bishop Auckland 0-1
Romford (2) v Kingstonian 1-5
South Bank v Marine 1-2
St Albans City v Wimbledon 1-4
Stanhope v Rawmarsh Welfare 3-2
Welton Rovers v Leyton 1-1
Whitehall Printeries v Evenwood Town 3-1
Worthing v Ilford 2-10
Wycombe Wanderers v Epsom Town 7-2
Yorkshire Amateur v Whitby United 3-1
r Leyton v Welton Rovers 2-1
r Portland United v Hampstead Town 1-0

Round Three

Bishop Auckland v Whitehall Printeries 3-1
Hitchin Town v Wimbledon 0-2
Ilford v Stanhope 5-1
Leyton v Bournemouth Gasworks Athletic 3-0
Marine v Maidenhead United 4-1
Portland United v Kingstonian 0-3
Stockton v Dulwich Hamlet 1-1
Yorkshire Amateur v Wycombe Wanderers 4-0
r Dulwich Hamlet v Stockton 3-0

Round Four

Dulwich Hamlet v Ilford 2-1
Kingstonian v Bishop Auckland 1-0
Marine v Leyton 3-0
Wimbledon v Yorkshire Amateur 2-2
r Yorkshire Amateur v Wimbledon 5-2

Semi Finals

Dulwich Hamlet v Kingstonian 1-0 N
Marine v Yorkshire Amateur 2-1 N

Final

Dulwich Hamlet v Marine 7-1 N

1932/33

Preliminary Round

13 Brentwood & Warley v Dagenham Town 1-3
Brightlingsea United v Crittall Athletic 3-6
Chelmsford v Leytonstone 2-1
Heybridge v 4th Divisional Signals Regiment 3-5e
South West Ham (2) v Tate Institute 3-2
18 Henley Town v Cowley 1-2
21 Brighton Mental Hospital v Eastbourne Comrades 6-3
Eastbourne v Wick 3-1
Hastings & St Leonards v Newhaven 8-1
Shoreham v Southwick 0-1
22 Bournemouth v Shaftesbury 3-2
Dorchester Town v Totton 2-6
24 Calne & Harris United v Purton 3-0
Chippenham Rovers v Swindon Victoria 8-5
Chippenham Town v Radstock Town 5-1
Devizes Town v Glastonbury 2-3
Paulton Rovers v Coleford Athletic 1-3
Salisbury Corinthians v Frome Town 2-3

Qualifying Round One

8 Morris Motors (Coventry) v Humber Hillman Rec. 1-2
10 Ely City v Warboys Town 5-2
Eynesbury Rovers v Chatteris Town 4-7e
March GE United v Chatteris Engineers 0-3
Pye Radio v Wisbech Town 0-4
Soham Rangers v March Town 4-2
St Neots & District v St Ives Town 5-1
11 Boulton & Paul v Diss Town 1-0
Cromer v Frosts Athletic 4-0
Great Yarmouth Town v North Walsham Town 2-1
Thetford Town v Norwich YMCA 3-4
12 Brantham Athletic v Leiston Works Athletic 5-3e
Bury Town v Woodbridge Town 5-1
Felixstowe Town v Kirkley 1-2e
Long Melford v Ipswich Town 2-7
Lowestoft Town v RAF Martlesham Heath 2-4
Orwell Works v Newmarket Town 3-1
RAF Felixstowe v Stowmarket 1-3
Sudbury Town v Walton United 5-1
13 Chelmsford v Dagenham Town 4-0
Clacton Town v 2nd Black Watch 9-1
Colchester Town v Harwich & Parkeston 1-6
Crittall Athletic v Parkeston Railway 9-1
Grays Athletic v Jurgens 1-8
Severalls Athletic v 4th Divisional Signals Regiment 1-3
South West Ham (2) v RA Shoeburyness 6-1
Tilbury v Custom House 5-2
14 Bexley v RM Deal 2-1
Bostall Heath v RM Chatham 5-1
Bromley v Woolwich Polytechnic 5-1
Cray Wanderers v Catford Wanderers 1-1e
Dover United v Beckenham 2-3
Maidstone United v Swanley Athletic 5-3
RN Depot v Callender Athletic 1-2
Woolwich Boro Council Ath. v Standard Telephones 6-3
15 Aquarius v PO Engineers 3-6e
Carshalton Athletic v Epsom Town 3-5
Leyland Motors v Sutton United 1-7
Merton v Dorking 4-3e
Redhill v Wills Sports 3-4e
Tooting & Mitcham United v Metropolitan Police 1-4
West Norwood v Beddington Corner 7-3
16 Civil Service v Wealdstone 0-1
Ealing Association v Southall 3-5
Hounslow Town v Old Lyonians 5-3
Old Latymerians v Polytechnic 7-3
Park Royal v Hendon Town 0-0e
Shepherds Bush (2) v Uxbridge Town 1-7
17 Aylesbury United v Bushey United 5-2
Luton Amateur v Vauxhall Motors wo/s
RAF Henlow v Watford BL 5-4
18 Banbury Harriers v Cowley 5-1
Gradwells Sports v Thame United 4-0
Littlemore v Headington United 2-4
Marlow v Stones Athletic 3-0
Morris Motors v Bicester Town 5-2
Newbury Town v Windsor & Eton 2-3
Slough v Osberton Radiator 9-0
Witney Town v Abingdon Town 6-0
19 Bishops Stortford v Hertford Town 3-4
Enfield v Finchley 7-3
Hoddesdon Town v Tufnell Park 2-3
Knebworth v Baldock Town 2-8
Old Johnians v Wood Green Town 0-1
Shredded Wheat v Stevenage Town 4-3
Welwyn Garden City v Ware 2-1
20 2nd Beds & Herts Regiment v RASC Aldershot 4-8
Basingstoke v Woking 2-4e
Courage & Co's Sports v Camberley & Yorktown 3-2
Godalming v 2nd Loyal Regt 1-3
RAMC Aldershot v Egham 4-2
Wellington Works v Walton-on-Thames 3-2
21 Bexhill v Horsham 2-2e
Bognor Regis v Littlehampton 3-4
Brighton Mental Hospital v East Grinstead 4-2
Hastings & St Leonards v Haywards Heath 6-1
Hollington United v Worthing 3-6e
Hove v Rock-a-Nore 2-2
Southwick v Eastbourne 2-1
Vernon Athletic v Broadwater 2-1
22 Blandford v Lymington 3-0
Bournemouth v HMS Excellent 2-4e
Bournemouth Transport v Osborne Athletic 5-2
Poole Town v Fareham Brotherhood 3-0
RAOC Hilsea v Ryde Sports 3-5
RM Portsmouth v Portsmouth Gas Co 2-6
South Hants Nomads v Gosport 0-1
Totton v Fareham 4-0
23 Cadbury Heath YMCA v Keynsham 2-6
Chalford v Warmley 2-1
Hanham Athletic v Mount Hill Enterprise 4-4e
Kingswood v Clevedon 4-2
St Philips Athletic v Listers 8-1
St Philips Marsh Adult School v Sneyd Park 4-2
Stonehouse v Weston-super-Mare 1-1e
Wesley Rangers v Gloucester City 3-0
24 Chippenham Rovers v Clandown 2-4
Frome Town v Chippenham Town 1-0
Melksham Town v Spencer Moulton 5-4
Minehead v Garrard Athletic 5-4e
Swindon Corinthians v Calne & Harris United 3-2
Trowbridge Town v Glastonbury 5-3
Wells City v Malmesbury Town 11-0
Westbury United v Coleford Athletic 3-0
14r Catford Wanderers v Cray Wanderers 3-1
16r Hendon Town v Park Royal 1-2
21r Horsham v Bexhill 7-1
r Rock-a-Nore v Hove 0-6
23r Mount Hill Enterprise v Hanham Athletic 4-2
r Weston-super-Mare v Stonehouse 6-1

Qualifying Round Two

1 Filey Town v Whitby Albion Rangers 2-2
Portrack Shamrocks v Cargo Fleet & Cochranes 2-1
South Bank East End v Pease & Partners n/a
2 1st Durham Light Infantry v Crookhall CW 4-1
Esh Winning v Chilton Colliery Recreation 5-0
Ferryhill Athletic v Trimdon Grange Colliery 2-0
Leasingthorne CW v Stanley United 0-4
3 Barnard Castle Athletic v Shildon Railway Athletic 0-1
Cockfield v Percy Main Amateurs 2-1e
Newcastle West End Amateurs v Shildon 0-4
West Auckland Town v Tow Law Town 3-2
4 Guiseley v Luddendenfoot 7-2
Hipperholme v Meltham Mills 1-2
Horsforth v Heptonstall Red Star 3-1
5 Formby v Preston GS OB 6-1
Harrowby v South Salford Amateurs 0-1
Orrell v Earle 2-4
Port Sunlight v Old Xaverians 1-2
6 Handsworth United Sports v Humber United 5-4
Sheffield Municipal Officers v Sheffield 5-2
7 Boots Athletic v Excelsior Foundry 5-5e
Nottingham Magdala Amateurs v Breaston n/a
Sneinton Church Institute v Leicestershire Nomads 1-3
Stapleford Brookhill v RAF Grantham 4-1
8 Badsey Rangers v Wolverhampton Amateurs 6-1
Birmingham Gas Officials v Red Hill Amateurs 1-1e
Malvern Holy Trinity v Headingley 4-3
Moor Green v Humber Hillman Recreation 6-1
9 Bletchley Town v Kempston Rovers 2-1
Daventry Town v Leighton United 3-1
Northampton Nomads v Mount Pleasant 3-1
Wolverton Town v Irchester United Sports 3-2
10 Chatteris Town v Soham Rangers 6-3
Histon Institute v Chatteris Engineers 1-4
St Neots & District v Ely City 6-2
Wisbech Town v Abbey United 11-4
11 Great Yarmouth Town v Boulton & Paul 0-0e
Norwich CEYMS v Norwich YMCA 3-2e
Norwich St Barnabas v Norwich Civil Service 7-2
Sheringham v Cromer 2-3e
12 Brantham Athletic v Ipswich Town 2-7
Bury Town v RAF Martlesham Heath 4-2
Orwell Works v Stowmarket 3-4
Sudbury Town v Kirkley 2-6
13 Chelmsford v Tilbury 9-0
Crittall Athletic v Clacton Town 5-2
Harwich & Parkeston v Jurgens 2-3
South West Ham (2) v 4th Divisional Signals Rgmt 1-3
14 Bostall Heath v Bexley 7-1
Bromley v Catford Wanderers 1-3
Callender Athletic v Maidstone United 4-3
Woolwich Borough Council Ath. v Beckenham 1-9
15 Epsom Town v Sutton United 4-1
Metropolitan Police v Reigate Priory 4-2
West Norwood v PO Engineers 2-5
Wills Sports v Merton 1-0

1932/33 to 1933/34

16	Hounslow Town v Park Royal	2-4
	Southall v Lyons	7-1
	Uxbridge Town v Old Latymerians	7-3
	Wealdstone v Staines Town	4-2
17	Apsley v Chesham United	4-3
	Aylesbury United v RAF Henlow	1-3
	Leavesden Mental Hospital v Luton Amateur	14-0
	Waterlows Dunstable v Berkhamsted Town	5-2
18	Gradwells Sports v Morris Motors	4-2
	Headington United v Marlow	1-7
	Windsor & Eton v Slough	1-2
	Witney Town v Banbury Harriers	3-3e
19	Enfield v Welwyn Garden City	7-1
	Hertford Town v Letchworth Town	3-5e
	Shredded Wheat v Wood Green Town	2-1
	Tufnell Park v Baldock Town	15-2
20	2nd Loyal Regt v Hersham	5-1
	Courage & Co's Sports v RASC Aldershot	0-1
	Guildford v Wellington Works	3-3e
	RAMC Aldershot v Woking	0-1
21	Brighton Mental Hospital v Worthing	1-5
	Hastings & St Leonards v Horsham	1-4
	Littlehampton v Hove	3-4
	Southwick v Vernon Athletic	5-2
22	Gosport v Bournemouth Transport	2-3
	Portsmouth Gas Co v Poole Town	0-9
	Ryde Sports v HMS Excellent	2-3
	Totton v Blandford	3-1
23	Chalford v Weston-super-Mare	3-4
	Mount Hill Enterprise v Keynsham	3-2
	St Philips Athletic v Kingswood	4-0
	St Philips Marsh Adult School v Wesley Rangers	5-1
24	Clandown v Westbury United	3-4
	Frome Town v Wells City	1-2
	Swindon Corinthians v Melksham Town	8-5
	Trowbridge Town v Minehead	3-2
1r	Whitby Albion Rangers v Filey Town	2-3
7r	Excelsior Foundry v Boots Athletic	6-2
8r	Red Hill Amateurs v Birmingham Gas Officials	0-12
11r	Boulton & Paul v Great Yarmouth Town	3-2
18r	Banbury Harriers v Witney Town	3-2
20r	Wellington Works v Guildford	4-1

Qualifying Round Three

1	Filey Town v Normanby Magnesite	1-2
	Portrack Shamrocks v South Bank East End	2-1e
2	Esh Winning v Ferryhill Athletic	1-4
	Stanley United v 1st Durham Light Infantry	3-2e
3	Cockfield v Shildon Railway Athletic	1-0
	Shildon v West Auckland Town	3-1
4	Guiseley v Farsley Celtic	6-2
	Horsforth v Meltham Mills	1-3
5	Earle v Old Xaverians	2-1
	South Salford Amateurs v Formby	4-1
6	Handsworth United Sports v Norton Woodseats	5-3
	Nether Edge Ams v Sheffield Municipal Officers	3-1
7	Leicestershire Nomads v Excelsior Foundry	2-4e
	Stapleford Brookhill v Nottingham Magdala Ams	3-1
8	Birmingham Gas Officials v Badsey Rangers	1-6
	Moor Green v Malvern Holy Trinity	3-1
9	Bletchley Town v Wolverton Town	2-10
	Daventry Town v Northampton Nomads	0-1
10	Chatteris Town v St Neots & District	2-3e
	Wisbech Town v Chatteris Engineers	5-4
11	Norwich CEYMS v Cromer	2-0
	Norwich St Barnabas v Boulton & Paul	1-2
12	Kirkley v Ipswich Town	0-3
	Stowmarket v Bury Town	4-2
13	4th Divisional Signals Regiment v Chelmsford	1-1e
	Jurgens v Crittall Athletic	2-0e
14	Bostall Heath v Callender Athletic	4-0
	Catford Wanderers v Beckenham	4-3e
15	Epsom Town v Wills Sports	3-1e
	PO Engineers v Metropolitan Police	0-2
16	Park Royal v Uxbridge Town	2-2e
	Southall v Wealdstone	5-0
17	RAF Henlow v Apsley	0-1
	Waterlows Dunstable v Leavesden Mental Hospital	0-3
18	Banbury Harriers v Slough	0-5
	Marlow v Gradwells Sports	4-1
19	Shredded Wheat v Enfield	2-6
	Tufnell Park v Letchworth Town	2-0
20	Wellington Works v RASC Aldershot	0-4
	Woking v 2nd Loyal Regt	5-1e
21	Horsham v Hove	4-0
	Worthing v Southwick	1-3e
22	Poole Town v HMS Excellent	0-3
	Totton v Bournemouth Transport	0-1
23	St Philips Athletic v Mount Hill Enterprise	1-3
	Weston-super-Mare v St Philips Marsh Adult School	4-3
24	Trowbridge Town v Wells City	2-1
	Westbury United v Swindon Corinthians	1-3
13r	Chelmsford v 4th Divisional Signals Regiment	4-4e
16r	Uxbridge Town v Park Royal	3-2
13r2	Chelmsford v 4th Divisional Signals Regiment	2-1

Qualifying Round Four

1	Normanby Magnesite v Portrack Shamrocks	2-2
2	Stanley United v Ferryhill Athletic	4-5
3	Cockfield v Shildon	0-0
4	Meltham Mills v Guiseley	4-5
5	South Salford Amateurs v Earle	1-1
6	Nether Edge Amateurs v Handsworth United Sports	4-1
7	Excelsior Foundry v Stapleford Brookhill	5-1
8	Badsey Rangers v Moor Green	3-0
9	Northampton Nomads v Wolverton Town	2-1
10	Wisbech Town v St Neots & District	5-2
11	Boulton & Paul v Norwich CEYMS	1-2
12	Stowmarket v Ipswich Town	5-2
13	Chelmsford v Jurgens	4-2
14	Catford Wanderers v Bostall Heath	4-1 v
15	Metropolitan Police v Epsom Town	5-2
16	Uxbridge Town v Southall	2-0
17	Apsley v Leavesden Mental Hospital	1-2
18	Slough v Marlow	8-2
19	Tufnell Park v Enfield	3-1
20	RASC Aldershot v Woking	2-2
21	Southwick v Horsham	1-1
22	Bournemouth Transport v HMS Excellent	1-3
23	Weston-super-Mare v Mount Hill Enterprise	1-0
24	Trowbridge Town v Swindon Corinthians	2-0
1r	Portrack Shamrocks v Normanby Magnesite	3-3e
3r	Shildon v Cockfield	2-1
5r	Earle v South Salford Amateurs	2-3
14r	Bostall Heath v Catford Wanderers	1-0
20r	Woking v RASC Aldershot	5-0
21r	Horsham v Southwick	2-2
1r2	Portrack Shamrocks v Normanby Magnesite	2-1
21r2	Horsham v Southwick	2-1

Round One

	Badsey Rangers v Players Athletic	1-1
	Barnet v Hampstead Town	4-0
	Bishop Auckland v Stockton	2-3
	Chelmsford v Bostall Heath	1-0
	Clapton v Cambridge Town	1-1
	Erith & Belvedere v Trowbridge Town	2-0
	Evenwood Town v Shildon	0-3
	Hayes v Norwich CEYMS	5-1
	Hitchin Town v Slough	2-2
	Horsham v HMS Excellent	5-1
	Maidenhead United v Ilford	2-4
	Manningham Mills v Guiseley	1-4
	Marine v Northern Nomads	7-0
	Metropolitan Police v Casuals	2-3
	Nether Edge Amateurs v Excelsior Foundry	3-1
	Oxford City v Barking	1-1
	Portland United v Kingstonian	2-2
	Portrack Shamrocks v Ferryhill Athletic	0-3
	Rawmarsh Welfare v Yorkshire Amateur	1-1
	Romford (2) v Leyton	1-1
	South Bank v Willington	3-2
	South Salford Amateurs v Whitehall Printeries	2-5
	St Albans City v Leavesden Mental Hospital	0-1
	Stowmarket v Bournemouth Gasworks Athletic	2-4
	Uxbridge Town v Dulwich Hamlet	1-2
	Walthamstow Avenue v Tufnell Park	1-1
	Welton Rovers v Nunhead	1-1
	Weston-super-Mare v Gorleston	3-2
	Whitby United v Stanhope	8-1
	Wisbech Town v Northampton Nomads	5-0
	Woking v London Caledonians	3-0
	Wycombe Wanderers v Wimbledon	1-2
r	Barking v Oxford City	0-2
r	Cambridge Town v Clapton	1-5
r	Kingstonian v Portland United	5-0
r	Leyton v Romford (2)	2-3a
r	Nunhead v Welton Rovers	7-1
r	Players Athletic v Badsey Rangers	1-2
r	Slough v Hitchin Town	5-1
r	Tufnell Park v Walthamstow Avenue	0-1
r	Yorkshire Amateur v Rawmarsh Welfare	1-0
r2	Leyton v Romford (2)	3-2

Round Two

	Badsey Rangers v Wisbech Town	3-1
	Barnet v Walthamstow Avenue	2-2a
	Casuals v Nunhead	0-1
	Dulwich Hamlet v Chelmsford	5-1
	Erith & Belvedere v Ilford	1-1a
	Ferryhill Athletic v Yorkshire Amateur	3-0
	Guiseley v Nether Edge Amateurs	2-1
	Leavesden Mental Hospital v Horsham	6-2
	Leyton v Kingstonian	1-3
	Oxford City v Clapton	1-2
	Slough v Woking	6-1
	South Bank v Marine	1-0
	Stockton v Shildon	2-0
	Weston-super-Mare v Bournemouth Gasworks Ath.	1-1
	Whitby United v Whitehall Printeries	2-2
	Wimbledon v Hayes	3-3
r	Barnet v Walthamstow Avenue	3-2
r	Bournemouth Gasworks Ath. v Weston-super-Mare	1-0
r	Erith & Belvedere v Ilford	3-2
r	Hayes v Wimbledon	3-2
r	Whitehall Printeries v Whitby United	1-1
r2	Whitehall Printeries v Whitby United	1-0 N

Round Three

	Erith & Belvedere v Leavesden Mental Hospital	2-1
	Ferryhill Athletic v Stockton	1-2
	Guiseley v Bournemouth Gasworks Athletic	1-2
	Hayes v Dulwich Hamlet	1-1
	Nunhead v Clapton	0-1
	Slough v Barnet	1-2
	South Bank v Kingstonian	1-2
	Whitehall Printeries v Badsey Rangers	3-0
r	Dulwich Hamlet v Hayes	4-0

Round Four

	Bournemouth Gasworks Ath. v Erith & Belvedere	2-0
	Kingstonian v Dulwich Hamlet	4-2
	Stockton v Barnet	2-1
	Whitehall Printeries v Clapton	8-3

Semi Finals

	Kingstonian v Whitehall Printeries	3-0 N
	Stockton v Bournemouth Gasworks Athletic	2-1 N

Final

	Kingstonian v Stockton	1-1 N
r	Kingstonian v Stockton	4-1 N

1933/34

Preliminary Round

13	2nd Kings Shropshire LI v South West Ham (2)	6-1
	Chelmsford v Port of London Authority	5-2
	Colchester Town v Brightlingsea United	7-0
	Jurgens v Severalls Athletic	11-0
14	UGBM Sports v Lloyds	4-0
	Whitstable v Deal Town	7-3
15	Streatham Town v Cranleigh	2-1
18	Sonning v Stokenchurch	wo/s
19	Hoxton Manor v Boxmoor St Johns	6-1
	Old Finchleians v Alexandra Park	3-2
21	Brighton Mental Hospital v Chichester	6-0
	Haywards Heath v Southwick	1-3
	Hollington United v Vernon Athletic	1-3
	Littlehampton v East Grinstead	6-4
	Wick v Rock-a-Nore	0-2
22	Bournemouth v Lymington	7-1
	Bournemouth Transport v Fareham	2-1
	Dorchester Town v Portsmouth Gas Co	3-4
	Osborne Athletic v Hamworthy	0-4
	Shaftesbury v HMS Excellent	1-7
24	Frome Town v Coleford Athletic	6-0
	Malmesbury Town v Melksham Town	4-3e
	Plymouth United v Tiverton Town	5-3e
	Purton v Swindon Victoria	3-2
	Salisbury Corinthians v Devizes Town	2-3
	Swindon Corinthians v Calne & Harris United	6-5
	Trowbridge Town v Warminster Town	5-2
	Wells City v Radstock Town	1-0
	Welton Rovers v Clandown	1-0

Qualifying Round One

1	Pease & Partners v South Bank East End	n/a
	Whitby Albion Rangers v Portrack Shamrocks	0-3
5	Liverpool West Derby Union v British Insulators SC	1-0
	Manchester Transport v Hipperholme	n/a
	Port Sunlight v Orrell	5-4
7	Boots Athletic v Ibstock Swifts	4-0
	Ibstock Penistone Rovers v Leicestershire Nomads	3-1
	Johnson & Barnes Athletic v Ransome & Marles	3-0
	Nottingham Magdala Amateurs v RAF Cranwell	1-4
10	Cambridge Town v Abbey United	9-1
	Chatteris Engineers v Wisbech Town	1-1
	March GE United v March Town	1-3
	Pye Radio v Histon Institute	4-5
	St Neots & District v Chatteris Town	2-2e
	Warboys Town v Soham Rangers	5-2
11	Cromer v Frosts Athletic	4-3
	Great Yarmouth Town v Norwich CEYMS	6-0
	King's Lynn v Wymondham	3-1
	Sheringham v Boulton & Paul	2-1
12	Brantham Athletic v RAF Martlesham Heath	4-7
	Felixstowe Town v Walton United	1-3
	Leiston Works Athletic v RAF Felixstowe	4-3
	Long Melford v Newmarket Town	3-5e
	Orwell Works v Kirkley	2-0
	Stowmarket v Lowestoft Town	1-4
	Sudbury Town v Bury Town	1-2
13	4th Divisional Signals Rgmt v Brentwood & Warley	1-3
	Barking v Custom House	3-2
	Chelmsford v Dagenham Town	5-0
	Clacton Town v Colchester Town	1-2
	Grays Athletic v Romford (2)	3-4
	Harwich & Parkeston v Crittall Athletic	1-2
	Heybridge v 2nd Kings Shropshire LI	1-3
	Jurgens v Tilbury	2-4

1933/34

14 Beckenham v Bexley 1-3
Bostall Heath v Woolwich Borough Council Ath. 5-2
Catford Wanderers v Swanley Athletic 3-0
RM Deal v Bromley 1-5
RN Depot v Standard Telephones 7-1
UGBM Sports v Maidstone United 1-3
Whitstable v Cray Wanderers 2-3
Woolwich Polytechnic v Callender Athletic 0-2
15 Beddington Corner v Aquarius 1-0
Dorking v PO Engineers 0-4
Epsom Town v Redhill 4-1
Merton v Leyland Motors 2-4
Reigate Priory v Streatham Town 2-1
Sutton United v Nunhead 2-0
Tooting & Mitcham United v Carshalton Athletic 0-3
West Norwood v Wills Sports 3-2
16 Golders Green v Civil Service 7-3
Hayes v Hounslow Town 2-1
Old Lyonians v Old Latymerians 3-1
Park Royal v Polytechnic 6-0
Shepherds Bush (2) v Uxbridge Town 1-3
Southall v Staines Town 5-0
Tufnell Park v Lyons 7-0
Wealdstone v Ealing Association 4-0
18 Abingdon Town v Marlow 4-7
Banbury Harriers v Morris Motors 1-3
Bicester Town v Sonning 6-2
Cowley v Windsor & Eton 2-1
Headington United v Witney Town 2-0
Newbury Town v Gradwells Sports 2-2e
Osberton Radiator v Littlemore 2-0
Thame United v Henley Town 0-4
19 Bishops Stortford v London Labour 6-0
Enfield v Old Finchleians 6-1
Hertford Town v Letchworth Town 4-2
Hoxton Manor v Ware 2-0
Shredded Wheat v Old Johnians 2-1
Stevenage Town v Hoddesdon Town 2-1
Welwyn Garden City v Knebworth 3-4
Wood Green Town v Baldock Town 4-0
20 Godalming v Courage & Co's Sports 1-3
Hersham v Guildford 2-3
Walton-on-Thames v Camberley & Yorktown 5-2
Woking v Wellington Works 4-2
21 Bexhill v Rock-a-Nore 7-2
Bognor Regis v Southwick 1-1e
Eastbourne v Worthing 3-0
Eastbourne Comrades v Shoreham 3-1
Horsham v Hastings & St Leonards 2-1e
Littlehampton v Brighton Mental Hospital 2-4
Newhaven v Hove 2-1e
Vernon Athletic v Broadwater 4-0
22 Bournemouth v Bournemouth Transport 3-1
HMS Excellent v RAOC Hilsea 0-2
HMS Victory v Blandford 6-0
Hamworthy v Gosport 1-2
Poole Town v RM Portsmouth 3-0
Portsmouth Gas Co v Swanage 6-2
Ryde Sports v Ringwood Town 3-4
Totton v Fareham Brotherhood 2-0
23 Chalford v Rose Green 4-3
Clevedon v Listers 4-1
Gloucester City v Stonehouse 8-0
Hanham Athletic v Wesley Rangers 8-1
Keynsham v Mount Hill Enterprise 5-1
Kingswood v St Philips Marsh Adult School 1-5
St Pancras (Knowle) v St Philips Athletic 5-1
24 Chippenham Rovers v Chippenham Town 3-1
Devizes Town v Frome Town 1-3
Malmesbury Town v Plymouth United 1-0
Minehead v Paulton Rovers 2-3
Swindon Corinthians v Wells City 5-3
Trowbridge Town v 2nd Loyal Regt 2-0
Welton Rovers v Spencer Moulton 4-1
Westbury United v Purton 5-0
10r Chatteris Engineers v Wisbech Town 1-4
r Chatteris Town v St Neots & District 0-2
18r Gradwells Sports v Newbury Town 3-1
21r Southwick v Bognor Regis 3-0

Qualifying Round Two

1 Cargo Fleet & Cochranes v Grangetown St Marys 1-6
Normanby Magnesite v South Bank St Peters 1-3
Portrack Shamrocks v Filey Town 5-4
South Bank East End v Redcar Works 4-3
2 1st Durham Light Infantry v Chilton Colliery Rec. 5-3
Crookhall CW v Stanley United 4-1
Trimdon Colliery United v Esh Winning 2-0
Trimdon Grange Colliery v Leasingthorne CW 5-1
3 South Hetton CW v Tow Law Town 4-2e
4 Shildon Railway Athletic v Barnard Castle Athletic 1-3e
West Auckland Town v Stanhope 1-2
5 Earle v Old Xaverians 3-0
Liverpool West Derby Union v Preston GS OB 6-1
Port Sunlight v Harrowby 6-2
South Salford Amateurs v Manchester Transport 3-0
6 Mexborough SS OB v Sheffield 3-1
Norton Woodseats v Marfleet 4-1
Rawmarsh Welfare v Humber United 3-1
Terrys v Kingston upon Hull OG 6-3
7 Boots Athletic v Players Athletic 1-6
Ibstock Penistone Rovers v Johnson & Barnes Ath 3-1
RAF Cranwell v Stapleford Brookhill 13-0
RAF Grantham v Excelsior Foundry 1-2e

8 Moor Green v Wolverhampton Amateurs 3-1
9 Daventry Town v Leighton United 1-5
Irchester United Sports v Kempston Rovers 2-1
Mount Pleasant v Northampton Nomads 5-2
Wolverton Town v Bletchley Town 3-0
10 Cambridge Town v Ely City 5-0
Histon Institute v Warboys Town 3-4
St Neots & District v St Ives Town 2-2a
Wisbech Town v March Town 7-0
11 Cromer v Norwich YMCA 6-0
Diss Town v Sheringham 2-3e
Great Yarmouth Town v North Walsham Town 6-0
Thetford Town v King's Lynn 2-1
12 Bury Town v Orwell Works 0-0e
Ipswich Town v Walton United 6-2
Lowestoft Town v Leiston Works Athletic 3-0
RAF Martlesham Heath v Newmarket Town 2-1
13 Brentwood & Warley v Romford (2) 2-3e
Chelmsford v 2nd Kings Shropshire LI 1-3
Colchester Town v Crittall Athletic 0-1
Tilbury v Barking 1-1e
14 Bromley v Catford Wanderers 1-2
Cray Wanderers v Bostall Heath 2-4
Maidstone United v Bexley 4-1
RN Depot v Callender Athletic 2-1
15 Beddington Corner v PO Engineers 0-4
Epsom Town v Carshalton Athletic 2-1
Reigate Priory v Leyland Motors 1-4
Sutton United v West Norwood 4-3
16 Hayes v Old Lyonians 3-1
Southall v Park Royal 1-0
Tufnell Park v Wealdstone 3-2
Uxbridge Town v Golders Green 2-3
17 Apsley v Waterlows Dunstable 4-2
Aylesbury United v Bushey United 6-1
RAF Henlow v Berkhamsted Town 7-0
18 Cowley v Bicester Town 1-2
Headington United v Marlow 0-3
Morris Motors v Henley Town 3-1
Osberton Radiator v Gradwells Sports 1-0
19 Bishops Stortford v Knebworth 6-0
Hertford Town v Stevenage Town 2-0e
Hoxton Manor v Enfield 1-2
Shredded Wheat v Wood Green Town 2-1
20 Egham v RAMC Aldershot 3-2
RASC Aldershot v Courage & Co's Sports 5-2
Walton-on-Thames v Basingstoke 0-2
Woking v Guildford 3-0
21 Bexhill v Newhaven 0-2
Eastbourne v Vernon Athletic 2-1e
Eastbourne Comrades v Brighton Mental Hospital 4-3
Southwick v Horsham 0-2
22 Bournemouth v Totton 3-4e
HMS Victory v RAOC Hilsea 1-2
Portsmouth Gas Co v Gosport 3-3e
Ringwood Town v Poole Town 1-7
23 Clevedon v St Pancras (Knowle) 1-2
Gloucester City v Chalford 4-2
Hanham Athletic v St Philips Marsh Adult School 2-0
Keynsham v Warmley Amateurs 5-2
24 Malmesbury Town v Frome Town 0-2
Swindon Corinthians v Trowbridge Town 4-1
Welton Rovers v Chippenham Rovers 5-1
Westbury United v Paulton Rovers 3-3e
10r St Ives Town v St Neots & District 0-2
12r Orwell Works v Bury Town 3-3e
13r Barking v Tilbury 4-3
22r Gosport v Portsmouth Gas Co 4-2e
24r Paulton Rovers v Westbury United 4-3e
12r2 Bury Town v Orwell Works 2-1 N

Qualifying Round Three

1 Portrack Shamrocks v South Bank St Peters 4-1
South Bank East End v Grangetown St Marys 0-1
2 1st Durham Light Infantry v Crookhall CW 4-0
Trimdon Grange Colliery v Trimdon Colliery United 2-1
3 Newcastle West End Amateurs v South Hetton CW 2-3
Witton Park Institute v Blackhill 1-1
4 Cockfield v Barnard Castle Athletic 2-1e
Shildon v Stanhope 2-2
5 Earle v Liverpool West Derby Union 1-3
Port Sunlight v South Salford Amateurs 2-1
6 Mexborough SS OB v Terrys 5-1
Rawmarsh Welfare v Norton Woodseats 5-0
7 Ibstock Penistone Rovers v Players Athletic 7-4e
RAF Cranwell v Excelsior Foundry 4-1
8 Malvern Holy Trinity v Headingley 6-1
Red Hill & Yardley Amateurs v Moor Green 1-4
9 Irchester United Sports v Leighton United 2-1
Wolverton Town v Mount Pleasant 1-2
10 St Neots & District v Wisbech Town 5-3
Warboys Town v Cambridge Town 2-2e
11 Cromer v Great Yarmouth Town 0-2
Sheringham v Thetford Town 1-0a
12 Ipswich Town v RAF Martlesham Heath 3-0
Lowestoft Town v Bury Town 4-1
13 Barking v Crittall Athletic 2-0
Romford (2) v 2nd Kings Shropshire LI 6-4
14 Catford Wanderers v Bostall Heath 0-3
RN Depot v Maidstone United 4-2
15 Epsom Town v Sutton United 1-2
Leyland Motors v PO Engineers 2-4

16 Hayes v Golders Green 1-3
Tufnell Park v Southall 4-2
17 Apsley v RAF Henlow 7-2
Aylesbury United v Watford BL 5-4
18 Morris Motors v Bicester Town 1-1e
Osberton Radiator v Marlow 2-1
19 Enfield v Bishops Stortford 5-1
Shredded Wheat v Hertford Town 0-2
20 Basingstoke v Egham 1-2
RASC Aldershot v Woking 0-3
21 Eastbourne Comrades v Horsham 2-3e
Newhaven v Eastbourne 2-0
22 Gosport v RAOC Hilsea 4-2e
Totton v Poole Town 3-5
23 Gloucester City v St Pancras (Knowle) 5-4
Keynsham v Hanham Athletic 1-1
24 Paulton Rovers v Swindon Corinthians 7-2
Welton Rovers v Frome Town 1-3
3r Blackhill v Witton Park Institute 1-0
4r Stanhope v Shildon 3-2
10r Cambridge Town v Warboys Town 7-0
11r Sheringham v Thetford Town 6-2
18r Bicester Town v Morris Motors 2-3
23r Hanham Athletic v Keynsham 1-2

Qualifying Round Four

1 Portrack Shamrocks v Grangetown St Marys 2-1
2 1st Durham Light Infantry v Trimdon Grange Colliery 4-2
3 South Hetton CW v Blackhill 1-0
4 Cockfield v Stanhope 2-0
5 Liverpool West Derby Union v Port Sunlight 5-2
6 Rawmarsh Welfare v Mexborough SS OB 5-1
7 Ibstock Penistone Rovers v RAF Cranwell 2-3
8 Moor Green v Malvern Holy Trinity 2-1
9 Mount Pleasant v Irchester United Sports 6-1
10 Cambridge Town v St Neots & District 0-2
11 Great Yarmouth Town v Sheringham 2-0
12 Ipswich Town v Lowestoft Town 3-1
13 Romford (2) v Barking 0-3
14 Bostall Heath v RN Depot 3-3
15 PO Engineers v Sutton United 0-2
16 Tufnell Park v Golders Green 2-1
17 Apsley v Aylesbury United 2-0
18 Morris Motors v Osberton Radiator 3-1
19 Enfield v Hertford Town 4-1
20 Egham v Woking 1-2
21 Newhaven v Horsham 0-2
22 Poole Town v Gosport 2-0
23 Keynsham v Gloucester City 3-1
24 Paulton Rovers v Frome Town 1-3
14r RN Depot v Bostall Heath 1-2

Round One

1st Durham Light Infantry v Whitby United 5-1
Badsey Rangers v RAF Cranwell 1-0
Barking v Tufnell Park 1-1
Barnet v Ipswich Town 4-1
Bishop Auckland v Willington 3-0
Bostall Heath v Leyton 1-2
Casuals v Ilford 1-1
Clapton v Leavesden Hospital 1-2
Dulwich Hamlet v Finchley 2-1
Hitchin Town v Chesham United 0-0
Horsham v Great Yarmouth Town 2-0
Keynsham v Frome Town 1-0
London Caledonians v Leytonstone 2-0
Marine v Cockfield 2-1
Metropolitan Police v Gorleston 2-1
Moor Green v Yorkshire Amateur 1-1
Morris Motors v Maidenhead United 1-2
Nether Edge Amateurs v Rawmarsh Welfare 2-5
Northern Nomads v Evenwood Town 3-3
Oxford City v Apsley 1-2
Poole Town v Portland United 1-2
Portrack Shamrocks v Stockton 1-1
Slough v Walthamstow Avenue 0-4
South Bank v Guiseley 2-0
South Hetton CW v Liverpool West Derby Union 2-1
St Albans City v Enfield 0-3
St Neots & District v Mount Pleasant 1-1
Sutton United v Erith & Belvedere 3-2
Weston-super-Mare v Bournemouth Gasworks Ath 0-0
Whitehall Printeries v Ferryhill Athletic 0-1
Wimbledon v Woking 2-1
Wycombe Wanderers v Kingstonian 0-1
r Barking v Tufnell Park 1-2
r Bournemouth Gasworks Ath v Weston-super-Mare 4-0
r Chesham United v Hitchin Town 6-3
r Evenwood Town v Northern Nomads 4-4
r Ilford v Casuals 0-3
r Mount Pleasant v St Neots & District 5-3
r Stockton v Portrack Shamrocks 0-1
r Yorkshire Amateur v Moor Green 2-0
r2 Evenwood Town v Northern Nomads 2-2
r3 Evenwood Town v Northern Nomads 4-0

Round Two

Apsley v Sutton United 1-4
Badsey Rangers v Portrack Shamrocks 1-0
Barnet v Horsham 4-2

1933/34 to 1934/35

	Bishop Auckland v Yorkshire Amateur	0-1
	Casuals v Tufnell Park	2-1
	Chesham United v Maidenhead United	7-1
	Dulwich Hamlet v Walthamstow Avenue	3-2
	Enfield v Leyton	1-1
	Evenwood Town v 1st Durham Light Infantry	2-1
	Kingstonian v Wimbledon	1-1
	London Caledonians v Leavesden Hospital	2-0
	Metropolitan Police v Keynsham	4-3
	Portland United v Bournemouth Gasworks Athletic	0-5
	Rawmarsh Welfare v Mount Pleasant	5-1
	South Bank v Marine	3-0
	South Hetton CW v Ferryhill Athletic	2-2
r	Ferryhill Athletic v South Hetton CW	0-3
r	Leyton v Enfield	1-1
r	Wimbledon v Kingstonian	3-0
r2	Leyton v Enfield	3-0 N

Round Three

	Badsey Rangers v Chesham United	1-3
	Barnet v Wimbledon	3-1
	Bournemouth Gasworks Athletic v Casuals	1-5
	Evenwood Town v South Bank	3-3
	London Caledonians v Rawmarsh Welfare	2-0
	Metropolitan Police v Yorkshire Amateur	4-1
	South Hetton CW v Leyton	1-3
	Sutton United v Dulwich Hamlet	1-3
r	South Bank v Evenwood Town	2-1

Round Four

	Barnet v London Caledonians	2-0
	Casuals v Dulwich Hamlet	1-2
	Metropolitan Police v Chesham United	4-0
	South Bank v Leyton	0-1

Semi Finals

	Dulwich Hamlet v Metropolitan Police	2-0 N
	Leyton v Barnet	2-0 N

Final

	Dulwich Hamlet v Leyton	2-1 N

1934/35

Preliminary Round

13	Barking v Eton Manor	3-1
	Ford Motors v 2nd Middlesex Regt	2-1
14	Bostall Heath v Sheppey United	3-2
	Callender Athletic v Bromley	1-3
	Deal Town v Woolwich Polytechnic	2-1
	Gravesend United v Betteshanger CW	5-2
	London Paper Mills v Erith & Belvedere	1-3
	Swanley Athletic v Catford Wanderers	1-1e
	UGBM Sports v RM Chatham	2-2
15	Barclays Bank v Banstead Mental Hospital	1-0
16	Acton v Brigade of Guards	1-0
	Finchley v Yiewsley	4-0
	Hayes v Pinner	3-1
	Hounslow Town v Staines Town	3-2
	Hoxton Manor v Uxbridge Town	2-3
	Old Lyonians v Southall	3-7
	Park Royal v Old Latymerians	13-0
	Wealdstone v Old Owens	3-2
21	Brighton Mental Hospital v Bexhill	1-1e
22	Bournemouth v HMS Victory	1-3
	Fareham v RM Portsmouth	0-4
	Ringwood Town v South Hants Nomads	4-4e
	Ryde Sports v Swanage	5-0
	Southern Railway (2) v Shaftesbury	5-1
	Totton v Winchester City	2-3
24	2nd Loyal Regt v Malmesbury Town	3-1
	Calne & Harris United v Warminster Town	2-6
	Chippenham Town v Swindon Corinthians	2-3
	Minehead v Weston-super-Mare	0-2
	Paulton Rovers v Timsbury Athletic	6-2
	Purton v Melksham Town	1-1e
	Spencer Moulton v Trowbridge Town	2-4
	Wells City v Coleford Athletic	8-0
	Westbury United v Salisbury Corinthians	3-1
14r	RM Chatham v UGBM Sports	3-1
r	Swanley Athletic v Catford Wanderers	0-2e
21r	Bexhill v Brighton Mental Hospital	3-4
22r	South Hants Nomads v Ringwood Town	0-1
24r	Melksham Town v Purton	5-0

Qualifying Round One

1	Cargo Fleet Works v Guisborough Brigantes	0-1
	Filey Town v South Bank St Peters	0-1
	Grangetown St Marys v Portrack Shamrocks	2-0e
	Scarborough Juniors v Thornaby St Patricks	2-3
	Smiths Dock Senior v Pease & Partners	3-2
	South Bank East End v Redcar Works	7-1e
	Thornaby v Clulows United	4-3
	Whitby Albion Rangers v Whitby United	1-3
2	Leasingthorne Village v Trimdon Grange Colliery	6-0
	Stanley United v Chilton Colliery Recreation	3-0
5	Bradford Rovers v Heptonstall Red Star	13-0
	British Insulators SC v Liverpool West Derby Union	5-2
	Harrowby v Old Xaverians	5-1
	Orrell v Earle	1-0
	South Salford Amateurs v Manchester Transport	n/a
	Whitehaven Athletic v Preston GS OB	4-1
	Wyke OB v Farsley Celtic	1-5
7	Ibstock Penistone Rovers v Players Athletic	4-2
	Ibstock Swifts v RAF Grantham	6-1
8	Boldmere St Michaels v Ledbury Town	11-2
10	Abbey United v Ely City	2-1
	March GE United v Histon Institute	4-4e
	March Town v Soham Rangers	8-4
	Newmarket Town v Eynesbury Rovers	3-1
	Pye Radio v St Neots & District	5-8
	Ramsey Town v Wisbech Town	1-5
	St Ives Town v Chatteris Town	3-3
	Warboys Town v Chatteris Town	0-1
11	Norwich CEYMS v Sheringham	3-0
	Norwich YMCA v Diss Town	3-0
12	Leiston Works Athletic v Kirkley	1-5
	RAF Felixstowe v Brantham Athletic	4-5
	RAF Martlesham Heath v Orwell Works	4-2
	Stowmarket v Sudbury Town	3-2e
	Walton United v Felixstowe Town	2-1
13	Clacton Town v Severalls Athletic	1-4
	Colchester Town v Chelmsford	2-1
	Crittall Athletic v Ford Motors	2-0e
	Dagenham Town v Custom House	0-0e
	Harwich & Parkeston v Clapton	3-0
	Heybridge v Grays Athletic	1-4
	Jurgens v Barking	2-3
	Tilbury v Brightlingsea United	2-0
14	Bostall Heath v Maidstone United	4-2
	Bromley v Beckenham	5-1
	Cray Wanderers v RM Chatham	4-2
	Erith & Belvedere v Woolwich Borough Council Ath.	3-2
	Lloyds v Bexley	1-3
	RM Deal v Gravesend United	6-1
	RN Depot v Deal Town	3-0
	Standard Telephones v Catford Wanderers	2-2
15	Carshalton Athletic v Aquarius	0-3
	Cranleigh v Wills Sports	3-4
	Epsom Town v Merton	4-1
	PO Engineers v Leyland Motors	3-1
	Redhill v Streatham Town	3-1
	Reigate Priory v Dorking	2-2e
	Tooting & Mitcham United v Barclays Bank	6-1
	West Norwood v Beddington Corner	2-1
16	Acton v Finchley	3-9
	Civil Service v Old Johnians	4-0
	Hayes v Ealing Association	3-1
	Hounslow Town v Southall	1-0
	Lyons v Old Finchleians	2-0
	Uxbridge Town v London Labour	11-1
	Wealdstone v Park Royal	1-5
	Wood Green Town v Polytechnic	3-1
17	Berkhamsted Town v RAF Halton	3-2
	Hazells Aylesbury v Leighton United	5-0
	Vauxhall Motors v Waterlows Dunstable	1-3
18	Banbury Harriers v Bicester Town	2-5
	Banbury Spencer v Henley Town	3-1
	Chipping Norton CA v Abingdon Town	3-2
	Cowley v Marlow	3-1
	Headington United v Slough	2-8
	Newbury Town v Osberton Radiator	2-1
	Thame United v Sonning	6-3
	Windsor & Eton v Witney Town	2-2e
19	Baldock Town v TocH	4-2
	Bishops Stortford v Welwyn Garden City	3-2
	Hitchin Town v Stevenage Town	3-0
	Hoddesdon Town v St Albans City	2-5
	Letchworth Town v Shredded Wheat	2-1
	Ware v Hertford Town	0-2
20	Egham v Woking	2-3
	Hersham v RAMC Aldershot	5-0
	Walton-on-Thames v Courage & Co's Sports	0-1
21	Chichester v Newhaven	0-4
	Eastbourne v Worthing	0-5
	Eastbourne Comrades v Haywards Heath	2-6
	Hastings & St Leonards v Wick	15-0
	Hove v Brighton Mental Hospital	1-7
	Littlehampton v Bognor Regis	2-1
	Shoreham v Vernon Athletic	3-2
	Southwick v East Grinstead	7-2
22	Blandford United v HMS Excellent	2-6
	Bournemouth Transport v HMS Victory	2-4
	Dorchester Town v Ryde Sports	1-11
	Hamworthy v Southern Railway (2)	1-4
	Portsmouth Gas Co v Poole Town	4-2
	RM Portsmouth v RAOC Hilsea	1-3
	Ringwood Town v Osborne Athletic	7-3
	Winchester City v Gosport	3-1
23	Bristol St George v Kingswood	4-2
	Chalford v St Pancras (Knowle)	3-4
	Hanham Athletic v National Smelting Co	2-0
	Keynsham v St Philips Athletic	6-1
	Mount Hill Enterprise v Gloucester City	3-4
	Rose Green v Cadbury Heath YMCA	2-0
	St Philips Marsh Adult School v Stonehouse	4-0
24	2nd Loyal Regt v Chippenham Rovers	2-0
	Clandown v Trowbridge Town	1-4e
	Frome Town v Westbury United	3-1
	Melksham Town v Devizes Town	5-2
	Paulton Rovers v Weston-super-Mare	4-0
	Radstock Town v Swindon Corinthians	2-1
	Swindon Victoria v Wells City	1-3
	Warminster Town v Welton Rovers	0-3
10r	Chatteris Town v St Ives Town	6-3e
r	Histon Institute v March GE United	4-5
13r	Dagenham Town v Custom House	3-1
14r	Catford Wanderers v Standard Telephones	6-1
15r	Dorking v Reigate Priory	2-1
18r	Witney Town v Windsor & Eton	4-1

Qualifying Round Two

1	Grangetown St Marys v South Bank St Peters	1-0
	Smiths Dock Senior v South Bank East End	1-3
	Thornaby v Thornaby St Patricks	2-1
	Whitby United v Guisborough Brigantes	2-0
2	4th Royal Tank Corps v 1st Durham Light Infantry	6-1
	Leasingthorne CW v Esh Winning	n/a
	Leasingthorne Village v Crookhall CW	3-2
	Trimdon Colliery United v Stanley United	n/a
3	Witton Park Institute v Tow Law Town	2-0
4	Barnard Castle Athletic v Stanhope	4-1
	Shildon Railway Athletic v Evenwood Town	1-3
	West Auckland Town v Woodland Celtic	3-1e
5	Farsley Celtic v Bradford Rovers	2-1
	Formby v Orrell	6-1
	Harrowby v British Insulators SC	1-6
	Whitehaven Athletic v South Salford Amateurs	4-4e
6	Humber United v Kingston upon Hull OG	4-1
	Mexborough SS OB v Brunswick Avenue OB	3-1
	Nether Edge Amateurs v Terrys	6-1
	Sheffield v Norton Woodseats	5-0
7	Boots Athletic v Stapleford Brookhill	7-1
	Ibstock Swifts v RAF Cranwell	2-1
	Leicestershire Nomads v Ibstock Penistone Rovers	0-3
	Magdala Amateurs v Excelsior Foundry	2-6
8	Badsey Rangers v Hereford City	1-8
	Boldmere St Michaels v Wolverhampton Amateurs	3-2
	Headingley v Stafford Old Edwardians	2-3
	Malvern Holy Trinity v Jack Moulds Athletic	0-5
10	Chatteris Engineers v Chatteris Town	2-4
	March GE United v Newmarket Town	2-3
	March Town v Wisbech Town	0-0
	St Neots & District v Abbey United	2-1
11	Boulton & Paul v Cromer	4-1
	Great Yarmouth Town v Norwich CEYMS	2-1
	Norwich YMCA v Thetford Town	1-2
	Wymondham v King's Lynn	1-2
12	Bury Town v RAF Martlesham Heath	4-4a
	Kirkley v Walton United	4-0
	Lowestoft Town v Ipswich Town	2-0
	Stowmarket v Brantham Athletic	15-2
13	Barking v Tilbury	1-0
	Dagenham Town v Crittall Athletic	3-1
	Grays Athletic v Colchester Town	0-2
	Harwich & Parkeston v Severalls Athletic	7-0
14	Bromley v Catford Wanderers	2-0
	Cray Wanderers v Erith & Belvedere	2-0
	RM Deal v Bexley	3-2e
	RN Depot v Bostall Heath	0-1
15	Epsom Town v Tooting & Mitcham United	3-0
	PO Engineers v Wills Sports	2-3
	Redhill v Aquarius	3-2
	West Norwood v Dorking	4-2
16	Finchley v Park Royal	2-1
	Hayes v Hounslow Town	8-0
	Uxbridge Town v Lyons	5-3
	Wood Green Town v Civil Service	3-0
17	Apsley v Bushey United	5-3
	Aylesbury United v RAF Henlow	3-0
	Hazells Aylesbury v Watford BL	3-1
	Waterlows Dunstable v Berkhamsted Town	3-4
18	Banbury Spencer v Chipping Norton CA	4-0
	Newbury Town v Slough	1-0
	Thame United v Cowley	5-6
	Witney Town v Bicester Town	0-1
19	Hertford Town v Knebworth	2-1
	Hitchin Town v Alexandra Park	5-2
	Letchworth Town v Baldock Town	1-1e
	St Albans City v Bishops Stortford	3-1
20	Courage & Co's Sports v RASC Aldershot	2-4
	Guildford v Wellington Works	3-4
	Horsham v Godalming	10-0
	Woking v Camberley & Yorktown	5-0
21	Haywards Heath v Littlehampton	3-2
	Newhaven v Southwick	3-0
	Shoreham v Brighton Mental Hospital	1-2
	Worthing v Hastings & St Leonards	1-2
22	HMS Excellent v Ringwood Town	2-1
	HMS Victory v Portsmouth Gas Co	3-1
	RAOC Hilsea v Winchester City	1-4
	Southern Railway (2) v Ryde Sports	2-1
23	Gloucester City v Bristol St George	7-2
	Hanham Athletic v Keynsham	2-3
	Rose Green v Clevedon	1-3
	St Pancras (Knowle) v St Philips Marsh Adult School	2-4

1934/35 to 1935/36

24	2nd Loyal Regt v Paulton Rovers	4-2
	Frome Town v Trowbridge Town	5-2
	Melksham Town v Radstock Town	0-3
	Wells City v Welton Rovers	1-2
2r	Stanley United v Trimdon Colliery United	1-0
5r	South Salford Amateurs v Whitehaven Athletic	wo/s
10r	Wisbech Town v March Town	2-1
12r	Bury Town v RAF Martlesham Heath	4-1
19r	Baldock Town v Letchworth Town	1-3e

Qualifying Round Three

1	South Bank East End v Thornaby	4-3e
	Whitby United v Grangetown St Marys	3-3e
2	Leasingthorne Village v 4th Royal Tank Corps	8-2
	Stanley United v Leasingthorne CW	6-2
3	Blackhill v Witton Park Institute	3-4
	Heaton Stannington v South Hetton CW	0-2
4	Cockfield v Barnard Castle Athletic	1-3
	Evenwood Town v West Auckland Town	1-1e
5	British Insulators SC v Formby	2-1
	South Salford Amateurs v Farsley Celtic	1-2
6	Humber United v Mexborough SS OB	7-1
	Nether Edge Amateurs v Sheffield	5-1
7	Ibstock Penistone Rovers v Excelsior Foundry	4-3
	Ibstock Swifts v Boots Athletic	2-1
8	Hereford City v Boldmere St Michaels	1-2
	Jack Moulds Athletic v Stafford Old Edwardians	2-1
9	Northampton Nomads v Wolverton Town	3-1
10	Newmarket Town v Wisbech Town	1-0a
	St Neots & District v Chatteris Town	6-2
11	Boulton & Paul v Thetford Town	1-0
	King's Lynn v Great Yarmouth Town	1-3
12	Kirkley v Bury Town	6-3e
	Lowestoft Town v Stowmarket	9-2
13	Colchester Town v Barking	1-4
	Harwich & Parkeston v Dagenham Town	4-2 v
14	Bromley v RM Deal	8-0
	Cray Wanderers v Bostall Heath	0-2
15	Redhill v West Norwood	3-1
	Wills Sports v Epsom Town	3-4e
16	Hayes v Finchley	4-4e
	Wood Green Town v Uxbridge Town	1-0 v
17	Berkhamsted Town v Aylesbury United	2-3
	Hazells Aylesbury v Apsley	4-2
18	Bicester Town v Banbury Spencer	2-3
	Newbury Town v Cowley	3-1
19	Hertford Town v St Albans City	1-5
	Hitchin Town v Letchworth Town	6-0
20	Hersham v Wellington Works	6-3
	Woking v RASC Aldershot	2-1
21	Hastings & St Leonards v Haywards Heath	4-2
	Newhaven v Brighton Mental Hospital	2-3
22	HMS Victory v HMS Excellent	2-1
	Winchester City v Southern Railway (2)	2-3
23	Clevedon v Keynsham	5-1
	Gloucester City v St Philips Marsh Adult School	2-2
24	2nd Loyal Regt v Welton Rovers	1-0
	Radstock Town v Frome Town	2-6
1r	Grangetown St Marys v Whitby United	4-3
4r	West Auckland Town v Evenwood Town	1-2
10r	Newmarket Town v Wisbech Town	3-0
13r	Dagenham Town v Harwich & Parkeston	0-4
16r	Finchley v Hayes	2-1
r	Uxbridge Town v Wood Green Town	2-0
23r	Gloucester City v St Philips Marsh Adult School	3-3a
23r2	Gloucester City v St Philips Marsh Adult School	4-3eN

Qualifying Round Four

1	South Bank East End v Grangetown St Marys	3-4
2	Stanley United v Leasingthorne Village	2-0
3	Witton Park Institute v South Hetton CW	2-1
4	Barnard Castle Athletic v Evenwood Town	2-2
5	Farsley Celtic v British Insulators SC	4-3
6	Nether Edge Amateurs v Humber United	2-2
7	Ibstock Penistone Rovers v Ibstock Swifts	2-1
8	Jack Moulds Athletic v Boldmere St Michaels	2-1
9	Mount Pleasant v Northampton Nomads	2-1
10	Newmarket Town v St Neots & District	1-1
11	Great Yarmouth Town v Boulton & Paul	6-0
12	Lowestoft Town v Kirkley	2-0
13	Barking v Harwich & Parkeston	0-1
14	Bostall Heath v Bromley	1-2
15	Redhill v Epsom Town	1-1
16	Uxbridge Town v Finchley	4-2 v
17	Aylesbury United v Hazells Aylesbury	3-1
18	Newbury Town v Banbury Spencer	0-3
19	St Albans City v Hitchin Town	0-2
20	Woking v Hersham	3-0
21	Hastings & St Leonards v Brighton Mental Hospital	4-2
22	HMS Victory v Southern Railway (2)	2-0
23	Gloucester City v Clevedon	5-2
24	Frome Town v 2nd Loyal Regt	5-2
4r	Evenwood Town v Barnard Castle Athletic	3-1
6r	Humber United v Nether Edge Amateurs	1-0
10r	St Neots & District v Newmarket Town	3-2
15r	Epsom Town v Redhill	3-1
16r	Finchley v Uxbridge Town	4-0

Round One

Aylesbury United v Sutton United	0-1
Barnet v Lowestoft Town	3-0
Bishop Auckland v Evenwood Town	3-0
Bournemouth Gasworks Athletic v Banbury Spencer	2-1
Bromley v Woking	2-1
Cambridge Town v St Neots & District	1-1
Chesham United v Harwich & Parkeston	2-0
Dulwich Hamlet v Horsham	3-2
Farsley Celtic v Whitehall Printeries	3-0
Gloucester City v Frome Town	0-3
Golders Green v Enfield	1-2
Grangetown St Marys v Ferryhill Athletic	2-1
Great Yarmouth Town v Walthamstow Avenue	1-3
Guiseley v Humber United	3-2
HMS Victory v Portland United	6-1
Hastings & St Leonards v Wycombe Wanderers	1-1
Hitchin Town v Finchley	1-1
Ibstock Penistone Rovers v Mount Pleasant	4-2
Ilford v London Caledonians	2-2
Leyton v Gorleston	2-1
Leytonstone v Leavesden Hospital	1-0
Maidenhead United v Nunhead	3-1
Metropolitan Police v Kingstonian	0-3
Moor Green v Jack Moulds Athletic	2-1
Northern Nomads v Marine	4-0
Oxford City v Casuals	0-1
Rawmarsh Welfare v Yorkshire Amateur	0-3
Romford (2) v Tufnell Park	7-0
Shildon v Witton Park Institute	3-0
South Bank v Stockton	1-0
Stanley United v Willington	1-0
Wimbledon v Epsom Town	2-0
r	Finchley v Hitchin Town	0-1
r	London Caledonians v Ilford	1-1
r	St Neots & District v Cambridge Town	1-5
r	Wycombe Wanderers v Hastings & St Leonards	4-2
r2	London Caledonians v Ilford	1-0 N

Round Two

Barnet v London Caledonians	2-3
Bishop Auckland v Grangetown St Marys	4-0
Bromley v Wycombe Wanderers	2-1
Chesham United v Wimbledon	0-2
Enfield v Maidenhead United	4-1
Farsley Celtic v Northern Nomads	2-0
Frome Town v Casuals	2-4
Guiseley v Moor Green	4-3
Hitchin Town v Sutton United	4-2
Ibstock Penistone Rovers v Cambridge Town	2-3
Kingstonian v Bournemouth Gasworks Athletic	4-1
Leyton v Romford (2)	2-3
Leytonstone v HMS Victory	0-0
Stanley United v South Bank	0-2
Walthamstow Avenue v Dulwich Hamlet	0-1
Yorkshire Amateur v Shildon	1-0
r	HMS Victory v Leytonstone	0-0
r2	HMS Victory v Leytonstone	3-3 N
r3	HMS Victory v Leytonstone	5-3 v
r4	HMS Victory v Leytonstone	2-1 N

Round Three

Bishop Auckland v Farsley Celtic	11-1
Dulwich Hamlet v London Caledonians	3-0
Enfield v South Bank	3-0
Guiseley v Cambridge Town	3-4
Hitchin Town v Casuals	0-1
Kingstonian v Yorkshire Amateur	3-0
Romford (2) v Bromley	1-2
Wimbledon v HMS Victory	3-0

Round Four

Bishop Auckland v Casuals	1-0
Bromley v Wimbledon	1-2
Dulwich Hamlet v Kingstonian	1-0
Enfield v Cambridge Town	4-2

Semi Finals

Bishop Auckland v Dulwich Hamlet	3-0 N
Wimbledon v Enfield	1-0 N

Final

Bishop Auckland v Wimbledon	0-0 N
r Bishop Auckland v Wimbledon	2-1 N

1935/36

Preliminary Round

7	Whitwick White Cross v Holbeach United	8-0
13	Brightlingsea United v Anglo (Purfleet)	1-2
	Harlow Town v Colchester Town	6-4
	Harwich & Parkeston v Crittall Athletic	4-4e
	Highgate v Gidea Park	4-0
	Hoffmann Ath (Chelmsford) v Briggs Motor Bodies	4-2
	Maldon & Heybridge v Dagenham Town	1-2e
	Saffron Walden Town v Tilbury	1-3
14	Deal Town v Bostall Heath	2-4
	Erith & Belvedere v Woolwich Polytechnic	5-0
	Gravesend United v Catford Wanderers	5-2
	London Paper Mills v Cray Wanderers	3-1
	Maidstone United v RM Deal	7-3
	Swanley Athletic v Dover	2-1
	Whitstable v Woolwich Borough Council Ath.	2-0
15	Beddington Corner v Leyland Motors	2-4
	West Norwood v Merton	4-0
16	Broomfield (1) v The Hook (Northaw) Sports	2-3
	Finchley v Ealing Association	8-3
	Hayesco Sports v Brigade of Guards	2-2
	Hoxton Manor v Old Latymerians	6-0
	London Welsh v Hounslow Town	1-2
	Old Lyonians v Old Johnians	1-0
	Southall v Park Royal	3-1
	Wealdstone v Old Owens	6-0
	Wood Green Town v Old Stationers	1-3
	Yiewsley v Lyons	2-3e
18	Marlow v Headington United	8-2
	Morris Motors v Pressed Steel	6-6e
	Thame United v Henley Town	1-4
21	Hastings & St Leonards v Shoreham	9-2
	Hove v Brighton Tramways	11-2
22	Blandford United v Hamworthy	3-1
	HMS Excellent v Winchester City	3-1
	Osborne Athletic v Bournemouth Transport	wo/s
	Totton v RM Portsmouth	3-1
23	Mount Hill Enterprise v Clevedon	2-0
	Tiverton Town v Timsbury Athletic	7-0
24	Salisbury Corinthians v Chippenham Rovers	5-0
	Swindon Corinthians v 2nd Loyal Regt	3-2
13r	Crittall Athletic v Harwich & Parkeston	1-2e
16r	Hayesco Sports v Brigade of Guards	1-0
18r	Pressed Steel v Morris Motors	9-2

Qualifying Round One

1	Normanby Magnesite v Smiths Dock	3-0
	Pease & Partners v Whitby Albion Rangers	3-3e
	Scarborough Juniors v Cargo Fleet Works	5-3
	South Bank East End v Portrack Shamrocks	2-1
	South Bank St Peters v Filey Town	4-2e
	Thornaby v North Ormesby	4-2
	Whitby United v Carlin How Athletic	3-1
4	Sunnybrow United v Wingate St Marys	1-0
5	Bromborough Pool v Harrowby	8-1
	Earle v Preston GS OB	5-0
	Earlestown Bohemians v Formby	5-3
	East Bierley v Bradford Rovers	3-7
	Liverpool West Derby Union v Old Xaverians	4-1
	Manchester Transport v Orrell	2-4
	Port Sunlight v ICI Alkali	1-2
	Ravensthorpe v Yeadon Celtic	3-1
7	Harrisons & Lewins v Boots Athletic	0-9
	Holwell Works v Nottingham Magdala Amateurs	5-1
	Ibstock Swifts v Excelsior Foundry	4-3e
	Leicestershire Nomads v Ibstock Penistone Rovers	1-3
	North Derbyshire Ramblers v Raleigh Athletic	1-5
	Players Athletic v Bourne Town	3-3
	RAF Cranwell v Whitwick White Cross	4-2
	Stapleford Brookhill v RAF Grantham	1-5
8	Ledbury Town v Baddesley OB	5-1
	Sutton Town v Shrewsbury Amateur	4-2
	Thynnes Athletic v Boldmere St Michaels	2-0
10	Abbey United v Histon Institute	2-1e
	Chatteris Engineers v United Cantabs	5-0
	Chatteris Town v Newmarket Town	2-5
	March Town v March GE United	3-6
	Soham Rangers v Pye Radio	5-1
	St Ives Town v Ramsey Town	1-0
	St Neots & District v Warboys Town	3-0
11	Frosts Athletic v Sheringham	4-1
	King's Lynn v Wymondham	9-0
	Thetford Town v Cromer	3-5
12	Bungay Town v Long Melford	9-0
	Ipswich Town v RAF Martlesham Heath	6-1
	Orwell Works v Felixstowe Town	5-2
13	Chelmsford v Clapton	1-2a
	Clacton Town v Highgate	3-0
	Dagenham Town v Eton Manor	3-2
	Ford Sports v Grays Athletic	1-2
	Harwich & Parkeston v Harlow Town	9-2
	Hoffmann Athletic (Chelmsford) v Custom House	2-0
	Jurgens v Tilbury	2-4
	Severalls Athletic v Anglo (Purfleet)	2-5

1935/36

14	Betteshanger CW v UGBM Sports	4-1
	Bexley v RM Chatham	wo/s
	Bostall Heath v RN Depot	1-2
	Callender Athletic v Erith & Belvedere	2-5
	Gravesend United v Beckenham	2-0
	London Paper Mills v Sheppey United	5-1
	Swanley Athletic v Maidstone United	1-6
	Whitstable v Standard Telephones	6-2
15	Banstead Mental Hospital v Aquarius	7-1
	Carshalton Athletic v Dorking	4-2
	Cranleigh v Sutton United	0-2
	Epsom Town v Reigate Priory	13-1
	Leyland Motors v Barclays Bank	5-1
	Redhill v Streatham Town	7-1
	Tooting & Mitcham United v West Norwood	2-1
	Wills Sports v PO Engineers	0-3
16	Civil Service v Old Finchleians	4-0
	Finchley v Pinner	3-1
	Hayes v Lyons	2-5
	Hounslow Town v Hayesco Sports	1-3e
	Hoxton Manor v The Hook (Northaw) Sports	4-1
	London Labour v Wealdstone	3-3e
	Old Lyonians v Old Stationers	3-1
	Southall v Polytechnic	7-1
17	Leavesden Hospital v Hazells Aylesbury	8-2
	Leighton United v Waterlows Dunstable	1-5
	RAF Halton v Bushey United	3-0
18	Abingdon Town v Cowley	3-4
	Banbury Harriers v Osberton Radiator	1-4
	Chipping Norton CA v Henley Town	4-5
	Marlow v Windsor & Eton	3-2
	Slough v Banbury Spencer	4-2
	Sonning v Pressed Steel	0-0e
	Witney Town v Newbury Town	4-1
	Wycombe Wanderers v Bicester Town	5-2
19	Hoddesdon Town v Alexandra Park	3-0
	Letchworth Town v Baldock Town	6-2
	Shredded Wheat v Ware	1-0
20	Courage & Co's Sports v Woking	2-6
	Egham v Thorneycroft Athletic	7-0
	Guildford v 2nd East Yorks Regt	2-5
	RAMC Aldershot v Hersham	4-2
21	Bexhill v Southwick	1-0
	Bognor Regis v Wick	6-0
	Eastbourne v Haywards Heath	2-1e
	Hastings & St Leonards v Eastbourne Comrades	3-1
	Littlehampton v Brighton Mental Hospital	2-5
	Newhaven v Hove	3-1
	Vernon Athletic v Chichester	2-1
	Worthing v East Grinstead	10-2
22	Blandford United v Osborne Athletic	6-1
	Bournemouth v Swanage	3-2
	HMS Excellent v Gosport	1-2
	Poole Town v East Cowes	7-3
	RAOC Hilsea v Dorchester Town	6-3
	South Hants Nomads v Portsmouth Gas Co	1-7
	Southern Railway (2) v Ringwood Town	6-0
	Totton v HMS Vernon	1-4
23	Cadbury Heath YMCA v Weston-super-Mare	4-1
	Chalford v Hanham Athletic	3-1
	Clandown v Minehead	5-0
	Coleford Athletic v Radstock Town	2-4
	Mount Hill Enterprise v Keynsham	7-4
	Paulton Rovers v Tiverton Town	4-3
	St Philips Athletic v St Pancras (Knowle)	0-5
	Wells City v Welton Rovers	4-3
24	5th Royal Tank Corps v Malmesbury Town	4-1
	Calne & Harris United v Spencer Moulton	2-4
	Chippenham Town v Devizes Town	2-0
	Shepton Mallet Town v Frome Town	2-5
	Swindon Victoria v Salisbury Corinthians	0-2
	Trowbridge Town v Purton	2-1
	Warminster Town v Swindon Corinthians	2-1
	Westbury United v Melksham Town	1-0
1r	Pease & Partners v Whitby Albion Rangers	3-2
7r	Bourne Town v Players Athletic	1-3
13r	Clapton v Chelmsford	4-2
16r	Wealdstone v London Labour	4-1
18r	Pressed Steel v Sonning	1-1a
18r2	Pressed Steel v Sonning	2-1

Qualifying Round Two

1	Scarborough Juniors v Thornaby	1-4
	South Bank St Peters v Normanby Magnesite	3-1
	Thornaby St Patricks v Pease & Partners	1-3
	Whitby United v South Bank East End	2-2
2	4th Royal Tank Corps v Stanley United	5-1
	Chilton Colliery Rec. v Trimdon Grange Colliery	2-1
	Leasingthorne Village v Leasingthorne CW	5-1
3	Heaton Stannington v Witton Park Institute	2-2
4	Brandon Social v Ferryhill Athletic	2-2
	Cockfield v Barnard Castle Athletic	2-0
	Evenwood Town v Newton Cap Bank	2-3
	Sunnybrow United v West Auckland Town	2-4
5	Bromborough Pool v ICI Alkali	3-6e
	Earlestown Bohemians v Liverpool W Derby Union	3-2
	Orrell v Earle	0-1
	Ravensthorpe v Bradford Rovers	3-2
6	Humber United v York Railway Institute	2-2e
	Kingston upon Hull OG v Withernsea OB	3-4
	Norton Woodseats v Brunswick Avenue OB	6-2
7	Boots Athletic v RAF Cranwell	1-2
	Holwell Works v RAF Grantham	4-2
	Players Athletic v Ibstock Swifts	4-1
	Raleigh Athletic v Ibstock Penistone Rovers	2-0
8	Badsey Rangers v Malvern Holy Trinity	4-1
	Jack Moulds Athletic v Thynnes Athletic	5-2
	Sutton Town v Hereford City	2-4e
	Wolverhampton Amateurs v Ledbury Town	2-5
10	Abbey United v Ely City	1-2
	Chatteris Engineers v Newmarket Town	4-1
	St Ives Town v Soham Rangers	0-2
	St Neots & District v March GE United	3-0
11	Gorleston v Frosts Athletic	5-0
	Great Yarmouth Town v Cromer	3-2
	King's Lynn v Norwich YMCA	4-0
	North Walsham Town v Norwich CEYMS	2-3
12	Bury Town v RAF Felixstowe	5-0
	Lowestoft Town v Bungay Town	4-1
	Orwell Works v Ipswich Town	1-10
	Stowmarket v Walton United	4-5
13	Clacton Town v Tilbury	1-5
	Clapton v Anglo (Purfleet)	3-1
	Grays Athletic v Harwich & Parkeston	1-3
	Hoffmann Athletic (Chelmsford) v Dagenham Town	0-1
14	Betteshanger CW v Bexley	3-6
	Gravesend United v Erith & Belvedere	1-3
	London Paper Mills v RN Depot	6-1
	Maidstone United v Whitstable	6-3
15	Epsom Town v Redhill	0-2
	Leyland Motors v Carshalton Athletic	5-0
	PO Engineers v Banstead Mental Hospital	4-1
	Sutton United v Tooting & Mitcham United	2-2
16	Civil Service v Old Lyonians	3-0
	Finchley v Hayesco Sports	2-2e
	Hoxton Manor v Lyons	2-0
	Southall v Wealdstone	7-0
17	Aylesbury United v Waterlows Dunstable	3-2
	Berkhamsted Town v Leavesden Hospital	0-1
	RAF Halton v Apsley	2-2
	RAF Henlow v Watford BL	4-0
18	Cowley v Witney Town	6-2
	Henley Town v Wycombe Wanderers	4-8
	Marlow v Slough	1-0
	Pressed Steel v Osberton Radiator	4-4e
19	Barnet v Shredded Wheat	5-2
	Bishops Stortford v Hoddesdon Town	2-4
	Letchworth Town v St Albans City	1-2e
	Stevenage Town v Hertford Town	0-2
20	Camberley & Yorktown v 2nd East Yorks Regt	2-1
	Godalming v Egham	1-2
	RAMC Aldershot v Woking	3-0
	Walton-on-Thames v RASC Aldershot	2-0
21	Brighton Mental Hospital v Bognor Regis	5-1
	Eastbourne v Bexhill	4-0
	Newhaven v Hastings & St Leonards	5-1
	Worthing v Vernon Athletic	4-1
22	Blandford United v Gosport	2-4
	Bournemouth v HMS Vernon	2-4
	Portsmouth Gas Co v Southern Railway (2)	4-1
	RAOC Hilsea v Poole Town	6-4
23	Cadbury Heath YMCA v St Pancras (Knowle)	0-1
	Chalford v Clandown	0-4
	Radstock Town v Mount Hill Enterprise	9-0
	Wells City v Paulton Rovers	1-2
24	Frome Town v Trowbridge Town	4-2
	Spencer Moulton v Chippenham Town	3-2
	Warminster Town v Salisbury Corinthians	1-3
	Westbury United v 5th Royal Tank Corps	6-1
1r	South Bank East End v Whitby United	3-3e
3r	Witton Park Institute v Heaton Stannington	1-2
4r	Ferryhill Athletic v Brandon Social	1-2
6r	York Railway Institute v Humber United	1-3
15r	Tooting & Mitcham United v Sutton United	0-4
16r	Hayesco Sports v Finchley	3-3e
17r	Apsley v RAF Halton	5-3e
18r	Osberton Radiator v Pressed Steel	2-1
1r2	South Bank East End v Whitby United	2-0
16r2	Finchley v Hayesco Sports	1-0 N

Qualifying Round Three

1	Pease & Partners v Thornaby	3-1
	South Bank St Peters v South Bank East End	2-3
2	Chilton Colliery Recreation v 4th Royal Tank Corps	3-4
	Leasingthorne Village v Crookhall CW	4-0
3	Heaton Stannington v Tow Law Town	6-1
	South Hetton CW v Dipton United	1-2
4	Brandon Social v West Auckland Town	0-4
	Newton Cap Bank v Cockfield	1-2
5	Earlestown Bohemians v Earle	7-1
	ICI Alkali v Ravensthorpe	2-2
6	Humber United v Sheffield	4-0
	Norton Woodseats v Withernsea OB	12-0
7	Holwell Works v RAF Cranwell	1-2
	Players Athletic v Raleigh Athletic	2-4
8	Hereford City v Badsey Rangers	1-4
	Jack Moulds Athletic v Ledbury Town	2-0
9	Daventry Town v Mount Pleasant	2-3
	Wolverton Town v Morris Motors (Coventry)	3-4
10	Chatteris Engineers v Ely City	12-0
	Soham Rangers v St Neots & District	3-2
11	Gorleston v Great Yarmouth Town	5-3
	King's Lynn v Norwich CEYMS	3-1
12	Ipswich Town v Walton United	3-1
	Lowestoft Town v Bury Town	5-1
13	Clapton v Dagenham Town	2-2
	Tilbury v Harwich & Parkeston	0-1
14	Bexley v Maidstone United	1-2
	Erith & Belvedere v London Paper Mills	0-3
15	Leyland Motors v PO Engineers	3-4
	Redhill v Sutton United	2-8
16	Finchley v Southall	2-5
	Hoxton Manor v Civil Service	2-0
17	Aylesbury United v RAF Henlow	2-0
	Leavesden Hospital v Apsley	2-0
18	Osberton Radiator v Cowley	1-3
	Wycombe Wanderers v Marlow	3-1
19	Hertford Town v Barnet	3-3
	Hoddesdon Town v St Albans City	6-1
20	Camberley & Yorktown v Walton-on-Thames	3-3
	RAMC Aldershot v Egham	3-1
21	Newhaven v Eastbourne	2-2
	Worthing v Brighton Mental Hospital	4-1
22	Portsmouth Gas Co v HMS Vernon	3-1
	RAOC Hilsea v Gosport	1-2
23	Paulton Rovers v Clandown	3-2
	Radstock Town v St Pancras (Knowle)	2-3
24	Spencer Moulton v Frome Town	2-5
	Westbury United v Salisbury Corinthians	2-4
5r	Ravensthorpe v ICI Alkali	0-1
13r	Dagenham Town v Clapton	0-1
19r	Barnet v Hertford Town	0-0e
20r	Walton-on-Thames v Camberley & Yorktown	2-1
21r	Eastbourne v Newhaven	4-1e
19r2	Barnet v Hertford Town	3-2 N

Qualifying Round Four

1	Pease & Partners v South Bank East End	2-1
2	4th Royal Tank Corps v Leasingthorne Village	7-0
3	Heaton Stannington v Dipton United	3-1
4	West Auckland Town v Cockfield	1-4
5	ICI Alkali v Earlestown Bohemians	1-1
6	Norton Woodseats v Humber United	2-0
7	RAF Cranwell v Raleigh Athletic	4-1
8	Badsey Rangers v Jack Moulds Athletic	3-0
9	Morris Motors (Coventry) v Mount Pleasant	3-2
10	Chatteris Engineers v Soham Rangers	8-3
11	King's Lynn v Gorleston	4-1
12	Ipswich Town v Lowestoft Town	2-0
13	Clapton v Harwich & Parkeston	3-1
14	London Paper Mills v Maidstone United	1-2
15	Sutton United v PO Engineers	5-3
16	Southall v Hoxton Manor	3-1
17	Leavesden Hospital v Aylesbury United	2-0
18	Wycombe Wanderers v Cowley	3-0
19	Hoddesdon Town v Barnet	2-4
20	RAMC Aldershot v Walton-on-Thames	3-1
21	Eastbourne v Worthing	2-4
22	Gosport v Portsmouth Gas Co	5-3
23	St Pancras (Knowle) v Paulton Rovers	2-0
24	Frome Town v Salisbury Corinthians	3-2
5r	Earlestown Bohemians v ICI Alkali	4-6

Round One

	Barking v Chesham United	6-1
	Cambridge Town v Chatteris Engineers	3-2
	Casuals v Horsham	4-1
	Clapton v Ilford	1-5
	Cockfield v 4th Royal Tank Corps	2-2
	Dulwich Hamlet v Metropolitan Police	5-1
	Farsley Celtic v Northern Nomads	3-2
	Golders Green v Leyton	2-2
	Gosport v Bournemouth Gasworks Athletic	2-1
	Grangetown St Marys v Willington	0-1
	Guiseley v Yorkshire Amateur	4-2
	HMS Victory v St Pancras (Knowle)	4-1
	Heaton Stannington v Pease & Partners	7-3
	Hitchin Town v Enfield	1-2
	ICI Alkali v Whitehall Printeries	4-3
	Ipswich Town v King's Lynn	6-1
	Leavesden Hospital v Kingstonian	2-2
	Leytonstone v London Caledonians	0-1
	Maidenhead United v RAMC Aldershot	4-4
	Maidstone United v Wimbledon	3-2
	Marine v Norton Woodseats	2-1
	Moor Green v Badsey Rangers	1-2
	Morris Motors (Coventry) v RAF Cranwell	1-1
	Oxford City v Sutton United	1-1
	Portland United v Frome Town	2-1
	Romford (2) v Barnet	6-2
	Shildon v Bishop Auckland	1-1
	Stockton v South Bank	2-0
	Uxbridge Town v Tufnell Park	4-1
	Walthamstow Avenue v Southall	3-3
	Worthing v Bromley	3-2
	Wycombe Wanderers v Nunhead	2-1
r	4th Royal Tank Corps v Cockfield	0-1
r	Bishop Auckland v Shildon	2-1
r	Kingstonian v Leavesden Hospital	7-0
r	Leyton v Golders Green	0-3
r	RAF Cranwell v Morris Motors (Coventry)	1-2
r	RAMC Aldershot v Maidenhead United	1-5
r	Southall v Walthamstow Avenue	5-2
r	Sutton United v Oxford City	4-1

1935/36 to 1936/37

Round Two

Barking v Golders Green	1-2
Bishop Auckland v Willington	2-1
Cambridge Town v Badsey Rangers	3-4
Cockfield v Guiseley	6-2
Dulwich Hamlet v Gosport	11-0
Enfield v Uxbridge Town	1-1
Farsley Celtic v Marine	1-8
HMS Victory v Maidenhead United	1-3
ICI Alkali v Morris Motors (Coventry)	6-2
Ilford v Portland United	6-0
Kingstonian v Ipswich Town	4-2
London Caledonians v Sutton United	0-2
Maidstone United v Romford (2)	0-7
Southall v Worthing	9-1
Stockton v Heaton Stannington	4-3
Wycombe Wanderers v Casuals	0-2
r Uxbridge Town v Enfield	2-4

Round Three

Casuals v Bishop Auckland	4-0
Cockfield v Kingstonian	4-2
ICI Alkali v Golders Green	4-2
Ilford v Enfield	5-0
Maidenhead United v Badsey Rangers	3-1
Romford (2) v Dulwich Hamlet	4-2
Southall v Marine	7-0
Stockton v Sutton United	1-2

Round Four

Casuals v ICI Alkali	3-0
Ilford v Cockfield	2-2
Maidenhead United v Southall	1-0
Romford (2) v Sutton United	4-1
r Cockfield v Ilford	3-7

Semi Finals

Casuals v Romford (2)	3-2 N
Ilford v Maidenhead United	4-1 N

Final

Casuals v Ilford	1-1 N
r Casuals v Ilford	2-0 N

1936/37

Extra Preliminary Round

2 Barnard Castle Athletic v West Auckland Town	2-6
Brandon Social v Leasingthorne Village	4-1e
Chilton Colliery Recreation v Etherley United	5-1
Evenwood Crusaders v Mackay's Sports	2-1e
Stanley United v 4th Royal Tank Corps	n/a
Tow Law Town v Leasingthorne CW	7-2
Witton Park Institute v Newton Cap Bank	5-2e
4 Tushingham Brick Works v Harrowby	4-3
6 Ransome & Marles v Netherfield Albion	3-1
16 Finchley v Old Finchleians	6-0
Northmet v Old Stationers	2-1
Old Johnians v Polytechnic	0-5
Old Latymerians v London Welsh	5-2
Old Lyonians v Alexandra Park	5-1
Yiewsley v Old Owens	wo/s
18 Banbury Harriers v Morris Motors	1-6
Banbury Spencer v Thatcham	6-1
Sonning v RAF Bicester	0-2
22 Fareham v Poole Town	0-1
HMS Dolphin v HMS Excellent	0-4
23 Clevedon v Cadbury Heath YMCA	4-2
St Philips Athletic v Chalford	1-3
Wells City v Paulton Rovers	4-3
Weston-super-Mare v Keynsham	0-4

Preliminary Round

2 4th Royal Tank Corps v Tow Law Town	2-1e
Billingham Synthonia v Ferryhill Station United	1-2
Brandon Social v Evenwood Crusaders	2-0
Chilton Colliery Recreation v Witton Park Institute	3-1
Darlington Amateurs v Wingate Celtic	3-2
Furness Athletic v Ferryhill Athletic	2-3
Rocket Athletic v Trimdon Grange Colliery	3-4
West Auckland Town v Crook	5-4
3 Cargo Fleet Works v Filey Town	2-3
Cleveland Works v Pease & Partners	n/a
Marske Rovers v Scarborough Juniors	3-1e
Normanby Magnesite v Thornaby St Patricks	6-0
Smiths Dock v Carlin How Athletic	n/a
South Bank St Peters v Whitby Albion Rangers	3-1
Thornaby v Portrack Shamrocks	4-3e
Whitby United v South Bank East End	2-5
4 Bromborough Pool v Formby	2-3
Earle v Orrell	2-0
East Bierley v Bradford Rovers	2-4
Golcar v Manchester Transport	4-0
Horbury v Crumpsall	7-1
Luddendenfoot v Ravensthorpe	2-4
Old Xaverians v Earlestown Bohemians	2-11
Tushingham Brick Works v Liverpool W Derby Union	2-3
6 Bourne Town v Leicestershire Nomads	1-3
Excelsior Foundry v Holbeach United	4-2e
Ibstock Penistone Rov. v N Derbyshire Ramblers	3-5
Johnson & Barnes Athletic v Boots Athletic	3-3e
RAF Grantham v Holwell Works	1-4
Ransome & Marles v Players Athletic	4-3e
Teversall &Silverhill Collieries v Nottm Magdala	2-1
Whitwick White Cross v RAF Cranwell	2-6
7 Bilston Borough v Stafford Old Edwardians	9-1
Droitwich OB v Wolverton Town	4-1
Hereford City v Mount Pleasant	1-7
Jack Moulds Athletic v Malvern Holy Trinity	5-1
Wolverhampton Amateurs v Northampton Nomads	1-10
8 Chatteris Engineers v Newmarket Town	2-0
March Town v Chatteris Town	1-1e
Pye Radio v Ramsey Town	1-2
United Cantabs v Abbey United	1-2
9 Holt United v Great Yarmouth Town	2-1
Norwich St Barnabas v North Walsham Town	1-1e
Thetford Town v Wymondham	2-1
10 Brantham Athletic v Walton United	1-2
Eastern Counties United v RAF Felixstowe	3-0
11 Briggs Motor Bodies v Grays Athletic	3-5e
CWS Silvertown v Dagenham Cables	7-1
Eton Manor v Gidea Park	2-0
Ford Sports v Highgate	6-0
12 Maldon & Heybridge v Clacton Town	1-6
13 Callender Athletic v Swanley Athletic	2-1
Cray Wanderers v Woolwich Borough Council Ath.	3-0
Erith & Belvedere v Bostall Heath	4-3
London Paper Mills v Catford Wanderers	5-0
Woolwich Polytechnic v UGBM Sports	3-2
14 Betteshanger CW v Deal Town	4-2
Chatham v RM Chatham	2-1e
Sheppey United v Aylesford Paper Mills	0-6
15 Aquarius v Merton	4-2
Banstead Mental Hospital v Epsom	1-6
Beddington Corner v West Norwood	1-4
Carshalton Athletic v Ewell & Stoneleigh	4-4 d
Leyland Motors v Streatham Town	2-1
PO Engineers v Cranleigh	6-3
Redhill v Barclays Bank	5-1
Tooting & Mitcham United v Reigate Priory	2-1
16 Broomfield (1) v Ealing Association	1-3
Finchley v Lyons	5-2
Hoxton Manor v Hounslow Town	1-3
Northmet v Old Latymerians	0-2
Pinner v Brigade of Guards	2-5
Wealdstone v Old Lyonians	9-0
Wood Green Town v Polytechnic	2-3e
Yiewsley v Hayesco Sports	2-4
17 Watford BL v Leighton United	0-15
18 Banbury Spencer v Headington United	4-1
Bicester Town v Slough	2-4
Cowley v Osberton Radiator	1-0
Morris Motors v RAF Bicester	9-1
Newbury Town v Witney Town	6-7
Pressed Steel v Abingdon Town	2-1e
Thame United v Marlow	2-4
Windsor & Eton v Henley Town	0-4
19 Baldock Town v Harlow Town	7-3
Stevenage Town v Epping Town	10-2
20 Brookwood Mental Hospital v 2nd East Yorks Regt	wo/s
Guildford v RASC Aldershot	1-8
RAMC Aldershot v Egham	5-1
Thorneycroft Athletic v Camberley & Yorktown	2-3
21 Bognor Regis v Littlehampton	0-4
Chichester v Eastbourne	5-1
Haywards Heath v Hove	2-4
Newhaven v East Grinstead	5-4
Southwick v Brighton Tramways	1-0
Vernon Athletic v Eastbourne Comrades	1-6
Wick v Bexhill	0-11
22 2nd Middlesex Regt v Bournemouth	5-1
Blandford United v Ringwood Town	3-1
Dorchester Town v Swanage	7-1
Hamworthy v Osborne Athletic	1-0
Poole Town v Sherborne Town	3-1
Portsmouth Gas Co v HMS Excellent	0-1
RAOC Hilsea v Winchester City	2-3e
Totton v HMS Vernon	3-1
23 Chalford v Radstock Town	2-8
Coleford Athletic v Mount Hill Enterprise	0-4
Keynsham v Hanham Athletic	7-1
Timsbury Athletic v Clandown	1-2
Tiverton Town v Wells City	1-3
Twerton St Michaels v St Pancras (Knowle)	0-3
Welton Rovers v Minehead	4-0
Weston-super-Mare UDC Employees v Clevedon	3-1
24 Chippenham Rovers v Calne & Harris United	3-6
Devizes Town v Wootton Bassett Town	8-4
Purton v Warminster Town	3-4e
Salisbury Corinthians v Melksham Town	6-1
Shepton Mallet Town v Chippenham Town	1-2
Swindon Victoria v Swindon Corinthians	1-2
6r Boots Athletic v Johnson & Barnes Athletic	5-2
8r Chatteris Town v March Town	1-5
9r North Walsham Town v Norwich St Barnabas	2-3

Qualifying Round One

2 Brandon Social v 4th Royal Tank Corps	3-2
Chilton Colliery Recreation v Darlington Amateurs	5-3
Ferryhill Athletic v Trimdon Grange Colliery	5-3
West Auckland Town v Ferryhill Station United	5-1
3 Cleveland Works v Marske Rovers	1-3
Filey Town v South Bank St Peters	3-0
South Bank East End v Carlin How Athletic	3-2
Thornaby v Normanby Magnesite	0-1
4 Earlestown Bohemians v Earle	1-2
Formby v Liverpool West Derby Union	3-4
Golcar v Horbury	2-0
Ravensthorpe v Bradford Rovers	1-1e
5 Fulwood v Sheffield	3-1
Humber United v unknown	n/a
6 Boots Athletic v Leicestershire Nomads	n/a
Excelsior Foundry v Ransome & Marles	1-6
North Derbyshire Ramblers v Holwell Works	4-1
RAF Cranwell v Teversall &Silverhill Collieries	3-0
7 Boldmere St Michaels v Droitwich OB	2-0
Morris Motors (Coventry) v Bilston Borough	1-0
Northampton Nomads v Jack Moulds Athletic	3-8
Sutton Town v Mount Pleasant	2-1
8 Histon Institute v Abbey United	4-1
March Town v St Ives Town	2-4
Ramsey Town v March GE United	2-4
Soham Rangers v Chatteris Engineers	5-2
9 Holt United v Cromer	2-0
Norwich St Barnabas v Frosts Athletic	1-3
Norwich YMCA v Norwich CEYMS	3-2e
Sheringham v Thetford Town	5-0
10 Bury Town v RAF Martlesham Heath	7-0
Orwell Works v Bungay Town	4-2
Stowmarket v Felixstowe Town	6-3
Walton United v Eastern Counties United	2-1
11 Dagenham Town v CWS Silvertown	3-2
Ford Sports v Eton Manor	3-3e
Jurgens v Anglo (Purfleet)	0-1
Tilbury v Grays Athletic	2-1
12 Chelmsford v Hoffmann Athletic (Chelmsford)	3-1
Crittall Athletic v Clacton Town	5-1
Saffron Walden Town v Brightlingsea United	3-2
Severalls Athletic v Colchester Town	0-1
13 Beckenham v Bexley	3-4
Erith & Belvedere v Callender Athletic	3-2
London Paper Mills v Standard Telephones	5-0
Woolwich Polytechnic v Cray Wanderers	3-0
14 Betteshanger CW v RM Deal	1-4
Gravesend United v Dover	6-3
RN Depot v Chatham	1-4
Whitstable v Aylesford Paper Mills	0-1
15 Carshalton Athletic v Aquarius	5-2e
Epsom v West Norwood	3-1
Redhill v Leyland Motors	4-2
Tooting & Mitcham United v PO Engineers	0-3
16 Ealing Association v Wealdstone	1-2
Finchley v Polytechnic	5-1
Hayesco Sports v Northmet	3-2
Hounslow Town v Brigade of Guards	1-1
17 Aylesbury United v Leighton United	2-0
Berkhamsted Town v RAF Halton	1-3
Bushey United v Hazells Aylesbury	1-2
RAF Henlow v Waterlows Dunstable	0-8
18 Banbury Spencer v Cowley	3-0
Henley Town v Marlow	3-6
Pressed Steel v Slough	0-2
Witney Town v Morris Motors	4-3
19 Hertford Town v Bishops Stortford	0-1
Hoddesdon Town v Stevenage Town	2-1
Letchworth Town v Hitchin Town	1-5
Ware v Baldock Town	2-1
20 Godalming v RASC Aldershot	0-5
Hersham v Brookwood Mental Hospital	4-2
RAMC Aldershot v Courage & Co's Sports	3-2e
Walton-on-Thames v Camberley & Yorktown	5-0
21 Chichester v Littlehampton	1-3
Newhaven v Hove	0-1
Shoreham v Eastbourne Comrades	5-2
Southwick v Bexhill	5-0
22 2nd Middlesex Regt v Winchester City	0-1
Dorchester Town v Blandford United	2-3
Hamworthy v Poole Town	1-4
Totton v HMS Excellent	2-0
23 Clandown v Keynsham	5-2
Radstock T v Weston-super-Mare UDC Employees	2-1e
St Pancras (Knowle) v Mount Hill Enterprise	5-3
Wells City v Welton Rovers	2-1
24 Calne & Harris United v Westbury United	1-7
Devizes Town v Chippenham Town	4-1
Salisbury Corinthians v Swindon Corinthians	3-1e
Warminster Town v Spencer Moulton	6-1
4r Bradford Rovers v Ravensthorpe	6-2
11r Eton Manor v Ford Sports	2-1
16r Hounslow Town v Brigade of Guards	1-0

1936/37 to 1937/38

Qualifying Round Two

1 Alnwick Alndale v Gosforth Amateurs	3-3
St Peters Albion v Dipton United	5-2
2 Brandon Social v Ferryhill Athletic	3-3e
West Auckland Town v Chilton Colliery Recreation	n/a
3 Filey Town v Marske Rovers	0-1
Normanby Magnesite v South Bank East End	2-2
4 Earle v Liverpool West Derby Union	2-1
Golcar v Bradford Rovers	1-2
5 Fulwood v Brunswick Avenue OB	6-2
Old Hullensians v Hull Nomads	1-2
6 Boots Athletic v Ransome & Marles	n/a
RAF Cranwell v North Derbyshire Ramblers	3-0
7 Boldmere St Michaels v Sutton Town	2-1
Morris Motors (Coventry) v Jack Moulds Athletic	3-1
8 Soham Rangers v Histon Institute	4-3
St Ives Town v March GE United	3-2
9 Frosts Athletic v Holt United	3-2
Sheringham v Norwich YMCA	0-2
10 Bury Town v Walton United	7-0
Orwell Works v Stowmarket	3-4
11 Dagenham Town v Anglo (Purfleet)	1-3
Eton Manor v Tilbury	2-1
12 Crittall Athletic v Colchester Town	4-0
Saffron Walden Town v Chelmsford	2-1
13 Erith & Belvedere v Woolwich Polytechnic	0-0
London Paper Mills v Bexley	2-0
14 Chatham v RM Deal	4-0
Gravesend United v Aylesford Paper Mills	0-1e
15 Epsom v PO Engineers	5-2e
Redhill v Carshalton Athletic	4-2
16 Finchley v Hayesco Sports	1-2e
Hounslow Town v Wealdstone	1-3
17 Aylesbury United v RAF Halton	2-0
Hazells Aylesbury v Waterlows Dunstable	3-5
18 Marlow v Slough	4-1
Witney Town v Banbury Spencer	2-4
19 Hitchin Town v Bishops Stortford	2-0e
Ware v Hoddesdon Town	0-4
20 Hersham v Walton-on-Thames	1-4
RASC Aldershot v RAMC Aldershot	5-3
21 Littlehampton v Shoreham	6-2
Southwick v Hove	2-1
22 Blandford United v Poole Town	1-4
Totton v Winchester City	1-1
23 Radstock Town v Wells City	1-3
St Pancras (Knowle) v Clandown	5-0
24 Warminster Town v Salisbury Corinthians	2-1
Westbury United v Devizes Town	1-5
1r Alnwick Alndale v Gosforth Amateurs	0-4
2r Ferryhill Athletic v Brandon Social	2-1
3r South Bank East End v Normanby Magnesite	3-0
13r Erith & Belvedere v Woolwich Polytechnic	2-1
22r Winchester City v Totton	3-2

Qualifying Round Three

1 St Peters Albion v Gosforth Amateurs	2-1
2 Ferryhill Athletic v West Auckland Town	0-1
3 South Bank East End v Marske Rovers	2-1
4 Earle v Bradford Rovers	4-0
5 Fulwood v Hull Nomads	5-2
6 Boots Athletic v RAF Cranwell	0-2
7 Morris Motors (Coventry) v Boldmere St Michaels	1-5
8 Soham Rangers v St Ives Town	4-0
9 Norwich YMCA v Frosts Athletic	2-4e
10 Bury Town v Stowmarket	3-1
11 Anglo (Purfleet) v Eton Manor	5-4
12 Crittall Athletic v Saffron Walden Town	10-1
13 London Paper Mills v Erith & Belvedere	5-1
14 Chatham v Aylesford Paper Mills	0-1
15 Redhill v Epsom	3-0
16 Wealdstone v Hayesco Sports	6-2
17 Waterlows Dunstable v Aylesbury United	3-3e
18 Banbury Spencer v Marlow	1-3
19 Hoddesdon Town v Hitchin Town	1-3
20 Walton-on-Thames v RASC Aldershot	2-1
21 Southwick v Littlehampton	2-1
22 Poole Town v Winchester City	3-1
23 Wells City v St Pancras (Knowle)	0-2
24 Devizes Town v Warminster Town	4-2
17r Aylesbury United v Waterlows Dunstable	4-3

Qualifying Round Four

Anglo (Purfleet) v Bury Town	2-1
Aylesbury United v Lowestoft Town	2-2
Boldmere St Michaels v Earle	4-1
Civil Service v London Paper Mills	1-2
Crittall Athletic v Leytonstone	4-2
Evenwood Town v Grangetown St Marys	6-1
Frome Town v St Pancras (Knowle)	2-4
Gorleston v King's Lynn	2-1
Gosport v Redhill	0-1
Hastings & St Leonards v Woking	3-1
Heaton Stannington v St Peters Albion	6-1
Leavesden Hospital v Hitchin Town	1-1
Maidstone United v Aylesford Paper Mills	1-1
Marlow v Chesham United	0-2
Metropolitan Police v Poole Town	5-1
Moor Green v Fulwood	5-1
Northern Nomads v Norton Woodseats	1-2
RAF Cranwell v Soham Rangers	9-1
Southwick v Worthing	1-2
St Albans City v Harwich & Parkeston	1-4
Walton-on-Thames v Devizes Town	4-2
Wealdstone v Frosts Athletic	3-0
West Auckland Town v South Bank	1-3
Whitehall Printeries v South Bank East End	1-2a
r Aylesford Paper Mills v Maidstone United	2-1
r Hitchin Town v Leavesden Hospital	5-4
r Lowestoft Town v Aylesbury United	3-0
r Whitehall Printeries v South Bank East End	0-1

Round One

Anglo (Purfleet) v Barking	3-2
Aylesford Paper Mills v Wimbledon	3-1
Barnet v Lowestoft Town	4-2
Boldmere St Michaels v Cambridge Town	3-0
Bromley v Horsham	3-2
Casuals v Oxford City	4-1
Clapton v HMS Victory	8-0
Crittall Athletic v Walthamstow Avenue	2-4
Enfield v Southall	2-5
Evenwood Town v South Bank	1-2
Gorleston v Wycombe Wanderers	0-0
Guiseley v South Bank East End	3-3
Hastings & St Leonards v B'mouth Gasworks Ath	0-4
Hayes v Walton-on-Thames	3-0
Heaton Stannington v Shildon	3-1
Hitchin Town v Dulwich Hamlet	2-4
ICI Alkali v Marine	3-0
Leyton v Worthing	8-4
London Paper Mills v Golders Green	3-2
Maidenhead United v Sutton United	1-3
Norton Woodseats v Badsey Rangers	5-2
Nunhead v Kingstonian	4-1
Portland United v Harwich & Parkeston	2-0
RAF Cranwell v Moor Green	0-1
Redhill v Metropolitan Police	0-2
Romford (2) v London Caledonians	3-0
St Pancras (Knowle) v Uxbridge	4-5
Stockton v Cockfield	3-1
Tufnell Park v Ilford	3-1
Wealdstone v Chesham United	4-0
Willington v Bishop Auckland	3-4
Yorkshire Amateur v Farsley Celtic	1-1
r Farsley Celtic v Yorkshire Amateur	0-1
r South Bank East End v Guiseley	5-2
r Wycombe Wanderers v Gorleston	3-2

Round Two

Aylesford Paper Mills v London Paper Mills	3-5
Bishop Auckland v South Bank East End	7-0
Bromley v Tufnell Park	5-1
Dulwich Hamlet v Casuals	1-0
Hayes v Anglo (Purfleet)	4-1
Leyton v Clapton	7-2
Metropolitan Police v Bournemouth Gasworks Ath	1-2
Moor Green v Boldmere St Michaels	6-0
Norton Woodseats v ICI Alkali	0-4
Romford (2) v Portland United	4-2
South Bank v Yorkshire Amateur	2-5
Stockton v Heaton Stannington	5-3
Sutton United v Barnet	2-1
Uxbridge v Wealdstone	1-3
Walthamstow Avenue v Southall	6-1
Wycombe Wanderers v Nunhead	4-2

Round Three

Bromley v Bournemouth Gasworks Athletic	4-0
Hayes v ICI Alkali	2-3
London Paper Mills v Leyton	0-1
Moor Green v Bishop Auckland	0-2
Romford (2) v Sutton United	3-4
Stockton v Wycombe Wanderers	4-1
Walthamstow Avenue v Yorkshire Amateur	3-1
Wealdstone v Dulwich Hamlet	1-1
r Dulwich Hamlet v Wealdstone	4-0

Round Four

Bromley v Stockton	4-1
Leyton v Bishop Auckland	3-2
Sutton United v ICI Alkali	3-2
Walthamstow Avenue v Dulwich Hamlet	1-2

Semi Finals

Dulwich Hamlet v Bromley	3-1 N
Leyton v Sutton United	1-1 N
r Leyton v Sutton United	2-1 N

Final

Dulwich Hamlet v Leyton	2-0 N

1937/38

Extra Preliminary Round

4 Bromborough Pool v Old Xaverians	3-1
Orrell v Tushingham Brick Works	0-3
Ravensthorpe v Horbury	2-4
15 Cobham v Venner Sports	1-1e
16 Old Finchleians v Ealing Association	4-3
Old Lyonians v Old Stationers	2-5
Pinner v Broomfield (1)	n/a
Roxonian v Civil Service	1-3
White City v Metropolitan Railway Athletic	4-4e
18 Marlow v Wallingford Town	5-1
22 Fareham v Hamworthy	6-2
HMS Vernon v Pennington St Marks	4-0
Poole Town v Sherborne Town	4-1
Portsmouth Gas Co v 2nd Middlesex Regt	8-4
Shaftesbury Town v Dorchester Town	3-3e
Winchester City v Bournemouth	4-2
23 Bedminster Down Sports v Clevedon	2-1
Cadbury Heath YMCA v Chalford	2-0
Kingswood v Keynsham	4-3
St Pancras (Knowle) v Tiverton Town	9-0
Weston-super-Mare v Radstock Town	1-3
Weston-super-Mare UDC Employees v Minehead	3-2
15r Venner Sports v Cobham	4-1
16r Metropolitan Railway Athletic v White City	2-3
22r Dorchester Town v Shaftesbury Town	6-0

Preliminary Round

2 Chilton Colliery Recreation v Newton Cap Bank	6-1
Crook v Ferryhill Athletic	2-5
Etherley United v West Auckland Town	2-4
Tow Law Town v Rocket Athletic	5-1
Washington Welfare v Leasingthorne CW	2-0
Witton Park Institute v Barnard Castle Athletic	3-4
3 Billingham Synthonia v South Bank East End	2-4
Filey Town v Scarborough Juniors	2-3
Furness Athletic v Marske Rovers	n/a
Normanby Magnesite v Billingham South	2-1
4 Bottom Boat v Urmston	1-2
Bromborough Pool v Liverpool West Derby Union	3-6
Earle v Earlestown Bohemians	3-2e
Harrowby v Formby	4-0
Heptonstall v Horbury	0-6
Manchester Transport v Whitkirk	n/a
Oulton Roseville v East Bierley	0-1
Stoneycroft v Tushingham Brick Works	5-4
6 Berridge Institute v Players Athletic	3-3
Coalville Town Amateur v Leicestershire Nomads	3-5e
Ibstock Penistone Rovers v Whitwick White Cross	1-4
RAF Cranwell v Nottingham Magdala Amateurs	n/a
7 Bilston Borough v Wolverhampton Amateurs	2-1e
Jack Moulds Athletic v Kettering United	1-0
Malvern Holy Trinity v Droitwich OB	0-4
Morris Motors (Coventry) v Sutton Town	2-4
Northampton Nomads v Thynnes Athletic	11-0
Stafford Old Edwardians v Nuneaton Borough	0-2
West Bromwich Amateurs v Mount Pleasant	1-2
9 Cromer v Fakenham Town	6-0
Frosts Athletic v Great Yarmouth Town	4-2
North Walsham Town v Holt United	3-6
Norwich CEYMS v Norwich YMCA	3-1e
10 Brantham Athletic v RAF Felixstowe	4-0
Stowmarket v Felixstowe Town	2-1
11 Briggs Motor Bodies v Highgate	2-1
CWS Silvertown v Tilbury	2-3
Esso v Ford Sports	3-2
Port of London Authority v Eton Manor	1-2
12 Crompton Parkinson v Severalls Athletic	1-3
Saffron Walden Town v Crittall Athletic	2-7
13 Erith & Belvedere v Bexley	5-3
14 Betteshanger CW v RM Deal	2-1
Gravesend United v Ramsgate Grenville	2-1
RN Depot v Dover	1-0
Sheppey United v Chatham	3-0
Whitstable v Maidstone United	2-3
15 Aquarius v Leyland Motors	1-3
Carshalton Athletic v Merton	4-3
Cranleigh v Barclays Bank	0-4
Epsom v Banstead Mental Hospital	2-2
Redhill v West Norwood	8-1
Tooting & Mitcham United v PO Engineers	2-2
Venner Sports v Reigate Priory	5-2
Wandsworth United v Ewell & Stoneleigh	2-0
16 Civil Service v Yiewsley	4-3
Hounslow Town v Brigade of Guards	1-1e
Hoxton Manor v Polytechnic	2-1
Lyons v Pinner	1-0
Northmet v Old Latymerians	7-1
Old Johnians v Old Finchleians	4-3
White City v Alexandra Park	2-1
Wood Green Town v Old Stationers	5-4
17 Apsley v Arlesey Town	1-0
Kings Langley v Bushey United	2-7

1937/38

18	Bicester Town v Newbury Town	6-4e
	Henley Town v Witney Town	8-1
	Marlow v Windsor & Eton	1-0
	Osberton Radiator v Headington United	3-6
	Pressed Steel v Banbury Harriers	6-2
	Slough v Abingdon Town	7-0
	Thame United v Morris Motors	1-3
	Thatcham v Cowley	5-4
19	Harlow Town v Baldock Town	4-1
	Hertford Town v Ware	3-3
20	4th Royal Tank Corps v Brookwood Mental Hospital	4-1
	Andover v Vickers Aviation	2-3
	Camberley & Yorktown v RAMC Aldershot	0-2
	RASC Aldershot v Walton-on-Thames	2-3
	Thorneycroft Athletic v Hersham	0-3
21	Bexhill v Haywards Heath	0-3
	East Grinstead v Vernon Athletic	9-2
	Eastbourne v Bognor Regis	3-2
	Hastings & St Leonards v Hove	8-0
	Littlehampton v Brighton Tramways	2-0
	Newhaven v Chichester	2-3
22	Blandford United v HMS Victory	4-7
	Fareham v Ringwood Town	3-1
	HMS Vernon v HMS Excellent	2-4
	Osborne Athletic v Portsmouth Gas Co	1-2
	Poole Town v Lymington	4-2
	Swanage v Dorchester Town	0-4
	Totton v Winchester City	4-2
	Wimborne v Ryde Sports	3-1
23	Bedminster Down Sports v Paulton Rovers	3-2
	Cadbury Heath YMCA v St Philips Marsh Adult Schl	5-1
	Farmborough v Hanham Athletic	3-4
	St Pancras (Knowle) v Clandown	1-2
	Timsbury Athletic v Kingswood	5-3
	Wells City v Mount Hill Enterprise	1-1e
	Welton Rovers v Radstock Town	1-3
	Weston-super-Mare UDCE v Twerton St Michaels	2-1
24	Calne & Harris United v Wootton Bassett Town	2-2
	Devizes Town v Salisbury Corinthians	4-3
	Melksham Town v Swindon Victoria	6-1
	Purton v Swindon Corinthians	n/a
	Spencer Moulton v Chippenham Town	2-4
6r	Players Athletic v Berridge Institute	2-1
15r	Epsom v Banstead Mental Hospital	3-2
r	PO Engineers v Tooting & Mitcham United	0-3
16r	Hounslow Town v Brigade of Guards	2-2
19r	Ware v Hertford Town	3-5
23r	Wells City v Mount Hill Enterprise	6-4
24r	Wootton Bassett Town v Calne & Harris United	2-0
16r2	Brigade of Guards v Hounslow Town	3-2 N

Qualifying Round One

2	Darlington Amateurs v Barnard Castle Athletic	2-1
	Ferryhill Athletic v Chilton Colliery Recreation	5-0
	Stanley United v West Auckland Town	0-1e
	Tow Law Town v Washington Welfare	3-3
3	Portrack Shamrocks v South Bank St Peters	3-2
	Smiths Dock v unknown	n/a
	South Bank East End v Normanby Magnesite	2-1
	Whitby United v Scarborough Juniors	5-0
4	Earle v Liverpool West Derby Union	4-2
	East Bierley v Horbury	3-1
	Manchester Transport v Urmston	0-5
	Stoneycroft v Harrowby	4-2
5	Hall Road Athletic v Brunswick Institute	1-4
	Rawmarsh Welfare v Old Hullensians	8-2
	Sheffield v Fulwood	1-2
6	Excelsior Foundry v Players Athletic	1-6
	Holwell Works v North Derbyshire Ramblers	2-1
	Netherfield Albion v Leicestershire Nomads	0-2
	RAF Cranwell v Whitwick White Cross	1-0
7	Hereford City v Droitwich OB	3-2
	Jack Moulds Athletic v Bilston Borough	3-2
	Northampton Nomads v Mount Pleasant	1-3
	Nuneaton Borough v Sutton Town	2-1
8	Abbey United v Histon Institute	5-1
	Newmarket Town v Warboys Town	7-3
	Pye Radio v Lakenheath	0-3
9	Cromer v Norwich St Barnabas	0-3
	Frosts Athletic v Wymondham	1-2
	Holt United v Norwich CEYMS	1-0
	Thetford Town v Sheringham	2-1
10	Brantham Athletic v Bungay Town	3-4
	Bury Town v Walton United	9-2
	Eastern Coachworks (Lowestoft) v Stowmarket	7-0
	Orwell Works v RAF Martlesham Heath	1-2
11	Dagenham Town v Eton Manor	0-0e
	Esso v Stork	0-2
	Grays Athletic v Briggs Motor Bodies	3-0
	Tilbury v Gidea Park	7-0
12	Chelmsford v Hoffmann Athletic (Chelmsford)	0-4
	Clacton Town v Brightlingsea United	2-0
	Crittall Athletic v Colchester Town	4-1
	Maldon & Heybridge v Severalls Athletic	2-2e
13	Beckenham v Erith & Belvedere	1-2
	Bostall Heath v Callender Athletic	1-2
	Catford Wanderers v Cray Wanderers	0-2
	Woolwich Polytechnic v UGBM Sports	0-2
14	Aylesford Paper Mills v Maidstone United	1-1e
	Betteshanger CW v Deal Town	1-2
	RM Chatham v Gravesend United	7-1
	RN Depot v Sheppey United	2-1
15	Epsom v Barclays Bank	6-4
	Redhill v Leyland Motors	1-1e
	Tooting & Mitcham United v Venner Sports	3-1
	Wandsworth United v Carshalton Athletic	2-0
16	Brigade of Guards v Lyons	2-1
	Civil Service v Hoxton Manor	1-0
	White City v Northmet	2-1
	Wood Green Town v Old Johnians	4-2
17	Apsley v Bushey United	3-2
	Aylesbury United v Berkhamsted Town	6-3
	Hazells Aylesbury v Waterlows Dunstable	0-8
	Leighton United v RAF Halton	3-4
18	Bicester Town v Headington United	1-2
	Henley Town v Morris Motors	5-3
	Pressed Steel v Marlow	2-3
	Slough v Thatcham	2-1
19	Hertford Town v Harlow Town	5-0
	Hoddesdon Town v Hitchin Town	2-4
	Letchworth Town v Epping Town	3-2
	Stevenage Town v Bishops Stortford	2-0
20	Guildford v Egham	6-2
	Hersham v Godalming	5-1
	RAMC Aldershot v Walton-on-Thames	7-5e
	Vickers Aviation v 4th Royal Tank Corps	0-3
21	Chichester v Littlehampton	1-6
	East Grinstead v Hollington United	6-3
	Hastings & St Leonards v Shoreham	11-2
	Haywards Heath v Eastbourne	3-1
22	Dorchester Town v Poole Town	0-2
	Fareham v HMS Victory	2-3
	Portsmouth Gas Co v Totton	3-0
	Wimborne v HMS Excellent	4-2
23	Cadbury Heath YMCA v Hanham Athletic	1-2
	Clandown v Timsbury Athletic	1-1
	Radstock Town v Bedminster Down Sports	3-2
	Weston-super-Mare UDC Employees v Wells City	3-4
24	Chippenham Town v Melksham Town	5-1
	Pewsey Young Men v Devizes Town	3-6
	Purton v Westbury United	1-0
	Wilts County Mental Hospital v Wootton Bassett T	5-2
2r	Washington Welfare v Tow Law Town	2-2e
11r	Eton Manor v Dagenham Town	1-1e
12r	Severalls Athletic v Maldon & Heybridge	1-1
14r	Maidstone United v Aylesford Paper Mills	1-4
15r	Leyland Motors v Redhill	1-3
23r	Timsbury Athletic v Clandown	3-6
2r2	Tow Law Town v Washington Welfare	2-1
11r2	Eton Manor v Dagenham Town	3-1 N
12r2	Severalls Athletic v Maldon & Heybridge	1-3

Qualifying Round Two

1	Alnwick Alndale v Bigges Main Celtic	4-7
	Newcastle West End v Gosforth Amateurs	0-2
2	Ferryhill Athletic v Darlington Amateurs	2-0
	Tow Law Town v West Auckland Town	1-3
3	Portrack Shamrocks v Whitby United	3-3e
	Smiths Dock v South Bank East End	1-4
4	Stoneycroft v Earle	2-3
	Urmston v East Bierley	3-2
5	Brunswick Avenue OB v Brunswick Institute	0-3
	Rawmarsh Welfare v Fulwood	2-1
6	Holwell Works v Players Athletic	0-3
	RAF Cranwell v Leicestershire Nomads	3-2e
7	Mount Pleasant v Jack Moulds Athletic	3-3
	Nuneaton Borough v Hereford City	7-1
8	Abbey United v Ramsey Town	3-1
	Lakenheath v Newmarket Town	1-2
9	Norwich St Barnabas v Thetford Town	3-1
	Wymondham v Holt United	2-2
10	Bungay Town v Eastern Coachworks (Lowestoft)	1-0
	Bury Town v RAF Martlesham Heath	5-3e
11	Grays Athletic v Eton Manor	1-2
	Tilbury v Stork	4-1
12	Clacton Town v Hoffmann Athletic (Chelmsford)	0-1
	Crittall Athletic v Maldon & Heybridge	9-2
13	Erith & Belvedere v Callender Athletic	6-0
	UGBM Sports v Cray Wanderers	1-4
14	RM Chatham v Deal Town	5-6e
	RN Depot v Aylesford Paper Mills	1-3
15	Epsom v Redhill	1-4
	Tooting & Mitcham United v Wandsworth United	3-1
16	Civil Service v Brigade of Guards	5-2
	Wood Green Town v White City	0-3
17	Apsley v Aylesbury United	4-3e
	RAF Halton v Waterlows Dunstable	2-3
18	Marlow v Headington United	4-3
	Slough v Henley Town	6-5e
19	Letchworth Town v Hertford Town	0-5
	Stevenage Town v Hitchin Town	2-4
20	Hersham v Guildford	3-2e
	RAMC Aldershot v 4th Royal Tank Corps	2-1
21	East Grinstead v Littlehampton	3-0
	Haywards Heath v Hastings & St Leonards	2-3
22	HMS Victory v Wimborne	3-1
	Portsmouth Gas Co v Poole Town	1-0
23	Radstock Town v Clandown	3-1e
	Wells City v Hanham Athletic	5-2
24	Purton v Chippenham Town	1-0
	Wilts County Mental Hospital v Devizes Town	1-2
3r	Whitby United v Portrack Shamrocks	n/a
7r	Jack Moulds Athletic v Mount Pleasant	3-1
9r	Holt United v Wymondham	4-1

Qualifying Round Three

1	Gosforth Amateurs v Bigges Main Celtic	n/a
2	Ferryhill Athletic v West Auckland Town	2-1
3	South Bank East End v Portrack Shamrocks	3-2
4	Urmston v Earle	3-1
5	Rawmarsh Welfare v Brunswick Institute	2-2e
6	Players Athletic v RAF Cranwell	4-3
7	Jack Moulds Athletic v Nuneaton Borough	4-1
8	Newmarket Town v Abbey United	2-1
9	Holt United v Norwich St Barnabas	3-2
10	Bury Town v Bungay Town	3-1
11	Eton Manor v Tilbury	3-0
12	Hoffmann Athletic (Chelmsford) v Crittall Athletic	0-6
13	Erith & Belvedere v Cray Wanderers	5-2
14	Aylesford Paper Mills v Deal Town	5-1
15	Tooting & Mitcham United v Redhill	3-1
16	Civil Service v White City	2-0
17	Apsley v Waterlows Dunstable	3-4
18	Marlow v Slough	2-2e
19	Hitchin Town v Hertford Town	3-0
20	RAMC Aldershot v Hersham	0-1
21	East Grinstead v Hastings & St Leonards	1-7
22	HMS Victory v Portsmouth Gas Co	1-1e
23	Wells City v Radstock Town	3-3
24	Devizes Town v Purton	0-1e
5r	Brunswick Institute v Rawmarsh Welfare	2-1
18r	Slough v Marlow	4-0
22r	Portsmouth Gas Co v HMS Victory	3-2
23r	Radstock Town v Wells City	9-1

Qualifying Round Four

	Aylesford Paper Mills v Civil Service	4-1
	Boldmere St Michaels v Norton Woodseats	2-1
	Brunswick Institute v Urmston	1-2
	Bury Town v Waterlows Dunstable	3-10
	Chesham United v Southwick	5-0
	Crittall Athletic v King's Lynn	7-1
	Erith & Belvedere v Tufnell Park	5-1
	Ferryhill Athletic v Evenwood Town	4-4
	Gorleston v Eton Manor	2-6
	Heaton Stannington v Bigges Main Celtic	3-1
	Hersham v Wealdstone	1-4
	Holt United v Leavesden Hospital	2-0
	Jack Moulds Athletic v Northern Nomads	2-2
	London Caledonians v Hastings & St Leonards	4-0
	London Paper Mills v Tooting & Mitcham United	2-3
	Lowestoft Town v Hitchin Town	4-2
	Newmarket Town v Players Athletic	3-1
	Portsmouth Gas Co v Frome Town	0-0
	Purton v Radstock Town	8-2
	Slough v Metropolitan Police	3-4
	South Bank v Whitehall Printeries	3-2
	South Bank East End v Grangetown St Marys	2-0
	St Albans City v Uxbridge	2-2
	Worthing v Gosport	3-1
r	Evenwood Town v Ferryhill Athletic	1-2
r	Frome Town v Portsmouth Gas Co	2-5
r	Northern Nomads v Jack Moulds Athletic	2-1
r	Uxbridge v St Albans City	1-1
r2	Uxbridge v St Albans City	3-2

Round One

	Aylesford Paper Mills v Enfield	2-2
	Barnet v Metropolitan Police	2-0
	Boldmere St Michaels v Badsey Rangers	1-1
	Bournemouth Gasworks Athletic v Leytonstone	0-1
	Crittall Athletic v Tooting & Mitcham United	4-2
	Dulwich Hamlet v Woking	7-0
	Erith & Belvedere v Worthing	3-0
	Eton Manor v Bromley	0-1
	Finchley v Casuals	4-1
	Golders Green v Barking	2-1
	Guiseley v Farsley Celtic	0-7
	Harwich & Parkeston v Portsmouth Gas Co	6-3
	Hayes v Leyton	4-5
	Heaton Stannington v Bishop Auckland	3-2
	Holt United v Oxford City	2-0
	Horsham v London Caledonians	4-1
	ICI Alkali v Yorkshire Amateur	0-1
	Kingstonian v Waterlows Dunstable	3-2
	Maidenhead United v Wimbledon	3-1
	Marine v Urmston	3-2
	Moor Green v Northern Nomads	2-1
	Newmarket Town v Cambridge Town	1-3
	Nunhead v Walthamstow Avenue	1-6
	Portland United v Wycombe Wanderers	1-4
	Purton v Lowestoft Town	0-2
	Romford (2) v Chesham United	4-2
	Shildon v South Bank	3-1
	South Bank East End v Ferryhill Athletic	1-4
	Southall v Ilford	1-5
	Sutton United v Wealdstone	2-0
	Uxbridge v Clapton	1-2
	Willington v Stockton	1-4
r	Badsey Rangers v Boldmere St Michaels	2-3
r	Enfield v Aylesford Paper Mills	1-2

1937/38 to 1938/39

Round Two

	Aylesford Paper Mills v Wycombe Wanderers	4-2
	Boldmere St Michaels v Marine	2-2
	Bromley v Clapton	4-2
	Dulwich Hamlet v Crittall Athletic	3-1
	Erith & Belvedere v Maidenhead United	1-0
	Ferryhill Athletic v Stockton	0-2
	Finchley v Harwich & Parkeston	0-2
	Golders Green v Leyton	0-2
	Heaton Stannington v Shildon	2-3
	Holt United v Barnet	0-2
	Horsham v Kingstonian	1-1
	Ilford v Lowestoft Town	4-2
	Moor Green v Cambridge Town	2-5
	Sutton United v Leytonstone	1-1
	Walthamstow Avenue v Romford (2)	1-1
	Yorkshire Amateur v Farsley Celtic	2-0
r	Kingstonian v Horsham	2-1
r	Leytonstone v Sutton United	3-1
r	Marine v Boldmere St Michaels	3-2
r	Romford (2) v Walthamstow Avenue	4-1

Round Three

	Aylesford Paper Mills v Cambridge Town	2-2
	Barnet v Stockton	3-0
	Erith & Belvedere v Leytonstone	2-2
	Ilford v Dulwich Hamlet	2-3
	Kingstonian v Shildon	1-2
	Leyton v Romford (2)	2-4
	Marine v Harwich & Parkeston	2-3
	Yorkshire Amateur v Bromley	1-2
r	Cambridge Town v Aylesford Paper Mills	1-3
r	Leytonstone v Erith & Belvedere	1-1e
r2	Erith & Belvedere v Leytonstone	3-1 N

Round Four

	Bromley v Shildon	4-1
	Dulwich Hamlet v Barnet	1-3
	Erith & Belvedere v Aylesford Paper Mills	4-2
	Harwich & Parkeston v Romford (2)	0-2

Semi Finals

	Bromley v Barnet	3-2 N
	Erith & Belvedere v Romford (2)	2-2 N
r	Erith & Belvedere v Romford (2)	4-2 N

Final

	Bromley v Erith & Belvedere	1-0 N

1938/39

Extra Preliminary Round

18	Banbury Spencer v Witney Town	6-0
	Redford Sports v Headington United	2-3
22	Gosport v Totton	1-2
	HMS Victory v Lymington	0-3
	Osborne Athletic v Fareham Casuals	5-3e
	Pennington St Marks v Shaftesbury Town	5-2
	Ryde Sports v Bridport	10-1
23	Brislington v Paulton Rovers	2-0
	Bristol St George v Weston-super-Mare UDCE	2-4
	Cadbury Heath YMCA v Wells City	1-2
	Hanham Athletic v Aero Engines	1-2
	Kingswood v Twerton St Michaels	0-7
	Newton Corinthians v Cinderford Town	3-5
	Peasedown Miners Welfare v Radstock Town	3-2
	Taunton Amateurs v St Philips Marsh Adult School	1-2
	Welton Rovers v Weston-super-Mare	5-2

Preliminary Round

2	Chilton Colliery Recreation v Washington Welfare	1-3
	Cockfield v Darlington Amateurs	4-1
	Lanchester Rangers v Darlington Rolling Mills	4-2
	Langley Park Villa v Barnard Castle Athletic	6-2
	Sacriston United v Crook	3-2e
	Stanley United v Rocket Athletic	9-1
	Tow Law Town v Witton Park Institute	1-2
	West Auckland Town v Crookhall Rovers	2-1
3	Billingham Synthonia v Scarborough Juniors	4-2
	Cargo Fleet Ironworks v Great Ayton United	5-2
	Furness Athletic v Smiths Dock	8-0
	Normanby Magnesite v South Bank East End	1-4
	South Bank St Peters v Grangetown St Marys	6-1
	Whitby United v Billingham South	2-0
4	Barnton Victoria v Ferguson Pailin	n/a
	Carlton United v Valley United	0-3
	Formby v Earle	4-3
	Harrowby v Liverpool West Derby Union	2-5
	Old Xaverians v Tushingham Brick Works	3-6
	Ravensthorpe v Oulton Roseville	0-2
	Urmston v East Bierley	4-3
	Whitkirk v Bottom Boat	4-1
6	Coalville Town Amateur v Bourne Town	5-4
	Leicestershire Nomads v Excelsior Foundry	5-0
	RAF Cranwell v Netherfield Albion	n/a
	Raleigh Athletic v Kettering United	4-1
	Sutton Town v Players Athletic	7-4
	Whitwick White Cross v Ibstock Penistone Rovers	3-2
7	Bridgnorth Town v Humber Hillman Recreation	5-2
	Daventry Town v Northampton Nomads	0-5
	Jack Moulds Athletic v West Bromwich Amateurs	4-2
	Malvern Holy Trinity v Hereford City Amateur	1-4
	Morris Motors (Coventry) v Cherry Orchard	6-0
	Mount Pleasant v Sutton Town	3-1
	Stafford Old Edwardians v Walsall Jolly Club	wo/s
	Wolverhampton Amateurs v Wesley Castle	3-2
9	Holt United v Norwich St Barnabas	5-1
	North Walsham Town v Norwich Electricity Works	2-1
11	Southend Corinthians v Grays Athletic	0-2
	Stork v Tilbury	0-2
14	Aylesford Paper Mills v RN Depot	6-1
	RM Chatham v Betteshanger CW	wo/s
	RM Deal v Ramsgate Grenville	5-2
15	Aquarius v Venner Sports	1-1e
	Banstead Hospital v Carshalton	1-0
	Carshalton Athletic v Leyland Motors	6-2
	Cranleigh v Reigate Priory	3-3e
	Epsom v Redhill	1-2e
	Nunhead v Cobham	6-1
	PO Engineers v Barclays Bank	6-0
16	Civil Service v Old Latymerians	5-1
	Harrow Town v Pinner	1-0
	Lyons v Northmet	3-0
	Old Finchleians v Ealing Association	0-2
	Old Lyonians v Hounslow Town	1-2
	Polytechnic v Old Stationers	3-0
	Wood Green Town v Old Johnians	5-2
	Yiewsley v Hoxton Manor	3-1
17	Apsley v Kings Langley	5-1
	Aylesbury United v Waterlows Dunstable	3-0
	Bushey United v Vauxhall Motors	0-1
	Watford BL v Luton Amateur	3-3
18	Banbury Spencer v Bicester Town	3-0
	Marlow v Abingdon Town	8-0
	Morris Motors v Banbury Harriers	5-0
	Pressed Steel v Henley Town	5-3
	Slough v Osberton Radiator	3-1
	Thame United v Newbury Town	2-5
	Wallingford Town v Headington United	3-2
	Windsor & Eton v Thatcham	1-0
19	Baldock Town v Hoddesdon Town	4-2
	Bishops Stortford v Arlesey Town	8-1
	Epping Town v Lyrn & Lahy Sports	3-2
	Harlow Town v Welwyn Garden City	1-3
	Hatfield United v Hertford Town	0-1
	Ware v Letchworth Town	4-4e
20	Brookwood Hospital v 4th Royal Tank Corps	2-4
	Camberley & Yorktown v RASC Aldershot	0-1
	Egham v Hersham	1-2
	Guildford v Walton-on-Thames	2-7
	RAMC Aldershot v Thorneycroft Athletic	5-1
21	Bognor Regis v East Grinstead	5-3
	Eastbourne v Brighton Tramways	2-1
	Eastbourne Comrades v Chichester	5-0
	Haywards Heath v Hove	3-1
	Newhaven v Bexhill	2-0
	Shoreham v Vernon Athletic	0-0e
22	Bournemouth v Portsmouth Gas Co	4-3
	Dorchester Town v Ringwood Town	5-3
	HMS Excellent v Pennington St Marks	6-0
	Osborne Athletic v Lymington	1-2
	Ryde Sports v Fareham	3-1
	Sherborne Town v Hamworthy	4-1
	Totton v Wimborne	4-2
	Winchester City v Poole Town	4-4e
23	Aero Engines v Keynsham	2-4
	Brislington v Mount Hill Enterprise	0-2
	Chalford v Twerton St Michaels	4-0
	Clandown v Timsbury Athletic	1-0
	Clevedon v Weston-super-Mare UDC Employees	2-1
	St Pancras (Knowle) v Peasedown Miners Welfare	2-1
	Wells City v St Philips Marsh Adult School	2-2
	Welton Rovers v Cinderford Town	5-2
24	Calne & Harris United v Pewsey Young Men	5-5
	Chippenham Town v Devizes Town	3-2
	Frome Town v Wootton Bassett Town	7-2
	Melksham Town v Swindon Corinthians	6-3
	Purton v Wilts County Mental Hospital	2-1e
	Spencer Moulton v Salisbury City	3-3e
	Swindon Victoria v Warminster Town	4-3
	Westbury United v Salisbury Corinthians	3-2
15r	Reigate Priory v Cranleigh	1-4
r	Venner Sports v Aquarius	4-1
17r	Luton Amateur v Watford BL	1-0
19r	Letchworth Town v Ware	4-2
21r	Shoreham v Vernon Athletic	0-1
22r	Poole Town v Winchester City	2-0
23r	St Philips Marsh Adult School v Wells City	1-4
24r	Pewsey Young Men v Calne & Harris United	6-2
r	Salisbury City v Spencer Moulton	2-3

Qualifying Round One

1	Bigges Main Celtic v Rosehill Athletic	n/a
	Newcastle West End v Wallsend St Lukes	3-4
	Wallsend Gordon v Gosforth Amateurs	2-1
2	Sacriston United v Cockfield	3-2e
	Stanley United v Lanchester Rangers	5-1
	Washington Welfare v Witton Park Institute	1-2
	West Auckland Town v Langley Park Villa	3-1
3	Portrack Shamrocks v Billingham Synthonia	2-1
	South Bank East End v Furness Athletic	5-0
	Thornaby v South Bank St Peters	2-7
	Whitby United v Cargo Fleet Works	3-1
4	Ferguson Pailin v Formby	4-1
	Liverpool W Derby Union v Tushingham Brick Works	1-3
	Urmston v Valley United	4-1
	Whitkirk v Oulton Roseville	4-1
5	Hall Road Athletic v Rawmarsh Welfare	1-5
	Old Hullensians v Sheffield	n/a
6	Chesterfield Ramblers v Holwell Works	3-3
	Leicestershire Nomads v Whitwick White Cross	4-2e
	Raleigh Athletic v Coalville Town Amateur	6-4
	Sutton Town v Netherfield Albion	2-4
7	Morris Motors (Coventry) v Bridgnorth Town	3-1
	Mount Pleasant v Northampton Nomads	4-1
	Stafford Old Edwardians v Hereford City Amateur	0-2
	Wolverhampton Amateurs v Jack Moulds Athletic	2-3
8	Histon Institute v Abbey United	5-1
	Lakenheath v Chatteris Town	5-0
	Warboys Town v Pye Radio	2-1
9	Fakenham Town v Frosts Athletic	6-4
	North Walsham Town v Holt United	3-6
	Thetford Town v Norwich YMCA	2-3
	Wymondham v Sheringham	9-2
10	Brantham Athletic v Walton United	5-1
	Eastern Coachworks (Lowestoft) v Bungay Town	5-1
	Felixstowe Town v RAF Martlesham Heath	2-4
	Orwell Works v RAF Felixstowe	13-1
11	Briggs Motor Bodies v Dagenham Town	4-1
	CWS Silvertown v Port of London Authority	5-2
	Ford Sports v Grays Athletic	3-3e
	Tilbury v Esso	5-1
12	Clacton Town v Saffron Walden Town	2-0
	Hoffmann Ath (Chelmsford) v Maldon & Heybridge	10-1
	Severalls Athletic v Crittall Athletic	0-5
13	Bostall Heath v Bexley	2-1
	Callender Athletic v Catford Wanderers	4-4e
	Cray Wanderers v Woolwich Polytechnic	3-4
14	Aylesford Paper Mills v Deal Town	7-1
	Chatham v Gravesend United	2-5
	Maidstone United v RM Deal	2-1
	Sheppey United v RM Chatham	3-2
15	Banstead Hospital v West Norwood	3-1
	Cranleigh v Carshalton Athletic	1-6
	Nunhead v Redhill	2-4e
	Venner Sports v PO Engineers	4-0
16	Ealing Association v Yiewsley	2-3
	Harrow Town v Civil Service	2-4
	Lyons v Wood Green Town	2-1
	Polytechnic v Hounslow Town	2-2e
17	Apsley v Vauxhall Motors	4-3
	Berkhamsted Town v Leighton United	5-2
	Hazells Aylesbury v Aylesbury United	3-5
	Luton Amateur v RAF Halton	3-1
18	Marlow v Morris Motors	6-1
	Newbury Town v Windsor & Eton	0-3
	Slough v Pressed Steel	2-1
	Wallingford Town v Banbury Spencer	0-0
19	Baldock Town v Epping Town	1-6
	Hertford Town v Bishops Stortford	4-0
	Hitchin Town v Stevenage Town	8-0
	Letchworth Town v Welwyn Garden City	4-3
20	4th Royal Tank Corps v Vickers Aviation	3-0
	Godalming v RAMC Aldershot	0-4
	Hersham v RASC Aldershot	1-2
	Walton-on-Thames v Andover	6-1
21	Bognor Regis v Haywards Heath	2-4
	Eastbourne Comrades v Eastbourne	4-2
	Hollington United v Newhaven	0-3
	Littlehampton v Vernon Athletic	2-1
22	Bournemouth v Sherborne Town	3-3
	Dorchester Town v Poole Town	2-3
	Ryde Sports v HMS Excellent	2-3e
	Totton v Lymington	3-0
23	Chalford v Wells City	3-5
	Clandown v Welton Rovers	3-2
	Clevedon v Keynsham	4-1
	St Pancras (Knowle) v Mount Hill Enterprise	4-0
24	Melksham Town v Pewsey Young Men	6-2
	Purton v Frome Town	4-1
	Spencer Moulton v Chippenham Town	1-2
	Westbury United v Swindon Victoria	4-1
6r	Holwell Works v Chesterfield Ramblers	4-0
11r	Grays Athletic v Ford Sports	1-2
13r	Catford Wanderers v Callender Athletic	4-1
16r	Hounslow Town v Polytechnic	3-1
18r	Banbury Spencer v Wallingford Town	8-0
22r	Sherborne Town v Bournemouth	3-1

1938/39

Qualifying Round Two

1	Wallsend Gordon v St Peters Albion	2-4
	Wallsend St Lukes v Bigges Main Celtic	5-0
2	Stanley United v Sacriston United	1-0
	Witton Park Institute v West Auckland Town	3-1
3	South Bank East End v Portrack Shamrocks	2-4
	South Bank St Peters v Whitby United	1-2
4	Ferguson Pailin v Tushingham Brick Works	2-1
	Urmston v Whitkirk	6-2
5	Brunswick Institute v Sheffield	3-2
	Fulwood v Rawmarsh Welfare	2-3
6	Holwell Works v Netherfield Albion	6-2
	Leicestershire Nomads v Raleigh Athletic	3-2
7	Jack Moulds Athletic v Mount Pleasant	3-1
	Morris Motors (Coventry) v Hereford City Amateur	2-0
8	Histon Institute v Warboys Town	6-0
	Newmarket Town v Lakenheath	5-0
9	Fakenham Town v Norwich YMCA	5-2
	Holt United v Wymondham	9-0
10	Brantham Athletic v Orwell Works	1-2
	Eastern Coachworks (L'toft) v RAF Martlesham Heath	6-2
11	Briggs Motor Bodies v CWS Silvertown	1-3
	Ford Sports v Tilbury	1-1e
12	Brightlingsea United v Clacton Town	2-2e
	Crittall Athletic v Hoffmann Athletic (Chelmsford)	2-1
13	Bostall Heath v UGB Charlton	0-3
	Catford Wanderers v Woolwich Polytechnic	5-3e
14	Aylesford Paper Mills v Maidstone United	2-3
	Gravesend United v Sheppey United	6-1
15	Banstead Hospital v Carshalton Athletic	1-0e
	Redhill v Venner Sports	3-0
16	Civil Service v Hounslow Town	2-3
	Lyons v Yiewsley	5-2
17	Aylesbury United v Luton Amateur	3-5
	Berkhamsted Town v Apsley	1-4
18	Banbury Spencer v Windsor & Eton	5-3
	Marlow v Slough	0-1
19	Epping Town v Hertford Town	3-1
	Letchworth Town v Hitchin Town	0-4
20	RAMC Aldershot v 4th Royal Tank Corps	0-2
	RASC Aldershot v Walton-on-Thames	7-1 v
21	Haywards Heath v Eastbourne Comrades	4-2
	Newhaven v Littlehampton	0-0
22	HMS Excellent v Poole Town	0-1
	Sherborne Town v Totton	2-2e
23	St Pancras (Knowle) v Clandown	2-1
	Wells City v Clevedon	1-4
24	Chippenham Town v Westbury United	6-1
	Purton v Melksham Town	4-5
11r	Tilbury v Ford Sports	0-3
12r	Clacton Town v Brightlingsea United	10-0
20r	Walton-on-Thames v RASC Aldershot	0-2
21r	Littlehampton v Newhaven	1-2
22r	Totton v Sherborne Town	3-0

Qualifying Round Three

1	Wallsend St Lukes v St Peters Albion	5-0
2	Witton Park Institute v Stanley United	3-2
3	Portrack Shamrocks v Whitby United	2-1e
4	Urmston v Ferguson Pailin	0-3
5	Rawmarsh Welfare v Brunswick Institute	5-1
6	Holwell Works v Leicestershire Nomads	4-1
7	Jack Moulds Athletic v Morris Motors (Coventry)	5-2
8	Histon Institute v Newmarket Town	5-1
9	Fakenham Town v Holt United	1-2
10	Eastern Coachworks (Lowestoft) v Orwell Works	0-2
11	Ford Sports v CWS Silvertown	6-2
12	Clacton Town v Crittall Athletic	3-1
13	UGB Charlton v Catford Wanderers	2-0
14	Gravesend United v Maidstone United	2-0
15	Redhill v Banstead Hospital	3-0
16	Lyons v Hounslow Town	0-1
17	Apsley v Luton Amateur	6-1
18	Banbury Spencer v Slough	0-1e
19	Epping Town v Hitchin Town	0-2
20	4th Royal Tank Corps v RASC Aldershot	1-2
21	Newhaven v Haywards Heath	1-3
22	Poole Town v Totton	3-2
23	Clevedon v St Pancras (Knowle)	3-2
24	Chippenham Town v Melksham Town	9-0

Qualifying Round Four

Apsley v Southwick	1-5
Chesham United v Worthing	3-2
Clevedon v Chippenham Town	1-1
Evenwood Town v Witton Park Institute	1-1
Ferryhill Athletic v Wallsend St Lukes	1-2
Ford Sports v Holt United	6-0
Gorleston v Clacton Town	2-1
Haywards Heath v Metropolitan Police	3-2
Heaton Stannington v Guiseley	2-4
Hitchin Town v Redhill	3-0
Holwell Works v Boldmere St Michaels	3-3
Horsham v St Albans City	3-3
Hounslow Town v UGB Charlton	4-2
Jack Moulds Athletic v Histon Institute	4-2
London Caledonians v Gravesend United	3-0
London Paper Mills v Finchley	2-1
Lowestoft Town v Eton Manor	1-1
Northern Nomads v Ferguson Pailin	2-3
Orwell Works v Leavesden Hospital	2-7
Oxford City v Slough	1-2
Poole Town v RASC Aldershot	0-1
Rawmarsh Welfare v Whitehall Printeries	1-1
Tooting & Mitcham United v Uxbridge	2-1
Willington v Portrack Shamrocks	6-3
r Boldmere St Michaels v Holwell Works	3-2
r Chippenham Town v Clevedon	3-2
r Eton Manor v Lowestoft Town	2-0
r St Albans City v Horsham	5-0
r Whitehall Printeries v Rawmarsh Welfare	0-1
r Witton Park Institute v Evenwood Town	0-1

Round One

Boldmere St Michaels v Moor Green	2-4
Cambridge Town v Jack Moulds Athletic	2-1
Chesham United v Enfield	1-1
Chippenham Town v Gorleston	1-3
Clapton v Maidenhead United	2-2
Dulwich Hamlet v Leytonstone	1-3
Erith & Belvedere v Barking	1-1
Eton Manor v Bromley	2-4
Farsley Celtic v Yorkshire Amateur	1-4
Ferguson Pailin v Marine	0-2
Harwich & Parkeston v Casuals	1-9
Hastings & St Leonards v Leavesden Hospital	4-1
Hitchin Town v Tooting & Mitcham United	1-1
ICI Alkali v Rawmarsh Welfare	2-0
Ilford v London Paper Mills	6-3
Kingstonian v Ford Sports	3-1
Leyton v Romford (2)	3-0
London Caledonians v Golders Green	0-0
Norton Woodseats v Badsey Rangers	9-0
Portland United v Sutton United	0-1
RASC Aldershot v Barnet	3-2
Shildon v Evenwood Town	7-0
South Bank v Guiseley	2-1
Southall v Hounslow Town	2-2
Southwick v Hayes	3-1
St Albans City v Haywards Heath	2-1
Wallsend St Lukes v Bishop Auckland	0-1
Walthamstow Avenue v Wealdstone	4-2
Willington v Stockton	2-1
Wimbledon v Bournemouth Gasworks Athletic	3-3
Woking v Tufnell Park	2-1
Wycombe Wanderers v Slough	1-5
r Barking v Erith & Belvedere	1-0
r Bournemouth Gasworks Athletic v Wimbledon	0-1
r Enfield v Chesham United	7-0
r Golders Green v London Caledonians	2-0
r Hounslow Town v Southall	1-1
r Maidenhead United v Clapton	1-0
r Tooting & Mitcham United v Hitchin Town	3-1
r2 Southall v Hounslow Town	2-2 N
r3 Hounslow Town v Southall	2-3 N

Round Two

Bromley v Southall	4-1
Cambridge Town v Marine	2-1
Golders Green v Southwick	2-1e
Hastings & St Leonards v Barking	4-3
Kingstonian v Gorleston	5-3e
Leyton v Casuals	1-0
Moor Green v Yorkshire Amateur	4-0
Norton Woodseats v ICI Alkali	2-1
RASC Aldershot v Enfield	1-3
Slough v St Albans City	0-3
South Bank v Bishop Auckland	1-7
Sutton United v Maidenhead United	4-1
Tooting & Mitcham United v Leytonstone	1-2
Walthamstow Avenue v Ilford	2-3
Willington v Shildon	2-0
Woking v Wimbledon	1-3

Round Three

Bishop Auckland v Leyton	2-0
Cambridge Town v Ilford	0-2
Kingstonian v Hastings & St Leonards	4-0
Leytonstone v Bromley	1-1
Norton Woodseats v Wimbledon	3-1
St Albans City v Enfield	2-1
Sutton United v Golders Green	4-2
Willington v Moor Green	1-0
r Bromley v Leytonstone	1-2

Round Four

Bishop Auckland v Ilford	3-1
St Albans City v Norton Woodseats	2-4
Sutton United v Leytonstone	0-2
Willington v Kingstonian	1-0

Semi Finals

Bishop Auckland v Leytonstone	0-0 N
Willington v Norton Woodseats	1-0 N
r Bishop Auckland v Leytonstone	2-1 N

Final

Bishop Auckland v Willington	3-0eN

1939/40 to 1944/45

No competition due to WWII

1945/46 to 1946/47

1945/46

Preliminary Round

21	Littlehampton Town v Bognor Regis Town	10-5
24	Chippenham Town v Swindon Victoria	4-1
	Devizes Town v Frome Town	0-6
	Swindon GWR Corinthians v Melksham Town	4-0
	Whiteheads v Westbury United	5-0

Qualifying Round One

5	Hull Amateurs v Brigham & Cowans	3-2
12	Apsley v Berkhamsted Town	4-5
	Aylesbury United v Kings Langley	10-1
	Bedford Avenue v Leighton United	3-2
	Luton Amateur v Vauxhall Motors	5-4e
13	Hatfield United v Hoddesdon Town	4-3
	Letchworth Town v Hertford Town	6-0
16	Callender Athletic v Catford Wanderers	0-1
	Deal Town v Sheppey United	1-6
17	Epsom v Banstead Hospital	0-1
18	Harrow Town v Lyons	10-1
	Hounslow Town v Yiewsley	3-2
	London Transport Central Buses v Edgware Town	0-10
	Pinner v Polytechnic	5-4
19	Headington United v Pressed Steel	4-1
	Osberton Radiator v Newbury Town	8-2
	Windsor & Eton v Henley Town	5-0
21	East Grinstead v Bexhill Town	wo/s
	Eastbourne v Haywards Heath	3-0
	Horsham v Hove	3-1
	Littlehampton Town v Newhaven	3-1
22	Totton v Dorchester Town	5-0
23	Clandown v Soundwell	2-2e
	Clevedon v Peasedown Miners Welfare	5-2
	Radstock Town v Hanham Athletic	4-3
	Welton Rovers v Paulton Rovers	0-5
24	Pewsey Young Men v Warminster Town	3-4
	Salisbury Corinthians v Purton	5-2
	Swindon GWR Corinthians v Chippenham Town	3-4
	Whiteheads v Frome Town	4-2
23r	Soundwell v Clandown	1-6

Qualifying Round Two

1	Rocket Athletic v Darlington Rolling Mills	n/a
	Washington Welfare v Brandon CW	1-6
3	Billingham Synthonia v Smiths Dock	n/a
5	Hull Amateurs v Thornhill Edge	3-2
7	Whitwick PCC v Coalville Town Amateur	1-4
12	Aylesbury United v Berkhamsted Town	2-2e
	Luton Amateur v Bedford Avenue	3-2
13	Letchworth Town v Hatfield United	5-1
	Welwyn Garden City v Stevenage Town	1-2
16	Catford Wanderers v RM Chatham	3-1
	Sheppey United v Woolwich Polytechnic	2-5
17	Merton v Epsom Town	1-3
	Redhill v Banstead Hospital	6-2
18	Harrow Town v Edgware Town	0-4
	Hounslow Town v Pinner	1-1e
19	Headington United v Windsor & Eton	3-1
	Osberton Radiator v Marlow	0-3
20	Vickers Aviation v Guildford	5-2
	Walton & Hersham v Stoke Recreation (Guildford)	6-0
21	East Grinstead v Littlehampton Town	1-2
	Horsham v Eastbourne	2-4
22	Ryde Sports v Gosport Borough Athletic	4-1
	Totton v HMS Excellent	3-3
23	Clevedon v Paulton Rovers	2-3
	Radstock Town v Clandown	2-1
24	Chippenham Town v Whiteheads	7-1
	Salisbury Corinthians v Warminster Town	3-2
12r	Berkhamsted Town v Aylesbury United	2-1
18r	Pinner v Hounslow Town	2-1
22r	HMS Excellent v Totton	3-8

Qualifying Round Three

1	Darlington Rolling Mills v Brandon CW	n/a
2	Crook Colliery Welfare v Wallsend St Lukes	3-1
3	Whitby v Billingham Synthonia	4-3a
4	Earle - Bye	
5	East Bierley v Hull Amateurs	1-4
6	Raleigh Athletic v Broomfield (2)	4-2
7	Holwell Works v Coalville Town Amateur	4-2
8	Bournville Athletic - Bye	
9	Abbey United v Newmarket Town	2-0
10	Lakenheath v King's Lynn	3-5
11	Leiston - Bye	
12	Luton Amateur v Berkhamsted Town	2-2a
13	Letchworth Town v Stevenage Town	2-1
14	Briggs Sports v Grays Athletic	1-2
15	Crittall Athletic v Hoffmann Athletic (Chelmsford)	5-2
16	Woolwich Polytechnic v Catford Wanderers	4-0
17	Redhill v Epsom Town	5-3
18	Pinner v Edgware Town	4-2
19	Headington United v Marlow	5-3a
20	Vickers Aviation v Walton & Hersham	0-5
21	Eastbourne v Littlehampton Town	6-0
22	Totton v Ryde Sports	5-2

23	Paulton Rovers v Radstock Town	3-2
24	Chippenham Town v Salisbury Corinthians	5-3
3r	Billingham Synthonia v Whitby	4-3
12r	Berkhamsted Town v Luton Amateur	2-3e
19r	Marlow v Headington United	6-2

Qualifying Round Four

Abbey United v Lowestoft Town	wo/s
Billingham Synthonia v Tow Law Town	n/a
Bournville Athletic v Boldmere St Michaels	4-2
Chesham United v Finchley	1-2
Crittall Athletic v Tooting & Mitcham United	3-1
Earle v Ferguson Pailin	1-2
Ford Sports v Pinner	5-0
Grays Athletic v Woolwich Polytechnic	8-3
Guiseley v Hull Amateurs	2-1
Hitchin Town v Luton Amateur	9-5
Holwell Works v Raleigh Athletic	0-2
King's Lynn v Leiston	6-0
Letchworth Town v Bishops Stortford	1-1
Morris Motors v Maidenhead United	2-5
Paulton Rovers v Chippenham Town	1-3
Players Athletic v Basford United	0-4
Slough United v Marlow	4-2
Southall v Eton Manor	8-0
Southwick v Totton	0-2
Stanley United v Brandon CW	4-4
Walton & Hersham v Redhill	11-0
West Auckland Town v Crook Colliery Welfare	1-2
Wood Green Town v Uxbridge	4-2
Worthing v Eastbourne	2-3
r Bishops Stortford v Letchworth Town	1-4
r Brandon CW v Stanley United	1-2

Round One

Abbey United v Hitchin Town	3-5
Bishop Auckland v Ferguson Pailin	7-1
Bournemouth Gasworks Athletic v Totton	2-5
Bromley v Barking	1-0
Chippenham Town v Slough United	1-5
Clapton v Enfield	2-1
Crook Colliery Welfare v Evenwood Town	5-3
Erith & Belvedere v Sutton United	2-2
Golders Green v Ford Sports	2-1
Guiseley v Billingham Synthonia	4-3
Hastings & St Leonards v Eastbourne	1-2
Hayes v Wealdstone	3-0
King's Lynn v Cambridge Town	4-1
Kingstonian v Wycombe Wanderers	1-1
Leyton v Tufnell Park	4-0
Marine v Basford United	5-2
Metropolitan Police v Letchworth Town	4-0
Moor Green v Bournville Athletic	2-0
Norton Woodseats v ICI Alkali	6-1
Oxford City v Maidenhead United	5-2
Raleigh Athletic v Rawmarsh Welfare	2-5
Romford (2) v Leytonstone	0-0
South Bank v Yorkshire Amateur	3-0
Southall v Grays Athletic	3-1
St Albans City v Ilford	0-3
Stanley United v Shildon	9-0
Walthamstow Avenue v Dulwich Hamlet	3-0
Walton & Hersham v Corinthian Casuals	3-2
Willington v Ferryhill Athletic	3-3
Wimbledon v Crittall Athletic	3-1
Woking v Finchley	2-1
Wood Green Town v Barnet	3-4
r Leytonstone v Romford (2)	3-5
r Sutton United v Erith & Belvedere	2-4
r Willington v Ferryhill Athletic	1-3
r Wycombe Wanderers v Kingstonian	10-1

Round Two

Barnet v Walton & Hersham	4-0
Bishop Auckland v Stanley United	3-0
Clapton v Erith & Belvedere	1-2
Eastbourne v Totton	5-2
Ferryhill Athletic v Crook Colliery Welfare	5-1
Golders Green v Leyton	1-3
Hayes v Bromley	0-4
Hitchin Town v King's Lynn	5-3
Ilford v Metropolitan Police	5-1
Marine v Rawmarsh Welfare	4-2
Moor Green v Norton Woodseats	4-1
Oxford City v Slough United	2-3
South Bank v Guiseley	3-1
Southall v Romford (2)	4-2
Wimbledon v Woking	5-2
Wycombe Wanderers v Walthamstow Avenue	1-1
r Walthamstow Avenue v Wycombe Wanderers	7-5

Round Three

Bromley v Walthamstow Avenue	0-0
Eastbourne v Erith & Belvedere	2-3
Hitchin Town v Barnet	2-5
Leyton v Southall	2-4
Marine v Ferryhill Athletic	4-1
Moor Green v Slough United	2-1
South Bank v Bishop Auckland	1-3
Wimbledon v Ilford	1-2
r Walthamstow Avenue v Bromley	2-1

Round Four

Barnet v Southall	4-3
Bishop Auckland v Moor Green	4-1
Ilford v Walthamstow Avenue	2-3e
Marine v Erith & Belvedere	2-1

Semi Finals

Barnet v Marine	1-0 N
Bishop Auckland v Walthamstow Avenue	2-1 N

Final

Barnet v Bishop Auckland	3-2 N

1946/47

Extra Preliminary Round

24	St Austell v Plymouth United	11-0

Preliminary Round

2	Barnard Castle v Etherley	5-3e
	Brandon CW v Wearmouth CW	3-1
	Chilton & Windlestone Senior Boys v Pont Institute	n/a
	Eden Colliery v Darlington Rolling Mills	n/a
	Rocket Athletic v Middleton Wanderers	5-2
	Shildon United v Langley Park	n/a
3	Smiths Dock v South Bank East End	n/a
4	Scalegill v Distington	6-0
5	Brunswick Institute v Hull Amateurs	1-4e
	Old Hullensians v Bradford Rovers	0-11
	Rothwell Athletic v Dawson Payne & Elliott Sports	2-3
6	Bentinck Welfare v Gedling Colliery	1-3
	Huthwaite CWS v Netherfield Albion	2-1
	Kiveton Park Colliery v Raleigh Athletic	2-1
	Parliament Street Methodists v Players Athletic	2-8
8	Boldmere St Michaels v Northampton Amateurs	7-0
	Lye Town v Coventry Amateur	2-4
	Raunds Town v Walsall Wood	1-7
	Rugby Town Amateur v Sheldon Town	7-2
10	Gorleston v Holt United	4-0
	Gothic v Lakenheath	3-2
	Wymondham Town v Great Yarmouth Town	5-6
13	Arlesey Town v Sawbridgeworth	5-1
	Biggleswade Town v De Havilland Hatfield	3-0
	Bishops Stortford v Crown & Manor	2-4
	Hatfield United v Welwyn Garden City	2-1
	Hertford Town v Harlow Town	3-3e
	Stevenage Town v Hoddesdon Town	0-9
	Wood Green Town v Letchworth Town	4-0
14	Eton Manor v Epping Town	3-1
	Ford Sports v West Thurrock Athletic	4-0
	London Transport Central Buses v Briggs Sports	0-3
	Tilbury v Port of London Authority	6-1
	Woodford Town v Upminster	4-1
16	Aylesford Paper Mills v Bexley	2-0
	Chatham v Foots Cray Social	0-3
	RM Chatham v Sheppey United	3-4
	RN Chatham v Lloyds	1-5
	Whitstable v Catford Wanderers	2-6
18	Acton Town v Old Latymerians	7-1
	Hounslow Town v Twickenham	9-3
	London Midland Athletic v Lyons	2-5
	Uxbridge v Civil Service	9-0
19	Henley Town v Headington United	1-5
	Maidenhead United v Pressed Steel	4-1
	Marlow v Osberton Radiator	11-0
	Morris Motors v Abingdon Town	1-2
	St Frideswides v Thame United	16-0
	Windsor & Eton v Metal & Produce Recovery Depot	3-1
	Wycombe Redfords v Bicester Town	1-3
21	Bexhill Town v Bognor Regis Town	2-0
	Eastbourne Comrades v Chichester	4-1
	Littlehampton Town v Haywards Heath	4-2
	Southwick v Horsham	3-9
22	Bournemouth v Portland United	0-4
	Sandown IofW v Bitterne Nomads	2-4
23	Clandown v Soundwell	3-0
	Clevedon v Bristol Aeroplane Co	6-3
	Hanham Athletic v St Pancras (Knowle)	2-0
	Paulton Rovers v Cinderford Town	3-2
	Peasedown Miners Welfare v Welton Rovers	3-1
	Radstock Town v Hoffmann Athletic (Stonehouse)	3-5
	Somerton Amateur v Watchet	6-3e
	St Philips Marsh Adult School v Odd Down	3-1
24	Calne & Harris United v Wilts County Mental Hospital	4-0
	Chippenham Town v Swindon Victoria	3-2
	Dilton Rovers v Wootton Bassett Town	1-3
	Melksham Town v Swindon GWR Corinthians	4-3
	Spencer Moulton v Frome Town	1-2e
	St Austell v Pewsey Young Men	4-0
	Warminster Town v Devizes Town	4-4e
	Westbury United v Purton	0-6
13r	Harlow Town v Hertford Town	1-0
24r	Warminster Town v Devizes Town	1-2

1946/47

Qualifying Round One

1 Ringtons Welfare v Percy Main Amateurs	2-4
2 Barnard Castle v Rocket Athletic	7-1
Brandon CW v Washington Welfare	2-0
Chilton&Windlestone Senior Boys v unknown	n/a
Tow Law Town v unknown	n/a
3 Cargo Fleet Works v Head Wrightsons	n/a
Portrack Shamrocks v Whitby	4-0
South Bank St Peters v Skinningrove Works	n/a
Whitby Albion Rangers v Smiths Dock	3-5a
4 Corinthians v Haig United	0-2
Parton United v Orrell	n/a
Penrith v Stoneycroft	7-2
Scalegill v Port Sunlight	3-1
5 Bradford Rovers v Brigham & Cowans	4-5
Broomhall Boys v Dawson Payne & Elliott Sports	1-3
Guiseley v Hull Amateurs	3-2e
Thornhill Edge v York Railway Institute	3-1
6 Boots Athletic v Huthwaite CWS	0-4
Fulwood v Kiveton Park Colliery	1-7
Maltby Main v Gedling Colliery	n/a
Players Athletic v New Houghton Villa	0-1
7 Midland Woodworking Sports v Coalville Town Ams	0-4
Whitwick Colliery v Whitwick White Cross	5-3
8 Boldmere St Michaels v Coventry Amateur	2-2
Michelin Athletic v Rootes Coventry	5-3a
Morris Motors (Coventry) v Hay Green	3-2
Walsall Wood v Rugby Town Amateur	3-1
9 Abbey United v Ely City	1-6
Bedford Avenue v Newmarket Town	2-0
Chatteris Town v Eynesbury Rovers	5-1
10 Gothic v City of Norwich School OBU	4-0
Great Yarmouth Town v Thetford Town	2-3
King's Lynn v Cromer	5-0
Sheringham v Gorleston	2-3
11 Eastern Coachworks (Lowestoft) v Bungay Town	2-3
Leiston v Lowestoft Town	2-6e
Stowuplands Corinthians v Bury Town	3-5
12 Berkhamsted Town v Wolverton Town	7-1
Chipperfield v Leighton United	2-1a
Kings Langley v Leavesden Hospital	1-4
Luton Amateur v Apsley	7-3
13 Arlesey Town v Biggleswade Town	4-2
Harlow Town v Hoddesdon Town	4-3
Ware v Hatfield United	2-5
Wood Green Town v Crown & Manor	4-2e
14 Briggs Sports v Eton Manor	2-1e
Dagenham British Legion v Woodford Town	0-1
Downshall Athletic v Ekco	3-6
Tilbury v Ford Sports	4-1
15 Harwich & Parkeston v Clacton Town	3-2
16 Aylesford Paper Mills v Foots Cray Social	1-2
Callender Athletic v Cray Wanderers	2-4
Catford Wanderers v Lloyds	1-5
Sheppey United v Thameside Amateurs	0-4
17 Epsom v Leyland Motors	9-0
Merton v Carshalton Athletic	1-5
PO Engineers (LTR) v Hawker Athletic	4-2
Redhill v Dorking	6-0
18 Acton Town v Lyons	3-5
Harrow Town v Polytechnic	1-0
Hounslow Town v Pinner	9-2
Yiewsley v Uxbridge	1-1a
19 Abingdon Town v St Frideswides	2-0
Maidenhead United v Oxford City	3-2
Marlow v Headington United	2-0
Windsor & Eton v Bicester Town	9-2
20 Camberley v Brookwood Hospital	7-2
21 Bexhill Town v Shoreham	1-4
East Grinstead v Hove	8-0
Eastbourne Comrades v Horsham	1-3
Littlehampton Town v Newhaven	5-0
22 Poole Town v Bitterne Nomads	3-1
Portland United v HMS Excellent	1-3
Ryde Sports v Lymington	3-1
Sherborne v Dorchester Town	0-4
23 Hanham Athletic v Clandown	1-2
Hoffmann Athletic (Stonehouse) v Clevedon	1-4
Paulton Rovers v Somerton Amateur	5-2
St Philips Marsh Adult Schl v Peasedown MW	1-4
24 Chippenham Town v Calne & Harris United	4-0
Frome Town v St Austell	1-6
Purton v Devizes Town	3-5
Wootton Bassett Town v Melksham Town	2-1
3r Smiths Dock v Whitby Albion Rangers	8-3
8r Coventry Amateur v Boldmere St Michaels	3-6e
r Michelin Athletic v Rootes Coventry	1-0
12r Leighton United v Chipperfield	1-3
18r Uxbridge v Yiewsley	6-3

Qualifying Round Two

1 Heaton Stannington v Sunnybrow CW	5-3
Wallsend St Lukes v Percy Main Amateurs	2-4
2 Chilton&Windlestone Senior Boys v Barnard Castle	5-0
Tow Law Town v Brandon CW	4-1e
3 Smiths Dock v unknown	n/a
South Bank St Peters v unknown	n/a
4 Penrith v Orrell	3-1
Scalegill v Haig United	2-2
5 Guiseley v Dawson Payne & Elliott Sports	3-2
Thornhill Edge v Brigham & Cowans	1-2
6 Huthwaite CWS v New Houghton Villa	2-1
Maltby Main v Kiveton Park Colliery	2-1
7 Coalville Town Amateur v Ibstock Penistone Rovers	7-1
Holwell Works v Whitwick Colliery	2-3
8 Morris Motors (Coventry) v Michelin Athletic	2-0
Walsall Wood v Boldmere St Michaels	2-0
9 Bedford Avenue v Histon Institute	2-0
Ely City v Chatteris Town	6-6e
10 Gorleston v Gothic	2-0
King's Lynn v Thetford Town	4-3
11 Bungay Town v Lowestoft Town	0-2
Bury Town v Ipswich Old Grammarians	4-0
12 Chipperfield v Luton Amateur	4-2
Leavesden Hospital v Berkhamsted Town	6-1
13 Harlow Town v Arlesey Town	1-4
Wood Green Town v Hatfield United	2-1
14 Tilbury v Briggs Sports	2-0
Woodford Town v Ekco	3-1e
15 Brentwood & Warley v Saffron Walden Town	5-1
Harwich & Parkeston v Hoffmann Ath (Chelmsford)	1-3
16 Cray Wanderers v Lloyds	6-3
Foots Cray Social v Thameside Amateurs	1-0
17 Carshalton Athletic v PO Engineers (LTR)	8-3
Redhill v Epsom	5-0
18 Hounslow Town v Harrow Town	3-1
Uxbridge v Lyons	4-1
19 Abingdon Town v Maidenhead United	0-3
Marlow v Windsor & Eton	5-5a
20 Guildford v Vickers Armstrong	2-6
Walton & Hersham v Camberley	9-3
21 Littlehampton Town v East Grinstead	4-3
Shoreham v Horsham	1-3
22 HMS Excellent v Poole Town	2-1
Ryde Sports v Dorchester Town	1-2
23 Clandown v Paulton Rovers	4-1
Peasedown Miners Welfare v Clevedon	6-0
24 St Austell v Devizes Town	3-2
Wootton Bassett Town v Chippenham Town	4-3
4r Haig United v Scalegill	2-1
9r Chatteris Town v Ely City	3-2
19r Windsor & Eton v Marlow	2-4

Qualifying Round Three

1 Heaton Stannington v Percy Main Amateurs	7-1
2 Tow Law Town v Chilton&Windlestone Senior Boys	n/a
3 South Bank St Peters v unknown	n/a
4 Penrith v Haig United	8-2
5 Guiseley v Brigham & Cowans	2-1
6 Huthwaite CWS v Maltby Main	5-4e
7 Coalville Town Amateur v Whitwick Colliery	4-1
8 Morris Motors (Coventry) v Walsall Wood	0-1
9 Bedford Avenue v Chatteris Town	4-2
10 Gorleston v King's Lynn	2-4
11 Bury Town v Lowestoft Town	1-1
12 Chipperfield v Leavesden Hospital	3-4
13 Wood Green Town v Arlesey Town	7-3
14 Tilbury v Woodford Town	7-0
15 Brentwood & Warley v Hoffmann Ath (Chelmsford)	3-1 D
16 Foots Cray Social v Cray Wanderers	2-1
17 Redhill v Carshalton Athletic	4-2
18 Uxbridge v Hounslow Town	2-6
19 Maidenhead United v Marlow	3-3
20 Walton & Hersham v Vickers Armstrong	5-2
21 Horsham v Littlehampton Town	2-5
22 Dorchester Town v HMS Excellent	3-2
23 Peasedown Miners Welfare v Clandown	4-1
24 St Austell v Wootton Bassett Town	9-0
11r Lowestoft Town v Bury Town	6-0
19r Marlow v Maidenhead United	2-1

Qualifying Round Four

Aylesbury United v Hounslow Town	0-3
Bournville Athletic v Huthwaite CWS	2-0
Crittall Athletic v Redhill	2-0
Dorchester Town v Totton	3-2
Edgware Town v Leavesden Hospital	1-2
Enfield v Slough United	3-2
Finchley v Marlow	5-1
Guiseley v Earle	3-1
Heaton Stannington v Billingham Synthonia	2-0
Hitchin Town v King's Lynn	8-0
Kingstonian v Erith & Belvedere	2-0
Lowestoft Town v Bedford Avenue	2-1
Maidstone United v Littlehampton Town	3-2
Sheffield v Coalville Town Amateur	1-2
St Albans City v Wood Green Town	1-1
St Austell v Peasedown Miners Welfare	2-2
Tow Law Town v Evenwood Town	6-1
Vauxhall Motors v Chesham United	4-2
Walsall Wood v Basford United	2-4
Walton & Hersham v Hoffmann Athletic (Chelmsford)	4-0
West Auckland Town v Penrith	1-1
Willington v South Bank St Peters	8-0
Woolwich Polytechnic v Foots Cray Social	3-1
Worthing v Tilbury	0-1
r Peasedown Miners Welfare v St Austell	3-1
r Penrith v West Auckland Town	4-4
r Wood Green Town v St Albans City	2-0
r2 Penrith v West Auckland Town	3-3eN
r3 Penrith v West Auckland Town	1-1aN
r4 Penrith v West Auckland Town	3-2eN

Round One

Barking v Hayes	1-2
Barnet v Woolwich Polytechnic	3-0
Bournville Athletic v Coalville Town Amateur	1-5
Cambridge Town v Hitchin Town	2-1
Corinthian Casuals v Bromley	1-3
Crook Colliery Welfare v Penrith	0-3
Dulwich Hamlet v Leyton	4-1
Eastbourne v Wimbledon	2-4
Ferryhill Athletic v Heaton Stannington	3-2
Finchley v Metropolitan Police	4-4
Gosport Borough Athletic v Dorchester Town	6-1
Grays Athletic v Tooting & Mitcham United	3-1
Hastings & St Leonards v Woking	1-3
Hounslow Town v Wealdstone	3-1
Ilford v Hendon	2-1
Kingstonian v Crittall Athletic	4-0
Maidstone United v Sutton United	2-1
Marine v ICI Alkali	3-0
Moor Green v Basford United	2-1
Peasedown Miners Welfare v B'mouth Gasworks Ath	2-1
Rawmarsh Welfare v Guiseley	3-5
Romford (2) v Clapton	0-3
Shildon v Bishop Auckland	1-1
Southall v Walton & Hersham	1-2
Tow Law Town v Stanley United	4-0
Tufnell Park v Leavesden Hospital	1-6
Vauxhall Motors v Lowestoft Town	0-1
Walthamstow Avenue v Leytonstone	2-3e
Willington v South Bank	2-1
Wood Green Town v Tilbury	1-3
Wycombe Wanderers v Enfield	3-3
Yorkshire Amateur v Norton Woodseats	1-2
r Bishop Auckland v Shildon	4-2
r Enfield v Wycombe Wanderers	5-2
r Metropolitan Police v Finchley	2-0

Round Two

Bishop Auckland v Marine	4-0
Bromley v Kingstonian	5-1
Dulwich Hamlet v Grays Athletic	3-3
Enfield v Walton & Hersham	3-0
Guiseley v Ferryhill Athletic	2-4
Hayes v Clapton	4-2
Hounslow Town v Maidstone United	3-0
Ilford v Barnet	0-3
Leavesden Hospital v Peasedown Miners Welfare	1-0
Leytonstone v Woking	3-1
Lowestoft Town v Gosport Borough Athletic	3-1
Metropolitan Police v Tilbury	0-1
Norton Woodseats v Moor Green	4-0
Tow Law Town v Coalville Town Amateur	3-2
Willington v Penrith	5-3
Wimbledon v Cambridge Town	2-1e
r Grays Athletic v Dulwich Hamlet	1-0

Round Three

Barnet v Hounslow Town	3-1
Ferryhill Athletic v Bromley	3-4
Hayes v Leytonstone	0-0
Lowestoft Town v Tow Law Town	1-0e
Norton Woodseats v Enfield	2-3
Tilbury v Leavesden Hospital	4-1
Willington v Bishop Auckland	1-6
Wimbledon v Grays Athletic	3-0
r Leytonstone v Hayes	2-1

Round Four

Barnet v Lowestoft Town	5-1
Bishop Auckland v Bromley	5-1
Leytonstone v Enfield	3-1
Wimbledon v Tilbury	8-4

Semi Finals

Leytonstone v Barnet	2-1eN
Wimbledon v Bishop Auckland	4-2 N

Final

Leytonstone v Wimbledon	2-1 N

1947/48

1947/48

Extra Preliminary Round

13 De Havilland Vampires v Cheshunt (2) 3-4
Epping Town v Letchworth Town 0-6
17 Pinner v Harrow Town 2-4
Wood Green Town v Corinthian Casuals 2-1
20 Huntley & Palmers v Chesham United 7-2
Marlow v Slough United 0-1
Pressed Steel v Abingdon Town 0-1
Slough Centre v Carpathians 0-4
Wallingford Town v Thame United 5-2
22 Spencer Moulton v Dilton Rovers 5-3
24 Bristol Aeroplane Co v Chalford 3-4
Crown Dynamos v Bristol St George 2-5
Ilfracombe Town v Plymouth United 2-3e
Mount Hill Enterprise v unknown n/a
Oak Villa v Heavitree United 4-2
Radstock Town v Ilminster Town 5-1
Shepton Mallet Town v Frome Town 2-1
Somerton Amateur v Hanham Athletic 5-1
St Austell v Truro City 8-0
St Blazey v Penzance 4-1
St Pancras (Knowle) v Soundwell 2-7
St Philips Marsh Adult School v Paulton Rovers 2-4
Welton Rovers v Cinderford Town 7-1

Preliminary Round

2 Howden-le-Wear v Eldon Albion 1-6
Royal Signals v Washington Welfare n/a
West Auckland Town v Chilton Athletic 2-1
3 Guisborough v Billingham Synthonia 1-4
Port Clarence v Portrack Shamrocks n/a
South Bank St Peters v Whitby 1-0
Whitby Albion Rangers v Cargo Fleet Works 5-1
4 Appleby v William Colliery 0-1
Cockermouth v Parton United 4-3
Derwent Rangers v Corinthians 3-2e
Haig United v Cleator Moor Celtic 4-7
Orrell v Stoneycroft 2-1
Port Sunlight v ICI Alkali 0-2
5 Brunswick Institute v Salts 2-5
Carlton United v York Railway Institute 6-3
6 Hallam v Dearne Athletic 3-0
Ilkeston Town Reserves v Huthwaite CWS 1-6
Maltby Main v Kiveton Park Colliery 1-4
Netherfield Albion v Raleigh Athletic 2-4
Players Athletic v Bentinck Welfare Colts 1-2
7 Peterborough Westwood Works v Northampton Ams 2-3
8 Badsey Rangers v Gaskill Chambers 2-1
Boldmere St Michaels v Staffordshire Casuals 5-0
Enfield Cycle Co v Rugby Town Amateur 3-11
Hay Green v Coventry Amateur 1-4
Leamington Southend v Bridgetts United 0-2
Sheldon Town v Craven Arms wo/s
Walsall Wood v Oswestry Town Reserves 9-1
9 March Town v Eynesbury Rovers 4-3
10 Cromer v King's Lynn 0-3
Holt United v Great Yarmouth Town 3-1
Sheringham v Gothic 5-4
11 Achilles v St Clements United 7-0
Leiston v Ipswich Electricity Supply 1-3
Stoke United v Ipswich Old Grammarians 5-0
Stowuplands Corinthians v Felixstowe United 1-1
Sudbury Town v Whitton United 2-4
12 Bedford Queens Works v Bedford Avenue 4-5
Leighton United v Kings Langley 5-0
Potton United v Wootton Blue Cross 1-0
Waterlows Dunstable v Luton Amateur 0-8
13 Arlesey Town v Crown & Manor 1-2
Biggleswade Town v Cheshunt (2) 1-2e
Bishops Stortford v Welwyn Garden City 4-3e
De Havilland Hatfield v Sawbridgeworth 2-5
Harlow Town v Hatfield United 0-1
Hoddesdon Town v Woodford Town 5-0
Royston Town v Letchworth Town 0-4
Ware v Stevenage Town 5-2
14 Dagenham British Legion v Ford Sports 1-2
Rainham Town v Leyton 0-3
Upminster v Eton Manor 2-0
16 Aylesford Paper Mills v Sheppey United 1-3
Cray Wanderers v RM Chatham 1-3
Tunbridge Wells v Thameside Amateurs 0-4
UGB Charlton v Faversham Town 4-0
17 Civil Service v Polytechnic 4-2
Edgware Town v Willesden 3-1
Edmonton Borough v Wood Green Town 6-0
Harrow Town v Wingate 4-3e
Tufnell Park v Lyons 4-3e
Uxbridge v Kingsbury Town 3-1
Wembley v Acton Town 4-4e
Yiewsley v Twickenham 5-1
19 East Grinstead v Chichester 2-0
Haywards Heath v Newhaven 2-1
Hove v Bexhill Town 7-1
Lancing Athletic v Shoreham 3-1
Littlehampton Town v Horsham 4-3

20 Aylesbury United v Henley Town 3-1
Headington United v Abingdon Town 5-2
Huntley & Palmers v Carpathians 3-2
Maidenhead United v Slough United 0-1
Metal & Produce R'very Depot v Osberton Radiators 1-5
Morris Motors v St Frideswides 1-2
Wallingford Town v Bicester Town 3-2
Windsor & Eton v Redford Sports 4-1e
22 Calne & Harris United v Westbury United 2-5
Chippenham Town v Devizes Town 2-7
Pewsey Vale v Melksham Town 3-1
Purton v Warminster Town 5-1
Salisbury v Chippenham United 7-0
Salisbury Corinthians v Swindon GWR Corinthians 5-1
Spencer Moulton v Wootton Bassett Town 1-2
Wilts County Mental Hospital v Swindon Victoria 1-3
23 Bitterne Nomads v Winchester City wo/s
Blandford United v Bournemouth 2-7
HMS Excellent v Portsmouth Electricity 2-3
Hamworthy v Longfleet St Marys 2-3
Portland United v Lymington 9-1
Sandown IofW v Fareham Town 0-4
24 Bristol St George v Odd Down 4-1
Chalford v Radstock Town 3-4
Clandown v Soundwell 10-4
Clevedon v Hoffmann Athletic (Stonehouse) 2-1
Paulton Rovers v Welton Rovers 2-0
Shepton Mallet Town v Somerton Amateur 4-3e
St Austell v Oak Villa 10-0
St Blazey v Plymouth United 5-1
11r Felixstowe United v Stowuplands Corinthians 2-4e
17r Acton Town v Wembley 1-3

Qualifying Round One

1 Wallsend St Lukes v Heaton Stannington 2-1
2 Darlington Rolling Mills v Sunnybrow CW 1-2
Eldon Albion v unknown n/a
Evenwood Town v West Auckland Town 3-1
Royal Signals v Wearmouth CW n/a
3 unknown v unknown n/a
Skinningrove Works v Billingham Synthonia 1-3
Smiths Dock v unknown n/a
Whitby Albion Rangers v South Bank St Peters 0-1
4 Cleator Moor Celtic v ICI Alkali 2-1
High Duty Alloys v Derwent Rangers 11-1
Newton YMCA v Orrell n/a
William Colliery v Cockermouth 4-1
5 Carlton United v Constable Street OB 3-1
Ravensthorpe v Bradford Rovers 1-3
Rothwell Athletic v Brigham & Cowans n/a
Salts v New Earswick 4-3
6 Bentinck Welfare Colts v Boots Athletic 0-0
Gedling Colliery v Raleigh Athletic 3-4
Huthwaite CWS v New Houghton Villa 3-1
Kiveton Park Colliery v Hallam 1-3
7 Northampton Amateurs v unknown n/a
Shepshed Albion v unknown n/a
Whitwick Colliery v Holwell Works 4-1
Whitwick White Cross v Ibstock Penistone Rovers 3-4
8 Badsey Rangers v Bridgetts United 0-1
Boldmere St Michaels v Sheldon Town 2-0
Coventry Amateur v Smethwick Highfield 1-0
Walsall Wood v Rugby Town Amateur 1-1
9 Ely City v Abbey United 0-4
March Town v Chatteris Town 4-2
St Ives Town v Oakham Rovers 6-0
St Neots & District v Newmarket Town 4-2e
10 Lakenheath v City of Norwich School OBU 2-1
Sheringham v Gorleston 3-6e
Thetford Town v King's Lynn 3-0
Wymondham Town v Holt United 2-4
11 Bungay Town v Ipswich Electricity Supply 2-3e
Bury Town v Achilles 0-1
EasternCoachworks(L'toft) v Stowuplands Corinthians 3-1
Stoke United v Whitton United 1-2
12 Bedford Avenue v Potton United 2-0
Berkhamsted Town v Hemel Hempstead Town 3-2
Luton Amateur v Leighton United 3-0
Wolverton Town v Chipperfield 5-0
13 Bishops Stortford v Crown & Manor 2-1
Cheshunt (2) v Ware 3-1
Hatfield United v Hoddesdon Town 1-3
Letchworth Town v Sawbridgeworth 7-0
14 Downshall Athletic v Upminster 1-3e
Ekco v London Transport Central Buses 1-4
Ford Sports v Leyton 0-1
West Thurrock Athletic v Briggs Sports 1-0e
15 Clacton Town v Harwich & Parkeston 1-2
Saffron Walden Town v Brentwood & Warley 1-4
16 Bexley v Thameside Amateurs 1-2
Foots Cray Social v Woolwich Polytechnic 2-1
RM Chatham v Callender Athletic 2-0
UGB Charlton v Sheppey United 0-0
17 Civil Service v Harrow Town 1-3
Edmonton Borough v Edgware Town 1-0
Uxbridge v Tufnell Park 4-1
Wembley v Yiewsley 6-4
18 Dorking v Leatherhead 0-4
Epsom v Carshalton Athletic 2-6
Merton v PO Telecomms 1-2
Redhill v Worcester Park 3-1

19 Bognor Regis Town v Littlehampton Town 2-3
East Grinstead v Eastbourne Comrades 4-1
Lancing Athletic v Haywards Heath 2-1
Southwick v Hove 6-0
20 Aylesbury United v Headington United 0-2
Slough United v Huntley & Palmers 1-3
Wallingford Town v St Frideswides 3-2e
Windsor & Eton v Osberton Radiator 8-2
21 Camberley v 3rd Training Battn RASC 2-5
Cobham v Guildford 1-3
Lagonda Sports v Vickers Armstrong 2-7
22 Pewsey Vale v Salisbury Corinthians 4-1e
Purton v Wootton Bassett Town 4-1e
Salisbury v Swindon Victoria 5-3
Westbury United v Devizes Town 2-0
23 Bitterne Nomads v Portsmouth Electricity 0-2
Dorchester Town v Longfleet St Marys 3-1
Portland United v Bournemouth 4-4e
Ryde Sports v Fareham Town 3-0
24 Bristol St George v Shepton Mallet Town 7-1
Paulton Rovers v Clandown 0-1
Radstock Town v Clevedon 1-2e
St Austell v St Blazey 3-1
6r Boots Athletic v Bentinck Welfare Colts 0-1
8r Rugby Town Amateur v Walsall Wood 1-2
16r Sheppey United v UGB Charlton n/a
23r Portland United v Bournemouth 4-1

Qualifying Round Two

1 Ringtons Welfare v East Tanfield CW 1-3
Wallsend St Lukes v Woodhorn CW 2-1
2 Eldon Albion v Evenwood Town 1-3
Sunnybrow CW v Royal Signals n/a
3 Smiths Dock v unknown n/a
South Bank St Peters v Billingham Synthonia 2-4
4 Cleator Moor Celtic v High Duty Alloys 4-2
William Colliery v Orrell 1-0
5 Carlton United v Bradford Rovers 1-4
Salts v Rothwell Athletic 3-2
6 Hallam v Raleigh Athletic 1-5
Huthwaite CWS v Bentinck Welfare Colts 3-0
7 Ibstock Penistone Rovers v Raunds Town 3-1
Whitwick Colliery v Shepshed Albion 3-0
8 Boldmere St Michaels v Coventry Amateur 5-0
Walsall Wood v Bridgetts United 2-2
9 Abbey United v St Ives Town 1-0
March Town v St Neots & District 0-1
10 Gorleston v Thetford Town 6-1
Lakenheath v Holt United 3-1
11 Ipswich Electricity Supply v Achilles 1-1e
Whitton United v Eastern Coachworks (Lowestoft) 2-3e
12 Luton Amateur v Berkhamsted Town 5-3e
Wolverton Town v Bedford Avenue 5-2
13 Cheshunt (2) v Bishops Stortford 1-1e
Letchworth Town v Hoddesdon Town 3-0
14 Leyton v Upminster 4-3e
West Thurrock Ath v London Transport Central Buses 2-1
15 Brantham Athletic v Colchester Casuals 3-1
Harwich & Parkeston v Brentwood & Warley 1-0
16 RM Chatham v Thameside Amateurs 2-3
Sheppey United v Foots Cray Social 2-0
17 Edmonton Borough v Uxbridge 1-2
Harrow Town v Wembley 9-0
18 Leatherhead v PO Telecomms 4-2e
Redhill v Carshalton Athletic 1-2
19 East Grinstead v Littlehampton Town 4-0
Southwick v Lancing Athletic 0-1
20 Headington United v Huntley & Palmers 2-3
Windsor & Eton v Wallingford Town 3-5e
21 Brookwood Hospital v 3rd Training Battn RASC 0-3
Vickers Armstrong v Guildford 4-0
22 Purton v Salisbury 1-1e
Westbury United v Pewsey Vale 0-2
23 Dorchester Town v Ryde Sports 1-1e
Portsmouth Electricity v Portland United 3-1
24 Clevedon v Clandown 3-2
St Austell v Bristol St George 4-1
8r Walsall Wood v Bridgetts United 1-2
11r Achilles v Ipswich Electricity Supply 2-1
13r Bishops Stortford v Cheshunt (2) 4-1
22r Salisbury v Purton 4-0
23r Ryde Sports v Dorchester Town 3-1

Qualifying Round Three

1 East Tanfield CW v Wallsend St Lukes 6-4
2 Evenwood Town v Royal Signals 3-6
3 Smiths Dock v Billingham Synthonia 4-1 v
4 Cleator Moor Celtic v William Colliery 1-2
5 Salts v Bradford Rovers 6-2
6 Raleigh Athletic v Huthwaite CWS 1-0
7 Whitwick Colliery v Ibstock Penistone Rovers 2-3
8 Boldmere St Michaels v Bridgetts United 4-0
9 St Neots & District v Abbey United 0-4
10 Lakenheath v Gorleston 0-4
11 Eastern Coachworks (Lowestoft) v Achilles 2-4
12 Wolverton Town v Luton Amateur 3-1
13 Bishops Stortford v Letchworth Town 2-3
14 Leyton v West Thurrock Athletic 2-2
15 Brantham Athletic v Harwich & Parkeston 0-2
16 Sheppey United v Thameside Amateurs 3-1

1947/48 to 1948/49

17	Uxbridge v Harrow Town	5-2
18	Leatherhead v Carshalton Athletic	1-0
19	East Grinstead v Lancing Athletic	2-5
20	Wallingford Town v Huntley & Palmers	4-8
21	3rd Training Battn RASC v Vickers Armstrong	8-1
22	Pewsey Vale v Salisbury	3-2
23	Ryde Sports v Portsmouth Electricity	2-4
24	Clevedon v St Austell	2-3
3r	Smiths Dock v Billingham Synthonia	0-1
14r	West Thurrock Athletic v Leyton	1-1
14r2	West Thurrock Athletic v Leyton	2-1 N

Qualifying Round Four

	Abbey United v Achilles	4-3e
	Billingham Synthonia v Salts	2-2
	Boldmere St Michaels v Sheffield	4-1
	Bournville Athletic v Ibstock Penistone Rovers	3-0
	Crook Colliery Welfare v Stanley United	2-3
	Eastbourne v 3rd Training Battn RASC	1-3
	Erith & Belvedere v Leatherhead	3-2
	Gorleston v Hitchin Town	1-0
	Harwich & Parkeston v Barking	1-4
	Huntley & Palmers v Finchley	3-1
	Lancing Athletic v Tooting & Mitcham United	1-2
	Oxford City v Letchworth Town	2-3
	Peasedown Miners Welfare v St Austell	1-2
	Penrith v William Colliery	9-1
	Pewsey Vale v Portsmouth Electricity	1-3
	Raleigh Athletic v Basford United	2-1
	Rawmarsh Welfare v Earle	1-1
	Royal Signals v East Tanfield CW	1-2
	Sheppey United v Metropolitan Police	2-5
	Totton v Bournemouth Gasworks Athletic	3-2
	Wealdstone v Uxbridge	3-1
	West Thurrock Athletic v Crittall Athletic	2-0
	Woking v Hastings & St Leonards	1-4
	Wolverton Town v Southall	1-0
r	Earle v Rawmarsh Welfare	3-2
r	Salts v Billingham Synthonia	2-3

Round One

	3rd Training Battn RASC v Barking	1-4
	Abbey United v Cambridge Town	0-1
	Bishop Auckland v Penrith	7-3
	Boldmere St Michaels v Coalville Town Amateur	7-0
	Bromley v Wimbledon	3-4e
	Clapton v Dulwich Hamlet	1-2
	Earle v Norton Woodseats	2-2e
	East Tanfield CW v Tow Law Town	2-1
	Erith & Belvedere v Leytonstone	0-1
	Ferryhill Athletic v South Bank	2-0
	Gorleston v Lowestoft Town	3-2
	Gosport Borough Athletic v Worthing	2-1
	Grays Athletic v Barnet	3-3e
	Guiseley v Yorkshire Amateur	4-5
	Hastings & St Leonards v Romford (2)	4-1
	Hayes v St Albans City	1-3
	Ilford v Hounslow Town	4-1
	Kingstonian v Hendon	1-2
	Letchworth Town v Huntley & Palmers	4-1
	Maidstone United v Walton & Hersham	0-5
	Metropolitan Police v Leavesden Hospital	3-2
	Moor Green v Bournville Athletic	2-1
	Poole Town v Totton	6-1
	Portsmouth Electricity v St Austell	6-2
	Raleigh Athletic v Marine	1-10
	Shildon v Willington	5-2
	Stanley United v Billingham Synthonia	0-0e
	Tilbury v West Thurrock Athletic	2-0
	Tooting & Mitcham United v Enfield	2-0
	Wealdstone v Sutton United	0-0e
	Wolverton Town v Vauxhall Motors	2-4
	Wycombe Wanderers v Walthamstow Avenue	2-1e
r	Barnet v Grays Athletic	4-1
r	Billingham Synthonia v Stanley United	0-1
r	Norton Woodseats v Earle	8-1
r	Sutton United v Wealdstone	3-4

Round Two

	Barnet v Metropolitan Police	7-2
	Dulwich Hamlet v Tilbury	6-1
	East Tanfield CW v Moor Green	2-1a
	Ferryhill Athletic v Bishop Auckland	0-6
	Hastings & St Leonards v Cambridge Town	0-5
	Hendon v Poole Town	3-1
	Ilford v Vauxhall Motors	2-1
	Letchworth Town v Gosport Borough Athletic	0-1
	Norton Woodseats v Marine	3-2e
	Portsmouth Electricity v Barking	2-3
	Shildon v Boldmere St Michaels	1-4
	St Albans City v Wycombe Wanderers	3-3e
	Stanley United v Yorkshire Amateur	1-4
	Tooting & Mitcham United v Leytonstone	0-2
	Walton & Hersham v Gorleston	2-1
	Wimbledon v Wealdstone	0-1
r	East Tanfield CW v Moor Green	2-3
r	Wycombe Wanderers v St Albans City	2-1

Round Three

	Barnet v Cambridge Town	6-0
	Bishop Auckland v Norton Woodseats	5-0
	Boldmere St Michaels v Gosport Borough Athletic	4-1
	Hendon v Barking	2-2e
	Ilford v Wycombe Wanderers	2-3
	Moor Green v Walton & Hersham	2-1e
	Wealdstone v Leytonstone	0-1
	Yorkshire Amateur v Dulwich Hamlet	2-3e
r	Barking v Hendon	0-3a
r2	Barking v Hendon	2-3 N

Round Four

	Barnet v Dulwich Hamlet	2-1
	Bishop Auckland v Wycombe Wanderers	6-2
	Boldmere St Michaels v Moor Green	1-0e
	Hendon v Leytonstone	1-4

Semi Finals

	Barnet v Boldmere St Michaels	2-0 N
	Leytonstone v Bishop Auckland	5-0 N

Final

	Leytonstone v Barnet	1-0 N

1948/49

Extra Preliminary Round

3	Ashmore Recreation v Billingham St Johns	n/a
	Bridlington Trinity United v Bridlington Central Uni	6-1
	Redcar Albion v Cochranes Sports	n/a
4	Moresby Welfare Centre v Arlecdon Red Rose	n/a
	Stork v Ward Street OB	n/a
8	Jack Moulds Athletic v Stratford on Avon Rangers	7-1
	Lockheed Leamington v Oakengates Youth	0-2
	Tangyes Recreation v Catherine-de-Barnes	4-0
	Warwick Town v Handsworth Wood	2-1
17	Camberley v Farnham Town	1-2
	Chertsey v Carshalton	5-1
	McLaren Sports v Worcester Park	5-3
18	Acton Town v Civil Service	6-1
	Harrow Town v Crown & Manor	5-2
	Kings Langley v Chipperfield	5-0
	Pinner v Kingsbury Town	3-1
	Polytechnic v Twickenham	8-0
	Rickmansworth Town v Willesden	2-1
	Ruislip Manor v Ruislip Manor	4-2e
	Wingate v Staines Town	2-0
	Wood Green Town v Southall	0-3
	Yiewsley v Dickinsons Apsley	5-0
19	Morris Motors v Thame United	4-1
	Osberton Radiator v Huntley & Palmers	2-6
	Pressed Steel v Abingdon Town	4-0
	Slough Town v Chesham United	3-2
	St Frideswides v Battle Athletic	1-2
	Windsor & Eton v NAC Athletic	6-2
21	Bournemouth Gasworks Ath v Whitehead Sports	wo/s
	Christchurch v Wimborne	2-4
	HMS Collingwood v Romsey Town	2-2
	Longfleet St Marys v Bridport	wo/s
	Thorneycroft Athletic v Botley	2-1
22	Coleford Athletic v Timsbury Athletic	4-3
	Devizes Town v Spencer Moulton	3-1
	Frome Town v Peasedown Miners Welfare	2-0
	Odd Down v Clandown	0-6
	Paulton Rovers v Welton Rovers	1-4
	Pewsey Vale v Corsham Town	6-1
	Salisbury Corinthians v Calne & Harris United	1-4
	Swindon Victoria v Warminster Town	5-0
	West End Rovers v Radstock Town	2-7
	Westbury United v Wootton Bassett Town	4-2e
23	Burnham United v Taunton Town	3-4
21r	Romsey Town v HMS Collingwood	3-0

Preliminary Round

2	Chilton Athletic v Stanhope	4-1
	Eldon Albion v Cockfield	8-5
	West Auckland Town v Broom Youth	4-0
3	Bridlington Trinity United v Head Wrightsons	4-2
	Furness Athletic v Cargo Fleet Works	2-8
	Guisborough v Ashmore Recreation	1-5
	North Skelton Athletic v Whitby Albion Rangers	8-0
	Portrack Shamrocks v Barkers Athletic	n/a
	South Bank East End v Skinningrove Works	2-4e
	South Bank St Peters v Smiths Dock	1-2
	Whitby Town v Redcar Albion	3-0
4	Cleator Moor Celtic v Calgarth	5-3
	Cockermouth v Frizington United	3-7
	Harrowby v ICI Alkali	1-5
	High Duty Alloys v Parton United	wo/s
	Manchester University v Stoneycroft	n/a
	Moresby Welfare Centre v Appleby	6-1
	Port Sunlight v Orrell	3-0
	UGB St Helens v Stork	6-7e
5	David Brown Athletic v North Ferriby United	6-3
	Salts v Farsley Celtic	2-0
6	Bolsover Colliery v Huthwaite CWS	0-1
	Chesterfield Ramblers v Players Athletic	1-5
	Maltby Main v Hallam	0-1
	Penistone Church v Basford United	3-4e
8	Coventry Amateur v Silhill	4-0
	Enfield Cycle Co v Walsall Wood	n/a
	Gaskill Chambers v Smethwick Highfield	0-2
	Jack Moulds Athletic v Evesham United	3-2
	Oakengates Youth v Badsey Rangers	3-6
	Sheldon Town v Warwick Town	1-6
	Staffordshire Casuals v Hay Green	6-3
	Tangyes Recreation v Oswestry Town	wo/s
9	Donnington United v St Ives Town	2-3e
	Ely City v Newmarket Town	1-2
	Ramsey Town v St Neots St Marys	2-1
	Sawston United v Histon Institute	2-9
	St Neots & District v March Town	wo/s
10	Carrow Works v South Lynn	4-0
11	Stoke United v Ipswich Old Grammarians	9-1
	Whitton United v Eastern Coachworks (Lowestoft)	4-3
12	Letchworth Town v Luton Amateur	1-4
	Marston Shelton Rovers v Baldock Town	4-1
	Royston Town v Waterlows Dunstable	3-0
	Stevenage Town v Biggleswade Town	6-3
	Wolverton Town v Bedford Queens Works	5-0
	Wootton Blue Cross v Bedford Avenue	9-0
13	Cheshunt (2) v Hoddesdon Town	2-1
	De Havilland Hatfield v Bishops Stortford	2-4
	Edmonton Borough v De Havilland Vampires	6-0
	Sawbridgeworth v Harlow Town	2-0
	Stansted v Epping Town	4-2
	Tufnell Park v Hatfield Town	1-0
	Woodford Town v Welwyn Garden City	7-0
14	Eton Manor v West Thurrock Athletic	2-2
	Ford Sports v Briggs Sports	2-4
	Rainham Town v Bata Sports	1-3
	Roneo v London Transport Central Buses	1-2
	Upminster v Leyton	0-2
16	Faversham Town v Woolwich Polytechnic	3-2
17	Brookwood Hospital v Cobham	2-3
	Carshalton Athletic v Dorking	2-3
	Chertsey v Epsom	2-2e
	Guildford v Merton	5-0
	Leatherhead v RASC	7-1
	McLaren Sports v Vickers Armstrong	1-0
	PO Telecomms v Farnham Town	0-2
	Redhill v RAMC Aldershot	3-0
18	Acton Town v Wembley	2-0
	Berkhamsted Town v Uxbridge	0-3
	Kings Langley v Ruislip Manor	3-1
	Lyons v Corinthian Casuals	1-2
	Polytechnic v Harrow Town	1-2
	Rickmansworth Town v Yiewsley	2-3
	Southall v Hemel Hempstead Town	1-3
	Wingate v Pinner	2-1
19	Bicester Town v Battle Athletic	5-5e
	Henley Town v Huntley & Palmers	1-9
	Marlow v Carpathians	1-2
	Metal & Produce Recovery Depot v Slough Town	1-4
	Pressed Steel v Aylesbury United	1-3
	Slough Centre v Morris Motors	6-1
	Wallingford Town v Headington United	1-6
	Windsor & Eton v Maidenhead United	1-3
20	Bexhill Town v Horsham	2-2
	Bognor Regis Town v Littlehampton Town	3-2
	Chichester City v Eastbourne Comrades	3-1
	East Grinstead v Newhaven	3-2
	Haywards Heath v Hove	5-1
21	Dorchester Town v Bournemouth Gasworks Athletic	3-2
	Fareham Town v Wimborne	1-1e
	HMS Excellent v Lymington	1-5
	Hamworthy v Blandford United	3-2
	Longfleet St Marys v Bournemouth	3-1e
	Romsey Town v Bitterne Nomads	n/a
	Thorneycroft Athletic v Portsmouth Electricity	4-8
	Totton v Portland United	0-1
22	Calne & Harris United v Purton	1-4
	Melksham Town v Clandown	2-0
	Pewsey Vale v Swindon BR Corinthians	3-2
	Radstock Town v Coleford Athletic	2-1
	Shepton Mallet Town v Salisbury	2-8
	Welton Rovers v Swindon Victoria	3-1
	Westbury United v Frome Town	0-3
	Wilts County Mental Hospital v Devizes Town	2-1
23	Bristol Aeroplane Co v Mount Hill Enterprise	2-4
	Bristol St George v Hoffmann Athletic (Stonehouse)	6-2
	Charlton Kings v Chalford	3-1
	Cinderford Town v Bridgwater Town	wo/s
	Clevedon v Taunton Town	6-3
	Somerton Amateur v Hanham Athletic	1-8
	St Philips Marsh Adult School v Ilminster Town	0-1
	Weston-super-Mare St Johns v Soundwell	2-3
24	Barnstaple Town v Ilfracombe Town	6-1
	Bugle v St Blazey	2-1
	Plymouth United v Heavitree United	2-2
	St Austell v Helston Athletic	2-1
	Wadebridge Town v Penzance	6-2
14r	Eton Manor v West Thurrock Athletic	4-2
17r	Epsom v Chertsey	2-1
19r	Battle Athletic v Bicester Town	5-7e
20r	Horsham v Bexhill Town	3-1
21r	Wimborne v Fareham Town	2-1
24r	Plymouth United v Heavitree United	0-1

1948/49

Qualifying Round One

1	Heaton Stannington v Washington Welfare	4-3
	Pont Institute v Woodhorn CW	3-0
	South Shields Ex Schoolboys v Wearmouth CW	0-2
2	Evenwood Town v Chilton Athletic	1-0
	Morris United v Eldon Albion	0-7
	Royal Signals v Trimdon Grange	n/a
	West Auckland Town v Howden-le-Wear	3-2
3	Ashmore Recreation v Smiths Dock	4-4e
	Bridlington Trinity United v Cargo Fleet Works	0-4
	Skinningrove Works v North Skelton Athletic	1-0
	Whitby Town v Portrack Shamrocks	4-1
4	Cleator Moor Celtic v Frizington United	4-4
	Moresby Welfare Centre v High Duty Alloys	2-1
	Port Sunlight v Stoneycroft	2-0
	Stork v ICI Alkali	6-2
5	David Brown Athletic v Brunswick Institute	n/a
	Hull Nomads v Bradford Rovers	1-8
	Rothwell Athletic v Ravensthorpe	5-2
	Salts v York Railway Institute	3-1
6	Basford United v Rawmarsh Welfare	2-1e
	Boots Athletic v Gedling Colliery	1-2
	Hallam v Raleigh Athletic	3-2
	Players Athletic v Huthwaite CWS	2-1
7	Holwell Works v Whitwick Colliery	wo/s
	Ibstock Penistone Rovers v Rugby Town Amateur	4-1
	Northampton Ams v Peterborough Westwood Works	4-0
	Shepshed Albion v Melton Town	5-6e
8	Coventry Amateur v Jack Moulds Athletic	2-5
	Tangyes Recreation v Staffordshire Casuals	2-0
	Walsall Wood v Smethwick Highfield	3-5
	Warwick Town v Badsey Rangers	3-6
9	Newmarket Town v Eynesbury Rovers	4-3
	Ramsey Town v Abbey United	3-3e
	St Ives Town v Chatteris Town	4-1
	St Neots & District v Histon Institute	2-4
10	Cromer v Carrow Works	0-1
	Diss Town v Sheringham	4-2
	Holt United v City of Norwich School OBU	4-4e
	Wymondham Town v Thetford Town	1-1e
11	Bungay Town v Stowmarket Corinthians	6-3
	Felixstowe United v Stoke United	1-3
	Ipswich Electricity Supply v Whitton United	3-7
	Leiston v Achilles	2-4
12	Arlesey Town v Marston Shelton Rovers	2-4e
	Leighton United v Wootton Blue Cross	2-2e
	Royston Town v Luton Amateur	3-2
	Wolverton Town v Stevenage Town	2-1
13	Cheshunt (2) v Woodford Town	7-2
	Edmonton Borough v Sawbridgeworth	4-0
	Tufnell Park v Stansted	2-1
	Ware v Bishops Stortford	2-1
14	Briggs Sports v Eton Manor	6-3
	Dagenham BL v London Transport Central Buses	1-0
	Ekco v Bata Sports	1-0
	Leyton v Downshall Athletic	5-0
15	Brentwood & Warley v Brightlingsea United	5-1
	Colchester Casuals v Brantham Athletic	2-4
	Hoffmann Ath (Chelmsford) v Harwich & Parkeston	4-2
16	Aylesford Paper Mills v UGB Charlton	7-2
	Callender Athletic v Sheppey United	2-4
	Faversham Town v Thameside Amateurs	1-2
	Foots Cray Social v Bexley	3-2
17	Cobham v Guildford	4-4e
	Farnham Town v Redhill	1-7
	Leatherhead v Epsom	4-1
	McLaren Sports v Dorking	2-2e
18	Acton Town v Yiewsley	0-6
	Hemel Hempstead Town v Corinthian Casuals	3-1
	Kings Langley v Harrow Town	0-2
	Wingate v Uxbridge	0-3
19	Aylesbury United v Bicester Town	4-1
	Headington United v Slough Town	1-4
	Huntley & Palmers v Carpathians	0-2
	Maidenhead United v Slough Centre	3-2
20	Bognor Regis Town v Haywards Heath	3-3
	East Grinstead v Horsham	0-3
	Shoreham v Lancing Athletic	0-5
	Southwick v Chichester City	4-3
21	Dorchester Town v Lymington	2-3
	Longfleet St Marys v Wimborne	0-1
	Portland United v Hamworthy	3-0
	Portsmouth Electricity v Bitterne Nomads	0-1
22	Melksham Town v Radstock Town	5-3
	Pewsey Vale v Frome Town	0-1e
	Salisbury v Welton Rovers	3-2
	Wilts County Mental Hospital v Purton	0-4
23	Bristol St George v Soundwell	2-3
	Charlton Kings v Clevedon	1-1
	Cinderford Town v Mount Hill Enterprise	4-1
	Hanham Athletic v Ilminster Town	2-1
24	Barnstaple Town v Oak Villa	4-0
	Bugle v Wadebridge Town	2-4
	St Austell v Tavistock	1-2
	Truro City v Heavitree United	7-6
3r	Smiths Dock v Ashmore Recreation	n/a
4r	Frizington United v Cleator Moor Celtic	1-2
9r	Abbey United v Ramsey Town	4-1
10r	Holt United v City of Norwich School OBU	5-1
r	Thetford Town v Wymondham Town	2-2e
12r	Wootton Blue Cross v Leighton United	4-1
17r	Dorking v McLaren Sports	4-2
r	Guildford v Cobham	0-2
20r	Bognor Regis Town v Haywards Heath	2-2
23r	Clevedon v Charlton Kings	5-1
10r2	Wymondham Town v Thetford Town	5-2
20r2	Haywards Heath v Bognor Regis Town	5-2 N

Qualifying Round Two

1	Heaton Stannington v Wallsend St Lukes	9-2
	Wearmouth CW v Pont Institute	n/a
2	Evenwood Town v Eldon Albion	4-1
	West Auckland Town v Trimdon Grange	2-3
3	Cargo Fleet Works v Whitby Town	1-3
	Smiths Dock v Skinningrove Works	n/a
4	Moresby Welfare Centre v Stork	1-4
	Port Sunlight v Cleator Moor Celtic	5-0
5	Bradford Rovers v Brunswick Institute	5-4
	Rothwell Athletic v Salts	1-1e
6	Basford United v Gedling Colliery	6-1
	Hallam v Players Athletic	2-0e
7	Ibstock Penistone Rovers v Northampton Amateurs	2-1
	Melton Town v Holwell Works	8-3
8	Badsey Rangers v Tangyes Recreation	3-6e
	Smethwick Highfield v Jack Moulds Athletic	5-2
9	Abbey United v Histon Institute	0-5
	St Ives Town v Newmarket Town	2-2e
10	Carrow Works v Diss Town	6-0
	Wymondham Town v Holt United	2-6
11	Achilles v Stoke United	2-1
	Whitton United v Bungay Town	0-2
12	Marston Shelton Rovers v Wootton Blue Cross	0-1
	Wolverton Town v Royston Town	4-2
13	Edmonton Borough v Ware	2-0
	Tufnell Park v Cheshunt (2)	1-2
14	Ekco v Briggs Sports	0-0
	Leyton v Dagenham British Legion	3-0
15	Brentwood & Warley v Saffron Walden Town	10-0
	Hoffmann Athletic (Chelmsford) v Brantham Athletic	1-5
16	Aylesford Paper Mills v Thameside Amateurs	1-4
	Sheppey United v Foots Cray Social	3-4
17	Dorking v Leatherhead	1-3
	Redhill v Cobham	3-0
18	Harrow Town v Uxbridge	1-2
	Yiewsley v Hemel Hempstead Town	4-1
19	Aylesbury United v Slough Town	1-3
	Maidenhead United v Carpathians	3-2
20	Haywards Heath v Horsham	6-3
	Lancing Athletic v Southwick	3-0
21	Bitterne Nomads v Portland United	0-0
	Lymington v Wimborne	5-2
22	Frome Town v Salisbury	4-1 v
	Purton v Melksham Town	4-1
23	Cinderford Town v Clevedon	3-8
	Hanham Athletic v Soundwell	2-4
24	Tavistock v Barnstaple Town	2-7
	Wadebridge Town v Truro City	4-5
5r	Salts v Rothwell Athletic	6-1
9r	Newmarket Town v St Ives Town	7-2
14r	Briggs Sports v Ekco	2-0
21r	Portland United v Bitterne Nomads	1-1e
22r	Salisbury v Frome Town	2-1e
21r2	Portland United v Bitterne Nomads	5-2 N

Qualifying Round Three

1	Heaton Stannington v Pont Institute	1-1
2	Evenwood Town v Trimdon Grange	2-3
3	Skinningrove Works v Whitby Town	0-1
4	Stork v Port Sunlight	3-1
5	Bradford Rovers v Salts	5-5
6	Hallam v Basford United	6-2
7	Ibstock Penistone Rovers v Melton Town	3-1
8	Smethwick Highfield v Tangyes Recreation	1-1e
9	Newmarket Town v Histon Institute	0-2
10	Carrow Works v Holt United	3-1
11	Bungay Town v Achilles	1-0
12	Wolverton Town v Wootton Blue Cross	2-3
13	Edmonton Borough v Cheshunt (2)	0-4
14	Briggs Sports v Leyton	5-1
15	Brentwood & Warley v Brantham Athletic	6-2
16	Foots Cray Social v Thameside Amateurs	3-4
17	Leatherhead v Redhill	2-2
18	Yiewsley v Uxbridge	1-0
19	Slough Town v Maidenhead United	0-2
20	Haywards Heath v Lancing Athletic	5-3
21	Lymington v Portland United	2-0
22	Salisbury v Purton	3-1e
23	Soundwell v Clevedon	1-3
24	Barnstaple Town v Truro City	3-1
1r	Pont Institute v Heaton Stannington	1-1
5r	Salts v Bradford Rovers	4-3
8r	Tangyes Recreation v Smethwick Highfield	1-2
17r	Redhill v Leatherhead	3-0
1r2	Pont Institute v Heaton Stannington	n/a

Qualifying Round Four

	Billingham Synthonia v Pont Institute	5-0
	Bournville Athletic v Earle	1-0
	Bungay Town v Brentwood & Warley	0-1
	Carrow Works v Briggs Sports	3-5
	Clevedon v Lymington	2-1
	Crittall Athletic v Lowestoft Town	1-1
	Enfield v Pegasus	1-3
	Grays Athletic v Romford (2)	0-1
	Hallam v Stork	1-2
	Hayes v Yiewsley	2-3
	Haywards Heath v Eastbourne	2-2e
	Histon Institute v Clapton	2-0
	Hitchin Town v Cheshunt (2)	2-0
	Hounslow Town v Wootton Blue Cross	4-1
	Leavesden Hospital v Finchley	2-4
	Maidenhead United v Worthing	2-1
	Penrith v Trimdon Grange	6-1
	Redhill v Maidstone United	1-0
	Salisbury v Barnstaple Town	5-2
	Salts v Ibstock Penistone Rovers	7-2
	Smethwick Highfield v Guiseley	5-3
	Thameside Amateurs - Bye	
	Tow Law Town v Willington	1-3e
	Whitby Town v Sheffield	1-3
r	Eastbourne v Haywards Heath	2-4
r	Lowestoft Town v Crittall Athletic	3-1

Round One

	Billingham Synthonia v Penrith	5-2
	Bournville Athletic v Brentwood & Warley	0-3
	Bromley v Maidenhead United	3-0
	Cambridge Town v Barnet	2-1
	Edgware Town v Briggs Sports	2-1 v
	Erith & Belvedere v Hounslow Town	3-1
	Ferryhill Athletic v Stork	3-2
	Finchley v Histon Institute	2-0
	Gosport Borough Athletic v Thameside Amateurs	1-2e
	Haywards Heath v Poole Town	1-2
	Hitchin Town v Romford (2)	2-4
	Ilford v Hendon	1-5
	Leytonstone v Vauxhall Motors	4-2
	Lowestoft Town v Boldmere St Michaels	1-2
	Marine - Bye	
	Moor Green v St Albans City	3-1
	Oxford City v Redhill	3-2
	Pegasus v Smethwick Highfield	4-1
	Ryde Sports v Clevedon	2-4
	Salts v Willington	3-5
	Sheffield v Yorkshire Amateur	1-2
	Shildon v Bishop Auckland	3-2
	South Bank v Norton Woodseats	1-2
	Stanley United v Crook Colliery Welfare	1-4
	Tilbury v Gorleston	2-0
	Tooting & Mitcham United v Metropolitan Police	0-2
	Walton & Hersham v Dulwich Hamlet	1-0
	Wealdstone v Walthamstow Avenue	2-0
	Wimbledon v Salisbury	2-1
	Woking v Kingstonian	3-1
	Wycombe Wanderers v Barking	5-5e
	Yiewsley v Sutton United	0-4
r	Barking v Wycombe Wanderers	2-0
r	Briggs Sports v Edgware Town	2-1e

Round Two

	Bromley v Wimbledon	6-1
	Clevedon v Billingham Synthonia	2-4
	Erith & Belvedere v Woking	4-0
	Finchley v Barking	2-3e
	Marine v Tilbury	3-1
	Moor Green v Ferryhill Athletic	3-1
	Oxford City v Leytonstone	1-6
	Pegasus v Brentwood & Warley	2-1
	Poole Town v Hendon	0-1
	Romford (2) v Briggs Sports	1-0
	Shildon v Thameside Amateurs	0-2
	Sutton United v Boldmere St Michaels	1-0e
	Walton & Hersham v Norton Woodseats	3-0
	Wealdstone v Metropolitan Police	1-1
	Willington v Cambridge Town	3-0
	Yorkshire Amateur v Crook Colliery Welfare	1-1
r	Crook Colliery Welfare v Yorkshire Amateur	4-2
r	Metropolitan Police v Wealdstone	1-3

Round Three

	Barking v Bromley	1-5
	Billingham Synthonia v Hendon	2-1
	Crook Colliery Welfare v Erith & Belvedere	2-2
	Leytonstone v Sutton United	7-0
	Marine v Walton & Hersham	4-1
	Romford (2) v Moor Green	5-1
	Wealdstone v Thameside Amateurs	2-0e
r	Erith & Belvedere v Crook Colliery Welfare	0-2
r	Pegasus v Willington	3-2

1948/49 to 1949/50

Round Four

Billingham Synthonia v Romford (2)	1-2
Crook Colliery Welfare v Marine	3-2e
Leytonstone v Wealdstone	0-0e
Pegasus v Bromley	3-4
r Wealdstone v Leytonstone	0-4

Semi Finals

Bromley v Leytonstone	0-0eN
Romford (2) v Crook Colliery Welfare	2-2eN
r Bromley v Leytonstone	2-0 N
r Romford (2) v Crook Colliery Welfare	3-0 N

Final

Bromley v Romford (2)	1-0 N

1949/50

Extra Preliminary Round

4 Earle v Orrell	wo/s
Formby v Harrowby	n/a
Hearts of Liddesdale v Aspatria Spartans	4-3
Hoylake Athletic v Stoneycroft	2-0
Liverpool Police v UGB St Helens	n/a
Old Blackburnians v Fulwood Amateur	2-0
Shap v Holme Head Works	0-2
12 Great Barford v Bedford Lynton Works	7-4
Harpenden Town v Bedford Police	8-1
Letchworth Town v Bedford Corinthians	4-0
Luton Amateur v Houghton Rangers	6-1
Royston Town v AC Sphinx	wo/s
Wolverton Town v Bedford St Cuthberts	8-0
Wootton Blue Cross v Percival Athletic	4-1
17 Banstead Athletic v Old Westminster Citizens	8-0
Carshalton Athletic v Staines Town	7-0
Surbiton Town v Vickers Armstrong	1-2
18 Chipperfield v Crown & Manor	2-4
Edgware Town v De Havilland Vampires	8-1
Hammersmith United v Lyons	2-0
Harrow Town v Rickmansworth Town	1-2
Kings Langley v Corinthian Casuals	1-3
Polytechnic v Leavesden Hospital	0-2
Ruislip Manor v Wood Green Town	3-0
Southall v Twickenham	2-0
Uxbridge v Civil Service	12-1
Wingate v Acton Town	4-0
Yiewsley v Kingsbury Town	3-0
19 Abingdon Town v Woodstock Town	1-2
Aylesbury United v Amersham Town	7-0
Chesham United v Witney Town	5-1
Huntley & Palmers v Dickinsons Apsley	3-4e
Marlow v Pressed Steel	9-4
Osberton Radiator v Berkhamsted Town	4-3
St Frideswides v Morris Motors	5-2
Thame United v Slough Town	1-3
Tring Town v Buckingham Town	1-3
Wallingford Town v Battle Athletic	2-1e
Windsor & Eton v Chipping Norton	2-2
21 HMS Excellent v Alton Town	2-5
Portsmouth Electricity v Winchester City	0-2
Swanage Town v Longfleet St Marys	1-6
22 Calne & Harris United v Roundway Hospital	3-0
Clandown v Swindon BR Corinthians	4-3
Corsham Town v Paulton Rovers	3-4
Farmborough v Warminster Town	1-2
Frome Town v Pewsey Vale	11-3
Odd Down v Devizes Town	1-8
Purton v Westbury United	3-0
Spencer Moulton v Timsbury Athletic	6-1
24 Camelford v Hall's Engineers	wo/s
Green Waves v Tamerton	2-6
RN Barracks v Nanpean Rovers	2-2
19r Chipping Norton v Windsor & Eton	1-3e
24r Nanpean Rovers v RN Barracks	4-3

Preliminary Round

2 Bearpark CW v Royal Signals	3-1
Langley Park CW v Philadelphia CW	n/a
Stanhope v Broom Youth	2-3
Stanley United v Eldon Albion	3-2
Tow Law Town v Howden-le-Wear	5-2
West Auckland Town v Trimdon Grange	1-3
3 Bridlington Trinity United v Cochranes Sports	2-4
Furness Athletic v Portrack Shamrocks	3-5
Lingdale Mines WM v Redcar Albion	n/a
North Skelton Athletic v Skinningrove Works	n/a
Rillington v Whitby Albion Rangers	3-2
South Bank East End v Bridlington Central United	5-3
South Bank St Peters v Cargo Fleet Works	2-0
Whitby Town v Barkers Athletic	4-0
4 Cleator Moor Celtic v Earle	2-1
Formby v Scalegill	4-2
Frizington United v Ward Street OB	3-6
Hearts of Liddesdale v Hoylake Athletic	5-0
ICI Alkali v Port Sunlight	0-2
Old Blackburnians v Manchester University	4-1
Stork v High Duty Alloys	wo/s
UGB St Helens v Holme Head Works	1-1
5 Fulford United v Leeds University YMI	n/a
Yeadon Celtic v Thackley	2-4
6 Ilkeston Town v Chesterfield Ramblers	1-7
Maltby Main v Basford United	n/a
Netherfield Albion v Cinderhill Colliery	7-2
Penistone Church v Players Athletic	3-1
RAF Cranwell v Parliament Street Methodists	0-3
Raleigh Athletic v British Ropes (Retford)	2-1
Sheepbridge v Bestwood Colliery	3-3
Stanton Ironworks v Boots Athletic	2-0
8 Hay Green v Catherine-de-Barnes	2-4
Jack Moulds Athletic v Badsey Rangers	3-1
Paget Rangers v Oakengates Youth	4-1
Sheldon Town v Evesham United	13-0
Silhill v Handsworth Wood	2-3
Tangyes Recreation v Michelin Athletic	n/a
9 Phorpes Sports v Wimblington OB	0-3
10 Carrow Works v Diss Town	6-2
North Walsham Town v Boulton & Paul	2-3
11 Churchmans Sports v Whitton United	2-4
Felixstowe United v Corton	1-3
Ipswich Electricity Supply v Beccles	4-2
12 Baldock Town v Arlesey Town	2-1
Bedford Avenue v Marston Shelton Rovers	2-1
Biggleswade Town v Bedford Queens Works	7-0
Great Barford v Wootton Blue Cross	1-1
Leighton United v Harpenden Town	6-4
Luton Amateur v Wolverton Town	0-7
Royston Town v Letchworth Town	0-9
Stevenage Town v Waterlows Dunstable	2-1
13 Edmonton Borough v Bishops Stortford	3-1
Epping Town v Harlow Town	1-2
Hatfield Town v De Havilland Hatfield	3-2e
Hoddesdon Town v Sawbridgeworth	1-2
Peartree OB v Hertford Town	1-2
Stansted v Ware	2-5
Welwyn Garden City v Cheshunt (2)	0-6
Woodford Town v Tufnell Park	4-2
14 Dagenham Cables v Eton Manor	3-1
Downshall Athletic v Roneo	wo/s
Leyton v Upminster	2-1
Rainham Town v Dagenham British Legion	2-3
Rainham WMC v Ford Sports	2-4
Thames Mills v London Transport Central Buses	0-2
West Thurrock Athletic v Chadwell Heath	2-1
15 Heybridge Swifts v Sudbury Town	1-3
16 Aylesford Paper Mills v Royal Ordnance	3-1
Bowater Lloyds v Sidcup United	11-2
Faversham Town v Tunbridge Wells	3-2
Foots Cray Social v Beckenham	2-3
Sheppey United v Maidstone United	3-1
17 Banstead Athletic v Worcester Park	9-2
Camberley v RAMC Aldershot	0-4e
Carshalton Athletic v Epsom	3-2
Chertsey v Leatherhead	1-3
Dorking v Cobham	0-1e
Farnham Town v RASC	5-0
Guildford v McLaren Sports	4-1
Vickers Armstrong v Merton	9-0
18 Edgware Town v Corinthian Casuals	1-0
Pinner v Wembley	0-1
Rickmansworth Town v Uxbridge	0-5
Ruislip Manor v Crown & Manor	0-6
Ruislip Town v Enfield	1-3
Willesden v Hammersmith United	3-1
Wingate v Leavesden Hospital	4-3
Yiewsley v Southall	1-0
19 Bicester Town v Osberton Radiator	2-3
Buckingham Town v Wallingford Town	2-0
Chesham United v Aylesbury United	3-2
Hemel Hempstead Town v Henley Town	2-0
NAC Athletic v Dickinsons Apsley	1-0
Slough Centre v Slough Town	2-1
Windsor & Eton v St Frideswides	3-1
Woodstock Town v Marlow	2-3
20 Bognor Regis Town v Bexhill Town	2-3e
Chichester City v Littlehampton Town	1-2
Hove v Eastbourne	1-6
Lancing Athletic v Horsham	1-2
Lewes v Newhaven	3-0
Southwick v East Grinstead	3-4
21 Fareham Town v Alton Town	3-2e
Gosport Borough Athletic v Portland United	1-0
Hamworthy v Totton	3-4e
Longfleet St Marys v Christchurch	6-1e
Lymington v Whitehead Sports	0-1e
Poole Town v Thorneycroft Athletic	4-1
Wimborne v Blandford United	2-1
Winchester City v Bournemouth	4-2
22 Calne & Harris United v Peasedown Miners Welfare	0-1
Coleford Athletic v Melksham Town	1-2
Frome Town v Swindon Victoria	3-1
Paulton Rovers v Devizes Town	5-2
Radstock Town v Purton	0-2
Shepton Mallet Town v Clandown	4-3
Warminster Town v Spencer Moulton	1-2
Wootton Bassett Town v Welton Rovers	2-1
23 Bristol St George v Burnham United	8-2
Cinderford Town v Chalford	9-0
Clevedon v Chard Town	3-1
Douglas (Bristol) v Weston-super-Mare St Johns	4-5
Hanham Athletic v Mount Hill Enterprise	2-1
Ilminster Town v Highbridge Town	3-3
Taunton v Soundwell	3-2
24 Bodmin Town v Tavistock	4-2
Bugle v Mousehole	2-2e
Camelford v Oak Villa	5-2
Millbrook Rangers v Heavitree United	2-3e
Nanpean Rovers v Plymouth United	3-1
St Blazey v Helston Athletic	0-1
Tamerton v Wadebridge Town	0-1
Truro City v St Austell	1-3
4r Holme Head Works v UGB St Helens	2-1
6r Bestwood Colliery v Sheepbridge	n/a
12r Wootton Blue Cross v Great Barford	2-1
23r Highbridge Town v Ilminster Town	2-4
24r Mousehole v Bugle	6-1

Qualifying Round One

1 South Shields Ex Schoolboys v Ringtons Welfare	0-2
Woodhorn CW v Washington Welfare	n/a
2 Bearpark CW v Broom Youth	2-3e
Chilton Athletic v Trimdon Grange	1-3
Cockfield v Tow Law Town	1-2
Stanley United v Langley Park CW	3-1
3 Portrack Shamrocks v North Skelton Athletic	2-1
Redcar Albion v Rillington	3-0
South Bank East End v Cochranes Sports	2-4e
Whitby Town v South Bank St Peters	4-2
4 Hearts of Liddesdale v Cleator Moor Celtic	6-4
Holme Head Works v Old Blackburnians	1-1
Port Sunlight v Formby	3-1
Stork v Ward Street OB	2-1
5 Bradford Rovers v Brunswick Institute	n/a
Guiseley v Ravensthorpe	4-2
North Ferriby United v unknown	n/a
Thackley v Farsley Celtic	3-1
6 Bestwood Colliery v Stanton Ironworks	1-2
Netherfield Albion v Maltby Main	5-3
Parliament Street Meths v Chesterfield Ramblers	4-2
Penistone Church v Raleigh Athletic	1-1
8 Catherine-de-Barnes v Staffordshire Casuals	3-0
Handsworth Wood v Walsall Wood	0-4
Sheldon Town v Paget Rangers	6-1
Tangyes Recreation v Jack Moulds Athletic	1-4
9 Doddington United v St Neots St Marys	4-2
Ramsey Town v St Ives Town	3-2
Sawston United v Ely City	2-6
Wimblington OB v Huntingdon United	5-3
10 Cromer v Carrow Works	3-2
Sheringham v Boulton & Paul	1-5
Thetford Town v South Lynn	2-1
Wymondham Town v City of Norwich School OBU	2-1
11 Achilles v Stoke United	4-1e
Eastern Coachworks (Lowestoft) v Corton	7-0
Ipswich Electricity Supply v Bungay Town	4-4e
Stowmarket v Whitton United	5-3
12 Leighton United v Baldock Town	1-2e
Stevenage Town v Biggleswade Town	0-1
Wolverton Town v Bedford Avenue	6-0
Wootton Blue Cross v Letchworth Town	3-4e
13 Cheshunt (2) v Sawbridgeworth	9-1
Edmonton Borough v Woodford Town	4-2
Harlow Town v Ware	1-3
Hertford Town v Hatfield Town	5-2
14 Dagenham British Legion v Bata Sports	3-1
Ford Sports v Dagenham Cables	1-2
Leyton v West Thurrock Athletic	0-1
London Transport Central Buses v Downshall Athletic	3-2
15 Brightlingsea United v Brantham Athletic	2-1
Colchester Casuals v Saffron Walden Town	0-2
Crittall Athletic v Hoffmann Athletic (Chelmsford)	8-0
Harwich & Parkeston v Sudbury Town	wo/s
16 Bowater Lloyds v Aylesford Paper Mills	6-1
Faversham Town v Callender Athletic	2-1
Sheppey United v Beckenham	3-0
Woolwich Polytechnic v Bexley	0-1
17 Carshalton Athletic v Cobham	3-4
Farnham Town v Vickers Armstrong	1-0
Guildford v Leatherhead	1-2
RAMC Aldershot v Banstead Athletic	0-4
18 Edgware Town v Willesden	5-0
Enfield v Wembley	4-0
Wingate v Crown & Manor	1-4
Yiewsley v Uxbridge	5-0
19 Chesham United v Buckingham Town	
Marlow v NAC Athletic	4-0
Osberton Radiator v Hemel Hempstead Town	2-3
Slough Centre v Windsor & Eton	2-2e

59

1949/50 to 1950/51

20	East Grinstead v Bexhill Town	6-0
	Eastbourne Comrades v Eastbourne	0-1
	Horsham v Littlehampton Town	1-0
	Lewes v Shoreham	2-0
21	Longfleet St Marys v Wimborne	4-5
	Poole Town v Winchester City	0-1
	Totton v Fareham Town	1-3
	Whitehead Sports v Gosport Borough Athletic	0-2
22	Frome Town v Melksham Town	3-1
	Paulton Rovers v Purton	1-2
	Shepton Mallet Town v Spencer Moulton	0-1
	Wootton Bassett Town v Peasedown Miners Welfare	1-0
23	Bristol St George v St Philips Marsh Adult School	1-0
	Cinderford Town v Clevedon	5-1
	Hanham Athletic v Weston-super-Mare St Johns	7-1
	Taunton v Ilminster	2-1
24	Camelford v Heavitree United	4-3
	Mousehole v Bodmin Town	3-2
	Nanpean Rovers v Wadebridge Town	0-1
	St Austell v Helston Athletic	2-0
4r	Old Blackburnians v Holme Head Works	4-1
6r	Raleigh Athletic v Penistone Church	4-0
11r	Bungay Town v Ipswich Electricity Supply	7-1
19r	Windsor & Eton v Slough Centre	4-0

Qualifying Round Two

1	Heaton Stannington v Ringtons Welfare	2-3
	Wallsend St Lukes v Washington Welfare	2-7
2	Stanley United v Trimdon Grange	7-4
	Tow Law Town v Broom Youth	4-2e
3	Cochranes Sports v Portrack Shamrocks	1-3
	Whitby Town v Redcar Albion	3-1
4	Hearts of Liddesdale v Port Sunlight	1-3
	Old Blackburnians v Stork	0-2
5	Bradford Rovers v Thackley	5-3e
	North Ferriby United v Guiseley	2-1
6	Parliament Street Methodists v Netherfield Albion	1-3
	Stanton Ironworks v Raleigh Athletic	3-0
7	Shepshed Albion v Coventry Amateur	2-3
	Warwick Town v Northampton Amateurs	1-1
8	Catherine-de-Barnes v Jack Moulds Athletic	3-5
	Sheldon Town v Walsall Wood	2-1
9	Doddington United v Ramsey Town	1-3
	Wimblington OB v Ely City	2-1e
10	Cromer v Thetford Town	4-1
	Wymondham Town v Boulton & Paul	3-0
11	Bungay Town v Achilles	1-0
	Eastern Coachworks (Lowestoft) v Stowmarket	3-3e
12	Baldock Town v Wolverton Town	2-3
	Letchworth Town v Biggleswade Town	4-1
13	Cheshunt (2) v Ware	5-1
	Edmonton Borough v Hertford Town	2-4
14	Dagenham British Legion v West Thurrock Athletic	2-1
	London Transport Central Buses v Dagenham Cables	2-2
15	Crittall Athletic v Saffron Walden Town	5-2
	Harwich & Parkeston v Brightlingsea United	9-2
16	Faversham Town v Bowater Lloyds	0-3
	Sheppey United v Bexley	8-0
17	Cobham v Farnham Town	0-2
	Leatherhead v Banstead Athletic	4-3
18	Edgware Town v Yiewsley	3-4
	Enfield v Crown & Manor	3-1
19	Buckingham Town v Hemel Hempstead Town	3-2
	Windsor & Eton v Marlow	4-0
20	East Grinstead v Horsham	3-1
	Eastbourne v Lewes	7-0
21	Gosport Borough Athletic v Winchester City	1-1
	Wimborne v Fareham Town	2-3
22	Frome Town v Spencer Moulton	6-4e
	Purton v Wootton Bassett Town	3-0
23	Bristol St George v Hanham Athletic	2-0
	Cinderford Town v Taunton	0-3
24	Mousehole v Wadebridge Town	1-3e
	St Austell v Heavitree United	2-1
7r	Northampton Amateurs v Warwick Town	1-2
11r	Stowmarket v Eastern Coachworks (Lowestoft)	7-0
14r	Dagenham Cables v London Transport Central Buses	3-0
21r	Winchester City v Gosport Borough Athletic	6-0

Qualifying Round Three

1	Ringtons Welfare v Washington Welfare	2-2e
2	Stanley United v Tow Law Town	0-1
3	Portrack Shamrocks v Whitby Town	2-2
4	Port Sunlight v Stork	0-2
5	North Ferriby United v Bradford Rovers	4-3
6	Netherfield Albion v Stanton Ironworks	3-2
7	Coventry Amateur v Warwick Town	2-1
8	Sheldon Town v Jack Moulds Athletic	2-3
9	Wimblington OB v Ramsey Town	1-4e
10	Wymondham Town v Cromer	1-3
11	Stowmarket v Bungay Town	2-5
12	Wolverton Town v Letchworth Town	1-0
13	Cheshunt (2) v Hertford Town	2-1
14	Dagenham British Legion v Dagenham Cables	1-2 v
15	Crittall Athletic v Harwich & Parkeston	2-0
16	Sheppey United v Bowater Lloyds	1-3
17	Farnham Town v Leatherhead	3-4
18	Enfield v Yiewsley	1-0
19	Buckingham Town v Windsor & Eton	2-5
20	East Grinstead v Eastbourne	0-3
21	Fareham Town v Winchester City	0-2

22	Purton v Frome Town	1-3
23	Bristol St George v Taunton	3-2
24	Wadebridge Town v St Austell	4-4e
1r	Washington Welfare v Ringtons Welfare	n/a
3r	Whitby Town v Portrack Shamrocks	5-2
14r	Dagenham British Legion v Dagenham Cables	0-5
24r	St Austell v Wadebridge Town	2-3

Qualifying Round Four

Bungay Town v Gorleston	0-0
Cheshunt (2) v Histon Institute	1-0
Coventry Amateur v Whitby Town	0-1
Crittall Athletic v Windsor & Eton	0-2
Cromer v Bowater Lloyds	2-2
Dagenham Cables v Clapton	1-3
Enfield v Hounslow Town	0-0
Frome Town v Ryde Sports	0-5
Hallam v Sheffield	2-4
Jack Moulds Athletic v Bournville Athletic	3-0
Leatherhead v Hayes	1-0a
Maidenhead United v Wycombe Wanderers	5-4a
Penrith v Netherfield Albion	2-0
Ramsey Town v Vauxhall Motors	1-7
Redhill v Eastbourne	2-1
Smethwick Highfield v Ibstock Penistone Rovers	3-0
South Bank v Salts	3-2
St Albans City v Briggs Sports	2-1
Tow Law Town v North Ferriby United	9-0
Wadebridge Town v Bristol St George	3-4
Washington Welfare v Stork	1-3
Winchester City v Salisbury	1-1
Wolverton Town v Lowestoft Town	4-1
Worthing v Grays Athletic	1-1
r Bowater Lloyds v Cromer	7-0
r Gorleston v Bungay Town	1-2
r Grays Athletic v Worthing	7-1
r Hounslow Town v Enfield	4-0
r Leatherhead v Hayes	2-1a
r Maidenhead United v Wycombe Wanderers	0-0
r Salisbury v Winchester City	6-5e
r2 Leatherhead v Hayes	1-3
r2 Wycombe Wanderers v Maidenhead United	2-1

Round One

Barking v Brentwood & Warley	6-4
Barnet v Woking	3-1
Billingham Synthonia v Crook Town	2-3
Bromley v Thameside Amateurs	11-2
Bungay Town v Wycombe Wanderers	0-4
Cambridge Town v Vauxhall Motors	1-1
Cheshunt (2) v Ryde Sports	2-1
Clapton v Haywards Heath	5-0
Dulwich Hamlet v Oxford City	2-1
Erith & Belvedere v Pegasus	1-1
Grays Athletic v Finchley	1-2
Hendon v Bowater Lloyds	3-0
Hitchin Town v Hayes	1-3
Hounslow Town v Tooting & Mitcham United	3-2
Ilford v Tilbury	0-0
Jack Moulds Athletic v Evenwood Town	2-3
Kingstonian v Wimbledon	0-2
Leytonstone v Bristol St George	2-0
Marine v Boldmere St Michaels	2-0
Moor Green v Smethwick Highfield	1-0
Norton Woodseats v Ferryhill Athletic	2-4
Penrith v Willington	0-2
Redhill v Bournemouth Gasworks Athletic	0-1
Romford v Windsor & Eton	3-2
Salisbury v Wealdstone	4-1
Sheffield v Yorkshire Amateur	3-2
South Bank v Bishop Auckland	0-2
St Albans City v Walton & Hersham	4-2
Sutton United v Wolverton Town	1-1
Tow Law Town v Stork	2-2
Walthamstow Avenue v Metropolitan Police	4-3
Whitby Town v Shildon	2-3
r Pegasus v Erith & Belvedere	5-2
r Stork v Tow Law Town	2-1
r Tilbury v Ilford	1-2
r Vauxhall Motors v Cambridge Town	0-4
r Wolverton Town v Sutton United	1-2

Round Two

Barking v Barnet	3-1
Bishop Auckland v Ilford	3-2e
Bournemouth Gasworks Athletic v Cambridge Town	0-2
Cheshunt (2) v Bromley	2-1
Evenwood Town v Moor Green	0-2
Finchley v Hendon	1-0
Hayes v Leytonstone	1-3
Marine v Shildon	2-0
Romford (2) v Clapton	0-1
Salisbury v Dulwich Hamlet	0-2
Sheffield v Wimbledon	2-3
St Albans City v Stork	1-0
Sutton United v Hounslow Town	0-1
Walthamstow Avenue v Pegasus	3-1
Willington v Ferryhill Athletic	3-1
Wycombe Wanderers v Crook Town	1-0

Round Three

Bishop Auckland v Moor Green	3-1
Cambridge Town v Leytonstone	1-3e
Clapton v Barking	1-2
Finchley v Marine	3-1
Hounslow Town v Walthamstow Avenue	3-1
St Albans City v Cheshunt (2)	5-2
Willington v Wimbledon	4-2
Wycombe Wanderers v Dulwich Hamlet	3-1

Round Four

Barking v Hounslow Town	5-2
Finchley v Bishop Auckland	1-3
Leytonstone v Willington	2-3
Wycombe Wanderers v St Albans City	4-1

Semi Finals

Bishop Auckland v Wycombe Wanderers	2-1 N
Willington v Barking	2-1 N

Final

Willington v Bishop Auckland	4-0 N

1950/51

Extra Preliminary Round

3	Smiths Dock v Head Wrightsons	n/a
4	Cleator Moor Celtic v Frizington United	0-1
	Hoylake Athletic v Lancashire Steel Recreation	2-0
	Rishton v ICI Alkali	2-2
	Threlkeld v Braithwaite	1-5
12	AC Sphinx v Bedford St Cuthberts	wo/s
	Bedford Corinthians v Marston Shelton Rovers	3-1e
	Bedford Queens Works v Luton Amateur	1-3
	Biggleswade Town v Stevenage Town	1-4
	Harpenden Town v Houghton Rangers	5-3
	Potton United v Bedford Lynton Works	9-0
	Royston Town v Dunstable Town (2)	1-1
	Waterlows Dunstable v Arlesey Town	1-3
17	Hawker Athletic v Skyways	1-0
18	Civil Service v Chipperfield	7-0
	Corinthian Casuals v Polytechnic	1-0
	Harrow Town v Kings Langley	2-2
19	Abingdon Town v Amersham Town	1-1
	Aylesbury United v Henley Town	5-1
	Berkhamsted Town v Thame United	8-1
	Buckingham Town v Witney Town	4-2
	Chesham United v Morris Motors	7-1
	Hemel Hempstead Town v NAC Athletic	4-0
	Huntley & Palmers v Bletchley Town	4-0
	Maidenhead United v St Frideswides	6-0
	Osberton Radiator v Slough Town	0-3
	Pressed Steel v Dickinsons Apsley	6-3
	Slough Centre v Didcot Town	2-1
	Tring Town v Chipping Norton	0-4
	Wallingford Town v Kidlington	2-5
	Woodstock Town v Bicester Town	2-4
21	Hamworthy v Longfleet St Marys	2-4
	Newtown United v Christchurch	7-1
	Portsmouth Electricity v HMS Excellent	1-2
	Shaftesbury v Swanage Town	5-1
	Thorneycroft Athletic v 2nd Training Battn RAOC	5-2e
22	Coleford Athletic v Odd Down	6-3
	Melksham Town v Calne & Harris United	1-1
	Paulton Rovers v Clandown	5-2
	Roundway Hospital v Devizes Town	1-7
	Shepton Mallet Town v Timsbury Athletic	2-5
	Swindon BR Corinthians v Westbury United	2-7
	Swindon Victoria v Pewsey Vale	2-1
	Warminster Town v Corsham Town	3-1e
23	Chard Town v Watchet Town	2-0
	Charlton Kings v Chalford	5-1
	Keynsham Town v High Littleton	5-0
	Taunton BR v Dulverton Town	3-2
24	Camelford v Mullion	5-3 v
	Nanpean Rovers v Saltash United	1-1
	St Dennis v Helston Athletic	4-3
	Truro City v Bodmin Town	3-3
4r	ICI Alkali v Rishton	n/a
12r	Dunstable Town (2) v Royston Town	2-1
18r	Kings Langley v Harrow Town	1-3
19r	Amersham Town v Abingdon Town	4-0
22r	Calne & Harris United v Melksham Town	1-2
24r	Bodmin Town v Truro City	5-5
r	Mullion v Camelford	2-5
r	Saltash United v Nanpean Rovers	6-2
24r2	Truro City v Bodmin Town	2-1 N

1950/51

Preliminary Round

2	Hartlepool Railway Athletic v Bearpark CW	1-1
	Langley Park CW v Wearmouth CW	3-2
	Royal Signals v West Auckland Town	2-0
	Stanhope v Eldon Albion	n/a
	Wolsingham Welfare v Chilton Athletic	6-1
3	Bridlington Central United v Skinningrove Works	6-0
	Bridlington Trinity United v Cochranes Sports	2-0
	Lingdale Mines WM v Head Wrightsons	n/a
	Portrack Shamrocks v Cargo Fleet Works	3-4
	South Bank East End v North Skelton Athletic	n/a
	South Bank St Peters v Furness Athletic	5-0
	Whitby Albion Rangers v Rillington	0-9
	Winterton Hospital v Redcar Albion	2-6
4	Fulwood Amateur v Formby	1-1
	Harrowby v Port Sunlight	1-4
	Hearts of Liddesdale v Braithwaite	5-2
	ICI Alkali v Holme Head Works	n/a
	Manchester University v Hoylake Athletic	5-4
	Old Blackburnians v UGB St Helens	6-0
	Stoneycroft v Frizington United	6-2
	Ward Street OB v Earle	1-1
5	Brunswick Institute v Yeadon Celtic	6-1
	Ravensthorpe v Leeds University YMI	n/a
	Thornhill Edge v Harrogate Town	1-1
6	Bestwood Colliery v Players Athletic	0-5
	Boots Athletic v Basford United	3-0
	Penistone Church v Gedling Colliery	0-1e
	RAF Cranwell v Cinderhill Colliery	4-5
	Rawmarsh Welfare v Maltby Main	7-2
8	Badsey Rangers v Silhill	2-1
	Handsworth Wood v Bretforton OB	2-0
	Walsall Wood v Birmingham City Transport	2-2
10	Carrow Works v Sheringham	1-8
	Dereham Town v Fakenham Town	5-2e
11	Beccles v Churchmans Sports	6-1
	Felixstowe United v Corton	2-1
	Waterside Works v Lakenheath	4-4
12	Baldock Town v Percival Athletic	3-2
	Bedford Corinthians v Arlesey Town	2-1
	Harpenden Town v Bedford Avenue	2-0
	Letchworth Town v Luton Amateur	1-0
	Shefford Town v Potton United	1-0
	Stevenage Town v AC Sphinx	7-0
	Vauxhall Motors v Dunstable Town (2)	5-1
	Wootton Blue Cross v Leighton United	1-4
13	Bishops Stortford v Hoddesdon Town	1-1
	Epping Town v Sawbridgeworth	5-1
	Harlow Town v Stansted	4-3
	Peartree OB v Hitchin Road OB	0-2
14	Bata Sports v Green & Silley Weir Athletic	5-0
	Dagenham v Storey Athletic	3-0
	Eton Manor v Dagenham British Legion	1-1
	Grays Athletic v West Thurrock Athletic	0-2
	Rainham Town v Leyton	0-2
	Upminster v Ford Sports	1-1
	Woodford Town v Downshall Athletic	7-0
15	Heybridge Swifts v Halstead Town	2-1
16	Callender Athletic v Royal Ordnance	4-0
	Foots Cray Social v Thameside Amateurs	6-1
	Maidstone United v Tunbridge Wells	2-2
	Sidcup United v Aylesford Paper Mills	0-4
	Woolwich Polytechnic v Beckenham	3-2
17	Carshalton Athletic v Guildford	7-1
	Chertsey Town v Dorking	2-1
	Cobham v Camberley	4-2
	Leatherhead v Hawker Athletic	3-0
	McLaren Sports v Farnham Town	2-4
	Surbiton Town v Epsom	2-4
	Vickers Armstrong v Banstead Athletic	3-1
	Worcester Park v Devas Institute	0-4 N
18	Corinthian Casuals v Enfield	0-2 N
	Edgware Town v Harrow Town	1-1
	Leavesden Hospital v Pinner	2-1
	Ruislip Manor v Yiewsley	0-8
	Tufnell Park Edmonton v Southall	5-3
	Uxbridge v Rickmansworth Town	4-1
	Wembley v Wood Green Town	5-3
	Willesden v Civil Service	2-4
19	Amersham Town v Huntley & Palmers	3-1
	Aylesbury United v Maidenhead United	1-1
	Bicester Town v Marlow	3-4
	Chesham United v Berkhamsted Town	2-1
	Chipping Norton v Buckingham Town	2-1
	Slough Centre v Pressed Steel	4-2
	Slough Town v Kidlington	3-0
	Windsor & Eton v Hemel Hempstead Town	2-2
20	Arundel v Bexhill Town	0-3
	Bognor Regis Town v Lancing Athletic	3-3
	Chichester City v Horsham	0-1
	Eastbourne v Brighton Old Grammarians	5-0
	Eastbourne Comrades v East Grinstead	2-2
	Lewes v Hove	2-4
	Littlehampton Town v Newhaven	2-5
	Shoreham v Southwick	0-3
21	Alton Town v Longfleet St Marys	5-1
	Blandford United v Lymington	1-4
	Bournemouth v Thorneycroft Athletic	3-0
	Gosport Borough Athletic v RAMC Aldershot	4-0
	Newtown United v HMS Excellent	2-1e
	Portland United v Pirelli General Cable Works	2-5
	Shaftesbury v Fareham Town	4-1
	Winchester City v Wimborne	3-0
22	Devizes Town v Timsbury Athletic	1-1
	Paulton Rovers v Frome Town	5-3
	Peasedown Miners Welfare v Melksham Town	5-2
	Radstock Town v Farmborough	6-2
	Spencer Moulton v Coleford Athletic	9-1
	Warminster Town v Swindon Victoria	4-0
	Welton Rovers v Purton	3-2
	Wootton Bassett Town v Westbury United	0-1
23	Charlton Kings v Burnham United	9-0
	Cinderford Town v Weston-super-Mare St Johns	7-0
	Douglas (Bristol) v Clevedon	1-9
	Hanham Athletic v Keynsham Town	0-2
	Highbridge Town v Ilminster Town	4-3
	Soundwell v Mount Hill Enterprise	4-2
	St Philips Marsh Adult School v Taunton BR	2-3
	Taunton v Chard Town	2-3
24	Camelford v Heavitree United	0-1
	Millbrook Rangers v Truro City	2-0 v
	Newquay v Oak Villa	4-4
	Saltash United v Plymouth United	5-0
	St Austell v Green Waves	1-0
	St Blazey v Tavistock	2-1
	St Dennis v Mousehole	5-1
	Wadebridge Town v Bugle	4-1
2r	Bearpark CW v Hartlepool Railway Athletic	n/a
4r	Earle v Ward Street OB	n/a
r	Formby v Fulwood Amateur	n/a
5r	Harrogate Town v Thornhill Edge	4-1
8r	Birmingham City Transport v Walsall Wood	0-2
11r	Lakenheath v Waterside Works	3-5
13r	Hoddesdon Town v Bishops Stortford	2-5
14r	Dagenham British Legion v Eton Manor	1-2
r	Ford Sports v Upminster	1-0
16r	Tunbridge Wells v Maidstone United	1-4
18r	Harrow Town v Edgware Town	0-4
19r	Hemel Hempstead Town v Windsor & Eton	2-0
r	Maidenhead United v Aylesbury United	3-0
20r	East Grinstead v Eastbourne Comrades	2-1
r	Lancing Athletic v Bognor Regis Town	3-11
22r	Timsbury Athletic v Devizes Town	2-3
24r	Oak Villa v Newquay	3-8
r	Truro City v Millbrook Rangers	4-1

Qualifying Round One

1	Whitley Bay v Seaton Delaval	2-1
2	Bearpark CW v Langley Park CW	3-0
	Royal Signals v Cockfield	3-0
	Stanhope v Wolsingham Welfare	2-8
	Tow Law Town v Stanley United	4-1
3	Cargo Fleet Works v Bridlington Central United	5-10e
	Head Wrightsons v Rillington	3-1
	North Skelton Athletic v Bridlington Trinity United	3-0
	South Bank St Peters v Redcar Albion	1-4
4	Hearts of Liddesdale v Old Blackburnians	2-4
	ICI Alkali v Formby	5-1
	Port Sunlight v Manchester University	2-2
	Stoneycroft v Ward Street OB	1-2
5	Bradford Rovers v Brunswick Institute	5-2
	Guiseley v Leeds University YMI	2-1
	Harrogate Town v Leeds University YMI	2-1
	Salts v North Ferriby United	2-1
6	Boots Athletic v Players Athletic	2-1
	Cinderhill Colliery v Stanton Ironworks	5-1
	Gedling Colliery v Rawmarsh Welfare	2-2
	Parliament Street Methodists v Netherfield Albion	0-2
7	Earl Shilton Institute v Melton Town	3-3
8	Evesham United v Staffordshire Casuals	2-1
	Paget Rangers v Handsworth Wood	5-1
	Smethwick Highfield v Badsey Rangers	4-1
	Walsall Wood v Sheldon Town	7-2
9	Ely City v Phorpes Sports	7-1
	Histon Institute v Atlas Sports	5-0
	Ramsey Town v St Neots St Marys	1-0
	Sawston United v Huntingdon United	1-5
10	Boulton & Paul v South Lynn	1-0
	Dereham Town v Cromer	0-5
	North Walsham Town v Wymondham Town	4-5
	Thetford Town v Sheringham	3-1
11	Beccles v Whitton United	2-1
	Ipswich Electricity Supply v Ipswich Wanderers	2-1
	Stowmarket v Felixstowe United	8-2
	Waterside Works v Eastern Coachworks (Lowestoft)	7-3
12	Bedford Corinthians v Baldock Town	1-1
	Harpenden Town v Shefford Town	3-0
	Letchworth Town v Vauxhall Motors	5-1
	Stevenage Town v Leighton United	8-1
13	Epping Town v Bishops Stortford	1-3
	Hatfield Town v Ware	2-0
	Hertford Town v Harlow Town	3-3
	Welwyn Garden City v Hitchin Road OB	0-2
14	Dagenham v Ford Sports	1-1
	Eton Manor v Dagenham Cables	2-0
	Leyton v Woodford Town	3-3
	West Thurrock Athletic v Bata Sports	1-3
15	Brightlingsea United v Harwich & Parkeston	0-2
	Crittall Athletic v Colchester Casuals	1-4
	Hoffmann Athletic (Chelmsford) v Brantham Athletic	2-1
	Saffron Walden Town v Heybridge Swifts	4-4
16	Callender Athletic v Sheppey United	0-0
	Faversham Town v Bexley	6-3
	Foots Cray Social v Maidstone United	0-2
	Woolwich Polytechnic v Aylesford Paper Mills	2-7
17	Carshalton Athletic v Farnham Town	7-1
	Chertsey Town v Vickers Armstrong	3-1
	Epsom v Cobham	7-2
	Leatherhead v Devas Institute	4-5
18	Edgware Town v Wembley	2-1
	Enfield v Uxbridge	2-1
	Leavesden Hospital v Civil Service	1-2
	Yiewsley v Tufnell Park Edmonton	2-1
19	Chipping Norton v Chesham United	2-2
	Maidenhead United v Hemel Hempstead Town	1-0
	Slough Centre v Marlow	6-0
	Slough Town v Amersham Town	2-0
20	Bexhill Town v Hove	1-1
	East Grinstead v Bognor Regis Town	3-1
	Newhaven v Eastbourne	2-3
	Southwick v Horsham	2-1
21	Gosport Borough Athletic v Alton Town	3-0
	Newtown United v Lymington	5-1
	Shaftesbury v Pirelli General Cable Works	1-4
	Winchester City v Bournemouth	3-1
22	Devizes Town v Welton Rovers	1-2
	Paulton Rovers v Peasedown Miners Welfare	3-2
	Spencer Moulton v Westbury United	0-3
	Warminster Town v Radstock Town	2-3
23	Chard Town v Soundwell	3-4
	Charlton Kings v Clevedon	0-3
	Cinderford Town v Keynsham Town	0-3
	Highbridge Town v Taunton BR	1-4
24	St Austell v Truro City	2-0
	St Blazey v Heavitree United	2-0
	St Dennis v Newquay	2-1
	Wadebridge Town v Saltash United	1-4
4r	Manchester University v Port Sunlight	1-0e
6r	Rawmarsh Welfare v Gedling Colliery	2-1
7r	Melton Town v Earl Shilton Institute	5-3
12r	Baldock Town v Bedford Corinthians	1-2e
13r	Harlow Town v Hertford Town	2-4
14r	Ford Sports v Dagenham	1-3
r	Woodford Town v Leyton	1-2
15r	Heybridge Swifts v Saffron Walden Town	1-0
16r	Sheppey United v Callender Athletic	8-0
19r	Chesham United v Chipping Norton	6-1
20r	Hove v Bexhill Town	1-1
20r2	Bexhill Town v Hove	3-2 N

Qualifying Round Two

1	Washington CW v Wallsend St Lukes	1-0
	Whitley Bay v Heaton Stannington	1-1
2	Bearpark CW v Wolsingham Welfare	5-2
	Royal Signals v Tow Law Town	0-0
3	Bridlington Central United v North Skelton Athletic	4-2
	Redcar Albion v Head Wrightsons	n/a
4	ICI Alkali v Ward Street OB	n/a
	Manchester University v Old Blackburnians	n/a
5	Guiseley v Bradford Rovers	2-0
	Harrogate Town v Salts	1-1
6	Cinderhill Colliery v Netherfield Albion	1-2
	Rawmarsh Welfare v Boots Athletic	2-2
7	Melton Town v Coventry Amateur	5-0
	Shepshed Albion v Ibstock Penistone Rovers	2-1
8	Paget Rangers v Evesham United	2-0
	Smethwick Highfield v Walsall Wood	4-1
9	Ely City v Histon Institute	1-7
	Ramsey Town v Huntingdon United	0-3
10	Boulton & Paul v Wymondham Town	2-2
	Thetford Town v Cromer	1-5
11	Beccles v Ipswich Electricity Supply	6-2
	Stowmarket v Waterside Works	3-3
12	Harpenden Town v Stevenage Town	0-4
	Letchworth Town v Bedford Corinthians	5-3
13	Hertford Town v Bishops Stortford	3-2
	Hitchin Road OB v Hatfield Town	1-5
14	Dagenham v Bata Sports	3-3
	Eton Manor v Leyton	1-1
15	Heybridge Swifts v Harwich & Parkeston	0-2
	Hoffmann Athletic (Chelmsford) v Colchester Casuals	0-3
16	Aylesford Paper Mills v Maidstone United	0-5
	Sheppey United v Faversham Town	2-1
17	Carshalton Athletic v Devas Institute	6-1
	Epsom v Chertsey Town	5-4
18	Enfield v Civil Service	8-1
	Yiewsley v Edgware Town	3-3
19	Chesham United v Maidenhead United	1-2
	Slough Town v Slough Centre	2-1
20	Bexhill Town v Eastbourne	0-4
	Southwick v East Grinstead	2-1
21	Newtown United v Gosport Borough Athletic	2-2
	Pirelli General Cable Works v Winchester City	0-1
22	Welton Rovers v Paulton Rovers	2-2
	Westbury United v Radstock Town	4-1
23	Clevedon v Taunton BR	5-1
	Keynsham Town v Soundwell	4-0
24	St Austell v St Blazey	3-1
	St Dennis v Saltash United	0-8
1r	Heaton Stannington v Whitley Bay	2-0
2r	Tow Law Town v Royal Signals	3-1
5r	Salts v Harrogate Town	0-1
6r	Boots Athletic v Rawmarsh Welfare	0-3
10r	Wymondham Town v Boulton & Paul	5-2
11r	Waterside Works v Stowmarket	1-0
14r	Bata Sports v Dagenham	1-3
r	Leyton v Eton Manor	0-1

1950/51 to 1951/52

18r Edgware Town v Yiewsley 3-1
21r Gosport Borough Athletic v Newtown United 7-0
22r Paulton Rovers v Welton Rovers 4-2

Qualifying Round Three

1 Heaton Stannington v Washington CW 2-2
2 Bearpark CW v Tow Law Town 3-2
3 Head Wrightsons v Bridlington Central United 2-5
4 Old Blackburnians v ICI Alkali 3-3e
5 Guiseley v Harrogate Town 1-1
6 Rawmarsh Welfare v Netherfield Albion 9-2
7 Melton Town v Shepshed Albion 4-1
8 Smethwick Highfield v Paget Rangers 4-1
9 Histon Institute v Huntingdon United 5-3
10 Cromer v Wymondham Town 7-2
11 Waterside Works v Beccles 1-5
12 Letchworth Town v Stevenage Town 4-1
13 Hertford Town v Hatfield Town 1-0
14 Dagenham v Eton Manor 3-1
15 Harwich & Parkeston v Colchester Casuals 2-1
16 Maidstone United v Sheppey United 0-1
17 Carshalton Athletic v Epsom 1-2
18 Edgware Town v Enfield 3-1
19 Slough Town v Maidenhead United 2-2
20 Southwick v Eastbourne 4-4
21 Gosport Borough Athletic v Winchester City 1-0
22 Westbury United v Paulton Rovers 3-2
23 Keynsham Town v Clevedon 3-5
24 St Austell v Saltash United 1-2
1r Washington CW v Heaton Stannington n/a
4r ICI Alkali v Old Blackburnians 1-2e
5r Harrogate Town v Guiseley 3-2e
19r Maidenhead United v Slough Town 0-3
20r Eastbourne v Southwick 3-0

Qualifying Round Four

Bearpark CW v Bridlington Central United 4-1
Beccles v Bungay Town 1-5
Bournemouth Gasworks Athletic v Salisbury 0-3
Bournville Athletic v Jack Moulds Athletic 2-2
Bowater Lloyds v Eastbourne 2-4
Brentwood & Warley v Wolverton Town 2-1
Briggs Sports v Tilbury 1-1
Edgware Town v Sutton United 4-0
Epsom v Dagenham 0-1
Harrogate Town v Rawmarsh Welfare 2-2
Hertford Town v Letchworth Town 1-1
Histon Institute v Cromer 5-3
Lowestoft Town v Harwich & Parkeston 2-3
Melton Town v Smethwick Highfield 2-3
Old Blackburnians v Sheffield 0-2
Penrith v Heaton Stannington 3-2
Redhill v Worthing 1-3
Ryde Sports v Gosport Borough Athletic 0-2
Saltash United v Clevedon 1-1
Sheppey United v Finchley 1-0
Slough Town v Haywards Heath 1-0
South Bank v Evenwood Town 0-1
Stork v Hallam 0-1
Westbury United v Bristol St George 5-1
r Clevedon v Saltash United 1-2
r Jack Moulds Athletic v Bournville Athletic 4-1
r Letchworth Town v Hertford Town 3-0
r Rawmarsh Welfare v Harrogate Town 4-1
r Tilbury v Briggs Sports 0-2

Round One

Barnet v Worthing 4-1
Billingham Synthonia v Norton Woodseats 2-1
Boldmere St Michaels v Hayes 0-0
Brentwood & Warley v Westbury United 1-1
Bromley v Dulwich Hamlet 5-0
Bungay Town v Histon Institute 4-3
Cambridge Town v Clapton 3-2
Cheshunt (2) v Dagenham 1-4
Crook Town v Yorkshire Amateur 2-0
Eastbourne v Barking 1-0
Edgware Town v Kingstonian 2-2
Evenwood Town v Bishop Auckland 0-2
Gosport Borough Athletic v Pegasus 3-4
Hallam v Whitby Town 1-2
Harwich & Parkeston v Hounslow Town 1-5
Hendon v Smethwick Highfield 2-0
Hitchin Town v St Albans City 1-0
Ilford v Briggs Sports 1-0
Jack Moulds Athletic v Woking 2-3
Leytonstone v Wealdstone 3-2
Metropolitan Police v Saltash United 4-2
Moor Green v Romford (2) 2-2
Oxford City v Erith & Belvedere 4-2
Rawmarsh Welfare v Ferryhill Athletic 2-2
Sheffield v Penrith 4-1
Shildon v Bearpark CW 2-1
Slough Town v Poole Town 4-1
Tooting & Mitcham United v Letchworth Town 7-1
Walton & Hersham v Salisbury 0-0
Willington v Marine 1-0
Wimbledon v Sheppey United 2-0
Wycombe Wanderers v Walthamstow Avenue 2-2

r Ferryhill Athletic v Rawmarsh Welfare 2-1
r Hayes v Boldmere St Michaels 5-0
r Kingstonian v Edgware Town 2-1
r Romford (2) v Moor Green 0-2
r Salisbury v Walton & Hersham 1-3
r Walthamstow Avenue v Wycombe Wanderers 3-0
r Westbury United v Brentwood & Warley 1-3

Round Two

Billingham Synthonia v Bromley 1-3
Bishop Auckland v Shildon 3-1
Brentwood & Warley v Ferryhill Athletic 5-1
Bungay Town v Hendon 0-3
Crook Town v Hounslow Town 4-2
Dagenham v Walthamstow Avenue 0-0
Eastbourne v Sheffield 2-2
Hitchin Town v Barnet 2-2
Ilford v Walton & Hersham 1-3
Leytonstone v Hayes 1-4
Oxford City v Metropolitan Police 4-2
Slough Town v Pegasus 1-3
Tooting & Mitcham United v Kingstonian 4-2
Whitby Town v Cambridge Town 1-1
Willington v Moor Green 3-1
Woking v Wimbledon 1-1
r Barnet v Hitchin Town 3-0
r Cambridge Town v Whitby Town 0-1
r Sheffield v Eastbourne 0-2
r Walthamstow Avenue v Dagenham 3-1
r Wimbledon v Woking 3-2

Round Three

Barnet v Eastbourne 6-1
Bishop Auckland v Whitby Town 7-2
Brentwood & Warley v Pegasus 2-3
Hayes v Bromley 0-2
Hendon v Walthamstow Avenue 0-0
Oxford City v Crook Town 2-2
Tooting & Mitcham United v Wimbledon 2-2
Willington v Walton & Hersham 0-1
r Crook Town v Oxford City 0-2
r Walthamstow Avenue v Hendon 0-2
r Wimbledon v Tooting & Mitcham United 2-2e
r2 Tooting & Mitcham United v Wimbledon 1-1e
r3 Wimbledon v Tooting & Mitcham United 3-1

Round Four

Barnet v Bromley 0-2
Bishop Auckland v Walton & Hersham 2-2
Oxford City v Pegasus 0-3
Wimbledon v Hendon 1-1
r Hendon v Wimbledon 2-0
r Walton & Hersham v Bishop Auckland 1-4

Semi Finals

Bishop Auckland v Bromley 3-2 N
Pegasus v Hendon 1-1 N
r Pegasus v Hendon 3-2 N

Final

Pegasus v Bishop Auckland 2-1 N

1951/52

Extra Preliminary Round

2 Durham University v Witton Park Institute 2-3
12 Marston Shelton Rovers v AC Sphinx 1-3
Royston Town v Potton United 1-11
Wootton Bassett Town v Dunstable Town (2) 3-3
18 Harrow Town v Hawker Athletic 1-0
Rainham Town v Vickers Armstrong 5-0
Wood Green Town v Bexley 2-1
20 Aylesbury United v Morris Motors 5-0
Bletchley Town v Kidlington 5-3
Chipping Norton v Osberton Radiator 6-1
Henley Town v Amersham Town 1-4
Marlow v Hemel Hempstead Town 0-1
NAC Athletic v Bicester Town 2-6
Pressed Steel v Tring Town 2-1
St Frideswides v Huntley & Palmers 0-3
Thame United v Didcot Town 1-3
Wallingford Town v Buckingham Town 6-3
Windsor & Eton v Abingdon Town 6-1
Woodstock Town v Witney Town 1-7
21 Basingstoke Town v HMS Excellent 3-4
Hamworthy v Bournemouth 4-1
Longfleet St Marys v Swanage Town 0-0
Shaftesbury v Portland United wo/s
Thorneycroft Athletic v RAMC Aldershot 1-6
22 Bulford United v Clandown 3-0
Devizes Town v Swindon Victoria 4-2
Farmborough v Purton 0-3
Melksham Town v Calne & Harris United 0-2
Shepton Mallet Town v Corsham Town 2-1
Swindon BR Corinthians v Odd Down 2-0
Warminster Town v Frome Town 0-5
Wootton Bassett Town v Peasedown Miners Welfare 4-3

23 Chalford v Taunton 1-4
Dulverton Town v Mount Hill Enterprise 1-2
Hanham Athletic v High Littleton 1-0
Watchet Town v Douglas (Bristol) 1-2
24 Liskeard Athletic v Looe 2-2
Tamerton v Plymouth United 3-3
12r Dunstable Town (2) v Wootton Bassett Town 0-2
21r Swanage Town v Longfleet St Marys 0-4
24r Looe v Liskeard Athletic 1-0
r Tamerton v Plymouth United 6-2

Preliminary Round

1 Hearts of Liddesdale v Appleby 3-1
Holme Head Works v Cleator Moor Celtic 1-2
Salterbeck v Threlkeld 3-1
Seaton Delaval v Vickers Armstrong (Newcastle) 5-1
2 Chilton Athletic v Wolsingham Welfare 0-6
Cockfield v Eldon Albion 2-3
Durham City v Wearmouth CW 6-1
Langley Park CW v Bearpark CW 1-2
Tow Law Town v Stanley United 1-2
Trimdon Grange v Howden-le-Wear 5-0
West Auckland Town v Hartlepool Railway Athletic 2-2
Witton Park Institute v Seaton Holy Trinity 5-1
3 Cochranes Sports v Filey Town n/a
Furness Athletic v Whitby Albion Rangers 5-2
Head Wrightsons v Cargo Fleet Works 1-1
Portrack Shamrocks v Smiths Dock 1-2
Skinningrove Works v Redcar Albion 0-4
South Bank St Peters v Winterton Hospital 3-2
4 Harrowby v Eastham Athletic 2-4
Lancashire Steel Recreation v Earle n/a
Old Blackburnians v Sandbach Ramblers 4-1
Southport Leyland Road v Runcorn Athletic 4-3 N
St Annes Athletic v Port Sunlight 2-4
5 Brunswick Institute v North Ferriby United n/a
Harrogate & District Railway v Ravensthorpe 5-2
Leeds University YMI v Yeadon Celtic 6-1
Rawdon OB v Thornhill Edge 0-2
6 Cinderhill Colliery v Basford United 1-1
Gedling Colliery v Rufford Colliery 12-1
Hampton Sports v Thurcroft Main n/a
Penistone Church v Maltby Main n/a
Players Athletic v Parliament Street Methodists 1-2
RAF Cranwell v Boots Athletic 5-2
Raleigh Athletic v British Ropes (Retford) n/a
Stanton Ironworks v Netherfield Albion 0-4
7 BL (Austin) v Loughborough College 1-6
Bournville Athletic v Sheldon Town 1-2
Catherine-de-Barnes v Sutton Coldfield Athletic 2-0
Coventry Amateur v Birmingham City Transport 2-2
Melton Town v Morris Sports (Loughborough) 5-1
Warwick Saltisford Rovers v Earl Shilton Institute 3-1
8 Whitchurch Alport v Fernhill Heath 2-2
10 Holt United v City of Norwich School OBU 0-3
North Walsham Town v Sheringham 4-0
11 Eastern Coachworks (Lowestoft) v Lakenheath 3-3
Leiston v Felixstowe United 4-0
Waterside Works v Churchmans Sports 2-1
Whitton United v Newmarket Town 5-0
12 Arlesey Town v Bedford Corinthians 5-2
Baldock Town v Stevenage Town 5-2
Houghton Rangers v Bedford Queens Works 8-1
Leighton United v Shelford Town 4-1
Letchworth Town v Vauxhall Motors 2-0
Luton Amateur v Bedford Avenue 3-1 N
Potton United v AC Sphinx 3-4
Waterlows Dunstable v Wootton Blue Cross 0-2
14 Callender Athletic v Woolwich Polytechnic 1-4
Crockenhill v Thameside Amateurs 2-0
15 Arundel v Brighton Old Grammarians 4-0
Lancing Athletic v Shoreham 2-1
16 Banstead Athletic v Chertsey Town 5-2
Camberley v Lewes 4-3
Crawley v Eastbourne Comrades 2-3
Dorking v East Grinstead 3-4
Haywards Heath v Horsham 2-1
Leatherhead v Cobham 4-3
Newhaven v Bexhill Town 1-6
Skyways v Guildford 4-2
17 Enfield v Hatfield Town 1-1
Harlow Town v Hertford Town 5-3
Kings Langley v Sawbridgeworth 7-0
Peartree OB v Leavesden Hospital 3-1
Tufnell Park Edmonton v Rickmansworth Town 1-1
Twickenham v Uxbridge 0-2
Ware v Hoddesdon Town 4-5
Welwyn Garden City v Bishops Stortford 0-1
18 Arlesey Town v Upminster 2-0
Eton Manor v Worcester Park 3-1
McLaren Sports v Bata Sports 0-4
Pinner v Harrow Town 1-2
Polytechnic v Ford Sports 3-2
Wembley v Leyton 2-2e
Willesden v Grays Athletic 1-5
Wood Green Town v Rainham Town 1-2
19 Civil Service v Dagenham 1-3
Dagenham British Legion v Southall 1-3
Malden Town v Surbiton Town 2-1
Royal Ordnance v Carshalton Athletic 1-1
West Thurrock Athletic v Foots Cray Social 3-3
Woodford Town v Epsom 5-1
Yiewsley v Devas Institute 5-0

1951/52

20	Amersham Town v Hemel Hempstead Town	1-2
	Aylesbury United v Wallingford Town	6-0
	Bicester Town v Slough Centre	4-5
	Bletchley Town v Witney Town	2-2
	Huntley & Palmers v Chesham United	5-2
	Maidenhead United v Wolverton Town & BR	2-2
	Pressed Steel v Chipping Norton	0-1
	Windsor & Eton v Didcot Town	4-1
21	Alton Town v Pirelli General Cable Works	5-2
	Bournemouth Gasworks Athletic v Longfleet St Marys	3-1
	Lymington v Blandford United	2-2
	Newtown United v Winchester City	0-5
	RAMC Aldershot v Totton	0-3
	Ryde Sports v Fareham Town	0-5
	Shaftesbury v Hamworthy	5-2
	Wimborne v HMS Excellent	3-5
22	Bulford United v Purton	1-1
	Calne & Harris United v Devizes Town	4-3
	Frome Town v Pewsey Vale	4-2
	Paulton Rovers v Roundway Hospital	3-1
	Shepton Mallet Town v Coleford Athletic	3-1
	Spencer Moulton v Radstock Town	1-5
	Timsbury Athletic v Welton Rovers	2-4
	Wootton Bassett Town v Swindon BR Corinthians	3-1
23	Bristol St George v Taunton BR	3-2
	Burnham United v Keynsham Town	1-3
	Chard Town v Weston-super-Mare St Johns	5-2
	Charlton Kings v Highbridge Town	2-1
	Cinderford Town v Clevedon	3-0
	Ilminster Town v Hanham Athletic	2-1
	Mount Hill Enterprise v Douglas (Bristol)	1-1
	St Philips Marsh Adult School v Taunton	1-1
24	Bugle v Tavistock	4-1
	Millbrook Rangers v Heavitree United	1-4
	Nanpean Rovers v Saltash United	0-4
	Newquay v Bodmin Town	6-0
	Oak Villa v Green Waves	3-0
	St Dennis v Truro City	wo/s
	Tamerton v Looe	0-5
	Wadebridge Town v Mullion	3-3
2r	West Auckland Town v Hartlepool Railway Athletic	2-2
3r	Cargo Fleet Works v Head Wrightsons	n/a
6r	Basford United v Cinderhill Colliery	n/a
r	British Ropes (Retford) v Raleigh Athletic	n/a
7r	Birmingham City Transport v Coventry Amateur	2-1
8r	Fernhill Heath v Whitchurch Alport	3-1
11r	Lakenheath v Eastern Coachworks (Lowestoft)	1-1
17r	Hatfield Town v Enfield	0-3
r	Rickmansworth Town v Tufnell Park Edmonton	4-2e
18r	Leyton v Wembley	3-3e
19r	Carshalton Athletic v Royal Ordnance	8-2
r	Foots Cray Social v West Thurrock Athletic	2-3
20r	Witney Town v Bletchley Town	0-4
r	Wolverton Town & BR v Maidenhead United	4-1
21r	Blandford United v Lymington	3-5e
22r	Purton v Bulford United	2-1
23r	Douglas (Bristol) v Mount Hill Enterprise	2-7
r	Taunton v St Philips Marsh Adult School	1-4
24r	Wadebridge Town v Mullion	9-0
2r2	West Auckland Town v Hartlepool Railway Athletic	1-6
11r2	Eastern Coachworks (Lowestoft) v Lakenheath	1-4 N
18r2	Wembley v Leyton	0-2 N

Qualifying Round One

1	Cleator Moor Celtic v Whitley Bay	1-3
	Hearts of Liddesdale v Seaton Delaval	1-0
	Heaton Stannington v Wallsend St Lukes	3-0
	Washington Welfare v Salterbeck	4-1
2	Durham City v Bearpark CW	0-2
	Hartlepool Railway Athletic v Witton Park Institute	5-3
	Stanley United v Eldon Albion	1-1
	Trimdon Grange v Wolsingham Welfare	0-3
3	Bridlington Central United v Smiths Dock	2-5
	Cochranes Sports v South Bank St Peters	1-5
	North Skelton Athletic v Head Wrightsons	3-3
	Redcar Albion v Furness Athletic	4-1
4	Earle v Eastham Athletic	n/a
	Manchester University v ICI Alkali	1-4
	Port Sunlight v Southport Leyland Road	8-2
	Stork v Old Blackburnians	6-2
5	Bradford Rovers v Guiseley	2-3
	Brunswick Institute v Harrogate Town	1-2
	Harrogate & District Railway v Thornhill Edge	6-0
	Salts v Leeds University YMI	3-3
6	Basford United v Penistone Church	0-3
	Gedling Colliery v Netherfield Albion	n/a
	Parliament Street Meths v British Ropes (Retford)	0-2
	RAF Cranwell v unknown	n/a
7	Catherine-de-Barnes v Loughborough College	1-4
	Paget Rangers v Birmingham City Transport	4-1
	Sheldon Town v Warwick Saltisford Rovers	2-6
	Shepshed Albion v Melton Town	2-1
8	Evesham United v Old Wulfrunians	1-2
	Fernhill Heath v Staffordshire Casuals	4-1
	Walsall Trinity v Bretforton OB	5-0
	Walsall Wood v Badsey Rangers	5-0
9	Atlas Sports v St Neots St Marys	6-1
	Higham Ferrers Town v Ely City	1-0
10	Boulton & Paul v Cromer	2-0
	North Walsham Town v Dereham Town	3-0
	Thetford Town v City of Norwich School OBU	5-5e
	Wymondham Town v Fakenham Town	2-3
11	Ipswich Electricity Supply v Lowestoft Town	0-2
	Stowmarket v Leiston	5-0
	Waterside Works v Beccles	4-0
	Whitton United v Lakenheath	3-2
12	Houghton Rangers v AC Sphinx	3-2
	Letchworth Town v Leighton United	7-1
	Luton Amateur v Arlesey Town	2-2
	Wootton Blue Cross v Baldock Town	5-2
13	Crittall Athletic v Halstead Town	3-1
14	Aylesford Paper Mills v Bowater Lloyds	n/a
	Crockenhill v Faversham Town	2-2
	Maidstone United v Beckenham	2-3
	Woolwich Polytechnic v Sidcup United	2-1e
15	Arundel v Littlehampton Town	1-0
	Lancing Athletic v Hove	9-0
	Southwick v Bognor Regis Town	1-2
	Worthing v Chichester City	1-2
16	Camberley v East Grinstead	2-4
	Eastbourne Comrades v Banstead Athletic	0-1
	Haywards Heath v Leatherhead	3-4
	Skyways v Bexhill Town	3-0
17	Enfield v Hoddesdon Town	1-2
	Kings Langley v Uxbridge	1-1
	Peartree OB v Harlow Town	4-0
	Rickmansworth Town v Bishops Stortford	5-4
18	Arlesey Town v Bata Sports	1-2
	Eton Manor v Grays Athletic	1-0
	Harrow Town v Leyton	1-3
	Polytechnic v Rainham Town	1-2
19	Malden Town v Dagenham	1-3
	Southall v Woodford Town	3-1
	West Thurrock Athletic v Bexleyheath & Welling	4-0
	Yiewsley v Carshalton Athletic	1-0
20	Aylesbury United v Slough Centre	2-1
	Hemel Hempstead Town v Chipping Norton	4-2
	Windsor & Eton v Huntley & Palmers	0-5
	Wolverton Town & BR v Bletchley Town	4-2
21	Bournemouth Gasworks Athletic v Winchester City	3-2
	Fareham Town v Totton	2-1
	HMS Excellent v Shaftesbury	3-4
	Lymington v Alton Town	2-1
22	Calne & Harris United v Paulton Rovers	5-2
	Purton v Frome Town	0-9
	Radstock Town v Welton Rovers	1-5
	Shepton Mallet Town v Wootton Bassett Town	4-1
23	Chard Town v Bristol St George	3-1
	Charlton Kings v Mount Hill Enterprise	1-2
	Ilminster Town v Cinderford Town	3-1
	Keynsham Town v St Philips Marsh Adult School	2-0
24	Bugle v Oak Villa	4-1
	Newquay v Saltash United	2-2
	St Dennis v Looe	3-11
	Wadebridge Town v Heavitree United	2-1
2r	Stanley United v Eldon Albion	1-5
3r	Head Wrightsons v North Skelton Athletic	6-1
5r	Leeds University YMI v Salts	4-4e
10r	Thetford Town v City of Norwich School OBU	0-4
12r	Arlesey Town v Luton Amateur	2-3e
14r	Faversham Town v Crockenhill	0-1
17r	Uxbridge v Kings Langley	5-1
24r	Saltash United v Newquay	5-1
5r2	Salts v Leeds University YMI	2-1 N

Qualifying Round Two

1	Heaton Stannington v Whitley Bay	1-1
	Washington Welfare v Hearts of Liddesdale	3-1
2	Bearpark CW v Wolsingham Welfare	4-5
	Eldon Albion v Hartlepool Railway Athletic	3-3
3	Head Wrightsons v South Bank St Peters	4-0
	Smiths Dock v Redcar Albion	3-3
4	ICI Alkali v Port Sunlight	5-2
	Stork v Earle	3-0
5	Guiseley v Harrogate Town	3-0
	Salts v Harrogate & District Railway	2-0
6	Gedling Colliery v Penistone Church	3-0
	RAF Cranwell v British Ropes (Retford)	1-2
7	Paget Rangers v Warwick Saltisford Rovers	7-1
	Shepshed Albion v Loughborough College	1-4
8	Old Wulfrunians v Walsall Trinity	1-4
	Walsall Wood v Fernhill Heath	2-1
9	Atlas Sports v Ramsey Town	1-3
	Histon Institute v Higham Ferrers Town	7-3
10	Boulton & Paul v City of Norwich School OBU	2-1
	Fakenham Town v North Walsham Town	3-3
11	Lowestoft Town v Waterside Works	2-1
	Stowmarket v Whitton United	1-0
12	Letchworth Town v Houghton Rangers	8-0
	Wootton Blue Cross v Luton Amateur	1-1
13	Crittall Athletic v Brantham Athletic	4-1
	Saffron Walden Town v Brightlingsea United	1-2
14	Beckenham v Woolwich Polytechnic	3-1
	Bowater Lloyds v Crockenhill	5-2
15	Bognor Regis Town v Lancing Athletic	1-3
	Chichester City v Arundel	0-1
16	East Grinstead v Banstead Athletic	0-2
	Leatherhead v Skyways	2-2
17	Hoddesdon Town v Uxbridge	0-3
	Peartree OB v Rickmansworth Town	2-1
18	Eton Manor v Rainham Town	1-0
	Leyton v Bata Sports	7-1
19	Southall v Dagenham	2-0
	Yiewsley v West Thurrock Athletic	2-2
20	Huntley & Palmers v Aylesbury United	0-4
	Wolverton Town & BR v Hemel Hempstead Town	4-1
21	Bournemouth Gasworks Athletic v Lymington	6-2
	Fareham Town v Shaftesbury	4-1
22	Frome Town v Calne & Harris United	2-0
	Welton Rovers v Shepton Mallet Town	2-0
23	Chard Town v Mount Hill Enterprise	4-1
	Ilminster Town v Keynsham Town	0-2
24	Bugle v Looe	5-0
	Saltash United v Wadebridge Town	3-2
1r	Whitley Bay v Heaton Stannington	3-2 N
2r	Hartlepool Railway Athletic v Eldon Albion	1-7
3r	Redcar Albion v Smiths Dock	4-4e
10r	North Walsham Town v Fakenham Town	0-3
12r	Luton Amateur v Wootton Blue Cross	1-1
16r	Skyways v Leatherhead	0-2
19r	West Thurrock Athletic v Yiewsley	0-1
3r2	Smiths Dock v Redcar Albion	n/a
12r2	Luton Amateur v Wootton Blue Cross	1-3 N

Qualifying Round Three

1	Whitley Bay v Washington Welfare	3-1
2	Wolsingham Welfare v Eldon Albion	1-1
3	Redcar Albion v Head Wrightsons	n/a
4	ICI Alkali v Stork	1-3
5	Guiseley v Salts	2-5
6	Gedling Colliery v British Ropes (Retford)	5-1
7	Paget Rangers v Loughborough College	1-0
8	Walsall Wood v Walsall Trinity	5-0
9	Ramsey Town v Histon Institute	0-3
10	Boulton & Paul v Fakenham Town	3-2
11	Lowestoft Town v Stowmarket	2-4
12	Wootton Blue Cross v Letchworth Town	2-3
13	Crittall Athletic v Brightlingsea United	5-2
14	Bowater Lloyds v Beckenham	3-4
15	Lancing Athletic v Arundel	0-0
16	Banstead Athletic v Leatherhead	0-0
17	Peartree OB v Uxbridge	5-5
18	Leyton v Eton Manor	1-0a
19	Southall v Yiewsley	7-1
20	Aylesbury United v Wolverton Town & BR	5-3
21	Bournemouth Gasworks Athletic v Fareham Town	0-0
22	Frome Town v Welton Rovers	7-1
23	Keynsham Town v Chard Town	5-1
24	Saltash United v Bugle	4-0
15r	Arundel v Lancing Athletic	3-2
16r	Leatherhead v Banstead Athletic	3-2
17r	Uxbridge v Peartree OB	4-4e
18r	Leyton v Eton Manor	3-1
21r	Bournemouth Gasworks Athletic v Fareham Town	2-1
17r2	Uxbridge v Peartree OB	6-0

Qualifying Round Four

	Arundel v Redhill	1-3
	Aylesbury United v Southall	1-2
	Beckenham v Tilbury	2-3
	Boulton & Paul v Stowmarket	0-2
	Cheshunt (2) v Finchley	7-3
	Edgware Town v Letchworth Town	1-1
	Frome Town v Gosport Borough Athletic	8-1
	Harwich & Parkeston v Bungay Town	3-1
	Histon Institute v Crittall Athletic	4-2
	Keynsham Town v Westbury United	1-1
	Leyton v Uxbridge	7-1
	Norton Woodseats v Hallam	4-1
	Paget Rangers v Walsall Wood	1-2
	Penrith v Evenwood Town	0-1
	Poole Town v Saltash United	2-4
	Rawmarsh Welfare v Gedling Colliery	5-1
	Salisbury v Bournemouth Gasworks Athletic	6-1
	Sheppey United v Metropolitan Police	3-0
	Smethwick Highfield v Jack Moulds Athletic	4-1
	South Bank v Head Wrightsons	3-3
	Stork v Salts	1-2
	Sutton United v Leatherhead	4-2
	Wealdstone v Corinthian Casuals	0-1
	Whitley Bay v Wolsingham Welfare	1-4
r	Head Wrightsons v South Bank	1-2
r	Letchworth Town v Edgware Town	2-0
r	Westbury United v Keynsham Town	0-2

Round One

	Barking v Hayes	4-0
	Billingham Synthonia v Evenwood Town	3-3
	Brentwood & Warley v Salisbury	2-1
	Briggs Sports v Sheppey United	6-2
	Cambridge City v Leyton	1-2
	Cheshunt (2) v Wycombe Wanderers	1-6
	Corinthian Casuals v Sutton United	2-1
	Eastbourne v Smethwick Highfield	3-0
	Erith & Belvedere v Tooting & Mitcham United	1-1
	Histon Institute v Boldmere St Michaels	1-2
	Hitchin Town v Ilford	2-2
	Kingstonian v Pegasus	0-4
	Letchworth Town v Bromley	0-5
	Moor Green v Dulwich Hamlet	0-1
	Norton Woodseats v Wolsingham Welfare	1-2
	Rawmarsh Welfare v Bishop Auckland	1-5 N
	Redhill v Harwich & Parkeston	5-1
	Saltash United v Oxford City	1-4

1951/52 to 1952/53

Salts v Crook Town	3-4
Sheffield v Shildon	4-2
Slough Town v Hendon	2-3
Southall v Leytonstone	4-1
St Albans City v Barnet	0-1
Stowmarket v Romford (2)	0-2
Tilbury v Frome Town	1-1
Walsall Wood v Walton & Hersham	2-3
Walthamstow Avenue v Hounslow Town	2-0
Whitby Town v South Bank	2-2
Willington v Marine	2-4
Wimbledon v Clapton	2-1
Woking v Keynsham Town	3-2
Yorkshire Amateur v Ferryhill Athletic	5-3
r Evenwood Town v Billingham Synthonia	1-1a
r Frome Town v Tilbury	1-1e
r Ilford v Hitchin Town	3-3a
r South Bank v Whitby Town	1-5
r Tooting & Mitcham United v Erith & Belvedere	0-1
r2 Billingham Synthonia v Evenwood Town	2-6 N
r2 Frome Town v Tilbury	2-5 N
r2 Ilford v Hitchin Town	3-1 N

Round Two

Barking v Corinthian Casuals	0-1
Barnet v Whitby Town	1-0
Boldmere St Michaels v Romford (2)	3-3
Brentwood & Warley v Eastbourne	3-1
Bromley v Yorkshire Amateur	2-0
Crook Town v Pegasus	1-1
Evenwood Town v Dulwich Hamlet	1-2
Hendon v Bishop Auckland	2-2
Ilford v Wimbledon	1-2
Oxford City v Leyton	0-1
Redhill v Walton & Hersham	0-1
Southall v Walthamstow Avenue	2-4
Tilbury v Sheffield	1-0
Woking v Marine	0-3
Wolsingham Welfare v Briggs Sports	0-0
Wycombe Wanderers v Erith & Belvedere	1-0
r Bishop Auckland v Hendon	5-1
r Briggs Sports v Wolsingham Welfare	4-0
r Pegasus v Crook Town	0-1
r Romford (2) v Boldmere St Michaels	4-0

Round Three

Barnet v Bromley	4-2
Bishop Auckland v Walton & Hersham	1-3
Briggs Sports v Brentwood & Warley	4-0
Corinthian Casuals v Wimbledon	0-3
Crook Town v Romford (2)	4-4
Leyton v Dulwich Hamlet	4-2
Tilbury v Walthamstow Avenue	0-2
Wycombe Wanderers v Marine	1-0
r Romford (2) v Crook Town	1-3

Round Four

Barnet v Wycombe Wanderers	2-0
Crook Town v Walton & Hersham	0-0
Leyton v Briggs Sports	3-1
Wimbledon v Walthamstow Avenue	0-0
r Walthamstow Avenue v Wimbledon	1-1
r Walton & Hersham v Crook Town	2-0
r2 Wimbledon v Walthamstow Avenue	0-3 N

Semi Finals

Leyton v Barnet	2-1 N
Walthamstow Avenue v Walton & Hersham	3-0 N

Final

Walthamstow Avenue v Leyton	2-1 N

1952/53

Extra Preliminary Round

2 Ashmore Recreation v Stockton Amateur	n/a
6 Heanor Town v Dunscroft Welfare	3-2
Lincoln City School OBU v Parkgate Welfare	n/a
12 Ampthill Town v Kempston Rovers	1-0
Shelford Town v Kents Athletic	2-2
16 Chertsey Town v Horley	4-3
Farnham Town v Eastbourne United	3-2
18 Edgware Town v Pinner	5-0
Eton Manor v Hornchurch & Upminster	3-2
Finchley v Grays Athletic	5-2
Rainham Town v Twickenham	5-0
Storey Athletic v Hawker Athletic	2-0
Wembley v Willesden	3-2
Yiewsley v Aveley	2-4
20 Aylesbury United v Osberton Radiator	5-1
Berkhamsted Town v Amersham Town	4-0
Bicester Town v Slough Centre	1-6
Chesham United v Marlow	5-2
Cranfield United v Pressed Steel	2-7
Didcot Town v Chipping Norton Town	3-2
Huntley & Palmers v Kidlington	4-1
Maidenhead United v Buckingham Town	14-1
NAC Athletic v Hemel Hempstead Town	1-2
St Frideswides v Henley Town	3-2
Thame United v Witney Town	1-3
Wallingford Town v Abingdon Town	5-0
Windsor & Eton v Morris Motors	4-2
Wolverton Town & BR v Woodstock Town	8-1
21 Alton Town v Ramsey Town	5-1
Bournemouth v Bournemouth Gasworks Athletic	3-2
East Cowes Victoria v Winchester City	0-3
Gosport Borough Athletic v Fareham Town	0-1
Ryde Sports v RAMC Aldershot	2-2
Thorneycroft Athletic v HMS Daedalus	1-3
22 Calne & Harris United v Warminster Town	0-1
Coleford United v Devizes Town	0-3
Corsham Town v Shepton Mallet Town	0-0
Melksham Town v Swindon Victoria	1-2
Radstock Town v Wootton Bassett Town	2-1
Spencer Moulton v Paulton Rovers	3-4
Westbury United v Roundway Hospital	7-4
23 Chard Town v Worle OB	2-2
Soundwell v High Littleton	3-1
24 Roche v St Just	4-3
12r Shelford Town v Kents Athletic	2-5
21r Ryde Sports v RAMC Aldershot	0-1
22r Shepton Mallet Town v Corsham Town	4-1
23r Worle OB v Chard Town	2-3e

Preliminary Round

1 Cleator Moor Celtic v Hearts of Liddesdale	5-0
Washington Welfare v Seaton Delaval	4-5
2 Bearpark CW v Langley Park CW	2-2
Cockfield v Seaton Holy Trinity	5-1
Durham City v West Auckland Town	3-2
Eldon Albion v Chilton Athletic	3-0
Howden-le-Wear v Ashmore Recreation	2-2
Stanhope v Durham University	0-4
Tow Law Town v Hartlepool Railway Athletic	8-0
Witton Park Institute v Stanley Unitied	1-3
3 Filey Town v Bridlington Central United	3-2
Head Wrightsons v Cargo Fleet Works	n/a
Pickering Town v Portrack Shamrocks	n/a
Skinningrove Works v Furness Athletic	5-0
Smiths Dock v Whitby Albion Rangers	6-1
South Bank St Peters v Cochranes Sports	6-0
Winterton Hospital v Redcar Albion	n/a
4 Blackpool Rangers v Manchester University	n/a
Eastham Athletic v Earle	2-8
Harrowby v ICI Alkali	0-6
Northern Nomads v Lancashire Steel Recreation	n/a
Old Blackburnians v Runcorn Athletic	6-0
Port Sunlight v Stoneycroft	0-1
St Annes Athletic v Atherton Colliery	5-1
Stork v Southport Leyland Road	10-0
5 Harrogate Town v Liversedge	2-2
Ossett Albion v Hull Old Grammarians	2-0
Thornhill Edge v Brunswick Institute	2-3
6 Gedling Colliery v Stanton Ironworks	8-0
Hallam v Hampton Sports	n/a
Parliament Street Meths v Lincoln City School OBU	1-0
Penistone Church v Netherfield Albion	2-2
Players Athletic v Boots Athletic	1-0
RAF Cranwell v Cinderhill Colliery	1-0
Raleigh Athletic v Heanor Town	2-2
Thurcroft Main v Basford United	2-3
7 Birmingham City Transport v Shepshed Albion	4-1
Earl Shilton Institute v Morris Motors (Coventry)	8-0
Enderby Town v Anstey Nomads	1-2
Ibstock Penistone Rovers v Paget Rangers	1-3
Loughborough College v Sheldon Town	n/a
Rootes Athletic v Knowle	wo/s
Syston St Peters v Cosby United	0-0
8 Richard Thomas & Baldwin v Badsey Rangers	wo/s
11 Achilles v Waterside Works	0-2
Bungay Town v Felixstowe United	7-2
Eastern Coachworks (Lowestoft) v Long Melford	0-4
Exning United v Churchmans Sports	4-3e
Lakenheath v Ipswich Electricity Supply	6-1
Lowestoft Town v Leiston	4-1
Whitton United v Beccles	2-2
12 Ampthill Town v Wootton Blue Cross	3-1
Baldock Town v Arlesey Town	3-1
Leighton United v Kents Athletic	2-1
Letchworth Town v AC Sphinx	0-5
Luton Amateur v Potton United	2-1
Royston Town v Bedford Avenue	6-5
Stevenage Town v Dunstable Town (2)	4-0
Vauxhall Motors v Bedford Corinthians	14-2
14 Bexley v Foots Cray	2-3
Callender Athletic v Whitstable	1-4
Cray Wanderers v Faversham Town	2-6
Crockenhill v Bexleyheath & Welling	2-5
Maidstone United v Aylesford Paper Mills	0-2
Woolwich Polytechnic v Thameside Amateurs	2-1e
15 Chichester City v Littlehampton Town	4-0
Southwick v Hove White Rovers	0-2
Wigmore Athletic v Whitehawk & Manor Farm OB	3-2
Worthing v Arundel	4-0
16 Bexhill Town v Farnham Town	2-0
Chertsey Town v Camberley	2-2
Cobham v East Grinstead	0-5
Crawley v Banstead Athletic	2-3
Haywards Heath v Leatherhead	0-2
Horsham v Guildford	9-1
Metropolitan Police v Lewes	3-0
Newhaven v Dorking	2-1
17 Bishops Stortford v Tufnell Park Edmonton	1-0
Enfield v Welwyn Garden City	5-1
Epping Town v Kings Langley	3-0
Harlow Town v Hatfield Town	2-5
Leavesden Hospital v Ware	2-6
Rickmansworth Town v Hertford Town	2-5
Sawbridgeworth v Hoddesdon Town	0-5
Stansted v Peartree OB	0-5
18 Edgware Town v Polytechnic	2-0
Eton Manor v Aveley	0-2
Ford Sports v McLaren Sports	2-2
Ruislip Manor v Rainham Town	2-2
Uxbridge v Harrow Town	5-2
Vickers Armstrong v Storey Athletic	3-1
Wembley v Downshall Athletic	2-0
Wood Green Town v Finchley	0-6
19 Carshalton Athletic v Dagenham British Legion	9-1
Dagenham v PO Engineers (LTR)	4-0
Dagenham Cables v Lathol Athletic	2-2
Epsom v Devas Institute	3-0
Malden Town v Civil Service	1-1e
Royal Ordnance v West Thurrock Athletic	1-2
Surbiton Town v Worcester Park	2-1
Woodford Town v Wingate	1-2
20 Bletchley Town v Berkhamsted Town	1-2
Didcot Town v Pressed Steel	2-2
Hemel Hempstead Town v Huntley & Palmers	1-2
Slough Centre v Chesham United	2-2
Tring Town v Maidenhead United	1-3
Wallingford Town v St Frideswides	0-0e
Windsor & Eton v Witney Town	1-1
Wolverton Town & BR v Aylesbury United	1-1
21 Blandford United v Alton Town	3-3
Bournemouth v Wimborne	3-1
Fareham Town v Shaftesbury	10-0
HMS Daedalus v Totton	n/a
HMS Excellent v Lymington	2-4
Longfleet St Marys v Winchester City	2-1
Pirelli General Cable Works v RAMC Aldershot	0-1
Swanage Town v Hamworthy	0-3
22 Devizes Town v Paulton Rovers	5-0
Farmborough v Clandown	0-5
Peasedown Miners Welfare v Radstock Town	2-1
Purton v Bulford United	4-2
Swindon BR Corinthians v Swindon Victoria	2-2
Warminster Town v Odd Down	4-2
Welton Rovers v Shepton Mallet Town	2-2
Westbury United v Pewsey Vale	9-0
23 Chard Town v Hanham Athletic	4-1
Charlton Kings v Watchet Town	0-2
Cinderford Town v Bristol St George	4-1
Clevedon v Ilminster Town	4-0
Highbridge Town v Weston-super-Mare St Johns	6-0
Mount Hill Enterprise v Soundwell	4-2
St Philips Marsh Adult School v Burnham United	3-0
Taunton BR v Douglas (Kingswood)	6-3
24 Camelford v Taunton	3-2
Dartmouth United v Bodmin Town	8-0
Heavitree United v St Dennis	6-1
Liskeard Athletic v Mullion	1-5
Looe v Roche	5-2
Mousehole v Oak Villa	5-2
Nanpean Rovers v Helston Athletic	5-1
Tavistock v Bugle	0-2
2r Ashmore Recreation v Howden-le-Wear	0-2
r Langley Park CW v Bearpark CW	0-3
5r Liversedge v Harrogate Town	3-1
6r Heanor Town v Raleigh Athletic	5-2
r Netherfield Albion v Penistone Church	3-5
7r Cosby United v Syston St Peters	0-4

64

1952/53

11r	Beccles v Whitton United	3-4
16r	Camberley v Chertsey Town	4-1
18r	McLaren Sports v Ford Sports	0-2
r	Rainham Town v Ruislip Manor	1-0
19r	Civil Service v Malden Town	0-3
r	Lathol Athletic v Dagenham Cables	2-4
20r	Aylesbury United v Wolverton Town & BR	2-4
r	Chesham United v Slough Centre	1-2
r	Pressed Steel v Didcot Town	4-0
r	St Frideswides v Wallingford Town	1-2
r	Witney Town v Windsor & Eton	4-1
21r	Alton Town v Blandford United	3-1
22r	Shepton Mallet Town v Welton Rovers	1-0
r	Swindon Victoria v Swindon BR Corinthians	1-2

Qualifying Round One

1	Appleby v Whitley Bay	0-5
	Cleator Moor Celtic v Salterbeck	2-1
	Holme Head Works v Wallsend St Lukes	5-6
	Seaton Delaval v Heaton Stannington	3-1
2	Cockfield v Stanley United	2-0
	Durham City v Tow Law Town	2-2 v
	Durham University v Bearpark CW	1-0
	Eldon Albion v Howden-le-Wear	2-5
3	North Skelton Athletic v Cargo Fleet Works	5-0
	Redcar Albion v Filey Town	5-3
	Smiths Dock v Skinningrove Works	4-2
	South Bank St Peters v Portrack Shamrocks	0-4
4	Earle v ICI Alkali	1-4
	Northern Nomads v unknown	n/a
	Stoneycroft v Old Blackburnians	1-3
	Stork v St Annes Athletic	1-2
5	Brunswick Institute v Ossett Albion	3-3
	Harrogate & District Railway v Guiseley	n/a
	Leeds University YMI v Bradford Rovers	0-4
	Liversedge v North Ferriby United	1-1
6	Gedling Colliery v Basford United	4-2
	Hallam v Parliament Street Methodists	6-2
	Penistone Church v Heanor Town	1-4
	Players Athletic v RAF Cranwell	5-3
7	Anstey Nomads v Coventry Amateur	7-0
	Earl Shilton Institute v Paget Rangers	2-1
	Rootes Athletic v Loughborough College	2-6
	Syston St Peters v Birmingham City Transport	4-1
8	Bournville Athletic v Old Wulfrunians	4-2
	Jack Moulds Athletic v Fernhill Heath	2-3
	Richard Thomas & Baldwin v Walsall Wood	1-3e
	Staffordshire Casuals v Walsall Trinity	6-3e
9	Ely City v Raunds Town	1-6
	St Neots St Marys v Atlas Sports	2-2
10	Boulton & Paul v Dereham Town	3-0
	Cromer v Holt United	2-4e
	Sheringham v Wymondham Town	0-1
	Thetford Town v Fakenham Town	2-2
11	Lakenheath v Bungay Town	4-0
	Lowestoft Town v Whitton United	0-2
	Waterside Works v Exning United	11-1
	Woodbridge Athletic v Long Melford	1-6
12	Baldock Town v Royston Town	3-0
	Luton Amateur v AC Sphinx	1-2
	Stevenage Town v Ampthill Town	8-1
	Vauxhall Motors v Leighton United	4-1
13	Brightlingsea United v Colchester Casuals	2-4
	Crittall Athletic v Brantham Athletic	2-2
14	Aylesford Paper Mills v Whitstable	1-0
	Bexleyheath & Welling v Beckenham	2-0
	Bowater Lloyds v Woolwich Polytechnic	7-1
	Foots Cray v Faversham Town	1-7
15	Lancing Athletic v Bognor Regis Town	1-0
	Shoreham v Hove White Rovers	2-2
	Wigmore Athletic v Chichester City	5-3
	Worthing v Brighton Old Corinthians	3-2e
16	Banstead Athletic v Horsham	3-3
	East Grinstead v Bexhill Town	4-1
	Metropolitan Police v Camberley	2-1
	Newhaven v Leatherhead	1-5
17	Epping Town v Bishops Stortford	1-4
	Hoddesdon Town v Hertford Town	5-2
	Peartree OB v Enfield	1-5
	Ware v Hatfield Town	5-3
18	Rainham Town v Finchley	3-3
	Uxbridge v Ford Sports	4-1
	Vickers Armstrong v Edgware Town	2-3
	Wembley v Aveley	2-1
19	Carshalton Athletic v Wingate	5-2
	Dagenham v Epsom	4-3
	Malden Town v Dagenham Cables	0-1
	Surbiton Town v West Thurrock Athletic	5-2
20	Berkhamsted Town v Wolverton Town & BR	4-2
	Pressed Steel v Maidenhead United	2-4
	Slough Centre v Huntley & Palmers	5-2
	Witney Town v Wallingford Town	3-2
21	Alton Town v Longfleet St Marys	6-0
	Bournemouth v RAMC Aldershot	1-4
	Fareham Town v HMS Daedalus	n/a
	Hamworthy v Lymington	4-4
22	Clandown v Purton	2-1
	Shepton Mallet Town v Peasedown Miners Welfare	3-0
	Warminster Town v Devizes Town	2-4
	Westbury United v Swindon BR Corinthians	6-0
23	Clevedon v St Philips Marsh Adult School	4-1
	Highbridge Town v Mount Hill Enterprise	2-3
	Taunton BR v Chard Town	1-1
	Watchet Town v Cinderford Town	2-4
24	Dartmouth United v Camelford	5-0
	Mousehole v Heavitree United	7-1
	Mullion v Bugle	0-5
	Nanpean Rovers v Looe	4-0
2r	Tow Law Town v Durham City	5-3eN
5r	North Ferriby United v Liversedge	1-2
r	Ossett Albion v Brunswick Institute	3-1
9r	Atlas Sports v St Neots St Marys	7-2e
10r	Fakenham Town v Thetford Town	1-3e
13r	Brantham Athletic v Crittall Athletic	1-3
15r	Shoreham v Hove White Rovers	6-1
16r	Horsham v Banstead Athletic	2-3
18r	Finchley v Rainham Town	2-0
21r	HMS Daedalus v Fareham Town	5-1
r	Lymington v Hamworthy	2-0e
23r	Chard Town v Taunton BR	6-1

Qualifying Round Two

1	Cleator Moor Celtic v Wallsend St Lukes	4-2
	Seaton Delaval v Whitley Bay	1-2
2	Cockfield v Durham University	4-0
	Tow Law Town v Howden-le-Wear	5-0
3	North Skelton Athletic v Portrack Shamrocks	n/a
	Smiths Dock v Redcar Albion	1-2e
4	ICI Alkali v Northern Nomads	4-2
	Old Blackburnians v St Annes Athletic	1-3
5	Liversedge v Bradford Rovers	4-2
	Ossett Albion v Harrogate & District Railway	0-1
6	Gedling Colliery v Hallam	1-4
	Players Athletic v Heanor Town	3-1
7	Anstey Nomads v Loughborough College	3-2
	Syston St Peters v Earl Shilton Institute	3-0
8	Fernhill Heath v Bournville Athletic	2-1
	Walsall Wood v Staffordshire Casuals	2-0
9	Atlas Sports v Higham Ferrers Town	2-5
	Ramsey Town v Raunds Town	4-0
10	Boulton & Paul v Thetford Town	2-0
	Holt United v Wymondham Town	2-1
11	Lakenheath v Long Melford	2-1
	Whitton United v Waterside Works	5-1
12	Baldock Town v Stevenage Town	0-7
	Vauxhall Motors v AC Sphinx	5-3
13	Crittall Athletic v Halstead Town	3-0
	Saffron Walden Town v Colchester Casuals	3-3e
14	Aylesford Paper Mills v Faversham Town	1-6
	Bexleyheath & Welling v Bowater Lloyds	6-0
15	Shoreham v Lancing Athletic	2-2
	Wigmore Athletic v Worthing	0-1
16	Banstead Athletic v Metropolitan Police	3-2
	Leatherhead v East Grinstead	2-3
17	Bishops Stortford v Ware	1-1
	Enfield v Hoddesdon Town	1-5
18	Edgware Town v Wembley	3-2
	Uxbridge v Finchley	1-3
19	Carshalton Athletic v Dagenham	1-1
	Surbiton Town v Dagenham Cables	1-3
20	Berkhamsted Town v Maidenhead United	2-1
	Slough Centre v Witney Town	6-0
21	Lymington v Alton Town	1-1
	RAMC Aldershot v HMS Daedalus	1-2
22	Clandown v Shepton Mallet Town	1-4
	Westbury United v Devizes Town	5-2
23	Cinderford Town v Chard Town	3-2
	Clevedon v Mount Hill Enterprise	6-0
24	Bugle v Nanpean Rovers	2-1
	Mousehole v Dartmouth United	0-5
13r	Saffron Walden Town v Colchester Casuals	3-5
15r	Lancing Athletic v Shoreham	4-0
17r	Ware v Bishops Stortford	4-2
19r	Dagenham v Carshalton Athletic	2-4
21r	Alton Town v Lymington	5-0

Qualifying Round Three

1	Cleator Moor Celtic v Whitley Bay	1-4
2	Tow Law Town v Cockfield	1-3
3	Portrack Shamrocks v Redcar Albion	3-1
4	St Annes Athletic v ICI Alkali	1-3
5	Liversedge v Harrogate & District Railway	0-8
6	Players Athletic v Hallam	0-2
7	Anstey Nomads v Syston St Peters	5-2
8	Fernhill Heath v Walsall Wood	2-5
9	Higham Ferrers Town v Ramsey Town	6-1
10	Holt United v Boulton & Paul	1-2
11	Whitton United v Lakenheath	3-3
12	Stevenage Town v Vauxhall Motors	2-3
13	Crittall Athletic v Colchester Casuals	5-1
14	Bexleyheath & Welling v Faversham Town	4-1
15	Lancing Athletic v Worthing	1-6
16	Banstead Athletic v East Grinstead	2-2
17	Ware v Hoddesdon Town	3-1
18	Edgware Town v Finchley	3-4
19	Carshalton Athletic v Dagenham Cables	3-0
20	Slough Centre v Berkhamsted Town	2-1
21	HMS Daedalus v Alton Town	2-2
22	Westbury United v Shepton Mallet Town	3-0
23	Cinderford Town v Clevedon	2-3
24	Dartmouth United v Bugle	3-2
11r	Lakenheath v Whitton United	2-3
16r	East Grinstead v Banstead Athletic	2-0e
21r	Alton Town v HMS Daedalus	1-2

Qualifying Round Four

	Anstey Nomads v Smethwick Town	4-0
	Cambridge City v Higham Ferrers Town	4-0
	Carshalton Athletic v Sheppey United	4-1
	Clapton v Hayes	0-5
	Clevedon v Salisbury	2-1
	Dartmouth United v HMS Daedalus	4-2
	East Grinstead v Sutton United	1-2
	Evenwood Town v Wolsingham Welfare	5-1
	Finchley v Cheshunt (2)	8-0
	Frome Town v Westbury United	2-2
	Harrogate & District Railway v Penrith	2-1
	Harwich & Parkeston v Crittall Athletic	2-2
	Histon v Boulton & Paul	4-1
	Hitchin Town v Slough Centre	3-1
	Norton Woodseats v ICI Alkali	3-3
	Portrack Shamrocks v Whitley Bay	1-2
	Saltash United v Keynsham Town	3-0
	Salts v Rawmarsh Welfare	2-1
	South Bank v Cockfield	2-6
	Tooting & Mitcham United v Worthing	5-1
	Walsall Wood v Hallam	1-1
	Ware v Vauxhall Motors	2-1
	Whitton United v Stowmarket	2-1
	Woking v Bexleyheath & Welling	5-0
r	Crittall Athletic v Harwich & Parkeston	0-2
r	Hallam v Walsall Wood	6-1
r	ICI Alkali v Norton Woodseats	2-0
r	Westbury United v Frome Town	1-2

Round One

	Barking v Kingstonian	3-1
	Brentwood & Warley v Corinthian Casuals	0-5
	Cambridge City v Anstey Nomads	2-1
	Carshalton Athletic v Ilford	1-0
	Clevedon v Briggs Sports	4-0
	Cockfield v Sheffield	3-2
	Dulwich Hamlet v Ware	3-2
	Eastbourne v Slough Town	1-4
	Ferryhill Athletic v ICI Alkali	1-2
	Finchley v Erith & Belvedere	2-0
	Harrogate & District Railway v Billingham Synthonia	2-1
	Hayes v Pegasus	2-4
	Hendon v Boldmere St Michaels	4-0
	Histon v Dartmouth United	3-3
	Hitchin Town v Wycombe Wanderers	0-0
	Leyton v Bromley	1-2
	Leytonstone v Frome Town	6-1
	Marine v Crook Town	1-0
	Redhill v Hallam	2-2
	Saltash United v Southall	2-2
	Salts v Willington	0-3
	Shildon v Bishop Auckland	2-7
	St Albans City v Romford (2)	4-4
	Sutton United v Hounslow Town	3-5
	Tooting & Mitcham United v Oxford City	5-0
	Walton & Hersham v Tilbury	1-0
	Wealdstone v Moor Green	1-1
	Whitby Town v Evenwood Town	2-3
	Whitton United v Harwich & Parkeston	1-1
	Wimbledon v Walthamstow Avenue	1-3
	Woking v Barnet	3-3
	Yorkshire Amateur v Whitley Bay	0-0
r	Barnet v Woking	2-0
r	Dartmouth United v Histon	3-2
r	Hallam v Redhill	1-1
r	Harwich & Parkeston v Whitton United	4-2
r	Moor Green v Wealdstone	1-6
r	Romford (2) v St Albans City	4-0
r	Southall v Saltash United	2-1
r	Whitley Bay v Yorkshire Amateur	0-2
r	Wycombe Wanderers v Hitchin Town	2-0
r2	Redhill v Hallam	0-2 N

Round Two

	Carshalton Athletic v Romford (2)	2-3
	Clevedon v Dartmouth United	5-0
	Corinthian Casuals v Finchley	4-1
	Hallam v Dulwich Hamlet	1-0 N
	Harwich & Parkeston v Harrogate & District Railway	3-2
	Hendon v Hounslow Town	1-2
	ICI Alkali v Leytonstone	2-3
	Marine v Evenwood Town	1-2
	Pegasus v Cockfield	5-0
	Slough Town v Barking	2-1
	Southall v Bishop Auckland	2-0
	Tooting & Mitcham United v Cambridge City	4-2
	Walthamstow Avenue v Wealdstone	0-0
	Willington v Bromley	2-1
	Wycombe Wanderers v Barnet	2-1
	Yorkshire Amateur v Walton & Hersham	1-2
r	Wealdstone v Walthamstow Avenue	1-0

1952/53 to 1953/54

Round Three

	Clevedon v Harwich & Parkeston	1-2
	Corinthian Casuals v Pegasus	0-1
	Hounslow Town v Tooting & Mitcham United	1-1
	Leytonstone v Hallam	3-1
	Southall v Wealdstone	3-0
	Walton & Hersham v Evenwood Town	3-1
	Willington v Slough Town	1-1
	Wycombe Wanderers v Romford (2)	0-5
r	Slough Town v Willington	3-2
r	Tooting & Mitcham United v Hounslow Town	2-1

Round Four

	Leytonstone v Harwich & Parkeston	3-4
	Slough Town v Pegasus	0-2
	Southall v Romford (2)	1-1
	Tooting & Mitcham United v Walton & Hersham	0-0
r	Romford (2) v Southall	1-2
r	Walton & Hersham v Tooting & Mitcham United	0-0
r2	Tooting & Mitcham United v Walton & Hersham	1-2 N

Semi Finals

	Harwich & Parkeston v Walton & Hersham	3-1 N
	Pegasus v Southall	1-1 N
r	Pegasus v Southall	2-1 N

Final

	Pegasus v Harwich & Parkeston	6-0 N

1953/54

Extra Preliminary Round

2	Langley Park CW v West Hartlepool St Josephs	2-7
	Spennymoor Amateur v West Auckland Town	3-4
7	Birm'gham City Trans. v Burgess Products (Hinckley)	3-7
12	Arlesey Town v Vauxhall Motors	5-3
	Kents Athletic v Bedford Avenue	1-3 N
	Leighton United v Stotfold	3-2
	Shefford Town v AC Delco	8-2
	Stevenage Town v Letchworth Town	4-3
16	Bexhill Town v Dorking	5-1
	Cobham v Metropolitan Police	0-1
	Horsham v Eastbourne United	0-1
18	Arlesey Town v Clapton	1-1
	Eton Manor v Wood Green Town	3-1
	Ford Sports v Uxbridge	2-4
	Harrow Town v West Thurrock Athletic	1-2
	McLaren Sports v Willesden	3-0
	Ruislip Manor v Hornchurch & Upminster	1-2
	Yiewsley v Woodford Town	3-2
20	Amersham Town v Marlow	6-4
	Buckingham Town v Osberton Radiator	3-3
	Chesham United v Bicester Town	5-4
	Huntley & Palmers v Wolverton Town & BR	3-3
	Maidenhead United v Cranfield United	3-2
	Newbury Town v Windsor & Eton	4-0
	Pressed Steel v Slough Centre	2-4
	Thame United v Abingdon Town	1-10
	Witney Town v St Frideswides	3-1
	Woodstock Town v NAC Athletic	4-0
21	Pirelli General Cable Works v East Cowes Victoria	1-4
	RAMC Aldershot v HMS Excellent	2-3
22	Paulton Rovers v Swindon BR Corinthians	6-3
	Peasedown Miners Welfare v Spencer Moulton	2-2
	Shepton Mallet Town v Calne & Harris United	5-1
	Wootton Bassett Town v Warminster Town	1-3
18r	Clapton v Arlesey Town	3-1
20r	Osberton Radiator v Buckingham Town	1-2
r	Wolverton Town & BR v Huntley & Palmers	3-1
22r	Spencer Moulton v Peasedown Miners Welfare	4-4e
22r2	Peasedown Miners Welfare v Spencer Moulton	2-0

Preliminary Round

1	Hearts of Liddesdale v Cleator Moor Celtic	2-4
	Penrith v Appleby	2-2
	Wallsend St Lukes v Bedlington Mechanics	7-1
2	Bearpark CW v Witton Park Institute	4-1
	Durham City v West Hartlepool St Josephs	8-3
	Eldon Albion v Wolsingham Welfare	1-6
	Esh Winning Albion v Chilton Athletic	1-1
	Hartlepool Railway Athletic v Ashmore Recreation	2-0
	Seaton Holy Trinity v Durham University	0-9
	Tow Law Town v Burnside United	6-2
	West Auckland Town v Stanley United	3-0
3	Bridlington Central United v Whitby Albion Rangers	4-0
	Furness Athletic v South Bank St Peters	n/a
	Head Wrightsons v Smiths Dock	n/a
	Redcar Albion v Cargo Fleet Works	5-1
	Skinningrove Works v Filey Town	1-5
4	Blackpool Rangers v Runcorn Athletic	2-5
	Harrowby v Eastham Athletic	0-5
	Newton v Manchester YMCA	5-2
	Old Blackburnians v Southport Leyland Road	4-0
	Port Sunlight v Stork	0-1
	St Annes Athletic v Stoneycroft	4-3
5	Harrogate Town v Guiseley	1-4
6	Basford United v Lincoln City School OBU	1-2
	Boots Athletic v Cinderhill Colliery	1-2
	Dunscroft Welfare v RAF Cranwell	3-3
	Gedling Colliery v Staveley Works	10-0
	Hampton Sports v Rawmarsh Welfare	2-6
	Parliament Street Methodists v Netherfield Albion	4-2
	Penistone Church v Atlas & Norfolk (Sheffield)	n/a
	Players Athletic v Raleigh Athletic	3-4
7	Anstey Nomads v Paget Rangers	4-3
	Burgess Products (Hinckley) v Sheldon Town	3-2
	Corby United v Coventry Amateur	2-2
	Earl Shilton Institute v Leicester Amateurs	2-3
	Enderby Town v Ibstock Penistone Rovers	2-3
	Loughborough College v Morris Sports (Loughboro)	0-1
	Oadby Town v Syston St Peters	2-2
	Shepshed Albion v Morris Motors (Coventry)	1-2
8	Fernhill Heath v Staffordshire Casuals	n/a
	Old Wulfrunians v Richard Thomas & Baldwin	3-0
11	Beccles v Bungay Town	3-2
	Exning United v Achilles	1-3
	Leiston v Felixstowe Town	3-1
	Lowestoft Town v Ipswich Electricity Supply	6-1
	Waterside Works v Newmarket Town	3-0
12	Baldock Town v Arlesey Town	3-1
	Bedford Corinthians v Shefford Town	1-3
	Berkhamsted Town v Stevenage Town	1-3
	Dunstable Town (2) v Hemel Hempstead Town	1-0
	Kempston Rovers v Bedford Avenue	0-1
	Leighton United v Potton United	1-3
	Waterlows Dunstable v Marston Shelton Rovers	0-5
	Wootton Blue Cross v Luton Amateur	1-1
14	Farnham Town v Cray Wanderers	3-2
	Foots Cray v Beckenham	7-2
	Sheppey United v Thameside Amateurs	6-1
15	Arundel v Lancing Athletic	1-5
	Brighton Old Corinthians v Southwick	4-1
	Chichester City v Worthing	4-11
	Wigmore Athletic v Littlehampton Town	7-1
16	Banstead Athletic v Lewes	7-0
	Chertsey Town v Farncombe	4-5
	Cuckfield v East Grinstead	1-1
	Eastbourne v Haywards Heath	1-2
	Farnham Town v Camberley	5-0
	Horley v Bexhill Town	1-1
	Leatherhead v Eastbourne United	1-0
	Newhaven v Metropolitan Police	3-2
17	Bishops Stortford v Hertford Town	3-1
	Enfield v Harlow Town	7-0
	Hatfield Town v Cheshunt (2)	0-2
	Kings Langley v Epping Town	6-0
	Rickmansworth Town v Leavesden Hospital	1-2
	Stansted v Welwyn Garden City	1-4
	Tufnell Park Edmonton v Hoddesdon Town	2-0
18	Bata Sports v Uxbridge	2-0
	Clapton v Eton Manor	4-1
	Edgware Town v Rainham Town	5-1
	Grays Athletic v McLaren Sports	3-0
	Storey Athletic v Downshall Athletic	wo/s
	Wembley v Hornchurch & Upminster	6-3
	West Thurrock Athletic v Polytechnic	3-2
	Yiewsley v Pinner	3-1
19	Epsom v Civil Service	5-0
	Malden Town v Royal Ordnance	4-0
	PO Engineers (LTR) v Dagenham Cables	3-3
	Surbiton Town v Devas Institute	3-1
	Vickers (Weybridge) v Worcester Park	1-2
20	Abingdon Town v Maidenhead United	0-8
	Aylesbury United v Wolverton Town & BR	4-3
	Chesham United v Buckingham Town	5-0
	Chipping Norton Town v Amersham Town	3-1
	Henley Town v Bletchley Town	3-4
	Newbury Town v Witney Town	2-1
	Slough Centre v Wallingford Town	4-2
	Woodstock Town v Kidlington	3-2
21	Bournemouth v Blandford United	1-0
	East Cowes Victoria v HMS Excellent	1-0
	Fareham Town v Gosport Borough Athletic	2-3
	Hamworthy v Longfleet St Marys	1-2
	Romsey Town v Alton Town	1-1
	Ryde Sports v Winchester City	2-2
	Swanage Town v Shaftesbury	2-3
	Totton v Lymington	2-2
22	Bulford United v Clandown	2-2
	Devizes Town v Peasedown Miners Welfare	1-1
	Melksham Town v Swindon Victoria	3-6
	Paulton Rovers v Corsham Town	9-1
	Pewsey Vale v Radstock Town	2-4
	Roundway Hospital v Westbury United	3-1
	Warminster Town v Purton	4-1
	Welton Rovers v Shepton Mallet Town	3-2
23	Ilminster Town v Mount Hill Enterprise	3-1
	St Philips Marsh Adult School v Chard Town	1-0
	Taunton BR v Bristol St George	0-3
	Worle OB v Hanham Athletic	3-2
24	Looe v Burraton	3-0
	St Dennis v Mullion	1-0
	St Just v Bugle	4-1
1r	Appleby v Penrith	3-3e
2r	Chilton Athletic v Esh Winning Albion	3-5
6r	RAF Cranwell v Dunscroft Welfare	n/a
7r	Coventry Amateur v Corby United	3-2
r	Syston St Peters v Oadby Town	1-3
12r	Luton Amateur v Wootton Blue Cross	1-1e
16r	Bexhill Town v Horley	3-0
r	East Grinstead v Cuckfield	4-2
19r	Dagenham Cables v PO Engineers (LTR)	2-1e
21r	Alton Town v Romsey Town	3-2
r	Lymington v Totton	4-0
r	Winchester City v Ryde Sports	2-0
22r	Clandown v Bulford United	1-5
r	Peasedown Miners Welfare v Devizes Town	3-2
1r2	Appleby v Penrith	2-3
12r2	Luton Amateur v Wootton Blue Cross	2-4eN

Qualifying Round One

1	Seaton Delaval v Holme Head Works	7-2
	Wallsend St Lukes v Cleator Moor Celtic	1-4
	Washington Welfare v Penrith	2-1
	Whitley Bay v Salterbeck	7-0
2	Durham City v West Auckland Town	2-2
	Durham University v Bearpark CW	1-6
	Esh Winning Albion v Hartlepool Railway Athletic	1-4
	Tow Law Town v Wolsingham Welfare	4-3
3	Bridlington Central United v Head Wrightsons	5-0
	South Bank v Filey Town	3-1e
	South Bank St Peters v North Skelton Athletic	0-3
	Winterton Hospital v Redcar Albion	2-3
4	Earle v Stork	n/a
	Old Blackburnians v Eastham Athletic	5-2
	Runcorn Athletic v Hoylake Athletic	1-2
	St Annes Athletic v Newton	1-2
5	Bradford Rovers v North Ferriby United	5-0
	Guiseley v Liversedge	3-3
	Leeds University YMI v Ossett Albion	2-4
	Thornhill Edge v Brunswick Institute	3-2
6	Dunscroft Welfare v Parliament Street Methodists	5-2
	Gedling Colliery v Penistone Church	7-3
	Lincoln City School OBU v Rawmarsh Welfare	1-5
	Raleigh Athletic v Cinderhill Colliery	3-1
7	Anstey Nomads v Coventry Amateur	4-2
	Burgess Products (Hinckley) v Leicester Amateurs	2-2
	Morris Motors (Cov'try) v Morris Sports (Loughboro)	2-0
	Oadby Town v Ibstock Penistone Rovers	1-1
8	Jack Moulds Athletic v Bournville Athletic	3-4
	Old Wulfrunians v Fernhill Heath	1-0
	Smethwick Town v Walsall Wood	4-1
	Sutton Coldfield Town v Walsall Trinity	0-3
9	Huntingdon United v Atlas Sports	0-1
	Raunds Town v Ramsey Town	4-1
	St Neots St Marys v Higham Ferrers Town	2-3
10	Dereham Town v Sheringham	2-3
	Downham Town v City of Norwich School OBU	2-4
	Holt United v Wymondham Town	5-0
	Thetford Town v Cromer	4-1
11	Eastern Coachworks (Lowestoft) v Beccles	0-2
	Lowestoft Town v Achilles	4-1
	Waterside Works v Ipswich Wanderers	2-2
	Woodbridge Athletic v Leiston	0-3
12	Baldock Town v Dunstable Town (2)	2-1
	Shefford Town v Bedford Avenue	6-0
	Stevenage Town v Potton United	4-3
	Wootton Blue Cross v Marston Shelton Rovers	0-0
13	Crittall Athletic v Colchester Casuals	7-1
	Halstead Town v Saffron Walden Town	4-1
14	Aylesford Paper Mills v Crockenhill	2-3
	Bexley v Maidstone United	0-5
	Foots Cray v Sheppey United	0-8
	Woolwich Polytechnic v Faversham Town	2-0
15	Brighton Old Corinthians v Bognor Regis Town	1-3
	Shoreham v Hove White Rovers	2-3
	Whitehawk & Manor Farm OB v Worthing	8-1
	Wigmore Athletic v Lancing Athletic	4-3
16	Banstead Athletic v Farnham Town	7-2
	Bexhill Town v Leatherhead	2-1
	East Grinstead v Farncombe	5-3
	Newhaven v Haywards Heath	1-0
17	Cheshunt (2) v Bishops Stortford	3-2
	Kings Langley v Leavesden Hospital	1-1
	Parkhill (Chingford) v Welwyn Garden City	2-2
	Tufnell Park Edmonton v Enfield	1-2
18	Clapton v Bata Sports	5-1
	Edgware Town v Yiewsley	3-4
	Grays Athletic v West Thurrock Athletic	4-1
	Wembley v Storey Athletic	1-5
19	Dagenham Cables v Dagenham British Legion	2-4
	Hawker Athletic v Surbiton Town	1-1
	Malden Town v Epsom	1-6
	Worcester Park v Lathol Athletic	4-1
20	Aylesbury United v Bletchley Town	2-0
	Chipping Norton Town v Woodstock Town	7-0
	Newbury Town v Maidenhead United	3-2
	Slough Centre v Chesham United	3-0
21	Alton Town v Shaftesbury	2-2
	Bournemouth v Winchester City	2-0
	East Cowes Victoria v Gosport Borough Athletic	4-0
	Lymington v Longfleet St Marys	6-1
22	Peasedown Miners Welfare v Bulford United	2-3
	Radstock Town v Swindon Victoria	2-1
	Warminster Town v Roundway Hospital	3-3
	Welton Rovers v Paulton Rovers	4-0
23	Bristol St George v Weston-super-Mare St Johns	9-0
	Keynsham Town v Soundwell	4-0
	St Philips Marsh Adult School v Cinderford Town	2-2
	Worle OB v Ilminster Town	6-2

1953/54 to 1954/55

24 Camelford v Tamerton 8-1
Heavitree United v St Just 3-2
Nanpean Rovers v Mousehole 2-1
St Dennis v Looe 2-3
2r West Auckland Town v Durham City 0-6
5r Liversedge v Guiseley 2-1
7r Burgess Products (Hinckley) v Leicester Amateurs 0-1
r Ibstock Penistone Rovers v Oadby Town 2-3
11r Waterside Works v Ipswich Wanderers 7-2
12r Marston Shelton Rovers v Wootton Blue Cross 1-5
17r Leavesden Hospital v Kings Langley 1-1e
r Welwyn Garden City v Parkhill (Chingford) 2-0
19r Surbiton Town v Hawker Athletic 1-0
21r Shaftesbury v Alton Town 2-7
22r Roundway Hospital v Warminster Town 4-2
23r Cinderford Town v St Philips Marsh Adult School 2-0
17r2 Leavesden Hospital v Kings Langley 4-2

Qualifying Round Two

1 Washington Welfare v Seaton Delaval 1-2
Whitley Bay v Cleator Moor Celtic 5-1
2 Bearpark CW v Durham City 1-2
Tow Law Town v Hartlepool Railway Athletic 3-0
3 Redcar Albion v North Skelton Athletic 2-5
South Bank v Bridlington Central United 1-3
4 Old Blackburnians v Hoylake Athletic 3-4
Stork v Newton 3-1
5 Ossett Albion v Bradford Rovers 3-5
Thornhill Edge v Liversedge 3-2
6 Raleigh Athletic v Gedling Colliery 3-6
Rawmarsh Welfare v Dunscroft Welfare 6-1
7 Anstey Nomads v Leicester Amateurs 7-2
Morris Motors (Coventry) v Oadby Town 0-2
8 Bournville Athletic v Walsall Trinity 1-2
Smethwick Town v Old Wulfrunians 1-0
9 Atlas Sports v Ely City 4-3
Higham Ferrers Town v Raunds Town 3-2
10 Holt United v City of Norwich School OBU 1-2
Thetford Town v Sheringham 4-0
11 Beccles v Lowestoft Town 0-1
Leiston v Waterside Works 4-2
12 Baldock Town v Shefford Town 2-3
Wootton Blue Cross v Stevenage Town 3-5
13 Brightlingsea United v Crittall Athletic 0-4
Halstead Town v Brantham Athletic 1-0
14 Maidstone United v Sheppey United 1-1
Woolwich Polytechnic v Crockenhill 4-2
15 Whitehawk & Manor Farm OB v Bognor Regis Town 3-2
Wigmore Athletic v Hove White Rovers 2-4
16 Banstead Athletic v Newhaven 4-1
Bexhill Town v East Grinstead 2-2
17 Enfield v Leavesden Hospital 4-2
Welwyn Garden City v Cheshunt (2) 2-2
18 Storey Athletic v Clapton 2-2
Yiewsley v Grays Athletic 0-2
19 Surbiton Town v Epsom 0-2
Worcester Park v Dagenham British Legion 3-1
20 Aylesbury United v Newbury Town 2-0
Slough Centre v Chipping Norton Town 2-4
21 Bournemouth v Alton Town 3-2
Lymington v East Cowes Victoria 1-2
22 Bulford United v Roundway Hospital 3-1
Radstock Town v Welton Rovers 2-5
23 Bristol St George v Cinderford Town 4-0
Keynsham Town v Worle OB 3-0
24 Heavitree United v Camelford 3-2
Nanpean Rovers v Looe 10-1
14r Sheppey United v Maidstone United 5-0
16r East Grinstead v Bexhill Town 4-2
17r Cheshunt (2) v Welwyn Garden City 6-2
18r Clapton v Storey Athletic 0-2

Qualifying Round Three

1 Whitley Bay v Seaton Delaval 3-2
2 Tow Law Town v Durham City 1-1
3 Bridlington Central United v North Skelton Athletic 2-0
4 Stork v Hoylake Athletic 1-1
5 Thornhill Edge v Bradford Rovers 7-0
6 Rawmarsh Welfare v Gedling Colliery 3-4
7 Oadby Town v Anstey Nomads 1-2
8 Smethwick Town v Walsall Trinity 3-2
9 Higham Ferrers Town v Atlas Sports 4-6
10 Thetford Town v City of Norwich School OBU 5-2
11 Lowestoft Town v Leiston 0-1
12 Shefford Town v Stevenage Town 1-1
13 Crittall Athletic v Halstead Town 4-0
14 Sheppey United v Woolwich Polytechnic 5-2
15 Whitehawk & Manor Farm OB v Hove White Rovers 5-0
16 East Grinstead v Banstead Athletic 0-8
17 Cheshunt (2) v Enfield 2-2
18 Storey Athletic v Grays Athletic 5-0
19 Epsom v Worcester Park 0-2
20 Aylesbury United v Chipping Norton Town 4-0
21 East Cowes Victoria v Bournemouth 6-1
22 Bulford United v Welton Rovers 4-3
23 Keynsham Town v Bristol St George 2-1
24 Nanpean Rovers v Heavitree United 5-1
2r Durham City v Tow Law Town 1-2
4r Hoylake Athletic v Stork 1-0
12r Stevenage Town v Shefford Town 5-0
17r Enfield v Cheshunt (2) 3-0

Qualifying Round Four

Atlas Sports v Dagenham 2-5
Banstead Athletic v Tilbury 4-3
Bournemouth Gasworks Ath v East Cowes Victoria 6-1
Brentwood & Warley v Worcester Park 5-2
Bulford United v Woking 1-4
Dartmouth United v Keynsham Town 3-2
Enfield v Stevenage Town 2-3
Gedling Colliery v Anstey Nomads 2-1
Histon v Briggs Sports 0-2
Hitchin Town v Oxford City 5-2
Leiston v Thetford Town 1-4
Nanpean Rovers v Saltash United 3-1
Northern Nomads v Hoylake Athletic 8-0
Norton Woodseats v Sheffield 1-3
Salts v Thornhill Edge 5-0
Sheppey United v Redhill 3-1
Smethwick Town v Boldmere St Michaels 4-2
Storey Athletic v Sutton United 2-2
Tow Law Town v Billingham Synthonia 1-1
Ware v Aylesbury United 2-0
Whitby Town v Ferryhill Athletic 2-3
Whitehawk & Manor Farm OB v Erith & Belvedere 3-3
Whitley Bay v Bridlington Central United 3-1
Whitton United v Crittall Athletic 2-2
r Billingham Synthonia v Tow Law Town 3-1e
r Crittall Athletic v Whitton United 2-1
r Erith & Belvedere v Whitehawk & Manor Farm OB 2-1e
r Sutton United v Storey Athletic 1-0

Round One

Banstead Athletic v Leytonstone 3-4
Barnet v Sutton United 7-0
Billingham Synthonia v Salts 4-4
Brentwood & Warley v Erith & Belvedere 1-6
Briggs Sports v Bournemouth Gasworks Athletic 3-1
Cambridge City v Barking 2-1
Cockfield v Whitley Bay 2-0
Dagenham v Bromley 1-2
Dartmouth United v St Albans City 1-3
Dulwich Hamlet v Slough Town 3-1
Evenwood Town v Hallam 0-1
Ferryhill Athletic v Marine 2-1
Finchley v Harwich & Parkeston 3-0
Gedling Colliery v Yorkshire Amateur 1-0
Harrogate & District Railway v Northern Nomads 2-2
Hayes v Carshalton Athletic 1-0
Hitchin Town v Crittall Athletic 4-0
Hounslow Town v Moor Green 5-1
ICI Alkali v Bishop Auckland 0-6
Leyton v Sheppey United 1-1
Pegasus v Clevedon 3-0
Romford (2) v Thetford Town 3-0
Sheffield v Willington 0-2
Shildon v Crook Town 0-3
Southall v Corinthian Casuals 0-2
Stevenage Town v Wimbledon 1-3
Walthamstow Avenue v Smethwick Town 2-1
Walton & Hersham v Ilford 3-0
Ware v Nanpean Rovers 6-2
Wealdstone v Hendon 3-3
Woking v Kingstonian 4-1
Wycombe Wanderers v Tooting & Mitcham United 5-0
r Hendon v Wealdstone 3-1
r Northern Nomads v Harrogate & District Railway 5-2
r Salts v Billingham Synthonia 5-2
r Sheppey United v Leyton 3-2

Round Two

Bishop Auckland v Ware 6-1
Bromley v Cockfield 2-1
Corinthian Casuals v Hallam 0-1
Dulwich Hamlet v Barnet 1-1
Finchley v Ferryhill Athletic 4-1
Gedling Colliery v Pegasus 1-6
Hendon v Hayes 4-2
Hitchin Town v Erith & Belvedere 1-0
Northern Nomads v Willington 3-3
Romford (2) v Crook Town 1-1
Salts v Hounslow Town 1-2
Sheppey United v Wimbledon 1-0
St Albans City v Briggs Sports 1-2
Walthamstow Avenue v Cambridge City 5-0
Walton & Hersham v Woking 3-1
Wycombe Wanderers v Leytonstone 0-0
r Barnet v Dulwich Hamlet 2-1
r Crook Town v Romford (2) 6-0
r Leytonstone v Wycombe Wanderers 0-0
r Willington v Northern Nomads 3-1
r2 Leytonstone v Wycombe Wanderers 1-2 N

Round Three

Barnet v Hitchin Town 1-1
Bishop Auckland v Hallam 5-0
Briggs Sports v Bromley 1-0
Crook Town v Walton & Hersham 5-0
Hendon v Finchley 1-1
Hounslow Town v Wycombe Wanderers 3-0
Pegasus v Willington 1-1
Walthamstow Avenue v Sheppey United 4-0

r Finchley v Hendon 2-1
r Hitchin Town v Barnet 3-1
r Willington v Pegasus 2-4

Round Four

Bishop Auckland v Hounslow Town 4-2
Briggs Sports v Pegasus 3-0
Crook Town v Hitchin Town 10-1
Finchley v Walthamstow Avenue 1-1
r Walthamstow Avenue v Finchley 1-0

Semi Finals

Bishop Auckland v Briggs Sports 5-1 N
Crook Town v Walthamstow Avenue 1-1 N
r Crook Town v Walthamstow Avenue 3-2 N

Final

Crook Town v Bishop Auckland 2-2eN
r Crook Town v Bishop Auckland 2-2 N
r2 Crook Town v Bishop Auckland 1-0 N

1954/55

Extra Preliminary Round

2 Bearpark CW v Craghead CW 2-4
Durham City v West Hartlepool St Josephs 2-2
6 Armthorpe Welfare v RAF Cranwell 1-2e
Basford United v Rawmarsh Welfare 0-4
Briggs Sports (Doncaster) v Stanton Ironworks n/a
Dunscroft Welfare v Parliament Street Methodists 4-1
Worthington Simpson v Boots Athletic 8-1
7 Birmingham City Transport v Syston St Peters 4-4
Coventry Amateur v Loughborough College 3-0
Ibstock Penistone Rovers v Oadby Town 2-2
Shepshed Albion v Paget Rangers 2-4
12 Arlesey Town v Bedford Avenue 2-3
Shefford Town v Letchworth Town 1-2
Vauxhall Motors v Royston Town 8-0
16 Camberley v Metropolitan Police 2-6
Farnham Town v Crawley 3-0
Haywards Heath v Bexhill Town 5-2
Horsham v Addlestone 7-1
Lewes v Dorking 1-1
Redhill v Farncombe 4-0
17 Enfield v Parkhill (Chingford) 4-1
18 Dagenham Cables v Wood Green Town 1-2
Edgware Town v Alexandra Park n/a
Ford Sports v Barkingside 4-0
Hornchurch & Upminster v Polytechnic 8-1
Rainham Town v Aveley 2-0
Wembley v Harrow Town 2-1
Wingate v Lathol Athletic 4-1
Woodford Town v West Thurrock Athletic 4-1
Yiewsley v Dagenham Park 4-0
20 Abingdon Town v Marlow 2-3
Amersham Town v NAC Athletic 5-2
Aylesbury United v Osberton Radiator 3-1
Bletchley Town v Huntley & Palmers 1-3
Buckingham Town v Oxford City 0-7
Chesham United v Bicester Town 2-0
Chipping Norton Town v Oxford YMCA 2-1
Didcot Town v Windsor & Eton 5-3
Kirtlington Sports v Wallingford Town 4-2
Maidenhead United v Cranfield United 4-0
Morris Motors v Woodstock Town 2-1
Newbury Town v St Frideswides 4-1
Pressed Steel v Slough Centre 2-2
Witney Town v Wokingham Town 3-3
Wolverton Town & BR v Henley Town 9-0
22 Clandown v Welton Rovers 3-0
Roundway Hospital v Wootton Bassett Town 4-3
Sharpness v Swindon BR Corinthians 4-2
Spencer Moulton v Peasedown Miners Welfare 0-2
Swindon Victoria v Purton 3-2
Westbury United v Corsham Town 7-0
2r Durham City v West Hartlepool St Josephs 3-4
7r Oadby Town v Ibstock Penistone Rovers 3-2
r Syston St Peters v Birmingham City Transport 3-2
16r Dorking v Lewes 9-1
20r Slough Centre v Pressed Steel 5-2
r Wokingham Town v Witney Town 3-2

Preliminary Round

1 Hearts of Liddesdale v Salterbeck 6-4
Washington CW v Seaton Delaval n/a
2 Chilton Athletic v Seaton Holy Trinity n/a
Cornsay Park Albion v West Hartlepool St Josephs 4-7
Langley Park CW v Esh Winning Albion 3-0
Spennymoor Amateur v Stockton Amateur n/a
Stanley United v Craghead CW 2-2
Tow Law Town v West Auckland Town 0-4
Witton Park Institute v Burnside United 1-2
Wolsingham Welfare v Durham University 5-0
3 Bridlington Central United v Bridlington Trinity United 1-4
Cargo Fleet Works v Whitby Albion Rangers 1-3
Head Wrightsons v South Bank 2-7
Redcar Albion v Winterton Hospital 0-1
Skinningrove Works v North Skelton Athletic 0-4

1954/55

4	Earle v Harrowby	n/a
	Eastham Athletic v Blackpool Metal Mechanics	1-5
	Hoylake Athletic v Southport Leyland Road	6-1
	Port Sunlight v Blackpool Rangers	1-2
	Runcorn Athletic v Stork	1-4
	St Annes Athletic v Newton	0-2
	Stockton Heath v Manchester University	4-1
	Stoneycroft v Old Blackburnians	5-1
5	Bradford Electricity v Guiseley	3-1
	Harrogate Town v Bradford Rovers	0-1
	Leeds University YMI v Liversedge	1-2
	Ossett Albion v Kingston Wolves	2-1
	Thackley v Thornhill Edge	3-1
6	Cinderhill Colliery v Hampton Sports	1-3
	Eastwood Town v Lincoln City School OBU	2-0
	Netherfield Albion v Dunscroft Welfare	3-2
	Norton Woodseats v Penistone Church	9-0
	Raleigh Athletic v Atlas & Norfolk (Sheffield)	6-1
	Rawmarsh Welfare v Stanton Ironworks	4-2
	Staveley Works v RAF Cranwell	n/a
	Worthington Simpson v Players Athletic	0-1
7	Barwell Athletic v Anstey Nomads	0-5
	Enderby Town v Earl Shilton Institute	4-3
	Oadby Town v Morris Sports (Loughborough)	2-0
	Quorn v Cosby United	1-1
	Rootes Athletic v Burgess Products (Hinckley)	1-0
	Sheldon Town v Coventry Amateur	0-2
	Stapenhill v Desford CW	7-3
	Syston St Peters v Paget Rangers	1-1
8	Bretforton OB v Walsall Trinity	3-7
11	Beccles v Exning United	wo/s
	Bungay Town v Ipswich Wanderers	4-2e
	Eastern Coachworks (Lowestoft) v Waterside Works	2-6
	Felixstowe Town v Woodbridge Athletic	5-4e
	Hadleigh United v Newmarket Town	1-4
	Leiston v Landseer	4-4
12	Baldock Town v Marston Shelton Rovers	4-1
	Berkhamsted Town v Leighton United	2-1
	Hemel Hempstead Town v Bedford Corinthians	wo/s
	Letchworth Town v Kempston Rovers	7-0
	Potton United v Wootton Blue Cross	2-2
	Stotfold v AC Delco	5-3
	Vauxhall Motors v Bedford Avenue	5-0
	Waterlows Dunstable v Tring Town	1-1
14	Bakers Sports v Crockenhill	1-2
	Bexley v Woolwich Polytechnic	1-1
	Bowater Lloyds v Foots Cray	1-5
	Maidstone United v Faversham Town	8-2
15	Arundel v Pulborough	2-3
	Bognor Regis Town v Southwick	6-1
	Lancing Athletic v Chichester City	3-1
	Littlehampton Town v Shoreham	3-2
	Whitehawk & Manor Farm v Brighton Old Gramm'ans	2-3
	Wigmore Athletic v Goldstone	3-1
	Worthing v Moulsecoomb Rovers	12-1
16	Chertsey Town v Redhill	2-4
	Corsham Town v Cuckfield	1-2
	Croydon Amateur v Metropolitan Police	1-7
	Dorking v Newhaven	1-1
	East Grinstead v Horley	1-2
	Eastbourne v Eastbourne United	3-0
	Haywards Heath v Farnham Town	2-4
	Leatherhead v Horsham	1-0
17	Boreham Wood v Bishops Stortford	1-5
	Cheshunt (2) v Harlow Town	0-0
	Epping Town v Tufnell Park Edmonton	1-0
	Hatfield Town v Stansted	1-2
	Hertford Town v Kings Langley	5-1
	Hoddesdon Town v Welwyn Garden City	2-2
	Leavesden Hospital v Enfield	1-2
	Rickmansworth Town v Crown & Manor	1-3
18	Brentwood & Warley v Tilbury	5-2
	Clapton v Yiewsley	1-1
	Edgware Town v Wood Green Town	4-4
	Ford Sports v Storey Athletic	2-2
	Hornchurch & Upminster v Willesden	4-0
	Pinner v Wingate	3-1
	Rainham Town v Bata Sports	3-0
	Woodford Town v Wembley	4-1
19	Epsom v Civil Service	6-1
	Hawker Athletic v Vickers (Weybridge)	1-0
	Kingsbury Town v Malden Town	1-1
	McLaren Sports v Twickenham	2-3
	Molesey v Devas Institute	5-2
	Royal Ordnance v PO Engineers (LTR)	4-5
	Ruislip Manor v Surbiton Town	4-0
	Worcester Park v Uxbridge	3-4
20	Aylesbury United v Marlow	8-3
	Didcot Town v Amersham Town	5-3
	Huntley & Palmers v Wolverton Town & BR	3-3
	Kidlington v Morris Motors	3-3
	Maidenhead United v Kirtlington Sports	9-1
	Newbury Town v Chesham United	2-1
	Oxford City v Wokingham Town	5-1
	Slough Centre v Chipping Norton Town	4-4
21	Fareham Town v Alton Town	2-3
	Hamworthy v Longfleet St Marys	3-2
	Lymington v Totton	0-2
	Ryde Sports v Gosport Borough Athletic	2-5
	Shaftesbury v Wimborne	3-4
	Swanage Town v Bournemouth	4-2
22	Bulford United v Westbury United	5-0
	Calne & Harris United v Devizes Town	0-5
	Clandown v Paulton Rovers	2-2
	Peasedown Miners Welfare v Roundway Hospital	3-2
	Pewsey Vale v Sharpness	0-2
	Radstock Town v Melksham Town	5-0
	Shepton Mallet Town v Warminster Town	1-1
	Sherston v Swindon Victoria	1-5
23	Cinderford Town v Bristol St George	5-0
	RAF Locking v Keynsham Town	0-5
	Soundwell v Chard Town	6-1
	Worle OB v Weston-super-Mare St Johns	3-1
2r	Craghead CW v Stanley United	3-1
7r	Cosby United v Quorn	4-2
r	Paget Rangers v Syston St Peters	5-1
11r	Landseer v Leiston	3-2
12r	Tring Town v Waterlows Dunstable	4-7
r	Wootton Blue Cross v Potton United	5-4e
14r	Woolwich Polytechnic v Bexley	2-1
16r	Newhaven v Dorking	3-3e
17r	Harlow Town v Cheshunt (2)	3-7
r	Welwyn Garden City v Hoddesdon Town	3-1
18r	Storey Athletic v Ford Sports	0-1
r	Wood Green Town v Edgware Town	3-3
r	Yiewsley v Clapton	1-3e
19r	Malden Town v Kingsbury Town	1-3
20r	Chipping Norton Town v Slough Centre	2-3e
r	Morris Motors v Kidlington	3-1
r	Wolverton Town & BR v Huntley & Palmers	6-0
22r	Paulton Rovers v Clandown	1-4
r	Warminster Town v Shepton Mallet Town	1-2
16r2	Newhaven v Dorking	2-4 N
18r2	Edgware Town v Wood Green Town	7-1

Qualifying Round One

1	Hearts of Liddesdale v Cleator Moor Celtic	4-1
	Penrith v Appleby	4-3
	Wallsend St Lukes v Heaton Stannington	3-0
	Washington CW v Hexham Hearts	2-0
2	Burnside United v West Hartlepool St Josephs	4-2
	Chilton Athletic v Spennymoor Amateur	5-2
	Langley Park CW v Wolsingham Welfare	3-2
	West Auckland Town v Craghead CW	9-0
3	South Bank v Bridlington Trinity United	6-0
	Whitby Albion Rangers v North Skelton Athletic	0-2
	Whitby Town v Winterton Hospital	3-1
4	Blackpool Metal Mechanics v Stoneycroft	n/a
	Hoylake Athletic v Blackpool Rangers	1-3
	Newton v Stockton Heath	2-0
	Stork v unknown	3-2
5	Bradford Rovers v Ossett Albion	1-4
	Ferrybridge Amateur v Liversedge	1-2
	North Ferriby United v Brunswick Institute	n/a
	Thackley v Bradford Electricity	4-2
6	Norton Woodseats v Eastwood Town	5-0
	Players Athletic v Netherfield Albion	1-2
	Raleigh Athletic v Hampton Sports	n/a
	Staveley Works v Rawmarsh Welfare	2-5
7	Cosby United v Anstey Nomads	0-2
	Coventry Amateur v Stapenhill	0-3
	Enderby Town v Oadby Town	1-1
	Rootes Athletic v Paget Rangers	2-1
8	Boldmere St Michaels v Walsall Trinity	2-6
	Bournville Athletic v Jack Moulds Athletic	0-1
	Fernhill Heath v Staffordshire Casuals	0-1
	Walsall Wood v Old Wulfrunians	2-1
9	Finedon Town v Histon	2-3
	Ramsey Town v Ely City	3-4
	Somersham Town v Higham Town	4-1
	St Neots St Marys v Huntingdon United	n/a
10	City of Norwich School OBU v Wymondham Town	3-3
	Downham Town v Cromer	5-2
	Holt United v North Walsham Town	3-3
11	Beccles v Waterside Works	6-2
	Felixstowe Town v Newmarket Town	1-4
	Landseer v Bungay Town	1-3
	Whitton United v Achilles	3-0
12	Berkhamsted Town v Vauxhall Motors	4-2
	Hemel Hempstead Town v Baldock Town	3-1
	Waterlows Dunstable v Letchworth Town	1-9
	Wootton Blue Cross v Stotfold	5-2
14	Beckenham v Cray Wanderers	1-3
	Foots Cray v Maidstone United	0-2
	RN Depot v Woolwich Polytechnic	0-3
	Thameside Amateurs v Crockenhill	1-1
15	Bognor Regis Town v Worthing	1-4
	Brighton Old Grammarians v Pulborough	6-2
	Lancing Athletic v Hove White Rovers	2-3
	Littlehampton Town v Wigmore Athletic	2-3
16	Dorking v Cuckfield	3-0
	Farnham Town v Metropolitan Police	2-2
	Leatherhead v Eastbourne	2-2
	Redhill v Horley	5-2
17	Cheshunt (2) v Hertford Town	2-2
	Crown & Manor v Enfield	1-5
	Epping Town v Bishops Stortford	2-3
	Stansted v Welwyn Garden City	3-5
18	Clapton v Edgware Town	1-0
	Ford Sports v Woodford Town	0-2
	Hornchurch & Upminster v Brentwood & Warley	2-0
	Rainham Town v Pinner	8-3
19	Hawker Athletic v Twickenham	2-2
	Kingsbury Town v Epsom	0-3
	Molesey v Uxbridge	1-1
	PO Engineers (LTR) v Ruislip Manor	2-5
20	Aylesbury United v Oxford City	6-3
	Maidenhead United v Wolverton Town & BR	3-1
	Morris Motors v Didcot Town	1-2
	Slough Centre v Newbury Town	1-1
21	Alton Town v Gosport Borough Athletic	4-3
	Swanage Town v Hamworthy	4-2
	Totton v Romsey Town	n/a
	Wimborne v Winchester City	4-2
22	Bulford United v Shepton Mallet Town	3-1
	Clandown v Radstock Town	3-1
	Peasedown Miners Welfare v Swindon Victoria	5-0
	Sharpness v Devizes Town	2-2
23	Hanham Athletic v Worle OB	2-4 N
	Ilminster Town v Mount Hill Enterprise	6-0
	Soundwell v Keynsham Town	0-0
	St Philips Marsh Adult School v Cinderford Town	3-0
24	Burraton v Saltash United	2-4
	Heavitree United v Mousehole	7-0
	Mullion v Bugle	3-2
	St Dennis v Camelford	5-2
4r	Blackpool Metal Mechanics v Stoneycroft	2-3
7r	Oadby Town v Enderby Town	1-2
10r	North Walsham Town v Holt United	0-1
r	Wymondham Town v City of Norwich School OBU	5-0
14r	Crockenhill v Thameside Amateurs	1-2
16r	Eastbourne v Leatherhead	2-0
r	Metropolitan Police v Farnham Town	4-1
17r	Hertford Town v Cheshunt (2)	2-2e
19r	Twickenham v Hawker Athletic	2-3e
r	Uxbridge v Molesey	2-1
20r	Newbury Town v Slough Centre	4-0
22r	Devizes Town v Sharpness	1-1
23r	Keynsham Town v Soundwell	5-2
17r2	Hertford Town v Cheshunt (2)	1-2 N
22r2	Devizes Town v Sharpness	3-1

Qualifying Round Two

1	Hearts of Liddesdale v Washington CW	3-1
	Wallsend St Lukes v Penrith	2-2
2	Chilton Athletic v Burnside United	1-2
	West Auckland Town v Langley Park CW	4-1
3	South Bank v Whitby Town	2-1
	South Bank St Peters v North Skelton Athletic	0-2
4	Newton v Stoneycroft	5-2
	Stork v Blackpool Rangers	3-2
5	North Ferriby United v Ossett Albion	2-3
	Thackley v Liversedge	3-2
6	Raleigh Athletic v Netherfield Albion	3-2
	Rawmarsh Welfare v Norton Woodseats	1-3
7	Anstey Nomads v Stapenhill	7-4
	Enderby Town v Rootes Athletic	0-2
8	Staffordshire Casuals v Walsall Trinity	2-1e
	Walsall Wood v Jack Moulds Athletic	1-0
9	Ely City v St Neots St Marys	2-0
	Somersham Town v Histon	2-7
10	Downham Town v Holt United	1-7
	Wymondham Town v Sheringham	6-2
11	Bungay Town v Newmarket Town	5-1
	Whitton United v Beccles	2-2
12	Berkhamsted Town v Hemel Hempstead Town	1-4
	Wootton Blue Cross v Letchworth Town	1-6
13	Brantham Athletic v Colchester Casuals	1-2
	Saffron Walden Town v Halstead Town	0-5
14	Cray Wanderers v Maidstone United	3-2
	Woolwich Polytechnic v Thameside Amateurs	0-1
15	Wigmore Athletic v Brighton Old Grammarians	2-4
	Worthing v Hove White Rovers	5-4
16	Dorking v Redhill	2-2
	Eastbourne v Metropolitan Police	0-5
17	Cheshunt (2) v Enfield	3-4
	Welwyn Garden City v Bishops Stortford	3-0
18	Hornchurch & Upminster v Rainham Town	1-3
	Woodford Town v Clapton	2-3
19	Epsom v Uxbridge	0-4
	Hawker Athletic v Ruislip Manor	0-2
20	Aylesbury United v Didcot Town	6-3
	Maidenhead United v Newbury Town	3-2
21	Swanage Town v Alton Town	2-4
	Wimborne v Totton	2-4
22	Bulford United v Peasedown Miners Welfare	5-3
	Clandown v Devizes Town	3-2
23	Ilminster Town v Keynsham Town	3-2
	Worle OB v St Philips Marsh Adult School	1-2
24	Heavitree United v St Dennis	5-2 v
	Mullion v Saltash United	1-5
1r	Penrith v Wallsend St Lukes	3-0
11r	Beccles v Whitton United	1-0
16r	Redhill v Dorking	4-3
24r	St Dennis v Heavitree United	2-1

Qualifying Round Three

1	Penrith v Hearts of Liddesdale	4-2
2	Burnside United v West Auckland Town	0-4
3	South Bank v North Skelton Athletic	3-1
4	Stork v Newton	3-0
5	Thackley v Ossett Albion	2-1

1954/55 to 1955/56

6 Raleigh Athletic v Norton Woodseats 0-10
7 Rootes Athletic v Anstey Nomads 2-5
8 Walsall Wood v Staffordshire Casuals 3-1
9 Ely City v Histon 0-4
10 Wymondham Town v Holt United 5-3
11 Bungay Town v Beccles 3-1
12 Letchworth Town v Hemel Hempstead Town 1-2
13 Halstead Town v Colchester Casuals 2-1
14 Thameside Amateurs v Cray Wanderers 3-2
15 Worthing v Brighton Old Grammarians 0-1
16 Metropolitan Police v Redhill 1-3
17 Enfield v Welwyn Garden City 6-0
18 Clapton v Rainham Town 1-1
19 Ruislip Manor v Uxbridge 2-3
20 Maidenhead United v Aylesbury United 1-3
21 Totton v Alton Town 1-2
22 Bulford United v Clandown 2-4
23 St Philips Marsh Adult School v Ilminster Town 2-2
24 St Dennis v Saltash United 2-5
18r Rainham Town v Clapton 0-4
23r Ilminster Town v St Philips Marsh Adult School 4-2

Qualifying Round Four

Anstey Nomads v Smethwick Town 5-0
Aylesbury United v Enfield 5-2
Billingham Synthonia v South Bank 5-0
Bournemouth Gasworks Athletic v Alton Town 2-2
Bungay Town v Wymondham Town 3-1
Clandown v Saltash United 1-2
Dagenham v Barking 1-0
Dartmouth United v Ilminster Town 9-0
Grays Athletic v Clapton 2-0
Harrogate & District Railway v Yorkshire Amateur 2-3
Harwich & Parkeston v Histon 2-1
ICI Alkali v Stork 2-3
Kingstonian v Thameside Amateurs 6-0
Leyton v Eton Manor 2-1
Nanpean Rovers v Clevedon 2-3
Redhill v Brighton Old Grammarians 2-2
Sheffield v Thackley 5-0
Slough Town v Uxbridge 3-3
Stevenage Town v Hemel Hempstead Town 4-2
Sutton United v Banstead Athletic 2-3
Thetford Town v Halstead Town 2-1
Walsall Wood v Norton Woodseats 2-2
West Auckland Town v Penrith 6-1
Whitley Bay v Shildon 0-0
r Alton Town v Bournemouth Gasworks Athletic 5-2
r Norton Woodseats v Walsall Wood 12-0
r Redhill v Brighton Old Grammarians 7-2
r Shildon v Whitley Bay 2-1
r Uxbridge v Slough Town 3-1

Round One

Alton Town v Banstead Athletic 2-1
Barnet v Hitchin Town 0-2
Bromley v Bungay Town 4-0
Cambridge City v Thetford Town 3-2
Carshalton Athletic v Leytonstone 3-1
Cockfield v Northern Nomads 1-2
Crook Town v Willington 0-1
Dartmouth United v Hendon 3-3
Dulwich Hamlet v Walton & Hersham 0-0
Erith & Belvedere v Harwich & Parkeston 2-0
Finchley v Southall 4-3
Gedling Colliery v Billingham Synthonia 3-3
Grays Athletic v Anstey Nomads 1-3
Hallam v Ferryhill Athletic 2-0
Ilford v Briggs Sports 1-0
Kingstonian v Aylesbury United 2-0
Leyton v Hayes 2-3
Marine v Shildon 0-1
Norton Woodseats v Salts 4-2
Pegasus v Dagenham 4-0
Redhill v Hounslow Town 3-3
Sheppey United v Saltash United 2-0
Stevenage Town v Corinthian Casuals 3-1
Stork v Bishop Auckland 1-3
Tooting & Mitcham United v Wimbledon 1-1
Uxbridge v Romford (2) 4-2
Walthamstow Avenue v Moor Green 4-0
Ware v Clevedon 3-2
West Auckland Town v Sheffield 2-2
Woking v St Albans City 2-1
Wycombe Wanderers v Wealdstone 1-1
Yorkshire Amateur v Evenwood Town 1-3
r Billingham Synthonia v Gedling Colliery 4-0
r Hendon v Dartmouth United 2-1
r Hounslow Town v Redhill 6-0
r Sheffield v West Auckland Town 1-4
r Walton & Hersham v Dulwich Hamlet 3-1
r Wealdstone v Wycombe Wanderers 1-2
r Wimbledon v Tooting & Mitcham United 4-3

Round Two

Alton Town v Uxbridge 3-1
Anstey Nomads v Hayes 1-2
Billingham Synthonia v Bromley 1-3
Bishop Auckland v Erith & Belvedere 5-0
Finchley v Sheppey United 0-0
Hallam v West Auckland Town 1-2
Hendon v Cambridge City 4-3
Hounslow Town v Hitchin Town 3-3
Ilford v Northern Nomads 2-2
Kingstonian v Walton & Hersham 3-2
Norton Woodseats v Carshalton Athletic 1-4
Shildon v Wimbledon 0-0
Stevenage Town v Pegasus 2-5
Walthamstow Avenue v Ware 11-0
Willington v Evenwood Town 1-2
Wycombe Wanderers v Woking 4-0
r Hitchin Town v Hounslow Town 1-2
r Ilford v Northern Nomads 2-1
r Sheppey United v Finchley 1-4
r Wimbledon v Shildon 2-1

Round Three

Alton Town v Carshalton Athletic 1-1
Evenwood Town v Finchley 2-3
Hayes v Wimbledon 0-2
Hounslow Town v Bromley 3-0
Kingstonian v Bishop Auckland 3-12
Pegasus v West Auckland Town 4-1
Walthamstow Avenue v Hendon 0-1
Wycombe Wanderers v Ilford 3-1
r Carshalton Athletic v Alton Town 4-3

Round Four

Bishop Auckland v Finchley 1-1
Carshalton Athletic v Hounslow Town 2-2
Wimbledon v Hendon 1-1
Wycombe Wanderers v Pegasus 0-0
r Finchley v Bishop Auckland 1-3
r Hendon v Wimbledon 4-1
r Hounslow Town v Carshalton Athletic 6-1
r Pegasus v Wycombe Wanderers 1-2

Semi Finals

Bishop Auckland v Wycombe Wanderers 1-0 N
Hendon v Hounslow Town 2-1 N

Final

Bishop Auckland v Hendon 2-0 N

1955/56

Extra Preliminary Round

2 Deerness Sports v Durham University 5-0
Stanhope Town v Esh Winning Albion n/a
Wolsingham Welfare v Langley Park CW 1-0
6 Armthorpe Welfare v Monk Bretton Colliery n/a
Atlas & Norfolk (Sheffield) v Netherfield Albion 2-1
Briggs Sports (Doncaster) v Basford United 2-0
Hampton Sports v Cinderhill Colliery 11-0
Thorncliffe Recreational v Rawmarsh Welfare 1-2
7 Barwell Athletic v Shepshed Albion 3-4
Desford CW v Morris Sports (Loughborough) 7-1
Measham Imperial v Birmingham City Transport 5-1
Paget Rangers v Coventry Amateur 4-1
Stapenhill v Oadby Town 3-2
12 Arlesey Town v Marston Shelton Rovers 8-2
Bedford Avenue v AC Delco 1-1
Cranfield United v Hemel Hempstead Town 0-4
Tring Town v Kempston Rovers 0-2
15 Croydon Amateur v Crawley 0-3
Eastbourne United v Cobham 9-5
Farncombe v Banstead Athletic 2-5
Horsham v East Grinstead 3-0
Metropolitan Police v Farnham Town 3-3
Newhaven v Leatherhead 1-0
17 Bishops Stortford v Chingford 4-2
Harris Lebus v Hoddesdon Town 3-0
20 Amersham Town v Bletchley & Wipac Sports 3-3
Bicester Town v Chesham United 1-1
Didcot Town v Abingdon Town 4-2
Kirtlington Sports v Huntley & Palmers 1-2
Maidenhead United v Slough Centre 2-2
Marlow v Buckingham Town 5-1
Morris Motors v Kidlington 2-2
Osberton Radiator v Chipping Norton Town 2-1
Oxford City v Henley Town 11-0
Pressed Steel v Woodstock Town 3-3
Slough Town v Oxford YMCA 5-0
Stokenchurch v Wallingford Town 0-6
Thame United v Wokingham Town 2-4
Windsor & Eton v NAC Athletic 4-2
Witney Town v St Frideswides 4-1
Wolverton Town & BR v Newbury Town 0-6
22 Bulford United v Roundway Hospital 6-0
Pinehurst Youth Centre v Devizes Town 6-1
Sharpness v Swindon BR Corinthians 1-0
Swindon Victoria v Radstock Town 6-1
Warminster Town v Spencer Moulton 0-1
Welton Rovers v Brimscombe 4-0
Westbury United v Wootton Bassett Town 6-1
12r AC Delco v Bedford Avenue 6-4
15r Farnham Town v Metropolitan Police 3-7
20r Bletchley & Wipac Sports v Amersham Town 2-0
r Chesham United v Bicester Town 3-3e
r Kidlington v Morris Motors 4-6
r Slough Centre v Maidenhead United 0-1
r Woodstock Town v Pressed Steel 0-2
20r2 Chesham United v Bicester Town 3-2e

Preliminary Round

1 Hearts of Liddesdale v Cowans Sheldon 1-2
Penrith v Cleator Moor Celtic 0-0
Seaton Sluice United v Wallsend St Lukes 2-2
Washington CW v Seaton Delaval wo/s
2 Bank Head United v Tow Law Town 3-2
Burnside United v Deerness Sports 1-0
Chilton Athletic v Stanley United 0-3
Craghead CW v Seaton Holy Trinity n/a
Durham County Constabulary v Bearpark CW 1-2
Heighington Amateur v Esh Winning Albion 6-3
Witton Park Institute v West Hartlepool St Josephs 3-2
Wolsingham Welfare v Durham City 4-5
3 Bridlington Central United v Head Wrightsons 2-0
Bridlington Trinity United v Whitby Albion Rangers 10-0
Cargo Fleet Works v Redcar Albion 3-4
North Skelton Athletic v Winterton Hospital 4-1
Wilton ICI v Skinningrove Works n/a
4 Blackpool Mechanics v Blackpool Rangers 1-3
Moreton v Runcorn Athletic 4-5
Newton v Middleton Amateurs 3-0
Old Blackburnians v Hoylake Athletic 0-3
Southport Leyland Road v Ainsdale Hesketh Park 2-0
St Annes Athletic v Earle 4-1
Stockton Heath v ICI Alkali 4-1
Stoneycroft v Port Sunlight 3-2
5 Brunswick Institute v Thackley n/a
Harrogate Town v Bradford Rovers 2-0
North Ferriby United v Harrogate & District Railway 1-6
6 Armthorpe Welfare v Players Athletic 1-0
Atlas & Norfolk (Sheffield) v Lincoln City School OB 1-2
Boots Athletic v Parliament Street Methodists 2-1
Briggs Sports (Doncaster) v Staveley Works 2-1
Eastwood Town v Hampton Sports 9-0
Hatford Main Welfare v Rawmarsh Welfare 0-3
Raleigh Athletic v Penistone Church 4-1
Worthington Simpson v RAF Cranwell 4-3
7 Cosby United v Sileby Town 1-3
Desford CW v Enderby Town 3-1
Earl Shilton Institute v Loughborough College 1-8
Ibstock Penistone Rovers v Syston St Peters 6-0
Shepshed Albion v Rootes Athletic 2-1
Smethwick Town v Measham Imperial 0-3
Stapenhill v Quorn 4-1
Wellington Victoria v Paget Rangers 0-0
8 Fernhill Heath v Jack Moulds Athletic 0-0
Malvern Town v Bournville Athletic 6-2
11 Colchester Casuals v Ipswich Wanderers 1-2
Crittall Athletic v Electric Supply & Transport 5-1
Hadleigh United v Leiston 0-6
Landseer v Waterside Works 3-3
Newmarket Town v Bury Town 2-6
Whitton United v Beccles 3-2
Woodbridge Athletic v Achilles 0-1
12 Arlesey Town v Wootton Blue Cross 3-3
Baldock Town v Vauxhall Motors 1-1
Berkhamsted Town v Leighton United 7-3
Hemel Hempstead Town v Potton United 5-1
Hunting Percival Athletic v Shelford Town 2-1
Letchworth Town v Stotfold 2-0
Royston Town v Kempston Rovers 2-6
Waterlows Dunstable v AC Delco 5-1
13 Cray Wanderers v Bakers Sports 6-3
Faversham Town v RN Depot 11-0
Foots Cray v Beckenham 4-2
Luton (Chatham) v Bowater Lloyds 5-3
Maidstone United v Callender Athletic 2-0
Thameside Amateurs v Crockenhill 2-2
Woolwich Polytechnic v Slade Green 1-0
14 Arundel v Brighton Old Grammarians 0-3
Bognor Regis Town v Goldstone 2-0
Chichester City v Moulsecoomb Rovers 0-1
Littlehampton Town v Hove White Rovers 2-2
Shoreham v Hastings Rangers 3-5
Whitehawk & Manor Farm OB v Chichester United 2-1
Wigmore Athletic v Lancing Athletic 1-2
Worthing v Southwick 2-1
15 APV Athletic v Newhaven 1-0
Banstead Athletic v Dorking 1-1
Camberley v London University 0-0
Chertsey Town v Haywards Heath 4-6
Eastbourne v Bexhill Town 1-0
Eastbourne United v Crawley 2-0
Horsham v Cuckfield 8-0
Metropolitan Police v Addlestone 4-1
16 Edgware Town v Pinner 3-0
Wingate v Wood Green Town 4-1
17 Bishops Stortford v Welwyn Garden City 5-1
Boreham Wood v Leavesden Hospital 5-1
Epping Town v Hatfield Town 5-1
Harlow Town v Harris Lebus 3-4
Hertford Town v Crown & Manor 2-0
Kings Langley v Stansted 3-4
Rickmansworth Town v Tufnell Park Edmonton 1-5
Saffron Walden Town v Cheshunt (2) 3-5

1955/56

18	Aveley v Dagenham Cables	4-1
	Basildon Town v Hornchurch & Upminster	5-2
	Brentwood & Warley v Bata Sports	2-1
	Dagenham v Ford Sports	4-2
	East Ham United v Rainham Town	2-2
	Lathol Athletic v Eton Manor	0-1
	Tilbury v Barking	1-1
	West Thurrock Athletic v Woodford Town	1-3
19	Civil Service v Hawker Athletic	1-2
	Epsom v Surbiton Town	10-0
	McLaren Sports v Vickers (Weybridge)	0-3
	Molesey v Worcester Park	4-3
	PO Engineers (LTR) v Devas Institute	0-0
	Ruislip Manor v Kingsbury Town	4-2
	Staines Town v Royal Ordnance	3-2
	Twickenham v Malden Town	3-3
20	Didcot Town v Newbury Town	1-2
	Maidenhead United v Osberton Radiator	7-2
	Marlow v Wallingford Town	3-1
	Morris Motors v Bletchley & Wipac Sports	2-0
	Oxford City v Slough Town	3-1
	Pressed Steel v Witney Town	1-1
	Windsor & Eton v Chesham United	5-1
	Wokingham Town v Huntley & Palmers	1-3
21	Fareham Town v Winchester City	1-1
	Hamworthy v Blandford United	2-2
	Lymington v Totton	2-2
	Ryde Sports v Romsey Town	6-0
	Swanage Town v Bournemouth Gasworks Athletic	1-4
	Thorneycroft v Gosport Borough Athletic	3-4
	Upwey & Broadway v Bournemouth	6-3
	Wimborne v Longfleet St Marys	7-1
22	Bulford United v Swindon Victoria	6-3
	Corsham Town v Sharpness	2-2
	Melksham Town v Welton Rovers	0-4
	Pewsey Vale v Clandown	4-4
	Pinehurst Youth Centre v Peasedown Miners Welf.	0-0
	Shepton Mallet Town v Paulton Rovers	6-4
	Spencer Moulton v Purton	0-1
	Westbury United v Calne & Harris United	4-1
23	Bristol St George v St Lukes College	4-3
	Keynsham Town v Ilminster Town	5-0
	Mount Hill Enterprise v Heavitree United	0-2
	Weston-super-Mare St Johns v Hanham Athletic	3-6
24	Liskeard Athletic v St Dennis	2-0
	Mousehole v St Austell	1-8
1r	Cleator Moor Celtic v Penrith	1-1e
r	Wallsend St Lukes v Seaton Sluice United	1-2e
7r	Paget Rangers v Wellington Victoria	2-4
8r	Jack Moulds Athletic v Fernhill Heath	5-0
11r	Waterside Works v Landseer	8-1
12r	Arlesey Town v Wootton Blue Cross	6-1
r	Vauxhall Motors v Baldock Town	2-4
13r	Crockenhill v Thameside Amateurs	7-2
14r	Littlehampton Town v Hove White Rovers	3-1
15r	Dorking v Banstead Athletic	2-1
r	London University v Camberley	0-1
18r	Barking v Tilbury	6-0
r	Rainham Town v East Ham United	4-2
19r	Malden Town v Twickenham	2-1
r	PO Engineers (LTR) v Devas Institute	1-3
20r	Witney Town v Pressed Steel	2-1
21r	Blandford United v Hamworthy	4-5e
r	Totton v Lymington	n/a
r	Winchester City v Fareham Town	2-0
22r	Clandown v Pewsey Vale	4-1
r	Peasedown Miners Welf. v Pinehurst Youth Centre	0-1
r	Sharpness v Corsham Town	4-1
1r2	Penrith v Cleator Moor Celtic	4-0 N

Qualifying Round One

1	Appleby v Cowans Sheldon	3-4
	Heaton Stannington v Whitley Bay	1-2
	Seaton Sluice United v Hexham Hearts	1-1
	Washington CW v Penrith	3-3
2	Bank Head United v Stanley United	0-3
	Bearpark CW v Burnside United	6-4
	Craghead CW v Heighington Amateur	7-0
	Durham City v Witton Park Institute	9-0
3	Bridlington Trinity United v Port Clarence SS	4-1
	North Skelton Athletic v Whitby Town	0-3
	Redcar Albion v Wilton ICI	0-0
	South Bank v Bridlington Central United	3-0
4	Blackpool Rangers v Newton	2-2
	Hoylake Athletic v Stockton Heath	3-2
	Runcorn Athletic v Stoneycroft	7-1
	St Annes Athletic v Southport Leyland Road	2-0
5	Harrogate & District Railway v Kingston Wolves	2-4
	Harrogate Town v Guiseley	3-2
	Ossett Albion v Liversedge	4-1
	Thornhill Edge v Thackley	5-1
6	Armthorpe Welfare v Boots Athletic	4-2
	Eastwood Town v Briggs Sports (Doncaster)	3-0
	Lincoln City School OBU v Raleigh Athletic	3-2
	Worthington Simpson v Rawmarsh Welfare	2-8
7	Desford CW v Ibstock Penistone Rovers	3-0
	Shepshed Albion v Wellington Victoria	1-2
	Sileby Town v Measham Imperial	1-2
	Stapenhill v Loughborough College	1-3
8	Jack Moulds Athletic v Walsall Trinity	2-4
	Lower Gornal Athletic v Staffordshire Casuals	4-1
	Malvern Town v Boldmere St Michaels	3-1
	Walsall Wood v Old Wulfrunians	3-2
9	Ely City v St Neots St Marys	5-0
	Higham Town v Eynesbury Rovers	wo/s
	Raunds Town v Finedon Town	0-6
	Somersham Town v Histon	1-4
10	Diss Town v Sheringham	2-4
	Holt United v City of Norwich School OBU	0-5
	North Walsham Town v Downham Town	5-4
	Wymondham Town v Cromer	1-1
11	Achilles v Ipswich Wanderers	3-3
	Brantham Athletic v Waterside Works	3-1
	Bury Town v Crittall Athletic	4-1
	Leiston v Whitton United	2-2
12	Arlesey Town v Berkhamsted Town	3-1
	Hemel Hempstead Town v Baldock Town	2-3
	Hunting Percival Athletic v Waterlows Dunstable	1-2
	Letchworth Town v Kempston Rovers	2-1
13	Bexley v Luton (Chatham)	0-1
	Crockenhill v Cray Wanderers	2-2
	Faversham Town v Maidstone United	1-0
	Woolwich Polytechnic v Foots Cray	1-3
14	Lancing Athletic v Brighton Old Grammarians	1-3
	Littlehampton Town v Bognor Regis Town	1-1
	Moulsecoomb Rovers v Hastings Rangers	1-2
	Worthing v Whitehawk & Manor Farm OB	3-2
15	Camberley v Eastbourne United	1-4
	Dorking v Haywards Heath	3-0
	Horsham v Eastbourne	3-5
	Metropolitan Police v APV Athletic	10-1
16	Edgware Town v Harrow Town	6-2
	Polytechnic v Wembley	1-5
	Wingate v Willesden	1-0
	Yiewsley v Wealdstone	3-3
17	Bishops Stortford v Cheshunt (2)	5-1
	Boreham Wood v Stansted	8-1
	Epping Town v Hertford Town	0-1
	Tufnell Park Edmonton v Harris Lebus	1-1
18	Aveley v Barking	2-3
	Basildon Town v Rainham Town	0-0
	Brentwood & Warley v Eton Manor	3-1
	Dagenham v Woodford Town	2-1
19	Epsom v Devas Institute	1-1
	Hawker Athletic v Ruislip Manor	1-1
	Malden Town v Staines Town	3-1
	Molesey v Vickers (Weybridge)	2-3
20	Marlow v Huntley & Palmers	3-2
	Morris Motors v Oxford City	1-7
	Windsor & Eton v Newbury Town	0-4
	Witney Town v Maidenhead United	1-1
21	Bournemouth Gasworks Athletic v Hamworthy	2-4
	Gosport Borough Athletic v Upwey & Broadway	8-1
	Ryde Sports v Wimborne	6-1
	Totton v Winchester City	1-1
22	Pinehurst Youth Centre v Clandown	3-1
	Purton v Welton Rovers	2-1
	Sharpness v Bulford United	4-3
	Westbury United v Shepton Mallet Town	1-1
23	Bristol St George v St Philips Marsh Adult School	3-1
	Chard Town v Soundwell	5-4
	Keynsham Town v Hanham Athletic	2-0
	Worle OB v Heavitree United	2-3
24	Burraton v Tamerton	1-2
	Camelford v Nanpean Rovers	1-1
	Liskeard Athletic v Bugle	2-0
	St Austell v Tavistock	wo/s
1r	Penrith v Washington CW	2-0
r	Seaton Sluice United v Hexham Hearts	2-5
3r	Wilton ICI v Redcar Albion	n/a
4r	Newton v Blackpool Rangers	2-0
10r	Cromer v Wymondham Town	5-1
11r	Achilles v Ipswich Wanderers	2-4
r	Whitton United v Leiston	5-1
13r	Cray Wanderers v Crockenhill	5-1
14r	Bognor Regis Town v Littlehampton Town	2-1
16r	Wealdstone v Yiewsley	0-1
17r	Harris Lebus v Tufnell Park Edmonton	2-3e
18r	Rainham Town v Basildon Town	2-1e
19r	Epsom v Devas Institute	2-1
r	Ruislip Manor v Hawker Athletic	5-1
20r	Maidenhead United v Witney Town	6-0
21r	Winchester City v Totton	3-1
22r	Shepton Mallet Town v Westbury United	2-1
24r	Nanpean Rovers v Camelford	1-4

Qualifying Round Two

1	Penrith v Hexham Hearts	7-0
	Whitley Bay v Cowans Sheldon	6-1
2	Durham City v Bearpark CW	3-1
	Stanley United v Craghead CW	3-1
3	Bridlington Trinity United v South Bank	1-7
	Redcar Albion v Whitby Town	2-3
4	Runcorn Athletic v Hoylake Athletic	0-2
	St Annes Athletic v Newton	0-2
5	Harrogate Town v Kingston Wolves	0-0
	Ossett Albion v Thornhill Edge	4-3
6	Armthorpe Welfare v Rawmarsh Welfare	3-1
	Eastwood Town v Lincoln City School OBU	1-1
7	Desford CW v Measham Imperial	2-3
	Wellington Victoria v Loughborough College	0-1
8	Malvern Town v Walsall Trinity	4-2
	Walsall Wood v Lower Gornal Athletic	2-1
9	Ely City v Finedon Town	2-2
	Higham Town v Histon	1-1
10	Cromer v North Walsham Town	2-5
	Sheringham v City of Norwich School OBU	4-2
11	Brantham Athletic v Ipswich Wanderers	1-2
	Whitton United v Bury Town	2-2
12	Baldock Town v Arlesey Town	5-0
	Waterlows Dunstable v Letchworth Town	0-5
13	Cray Wanderers v Luton (Chatham)	8-2
	Faversham Town v Foots Cray	3-0
14	Bognor Regis Town v Worthing	3-5
	Brighton Old Grammarians v Hastings Rangers	4-2
15	Dorking v Eastbourne	4-2
	Metropolitan Police v Eastbourne United	0-3
16	Edgware Town v Yiewsley	5-3
	Wembley v Wingate	1-3
17	Boreham Wood v Bishops Stortford	1-2
	Hertford Town v Tufnell Park Edmonton	3-0
18	Brentwood & Warley v Barking	2-2
	Rainham Town v Dagenham	2-3
19	Epsom v Malden Town	2-1
	Ruislip Manor v Vickers (Weybridge)	5-3
20	Maidenhead United v Oxford City	5-1
	Newbury Town v Marlow	3-2
21	Gosport Borough Athletic v Winchester City	1-2
	Hamworthy v Ryde Sports	3-4
22	Pinehurst Youth Centre v Shepton Mallet Town	3-1
	Purton v Sharpness	0-1
23	Bristol St George v Heavitree United	2-3
	Chard Town v Keynsham Town	2-3
24	St Austell v Camelford	2-0
	Tamerton v Liskeard Athletic	6-2
5r	Harrogate Town v Kingston Wolves	4-1
6r	Eastwood Town v Lincoln City School OBU	2-0
9r	Finedon Town v Ely City	1-2e
r	Histon v Higham Town	3-1
11r	Bury Town v Whitton United	4-1
18r	Barking v Brentwood & Warley	3-1

Qualifying Round Three

1	Penrith v Whitley Bay	3-1
2	Durham City v Stanley United	2-1
3	Whitby Town v South Bank	1-3
4	Newton v Hoylake Athletic	4-1
5	Harrogate Town v Ossett Albion	1-4
6	Eastwood Town v Armthorpe Welfare	7-0
7	Measham Imperial v Loughborough College	2-3
8	Malvern Town v Walsall Wood	5-0
9	Histon v Ely City	0-0
10	Sheringham v North Walsham Town	4-1
11	Bury Town v Ipswich Wanderers	3-1
12	Letchworth Town v Baldock Town	5-0
13	Cray Wanderers v Faversham Town	1-3
14	Worthing v Brighton Old Grammarians	5-1
15	Eastbourne United v Dorking	3-2
16	Edgware Town v Wingate	2-2
17	Hertford Town v Bishops Stortford	2-1
18	Barking v Dagenham	0-4
19	Epsom v Ruislip Manor	3-1
20	Maidenhead United v Newbury Town	0-2
21	Winchester City v Ryde Sports	0-2
22	Sharpness v Pinehurst Youth Centre	2-1
23	Heavitree United v Keynsham Town	1-4
24	St Austell v Tamerton	2-0
9r	Ely City v Histon	2-1
16r	Wingate v Edgware Town	3-0

Qualifying Round Four

	Anstey Nomads v Eastwood Town	1-1
	Dagenham v Leyton	1-1
	Dartmouth United v Clevedon	1-1
	Ely City v Bury Town	3-2
	Faversham Town v Eastbourne United	1-2
	Grays Athletic v Briggs Sports	2-4
	Harwich & Parkeston v Bungay Town	4-2
	Hertford Town v Aylesbury United	1-1
	Letchworth Town v Newbury Town	2-2
	Malvern Town v Loughborough College	3-1
	Moor Green v Gedling Colliery	2-4
	Newton v Sheffield	1-0
	Ossett Albion v Yorkshire Amateur	1-1
	Penrith v Cuckfield	4-3
	Redhill v Epsom	2-1
	Ryde Sports v Alton Town	2-4
	Saltash United v Keynsham Town	3-3
	Sharpness v St Austell	1-3
	South Bank v Durham City	2-3
	Stevenage Town v Enfield	1-1
	Stork v Marine	3-1
	Sutton United v Worthing	3-0
	Thetford Town v Sheringham	4-0
	Wingate v Uxbridge	0-4
r	Aylesbury United v Hertford Town	1-3
r	Clevedon v Dartmouth United	8-1
r	Eastwood Town v Anstey Nomads	2-1
r	Enfield v Stevenage Town	1-0
r	Keynsham Town v Saltash United	3-2
r	Leyton v Dagenham	0-1
r	Newbury Town v Letchworth Town	1-3
r	Yorkshire Amateur v Ossett Albion	2-1

1955/56 to 1956/57

Round One

Bishop Auckland v Crook Town	1-1
Briggs Sports v Romford (2)	2-0
Cambridge City v Thetford Town	2-2
Clevedon v Carshalton Athletic	2-2
Corinthian Casuals v Sheppey United	4-1
Dulwich Hamlet v Harwich & Parkeston	3-1
Durham City v Newton	5-1
Eastwood Town v Shildon	0-1
Ely City v Alton Town	0-3
Enfield v Wimbledon	1-1
Hallam v West Auckland Town	2-3
Hertford Town v Eastbourne United	3-2
Hitchin Town v Keynsham Town	8-1
Hounslow Town v Ware	5-1
Ilford v Erith & Belvedere	1-1
Kingstonian v Bromley	3-1
Letchworth Town v St Albans City	1-1
Northern Nomads v Gedling Colliery	2-2
Norton Woodseats v Malvern Town	3-2
Pegasus v Barnet	2-0
Penrith v Billingham Synthonia	1-3
Salts v Yorkshire Amateur	2-1
Southall v Uxbridge	2-0
St Austell v Redhill	2-1
Stork v Ferryhill Athletic	2-2
Sutton United v Clapton	1-1
Tooting & Mitcham United v Hendon	2-1
Walthamstow Avenue v Hayes	1-1
Walton & Hersham v Finchley	2-7
Willington v Evenwood Town	4-2
Woking v Leytonstone	0-0
Wycombe Wanderers v Dagenham	4-1
r Carshalton Athletic v Clevedon	3-1
r Clapton v Sutton United	3-2
r Crook Town v Bishop Auckland	3-4
r Erith & Belvedere v Ilford	3-1
r Ferryhill Athletic v Stork	1-0
r Gedling Colliery v Northern Nomads	4-2
r Hayes v Walthamstow Avenue	4-1
r Leytonstone v Woking	2-0
r St Albans City v Letchworth Town	2-0
r Thetford Town v Cambridge City	1-3
r Wimbledon v Enfield	3-1

Round Two

Alton Town v Southall	1-4
Briggs Sports v Hitchin Town	0-2
Corinthian Casuals v Wimbledon	3-2
Dulwich Hamlet v Clapton	1-0
Durham City v Norton Woodseats	1-2
Ferryhill Athletic v Shildon	2-2
Gedling Colliery v Bishop Auckland	1-4
Hayes v Finchley	2-3
Hertford Town v Kingstonian	0-3
Hounslow Town v Erith & Belvedere	2-2
Pegasus v Wycombe Wanderers	1-2
Salts v Billingham Synthonia	3-2
St Albans City v Cambridge City	4-1
St Austell v Carshalton Athletic	2-1
Tooting & Mitcham United v Leytonstone	2-0
West Auckland Town v Willington	2-1
r Erith & Belvedere v Hounslow Town	1-2
r Shildon v Ferryhill Athletic	2-4

Round Three

Ferryhill Athletic v Bishop Auckland	0-1
Finchley v Hounslow Town	2-0
Hitchin Town v Wycombe Wanderers	1-0
Kingstonian v St Austell	4-0
Norton Woodseats v Dulwich Hamlet	2-5
St Albans City v Corinthian Casuals	0-1
Tooting & Mitcham United v Southall	2-1
West Auckland Town v Salts	5-4

Round Four

Corinthian Casuals v Hitchin Town	3-3
Finchley v Bishop Auckland	0-4
Kingstonian v Tooting & Mitcham United	3-0
West Auckland Town v Dulwich Hamlet	0-0
r Dulwich Hamlet v West Auckland Town	3-0
r Hitchin Town v Corinthian Casuals	0-5

Semi Finals

Bishop Auckland v Kingstonian	5-1 N
Corinthian Casuals v Dulwich Hamlet	3-1 N

Final

Bishop Auckland v Corinthian Casuals	1-1 N
r Bishop Auckland v Corinthian Casuals	4-1 N

1956/57

Extra Preliminary Round

2 Bank Head United v Langley Park CW	5-2
Esh Winning Alb v Darlington &Simpson Rolling Mill	6-0
Heighington Amateur v Wingate Welfare	n/a
Highgate United (Newcastle) v Stockton	2-3
Seaton Holy Trinity v New Brancepeth CW	n/a
4 East Chorlton Ams v Unit Construction (Liverpool)	n/a
Port Sunlight v Shell	5-2
6 Armthorpe Welfare v Worthington Simpson	3-2
Aspley OB v Pilkington Recreation	n/a
Basford United v Raleigh Athletic	0-4
Brodsworth Main v Ollerton Colliery	1-3
Lincoln Clayton v Boots Athletic	3-4
7 Baddesley Colliery v Birmingham City Transport	6-4e
Bentley Engineering v Sileby Town	3-1
Ibstock Penistone Rovers v Cosby United	0-2
Leicester Amateurs v Wellington Victoria	1-3
Measham Imperial v Stapenhill	4-1
Morris Sports (Loughborough) v Paget Rangers	1-1
Wilmorton & Alvaston v Lucas Great King Street	n/a
12 AC Delco v Hunting Percival Athletic	3-2
Baldock Town v Potton United	wo/s
Leighton United v Kempston Rovers	3-5
Royston Town v Stotfold	3-1
15 Moulsecoomb Rovers v Lancing Athletic	0-1
Old Varndonians v Hastings & St Leonards	5-2
16 Croydon Amateur v Cobham	3-0
Dorking v APV Athletic	7-0
Eastbourne v Haywards Heath	7-0
Farncombe v Newhaven	2-0
Farnham Town v Lewes	2-1
18 Basildon Town v Aveley	2-2
East Ham United v Woodford Town	5-1
Hornchurch & Upminster v Ford Sports	2-2
19 PO Engineers (LTR) v Malden Town	0-0
20 Maidenhead United v Witney Town	5-1
Marlow v Abingdon Town	4-0
NAC Athletic v Thame United	5-3
Newbury Town v Buckingham Town	7-0
Osberton Radiator v Henley Town	2-1
Oxford City v Amersham Town	6-0
Oxford YMCA v Kidlington	4-2
Pressed Steel v St Frideswides	4-0
Slough Town v Windsor & Eton	3-0
Stokenchurch v Kirtlington Sports	4-0
Wokingham Town v Bicester Town	6-0
Woodstock Town v Wallingford Town	3-0
22 Brimscombe v Peasedown Miners Welfare	7-2
Calne & Harris United v Timsbury Athletic	4-1
Pewsey Vale v Corsham Town	4-3
Purton v Welton Rovers	1-1
Shepton Mallet Town v Roundway Hospital	5-4
Spencer Moulton v Downton	1-3
Warminster Town v Radstock Town	4-4
Westbury United v Clandown	0-0
7r Paget Rangers v Morris Sports (Loughborough)	3-0
18r Aveley v Basildon Town	1-0
r Hornchurch & Upminster v Ford Sports	6-0
19r Malden Town v PO Engineers (LTR)	5-1
22r Clandown v Westbury United	3-1
r Radstock Town v Warminster Town	2-4
r Welton Rovers v Purton	4-2

Preliminary Round

1 Cleator Moor Celtic v Appleby	3-2
Cowans Sheldon v Salterbeck	4-3
Wallsend St Lukes v Heaton Stannington	2-0
2 Bank Head United v Esh Winning Albion	2-2
Burnside United v Chilton Athletic	4-5
Cockfield v Craghead CW	2-0
New Brancepeth CW v Stockton	0-2
Stanhope Town v Wolsingham Welfare	2-1
Stanley United v Tow Law Town	2-1
West Hartlepool St Josephs v Witton Park	6-3
Wingate Welfare v Bearpark CW	8-1
3 Bridlington Trinity United v Skinningrove Works	7-1
Whitby Town v Winterton Hospital	4-1
4 Ainsdale Hesketh Park v Stoneycroft	n/a
Blackpool Rangers v Runcorn Athletic	1-4
East Chorlton Amateur v Blackpool Mechanics	3-2
ICI Alkali v Hoylake Athletic	4-1
Marine v Southport Leyland Road	2-0
Moreton v Earle	n/a
Old Blackburnians v St Annes Athletic	1-2
Port Sunlight v Stockton Heath	2-2
5 Christ Church OB Harrogate v North Ferriby United	1-5
Harrogate Town v Methley United	2-3e
Liversedge v East End Park WMC	0-4
Ossett Albion v Harrogate & District Railway	2-2
Rothwell Athletic v Guiseley	2-0
Thornhill Edge v Thackley	3-3
6 Armthorpe Welfare v Lincoln City School OBU	1-3
Atlas & Norfolk (Sheffield) v Sheffield	3-2
Boots Athletic v Ollerton Colliery	3-4
Hampton Sports v Monk Bretton Colliery	3-1
Parliament Street Methodists v Staveley Works	0-3
Penistone Church v Players Athletic	7-0
Raleigh Athletic v Aspley OB	4-6
Thorncliffe Recreational v RAF Cranwell	7-1
7 Anstey Nomads v Smethwick Town	0-1
Baddesley Colliery v Wellington Victoria	4-2
Barwell Athletic v Paget Rangers	2-0
Bentley Engineering v Cosby United	2-1
Lucas Great King Street v Enderby Town	1-5
Measham Imperial v Coventry Amateur	5-0
Oadby Town v Earl Shilton Institute	3-2
Shepshed Albion v Loughborough College	3-1
8 Bournville Athletic v Fernhill Heath	4-3
Stratford Town v Walsall Trinity	2-0
Walsall Wood v Goodyear Sports (Wolverhampton)	4-1
11 Bungay Town v Brantham Athletic	2-1
Bury Town v Crittall Athletic	4-2
Hadleigh United v Achilles	3-4
Ipswich Electricity Supply v Woodbridge Athletic	8-2
Landseer Youth v Ipswich Wanderers	1-2
Lowestoft Town v Beccles	3-3
Newmarket Town v Whitton United	4-1
Waterside Works v Leiston	2-3
12 Baldock Town v Kempston Rovers	2-2
Hemel Hempstead Town v Arlesey Town	1-1
Royston Town v AC Delco	2-3
Stevenage Town v Shefford Town	2-1
Tring Town v Marston Shelton Rovers	4-1e
Vauxhall Motors v Berkhamsted Town	4-1
Waterlows Dunstable v Cranfield United	2-2
Wootton Blue Cross v Bedford Avenue	4-2
13 Edgware Town v Wembley	1-1
Polytechnic v Yiewsley	0-7
14 Beckenham v Luton (Chatham)	3-0
Bexley v Foots Cray	1-1
Cray Wanderers v Slade Green	4-2
Crockenhill v Bowater Lloyds	5-0
Faversham Town v Thameside Amateurs	7-1
Herne Bay v Maidstone United	1-2
Woolwich Polytechnic v Bakers Sports	4-1
15 Brighton Old Grammarians v Hastings Rangers	5-2
Hove Town v Chichester United	5-0
Lancing Athletic v Bognor Regis Town	4-0
Shoreham v Littlehampton Town	3-4
Southwick v Old Varndonians	5-1
Whitehawk & Manor Farm OB v Goldstone	9-0
Wigmore Athletic v Arundel	5-3
Worthing v Chichester City	0-3
16 Banstead Athletic v Horsham	2-1
Bexhill Town v Addlestone	6-1
Chertsey Town v Cuckfield	10-0
Croydon Amateur v Crawley	5-1
East Grinstead v Camberley	5-2
Eastbourne v Farnham Town	2-1
Farncombe v Dorking	3-0
Leatherhead v Metropolitan Police	4-1
17 Crown & Manor v Boreham Wood	2-4
Epping Town v Welwyn Garden City	2-2
Finsbury v Bishops Stortford	0-3
Harlow Town v Hatfield Town	2-4
Leavesden Hospital v Rickmansworth Town	1-5
Saffron Walden Town v Kings Langley	0-5
Stansted v Hoddesdon Town	5-3
Tufnell Park Edmonton v Cheshunt (2)	3-1
18 Aveley v Grays Athletic	1-5
Bata Sports v Barking	0-5
Dagenham Cables v Barkingside	1-2
Eton Manor v Chingford	5-0
Hornchurch & Upminster v East Ham United	2-1
Leyton v Tilbury	2-0
Rainham Town v Brentwood & Warley	1-1
West Thurrock Athletic v Lathol Athletic	1-1
19 Civil Service v Ruislip Manor	0-6
Hawker Athletic v Devas Institute	2-4
London University v Twickenham	2-5
Malden Town v Epsom	0-2
Staines Town v Molesey	2-1
Surbiton Town v Petter & Bryce Sports	1-1
Vickers (Weybridge) v Kingsbury Town	4-0
Worcester Park v ROF (SA)	4-2
20 Aylesbury United v Pressed Steel	3-1
Bletchley & Wipac Sports v Maidenhead United	2-4
Chesham United v NAC Athletic	8-2
Marlow v Newbury Town	4-1
Osberton Radiator v Oxford YMCA	3-1
Oxford City v Woodstock Town	2-0
Stokenchurch v Slough Town	1-3
Wokingham Town v Didcot Town	3-2
21 Blandford United v Bournemouth Gasworks Athletic	1-5
Gosport Borough Athletic v Thorneycroft	5-1
HMS Collingwood v Winchester City	0-2
Lymington v Bournemouth	0-6
Ryde Sports v Pirelli General Cable Works	1-3
Swanage Town v Upwey & Broadway	4-0
Totton v Fareham Town	3-7
Wimborne v Hamworthy	0-2

71

1956/57

22	Clandown v Swindon BR Corinthians	2-5
	Devizes Town v Pinehurst Youth Centre	4-1
	Downton v Melksham Town	2-2
	Shepton Mallet Town v Pewsey Vale	4-0
	Swindon Victoria v Calne & Harris United	2-0
	Warminster Town v Bulford United	2-3
	Welton Rovers v Brimscombe	4-2
	Wootton Bassett Town v Paulton Rovers	1-2
23	Chard Town v Mount Hill Enterprise	1-5
	Worle OB v Bristol St George	3-1
24	Looe v Chelston	2-4
	Newton Abbott Spurs v Burraton	3-2
	Saltash United v Nanpean Rovers	6-4
2r	Esh Winning Albion v Bank Head United	1-1e
4r	Stockton Heath v Port Sunlight	4-3
5r	Harrogate & District Railway v Ossett Albion	2-4
r	Thackley v Thornhill Edge	2-4
8r	Stratford Town v Walsall Trinity	5-0
11r	Beccles v Lowestoft Town	2-4e
12r	Arlesey Town v Hemel Hempstead Town	1-3
r	Cranfield United v Waterlows Dunstable	1-3
r	Kempston Rovers v Baldock Town	1-3e
13r	Wembley v Edgware Town	1-0
14r	Foots Cray v Bexley	1-0
17r	Welwyn Garden City v Epping Town	2-1
18r	Brentwood & Warley v Rainham Town	4-1
r	Lathol Athletic v West Thurrock Athletic	1-2
19r	Petter & Bryce Sports v Surbiton Town	1-2
22r	Melksham Town v Downton	6-3
2r2	Esh Winning Albion v Bank Head United	4-1

Qualifying Round One

1	Cleator Moor Celtic v Seaton Sluice United	2-2
	Cowans Sheldon v Hearts of Liddesdale	6-3
	Shap v Washington CW	4-1
	Whitley Bay v Wallsend St Lukes	3-1
2	Esh Winning Albion v Cockfield	2-0
	Stanhope Town v Stanley United	0-4
	West Hartlepool St Josephs v Stockton	0-3
	Wingate Welfare v Chilton Athletic	6-2
3	Bridlington Trinity United v Whitby Town	2-7
	North Skelton Athletic v Bridlington Central United	2-0
	Redcar Albion v South Bank	4-0
	Whitby Albion Rangers v Cargo Fleet Works	1-6
4	East Chorlton Amateur v Runcorn Athletic	2-4
	Moreton v Marine	3-3
	St Annes Athletic v ICI Alkali	2-2
	Stockton Heath v Stoneycroft	5-1
5	East End Park WMC v Brunswick Institute	5-1
	North Ferriby United v Thornhill Edge	0-1
	Ossett Albion v Bradford Rovers	1-2
	Rothwell Athletic v Methley United	2-2
6	Atlas & Norfolk (Sheffield) v Aspley OB	4-3
	Lincoln City School OBU v Penistone Church	2-2
	Ollerton Colliery v Staveley Works	n/a
	Thorncliffe Recreational v Hampton Sports	3-2
7	Barwell Athletic v Baddesley Colliery	0-1
	Bentley Engineering v Shepshed Albion	7-1
	Enderby Town v Oadby Town	0-4
	Smethwick Town v Measham Imperial	3-1
8	Boldmere St Michaels v Stratford Town	0-0
	Bournville Athletic v Walsall Wood	0-4
	Jack Moulds Athletic v Moor Green	1-2
	Old Wulfrunians v Staffordshire Casuals	5-1
9	Higham Town v Sutton Bridge United	1-4
	Histon v Raunds Town	6-0
	Somersham Town v Finedon Town	2-2
	Wolverton Town & BR v St Neots St Marys	5-1
10	Cromer v Sheringham	2-4
	Diss Town v City of Norwich School OBU	4-1
	North Walsham Town v Wymondham Town	1-2
11	Achilles v Ipswich Wanderers	4-4
	Bury Town v Lowestoft Town	7-3
	Ipswich Electricity Supply v Leiston	3-0
	Newmarket Town v Bungay Town	1-1
12	AC Delco v Hemel Hempstead Town	2-4
	Stevenage Town v Waterlows Dunstable	3-0
	Tring Town v Wootton Blue Cross	2-3
	Vauxhall Motors v Baldock Town	2-2
13	Wealdstone v Pinner	5-0
	Wembley v Yiewsley	1-1
	Willesden v Harrow Town	2-1
	Wood Green Town v Wingate	3-1
14	Callender Athletic v Beckenham	2-7
	Cray Wanderers v Maidstone United	2-7
	Faversham Town v Crockenhill	6-1
	Foots Cray v Woolwich Polytechnic	2-1
15	Hove Town v Littlehampton Town	0-2
	Lancing Athletic v Brighton Old Grammarians	0-2
	Southwick v Chichester City	3-1
	Wigmore Athletic v Whitehawk & Manor Farm OB	4-4
16	Banstead Athletic v Farncombe	2-1
	Croydon Amateur v Leatherhead	0-1
	East Grinstead v Bexhill Town	2-3
	Eastbourne v Chertsey Town	3-1
17	Boreham Wood v Kings Langley	5-1
	Stansted v Bishops Stortford	0-4
	Tufnell Park Edmonton v Hatfield Town	1-0
	Welwyn Garden City v Rickmansworth Town	3-1
18	Eton Manor v West Thurrock Athletic	4-0
	Grays Athletic v Barkingside	2-1
	Hornchurch & Upminster v Barking	1-1
	Leyton v Brentwood & Warley	2-0
19	Epsom v Devas Institute	10-1
	Ruislip Manor v Vickers (Weybridge)	2-2
	Staines Town v Twickenham	0-1
	Surbiton Town v Worcester Park	1-1
20	Aylesbury United v Osberton Radiator	4-0
	Oxford City v Maidenhead United	2-3
	Slough Town v Chesham United	2-2
	Wokingham Town v Marlow	0-3
21	Blandford United v Gosport Borough Athletic	1-1
	Bournemouth v Swanage Town	3-0
	Hamworthy v Fareham Town	3-5
	Pirelli General Cable Works v Winchester City	2-3
22	Devizes Town v Swindon BR Corinthians	3-1
	Melksham Town v Bulford United	2-2
	Shepton Mallet Town v Paulton Rovers	3-2
	Swindon Victoria v Welton Rovers	3-0
23	Heavitree United v Hanham Athletic	1-2
	Ilminster Town v Soundwell	4-0
	St Philips Marsh Adult School v St Lukes College	0-2
	Worle OB v Mount Hill Enterprise	3-2
24	Camelford v Dartmouth United	3-3
	Liskeard Athletic v Tamerton	5-4e
	Saltash United v Newton Abbott Spurs	6-2
	St Dennis v Chelston	2-5
1r	Seaton Sluice United v Cleator Moor Celtic	1-5
4r	ICI Alkali v St Annes Athletic	3-2
r	Marine v Moreton	4-1
5r	Methley United v Rothwell Athletic	2-1
6r	Penistone Church v Lincoln City School OBU	3-4
8r	Stratford Town v Boldmere St Michaels	0-1
9r	Finedon Town v Somersham Town	3-5
11r	Bungay Town v Newmarket Town	2-1
r	Ipswich Wanderers v Achilles	5-0
12r	Baldock Town v Vauxhall Motors	3-2e
13r	Yiewsley v Wembley	4-2
15r	Whitehawk & Manor Farm OB v Wigmore Athletic	6-2
18r	Barking v Hornchurch & Upminster	1-1e
19r	Vickers (Weybridge) v Ruislip Manor	2-4
r	Worcester Park v Surbiton Town	2-0
20r	Chesham United v Slough Town	2-1
21r	Gosport Borough Athletic v Blandford United	4-1
22r	Bulford United v Melksham Town	2-4
24r	Dartmouth United v Camelford	2-3
18r2	Barking v Hornchurch & Upminster	1-0 N

Qualifying Round Two

1	Cleator Moor Celtic v Cowans Sheldon	2-2
	Shap v Whitley Bay	1-7
2	Esh Winning Albion v Stockton	2-4
	Stanley United v Wingate Welfare	1-2
3	Redcar Albion v North Skelton Athletic	4-1
	Whitby Town v Cargo Fleet Works	4-0
4	Marine v ICI Alkali	1-1
	Stockton Heath v Runcorn Athletic	2-4
5	East End Park WMC v Thornhill Edge	3-0
	Methley United v Bradford Rovers	2-4
6	Ollerton Colliery v Atlas & Norfolk (Sheffield)	1-1
	Thorncliffe Recreational v Lincoln City School OBU	4-2
7	Bentley Engineering v Baddesley Colliery	1-3
	Smethwick Town v Oadby Town	4-1
8	Boldmere St Michaels v Old Wulfrunians	7-0
	Moor Green v Walsall Wood	1-2
9	Histon v Wolverton Town & BR	2-3
	Sutton Bridge United v Somersham Town	3-1
10	Holt United v Wymondham Town	3-0
	Sheringham v Diss Town	1-3
11	Bungay Town v Bury Town	1-2
	Ipswich Electricity Supply v Ipswich Wanderers	3-2
12	Baldock Town v Hemel Hempstead Town	1-5
	Stevenage Town v Wootton Blue Cross	2-2
13	Willesden v Wealdstone	1-2
	Yiewsley v Wood Green Town	3-0
14	Foots Cray v Beckenham	2-1
	Maidstone United v Faversham Town	8-3
15	Southwick v Brighton Old Grammarians	3-1
	Whitehawk & Manor Farm OB v Littlehampton Town	4-2
16	Banstead Athletic v Eastbourne	5-3
	Leatherhead v Bexhill Town	4-1
17	Bishops Stortford v Boreham Wood	4-1
	Welwyn Garden City v Tufnell Park Edmonton	4-2
18	Grays Athletic v Barking	1-1
	Leyton v Eton Manor	3-1
19	Epsom v Twickenham	3-2
	Ruislip Manor v Worcester Park	6-3
20	Aylesbury United v Chesham United	2-0
	Maidenhead United v Marlow	2-1
21	Bournemouth v Fareham Town	0-2
	Winchester City v Gosport Borough Athletic	1-1
22	Devizes Town v Melksham Town	5-0
	Swindon Victoria v Shepton Mallet Town	0-3
23	St Lukes College v Ilminster Town	1-1
	Worle OB v Hanham Athletic	3-1
24	Liskeard Athletic v Chelston	4-2
	Saltash United v Camelford	6-1
1r	Cowans Sheldon v Cleator Moor Celtic	2-3
4r	ICI Alkali v Marine	0-4
6r	Atlas & Norfolk (Sheffield) v Ollerton Colliery	2-4
12r	Wootton Blue Cross v Stevenage Town	1-4
18r	Barking v Grays Athletic	1-3
23r	Ilminster Town v St Lukes College	1-4

Qualifying Round Three

1	Cleator Moor Celtic v Whitley Bay	2-5
2	Stockton v Wingate Welfare	2-1
3	Redcar Albion v Whitby Town	2-2
4	Marine v Runcorn Athletic	2-1
5	Bradford Rovers v East End Park WMC	3-2
6	Ollerton Colliery v Thorncliffe Recreational	1-0
7	Baddesley Colliery v Smethwick Town	2-3
8	Boldmere St Michaels v Walsall Wood	3-0
9	Wolverton Town & BR v Sutton Bridge United	1-1
10	Holt United v Diss Town	3-1
11	Bury Town v Ipswich Electricity Supply	1-4
12	Stevenage Town v Hemel Hempstead Town	0-1
13	Yiewsley v Wealdstone	3-2
14	Maidstone United v Foots Cray	3-0
15	Whitehawk & Manor Farm OB v Southwick	0-1
16	Leatherhead v Banstead Athletic	2-1
17	Welwyn Garden City v Bishops Stortford	3-3
18	Leyton v Grays Athletic	2-1
19	Ruislip Manor v Epsom	1-6
20	Maidenhead United v Aylesbury United	2-1
21	Winchester City v Fareham Town	1-1
22	Devizes Town v Shepton Mallet Town	4-0
23	Worle OB v St Lukes College	1-0
24	Saltash United v Liskeard Athletic	5-2
3r	Whitby Town v Redcar Albion	6-0
9r	Sutton Bridge United v Wolverton Town & BR	0-3
17r	Bishops Stortford v Welwyn Garden City	4-1
21r	Fareham Town v Winchester City	1-2

Qualifying Round Four

	Barnet v Enfield	1-3
	Clevedon v Keynsham Town	2-1
	Dagenham v Leyton	1-1
	Eastbourne United v Maidstone United	3-2
	Eastwood Town v Boldmere St Michaels	2-1
	Hemel Hempstead Town v Uxbridge	3-1
	Holt United v Thetford Town	2-1
	Ipswich Electricity Supply v Harwich & Parkeston	0-6
	Leatherhead v Redhill	1-5
	Malvern Town v Smethwick Town	2-0
	Northern Nomads v Newton	0-1
	Ollerton Colliery v Hallam	1-4
	Penrith v Whitley Bay	1-3
	Sheppey United v Epsom	0-0
	Southwick v Sutton United	1-3
	Stork v Marine	4-1
	Walton & Hersham v Letchworth Town	1-1
	Ware v Bishops Stortford	4-2
	Whitby Town v Stockton	4-5
	Winchester City v Devizes Town	1-1
	Wolverton Town & BR v Ely City	2-5
	Worle OB v Saltash United	1-4
	Yiewsley v Maidenhead United	2-0
	Yorkshire Amateur v Bradford Rovers	2-2
r	Bradford Rovers v Yorkshire Amateur	3-4
r	Devizes Town v Winchester City	2-3
r	Epsom v Sheppey United	2-3
r	Letchworth Town v Walton & Hersham	3-5
r	Leyton v Dagenham	1-1e
r2	Dagenham v Leyton	1-4 N

Round One

	Alton Town v Carshalton Athletic	4-1
	Bishop Auckland v Norton Woodseats	1-0
	Bromley v Tooting & Mitcham United	2-2
	Cambridge City v Dulwich Hamlet	1-1
	Clapton v Leyton	0-0
	Clevedon v Wimbledon	1-1
	Eastwood Town v Salts	2-4
	Ely City v Erith & Belvedere	2-2
	Enfield v Yiewsley	0-1
	Gedling Colliery v Hallam	1-0
	Harwich & Parkeston v Briggs Sports	1-4
	Hayes v Holt United	5-0
	Hertford Town v Corinthian Casuals	1-2
	Hitchin Town v Redhill	2-1
	Hounslow Town v Leytonstone	2-1
	Malvern Town v Billingham Synthonia	1-5
	Newton v Ferryhill Athletic	2-3
	Pegasus v Romford (2)	1-2
	Saltash United v Kingstonian	2-4
	Sheppey United v Hemel Hempstead Town	3-0
	Shildon v Willington	2-3
	St Albans City v Wycombe Wanderers	1-4
	St Austell v Eastbourne United	0-2
	Stockton v Crook Town	0-3
	Stork v Evenwood Town	0-1
	Sutton United v Finchley	1-0
	Walthamstow Avenue v Woking	1-1
	Walton & Hersham v Ilford	1-4
	Ware v Hendon	1-1
	West Auckland Town v Durham City	2-0
	Whitley Bay v Yorkshire Amateur	3-0
	Winchester City v Southall	2-1
r	Dulwich Hamlet v Cambridge City	3-0
r	Erith & Belvedere v Ely City	7-3
r	Hendon v Ware	4-0
r	Leyton v Clapton	1-2
r	Tooting & Mitcham United v Bromley	4-3
r	Wimbledon v Clevedon	4-3
r	Woking v Walthamstow Avenue	2-3

1956/57 to 1957/58

Round Two

	Alton Town v Hounslow Town	1-2
	Billingham Synthonia v West Auckland Town	1-1
	Bishop Auckland v Gedling Colliery	5-1
	Briggs Sports v Hendon	4-3
	Corinthian Casuals v Eastbourne United	2-2
	Erith & Belvedere v Sutton United	1-2
	Evenwood Town v Whitley Bay	2-1
	Hitchin Town v Dulwich Hamlet	1-5
	Ilford v Wimbledon	4-2
	Salts v Ferryhill Athletic	0-1
	Tooting & Mitcham United v Sheppey United	2-0
	Walthamstow Avenue v Romford (2)	2-2
	Willington v Crook Town	1-2
	Winchester City v Hayes	1-2
	Wycombe Wanderers v Clapton	4-2
	Yiewsley v Kingstonian	0-1
r	Eastbourne United v Corinthian Casuals	0-2
r	Romford (2) v Walthamstow Avenue	0-4
r	West Auckland Town v Billingham Synthonia	3-2

Round Three

	Briggs Sports v Bishop Auckland	0-1
	Crook Town v Evenwood Town	1-1
	Hayes v Ferryhill Athletic	1-1
	Ilford v Walthamstow Avenue	4-0
	Kingstonian v Dulwich Hamlet	5-1
	Tooting & Mitcham United v Sutton United	1-1
	West Auckland Town v Corinthian Casuals	0-2
	Wycombe Wanderers v Hounslow Town	3-1
r	Evenwood Town v Crook Town	1-2
r	Ferryhill Athletic v Hayes	3-4
r	Sutton United v Tooting & Mitcham United	0-3

Round Four

	Crook Town v Bishop Auckland	2-2
	Ilford v Wycombe Wanderers	3-3
	Kingstonian v Hayes	1-1
	Tooting & Mitcham United v Corinthian Casuals	1-3
r	Bishop Auckland v Crook Town	2-0
r	Hayes v Kingstonian	1-0
r	Wycombe Wanderers v Ilford	2-0

Semi Finals

Bishop Auckland v Hayes	2-0 N
Wycombe Wanderers v Corinthian Casuals	4-2 N

Final

Bishop Auckland v Wycombe Wanderers	3-1 N

1957/58

Extra Preliminary Round

2	Heighington Amateur v Crookhall CW	n/a
4	Blackpool Mechanics v East Chorlton Amateur	3-1
	Blackpool Rangers v Unit Construction (Liverpool)	0-1
	Earle v Southport Leyland Road	n/a
	Marine v Manchester University	7-1
	Port Sunlight v Northern Nomads	2-1
	St Annes Athletic v Ainsdale Hesketh Park	5-1
6	Arnold St Marys v Linby Colliery	n/a
	Claycross & Danesmoor v Atlas & Norfolk (Sheffield)	3-2
	Hampton Sports v Armthorpe Welfare	n/a
	Lincoln Clayton v Penistone Church	3-2
	Old Mexburians v RAF Cranwell	4-2
	Ollerton Colliery v Raleigh Athletic	2-2
	Pilkington Recreation v Boots Athletic	4-4
	Players Athletic v Aspley OB	0-4
	Thurcroft Main v Lincoln City School OBU	3-1
7	Anstey Nomads v Dainite Sports	wo/s
	Baddesley Colliery v Oadby Town	2-0
	Barwell Athletic v Loughborough College	1-3
	Ibstock Penistone Rovers v Midland Woodworking	2-2
	Lucas Great King Street v Stapenhill	1-3
12	Arlesey Town v Shefford Town	4-1
	Hemel Hempstead Town v Waterlows Dunstable	2-0
15	Bognor Regis Town v Old Varndonians	1-2
	Worthing v Goldstone	1-2
16	APV Athletic v Horsham	2-5
	Banstead Athletic v Camberley	1-2
	East Grinstead v Addlestone	4-1
	Farnham Town v Bexhill Town	3-2
	Leatherhead v Cobham	4-1
	Newhaven v Cuckfield	6-1
17	Harlow Town v Barnet	0-3
18	Barking v Grays Athletic	2-2
	Chingford v West Thurrock Athletic	4-2
20	Abingdon Town v Wokingham Town	1-3
	Aylesbury United v Oxford City	1-0
	Bicester Town v Newbury Town	2-2
	Bletchley & Wipac Sports v Osberton Radiator	3-2
	Buckingham Town v Chesham United	1-4
	Chipping Norton Town v Maidenhead United	0-3
	Didcot Town v Stokenchurch	1-0
	Henley Town v Morris Motors	3-3
	Kidlington v Thame United	3-2
	Marlow v Amersham Town	12-1
	NAC Athletic v Huntley & Palmers	1-2
	Slough Town v Wolvercote	6-0
	Wallingford Town v St Frideswides	0-1
	Windsor & Eton v Kirtlington Sports	1-0
	Witney Town v Oxford YMCA	4-0
	Woodstock Town v Pressed Steel	1-1
22	Bulford United v Bromham	4-2
	Clandown v Swindon Victoria	3-1
	Downton v Sharpness	2-3
	Hoffmann Athletic (Stonehouse) v Shepton Mallet T	0-1
	Paulton Rovers v Pewsey Vale	4-1
	Purton v Calne & Harris United	1-2
	Radstock Town v Melksham Town	7-5
	Spencer Moulton v Roundway Hospital	4-3
	Swindon BR Corinthians v Brimscombe	0-6
	Westbury United v Peasedown Miners Welfare	3-3
6r	Boots Athletic v Pilkington Recreation	5-2
r	Raleigh Athletic v Ollerton Colliery	1-5
7r	Midland Woodworking v Ibstock Penistone Rovers	3-2
18r	Grays Athletic v Barking	1-2
20r	Morris Motors v Henley Town	2-1
r	Newbury Town v Bicester Town	8-0
r	Pressed Steel v Woodstock Town	2-1
22r	Peasedown Miners Welfare v Westbury United	0-5

Preliminary Round

1	Hearts of Liddesdale v Appleby	7-0
	Shap v Penrith	1-1
	Wallsend St Lukes v Seaton Sluice United	n/a
2	Esh Winning Albion v Bank Head United	6-4
	Heighington Ams v Darlington &Simpson Rolling Mill	5-2
	New Brancepeth CW v Highgate United (Newcastle)	0-2
	Seaton Holy Trinity v Langley Park CW	2-6
	Stanley United v Chilton Athletic	4-1
	Wingate Welfare v Cockfield	2-6
	Witton Park v Tow Law Town	2-3
	Wolsingham Welfare v Burnside United	4-1
4	Hoylake Athletic v Port Sunlight	4-0
	ICI Alkali v Marine	3-3
	Manchester YMCA v Blackpool Mechanics	3-0
	Runcorn Athletic v Moreton	5-0
	Shell v Old Blackburnians	5-3
	St Annes Athletic v Southport Leyland Road	4-0
	Whitchurch Alport v Stockton Heath	4-0
5	Brunswick Institute v Harrogate & District Railway	1-3
	Carlton United v Harrogate Town	2-1
	Kingston Wolves v Bradford Rovers	2-1
	Liversedge v Ossett Albion	2-0
	North Ferriby United v Methley United	1-6
	Thackley v Swillington MW	0-3
6	Armthorpe Welfare v Basford United	4-0
	Arnold St Marys v Claycross & Danesmoor	1-2
	Aspley OB v Ollerton Colliery	1-0
	British Ropes (Retford) v Sheffield	0-7
	Brodsworth Main v Old Mexburians	6-1
	Parliament Street Methodists v Boots Athletic	4-2
	Thorncliffe Recreational v Lincoln Clayton	7-1
	Thurcroft Main v Grantham St Johns	2-7
7	Coventry Amateur v Baddesley Colliery	4-1
	Earl Shilton Institute v Measham Imperial	2-1
	Midland Woodworking v Corby United	4-2
	Paget Rangers v Enderby Town	1-1
	Quorn v Anstey Nomads	3-5
	Shepshed Albion v Loughborough College	0-4
	Smethwick Town v Stapenhill	0-1
	Wellington Victoria v Sileby Town	1-2
8	Boldmere St Michaels v Old Wulfrunians	4-1
	Jack Moulds Athletic v Stratford Town	n/a
	Moor Green v Staffordshire Casuals	5-0
11	Beccles v Ipswich Wanderers	4-1
	Brantham Athletic v Leiston	5-2
	Bury Town v Hadleigh United	9-1
	Crittall Athletic v Newmarket Town	2-2
	Ipswich Electricity Supply v Whitton United	0-5
	Landseer Youth v Achilles	0-9
12	Hemel Hempstead Town v Berkhamsted Town	1-1
	Hunting Percival Athletic v Marston Shelton Rovers	1-3
	Letchworth Town v AC Delco	5-3
	Royston Town v Leighton United	0-3
	Stevenage Town v Baldock Town	0-0
	Tring Town v Bedford Avenue	3-4
	Vauxhall Motors v Stotfold	6-1
13	Polytechnic v Wood Green Town	2-2
	Wingate v Wealdstone	1-4
14	Beckenham v Luton (Chatham)	1-3
	Herne Bay v Cray Wanderers	3-1
	Maidstone United v Bexley	9-0
	Thameside Amateurs v Callender Athletic	4-1
	Woolwich Polytechnic v Foots Cray	1-0
15	Goldstone v Chichester United	7-3
	Hastings & St Leonards v Old Varndonians	3-3
	Hove Town v Arundel	3-4
	Lancing Athletic v Moulsecoomb Rovers	4-2
	Littlehampton Town v Hastings Rangers	5-0
	Shoreham v Brighton Old Grammarians	2-3
	Whitehawk v Chichester City	7-3
	Wigmore Athletic v Southwick	3-0
16	Chertsey Town v Leatherhead	2-4
	Crawley v Dorking	1-1
	Eastbourne v Croydon Amateur	1-1
	Farncombe v Horsham	3-6
	Farnham Town v East Grinstead	5-1
	Haywards Heath v Metropolitan Police	3-4
	Lewes v Camberley	2-2
	Newhaven v Three Bridges United	0-0
17	Barnet v Epping Town	9-0
	Finsbury v Bishops Stortford	0-6
	Harpenden Town v Boreham Wood	3-0
	Hatfield Town v Kings Langley	2-1
	Leavesden Hospital v Hoddesdon Town	2-4
	Rickmansworth Town v Cheshunt (2)	3-0
	Tufnell Park Edmonton v Crown & Manor	2-1
	Welwyn Garden City v Saffron Walden Town	1-2
18	Brentwood & Warley v Barking	4-1
	Chingford v Bata Sports	3-1
	Dagenham Cables v Eton Manor	2-7
	Ford Sports v East Ham United	2-1
	Hornchurch & Upminster v Barkingside	3-1
	Rainham Town v Basildon Town	2-1
	Tilbury v Lathol Athletic	4-2e
	Woodford Town v Aveley	2-3
19	Civil Service v Molesey	0-2
	London University v ROF (SA)	2-2
	PO Engineers (LTR) v Ruislip Manor	1-3
	Petter & Bryce Sports v Devas Institute	4-2
	Staines Town v Kingsbury Town	1-1
	Surbiton Town v Worcester Park	4-2
	Twickenham v Malden Town	0-2
	Vickers (Weybridge) v Epsom	0-7
20	Aylesbury United v Kidlington	3-0
	Chesham United v Maidenhead United	0-1
	Didcot Town v Bletchley & Wipac Sports	8-0
	Huntley & Palmers v Wokingham Town	0-4
	Morris Motors v Windsor & Eton	1-7
	Pressed Steel v Newbury Town	0-7
	Slough Town v St Frideswides	5-0
	Witney Town v Marlow	1-1
21	Blandford United v Swanage Town	wo/s
	Bournemouth v Bournemouth Gasworks Athletic	0-3
	Gosport Borough Athletic v Fareham Town	2-1
	Thorneycroft v Totton	1-1
	Wimborne v Hamworthy	1-3
22	Calne & Harris United v Bulford United	3-1
	Clandown v Radstock Town	1-3
	Corsham Town v Westbury United	2-0
	Devizes Town v Shepton Mallet Town	5-0
	Sharpness v Spencer Moulton	7-3
	Warminster Town v Brimscombe	6-2
	Welton Rovers v Pinehurst Youth Centre	1-2
	Wootton Bassett Town v Paulton Rovers	2-2
23	Bristol St George v Worle OB	0-0
	Chard Town v Eden Grove OB	0-5
	Keynsham Town v St Philips Marsh Adult School	0-2
	Pucklechurch v Hanham Athletic	0-1
	Soundwell v Heavitree United	3-0
1r	Penrith v Shap	4-2
4r	Marine v ICI Alkali	5-0
7r	Enderby Town v Paget Rangers	0-2
11r	Newmarket Town v Crittall Athletic	2-1
12r	Baldock Town v Stevenage Town	1-0
r	Berkhamsted Town v Hemel Hempstead Town	1-2e
13r	Wood Green Town v Polytechnic	2-0
15r	Hastings & St Leonards v Old Varndonians	3-3e
16r	Camberley v Lewes	3-0
r	Croydon Amateur v Eastbourne	0-2
r	Dorking v Crawley	3-2
r	Newhaven v Three Bridges United	2-1
19r	Kingsbury Town v Staines Town	4-2
r	ROF (SA) v London University	1-4
20r	Marlow v Witney Town	6-4
21r	Totton v Thorneycroft	2-4e
22r	Paulton Rovers v Wootton Bassett Town	4-2e
23r	Worle OB v Bristol St George	3-4
15r2	Old Varndonians v Hastings & St Leonards	wo/s

Qualifying Round One

1	Cleator Moor Celtic v Penrith	2-9
	Gretna v Seaton Sluice United	1-1
	Hearts of Liddesdale v Washington CW	0-3
	Heaton Stannington v Kirkby Stephen	5-1
2	Cockfield v Stanley United	2-3
	Esh Winning Albion v Heighington Amateur	4-3
	Highgate United (Newcastle) v Tow Law Town	2-2
	Langley Park CW v Wolsingham Welfare	3-3
3	Bridlington Trinity United v Whitby Town	1-1
	North Skelton Athletic v Cargo Fleet Works	2-5
	South Bank v Redcar Albion	2-5
	Winterton Hospital v Bridlington Central United	2-3
4	Manchester YMCA v Unit Construction (Liverpool)	n/a
	Marine v St Annes Athletic	3-1
	Runcorn Athletic v Whitchurch Alport	2-0
	Shell v Hoylake Athletic	2-2

1957/58

5 Carlton United v Kingston Wolves	3-3
Guiseley v Harrogate & District Railway	5-3
Liversedge v Thornhill Edge	3-1
Methley United v Swillington MW	2-0
6 Armthorpe Welfare v Sheffield	4-1
Brodsworth Main v Grantham St Johns	3-2
Claycross & Danesmoor v Aspley OB	2-5
Thorncliffe Recreational v Parliament Street Meths	5-1
7 Coventry Amateur v Midland Woodworking	2-3
Earl Shilton Institute v Sileby Town	3-2
Paget Rangers v Anstey Nomads	4-1
Stapenhill v Loughborough College	2-4
8 Bournville Athletic v Boldmere St Michaels	2-1
Fernhill Heath v Walsall Trinity	1-0
Moor Green v Alvechurch	7-0
Walsall Wood v Jack Moulds Athletic	3-3
9 Histon v Ramsey Town	6-1
Raunds Town v St Neots St Marys	0-4
Sutton Bridge United v Somersham Town	3-2
Wolverton Town & BR v Finedon Town	11-0
10 Cromer v Diss Town	2-1e
Sheringham v City of Norwich School OBU	2-3e
Thetford Town v North Walsham Town	1-3
11 Beccles v Newmarket Town	3-1
Brantham Athletic v Achilles	2-0
Bungay Town v Bury Town	8-1
Whitton United v Waterside Works	3-0
12 Arlesey Town v Hemel Hempstead Town	5-0
Bedford Avenue v Baldock Town	1-5
Leighton United v Letchworth Town	4-2
Marston Shelton Rovers v Vauxhall Motors	2-4
13 Harrow Town v Edgware Town	5-2
Wealdstone v Willesden	3-2
Wembley v Pinner	2-1
Wood Green Town v Uxbridge	2-5
14 Crockenhill v Luton (Chatham)	4-0
Faversham Town v Maidstone United	1-2
Herne Bay v Woolwich Polytechnic	n/a
Thameside Amateurs v Slade Green	1-2
15 Lancing Athletic v Arundel	2-1e
Littlehampton Town v Wigmore Athletic	4-4
Old Varndonians v Goldstone	2-1
Whitehawk v Brighton Old Grammarians	7-0
16 Camberley v Horsham	0-3
Dorking v Metropolitan Police	5-1
Eastbourne v Newhaven	2-0
Leatherhead v Farnham Town	0-1
17 Bishops Stortford v Barnet	1-4
Hatfield Town v Saffron Walden Town	4-0
Hoddesdon Town v Harpenden Town	2-0
Tufnell Park Edmonton v Rickmansworth Town	4-1
18 Brentwood & Warley v Chingford	2-1
Eton Manor v Tilbury	3-0
Ford Sports v Aveley	2-2
Rainham Town v Hornchurch & Upminster	0-0
19 London University v Epsom	0-7
Malden Town v Kingsbury Town	6-0
Petter & Bryce Sports v Molesey	1-4
Ruislip Manor v Surbiton Town	6-1
20 Maidenhead United v Marlow	3-2
Slough Town v Didcot Town	7-0
Windsor & Eton v Aylesbury United	2-0
Wokingham Town v Newbury Town	2-2
21 Bournemouth Gasworks Athletic v Thorneycroft	2-1
Gosport Borough Athletic v Upwey & Broadway	4-0
Hamworthy v Blandford United	2-0
Ryde Sports v Pirelli General Cable Works	1-1
22 Calne & Harris United v Radstock Town	1-0
Corsham Town v Paulton Rovers	0-1
Sharpness v Pinehurst Youth Centre	2-0
Warminster Town v Devizes Town	1-3
23 Exmouth Town v Hanham Athletic	2-2
Ilminster Town v Bristol St George	1-2
Mount Hill Enterprise v Eden Grove OB	2-0
Soundwell v St Philips Marsh Adult School	2-2
24 Camelford v Tamerton	2-2
Dartmouth United v Chelston	8-2
Nanpean Rovers v Liskeard Athletic	2-0
Newton Abbott Spurs v Burraton	3-1
1r Seaton Sluice United v Gretna	2-0
2r Tow Law Town v Highgate United (Newcastle)	2-2e
r Wolsingham Welfare v Langley Park CW	3-1
3r Whitby Town v Bridlington Trinity United	4-3
4r Hoylake Athletic v Shell	3-2
5r Kingston Wolves v Carlton United	2-1
8r Jack Moulds Athletic v Walsall Wood	1-2e
15r Wigmore Athletic v Littlehampton Town	5-2
18r Aveley v Ford Sports	3-0
r Hornchurch & Upminster v Rainham Town	3-0
20r Newbury Town v Wokingham Town	1-2e
21r Pirelli General Cable Works v Ryde Sports	3-2
23r Exmouth Town v Hanham Athletic	0-4
r St Philips Marsh Adult School v Soundwell	4-0
24r Camelford v Tamerton	4-3
2r2 Tow Law Town v Highgate United (Newcastle)	5-1

Qualifying Round Two

1 Heaton Stannington v Washington CW	2-1
Seaton Sluice United v Penrith	0-3
2 Tow Law Town v Stanley United	2-4
Wolsingham Welfare v Esh Winning Albion	5-1
3 Bridlington Central United v Redcar Albion	2-7
Whitby Town v Cargo Fleet Works	4-1
4 Marine v Hoylake Athletic	2-0
Runcorn Athletic v Unit Construction (Liverpool)	7-3
5 Guiseley v Kingston Wolves	3-3
Liversedge v Methley United	2-3
6 Armthorpe Welfare v Thorncliffe Recreational	3-1
Brodsworth Main v Aspley OB	4-1
7 Earl Shilton Institute v Loughborough College	1-7
Paget Rangers v Midland Woodworking	7-1
8 Moor Green v Bournville Athletic	1-1
Walsall Wood v Fernhill Heath	5-2
9 Sutton Bridge United v Histon	1-3
Wolverton Town & BR v St Neots St Marys	10-1
10 Cromer v North Walsham Town	4-2
Wymondham Town v City of Norwich School OBU	3-2e
11 Bungay Town v Beccles	6-0
Whitton United v Brantham Athletic	2-0
12 Baldock Town v Leighton United	6-3
Vauxhall Motors v Arlesey Town	7-1
13 Wealdstone v Harrow Town	5-2
Wembley v Uxbridge	0-4
14 Crockenhill v Slade Green	2-2
Maidstone United v Herne Bay	4-3
15 Whitehawk v Lancing Athletic	7-1
Wigmore Athletic v Old Varndonians	2-1
16 Dorking v Farnham Town	1-2
Horsham v Eastbourne	1-6
17 Hatfield Town v Barnet	1-6
Tufnell Park Edmonton v Hoddesdon Town	2-2
18 Eton Manor v Brentwood & Warley	1-2
Hornchurch & Upminster v Aveley	0-2
19 Malden Town v Epsom	2-4
Ruislip Manor v Molesey	2-4
20 Slough Town v Wokingham Town	2-2
Windsor & Eton v Maidenhead United	1-2
21 B'mouth Gasworks Ath v Pirelli General Cables Wks	3-3
Hamworthy v Gosport Borough Athletic	4-3
22 Devizes Town v Paulton Rovers	9-0
Sharpness v Calne & Harris United	7-2
23 Bristol St George v Hanham Athletic	1-3
Mount Hill Enterprise v St Philips Marsh Adult Sch.	5-1
24 Nanpean Rovers v Camelford	2-5
Newton Abbott Spurs v Dartmouth United	2-3
5r Kingston Wolves v Guiseley	3-1
8r Bournville Athletic v Moor Green	2-4
14r Slade Green v Crockenhill	2-3
17r Hoddesdon Town v Tufnell Park Edmonton	2-1
20r Wokingham Town v Slough Town	2-0
21r Pirelli General Cable Wks v B'mouth Gasworks Ath	6-3

Qualifying Round Three

1 Penrith v Heaton Stannington	1-2
2 Stanley United v Wolsingham Welfare	4-1
3 Redcar Albion v Whitby Town	1-1
4 Marine v Runcorn Athletic	0-4
5 Kingston Wolves v Methley United	1-7
6 Armthorpe Welfare v Brodsworth Main	4-1
7 Loughborough College v Paget Rangers	1-2e
8 Walsall Wood v Moor Green	3-0
9 Histon v Wolverton Town & BR	5-4
10 Cromer v Wymondham Town	0-1
11 Whitton United v Bungay Town	0-1
12 Baldock Town v Vauxhall Motors	2-4
13 Uxbridge v Wealdstone	1-1
14 Maidstone United v Crockenhill	7-1
15 Whitehawk v Wigmore Athletic	0-0
16 Eastbourne v Farnham Town	4-2
17 Hoddesdon Town v Barnet	1-4
18 Aveley v Brentwood & Warley	1-1
19 Epsom v Molesey	1-1
20 Wokingham Town v Maidenhead United	1-0
21 Hamworthy v Pirelli General Cable Works	1-3
22 Devizes Town v Sharpness	1-0
23 Mount Hill Enterprise v Hanham Athletic	2-2
24 Camelford v Dartmouth United	4-1
3r Whitby Town v Redcar Albion	2-4
13r Wealdstone v Uxbridge	1-2
15r Wigmore Athletic v Whitehawk	2-1
18r Brentwood & Warley v Aveley	1-4
19r Molesey v Epsom	1-5
23r Hanham Athletic v Mount Hill Enterprise	1-0

Qualifying Round Four

Armthorpe Welfare v Methley United	1-3
Cambridge City v Wymondham Town	5-1
Carshalton Athletic v Maidstone United	1-1
Clevedon v Saltash United	0-0
Dagenham v Leyton	2-0
Devizes Town v Pirelli General Cable Works	3-2
Eastbourne v Epsom	3-2
Ely City v Histon	2-4
Enfield v Wigmore Athletic	3-0
Hallam v Stork	2-2
Harwich & Parkeston v Aveley	1-1
Hertford Town v Barnet	2-4
Holt United v Bungay Town	1-2
Malvern Town v Eastwood Town	1-5
Paget Rangers v Walsall Wood	2-4
Redcar Albion v Durham City	2-3
Redhill v Walton & Hersham	1-2
Runcorn Athletic v Newton	0-0
St Austell v Camelford	7-2
Stanley United v Heaton Stannington	2-1

Stockton v Shildon	3-2
Ware v Vauxhall Motors	1-1
Winchester City v Hanham Athletic	1-0
Wokingham Town v Uxbridge	5-2
r Aveley v Harwich & Parkeston	2-0
r Maidstone United v Carshalton Athletic	2-0
r Newton v Runcorn Athletic	4-4
r Saltash United v Clevedon	4-2
r Stork v Hallam	3-0
r Vauxhall Motors v Ware	5-3
r2 Newton v Runcorn Athletic	2-1

Round One

Alton Town v Walton & Hersham	3-1
Billingham Synthonia v Eastwood Town	3-0
Bromley v Cambridge City	2-0
Bungay Town v Kingstonian	6-5
Clapton v Southall	2-1
Devizes Town v St Albans City	3-1
Durham City v Methley United	6-0
Erith & Belvedere v Romford (2)	3-1
Evenwood Town v Ferryhill Athletic	1-1
Finchley v Eastbourne United	2-1
Gedling Colliery v Willington	0-2
Hendon v Dulwich Hamlet	5-1
Hitchin Town v Corinthian Casuals	0-1
Ilford v Eastbourne	2-1
Maidstone United v Dagenham	0-2
Saltash United v Briggs Sports	1-2
Salts v Stanley United	3-2
Sheppey United v Barnet	1-3
St Austell v Hayes	0-2
Stockton v Newton	4-0
Stork v Bishop Auckland	1-1
Vauxhall Motors v Hounslow Town	3-1
Walsall Wood v West Auckland Town	0-3
Walthamstow Avenue v Pegasus	2-2
Whitley Bay v Crook Town	2-4
Wimbledon v Tooting & Mitcham United	0-5
Winchester City v Enfield	1-0
Woking v Aveley	6-1
Wokingham Town v Histon	4-0
Wycombe Wanderers v Leytonstone	2-0
Yiewsley v Sutton United	3-1
Yorkshire Amateur v Norton Woodseats	1-3
r Bishop Auckland v Stork	3-2
r Ferryhill Athletic v Evenwood Town	2-1
r Pegasus v Walthamstow Avenue	3-1

Round Two

Barnet v Yiewsley	6-0
Billingham Synthonia v Willington	1-2
Bishop Auckland v Tooting & Mitcham United	2-0
Bungay Town v Ilford	0-4
Clapton v Bromley	1-2
Corinthian Casuals v Salts	10-0
Crook Town v Briggs Sports	3-0
Dagenham v Hayes	0-0
Devizes Town v Vauxhall Motors	1-7
Finchley v Alton Town	3-1
Hendon v Woking	1-3
Norton Woodseats v Wokingham Town	2-2
Pegasus v Ferryhill Athletic	0-2
Stockton v Durham City	0-0
West Auckland Town v Erith & Belvedere	3-0
Wycombe Wanderers v Winchester City	6-0
r Durham City v Stockton	3-4
r Hayes v Dagenham	3-0
r Wokingham Town v Norton Woodseats	1-0

Round Three

Bromley v Vauxhall Motors	1-3
Crook Town v Corinthian Casuals	2-2
Ferryhill Athletic v Barnet	3-3
Finchley v Willington	3-0
Ilford v Wycombe Wanderers	2-1
Stockton v Bishop Auckland	2-1
Woking v Hayes	5-1
Wokingham Town v West Auckland Town	4-2 v
r Barnet v Ferryhill Athletic	4-2
r Corinthian Casuals v Crook Town	1-2
r West Auckland Town v Wokingham Town	2-3

Round Four

Barnet v Stockton	4-1
Crook Town v Wokingham Town	3-2
Ilford v Vauxhall Motors	3-0
Woking v Finchley	3-2

Semi Finals

Ilford v Crook Town	1-0 N
Woking v Barnet	1-1 N
r Woking v Barnet	3-2 N

Final

Woking v Ilford	3-0 N

1958/59

1958/59

Extra Preliminary Round

4	Ainsdale Hesketh Park v Middleton Amateurs	0-8 N
	Earle v Manchester YMCA	n/a
	East Chorlton Amateur v Runcorn Athletic	3-2
6	Lincoln City School OBU v Grantham St Johns	2-1
8	Fernhill Heath v Alvechurch	n/a
16	Kings Langley v Hoddesdon Town	0-1
	Ware v Leavesden Hospital	2-0
17	Ford Sports v East Ham United	0-4
20	Oxford City v NAC Athletic	10-0
22	Bulford United v Westcott Youth Centre	3-1
	Clandown v Pinehurst Youth Centre	2-1
	Corsham Town v Warminster Town	1-8
23	Clevedon v Lydbrook Athletic	3-4
	Paulton Rovers v Eden Grove OB	3-0
	Peasedown Miners Welfare v Shepton Mallet Town	1-5

Preliminary Round

1	Bank Head United v Burnside United	5-4
	Burradon Welfare v Naval Yard (Walker)	2-2
	Carlisle BR v Penrith	1-2
	Shap v Salterbeck	2-1
	Wallsend Rising Sun v Wallsend St Lukes	4-3
	Washington CW v Heaton Stannington	1-1
2	Cockfield v Witton Park	2-1
	Darlington &Simpson Rolling Mill v Wolsingham Welf	3-2
	Esh Winning Albion v Annfield Plain	1-3
	Langley Park CW v Highgate United (Newcastle)	2-0
	Shildon v Throston Wanderers	5-1
	Tow Law Town v Heighington Amateur	5-1
	Wingate Welfare v Crookhall CW	4-1
3	Bridlington Trinity United v Reckitt & Sons	2-1
	Brunswick Institute v Kingston Wolves	0-1
	South Bank v Cleveland Mines	3-2
4	Earle v Stockton Heath	0-4
	East Chorlton Amateur v Harrowby	4-1
	Hoylake Athletic v Manchester University	4-4
	ICI Alkali v Middleton Amateurs	5-3
	Marine v Port Sunlight	3-2
	Middlewich Athletic v Shell	4-1
	Old Blackburnians v Blackpool Mechanics	1-2
5	Armthorpe Welfare v Brodsworth Main	7-3
	Bradford Rovers v Grange OB (Leeds)	1-1
	Farsley Celtic v Thackley	3-1
	Harrogate Town v Harrogate & District Railway	1-4
	Liversedge v Thorncliffe Recreational	1-0
	Ossett Albion v Guiseley	4-2
	Penistone Church v Swillington MW	2-2
	Thornhill Edge v Thurcroft Welfare	1-10
6	Aspley OB v RAF Cranwell	n/a
	Boots Athletic v Sheffield	1-2
	British Ropes (Retford) v Lincoln City School OBU	2-5
	Ericsson Athletic v Raleigh Athletic	1-1
	Hallam v Arnold St Marys	6-1
	Lincoln Clayton v Hampton Sports	2-0
	Parliament Street Methodists v Basford United	3-0
	Players Athletic v Claycross & Danesmoor	wo/s
7	Anstey Nomads v Baddesley Colliery	5-4
	Barwell Athletic v Sileby Town	2-4e
	Coventry Amateur v Wellington Victoria	1-5
	Earl Shilton Institute v Boldmere St Michaels	5-2
	Ibstock Penistone Rovers v Shepshed Albion	6-1
	Oadby Town v Loughborough College	1-2
	Paget Rangers v Stapenhill	1-1
	Quorn v Corby United	6-3
8	Allens Cross v Stratford Town	1-2
	Cresconians v Metal Box Company (Worcester)	n/a
	Jack Moulds Athletic v Bournville Athletic	5-1
	Malvern Town v Fernhill Heath	6-3
	Moor Green v Sankey of Wellington	3-2
	Smethwick Town v Old Wulfrunians	5-2
	Wrockwardine Wood v Walsall Trinity	1-1
9	Cromer v North Walsham Town	2-1
	Desborough Town v Somersham Town	4-0
	Great Yarmouth Town v Holt United	3-1
	Ramsey Town v Finedon Town	1-1
	Raunds Town v St Neots St Marys	6-0
	Thetford Town v City of Norwich School OBU	1-1
	Wymondham Town v Sheringham	2-1
10	Beccles v Brantham Athletic	11-4
	Beccles Caxton v Newmarket Town	2-3
	Hadleigh United v Waterside Works	1-2
	Harwich & Parkeston v Achilles	7-1
	Landseer Youth v Leiston	6-4
11	AC Delco v Tring Town	0-2
	Arlesey Town v Baldock Town	2-1
	Hemel Hempstead Town v Waterlows Dunstable	3-2
	Leighton United v Luton Skefco Athletic	1-2
	Letchworth Town v Stevenage Town	2-0
	Royston Town v Marston Shelton Rovers	2-3
	Shefford Town v Berkhamsted Town	2-0
	Stotfold v Bedford Avenue	7-2
12	Edgware Town v Old Finchleians	4-0
	Harrow Town v Wembley	4-2
	Kingsbury Town v Finsbury	2-2
	Polytechnic v Pinner	6-2
	Ruislip Manor v Wingate	2-1
	Twickenham v Wood Green Town	5-2
	Willesden v Staines Town	2-2
13	Bexley v Brentstonians	1-4
	Callender Athletic v Beckenham	2-3
	Herne Bay v Crockenhill	6-3
	Woolwich Polytechnic v Slade Green	1-1
14	Arundel v Hove Town	1-1
	Bognor Regis Town v Wigmore Athletic	1-3
	Chichester City v Brighton Old Grammarians	5-0
	Hastings & St Leonards v Southwick	0-3
	Lancing Athletic v Shoreham	1-1
	Littlehampton Town v Moulsecoomb Rovers	3-1
	Old Varndonians v Goldstone	2-2
	Worthing v Hastings Rangers	7-1
15	Camberley v Bexhill Town	1-3
	Crawley v Newhaven	3-0
	Dorking v Three Bridges United	6-2
	East Grinstead v Banstead Athletic	1-1
	Farncombe v Lewes	2-1
	Haywards Heath v Farnham Town	3-1
	Metropolitan Police v Cockfield	8-0
16	Bishops Stortford v Saffron Walden Town	6-0
	Cheshunt (2) v Welwyn Garden City	3-1
	Crown & Manor v Hoddesdon Town	3-3
	Epping Town v Rickmansworth Town	0-2
	Harpenden Town v Harlow Town	3-5
	Hatfield Town v Boreham Wood	0-4
	Stansted v Hertford Town	6-4
	Ware v Tufnell Park Edmonton	4-3
17	Barking v Barkingside	7-1
	Basildon Town v Tilbury	0-5
	Bata Sports v Lathol Athletic	2-1
	Brentwood & Warley v Woodford Town	2-0
	Chingford v East Ham United	1-5
	Dagenham v Rainham Town	0-2
	Hornchurch & Upminster v Eton Manor	1-1
	Leyton v West Thurrock Athletic	1-0
18	Addlestone v Worcester Park	4-2
	Chertsey Town v Cobham	1-1
	Epsom v Vickers (Weybridge)	5-2
	Leatherhead v Whitehawk	3-0
	Malden Town v Carshalton Athletic	1-5
	Molesey v Surbiton Town	0-0
	Petter & Bryce Sports v PO Engineers (LTR)	1-3
	ROF (SA) v Civil Service	1-0
19	Bletchley Town v Aylesbury United	1-6
	Chesham United v Wokingham Town	1-1
	Huntley & Palmers v Wolverton Town & BR	4-1
	Marlow v Amersham Town	7-2
	Newbury Town v Wallingford Town	7-2
	Stokenchurch v Slough Town	2-3
	Windsor & Eton v Henley Town	3-0
20	Abingdon Town v Witney Town	4-0
	Didcot Town v Woodstock Town	4-0
	Kidlington v Oxford City	2-5
	Morris Motors v St Frideswides	4-3
	Oxford University Press v Wantage Town	3-3
	Oxford YMCA v Osberton Radiator	4-1 N
	Pressed Steel v Bicester Town	5-5
	South Oxford United v Wolvercote	4-0
21	Bournemouth v Upwey & Broadway	1-1
	Bournemouth Gasworks Athletic v Hamworthy	2-5
	Chard Town v Blandford United	4-0 D
	Fareham Town v Gosport Borough Athletic	2-1
	Lymington v Swaythling Athletic	0-3
	Ryde Sports v Waterlooville	4-3
	Totton v Pirelli General Cable Works	4-1
	Wimborne v Ilminster Town	2-8
22	Calne & Harris United v Swindon BR Corinthians	5-3
	Clandown v Westbury United	0-6
	Melksham Town v Wootton Bassett Town	3-0
	Pewsey Vale v Bulford United	3-4
	Purton v Swindon Victoria	3-1
	Spencer Moulton v Radstock Town	1-4
	Warminster Town v Amesbury	4-0
	Welton Rovers v Bromham	3-0
23	Brimscombe v Mount Hill Enterprise	1-5
	Bristol St George v Lydbrook Athletic	2-6
	Hanham Athletic v Pucklechurch	0-1
	Keynsham Town v Hoffmann Athletic (Stonehouse)	4-4
	Paulton Rovers v Soundwell	1-2
	Sharpness v Worle OB	3-1
	Shepton Mallet Town v Bristol Mental Hospital	1-3
	Watchet Town v St Philips Marsh Adult School	3-1
24	Camelford United v Heavitree United	1-1
	Nanpean Rovers v Burraton	4-0
1r	Heaton Stannington v Washington CW	2-5
r	Naval Yard (Walker) v Burradon Welfare	n/a
4r	Manchester University v Hoylake Athletic	2-1
5r	Grange OB (Leeds) v Bradford Rovers	1-2
r	Swillington MW v Penistone Church	11-1
6r	Raleigh Athletic v Ericsson Athletic	2-1
7r	Stapenhill v Paget Rangers	5-1
8r	Wrockwardine Wood v Walsall Trinity	2-3
9r	Finedon Town v Ramsey Town	2-5
r	Thetford Town v City of Norwich School OBU	1-2
12r	Finsbury v Kingsbury Town	2-3
r	Staines Town v Willesden	1-2
13r	Slade Green v Woolwich Polytechnic	4-1
14r	Arundel v Hove Town	5-1
r	Goldstone v Old Varndonians	0-1 N
r	Shoreham v Lancing Athletic	2-3
15r	Banstead Athletic v East Grinstead	4-2
16r	Hoddesdon Town v Crown & Manor	6-2
17r	Eton Manor v Hornchurch & Upminster	0-1
18r	Cobham v Chertsey Town	4-2
r	Molesey v Surbiton Town	9-0
19r	Wokingham Town v Chesham United	3-0
20r	Bicester Town v Pressed Steel	3-2
r	Wantage Town v Oxford University Press	7-7
21r	Upwey & Broadway v Bournemouth	2-4
23r	Hoffmann Athletic (Stonehouse) v Keynsham Town	2-3
24r	Heavitree United v Camelford United	8-2
20r2	Wantage Town v Oxford University Press	3-3e
20r3	Oxford University Press v Wantage Town	1-4

Qualifying Round One

1	Appleby v Shap	2-8
	Bank Head United v Wallsend Rising Sun	0-5
	Penrith v Hearts of Liddesdale	8-3
	Washington CW v Naval Yard (Walker)	2-3
2	Darlington &Simpson Rolling Mill v Annfield Plain	1-4
	New Brancepeth CW v Cockfield	2-3
	Shildon v Langley Park CW	3-1
	Tow Law Town v Wingate Welfare	4-3
3	Bridlington Trinity United v Bridlington Central Uni	1-2
	North Ferriby United v Kingston Wolves	1-2
	Redcar Albion v South Bank	0-1
	Whitby Town v Cargo Fleet Works	2-0
4	Blackpool Mechanics v Middlewich Athletic	3-6
	ICI Alkali v Marine	3-2
	Manchester University v East Chorlton Amateur	n/a
	Northern Nomads v Stockton Heath	1-1
5	Bradford Rovers v Ossett Albion	2-3
	Harrogate & District Railway v Farsley Celtic	0-4
	Liversedge v Swillington MW	2-1
	Thurcroft Welfare v Armthorpe Welfare	2-1
6	Lincoln Clayton v Raleigh Athletic	4-1
	Parliament Street Methodists v RAF Cranwell	2-1
	Players Athletic v Lincoln City School OBU	2-4
	Sheffield v Hallam	2-5
7	Earl Shilton Institute v Ibstock Penistone Rovers	2-2
	Loughborough College v Stapenhill	6-2
	Quorn v Sileby Town	0-4
	Wellington Victoria v Anstey Nomads	3-0
8	Jack Moulds Athletic v Stratford Town	1-3
	Malvern Town v Smethwick Town	1-0
	Moor Green v Staffordshire Casuals	4-0
	Walsall Trinity v unknown	n/a
9	Cromer v City of Norwich School OBU	1-3
	Ramsey Town v Sutton Bridge United	6-5
	Raunds Town v Desborough Town	2-4
	Wymondham Town v Great Yarmouth Town	4-3
10	Harwich & Parkeston v Waterside Works	2-0
	Landseer Youth v Ipswich Wanderers	2-3
	Newmarket Town v Beccles	1-0
	Whitton United v Crittall Athletic	3-0
11	Hemel Hempstead Town v Arlesey Town	1-0
	Letchworth Town v Luton Skefco Athletic	4-1
	Marston Shelton Rovers v Tring Town	1-3
	Shefford Town v Stotfold	0-6
12	Harrow Town v Willesden	2-2
	Polytechnic v Kingsbury Town	1-3
	Twickenham v Edgware Town	4-2
	Wealdstone v Ruislip Manor	2-2
13	Beckenham v Brentstonians	0-3
	Herne Bay v Luton (Chatham)	6-1
	Slade Green v Cray Wanderers	1-1
	Thameside Amateurs v Faversham Town	2-7
14	Arundel v Lancing Athletic	2-3
	Littlehampton Town v Wigmore Athletic	2-3
	Southwick v Old Varndonians	3-4
	Worthing v Chichester City	3-2
15	Bexhill Town v Haywards Heath	5-0
	Dorking v Banstead Athletic	1-1
	Farncombe v Metropolitan Police	1-6
	Horsham v Crawley	2-1
16	Boreham Wood v Bishops Stortford	2-2
	Cheshunt (2) v Stansted	3-4
	Harlow Town v Ware	2-3
	Hoddesdon Town v Rickmansworth Town	2-0
17	Bata Sports v Tilbury	2-8
	Brentwood & Warley v Barking	0-1
	East Ham United v Rainham Town	1-2
	Hornchurch & Upminster v Leyton	9-0
18	Carshalton Athletic v Molesey	7-2
	Epsom v Cobham	3-0
	Leatherhead v ROF (SA)	3-1
	PO Engineers (LTR) v Addlestone	3-5
19	Aylesbury United v Slough Town	2-0
	Huntley & Palmers v Marlow	4-2
	Newbury Town v Windsor & Eton	1-0
	Thame United v Wokingham Town	0-6
20	Bicester Town v Abingdon Town	2-6
	Didcot Town v Wantage Town	2-2
	Oxford City v Morris Motors	12-2
	Oxford YMCA v South Oxford United	4-1
21	Fareham Town v Ryde Sports	4-4
	Hamworthy v Bournemouth	2-1
	Ilminster Town v Blandford United	1-3
	Totton v Swaythling Athletic	3-2

1958/59 to 1959/60

22 Bulford United v Purton	1-2
Calne & Harris United v Welton Rovers	4-4
Melksham Town v Warminster Town	1-1
Radstock Town v Westbury United	1-2
23 Keynsham Town v Soundwell	1-0
Lydbrook Athletic v Pucklechurch	3-0
Mount Hill Enterprise v Watchet Town	0-0
Sharpness v Bristol Mental Hospital	2-1
24 Bugle v Dartmouth United	5-0
Heavitree United v Nanpean Rovers	5-2
Liskeard Athletic v Chelston	0-4
Looe v Exmouth Town	3-1
4r Stockton Heath v Northern Nomads	4-1
7r Ibstock Penistone Rovers v Earl Shilton Institute	2-0
12r Ruislip Manor v Wealdstone	0-4
r Willesden v Harrow Town	1-2
13r Cray Wanderers v Slade Green	1-2
15r Banstead Athletic v Dorking	1-3
16r Bishops Stortford v Boreham Wood	4-0
20r Wantage Town v Didcot Town	1-2
21r Ryde Sports v Fareham Town	2-4
22r Warminster Town v Melksham Town	2-3
r Welton Rovers v Calne & Harris United	1-0
23r Watchet Town v Mount Hill Enterprise	1-3

Qualifying Round Two

1 Penrith v Shap	7-1
Wallsend Rising Sun v Naval Yard (Walker)	6-1
2 Shildon v Cockfield	4-3
Tow Law Town v Annfield Plain	1-0
3 Bridlington Central United v Kingston Wolves	6-2
Whitby Town v South Bank	9-1
4 Manchester University v ICI Alkali	0-0
Stockton Heath v Middlewich Athletic	3-1
5 Farsley Celtic v Liversedge	2-1
Ossett Albion v Thurcroft Welfare	4-1
6 Hallam v Lincoln City School OBU	4-1
Lincoln Clayton v Parliament Street Methodists	2-2
7 Loughborough College v Sileby Town	7-0
Wellington Victoria v Ibstock Penistone Rovers	0-4
8 Malvern Town v Walsall Trinity	3-1
Stratford Town v Moor Green	2-4
9 Desborough Town v City of Norwich School OBU	0-7
Wymondham Town v Ramsey Town	4-0
10 Harwich & Parkeston v Ipswich Wanderers	10-0
Whitton United v Newmarket Town	3-3
11 Letchworth Town v Stotfold	0-4
Tring Town v Hemel Hempstead Town	0-0
12 Harrow Town v Kingsbury Town	5-1
Wealdstone v Twickenham	2-1
13 Faversham Town v Brentstonians	6-1
Slade Green v Herne Bay	2-2
14 Lancing Athletic v Old Varndonians	2-0
Wigmore Athletic v Worthing	3-3
15 Horsham v Dorking	2-2
Metropolitan Police v Bexhill Town	3-2
16 Hoddesdon Town v Bishops Stortford	0-4
Ware v Stansted	1-0
17 Hornchurch & Upminster v Barking	1-0
Rainham Town v Tilbury	3-2
18 Addlestone v Epsom	4-2
Carshalton Athletic v Leatherhead	5-1
19 Newbury Town v Aylesbury United	5-1
Wokingham Town v Huntley & Palmers	6-0
20 Oxford City v Abingdon Town	4-1
Oxford YMCA v Didcot Town	0-0
21 Blandford United v Totton	2-2
Fareham Town v Hamworthy	3-3
22 Purton v Welton Rovers	1-1
Westbury United v Melksham Town	2-4
23 Keynsham Town v Sharpness	7-0
Lydbrook Athletic v Mount Hill Enterprise	7-1
24 Chelston v Heavitree United	0-3
Looe v Bugle	1-1
4r ICI Alkali v Manchester University	4-2e
6r Parliament Street Methodists v Lincoln Clayton	2-4
10r Newmarket Town v Whitton United	3-0
11r Hemel Hempstead Town v Tring Town	0-1
13r Herne Bay v Slade Green	5-0
14r Worthing v Wigmore Athletic	0-3
15r Dorking v Horsham	3-3
20r Didcot Town v Oxford YMCA	6-3
21r Hamworthy v Fareham Town	0-2
r Totton v Blandford United	4-3
22r Welton Rovers v Purton	4-0
24r Bugle v Looe	4-2
15r2 Horsham v Dorking	5-0

Qualifying Round Three

1 Wallsend Rising Sun v Penrith	6-2
2 Shildon v Tow Law Town	1-0
3 Bridlington Central United v Whitby Town	1-5
4 ICI Alkali v Stockton Heath	4-1
5 Ossett Albion v Farsley Celtic	4-0
6 Hallam v Lincoln Clayton	10-3
7 Ibstock Penistone Rovers v Loughborough College	1-3
8 Malvern Town v Moor Green	0-4
9 Wymondham Town v City of Norwich School OBU	1-2
10 Newmarket Town v Harwich & Parkeston	1-4
11 Stotfold v Tring Town	3-0
12 Wealdstone v Harrow Town	2-3

13 Faversham Town v Herne Bay	3-1
14 Lancing Athletic v Wigmore Athletic	1-1
15 Horsham v Metropolitan Police	3-1
16 Bishops Stortford v Ware	3-2
17 Rainham Town v Hornchurch & Upminster	1-2
18 Carshalton Athletic v Addlestone	3-0
19 Wokingham Town v Newbury Town	2-4
20 Oxford City v Didcot Town	4-1
21 Fareham Town v Totton	5-0
22 Welton Rovers v Melksham Town	1-1
23 Lydbrook Athletic v Keynsham Town	2-2
24 Heavitree United v Bugle	5-2
14r Wigmore Athletic v Lancing Athletic	2-1
22r Melksham Town v Welton Rovers	1-3
23r Keynsham Town v Lydbrook Athletic	0-3

Qualifying Round Four

25 Yorkshire Amateur v Ossett Albion	3-1
Bungay Town v Harwich & Parkeston	2-2
Carshalton Athletic v Hornchurch & Upminster	1-1
Devizes Town v Welton Rovers	1-0
Eastbourne v Stotfold	0-1
Eastwood Town v Loughborough College	2-2
Fareham Town v Lydbrook Athletic	4-0
Faversham Town v Aveley	2-2
Heavitree United v Saltash United	0-1
Horsham v Harrow Town	1-3
Maidenhead United v Uxbridge	1-2
Maidstone United v Bishops Stortford	3-1
Methley United v Whitby Town	1-3
Newbury Town v Leytonstone	1-1
Newton v Hallam	0-2
Oxford City v St Albans City	6-1
Redhill v Enfield	2-0
Sheppey United v Grays Athletic	3-1
Stanley United v Shildon	3-3
Stork v ICI Alkali	0-1
Walsall Wood v Moor Green	3-1
Whitley Bay v Wallsend Rising Sun	4-2
Wigmore Athletic v Southall	0-4
Wymondham Town v Histon	0-3
r Aveley v Faversham Town	1-4
r Harwich & Parkeston v Bungay Town	8-0
r Hornchurch & Upminster v Carshalton Athletic	0-0e
r Leytonstone v Newbury Town	4-0
r Loughborough College v Eastwood Town	4-1
r Shildon v Stanley United	3-1
r2 Carshalton Athletic v Hornchurch & Upminster	4-2e

Round One

Alton Town v Histon	2-1
Barnet v Sheppey United	4-0
Billingham Synthonia v Evenwood Town	0-4
Briggs Sports v Maidstone United	0-0
Carshalton Athletic v Wimbledon	2-0
Corinthian Casuals v Harrow Town	1-1
Dulwich Hamlet v Saltash United	4-0
Durham City v Yorkshire Amateur	0-2
Eastbourne United v Harwich & Parkeston	0-0
Fareham Town v Clapton	2-2
Ferryhill Athletic v Crook Town	1-2
Finchley v Bromley	0-2
Gedling Colliery v Hallam	0-2
Hayes v Dagenham	1-0
Hitchin Town v Faversham Town	1-0
Hounslow Town v Wycombe Wanderers	1-1a
Norton Woodseats v Whitby Town	2-5
Oxford City v Ilford	3-1
Pegasus v Kingstonian	1-0
Redhill v Woking	6-3
Romford (2) v Leytonstone	0-1
Salts v Loughborough College	2-1
Southall v Sutton United	0-0
Stockton v Shildon	3-3
Stotfold v Erith & Belvedere	1-3
Vauxhall Motors v Hendon	1-3
Walthamstow Avenue v Devizes Town	3-1
Walton & Hersham v Uxbridge	0-2
West Auckland Town v ICI Alkali	2-3
Whitley Bay v Bishop Auckland	1-3
Willington v Walsall Wood	1-0
Winchester City v Tooting & Mitcham United	1-5
r Clapton v Fareham Town	3-1
r Harrow Town v Corinthian Casuals	1-3
r Harwich & Parkeston v Eastbourne United	4-2
r Hounslow Town v Wycombe Wanderers	2-4
r Maidstone United v Briggs Sports	1-2
r Shildon v Stockton	2-0
r Sutton United v Southall	0-3

Round Two

Alton Town v Hayes	3-1
Barnet v Willington	8-4
Bishop Auckland v Pegasus	0-0
Briggs Sports v Whitby Town	2-1
Corinthian Casuals v Hitchin Town	4-1
Erith & Belvedere v Crook Town	2-5
Evenwood Town v Hallam	2-2
Harwich & Parkeston v Yorkshire Amateur	0-0
Hendon v Tooting & Mitcham United	2-0

ICI Alkali v Oxford City	3-7
Leytonstone v Carshalton Athletic	2-0
Salts v Uxbridge	3-1
Shildon v Clapton	5-3
Southall v Redhill	0-1
Walthamstow Avenue v Bromley	4-0
Wycombe Wanderers v Dulwich Hamlet	2-1
r Hallam v Evenwood Town	2-0a
r Pegasus v Bishop Auckland	0-0
r Yorkshire Amateur v Harwich & Parkeston	3-2
r2 Bishop Auckland v Pegasus	1-0 N
r2 Hallam v Evenwood Town	4-3

Round Three

Alton Town v Leytonstone	0-3
Barnet v Wycombe Wanderers	2-2
Bishop Auckland v Redhill	3-2
Crook Town v Oxford City	5-2
Hallam v Hendon	0-1
Salts v Briggs Sports	2-3
Shildon v Corinthian Casuals	5-0
Walthamstow Avenue v Yorkshire Amateur	4-0
r Wycombe Wanderers v Barnet	0-1

Round Four

Barnet v Bishop Auckland	2-1
Briggs Sports v Crook Town	0-3
Leytonstone v Hendon	3-3
Shildon v Walthamstow Avenue	1-1
r Hendon v Leytonstone	1-2
r Walthamstow Avenue v Shildon	3-1

Semi Finals

Barnet v Walthamstow Avenue	0-0 N
Crook Town v Leytonstone	2-0 N
r Barnet v Walthamstow Avenue	2-0 N

Final

Crook Town v Barnet	3-2 N

1959/60

Extra Preliminary Round

16 Cheshunt (2) v Leavesden Hospital	2-0
19 Maidenhead United v Slough Town	3-0
20 Abingdon Town v Pressed Steel	4-0

Preliminary Round

1 Shankhouse v Heaton Stannington	1-4
Wallsend Rising Sun v Cornsay Park Albion	2-1
Washington CW v Annfield Plain	2-2
2 Darlington & Simpson Rolling Mill v Highgate United	1-4
West View Albion v West Hartlepool St Josephs	2-0
3 Appleby v Carlisle BR	1-7
Blackpool Mechanics v Manchester University	1-1
Blackpool Rangers v Ainsdale Hesketh Park	3-0
Cleator Moor Celtic v Penrith	0-5
East Chorlton Amateur v Manchester YMCA	4-3
4 Guinness Exports v Norley United	0-0
Hoylake Athletic v Newton	0-3
Middlewich Athletic v Middleton Amateurs	1-0
Northern Nomads v Marine	1-1
Runcorn Athletic v Earle	4-1
Shell v Harrowby	1-0
Stork v Stockton Heath	1-0
5 Armthorpe Welfare v Kingston Wolves	1-0
Bradford Rovers v Doncaster United Amateurs	1-3
Guiseley v Liversedge	1-3
Methley United v Fryston CW	4-2
Penistone Church v Reckitt & Sons	3-1
Thackley v Harrogate & District Railway	1-3
Thorncliffe Recreational v Swillington MW	1-4
Thurcroft Welfare v Brunswick Institute	2-0
6 Basford United v Lincoln City School OBU	2-1
Boots Athletic v Players Athletic	1-3
Eastwood Town v Nottingham University	10-0
Grantham St Johns v Aspley OB	1-2
Parliament Street Methodists v Hampton Sports	0-2
RAF Cranwell v Swallownest CW	n/a
Raleigh Athletic v Arnold St Marys	n/a
Sheffield v Appleby Frodingham Works	4-3
7 Boldmere St Michaels v Wellington Victoria	2-1
Coventry Amateur v Quorn	3-0
Darlaston v Bentley Engineering	0-2
Ibstock Penistone Rovers v Sileby Town	5-5
Morris Sports (Loughborough) v Ericsson Athletic	5-2
Oadby Town v Cosby United	3-1
Shepshed Albion v Paget Rangers	1-4
Stapenhill v Baddesley Colliery	2-1
8 Allens Cross v Pershore United	1-2
Bournville Athletic v Wrockwardine Wood	3-4
Jack Moulds Athletic v Sankey of Wellington	1-6
Malvern Town v Lower Gornal Athletic	3-0
Metal Box Co (W'cester) v Staffordshire Casuals	4-4
Moor Green v Fernhill Heath	5-0
Smethwick Town v Old Wulfrunians	8-2
Stratford Town v Alvechurch	7-2

1959/60

9	City of Norwich School OBU v Great Yarmouth Town	1-0
	Cromer v Sheringham	2-1
	Holt United v Thetford Town	1-2
10	Beccles v Ipswich Wanderers	2-2
	Leiston v Hadleigh United	2-3
	Waterside Works v Achilles	3-4
	Whitton United v Landseer Youth	2-1
11	Arlesey Town v AC Delco	7-2
	Hemel Hempstead Town v Shefford Town	3-0
	Leighton United v Stotfold	1-3
	Letchworth Town v Napier/English Electric	5-1
	Marston Shelton Rovers v Berkhamsted Town	1-1
	Stevenage Town v Royston Town	2-1
	Tring Town v Baldock Town	2-1
	Waterlows Dunstable v Bedford Avenue	4-0
12	Civil Service v Old Owens	2-3
	Edgware Town v Wood Green Town	1-0
	Polytechnic v Barclays Bank	4-1
	Ruislip Manor v Kingsbury Town	4-0
	Twickenham v Old Finchleians	4-3
	Wembley v Staines Town	1-3
	Willesden v Pinner	4-0
	Wingate v Rayners Lane	1-1
13	Brentstonians v Bexley	6-0
	Faversham Town v Callender Athletic	5-0
	Herne Bay v Beckenham	3-2
	Thameside Amateurs v Crockenhill	1-4
	Woolwich Polytechnic v Slade Green	1-1
14	Bognor Regis Town v Worthing	1-1
	Eastbourne v Arundel	0-1
	Goldstone v Moulsecoomb Rovers	1-3
	Lancing Athletic v Littlehampton Town	5-0
	Newhaven v Hastings & St Leonards	0-3
	Southwick v Brighton Old Grammarians	0-3
	Wigmore Athletic v Chichester City	1-3e
15	Banstead Athletic v Sidley United	2-2
	Bexhill Town v Three Bridges United	4-1
	Camberley v Whyteleafe	3-0
	Croydon Amateur v Haywards Heath	3-1
	Dorking v Metropolitan Police	1-0
	East Grinstead v APV Athletic	2-2
	Farncombe v Crawley Town	0-1
	Horsham v Farnham Town	4-0
16	Crown & Manor v Boreham Wood	3-0
	Harlow Town v Ware	1-2
	Hatfield Town v Saffron Walden Town	4-2
	Hertford Town v Tufnell Park Edmonton	2-1
	Hoddesdon Town v Cheshunt (2)	1-2
	Kings Langley v Harpenden Town	1-1
	Stansted v Rickmansworth Town	9-2
	Welwyn Garden City v Epping Town	2-1
17	Barking v Grays Athletic	3-3
	Bata Sports v Woodford Town	1-4
	Dagenham Cables v Tilbury	0-8
	East Ham United v Aveley	0-1
	Eton Manor v Brentwood & Warley	3-1
	Leyton v Chingford	2-1
	Rainham Town v Hornchurch & Upminster	1-1
	West Thurrock Athletic v Barkingside	0-2
18	Addlestone v Merton	3-0
	Chertsey Town v Vickers (Weybridge)	4-3
	Epsom v Worcester Park	3-0
	Leatherhead v Ulysses	1-1
	Molesey v Petters Sports	3-0
	ROF (SA) v Malden Town	0-1
	Whitehawk v Cobham	2-1
19	Aylesbury United v Wolverton Town & BR	6-1
	Chesham United v Stokenchurch	2-0
	Hungerford Town v Bletchley Town	6-2
	Huntley & Palmers v Maidenhead United	0-5
	Marlow v Bletchley Town	4-5
	Thame United v Newbury Town	3-3
	Windsor & Eton v Henley Town	6-2
	Wokingham Town v Amersham Town	4-1
20	Didcot Town v Wolvercote	3-0
	Morris Motors v St Frideswides	1-1
	NAC Athletic v Wantage Town	2-5
	Osberton Radiator v Abingdon Town	1-0
	Oxford University Press v Kidlington	1-2
	Oxford YMCA v South Oxford United	2-1
	Wallingford Town v Marston United	5-3e
	Witney Town v Bicester Town	3-2
21	Fareham Town v Netley Sports	2-2
	Hamworthy v Chard Town	wo/s
	Ilminster Town v Lymington	2-5
	Shepton Mallet Town v Amesbury	2-4
	Swaythling Athletic v Gosport Borough Athletic	0-2
	Totton v Pirelli General Cable Works	0-0
	Upwey & Broadway v Blandford United	n/a
	Waterlooville v Ryde Sports	4-0
22	Bulford United v Bromham	4-4
	Calne & Harris United v Westcott Youth Centre	8-2
	Clandown v Wootton Bassett Town	1-1
	Pewsey Vale v Warminster Town	2-2
	Pinehurst Youth Centre v Westbury United	5-1
	Radstock Town v Gorse Hill United	1-0
	Spencer Moulton v Melksham Town	2-5
	Welton Rovers v Swindon BR Corinthians	3-1 N
23	Brimscombe v Worle OB	3-1
	Bristol Mental Hospital v Bristol St George	1-2
	Keynsham Town v Sharpness	6-1
	Lydbrook Athletic v Wells City	2-1
	Mount Hill Enterprise v Clevedon	0-3
	Peasedown Miners Welfare v Hanham Athletic	2-3
	Soundwell v Eden Grove OB	4-3
	St Philips Marsh Adult School v Paulton Rovers	0-3
24	Looe v Dartmouth United	3-3
1r	Annfield Plain v Washington CW	1-1e
3r	Manchester University v Blackpool Mechanics	2-4e
4r	Marine v Northern Nomads	5-1
r	Norley United v Guinness Exports	0-1
r	Stockton Heath v Stork	1-0
7r	Sileby Town v Ibstock Penistone Rovers	0-1
8r	Staffordshire Casuals v Metal Box Co (Worcester)	n/a
10r	Ipswich Wanderers v Beccles	3-5e
11r	Berkhamsted Town v Marston Shelton Rovers	6-1
12r	Rayners Lane v Wingate	1-3
13r	Slade Green v Woolwich Polytechnic	4-3e
14r	Worthing v Bognor Regis Town	3-1
15r	APV Athletic v East Grinstead	3-1
r	Sidley United v Banstead Athletic	1-3
16r	Harpenden Town v Kings Langley	4-1
17r	Grays Athletic v Barking	3-1
r	Hornchurch & Upminster v Rainham Town	3-0
18r	Ulysses v Leatherhead	0-3
19r	Newbury Town v Thame United	7-0
20r	St Frideswides v Morris Motors	2-3
21r	Fareham Town v Netley Sports	1-0
r	Pirelli General Cable Works v Totton	1-0
22r	Bromham v Bulford United	4-2
r	Warminster Town v Pewsey Vale	1-2
r	Wootton Bassett Town v Clandown	2-0
24r	Dartmouth United v Looe	7-2
1r2	Annfield Plain v Washington CW	2-1

Qualifying Round One

1	Annfield Plain v Heaton Stannington	2-3
	Langley Park CW v Seaton Delaval	5-1
	Stanley United v Wallsend Rising Sun	3-0
	Tow Law Town v Naval Yard (Walker)	3-0
2	Bridlington Town v Redcar Albion	0-4
	Bridlington Trinity United v Wensleydale Wanderers	5-1
	Highgate United (Newcastle) v Cockfield	4-0
	West View Albion v South Bank	2-1
3	Blackpool Mechanics v Blackpool Rangers	1-3
	Carlisle BR v Kirkby Stephen	6-1
	East Chorlton Amateur v Old Blackburnians	3-0
	Penrith v Hearts of Liddesdale	3-2
4	Marine v Guinness Exports	3-2
	Middlewich Athletic v Runcorn Athletic	4-3
	Port Sunlight v Newton	2-2
	Shell v Stockton Heath	0-3
5	Doncaster United Amateurs v Methley United	4-1
	Liversedge v Armthorpe Welfare	3-2
	Penistone Church v Thurcroft Welfare	0-2
	Swillington MW v Harrogate & District Railway	8-2
6	Basford United v Hampton Sports	2-4
	RAF Cranwell v Aspley OB	n/a
	Raleigh Athletic v Players Athletic	n/a
	Sheffield v Eastwood Town	3-0
7	Boldmere St Michaels v Ibstock Penistone Rovers	2-0
	Coventry Amateur v Paget Rangers	0-1
	Morris Sports (Loughboro) v Bentley Engineering	0-2
	Oadby Town v Stapenhill	3-1
8	Malvern Town v Pershore United	1-3
	Moor Green v Stratford Town	3-2
	Sankey of Wellington v Smethwick Town	3-3
	Wrockwardine Wood v Staffordshire Casuals	3-1
9	Cromer v City of Norwich School OBU	1-3
	Desborough Town v Sutton Bridge United	2-0
	Ramsey Town v Somersham Town	wo/s
	Thetford Town v Wymondham Town	2-0
10	Crittall Athletic v Achilles	5-0
	Ipswich Electricity Supply v Brantham Athletic	3-2
	Orwell Works v Hadleigh United	6-0
	Whitton United v Beccles	3-4
11	Berkhamsted Town v Tring Town	1-0
	Hemel Hempstead Town v Stevenage Town	2-1
	Letchworth Town v Arlesey Town	5-0
	Waterlows Dunstable v Stotfold	3-6
12	Edgware Town v Willesden	1-6
	Polytechnic v Old Owens	2-0
	Ruislip Manor v Wingate	0-2
	Staines Town v Twickenham	5-0
13	Cray Wanderers v Herne Bay	5-1
	Mottingham v Brentstonians	1-2
	Slade Green v Faversham Town	1-5
	Whitstable v Crockenhill	2-1
14	Chichester City v Worthing	2-2
	Lancing Athletic v Brighton Old Grammarians	3-1
	Moulsecoomb Rovers v Arundel	0-8 N
	Shoreham v Hastings & St Leonards	6-0
15	APV Athletic v Banstead Athletic	6-2
	Camberley v Dorking	2-3
	Crawley Town v Bexhill Town	0-2
	Croydon Amateur v Horsham	0-4
16	Cheshunt (2) v Crown & Manor	0-2
	Harpenden Town v Welwyn Garden City	4-1
	Hatfield Town v Stansted	4-2
	Ware v Hertford Town	2-0
17	Aveley v Grays Athletic	1-3
	Eton Manor v Barkingside	2-2
	Leyton v Hornchurch & Upminster	1-0
	Woodford Town v Tilbury	2-2
18	Epsom v Chertsey Town	2-3
	Leatherhead v Surbiton Town	8-0
	Malden Town v Addlestone	0-2
	Molesey v Whitehawk	0-2
19	Aylesbury United v Windsor & Eton	2-2
	Bletchley Town v Wokingham Town	2-7
	Chesham United v Newbury Town	0-0
	Maidenhead United v Hungerford Town	4-1
20	Didcot Town v Wantage Town	6-1
	Kidlington v Witney Town	0-2
	Morris Motors v Oxford YMCA	2-2
	Osberton Radiator v Wallingford Town	1-2
21	Amesbury v Blandford United	0-3
	Fareham Town v Pirelli General Cable Works	5-2
	Gosport Borough Athletic v Waterlooville	0-5
	Lymington v Hamworthy	2-2
22	Melksham Town v Calne & Harris United	1-3
	Pewsey Vale v Welton Rovers	0-4
	Radstock Town v Bromham	4-2
	Wootton Bassett Town v Pinehurst Youth Centre	1-1
23	Brimscombe v Keynsham Town	3-0
	Clevedon v Soundwell	2-1
	Lydbrook Athletic v Bristol St George	3-0
	Paulton Rovers v Hanham Athletic	4-1
24	Burraton v Liskeard Athletic	wo/s
	Heavitree United v Bugle	3-2
	Nanpean Rovers v Chelston	3-1
	Penzance v Dartmouth United	4-2
4r	Newton v Port Sunlight	4-2e
8r	Smethwick Town v Sankey of Wellington	2-1
14r	Worthing v Chichester City	4-3
17r	Barkingside v Eton Manor	3-5
r	Tilbury v Woodford Town	3-4e
19r	Newbury Town v Chesham United	2-2e
r	Windsor & Eton v Aylesbury United	1-3
20r	Morris Motors v Oxford YMCA	1-2
21r	Hamworthy v Lymington	5-1
22r	Pinehurst Youth Centre v Wootton Bassett Town	1-3
19r2	Chesham United v Newbury Town	1-2 N

Qualifying Round Two

1	Langley Park CW v Heaton Stannington	1-0
	Stanley United v Tow Law Town	8-2
2	Bridlington Trinity United v West View Albion	3-1
	Highgate United (Newcastle) v Redcar Albion	5-2
3	Blackpool Rangers v Penrith	2-1
	Carlisle BR v East Chorlton Amateur	4-5
4	Middlewich Athletic v Marine	2-4
	Stockton Heath v Newton	1-3
5	Doncaster United Amateurs v Thurcroft Welfare	4-0
	Swillington MW v Liversedge	4-1
6	Hampton Sports v Aspley OB	2-4
	Sheffield v Raleigh Athletic	4-0
7	Bentley Engineering v Boldmere St Michaels	0-1
	Paget Rangers v Oadby Town	2-5
8	Pershore United v Wrockwardine Wood	3-0
	Smethwick Town v Moor Green	2-6
9	Desborough Town v City of Norwich School OBU	0-2
	Thetford Town v Ramsey Town	6-2
10	Beccles v Orwell Works	3-1
	Crittall Athletic v Ipswich Electricity Supply	3-2
11	Berkhamsted Town v Hemel Hempstead Town	4-0
	Stotfold v Letchworth Town	1-2
12	Willesden v Polytechnic	3-0
	Wingate v Staines Town	1-3
13	Cray Wanderers v Brentstonians	5-2
	Faversham Town v Whitstable	2-2
14	Lancing Athletic v Arundel	4-1
	Shoreham v Worthing	1-8
15	Bexhill Town v Horsham	2-3
	Dorking v APV Athletic	7-2
16	Harpenden Town v Hatfield Town	1-0
	Ware v Crown & Manor	3-1
17	Eton Manor v Leyton	0-1
	Woodford Town v Grays Athletic	1-5
18	Addlestone v Whitehawk	1-0
	Leatherhead v Chertsey Town	2-2
19	Aylesbury United v Maidenhead United	0-1
	Wokingham Town v Newbury Town	4-1
20	Didcot Town v Wallingford Town	4-2
	Witney Town v Oxford YMCA	3-0
21	Hamworthy v Fareham Town	1-1
	Waterlooville v Blandford United	2-1
22	Calne & Harris United v Welton Rovers	1-7
	Wootton Bassett Town v Radstock Town	2-2
23	Brimscombe v Lydbrook Athletic	0-3
	Clevedon v Paulton Rovers	5-3
24	Nanpean Rovers v Heavitree United	0-2
	Penzance v Burraton	4-0
13r	Whitstable v Faversham Town	0-4
18r	Chertsey Town v Leatherhead	1-2
21r	Fareham Town v Hamworthy	5-0
22r	Radstock Town v Wootton Bassett Town	2-2e
22r2	Wootton Bassett Town v Radstock Town	3-1 N

1959/60 to 1960/61

Qualifying Round Three

1 Stanley United v Langley Park CW	4-0
2 Highgate United (Newcastle) v Bridlington Trinity U	0-5
3 East Chorlton Amateur v Blackpool Rangers	n/a
4 Newton v Marine	1-3
5 Doncaster United Amateurs v Swillington MW	3-2
6 Sheffield v Aspley OB	4-1
7 Boldmere St Michaels v Oadby Town	1-1
8 Pershore United v Moor Green	0-1
9 Thetford Town v City of Norwich School OBU	2-2
10 Crittall Athletic v Beccles	1-5
11 Letchworth Town v Berkhamsted Town	6-0
12 Willesden v Staines Town	1-1
13 Cray Wanderers v Faversham Town	1-3
14 Worthing v Lancing Athletic	3-0
15 Dorking v Horsham	2-4
16 Ware v Harpenden Town	4-1
17 Grays Athletic v Leyton	6-4
18 Leatherhead v Addlestone	8-0
19 Maidenhead United v Wokingham Town	3-1
20 Didcot Town v Witney Town	3-0
21 Fareham Town v Waterlooville	0-3
22 Wootton Bassett Town v Welton Rovers	3-3
23 Lydbrook Athletic v Clevedon	0-2
24 Heavitree United v Penzance	1-1
7r Oadby Town v Boldmere St Michaels	1-0
9r City of Norwich School OBU v Thetford Town	2-4
12r Staines Town v Willesden	5-2
22r Welton Rovers v Wootton Bassett Town	7-1
24r Penzance v Heavitree United	1-0

Qualifying Round Four

Beccles v Thetford Town	3-1
Bishops Stortford v Histon	0-4
Bungay Town v Harwich & Parkeston	0-1
Clevedon v Penzance	3-2
Devizes Town v Welton Rovers	3-2
Doncaster United Amateurs v Gedling CW	2-1
East Chorlton Amateur v Marine	2-4
Eastbourne United v Maidstone United	2-4
Enfield v Didcot Town	6-0
Faversham Town v Carshalton Athletic	0-1
Grays Athletic v St Albans City	2-1
Hallam v ICI Alkali	5-0
Harrow Town v Maidenhead United	1-2
Leatherhead v Sheppey United	2-0
Letchworth Town v Ware	4-3
Loughborough College v Walsall Wood	5-2
Oadby Town v Moor Green	2-8
Sheffield v Bridlington Trinity United	4-0
Vauxhall Motors v Staines Town	1-1
Waterlooville v Horsham	1-1
Wealdstone v Oxford City	3-2
Whitby Town v Durham City	3-1
Whitley Bay v Stanley United	2-5
Worthing v Walton & Hersham	5-2
r Horsham v Waterlooville	2-4
r Staines Town v Vauxhall Motors	0-2

Round One

Alton Town v Pegasus	1-2
Barnet v Hayes	1-1
Beccles v Enfield	1-6
Bromley v Wealdstone	5-1
Clevedon v Ilford	2-1
Corinthian Casuals v Tooting & Mitcham United	2-2
Devizes Town v Finchley	1-1
Ferryhill Athletic v Sheffield	1-0
Ford United v Woking	2-0
Hallam v Willington	4-3
Hendon v Vauxhall Motors	3-0
Histon v Kingstonian	0-3
Hitchin Town v Harwich & Parkeston	1-3
Hounslow Town v Wycombe Wanderers	3-0
Letchworth Town v Grays Athletic	2-1
Leytonstone v Winchester City	3-0
Maidenhead United v Sutton United	1-1
Maidstone United v Erith & Belvedere	2-3
Marine v Moor Green	3-1
Norton Woodseats v Bishop Auckland	1-0
Redhill v Leatherhead	1-1
Salts v Whitby Town	1-0
Shildon v Billingham Synthonia	4-4
Stanley United v Loughborough College	5-0
Stockton v Evenwood Town	0-0
Uxbridge v Clapton	4-1
Walthamstow Avenue v Dagenham	2-1
Waterlooville v Carshalton Athletic	0-1
West Auckland Town v Doncaster United Amateurs	1-0
Wimbledon v Dulwich Hamlet	1-0
Worthing v Southall	1-2
Yorkshire Amateur v Crook Town	0-3
r Billingham Synthonia v Shildon	1-2
r Evenwood Town v Stockton	3-1
r Finchley v Devizes Town	4-0
r Hayes v Barnet	3-2
r Leatherhead v Redhill	0-1
r Sutton United v Maidenhead United	2-3
r Tooting & Mitcham United v Corinthian Casuals	3-1

Round Two

Bromley v West Auckland Town	1-1
Carshalton Athletic v Stanley United	3-1
Erith & Belvedere v Shildon	2-7
Evenwood Town v Walthamstow Avenue	2-2
Ferryhill Athletic v Marine	1-0
Finchley v Southall	1-1
Ford United v Salts	4-0
Hallam v Crook Town	2-6 N
Harwich & Parkeston v Tooting & Mitcham United	1-3
Hayes v Clevedon	6-2
Hendon v Wimbledon	2-1
Hounslow Town v Enfield	2-2
Kingstonian v Letchworth Town	5-2
Leytonstone v Redhill	1-2
Norton Woodseats v Pegasus	4-1
Uxbridge v Maidenhead United	1-4
r Enfield v Hounslow Town	3-2
r Southall v Finchley	2-2
r Walthamstow Avenue v Evenwood Town	2-0
r West Auckland Town v Bromley	3-0
r2 Finchley v Southall	3-3 N
r3 Southall v Finchley	4-1

Round Three

Carshalton Athletic v Norton Woodseats	3-0
Crook Town v Walthamstow Avenue	1-0
Ford United v Hayes	0-0
Kingstonian v Ferryhill Athletic	3-3
Maidenhead United v West Auckland Town	1-2
Redhill v Hendon	0-6
Shildon v Enfield	1-3
Tooting & Mitcham United v Southall	1-1
r Ferryhill Athletic v Kingstonian	2-4
r Hayes v Ford United	5-3
r Southall v Tooting & Mitcham United	1-0

Round Four

Crook Town v Hayes	2-1
Kingstonian v Carshalton Athletic	4-0
Southall v Enfield	0-1
West Auckland Town v Hendon	1-1
r Hendon v West Auckland Town	2-0

Semi Finals

Hendon v Enfield	2-0 N
Kingstonian v Crook Town	2-1 N

Final

Hendon v Kingstonian	2-1 N

1960/61

Extra Preliminary Round

5 Reckitt & Sons v Ossett Albion	2-10
6 Gedling CW v Parliament Street Methodists	n/a
Lenton Gregory v Bilsthorpe Colliery	n/a
Netherfield Albion v Nottingham University	wo/s
Raleigh Athletic v Rufford Colliery	n/a
18 Walton & Hersham v ROF (SA)	5-0
19 Slough Town v Amersham Town	10-1
22 Clandown v Timsbury Athletic	0-0
Swindon Victoria v Wootton Bassett Town	0-5
22r Timsbury Athletic v Clandown	1-2

Preliminary Round

2 Highgate United (Newcastle) v Tow Law Town	4-2
3 Appleby v Hearts of Liddesdale	1-3
Blackpool Rangers v Ainsdale Hesketh Park	n/a
Penrith v Cleator Moor Celtic	4-0
Whalley Range Amateur v Blackpool Mechanics	n/a
4 Hoylake Athletic v Newton	2-2
Middlewich Athletic v Northern Nomads	2-6
Moreton v Earle	2-3
Port Sunlight v Guinness Exports	1-1
Runcorn Athletic v Shell	3-0
Stockton Heath v ICI Alkali	0-0
Stork v Middleton Amateurs	4-1
5 Bradford Rovers v Ossett Albion	1-3
Doncaster United Ams v Thorncliffe Recreational	4-0
Harrogate & District Railway v Kingston Wolves	3-1
Penistone Church v Hull Amateurs	3-0
Rawmarsh Welfare v Guiseley	1-4
Swillington MW v Fryston CW	5-2
Thackley v Brunswick Institute	4-1
Thurcroft Welfare v Swallownest CW	wo/s
6 Boots Athletic v Basford United	3-0
Eastwood Town v unknown	n/a
Ericsson Athletic v RAF Cranwell	1-0
Gedling CW v Aspley OB	3-2
Lincoln City School OBU v Bestwood Colliery	1-2
Netherfield Albion v Raleigh Athletic	n/a
Players Athletic v Radford & Wollaton	n/a
Worthington Simpson v Grantham St Johns	n/a
7 Cosby United v Baddesley Colliery	7-1
Darlaston v Wellington Victoria	7-0
Oadby Town v Boldmere St Michaels	2-0
8 Lower Gornal Athletic v Staffordshire Casuals	2-0
Malvern Town v Fernhill Heath	3-1
Smethwick Town v Walsall Wood	0-0
Stratford Town v Alvechurch	4-1
Wrockwardine Wood v Bournville Athletic	4-4
9 City of Norwich School OBU v Dereham Town	3-1
Desborough Town v Eynesbury Rovers	3-3
Gorleston v Cromer	3-3e
Thetford Town v Sheringham	6-0
Wymondham Town v North Walsham Town	3-1
10 Brantham Athletic v Halstead Town	1-7
Crittall Athletic v Whitton United	0-1
Hadleigh United v Achilles	5-4
11 Baldock Town v Electrolux	6-1
Berkhamsted Town v Stevenage Town	1-1
Hemel Hempstead Town v Royston Town	8-2
Marston Shelton Rovers v Letchworth Town	1-10
Napier/English Electric v Luton Skefco Athletic	1-2
Shefford Town v Bedford Avenue	3-2
Shillington v Leighton United	2-1
Tring Town v Stotfold	3-1
12 Civil Service v Pinner	6-3
Edgware Town v Hampton	3-1
Ruislip Manor v Polytechnic	2-3
Staines Town v Harrow Town	0-2
Twickenham v Old Owens	6-1
Wembley v Kingsbury Town	6-3
Willesden v Old Finchleians	2-0
Wood Green Town v Wingate	1-2
13 Beckenham v Bexley	1-2
Cray Wanderers v Whitstable	5-0
Herne Bay v Crockenhill	5-2
Thameside Amateurs v Woolwich Polytechnic	n/a
14 Arundel v Goldstone	5-0
Bognor Regis Town v Eastbourne United	1-4
Chichester City v Southwick	7-0
Eastbourne v Newhaven	4-1
Lewes v Moulsecoomb Rovers	3-0
Littlehampton Town v Lancing Athletic	1-3
Shoreham v Brighton Old Grammarians	3-0
Worthing v Wigmore Athletic	3-1
15 Camberley v Farncombe	0-2
Crawley Town v Banstead Athletic	4-2
Dorking v Three Bridges United	5-0
East Grinstead v Metropolitan Police	1-1
Haywards Heath v Farnham Town	2-6
Horsham v Bexhill Town	3-2
Reigate Priory v Whyteleafe	4-4
Sidley United v Croydon Amateur	4-5
16 Crown & Manor v Hertford Town	3-6
Edmonton (2) v Boreham Wood	6-2
Harlow Town v Saffron Walden Town	2-0
Harpenden Town v Stansted	1-3
Hatfield Town v Rickmansworth Town	3-1
Kings Langley v Hoddesdon Town	0-1
Leavesden Hospital v Cheshunt (2)	5-0
Ware v Welwyn Garden City	2-0
17 Barkingside v East Ham United	0-5
Bata Sports v Aveley	1-2
Chingford v West Thurrock Athletic	5-2
Dagenham Cables v Rainham Town	1-5
Epping Town v Woodford Town	0-4
Hornchurch & Upminster v Eton Manor	5-1
Leyton v Barking	2-1
Tilbury v Brentwood & Warley	1-0
18 Addlestone v Malden Town	4-2
Chertsey Town v Walton & Hersham	4-4
Cobham v Ulysses	2-1
Epsom v Whitehawk	3-2
Leatherhead v Surbiton Town	wo/s
Molesey v Merton	7-0
Petters Sports v Cobham	0-2
Vickers (Weybridge) v Worcester Park	2-2
19 Aylesbury United v Hungerford Town	2-3
Bletchley Town v Slough Town	1-2
Chesham United v Windsor & Eton	2-1
Henley Town v Stokenchurch	3-0
Marlow v Huntley & Palmers	1-1
Newbury Town v Thatcham	6-2
Thame United v Bletchley United	4-1
Wolverton Town & BR v Wokingham Town	4-0
20 Bicester Town v Didcot Town	2-2
Kidlington v South Oxford United	2-3
Morris Motors v Oxford YMCA	4-1
NAC Athletic v Wolvercote	4-2
Oxford University Press v Pressed Steel	6-1
Wallingford Town v Wantage Town	6-1
Witney Town v Abingdon Town	0-0
21 Blandford United v Hamworthy	5-6
Bournemouth v Shepton Mallet Town	4-2
Gosport Borough Athletic v Waterlooville	3-2
Pirelli General Cable Works v Totton	4-3
Ryde Sports v Netley Sports	2-3
Swaythling Athletic v Fareham Town	0-1
22 Box Rovers v Pewsey Vale	6-3
Bromham v Wootton Bassett Town	2-1
Melksham Town v Swindon BR Corinthians	3-2
Radstock Town v Pinehurst Youth Centre	1-0
Spencer Moulton v Clandown	1-5
Warminster Town v Calne & Harris United	4-1
Welton Rovers v Gorse Hill United	8-0
Westbury United v Westcott Youth Centre	6-2

1960/61

23	Brimscombe v Chalford	1-1
	Bristol St George v Lydbrook Athletic	2-3
	Keynsham Town v St Philips Marsh Adult School	2-3
	Paulton Rovers v Mount Hill Enterprise	2-3
	Peasedown Miners Welf. v Hoffmann Ath (Stonehse)	6-2
	Sharpness v Glenside Hospital	6-2
	Soundwell v Hanham Athletic	2-3
	Worle OB v Wells City	0-4
4r	ICI Alkali v Stockton Heath	4-1
r	Newton v Hoylake Athletic	2-0
r	Port Sunlight v Guinness Exports	0-2
8r	Bournville Athletic v Wrockwardine Wood	0-2
r	Walsall Wood v Smethwick Town	2-1
9r	Cromer v Gorleston	0-1
r	Eynesbury Rovers v Desborough Town	5-2
11r	Stevenage Town v Berkhamsted Town	9-3e
12r	Wingate v Wood Green Town	1-2
15r	Metropolitan Police v East Grinstead	2-0
r	Whyteleafe v Reigate Priory	6-1
18r	Vickers (Weybridge) v Worcester Park	2-1
r	Walton & Hersham v Chertsey Town	3-1
19r	Huntley & Palmers v Marlow	2-1e
20r	Abingdon Town v Witney Town	4-2
r	Didcot Town v Bicester Town	1-2
23r	Chalford v Brimscombe	1-0a
23r2	Chalford v Brimscombe	3-2

Qualifying Round One

1	Heaton Stannington v Washington Glebe Welfare	n/a
	Naval Yard (Walker) v Washington CW	n/a
	Shankhouse v Morriston Busty CW	4-3
	Wallsend St Lukes Institute v Annfield Plain	2-6
2	Cockfield v West Hartlepool St Josephs	4-2
	Hamsteels CW v South Bank	4-10
	Langley Park CW v Durham City	4-0
	Spennymoor United v Highgate United (Newcastle)	2-1
3	East Chorlton Amateur v Manchester YMCA	n/a
	Old Blackburnians v Manchester University	1-4
	Penrith v Hearts of Liddesdale	7-1
	Whalley Range Amateur v unknown	n/a
4	ICI Alkali v Earle	4-0
	Newton v Guinness Exports	0-1
	Runcorn Athletic v Northern Nomads	0-5
	Stork v Harrowby	2-1
5	Guiseley v Thackley	2-3
	Harrogate & District Railway v Doncaster United Ams	3-0
	Ossett Albion v Penistone Church	1-2
	Thurcroft Welfare v Swillington MW	1-2
6	Boots Athletic v Players Athletic	6-0
	Ericsson Athletic v Grantham St Johns	4-1
	Gedling CW v Bestwood Colliery	n/a
	Raleigh Athletic v Eastwood Town	2-6
7	Anstey Nomads v Quorn	5-2
	Cosby United v Stapenhill	1-4
	Coventry Amateur v Darlaston	2-2
	Paget Rangers v Oadby Town	0-1
8	Jack Moulds Athletic v Wrockwardine Wood	5-2
	Lower Gornal Athletic v Old Wulfrunians	4-1
	Malvern Town v Stratford Town	1-3
	Walsall Wood v Pershore United	1-3
9	Great Yarmouth Town v City of Norwich School OBU	2-1
	Ramsey Town v Eynesbury Rovers	2-3
	Thetford Town v Diss Town	0-1
	Wymondham Town v Gorleston	2-7
10	Beccles v Whitton United	0-3
	Bungay Town v Landseer Youth	1-1
	Hadleigh United v Ipswich Wanderers	3-3
	Halstead Town v Leiston	3-2
11	Baldock Town v Luton Skefco Athletic	2-1
	Letchworth Town v Stevenage Town	7-0
	Shillington v Shefford Town	0-0
	Tring Town v Hemel Hempstead Town	1-1
12	Civil Service v Wembley	0-5
	Edgware Town v Harrow Town	5-2
	Polytechnic v Willesden	0-3
	Wood Green Town v Twickenham	7-3
13	Brentstonians v Bexley	4-2
	Cray Wanderers v Callender Athletic	0-0
	Luton (Chatham) v Herne Bay	0-8
	Woolwich Polytechnic v Slade Green	4-2
14	Arundel v Shoreham	1-2
	Eastbourne United v Lewes	6-2
	Lancing Athletic v Chichester City	0-2
	Worthing v Eastbourne	4-0
15	Crawley Town v Horsham	2-3
	Farncombe v Croydon Amateur	2-2
	Farnham Town v Dorking	1-6
	Whyteleafe v Metropolitan Police	2-1
16	Edmonton (2) v Leavesden Hospital	1-2
	Hertford Town v Harlow Town	4-1
	Hoddesdon Town v Stansted	5-2
	Ware v Hatfield Town	2-2
17	Aveley v Leyton	6-1
	East Ham United v Tilbury	1-5
	Hornchurch & Upminster v Chingford	8-0
	Woodford Town v Rainham Town	2-1
18	Addlestone v Cobham	2-2
	Molesey v Epsom	3-0
	Vickers (Weybridge) v Leatherhead	4-3
	Walton & Hersham v Petters Sports	7-1
19	Hungerford Town v Thame United	2-1
	Huntley & Palmers v Chesham United	3-5
	Slough Town v Newbury Town	3-5
	Wolverton Town & BR v Henley Town	11-1
20	Abingdon Town v Bicester Town	1-1
	Morris Motors v South Oxford United	3-0
	NAC Athletic v Marston United	4-2
	Wallingford Town v Oxford University Press	4-0
21	Amesbury v Ilminster Town	3-4
	Gosport Borough Athletic v Netley Sports	0-2
	Hamworthy v Bournemouth	4-4
	Pirelli General Cable Works v Fareham Town	2-5
22	Box Rovers v Warminster Town	0-6
	Bromham v Clandown	1-6
	Radstock Town v Welton Rovers	1-0
	Westbury United v Melksham Town	1-0
23	Chalford v Peasedown Miners Welfare	2-2
	Lydbrook Athletic v Sharpness	6-3
	Mount Hill Enterprise v Hanham Athletic	3-1
	Wells City v St Philips Marsh Adult School	2-5
24	Dartmouth United v Saltash United	1-2
	Penzance v Chelston	7-0
7r	Darlaston v Coventry Amateur	3-0
10r	Bungay Town v Landseer Youth	4-4
r	Hadleigh United v Ipswich Wanderers	2-3
11r	Hemel Hempstead Town v Tring Town	0-1
r	Shefford Town v Shillington	3-0
13r	Callender Athletic v Cray Wanderers	1-4
15r	Croydon Amateur v Farncombe	3-0
16r	Hatfield Town v Ware	1-1
18r	Cobham v Addlestone	3-5
20r	Bicester Town v Abingdon Town	1-1
21r	Bournemouth v Hamworthy	0-2
23r	Peasedown Miners Welfare v Chalford	3-2
10r2	Bungay Town v Landseer Youth	wo/s
16r2	Hatfield Town v Ware	2-1
20r2	Bicester Town v Abingdon Town	1-3 N

Qualifying Round Two

1	Annfield Plain v Shankhouse	5-1
	Washington Glebe Welfare v Washington CW	3-0
2	Cockfield v South Bank	2-3
	Spennymoor United v Langley Park CW	4-1
3	Manchester YMCA v Whalley Range Amateur	1-1
	Penrith v Manchester University	3-0
4	Northern Nomads v ICI Alkali	2-4
	Stork v Guinness Exports	4-2
5	Harrogate & District Railway v Penistone Church	6-2
	Thackley v Swillington MW	1-3
6	Boots Athletic v Eastwood Town	2-2
	Gedling CW v Ericsson Athletic	2-2
7	Oadby Town v Darlaston	3-0
	Stapenhill v Anstey Nomads	2-0
8	Jack Moulds Athletic v Stratford Town	1-3
	Pershore United v Lower Gornal Athletic	3-1
9	Gorleston v Eynesbury Rovers	1-2
	Great Yarmouth Town v Diss Town	3-2
10	Bungay Town v Whitton United	4-1
	Halstead Town v Ipswich Wanderers	6-3
11	Baldock Town v Tring Town	3-3
	Shefford Town v Letchworth Town	2-1
12	Edgware Town v Wood Green Town	2-3
	Wembley v Willesden	1-2
13	Brentstonians v Woolwich Polytechnic	1-3
	Cray Wanderers v Herne Bay	2-2
14	Eastbourne United v Worthing	0-0
	Shoreham v Chichester City	3-7
15	Croydon Amateur v Dorking	1-1
	Horsham v Whyteleafe	8-1
16	Hertford Town v Hoddesdon Town	7-1
	Leavesden Hospital v Hatfield Town	1-0
17	Aveley v Woodford Town	0-2
	Tilbury v Hornchurch & Upminster	0-3
18	Addlestone v Molesey	3-5
	Walton & Hersham v Vickers (Weybridge)	3-1
19	Hungerford Town v Chesham United	1-3
	Newbury Town v Wolverton Town & BR	4-3
20	Morris Motors v Abingdon Town	2-5
	Wallingford Town v NAC Athletic	4-3
21	Hamworthy v Netley Sports	2-3
	Ilminster Town v Fareham Town	2-2
22	Clandown v Westbury United	1-1
	Warminster Town v Radstock Town	3-7
23	Lydbrook Athletic v Mount Hill Enterprise	4-1
	Peasedown Miners Welf v St Philips Marsh Adult Scl	1-4
24	Heavitree United v Saltash United	1-3
	Nanpean Rovers v Penzance	2-1
3r	Whalley Range Amateur v Manchester YMCA	4-3e
6r	Eastwood Town v Boots Athletic	3-2
r	Ericsson Athletic v Gedling CW	2-6
11r	Tring Town v Baldock Town	5-2
13r	Herne Bay v Cray Wanderers	2-1
14r	Worthing v Eastbourne United	2-1
15r	Dorking v Croydon Amateur	4-3
21r	Fareham Town v Ilminster Town	1-0
22r	Westbury United v Clandown	4-3

Qualifying Round Three

1	Annfield Plain v Washington Glebe Welfare	2-0
2	Spennymoor United v South Bank	5-2
3	Penrith v Whalley Range Amateur	3-2
4	ICI Alkali v Stork	3-4
5	Swillington MW v Harrogate & District Railway	1-4
6	Gedling CW v Eastwood Town	2-2
7	Oadby Town v Stapenhill	3-2
8	Stratford Town v Pershore United	5-0
9	Eynesbury Rovers v Great Yarmouth Town	2-4
10	Bungay Town v Halstead Town	2-1
11	Tring Town v Shefford Town	1-1
12	Wood Green Town v Willesden	3-2
13	Herne Bay v Woolwich Polytechnic	0-1
14	Worthing v Chichester City	2-4
15	Horsham v Dorking	6-4
16	Leavesden Hospital v Hertford Town	0-1
17	Woodford Town v Hornchurch & Upminster	1-1
18	Walton & Hersham v Molesey	9-2
19	Newbury Town v Chesham United	3-2
20	Abingdon Town v Wallingford Town	3-1
21	Fareham Town v Netley Sports	2-0
22	Westbury United v Radstock Town	5-1
23	St Philips Marsh Adult School v Lydbrook Athletic	1-3
24	Saltash United v Nanpean Rovers	3-2e
6r	Eastwood Town v Gedling CW	6-2
11r	Shefford Town v Tring Town	3-3
17r	Hornchurch & Upminster v Woodford Town	1-2
11r2	Tring Town v Shefford Town	5-0

Qualifying Round Four

	Alton Town v Winchester City	4-1
	Annfield Plain v Whitley Bay	1-3
	Chichester City v Horsham	1-0
	Faversham Town v Maidstone United	1-4
	Great Yarmouth Town v Bungay Town	1-3
	Harrogate & District Railway v Stork	3-0
	Hertford Town v St Albans City	4-2
	Histon v Bishops Stortford	2-5
	Loughborough College v Moor Green	10-5
	Lydbrook Athletic v Fareham Town	1-2
	Maidenhead United v Oxford City	3-1
	Marine v Penrith	2-3
	Newbury Town v Abingdon Town	3-1
	Saltash United v Clevedon	0-4
	Sheffield v Eastwood Town	0-0
	Spennymoor United v Stanley United	1-5
	Stockton v Whitby Town	2-1
	Stratford Town v Oadby Town	3-2
	Sutton United v Woolwich Polytechnic	6-1
	Vauxhall Motors v Tring Town	1-0
	Walton & Hersham v Sheppey United	5-2
	Westbury United v Devizes Town	2-0
	Wood Green Town v Wealdstone	0-8
	Woodford Town v Grays Athletic	0-2
r	Eastwood Town v Sheffield	2-1

Round One

	Bungay Town v Leytonstone	0-0
	Carshalton Athletic v Hendon	2-2
	Clapton v Hayes	3-1
	Corinthian Casuals v Hertford Town	3-2
	Crook Town v Stanley United	1-1
	Dulwich Hamlet v Redhill	4-0
	Erith & Belvedere v Pegasus	3-3
	Evenwood Town v Ferryhill Athletic	1-2
	Grays Athletic v Finchley	2-3
	Hallam v Stratford Town	0-1a
	Harwich & Parkeston v Barnet	3-2
	Hitchin Town v Ford United	4-0
	Hounslow Town v Fareham Town	2-0
	Ilford v Sutton United	2-5
	Kingstonian v Maidstone United	1-3
	Loughborough College v Salts	6-1
	Maidenhead United v Alton Town	1-2
	Norton Woodseats v Eastwood Town	2-2
	Shildon v Billingham Synthonia	2-0
	Southall v Newbury Town	5-1
	Stockton v Penrith	0-3
	Tooting & Mitcham United v Bromley	2-3
	Uxbridge v Dagenham	0-0
	Walthamstow Avenue v Bishops Stortford	3-0
	Walton & Hersham v Clevedon	10-0
	Wealdstone v Enfield	1-2
	Westbury United v Vauxhall Motors	0-0
	Whitley Bay v Harrogate & District Railway	4-2
	Willington v Bishop Auckland	1-1
	Woking v Chichester City	6-2
	Wycombe Wanderers v Wimbledon	1-2
	Yorkshire Amateur v West Auckland Town	0-3
r	Bishop Auckland v Willington	3-1
r	Dagenham v Uxbridge	1-2
r	Eastwood Town v Norton Woodseats	2-3
r	Hallam v Stratford Town	0-0
r	Hendon v Carshalton Athletic	2-1
r	Leytonstone v Bungay Town	5-0
r	Pegasus v Erith & Belvedere	2-0eN
r	Stanley United v Crook Town	2-0
r	Vauxhall Motors v Westbury United	1-4
r2	Stratford Town v Hallam	0-2

1960/61 to 1961/62

Round Two

Alton Town v Ferryhill Athletic	1-2
Bromley v Pegasus	1-1
Corinthian Casuals v Norton Woodseats	5-0
Enfield v Maidstone United	0-2
Harwich & Parkeston v Dulwich Hamlet	7-1
Hendon v Walthamstow Avenue	0-0a
Hitchin Town v Southall	3-2
Leytonstone v Uxbridge	3-0
Loughborough College v Bishop Auckland	3-1
Stanley United v Penrith	1-1
Sutton United v Finchley	1-1
Walton & Hersham v Shildon	5-0
West Auckland Town v Clapton	3-1
Westbury United v Hallam	1-2
Whitley Bay v Hounslow Town	3-1
Woking v Wimbledon	1-5
r Finchley v Sutton United	0-2
r Hendon v Walthamstow Avenue	0-2 N
r Pegasus v Bromley	1-2
r Penrith v Stanley United	3-2

Round Three

Harwich & Parkeston v Walthamstow Avenue	2-7
Hitchin Town v Ferryhill Athletic	3-2
Leytonstone v Hallam	1-1
Loughborough College v Corinthian Casuals	2-1
Maidstone United v Walton & Hersham	0-1
Penrith v West Auckland Town	1-1
Sutton United v Bromley	3-1
Wimbledon v Whitley Bay	3-3
r Hallam v Leytonstone	0-3
r West Auckland Town v Penrith	2-2
r Whitley Bay v Wimbledon	2-2
r2 West Auckland Town v Penrith	1-0 N
r2 Wimbledon v Whitley Bay	6-1 N

Round Four

Hitchin Town v Loughborough College	5-1
Leytonstone v Sutton United	2-0
West Auckland Town v Walton & Hersham	4-1
Wimbledon v Walthamstow Avenue	0-1

Semi Finals

Walthamstow Avenue v Hitchin Town	1-0 N
West Auckland Town v Leytonstone	3-1 N

Final

Walthamstow Avenue v West Auckland Town	2-1 N

1961/62

Preliminary Round

3 Ainsdale Hesketh Park v Manchester YMCA	n/a
Appleby v Cleator Moor Celtic	1-4
Chapel Town v Old Blackburnians	5-2e
East Chorlton Amateur v Whalley Range Amateur	n/a
Hearts of Liddesdale v Shap	n/a
Manchester University v Blackpool Mechanics	n/a
4 Harrowby v Moreton	1-2
Hoylake Athletic v Middlewich Athletic	3-1
ICI Alkali v Runcorn Athletic	5-1
Marine v Newton	4-1
Port Sunlight v Middleton Amateurs	7-2
Warrington Town v Guinness Exports	1-1
5 Bradford Rovers v Penistone Church	8-1
Brunswick Institute v Thackley	0-5
Manningham Mills v Guiseley	2-5
Sheffield v Hull Amateurs	3-0
Thurcroft Welfare v Harrogate & District Railway	1-2
6 Basford United v Parliament Street Methodists	0-1
Bestwood Colliery v Netherfield Albion	3-1
Bulwell Forest Villa v Boots Athletic	2-5
Lincoln United v Swallownest CW	1-2
Players Athletic v Mapperley	4-6
Raleigh Athletic v RAF Cranwell	2-2
Rufford Colliery v Bilsthorpe Colliery	3-0
Worthington Simpson v Gedling CW	1-1
7 Anstey Nomads v Oadby Town	0-0
Boldmere St Michaels v Quorn	2-1
Newfoundpool WMC v Coventry Amateur	2-1
Paget Rangers v Ericsson Athletic	1-4
Wellington Victoria v Darlaston	wo/s
8 Alvechurch v Malvern Town	5-2
Bournville Athletic v Staffordshire Casuals	3-0
Cresconians v Netherton Town	1-1
Jack Moulds Athletic v Old Wulfrunians	7-2
Lower Gornal Athletic v Smethwick Town	6-3
Wrockwardine Wood v Badsey Rangers	7-4

9 Cromer v Sheringham	3-2
Gorleston v Thetford Town	2-3
Gothic v Wymondham Town	3-0
Histon v Ramsey Town	2-2
North Walsham Town v Diss Town	2-1
Stowmarket v Desborough Town	wo/s
11 Buntingford Town v Baldock Town	1-3
Hemel Hempstead Town v Letchworth Town	2-1
Leighton United v Electrolux	2-3
Royston Town v Berkhamsted Town	1-2
Shillington v Bedford Avenue	2-5
Stotfold v Shelford Town	2-0
Tring Town v Stevenage Town	0-1
12 Chalfont National v Ruislip Manor	2-2
Civil Service v Chalfont St Peter	0-2
Hampton v Twickenham	3-2
Harrow Town v Staines Town	3-3
Rayners Lane v Polytechnic	1-2
Wembley v Edgware Town	2-1
Willesden v Wingate	3-4
Wood Green Town v Kingsbury Town	0-5
13 Bexley v Midland Bank	1-4
Brentstonians v Slade Green Athletic	1-3
Callender Athletic v Luton (Chatham)	wo/s
Crockenhill v Herne Bay	3-3
Faversham Town v Cray Wanderers	2-1
Whitstable v Sheppey United	2-5
Woolwich Polytechnic v Thameside Amateurs	7-1
14 Arundel v Haywards Heath	1-6
Bognor Regis Town v Worthing	2-3
Eastbourne v Moulsecoomb Rovers	14-1
Eastbourne United v Littlehampton Town	3-2
Newhaven v Brighton Old Grammarians	3-5
Shoreham v Southwick	2-4
Whitehawk v Lancing Athletic	3-4
Wigmore Athletic v Goldstone	5-2
15 Banstead Athletic v Three Bridges United	1-1
Camberley v Farncombe	2-1
Carshalton Athletic v East Grinstead	6-1
Farnham Town v Bexhill Town	5-0
Frimley Green v Croydon Amateur	1-4
Horsham v Metropolitan Police	9-2
Sidley United v Crawley Town	2-3
Whyteleafe v Dorking	2-5
16 Boreham Wood v Crown & Manor	1-4
Epping Town v Saffron Walden Town	1-4
Hatfield Town v Kings Langley	0-2
Hoddesdon Town v Harpenden Town	7-2
Leavesden Hospital v Harlow Town	2-0
Ware v Stansted	4-2
Welwyn Garden City v Rickmansworth Town	1-1
17 Barking v Eton Manor	1-3
Barkingside v Edmonton (2)	0-2
Brentwood & Warley v Tilbury	0-1
Chingford v Hornchurch	0-1
East Ham United v Rainham Town	3-2
Woodford Town v Aveley	1-1
18 Chertsey Town v Molesey	3-2
Cobham v Ulysses	0-2
Epsom & Ewell v Petters Sports	5-3
Leatherhead v ROF (SA)	7-0
Malden Town v Chobham	2-2
Vickers (Weybridge) v Addlestone	2-4
19 Amersham Town v Wokingham Town	0-10
Bletchley United v Newbury Town	3-1
Chesham United v Marlow	6-0
Hazells Aylesbury v Hungerford Town	1-3
Slough Town v Aylesbury United	1-2
Stokenchurch v Thame United	0-4
Windsor & Eton v Henley Town	17-0
Wolverton Town & BR v Huntley & Palmers	2-3
20 Abingdon Town v Alcan Industries	5-1
Easington Sports v Kidlington	7-0
Moreton Town v Witney Town	3-2
Oxford University Press v Viking Sports	3-6
Oxford YMCA v Quarry Nomads	1-2
Pressed Steel v Wallingford Town	2-0
Wantage Town v Bicester Town	2-7
Wolvercote v Marston United	3-5
21 Gosport Borough Athletic v Netley Sports	4-2
Hamworthy v Ilminster Town	0-0
Pirelli General Cable Works v Totton	4-1
Shepton Mallet Town v Amesbury	7-2
22 Bromham v Melksham Town	0-3
Calne & Harris United v Swindon BR Corinthians	4-2
Devizes Town v Warminster Town	6-0
Swindon Victoria v Pinehurst Youth Centre	1-1
Westcott Youth Centre v Pewsey Vale	3-4
23 Brimscombe v Wells City	3-2
Bristol St George v Keynsham Town	1-1
Glenside Hospital v Paulton Rovers	2-4
Peasedown Miners Welfare v Chalford	4-2
Soundwell v Hoffmann Athletic (Stonehouse)	6-1
St Philips Marsh Adult School v Sharpness	5-1
Worle OB v Lydbrook Athletic	0-5
4r Guinness Exports v Warrington Town	1-0
6r Gedling CW v Worthington Simpson	3-2
r Raleigh Athletic v RAF Cranwell	1-4
7r Oadby Town v Anstey Nomads	3-0
8r Netherton Town v Cresconians	3-0
9r Ramsey Town v Histon	1-2
12r Ruislip Manor v Chalfont National	8-1
r Staines Town v Harrow Town	4-3e

13r Herne Bay v Crockenhill	6-0
15r Three Bridges United v Banstead Athletic	0-1
16r Rickmansworth Town v Welwyn Garden City	2-4
17r Aveley v Woodford Town	5-0
18r Malden Town v Chobham	3-0e
21r Ilminster Town v Hamworthy	0-1
22r Pinehurst Youth Centre v Swindon Victoria	4-1
23r Keynsham Town v Bristol St George	2-1

Qualifying Round One

1 Heaton Stannington v Naval Yard (Walker)	1-3
Seaton Delaval v Morriston Busty CW	4-3
Washington CW v Shankhouse	1-3
2 Cockfield v West Hartlepool St Josephs	4-1
Langley Park CW v Highgate United (Newcastle)	0-1
South Bank v Durham City	4-4
Spennymoor United v Tow Law Town	3-3
3 unknown v Heys Old Boys	n/a
Blackpool Rangers v Ainsdale Hesketh Park	4-1
Cleator Moor Celtic v Hearts of Liddesdale	1-4
East Chorlton Amateur v Chapel Town	n/a
4 Guinness Exports v Port Sunlight	1-0
Hoylake Athletic v Northern Nomads	1-3
ICI Alkali v Moreton	2-0
Marine v Stork	0-2
5 Guiseley v Doncaster United Amateurs	3-3
Ossett Albion v Bradford Rovers	4-2
Sheffield v Harrogate & District Railway	2-2
Thackley v Thorncliffe Recreational	3-5
6 Bestwood Colliery v RAF Cranwell	0-2
Boots Athletic v Swallownest CW	1-2
Mapperley v Gedling CW	2-3
Rufford Colliery v Parliament Street Methodists	2-2
7 Boldmere St Michaels v Stapenhill	1-0
Ericsson Athletic v Wellington Victoria	4-2
Moor Green v Oadby Town	2-0
Newfoundpool WMC v Cosby United	5-0
8 Bournville Athletic v Netherton Town	2-1
Jack Moulds Athletic v Walsall Wood	2-1
Pershore United v Alvechurch	1-2
Wrockwardine Wood v Lower Gornal Athletic	2-1
9 Dereham Town v Cromer	2-1
Histon v Stowmarket	1-0
North Walsham Town v City of Norwich School OBU	0-4
Thetford Town v Gothic	1-4
10 Crittall Athletic v Beccles	wo/s
Halstead Town v Landseer Youth	2-0
Leiston v Brantham Athletic	1-3
Whitton United v Achilles	2-0
11 Berkhamsted Town v Baldock Town	3-1
Electrolux v Stotfold	1-4
Hemel Hempstead Town v Stevenage Town	3-0
Waterlows Dunstable v Bedford Avenue	5-4
12 Kingsbury Town v Hampton	6-6
Polytechnic v Chalfont St Peter	1-5
Staines Town v Wingate	1-3
Wembley v Ruislip Manor	2-1
13 Callender Athletic v Midland Bank	1-2
Faversham Town v Sheppey United	2-3
Herne Bay v Woolwich Polytechnic	2-1
Slade Green Athletic v Beckenham	2-2
14 Eastbourne United v Southwick	6-0
Haywards Heath v Worthing	1-4
Lancing Athletic v Brighton Old Grammarians	1-2
Wigmore Athletic v Eastbourne	0-1
15 Carshalton Athletic v Horsham	8-2
Crawley Town v Camberley	1-0
Croydon Amateur v Banstead Athletic	6-0
Farnham Town v Dorking	2-6
16 Hoddesdon Town v Welwyn Garden City	0-2
Kings Langley v Ware	1-1
Leavesden Hospital v Crown & Manor	1-0
Saffron Walden Town v Cheshunt (2)	2-8
17 Aveley v East Ham United	2-0
Hornchurch v West Thurrock Athletic	6-0
Leyton v Edmonton (2)	1-0
Tilbury v Eton Manor	1-1
18 Addlestone v Leatherhead	1-1
Chertsey Town v Ulysses	0-0
Epsom & Ewell v Worcester Park	2-0
Reigate Priory v Malden Town	2-8
19 Aylesbury United v Huntley & Palmers	2-0
Chesham United v Thame United	2-1
Hungerford Town v Wokingham Town	1-6
Windsor & Eton v Bletchley United	4-0
20 Abingdon Town v Pressed Steel	3-2
Bicester Town v Viking Sports	2-3
Easington Sports v Moreton Town	2-3
Quarry Nomads v Marston United	6-4
21 Hamworthy v Shepton Mallet Town	0-1
Pirelli General Cable Works v Swaythling Athletic	3-2
Ryde Sports v Gosport Borough Athletic	2-7
Winchester City v Bournemouth	4-2
22 Devizes Town v Welton Rovers	3-8
Melksham Town v Gorse Hill United	6-1
Pinehurst Youth Centre v Pewsey Vale	4-1
Radstock Town v Calne & Harris United	0-1
23 Hanham Athletic v St Philips Marsh Adult School	3-2
Keynsham Town v Brimscombe	4-0
Peasedown Miners Welfare v Lydbrook Athletic	1-4
Soundwell v Paulton Rovers	4-3

1961/62 to 1962/63

24	Heavitree United v Nanpean Rovers	2-5
	Liskeard Athletic v Saltash United	4-4
	Penzance v Plymouth City Engineers Dept	8-3
	Woodlands v Chelston	2-1e
2r	Durham City v South Bank	1-4
r	Tow Law Town v Spennymoor United	2-0
5r	Doncaster United Amateurs v Guiseley	3-1
r	Harrogate & District Railway v Sheffield	3-2
6r	Parliament Street Methodists v Rufford Colliery	n/a
12r	Hampton v Kingsbury Town	3-1
13r	Beckenham v Slade Green Athletic	1-1
16r	Ware v Kings Langley	1-2
17r	Eton Manor v Tilbury	2-4
18r	Chertsey Town v Ulysses	2-1
r	Leatherhead v Addlestone	1-3
24r	Saltash United v Liskeard Athletic	14-3
13r2	Slade Green Athletic v Beckenham	3-2 N

Qualifying Round Two

1	Shankhouse v Seaton Delaval	2-2
	Wallsend Rising Sun v Naval Yard (Walker)	n/a
2	South Bank v Highgate United (Newcastle)	5-0
	Tow Law Town v Cockfield	5-2
3	Blackpool Rangers v Heys Old Boys	2-2
	East Chorlton Amateur v Hearts of Liddesdale	n/a
4	Guinness Exports v Stork	4-2
	Northern Nomads v ICI Alkali	4-0
5	Doncaster United Ams v Thorncliffe Recreational	2-3
	Ossett Albion v Harrogate & District Railway	1-0
6	Gedling CW v Parliament Street Methodists	1-0
	RAF Cranwell v Swallownest CW	n/a
7	Moor Green v Ericsson Athletic	7-1
	Newfoundpool WMC v Boldmere St Michaels	0-3
8	Alvechurch v Bournville Athletic	3-0
	Wrockwardine Wood v Jack Moulds Athletic	3-0
9	City of Norwich School OBU v Dereham Town	3-0
	Histon v Gothic	1-1
10	Crittall Athletic v Brantham Athletic	2-3
	Whitton United v Halstead Town	1-2
11	Hemel Hempstead Town v Stotfold	5-0
	Waterlows Dunstable v Berkhamsted Town	1-3
12	Hampton v Wembley	1-2
	Wingate v Chalfont St Peter	2-1
13	Herne Bay v Sheppey United	5-1
	Slade Green Athletic v Midland Bank	4-1
14	Eastbourne v Brighton Old Grammarians	4-2
	Worthing v Eastbourne United	2-1
15	Crawley Town v Dorking	2-5
	Croydon Amateur v Carshalton Athletic	0-2
16	Cheshunt (2) v Leavesden Hospital	4-2
	Kings Langley v Welwyn Garden City	2-1
17	Hornchurch v Aveley	0-1
	Tilbury v Leyton	2-2
18	Chertsey Town v Malden Town	2-5
	Epsom & Ewell v Addlestone	1-3
19	Windsor & Eton v Aylesbury United	3-1
	Wokingham Town v Chesham United	0-3
20	Moreton Town v Abingdon Town	1-6
	Viking Sports v Quarry Nomads	0-4
21	Gosport Borough Athletic v Shepton Mallet Town	3-0
	Pirelli General Cable Works v Winchester City	5-1
22	Pinehurst Youth Centre v Calne & Harris United	4-1
	Welton Rovers v Melksham Town	2-0
23	Keynsham Town v Hanham Athletic	3-1
	Soundwell v Lydbrook Athletic	4-6
24	Saltash United v Nanpean Rovers	4-5
	Woodlands v Penzance	2-3
1r	Naval Yard (Walker) v Wallsend Rising Sun	1-4
r	Seaton Delaval v Shankhouse	0-1
3r	Blackpool Rangers v Heys Old Boys	0-4
9r	Gothic v Histon	5-0
17r	Leyton v Tilbury	3-1

Qualifying Round Three

1	Shankhouse v Wallsend Rising Sun	3-1
2	Tow Law Town v South Bank	0-0
3	East Chorlton Amateur v Heys Old Boys	n/a
4	Guinness Exports v Northern Nomads	0-1
5	Thorncliffe Recreational v Ossett Albion	0-2
6	Swallownest CW v Gedling CW	3-0
7	Boldmere St Michaels v Moor Green	2-3
8	Wrockwardine Wood v Alvechurch	2-4
9	City of Norwich School OBU v Gothic	1-3
10	Brantham Athletic v Halstead Town	2-0
11	Hemel Hempstead Town v Berkhamsted Town	4-1
12	Wembley v Wingate	3-4
13	Herne Bay v Slade Green Athletic	2-2
14	Eastbourne v Worthing	5-3
15	Dorking v Carshalton Athletic	3-4
16	Kings Langley v Cheshunt (2)	0-4
17	Leyton v Aveley	2-3
18	Malden Town v Addlestone	8-2
19	Windsor & Eton v Chesham United	2-2
20	Abingdon Town v Quarry Nomads	1-0
21	Gosport Borough Ath v Pirelli General Cable Works	4-1
22	Pinehurst Youth Centre v Welton Rovers	1-2
23	Lydbrook Athletic v Keynsham Town	2-1
24	Penzance v Nanpean Rovers	3-0
2r	South Bank v Tow Law Town	0-1
13r	Slade Green Athletic v Herne Bay	0-1
19r	Chesham United v Windsor & Eton	0-3

Qualifying Round Four

	Alvechurch v Stratford Town	0-0
	Bishops Stortford v Brantham Athletic	3-2
	Cheshunt (2) v Hemel Hempstead Town	1-3
	Chichester City v Eastbourne	1-3
	Clevedon v Welton Rovers	2-2
	Eastwood Town v Moor Green	3-2
	Fareham Town v Alton Town	2-1
	Ford United v Grays Athletic	4-2
	Gothic v Bungay Town	4-3
	Herne Bay v Erith & Belvedere	0-7
	Heys Old Boys v Northern Nomads	2-3
	Lydbrook Athletic v Penzance	2-2
	Maidenhead United v Oxford City	3-2
	Malden Town v Carshalton Athletic	0-1
	Ossett Albion v Swallownest CW	6-2
	Penrith v Tow Law Town	3-2
	Salts v Yorkshire Amateur	2-3
	Shankhouse v Billingham Synthonia	0-1
	St Albans City v Hertford Town	2-0
	Stockton v Whitby Town	2-3
	Vauxhall Motors v Wingate	2-2
	Wealdstone v Aveley	5-0
	Westbury United v Gosport Borough Athletic	7-3
	Windsor & Eton v Abingdon Town	1-1
r	Abingdon Town v Windsor & Eton	2-4
r	Penzance v Lydbrook Athletic	0-1
r	Stratford Town v Alvechurch	1-2
r	Welton Rovers v Clevedon	5-0
r	Wingate v Vauxhall Motors	0-2

Round One

	Barnet v Sutton United	1-2
	Bishop Auckland v Whitby Town	2-0
	Bishops Stortford v Gothic	3-0
	Bromley v Fareham Town	2-0
	Carshalton Athletic v Leytonstone	0-2
	Clapton v Hounslow Town	2-2
	Corinthian Casuals v Woking	2-3
	Crook Town v Ossett Albion	1-0
	Dagenham v Hitchin Town	6-2
	Eastbourne v Kingstonian	2-0
	Eastwood Town v Norton Woodseats	4-0
	Evenwood Town v Stanley United	1-3
	Hallam v Yorkshire Amateur	1-2
	Hemel Hempstead T v Tooting & Mitcham United	1-3
	Ilford v Wimbledon	0-1
	Lydbrook Athletic v Westbury United	2-1
	Maidenhead United v Wealdstone	3-1
	Maidstone United v Harwich & Parkeston	2-0
	Pegasus v Hendon	0-0
	Penrith v Billingham Synthonia	2-1
	Redhill v Enfield	0-2
	Shildon v Alvechurch	1-0
	St Albans City v Welton Rovers	6-0
	Uxbridge v Finchley	1-1
	Vauxhall Motors v Dulwich Hamlet	0-2
	Walthamstow Avenue v Ford United	0-2
	Walton & Hersham v Hayes	1-0
	West Auckland Town v Northern Nomads	2-1
	Whitley Bay v Ferryhill Athletic	1-1
	Willington v Loughborough College	1-2
	Windsor & Eton v Southall	1-1
	Wycombe Wanderers v Erith & Belvedere	2-1
r	Finchley v Uxbridge	1-0
r	Hendon v Pegasus	6-1
r	Hounslow Town v Clapton	3-0
r	Southall v Windsor & Eton	0-1

Round Two

	Bishop Auckland v Lydbrook Athletic	5-0
	Bishops Stortford v West Auckland Town	0-4
	Bromley v Yorkshire Amateur	3-1
	Crook Town v Windsor & Eton	2-1
	Eastbourne v Woking	0-1
	Eastwood Town v Finchley	1-2
	Hendon v St Albans City	0-3 N
	Hounslow Town v Dulwich Hamlet	6-1
	Loughborough College v Maidenhead United	4-0
	Maidstone United v Walton & Hersham	0-2
	Penrith v Leytonstone	0-0
	Shildon v Enfield	1-2
	Stanley United v Whitley Bay	2-1
	Sutton United v Wycombe Wanderers	1-4
	Tooting & Mitcham United v Dagenham	1-2
	Wimbledon v Ford United	6-0
r	Leytonstone v Penrith	1-0

Round Three

	Bishop Auckland v Loughborough College	2-0
	Dagenham v Crook Town	0-0
	Enfield v St Albans City	0-0
	Finchley v Hounslow Town	0-0
	Stanley United v West Auckland Town	2-4
	Walton & Hersham v Bromley	2-3
	Wimbledon v Wycombe Wanderers	1-0
	Woking v Leytonstone	1-1
r	Crook Town v Dagenham	2-1
r	Hounslow Town v Finchley	2-0
r	Leytonstone v Woking	1-0
r	St Albans City v Enfield	1-2

Round Four

	Bromley v Hounslow Town	1-1
	Crook Town v Wimbledon	2-0
	Leytonstone v Bishop Auckland	1-2
	West Auckland Town v Enfield	0-0
r	Enfield v West Auckland Town	0-1
r	Hounslow Town v Bromley	2-1

Semi Finals

	Crook Town v West Auckland Town	2-0 N
	Hounslow Town v Bishop Auckland	2-1 N

Final

	Crook Town v Hounslow Town	1-1 N
r	Crook Town v Hounslow Town	4-0 N

1962/63

Preliminary Round

3	Appleby v Hearts of Liddesdale	0-2
	Blackpool Mechanics v Heys Old Boys	2-3
	Blackpool Rangers v East Chorlton Amateur	3-1
	Kendal United v Cleator Moor Celtic	2-2
	Manchester University v Whalley Range Amateur	1-2
	Manchester YMCA v Old Salfordians	1-0
	Old Blackburnians v Monarch United	2-2
4	Newton v Warrington Town	1-0
	Port Sunlight v Earle	4-1
	Skelmersdale United v Middleton Amateurs	5-1
5	Guiseley v Penistone Church	5-1
	Thackley v Harrogate & District Railway	1-0
	Thurcroft Welfare v Hull Amateurs	0-2
6	Basford United v Rufford Colliery	3-2
	Bestwood Colliery v Shirebrook	wo/s
	Gedling CW v Hyson Green OB	2-0
	Mapperley v Boots Athletic	0-1
	Players Athletic v Bulwell Forest Villa	1-9
	RAF Cranwell v Netherfield Albion	3-2
	Raleigh Athletic v Bilsthorpe Colliery	2-0
	Worthington Simpson v Parliament Street Meths	2-0
7	Coventry Amateur v Quorn	4-3
	Ericsson Athletic v Paget Rangers	2-4
	Loughborough College v Boldmere St Michaels	5-1
	Lutterworth Town v Anstey Nomads	0-4
	Stapenhill v Moor Green	2-3
	Wellington Victoria v Shepshed Albion	1-0
8	Lower Gornal Athletic v Walsall Wood	3-0
	Malvern Town v Cresconians	4-2
	Pershore United v Jack Moulds Athletic	4-0
	Stratford Town v Smethwick Town	3-1
9	Cromer v Gothic	2-1
	Dereham Town v Gorleston	0-3
	Histon v Thetford Town	2-3
	St Ives Town v Ramsey Town	4-2
10	Brantham Athletic v Achilles	3-0
	Bungay Town v Halstead Town	4-2
11	Baldock Town v Stotfold	1-2
	Hemel Hempstead Town v Arlesey Town	6-0
	Leighton United v Buntingford Town	2-3
	Napier/English Electric v Bedford Avenue	3-2
	Shefford Town v Electrolux	4-1
	Shillington v Letchworth Town	1-6
	Stevenage Town v Berkhamsted Town	2-1
	Tring Town v Royston Town	3-0
12	Civil Service v Kingsbury Town	1-1
	Edgware Town v Harrow Town	0-0
	Rayners Lane v Willesden	2-2
	Ruislip Manor v Wembley	3-0
	Wingate v Twickenham	5-0
	Wood Green Town v Hampton	1-4
13	Bexley v Whitstable	4-2
	Brentstonians v Beckenham	2-3
	Faversham Town v Aylesford Paper Mills	2-0
	Herne Bay v Cray Wanderers	1-2
	Sheppey United v Crockenhill	4-0
	Slade Green Athletic v Luton (Chatham)	5-0
	Thameside Amateurs v Callender Athletic	2-3
	Woolwich Polytechnic v Midland Bank	2-1
14	Arundel v Brighton Old Grammarians	1-2
	Bexhill Town v Newhaven	1-1
	Bognor Regis Town v Worthing	4-3
	Lancing Athletic v Chichester City	2-5
	Littlehampton Town v Goldstone	10-1
	Shoreham v Haywards Heath	8-7
	Southwick v Moulsecoomb Rovers	3-1
	Wigmore Athletic v Eastbourne United	2-5
15	Camberley v Reigate Priory	3-1
	Croydon Amateur v Farnham Town	wo/s
	Farncombe v East Grinstead	2-0
	Frimley Green v Sidley United	1-2
	Horsham v Three Bridges United	5-2
16	Cheshunt (2) v Epping Town	6-1
	Harlow Town v Boreham Wood	4-1
	Hatfield Town v Saffron Walden Town	2-1
	Hoddesdon Town v Rickmansworth Town	11-4
	Ware v Crown & Manor	1-1
	Welwyn Garden City v Leavesden Hospital	1-0

1962/63

17	Aveley v Chingford	3-1
	Barking v Brentwood & Warley	2-0
	Edmonton (2) v Tilbury	0-0
	Eton Manor v Rainham Town	3-2
	West Thurrock Athletic v Leyton	1-6
	Woodford Town v Barkingside	6-3
18	Addlestone v Worcester Park	6-0
	Chertsey Town v West Wickham	9-4
	Epsom & Ewell v ROF (SA)	6-2
	Leatherhead v Hermes	3-1
	Malden Town v Cobham	3-1
	Molesey v Ulysses	3-0
	Vickers (Weybridge) v Petters Sports	2-4
	Whitehawk v Chobham	2-0
19	Amersham Town v Chesham United	1-9
	Aylesbury United v Huntley & Palmers	4-1
	Chalfont St Peter v Stokenchurch	3-2
	Didcot Town v Wolverton Town & BR	5-1
	Henley Town v Hungerford Town	3-2
	Slough Town v Newbury Town	2-4
	Wokingham Town v Hazells Aylesbury	3-0
20	Easington Sports v Viking Sports	4-2
	Kidlington v Chipping Norton Town	3-4
	Marston United v Bicester Town	1-2
	Oxford City v Alcan Industries	15-1
	Thame United v Witney Town	5-0
	Wallingford Town v Oxford University Press	4-3
	Wantage Town v Abingdon Town	0-3
	Wolvercote v Pressed Steel	2-5
21	Brockenhurst v Alton Town	3-4
	Gosport Borough Athletic v Hamworthy	6-0
	Pirelli General Cable Works v Totton	1-4
	Ryde Sports v Winchester City	2-1
	Waterlooville v Netley Sports	3-2
22	Bromham v Marlborough Town	2-1
	Calne & Harris United v Pinehurst Youth Centre	1-3
	Melksham Town v Gorse Hill United	3-2
	Radstock Town v Warminster Town	5-1
	Swindon BR Corinthians v Westcott Youth Centre	1-0
23	Hanham Athletic v Clevedon	3-3
	Hoffmann Athletic (Stonehouse) v Brimscombe	1-0
	Iron Acton v Wells City	5-1
	Moreton Town v Forest Green Rovers	2-3
	Paulton Rovers v Worle OB	5-1
	Sharpness v Keynsham Town	4-1
	St Philips Marsh Adult School v Chalford	4-1
3r	Cleator Moor Celtic v Kendal United	0-3
r	Old Blackburnians v Monarch United	5-3
12r	Harrow Town v Edgware Town	5-0
r	Kingsbury Town v Civil Service	1-2
r	Willesden v Rayners Lane	1-0
14r	Newhaven v Bexhill Town	2-0
16r	Crown & Manor v Ware	0-1
17r	Tilbury v Edmonton (2)	2-1
23r	Clevedon v Hanham Athletic	1-2

Qualifying Round One

1	Morriston Busty CW v Naval Yard (Walker)	3-3
	North Eastern Marine v Shankhouse	1-1
	Wallsend Corinthians v Heaton Stannington	n/a
2	Cockfield v Langley Park CW	1-4
	Durham City v South Bank	1-0
	Spennymoor United v West Hartlepool St Josephs	6-1
	Tow Law Town v Redcar Albion	5-1
3	Hearts of Liddesdale v Kendal United	0-0
	Heys Old Boys v Old Blackburnians	4-0
	Manchester YMCA v Blackpool Rangers	n/a
	Whalley Range Amateur v Chapel Town	n/a
4	ICI Alkali v Newton	3-0
	Port Sunlight v Ashville	3-3
	Skelmersdale United v Marine	1-0
	Stork v Guinness Exports	1-2
5	Bradford Rovers v Hull Amateurs	1-3
	Guiseley v Doncaster United Amateurs	0-1
	Sheffield v Salts	6-1
	Swallownest CW v Thackley	1-2
6	Boots Athletic v Basford United	4-4
	Gedling CW v Bulwell Forest Villa	2-0
	Raleigh Athletic v RAF Cranwell	n/a
	Worthington Simpson v Bestwood Colliery	0-3
7	Coventry Amateur v Wellington Victoria	2-2
	Loughborough College v Anstey Nomads	n/a
	Newfoundpool WMC v Moor Green	2-2
	Paget Rangers v Cosby United	2-0
8	Malvern Town v Bournville Athletic	3-1
	Old Wulfrunians v English Electric (Stafford)	n/a
	Stratford Town v Pershore United	5-0
	Sutton Coldfield Town v Lower Gornal Athletic	2-4
9	City of Norwich School OBU v North Walsham Town	1-1
	Cromer v Sheringham	2-2
	Gorleston v Wymondham Town	6-0
	Thetford Town v St Ives Town	1-1
10	Bungay Town v Crittall Athletic	1-2e
	Diss Town v Landseer Youth	4-3
	Ipswich Electricity Supply v Whitton United	0-4
	Leiston v Brantham Athletic	3-0
11	Buntingford Town v Stotfold	1-3
	Hemel Hempstead Town v Shefford Town	6-0
	Stevenage Town v Letchworth Town	0-2
	Tring Town v Napier/English Electric	3-0
12	Civil Service v Harrow Town	0-4
	Ruislip Manor v Polytechnic	5-2
	Staines Town v Wingate	7-2
	Willesden v Hampton	1-2
13	Callender Athletic v Slade Green Athletic	0-2
	Cray Wanderers v Bexley	4-3
	Faversham Town v Sheppey United	2-0
	Woolwich Polytechnic v Beckenham	3-0
14	Chichester City v Shoreham	4-1
	Eastbourne United v Southwick	5-0
	Littlehampton Town v Bognor Regis Town	2-4
	Newhaven v Brighton Old Grammarians	5-2
15	Banstead Athletic v Farncombe	2-2
	Camberley v Dorking	1-4
	Croydon Amateur v Sidley United	2-1
	Metropolitan Police v Horsham	0-1
16	Harlow Town v Cheshunt (2)	3-0
	Hatfield Town v Ware	0-2
	Hoddesdon Town v Harpenden Town	4-2
	Kings Langley v Welwyn Garden City	1-2
17	Aveley v Barking	1-2
	Eton Manor v East Ham United	3-0
	Hornchurch v Leyton	2-0
	Tilbury v Woodford Town	1-1
18	Leatherhead v Epsom & Ewell	3-2
	Malden Town v Addlestone	4-2
	Petters Sports v Chertsey Town	1-3
	Whitehawk v Molesey	1-2
19	Aylesbury United v Didcot Town	4-0
	Chalfont St Peter v Wokingham Town	2-4
	Chesham United v Newbury Town	5-1
	Marlow v Henley Town	2-0
20	Abingdon Town v Wallingford Town	0-1
	Bicester Town v Thame United	4-0
	Chipping Norton Town v Easington Sports	3-0
	Oxford City v Pressed Steel	6-1
21	Alton Town v Bournemouth	5-1
	Gosport Borough Athletic v Bitterne Nomads	3-2
	Swaythling Athletic v Ryde Sports	2-3
	Waterlooville v Totton	5-2
22	Amesbury v Melksham Town	2-4
	Bromham v Devizes Town	1-0
	Pinehurst Youth Centre v Radstock Town	7-2
	Swindon Victoria v Swindon BR Corinthians	3-1
23	Bristol St George v Sharpness	0-0
	Hanham Athletic v St Philips Marsh Adult School	0-2
	Hoffmann Athletic (Stonehouse) v Iron Acton	2-2
	Paulton Rovers v Forest Green Rovers	2-2
24	Chelston v Liskeard Athletic	6-3
	Torpoint Athletic v Heavitree United	3-2
1r	Naval Yard (Walker) v Morriston Busty CW	2-4
r	Shankhouse v North Eastern Marine	0-1e
3r	Kendal United v Hearts of Liddesdale	1-3
4r	Ashville v Port Sunlight	1-4
6r	Basford United v Boots Athletic	2-3
r	RAF Cranwell v Raleigh Athletic	n/a
7r	Moor Green v Newfoundpool WMC	0-1
r	Wellington Victoria v Coventry Amateur	1-1e
9r	North Walsham Town v City of Norwich School OBU	0-5
r	Sheringham v Cromer	2-1
r	St Ives Town v Thetford Town	0-2
15r	Farncombe v Banstead Athletic	1-0
17r	Woodford Town v Tilbury	2-4
23r	Forest Green Rovers v Paulton Rovers	7-1
r	Iron Acton v Hoffmann Athletic (Stonehouse)	1-2
r	Sharpness v Bristol St George	5-3
7r2	Coventry Amateur v Wellington Victoria	3-2eN

Qualifying Round Two

1	Highgate United (Newcastle) v Morriston Busty CW	3-4
	North Eastern Marine v Wallsend Corinthians	1-1
2	Durham City v Langley Park CW	2-0
	Tow Law Town v Spennymoor United	1-0
3	Blackpool Rangers v Heys Old Boys	3-1
	Chapel Town v Hearts of Liddesdale	n/a
4	ICI Alkali v Guinness Exports	0-2
	Skelmersdale United v Port Sunlight	7-2
5	Doncaster United Amateurs v Thackley	3-2
	Sheffield v Hull Amateurs	5-2
6	Boots Athletic v Gedling CW	1-1
	RAF Cranwell v Bestwood Colliery	n/a
7	Loughborough College v Newfoundpool WMC	3-3
	Paget Rangers v Coventry Amateur	0-2
8	Lower Gornal Athletic v Old Wulfrunians	4-2
	Malvern Town v Stratford Town	1-4
9	Gorleston v City of Norwich School OBU	4-2
	Thetford Town v Sheringham	2-2
10	Crittall Athletic v Leiston	4-2
	Whitton United v Diss Town	2-1
11	Hemel Hempstead Town v Letchworth Town	2-2
	Stotfold v Tring Town	0-1
12	Hampton v Harrow Town	1-1
	Ruislip Manor v Staines Town	2-3
13	Cray Wanderers v Woolwich Polytechnic	3-2
	Faversham Town v Slade Green Athletic	3-0
14	Bognor Regis Town v Newhaven	2-1
	Chichester City v Eastbourne United	4-4
15	Croydon Amateur v Farncombe	2-0
	Dorking v Horsham	3-0
16	Hoddesdon Town v Welwyn Garden City	2-1
	Ware v Harlow Town	1-3
17	Eton Manor v Hornchurch	1-3
	Tilbury v Barking	1-3
18	Leatherhead v Molesey	6-3
	Malden Town v Chertsey Town	2-0
19	Chesham United v Marlow	5-0
	Wokingham Town v Aylesbury United	4-1
20	Bicester Town v Oxford City	2-2
	Chipping Norton Town v Wallingford Town	3-2
21	Alton Town v Ryde Sports	5-3
	Waterlooville v Gosport Borough Athletic	0-1
22	Bromham v Swindon Victoria	1-0e
	Pinehurst Youth Centre v Melksham Town	2-2
23	Hoffmann Athletic (Stonehouse) v Forest Green Rov.	4-2
	St Philips Marsh Adult School v Sharpness	4-3
24	Chelston v EEM Dept (Devonport)	1-2
	Saltash United v Torpoint Athletic	1-5
1r	North Eastern Marine v Wallsend Corinthians	2-3
6r	Gedling CW v Boots Athletic	1-6
7r	Newfoundpool WMC v Loughborough College	1-4
9r	Sheringham v Thetford Town	1-2
11r	Letchworth Town v Hemel Hempstead Town	3-1
12r	Harrow Town v Hampton	1-2
14r	Eastbourne United v Chichester City	3-0
20r	Oxford City v Bicester Town	9-2
22r	Melksham Town v Pinehurst Youth Centre	1-2

Qualifying Round Three

1	Wallsend Corinthians v Morriston Busty CW	3-3
2	Tow Law Town v Durham City	2-2
3	Blackpool Rangers v Chapel Town	n/a
4	Guinness Exports v Skelmersdale United	1-0
5	Sheffield v Doncaster United Amateurs	1-4
6	Bestwood Colliery v Boots Athletic	4-2
7	Loughborough College v Coventry Amateur	4-0
8	Lower Gornal Athletic v Stratford Town	1-3
9	Gorleston v Thetford Town	2-1
10	Whitton United v Crittall Athletic	3-1
11	Tring Town v Letchworth Town	1-1
12	Staines Town v Hampton	3-0
13	Cray Wanderers v Faversham Town	7-1
14	Bognor Regis Town v Eastbourne United	2-2
15	Dorking v Croydon Amateur	0-4
16	Hoddesdon Town v Harlow Town	2-2
17	Hornchurch v Barking	2-4
18	Malden Town v Leatherhead	2-4
19	Chesham United v Wokingham Town	0-0
20	Oxford City v Chipping Norton Town	7-0
21	Alton Town v Gosport Borough Athletic	2-1
22	Bromham v Pinehurst Youth Centre	5-5
23	Hoffmann Ath (St'house) v St Philips Marsh Ad. Schl	1-3
24	Torpoint Athletic v EEM Dept (Devonport)	0-2
1r	Morriston Busty CW v Wallsend Corinthians	2-3a
2r	Durham City v Tow Law Town	1-7
11r	Letchworth Town v Tring Town	5-2
14r	Eastbourne United v Bognor Regis Town	3-1
16r	Harlow Town v Hoddesdon Town	3-0
19r	Wokingham Town v Chesham United	0-2
22r	Pinehurst Youth Centre v Bromham	4-0
1r2	Morriston Busty CW v Wallsend Corinthians	4-4e
1r3	Morriston Busty CW v Wallsend Corinthians	2-3 N

Qualifying Round Four

	Alton Town v Fareham Town	2-1
	Barking v Ilford	2-1
	Blackpool Rangers v Doncaster United Amateurs	1-1
	Carshalton Athletic v Leatherhead	1-4
	Cray Wanderers v Erith & Belvedere	3-2
	EEM Dept (Devonport) v Pinehurst Youth Centre	0-3
	Eastbourne v Croydon Amateur	5-2
	Eastbourne United v Redhill	3-0
	Evenwood Town v Willington	0-1
	Grays Athletic v Whitton United	6-0
	Guinness Exports v Northern Nomads	2-0
	Harwich & Parkeston v Gorleston	6-1
	Hertford Town v Harlow Town	1-2
	Letchworth Town v Wealdstone	2-1
	Loughborough College v Alvechurch	2-0
	Ossett Albion v Billingham Synthonia	0-4
	Oxford City v Chesham United	1-1
	Pegasus v Windsor & Eton	1-3
	St Philips Marsh Adult School v Lydbrook Athletic	2-3
	Stratford Town v Bestwood Colliery	5-0
	Tow Law Town v Stockton	3-2
	Vauxhall Motors v Staines Town	6-2
	Welton Rovers v Westbury United	4-0
	Whitby Town v Wallsend Corinthians	3-3
r	Chesham United v Oxford City	3-2
r	Doncaster United Amateurs v Blackpool Rangers	1-3
r	Whitby Town v Wallsend Corinthians	5-0

Round One

	Alton Town v Eastbourne United	2-1
	Barking v Hendon	1-0
	Barnet v Cray Wanderers	3-0 N
	Bishops Stortford v Vauxhall Motors	1-0a
	Chesham United v Corinthian Casuals	2-0 N
	Dagenham v Leytonstone	1-2
	Dulwich Hamlet v Hitchin Town	1-2
	Ferryhill Athletic v Hallam	4-1
	Finchley v Enfield	0-6
	Ford United v Maidstone United	0-1
	Harlow Town v Letchworth Town	1-1
	Harwich & Parkeston v Walton & Hersham	3-3

1962/63 to 1963/64

Hayes v Maidenhead United	4-0
Hounslow Town v Kingstonian	1-3
Leatherhead v Pinehurst Youth Centre	3-0
Loughborough College v Billingham Synthonia	3-0
Lydbrook Athletic v Woking	0-1 N
Shildon v Bishop Auckland	1-5
Stanley United v Penrith	1-4
Stratford Town v Guinness Exports	1-1
Sutton United v Clapton	4-1
Tooting & Mitcham United v St Albans City	2-1
Tow Law Town v Whitley Bay	0-0 N
Walthamstow Avenue v Grays Athletic	2-1
Welton Rovers v Bromley	3-2
West Auckland Town v Blackpool Rangers	2-3aN
Whitby Town v Crook Town	3-3
Willington v Norton Woodseats	1-3
Wimbledon v Southall	3-3
Windsor & Eton v Eastbourne	0-3
Wycombe Wanderers v Uxbridge	2-0
Yorkshire Amateur v Eastwood Town	2-1
r Bishops Stortford v Vauxhall Motors	5-2
r Crook Town v Whitby Town	2-1
r Guinness Exports v Stratford Town	0-1
r Letchworth Town v Harlow Town	2-2
r Southall v Wimbledon	0-3
r Walton & Hersham v Harwich & Parkeston	1-0
r West Auckland Town v Blackpool Rangers	5-1 N
r Whitley Bay v Tow Law Town	2-1 N
r2 Letchworth Town v Harlow Town	3-2

Round Two

Alton Town v Letchworth Town	3-1
Barnet v Kingstonian	2-0
Bishop Auckland v West Auckland Town	1-3
Bishops Stortford v Norton Woodseats	6-2
Chesham United v Wimbledon	1-3
Crook Town v Walthamstow Avenue	0-0a
Eastbourne v Yorkshire Amateur	1-1
Enfield v Ferryhill Athletic	2-0
Leatherhead v Hitchin Town	1-4
Leytonstone v Loughborough College	5-1
Maidstone United v Sutton United	2-2
Stratford Town v Penrith	2-1
Tooting & Mitcham United v Welton Rovers	11-0
Whitley Bay v Hayes	2-2
Woking v Walton & Hersham	1-2
Wycombe Wanderers v Barking	3-2
r Crook Town v Walthamstow Avenue	3-0
r Hayes v Whitley Bay	3-0
r Sutton United v Maidstone United	6-0
r Yorkshire Amateur v Eastbourne	1-0

Round Three

Alton Town v Crook Town	2-1
Barnet v Wimbledon	0-1
Enfield v Tooting & Mitcham United	3-2
Hayes v Walton & Hersham	3-2
Hitchin Town v Wycombe Wanderers	3-2
Leytonstone v Yorkshire Amateur	5-1
Sutton United v Stratford Town	4-0
West Auckland Town v Bishops Stortford	0-0
r Bishops Stortford v West Auckland Town	1-0

Round Four

Hitchin Town v Hayes	2-2
Leytonstone v Enfield	4-0
Sutton United v Alton Town	1-0
Wimbledon v Bishops Stortford	1-0
r Hayes v Hitchin Town	0-1

Semi Finals

Sutton United v Hitchin Town	4-0 N
Wimbledon v Leytonstone	2-1 N

Final

Wimbledon v Sutton United	4-2 N

1963/64

Extra Preliminary Round

3 Kendal United v Hearts of Liddesdale	2-1

Preliminary Round

3 Bury Amateur v Manchester YMCA	1-1
Chapel Town v Heys Old Boys	n/a
Kendal United v Appleby	5-1
Lytham St Annes v Old Blackburnians	2-0
Manchester University v Formby	3-2
Old Boltonians v East Chorlton Amateur	n/a
Padiham v Chloride Recreation	1-2
Whalley Range Amateur v Old Salfordians	n/a
4 Ainsdale Hesketh Park v Port Sunlight	1-1
Guinness Exports v Northern Nomads	3-1
ICI Alkali v Earle	1-4
Linotype & Machinery v Unit Construction (Liverpool)	2-1
Marine v Ashville	3-1
Skelmersdale United v Middleton Amateurs	2-2
Stork v Newton	0-2
Warrington Town v Moreton	1-1
5 Doncaster United Amateurs v Hull Amateurs	1-0
Guiseley v Ossett Albion	1-4
Penistone Church v Harrogate & District Railway	5-4
Salts v Thurcroft Welfare	3-0
Sheffield v Kingburn Athletic	3-2
Thorncliffe Recreational v Thackley	0-6
6 Bestwood Colliery v Rufford Colliery	n/a
Boots Athletic v Chandos OB	4-2
Clipstone Welfare v Mapperley	1-2
Gedling CW v Bulwell Forest Villa	1-9
Parliament Street Methodists v Raleigh Athletic	0-3
Players Athletic v Netherfield Albion	n/a
RAF Cranwell v Worthington Simpson	2-1
7 Ericsson Athletic v Staffordshire Casuals	4-2
Lutterworth Town v Cosby United	5-2
Paget Rangers v Quorn	5-2
8 English Electric (Stafford) v Old Wulfrunians	5-1
Pershore United v Bournville Athletic	6-3
Walsall Wood v Malvern Town	0-1
Wrockwardine Wood v Smethwick Highfield	3-1
9 North Walsham Town v Gorleston	3-1
Ramsey Town v St Ives Town	1-3
11 Arlesey Town v Shillington	5-2
Buntingford Town v Leighton Town	0-5
Shefford Town v Baldock Town	2-0
Tring Town v Hemel Hempstead Town	3-1
12 Civil Service v Twickenham	2-0
Harrow Town v Rayners Lane	2-1
Kingsbury Town v Edgware Town	0-7
Ruislip Manor v Polytechnic	3-0
Staines Town v Wood Green Town	3-4
Wingate v Willesden	2-3
13 Beckenham v Slade Green Athletic	2-0
Cray Wanderers v Midland Bank	2-1
Faversham Town v Callender Athletic	3-2
Sheppey United v Herne Bay	0-5
Whitstable v Crockenhill	1-2
14 Bognor Regis Town v Wigmore Athletic	0-0
Hastings Rangers v Brighton Old Grammarians	8-1
Haywards Heath v Chichester City	5-1
Newhaven v Littlehampton Town	8-1
Seaford Town v Lancing Athletic	5-4
Shoreham v Worthing	1-5
Southwick v Moulsecoomb Rovers	6-2
15 Bexhill Town v Sidley United	2-2
Camberley v Redhill	0-4
Dorking v Croydon Amateur	2-0
Frimley Green v Reigate Priory	6-0
Horsham v Farncombe	2-0
Metropolitan Police v Three Bridges United	4-1
Whyteleafe v East Grinstead	1-1
16 Boreham Wood v Leavesden Hospital	2-4
Epping Town v Hatfield Town	2-0
Harlow Town v Cheshunt (2)	3-0
Hoddesdon Town v Harpenden Town	1-2
Kings Langley v Ware	1-1
Welwyn Garden City v Saffron Walden Town	4-1
17 Aveley v Rainham Town	4-2
Edmonton (2) v Brentwood & Warley	5-0
Hornchurch v Chingford	7-0
Leyton v Eton Manor	1-1
West Thurrock Athletic v East Ham United	2-2
18 Carshalton Athletic v ROF (SA)	7-1
Chobham v Malden Town	4-0
Cobham v Hermes	1-3
Molesey v Epsom & Ewell	2-0
Petters Sports v Vickers (Weybridge)	4-0
Whitehawk v West Wickham	4-0
19 Chalfont St Peter v Slough Town	1-1
Henley Town v Marlow	1-1
Newbury Town v Didcot Town	3-2
Wolverton Town & BR v Huntley & Palmers	4-1
20 Easington Sports v Chipping Norton Town	1-0
Wallingford Town v Thame United	5-2
21 Bournemouth v Pirelli General Cable Works	3-2
Fareham Town v Swaythling Athletic	4-1
Hamworthy v Brockenhurst	0-6
Ryde Sports v Netley Sports	1-0
Waterlooville v Gosport Borough Athletic	3-0
22 Bromham v Devizes Town	5-2
Dowty New Mendip v Radstock Town	3-2
Gorse Hill United v Amesbury	n/a
Marlborough Town v Swindon Victoria	1-3
Shepton Mallet Town v West Lavington	6-1
Warminster Town v Pinehurst Youth Centre	1-2
Westbury United v Calne & Harris United	2-1
Westcott Youth Centre v Melksham Town	1-2
23 Brimscombe v Wells City	1-2
Clevedon v Gloucester City YMCA	8-3
Hanham Athletic v Forest Green Rovers	2-1
Ilminster Town v Hoffmann Athletic (Stonehouse)	1-2
Sharpness v Worle OB	4-2
St Philips Marsh Adult School v Iron Acton	n/a
3r Manchester YMCA v Bury Amateur	0-1
4r Moreton v Warrington Town	1-2
r Port Sunlight v Ainsdale Hesketh Park	7-2
r Skelmersdale United v Middleton Amateurs	3-2
14r Wigmore Athletic v Bognor Regis Town	1-3
15r Sidley United v Bexhill Town	2-0
r Whyteleafe v East Grinstead	1-3
16r Ware v Kings Langley	3-0
17r East Ham United v West Thurrock Athletic	0-4
r Eton Manor v Leyton	2-1
19r Marlow v Henley Town	2-1
r Slough Town v Chalfont St Peter	5-1

Qualifying Round One

1 Highgate United (Newcastle) v Seaton Delaval	2-0
Newcastle University v North Eastern Marine	3-0
Shankhouse v Blyth YMCA	5-4
Wallsend Corinthians v North Shields	1-2
2 Consett v South Bank	1-2
Durham City v Spennymoor United	0-0
Stockton v West Hartlepool St Josephs	4-1
3 Bury Amateur v Old Boltonians	2-5
Chloride Recreation v Whalley Range Amateur	2-4
Kendal United v Lytham St Annes	1-1
Manchester University v Heys Old Boys	n/a
4 Marine v Earle	6-0
Newton v Port Sunlight	1-5
Skelmersdale United v Linotype & Machinery	9-3
Warrington Town v Guinness Exports	1-4
5 Doncaster United Amateurs v Sheffield	0-5
Ossett Albion v Thackley	2-1
Penistone Church v Bradford Rovers	n/a
Salts v Swallownest CW	1-1
6 Bestwood Colliery v Boots Athletic	n/a
Bulwell Forest Villa v Mapperley	5-0
Players Athletic v Basford United	n/a
Raleigh Athletic v RAF Cranwell	n/a
7 Anstey Nomads v Moor Green	0-4
Boldmere St Michaels v Lutterworth Town	3-0
Coventry Amateur v Ericsson Athletic	n/a
Paget Rangers v Stapenhill	3-2
8 Alvechurch v Pershore United	3-0
English Electric (Stafford) v Sutton Coldfield Town	3-0
Malvern Town v Cresconians	4-3
Wrockwardine Wood v Jack Moulds Athletic	1-0
9 Cromer v Desborough Town	2-1
North Walsham Town v Wymondham Town	5-1
Sheringham v Histon	5-2
St Ives Town v Thetford Town	2-0
10 Brantham Athletic v Leiston	3-1
Bungay Town v Stowmarket	3-3
Landseer Youth v Achilles	0-1
Orwell Works v Whitton United	2-1e
11 Arlesey Town v Electrolux	4-1
Berkhamsted Town v Tring Town	1-0
Leighton Town v Stotfold	2-2
Tottenhoe v Shefford Town	2-2
12 Edgware Town v Willesden	5-1
Harrow Town v Civil Service	1-0
Ruislip Manor v Hampton	0-3
Wood Green Town v Wembley	0-6
13 Beckenham v Herne Bay	0-8
Bexley v Crockenhill	2-2
Cray Wanderers v Woolwich Polytechnic	1-1
Faversham Town v Thameside Amateurs	3-0
14 Bognor Regis Town v Hastings Rangers	5-1
Haywards Heath v Seaford Town	2-4
Newhaven v Arundel	1-4
Southwick v Worthing	0-6
15 Dorking v East Grinstead	3-0
Frimley Green v Metropolitan Police	3-2
Horsham v Banstead Athletic	1-2
Sidley United v Redhill	0-1
16 Epping Town v Leavesden Hospital	0-3
Harlow Town v Welwyn Garden City	2-2
Harpenden Town v Crown & Manor	1-1
Ware v Rickmansworth Town	12-3
17 Aveley v Eton Manor	4-0
Barkingside v West Thurrock Athletic	0-3
Edmonton (2) v Tilbury	1-2
Hornchurch v Woodford Town	3-0

1963/64 to 1964/65

18	Chobham v Carshalton Athletic	0-0
	Hermes v Whitehawk	2-2
	Molesey v Addlestone	2-1
	Petters Sports v Ulysses	4-2
19	Aylesbury United v Newbury Town	3-0
	Hazells Aylesbury v Wolverton Town & BR	5-2
	Marlow v Wokingham Town	0-4
	Slough Town v Hungerford Town	6-0
20	Bicester Town v Wantage Town	4-1
	Oxford City v Easington Sports	10-1
	Pressed Steel v Abingdon Town	1-3
	Wallingford Town v Witney Town	2-2
21	Bournemouth v Winchester City	2-0
	Brockenhurst v Totton	5-4
	Fareham Town v Ryde Sports	7-0
	Waterlooville v Bitterne Nomads	4-2
22	Bromham v Amesbury	7-3
	Melksham Town v Westbury United	2-4
	Pinehurst Youth Centre v Dowty New Mendip	5-2
	Shepton Mallet Town v Swindon Victoria	3-1
23	unknown v Bristol St George	n/a
	Hanham Athletic v Hoffmann Athletic (Stonehouse)	4-1
	Keynsham Town v Sharpness	3-1
	Wells City v Clevedon	5-5
24	Chelston v Heavitree United	1-3
	Liskeard Athletic v EEM Dept (Devonport)	3-2
2r	Spennymoor United v Durham City	7-1
3r	Lytham St Annes v Kendal United	3-5
5r	Swallownest CW v Salts	0-2
10r	Stowmarket v Bungay Town	5-0
11r	Shefford Town v Tottenhoe	4-2
r	Stotfold v Leighton Town	2-3
13r	Cray Wanderers v Woolwich Polytechnic	1-3
r	Crockenhill v Bexley	5-3
16r	Crown & Manor v Harpenden Town	2-4
r	Welwyn Garden City v Harlow Town	1-2
18r	Carshalton Athletic v Chobham	3-0
r	Whitehawk v Hermes	3-1
20r	Witney Town v Wallingford Town	3-0
23r	Clevedon v Wells City	6-1

Qualifying Round Two

1	North Shields v Newcastle University	4-0
	Shankhouse v Highgate United (Newcastle)	5-0
2	Langley Park CW v Spennymoor United	1-2
	Stockton v South Bank	2-1
3	Kendal United v Whalley Range Amateur	4-0
	Old Boltonians v Heys Old Boys	n/a
4	Marine v Guinness Exports	1-3
	Skelmersdale United v Port Sunlight	3-2
5	Ossett Albion v Bradford Rovers	4-1
	Salts v Sheffield	1-3
6	Basford United v RAF Cranwell	n/a
	Boots Athletic v Bulwell Forest Villa	n/a
7	Boldmere St Michaels v Moor Green	0-1
	Paget Rangers v Ericsson Athletic	8-2
8	Alvechurch v Wrockwardine Wood	2-0
	English Electric (Stafford) v Malvern Town	0-2
9	North Walsham Town v Cromer	3-4
	St Ives Town v Sheringham	1-4
10	Brantham Athletic v Stowmarket	1-5
	Orwell Works v Achilles	2-1e
11	Arlesey Town v Shefford Town	2-2
	Leighton Town v Berkhamsted Town	2-2
12	Hampton v Edgware Town	4-4
	Wembley v Harrow Town	0-1
13	Faversham Town v Herne Bay	2-5
	Woolwich Polytechnic v Crockenhill	1-3
14	Arundel v Worthing	1-1
	Seaford Town v Bognor Regis Town	3-1
15	Banstead Athletic v Frimley Green	3-2
	Dorking v Redhill	0-1
16	Harpenden Town v Harlow Town	1-2
	Ware v Leavesden Hospital	3-0
17	Hornchurch v West Thurrock Athletic	0-1
	Tilbury v Aveley	1-3
18	Molesey v Whitehawk	3-1
	Petters Sports v Carshalton Athletic	0-4
19	Slough Town v Aylesbury United	3-0
	Wokingham Town v Hazells Aylesbury	1-1
20	Bicester Town v Oxford City	3-3
	Witney Town v Abingdon Town	2-0
21	Bournemouth v Waterlooville	1-3
	Brockenhurst v Fareham Town	1-1
22	Shepton Mallet Town v Pinehurst Youth Centre	1-4
	Westbury United v Bromham	1-7
23	Bristol St George v Keynsham Town	n/a
	Hanham Athletic v Clevedon	2-1
24	Saltash United v Liskeard Athletic	1-1
	Torpoint Athletic v Heavitree United	12-0
6r	Bulwell Forest Villa v Boots Athletic	2-0
11r	Berkhamsted Town v Leighton Town	8-1
r	Shefford Town v Arlesey Town	1-0
12r	Edgware Town v Hampton	3-1
14r	Worthing v Arundel	4-3
19r	Hazells Aylesbury v Wokingham Town	0-5
20r	Oxford City v Bicester Town	4-3
21r	Fareham Town v Brockenhurst	4-1
24r	Liskeard Athletic v Saltash United	2-3

Qualifying Round Three

1	North Shields v Shankhouse	5-2
2	Stockton v Spennymoor United	2-6
3	Heys Old Boys v Kendal United	1-4 v
4	Guinness Exports v Skelmersdale United	2-0
5	Ossett Albion v Sheffield	3-0
6	Bulwell Forest Villa v RAF Cranwell	1-3
7	Moor Green v Paget Rangers	2-2
8	Alvechurch v Malvern Town	5-4
9	Sheringham v Cromer	2-1
10	Orwell Works v Stowmarket	0-4
11	Berkhamsted Town v Shefford Town	3-1
12	Harrow Town v Edgware Town	2-1
13	Crockenhill v Herne Bay	2-4
14	Worthing v Seaford Town	0-1
15	Banstead Athletic v Redhill	0-3
16	Ware v Harlow Town	0-2
17	West Thurrock Athletic v Aveley	1-2
18	Carshalton Athletic v Molesey	2-0
19	Wokingham Town v Slough Town	4-1
20	Witney Town v Oxford City	1-4
21	Waterlooville v Fareham Town	1-1
22	Pinehurst Youth Centre v Bromham	4-0
23	Bristol St George v Hanham Athletic	3-3
24	Torpoint Athletic v Saltash United	5-1
3r	Heys Old Boys v Kendal United	3-2 N
7r	Paget Rangers v Moor Green	3-2
21r	Fareham Town v Waterlooville	6-1
23r	Hanham Athletic v Bristol St George	2-1

Qualifying Round Four

	Alvechurch v Paget Rangers	4-0
	Aveley v Letchworth Town	3-1
	Barking v Harwich & Parkeston	3-6
	Blackpool Rangers v Heys Old Boys	2-4
	Carshalton Athletic v Eastbourne United	3-1
	Chesham United v Fareham Town	3-6
	Eastwood Town v RAF Cranwell	10-3
	Evenwood Town v Tow Law Town	3-0
	Grays Athletic v Harlow Town	2-1
	Guinness Exports v Hallam	1-1
	Harrow Town v Herne Bay	7-0
	Hertford Town v Berkhamsted Town	1-2
	Ilford v Ford United	2-3
	Leatherhead v Redhill	2-0
	Ossett Albion v Whitby Town	1-1
	Pinehurst Youth Centre v Hanham Athletic	1-2
	Spennymoor United v Billingham Synthonia	2-1
	Stowmarket v Sheringham	3-1
	Torpoint Athletic v Lydbrook Athletic	4-1
	Uxbridge v Erith & Belvedere	2-1
	Vauxhall Motors v Wealdstone	0-4
	Willington v North Shields	2-2
	Windsor & Eton v Seaford Town	4-1
	Wokingham Town v Oxford City	2-3
r	Hallam v Guinness Exports	3-4
r	North Shields v Willington	1-2
r	Whitby Town v Ossett Albion	1-0

Round One

	Alton Town v Hayes	1-2
	Alvechurch v Penrith	1-1
	Aveley v Windsor & Eton	2-4
	Berkhamsted Town v Harrow Town	2-2
	Bishop Auckland v Whitley Bay	4-4
	Bishops Stortford v Ford United	2-1
	Bromley v Corinthian Casuals	2-0
	Clapton v Hanham Athletic	1-0
	Crook Town v Stanley United	1-1
	Dagenham v Woking	0-0
	Eastbourne v Walthamstow Avenue	0-5
	Enfield v Finchley	2-1
	Fareham Town v Hendon	1-0
	Ferryhill Athletic v Norton Woodseats	3-0
	Grays Athletic v Southall	2-2
	Harwich & Parkeston v Leatherhead	4-2
	Heys Old Boys v West Auckland Town	2-2
	Hitchin Town v Tooting & Mitcham United	1-2
	Hounslow Town v Barnet	1-4
	Kingstonian v Stowmarket	1-0
	Leytonstone v Maidstone United	2-0
	Loughborough College v Eastwood Town	1-6
	Shildon v Evenwood Town	2-3
	Spennymoor United v Stratford Town	3-0
	Sutton United v Oxford City	0-0
	Uxbridge v St Albans City	2-6
	Walton & Hersham v Torpoint Athletic	5-4
	Wealdstone v Carshalton Athletic	1-1
	Whitby Town v Yorkshire Amateur	7-0
	Willington v Guinness Exports	2-4
	Wimbledon v Maidenhead United	4-0
	Wycombe Wanderers v Dulwich Hamlet	3-0
r	Carshalton Athletic v Wealdstone	3-1
r	Harrow Town v Berkhamsted Town	2-1
r	Oxford City v Sutton United	1-2
r	Penrith v Alvechurch	2-0
r	Southall v Grays Athletic	0-2
r	Stanley United v Crook Town	1-5
r	West Auckland Town v Heys Old Boys	3-0
r	Whitley Bay v Bishop Auckland	1-0
r	Woking v Dagenham	3-1

Round Two

	Bromley v Sutton United	1-1
	Clapton v Barnet	0-1
	Eastwood Town v Woking	2-1
	Ferryhill Athletic v Bishops Stortford	3-1
	Guinness Exports v Kingstonian	0-1
	Harrow Town v Carshalton Athletic	1-5
	Harwich & Parkeston v Evenwood Town	0-2
	Hayes v Crook Town	0-0
	Penrith v Grays Athletic	0-2
	Spennymoor United v Leytonstone	2-1
	St Albans City v Whitby Town	0-2
	Walthamstow Avenue v Tooting & Mitcham United	1-1
	Walton & Hersham v Enfield	0-1
	West Auckland Town v Fareham Town	2-0
	Wimbledon v Windsor & Eton	2-1
	Wycombe Wanderers v Whitley Bay	4-2
r	Crook Town v Hayes	3-1
r	Sutton United v Bromley	3-0
r	Tooting & Mitcham United v Walthamstow Avenue	2-2
r2	Tooting & Mitcham United v Walthamstow Avenue	1-1
r3	Walthamstow Avenue v Tooting & Mitcham United	3-1

Round Three

	Barnet v Sutton United	2-2
	Carshalton Athletic v Walthamstow Avenue	1-1
	Eastwood Town v Whitby Town	0-2
	Enfield v Wimbledon	2-0
	Evenwood Town v Ferryhill Athletic	0-3
	Grays Athletic v Kingstonian	1-2
	West Auckland Town v Crook Town	0-0
	Wycombe Wanderers v Spennymoor United	2-2
r	Crook Town v West Auckland Town	1-0
r	Spennymoor United v Wycombe Wanderers	2-1
r	Sutton United v Barnet	1-2
r	Walthamstow Avenue v Carshalton Athletic	2-1

Round Four

	Enfield v Whitby Town	3-0
	Ferryhill Athletic v Kingstonian	0-1 N
	Spennymoor United v Barnet	2-5 N
	Walthamstow Avenue v Crook Town	1-1 N
r	Crook Town v Walthamstow Avenue	3-0

Semi Finals

	Crook Town v Barnet	2-1 N
	Enfield v Kingstonian	0-0 N
r	Enfield v Kingstonian	3-2 N

Final

	Crook Town v Enfield	2-1 N

1964/65

Preliminary Round

3	Blackpool Rangers v Whalley Range Amateur	2-3
	Manchester YMCA v Chapel Town	5-2
	Old Blackburnians v Old Salfordians	2-1
4	Ainsdale Hesketh Park v Middleton Amateurs	1-0
	Linotype & Machinery v ICI Alkali	2-3
	Moreton v Ashville	2-1
	Northern Nomads v Marine	1-2
	Port Sunlight v Harrowby	5-0
	Skelmersdale United v Stork	3-0
	Warrington Town v Old Altrinchamians	0-1
5	Bradford Rovers v Maltby MW	3-1
	Harrogate & District Railway v Leeds University	2-1
	Kingburn Athletic v Doncaster United Amateurs	1-1
	Leeds Ashley Road v Guiseley	2-3
	Ossett Albion v Altofts	1-1
	Salts v Swallownest CW	2-0
	Thackley v Harrogate Town	1-1
8	Pershore United v Sutton Coldfield Town	5-0
11	Arlesey Town v Vauxhall Motors	3-2
	Buntingford Town v Sandy Albions	1-1
	Hemel Hempstead Town v Baldock Town	3-1
	Letchworth Town v Berkhamsted Town	4-2
	Shefford Town v Chesham United	1-4
	Shillington v Stotfold	1-1
	Tring Town v Hertford Town	0-7
12	Civil Service v Kingsbury Town	4-2
	Edgware Town v Hampton	0-2
	Feltham v Rayners Lane	6-3
	Ruislip Manor v Staines Town	0-2
	Wembley v Twickenham	3-0
	Willesden v Wood Green Town	2-2
13	Faversham Town v Orpington Athletic	0-5
	Herne Bay v Beckenham	7-2
	Whitstable v Callender Athletic	1-1
	Woolwich Polytechnic v Slade Green Athletic	3-1
14	Arundel v Worthing	2-3
	Farnham Town v Horsham	1-3
	Lancing Athletic v Seaford Town	2-5
	Selsey v Chichester City	1-0
	Shoreham v Eastbourne United	0-6
	Wigmore Athletic v Littlehampton Town	1-1

1964/65

15 Banstead Athletic v Redhill 1-0
Bexhill Town v Camberley 9-0
Croydon Amateur v East Grinstead 6-0
Frimley Green v Farncombe 1-0
Metropolitan Police v Three Bridges United 1-0
Sidley United v Dorking 1-1
Whyteleafe v Reigate Priory 3-1
16 Kings Langley v Boreham Wood 2-3
Leavesden Hospital v Cheshunt (2) 2-1
Ware v Saffron Walden Town 5-1
Welwyn Garden City v Epping Town 1-3
17 Leyton v Edmonton (2) 5-1
Rainham Town v Tilbury 1-1
West Thurrock Athletic v Brentwood & Warley 3-1
18 Addlestone v Cobham 1-0
BAC Weybridge v Chobham 2-0
Malden Town v Molesey 1-1
Petters Sports v ROF (SA) 3-1
Ulysses v Whitehawk 2-0
Westfield v Hermes 5-1
19 Bracknell Town v Chalfont St Peter 2-4
Slough Town v Hungerford Town 14-1
Wokingham Town v Wolverton Town & BR 4-2
20 Moreton Town v Abingdon Town 0-2
Wallingford Town v Kidlington 3-1
Wantage Town v Witney Town 0-6
21 Gosport Borough Athletic v Sholing Sports 4-0
Hamworthy v Winchester City 2-3
22 Devizes Town v Box Hill Sports 7-1
Ferndale Youth Centre v Bromham 3-1
Highworth Town v Wootton Bassett Town 1-8
Melksham Town v Shepton Mallet Town 2-2
Swindon Victoria v Warminster Town 1-1
Westbury United v Marlborough Town 1-3
23 Clevedon v Brimscombe 4-4
Ilminster Town v Bristol St George 1-1
Keynsham Town v Forest Green Rovers 3-0
Sharpness v Soundwell 1-1
St Philips Marsh Adult School v Hanham Athletic 1-0
Wells City v Lydbrook Athletic 0-3
Wincombe v Gloucester City YMCA 1-4
5r Altofts v Ossett Albion 1-0
r Doncaster United Amateurs v Kingburn Athletic 0-1
r Harrogate Town v Thackley 0-5
11r Sandy Albions v Buntingford Town 3-0
r Stotfold v Shillington 2-5
12r Wood Green Town v Willesden 4-1
13r Callender Athletic v Whitstable 5-1e
14r Littlehampton Town v Wigmore Athletic 2-0
15r Dorking v Sidley United 0-2
17r Tilbury v Rainham Town 1-0
18r Molesey v Malden Town 0-4
22r Shepton Mallet Town v Melksham Town 3-1
r Warminster Town v Swindon Victoria 4-1
23r Brimscombe v Clevedon 2-1
r Bristol St George v Ilminster Town 1-1
r Soundwell v Sharpness 1-4
23r2 Bristol St George v Ilminster Town 0-0e
23r3 Bristol St George v Ilminster Town 3-0

Qualifying Round One

1 Hearts of Liddesdale v Wallsend 4-2
Heaton Stannington v Newcastle University 3-5
Naval Yard (Walker) v Blyth Spartans 1-3
North Eastern Marine v North Shields 0-10
2 Consett v West Hartlepool St Josephs 3-1
Durham City v Billingham Synthonia 1-1
Langley Park CW v South Bank 1-2
Tow Law Town v Stockton 3-1
3 Bury Amateur v Chloride Recreation 1-1
Manchester YMCA v East Chorlton Amateur 2-1
Old Blackburnians v Chadderton 1-0
Whalley Range Amateur v Manchester University 4-0
4 Ainsdale Hesketh Park v Skelmersdale United 0-6
Marine v Old Altrinchamians 5-1
Moreton v Newton 2-3
Port Sunlight v ICI Alkali 5-1
5 Altofts v Bradford Rovers 8-2
Guiseley v Salts 6-3
Harrogate & District Railway v Hull Amateurs 5-0
Kingburn Athletic v Thackley 2-4
6 Bulwell Forest Villa v Basford United 3-2
Hallam v Nottingham University 2-7
Players Athletic v Sheffield 0-1
7 Coventry Amateur v Staffordshire Casuals 5-0
Lutterworth Town v Anstey Nomads 6-2
Moor Green v Paget Rangers 4-0
Stapenhill v Boldmere St Michaels wo/s
8 Bournville Athletic v Pershore United 3-2
Eastwood Hanley v Walsall Wood 0-2
Jack Moulds Athletic v Old Wulfrunians 3-1
Pegasus Juniors v Wrockwardine Wood 1-4
9 Cromer v Wymondham Town 8-1
Gorleston v City of Norwich School OBU 4-4e
Ramsey Town v Histon 3-3
10 Ipswich Electricity Supply v Achilles 6-0
Leiston v Bungay Town 2-3
Stowmarket v Brantham Athletic 4-1
11 Chesham United v Arlesey Town 2-0
Hemel Hempstead Town v Hertford Town 2-2
Letchworth Town v Shillington 6-2
Sandy Albions v Electrolux 4-0

12 Feltham v Polytechnic 4-2
Hampton v Civil Service 2-1
Staines Town v Wingate 2-4
Wood Green Town v Wembley 0-3
13 Callender Athletic v Midland Bank 3-2
Cray Wanderers v Bexley 3-0
Herne Bay v Woolwich Polytechnic 4-0
Orpington Athletic v Crockenhill 4-1
14 Littlehampton Town v Southwick 2-2
Seaford Town v Bognor Regis Town 3-2
Selsey v Eastbourne United 0-3
Worthing v Brighton Old Grammarians 11-1
15 Croydon Amateur v Banstead Athletic 4-1
Frimley Green v Horsham 3-2
Sidley United v Bexhill Town 4-2e
Whyteleafe v Metropolitan Police 1-4
16 Boreham Wood v Hoddesdon Town 0-0
Crown & Manor v Harpenden Town 4-1
Epping Town v Rickmansworth Town 4-1
Ware v Leavesden Hospital 1-3
17 Chingford v East Ham United 0-1
Leyton v Eton Manor 4-3
Tilbury v Barkingside 4-0
West Thurrock Athletic v Hornchurch 1-3
18 BAC Weybridge v Addlestone 1-0
Malden Town v West Wickham 4-4
Ulysses v Petters Sports 2-2
Westfield v Epsom & Ewell 0-1
19 Aylesbury United v Wokingham Town 4-2
Chalfont St Peter v Newbury Town 2-0
Didcot Town v Hazells Aylesbury 3-0
Slough Town v Huntley & Palmers 5-0
20 Abingdon Town v Thame United 2-2
Bicester Town v Chipping Norton Town 5-3
Morris Motors v Witney Town 1-2
Wallingford Town v Pressed Steel 1-0
21 Gosport Borough Athletic v Totton 5-0
Longfleet St Marys v Waterlooville 0-3
Pirelli General Cable Works v Swaythling Athletic 3-1
Winchester City v Netley Sports 5-4
22 Devizes Town v Calne Town 4-1
Marlborough Town v Warminster Town 2-2
Shepton Mallet Town v Westcott Youth Centre 11-1
Wootton Bassett Town v Ferndale Youth Centre 1-2
23 Bristol St George v Iron Acton 5-1
Gloucester City YMCA v Sharpness 1-9
Keynsham Town v Lydbrook Athletic 0-1
St Philips Marsh Adult School v Brimscombe 4-0
24 Torpoint Athletic v Nanpean Rovers 4-1
2r Billingham Synthonia v Durham City 4-2
3r Chloride Recreation v Bury Amateur 3-1
9r City of Norwich School OBU v Gorleston 3-2
r Histon v Ramsey Town 5-0
11r Hertford Town v Hemel Hempstead Town 1-0
14r Southwick v Littlehampton Town 2-1
16r Hoddesdon Town v Boreham Wood 0-1
18r Malden Town v West Wickham 1-3
r Petters Sports v Ulysses 3-0
20r Thame United v Abingdon Town 6-2
22r Warminster Town v Marlborough Town 4-0

Qualifying Round Two

1 Blyth Spartans v Newcastle University 4-3
Hearts of Liddesdale v North Shields 2-4
2 Billingham Synthonia v Consett 2-2
Tow Law Town v South Bank 3-1
3 Manchester YMCA v Chloride Recreation 2-5
Old Blackburnians v Whalley Range Amateur 3-2
4 Port Sunlight v Marine 0-1
Skelmersdale United v Newton 2-0
5 Altofts v Thackley 2-2
Guiseley v Harrogate & District Railway 2-5
6 Bulwell Forest Villa v Raleigh Athletic 1-3
Sheffield v Nottingham University 1-4
7 Coventry Amateur v Stapenhill 0-2
Lutterworth Town v Moor Green 2-4
8 Bournville Athletic v Wrockwardine Wood 1-4
Walsall Wood v Jack Moulds Athletic 5-5e
9 City of Norwich School OBU v Cromer 1-4
Histon v St Ives Town 4-0
10 Ipswich Electricity Supply v Whitton United 3-3
Stowmarket v Bungay Town 6-1
11 Letchworth Town v Hertford Town 0-6
Sandy Albions v Chesham United 0-1
12 Wembley v Hampton 1-4
Wingate v Feltham 3-0
13 Callender Athletic v Orpington Athletic 2-1
Herne Bay v Cray Wanderers 3-1
14 Eastbourne United v Seaford Town 3-1
Southwick v Worthing 2-3
15 Croydon Amateur v Sidley United 4-0
Frimley Green v Metropolitan Police 1-3
16 Epping Town v Boreham Wood 1-1
Leavesden Hospital v Crown & Manor 2-1
17 Hornchurch v Leyton 0-2
Tilbury v East Ham United 6-2
18 Epsom & Ewell v West Wickham 3-1
Petters Sports v BAC Weybridge 1-4
19 Aylesbury United v Didcot Town 0-1
Chalfont St Peter v Slough Town 2-1
20 Thame United v Wallingford Town 3-1
Witney Town v Bicester Town 2-3

21 Waterlooville v Gosport Borough Athletic 1-0
Winchester City v Pirelli General Cable Works 2-6
22 Shepton Mallet Town v Devizes Town 1-3
Warminster Town v Ferndale Youth Centre 3-4
23 Bristol St George v St Philips Marsh Adult School 2-2
Sharpness v Lydbrook Athletic 7-2
24 St Lukes College v Falmouth Docks 6-0
Torpoint Athletic v EEM Dept (Devonport) 3-0
2r Consett v Billingham Synthonia 3-1
5r Thackley v Altofts 4-1
8r Jack Moulds Athletic v Walsall Wood 3-6
10r Whitton United v Ipswich Electricity Supply 3-1
16r Boreham Wood v Epping Town 0-1
23r St Philips Marsh Adult School v Bristol St George 1-2

Qualifying Round Three

1 North Shields v Blyth Spartans 1-4
2 Tow Law Town v Consett 3-0
3 Chloride Recreation v Old Blackburnians 1-1
4 Marine v Skelmersdale United 1-4
5 Thackley v Harrogate & District Railway 1-0
6 Raleigh Athletic v Nottingham University 2-4
7 Stapenhill v Moor Green 0-5
8 Walsall Wood v Wrockwardine Wood 3-4
9 Cromer v Histon 7-2
10 Stowmarket v Whitton United 3-0
11 Chesham United v Hertford Town 0-5
12 Wingate v Hampton 0-2
13 Callender Athletic v Herne Bay 3-2
14 Worthing v Eastbourne United 1-4
15 Metropolitan Police v Croydon Amateur 1-2
16 Epping Town v Leavesden Hospital 1-1
17 Leyton v Tilbury 1-1
18 Epsom & Ewell v BAC Weybridge 1-2
19 Chalfont St Peter v Didcot Town 3-4
20 Thame United v Bicester Town 4-1
21 Waterlooville v Pirelli General Cable Works 0-0
22 Devizes Town v Ferndale Youth Centre 4-2
23 Bristol St George v Sharpness 4-2
24 St Lukes College v Torpoint Athletic 1-1
3r Old Blackburnians v Chloride Recreation 2-1
16r Leavesden Hospital v Epping Town 1-2
17r Tilbury v Leyton 0-2
21r Pirelli General Cable Works v Waterlooville 0-2
24r Torpoint Athletic v St Lukes College 3-3
24r2 Torpoint Athletic v St Lukes College 3-2

Qualifying Round Four

Alvechurch v Stratford Town 4-0
BAC Weybridge v Leatherhead 1-4
Callender Athletic v Erith & Belvedere 3-1
Cromer v Stowmarket 1-3
Devizes Town v Bristol St George 3-2
Didcot Town v Wealdstone 1-2
Dulwich Hamlet v Harlow Town 3-1
Eastbourne United v Croydon Amateur 1-2
Epping Town v Harrow Town 0-0
Fareham Town v Waterlooville 6-0
Ford United v Leyton 2-1
Hounslow Town v Hampton 2-1
Ilford v Barking 1-0
Moor Green v Wrockwardine Wood 2-2
Norton Woodseats v Nottingham University 3-2
Old Blackburnians v Skelmersdale United 0-8
Oxford City v Hertford Town 2-2
Prestwich Heys v Guinness Exports 3-3
Southall v Thame United 4-2
Stanley United v Thackley 2-2
Torpoint Athletic v Pinehurst Youth Centre 3-1
Tow Law Town v Blyth Spartans 2-0
Uxbridge v Aveley 0-2
Willington v Shildon 2-1
r Guinness Exports v Prestwich Heys 2-3
r Harrow Town v Epping Town 9-0
r Hertford Town v Oxford City 1-2
r Thackley v Stanley United 3-0
r Wrockwardine Wood v Moor Green 1-3

Round One

Alvechurch v Norton Woodseats 2-0
Aveley v Dulwich Hamlet 0-1
Bishop Auckland v Loughborough College 2-1
Callender Athletic v Kingstonian 0-10
Corinthian Casuals v Harwich & Parkeston 0-1
Crook Town v Willington 0-1
Croydon Amateur v Clapton 1-1
Eastbourne v Leatherhead 2-1
Eastwood Town v Evenwood Town 2-1
Enfield v Dagenham 3-2
Fareham Town v Carshalton Athletic 1-2
Ford United v Maidenhead United 2-2
Hayes v Harrow Town 4-4 v
Hitchin Town v Devizes Town 5-0
Hounslow Town v Alton Town 10-0
Ilford v Bishops Stortford 0-2
Leytonstone v Wycombe Wanderers 2-2
Maidstone United v Barnet 1-4
Oxford City v Southall 6-0
Spennymoor United v Skelmersdale United 3-0
Stowmarket v St Albans City 0-1

1964/65 to 1965/66

Sutton United v Hendon	1-2
Thackley v Penrith	0-2
Tooting & Mitcham United v Walthamstow Avenue	1-1
Tow Law Town v Ferryhill Athletic	1-2
Walton & Hersham v Torpoint Athletic	1-1
Wealdstone v Grays Athletic	3-0
Whitby Town v Moor Green	3-2
Whitley Bay v West Auckland Town	4-3
Windsor & Eton v Finchley	1-1
Woking v Bromley	2-2
Yorkshire Amateur v Prestwich Heys	2-3
r Bromley v Woking	2-1
r Clapton v Croydon Amateur	0-1
r Finchley v Windsor & Eton	5-1
r Hayes v Harrow Town	3-1
r Maidenhead United v Ford United	3-1
r Torpoint Athletic v Walton & Hersham	4-2
r Walthamstow Avenue v Tooting & Mitcham United	1-0
r Wycombe Wanderers v Leytonstone	0-2

Round Two

Alvechurch v Walthamstow Avenue	2-1
Bishop Auckland v Wealdstone	2-4
Bishops Stortford v Maidenhead United	4-1
Carshalton Athletic v Hounslow Town	4-1
Croydon Amateur v St Albans City	1-2
Dulwich Hamlet v Whitley Bay	1-2
Eastbourne v Whitby Town	0-2
Eastwood Town v Prestwich Heys	5-3
Enfield v Barnet	1-1
Finchley v Hayes	4-0
Hendon v Leytonstone	5-1
Hitchin Town v Oxford City	2-2
Kingstonian v Spennymoor United	11-2
Penrith v Ferryhill Athletic	1-3
Torpoint Athletic v Harwich & Parkeston	0-4
Willington v Bromley	2-4
r Barnet v Enfield	2-3
r Oxford City v Hitchin Town	3-1

Round Three

Alvechurch v Wealdstone	4-1
Bromley v Kingstonian	0-0
Eastwood Town v Enfield	2-3
Ferryhill Athletic v Finchley	1-2
Harwich & Parkeston v Bishops Stortford	0-0
Hendon v Carshalton Athletic	5-1
Oxford City v Whitby Town	1-2
St Albans City v Whitley Bay	0-1
r Bishops Stortford v Harwich & Parkeston	1-2
r Kingstonian v Bromley	4-2

Round Four

Alvechurch v Enfield	1-3
Harwich & Parkeston v Whitby Town	0-0
Kingstonian v Finchley	0-2
Whitley Bay v Hendon	1-3
r Whitby Town v Harwich & Parkeston	3-2

Semi Finals

Hendon v Finchley	4-1 N
Whitby Town v Enfield	2-1 N

Final

Hendon v Whitby Town	3-1 N

1965/66

Preliminary Round

3 Curzon Amateur v Old Altrinchamians	1-2
East Chorlton Amateur v Chadderton	2-4
4 Ashville v Ainsdale Hesketh Park	2-3
Guinness Exports v Port Sunlight	5-0
Marine v Newton	1-0
Stork v Winnington Park	3-0
Warrington Town v Middleton Amateurs	5-1
5 Guiseley v Swallownest CW	3-3
Harrogate & District Railway v Bradford Rovers	7-2
Harrogate Town v Doncaster United Amateurs	2-2
Kingburn Athletic v Hull Amateurs	1-1
Leeds Ashley Road v Salts	2-1
Ossett Albion v Altofts	4-2
7 Anstey Nomads v Smethwick Highfield	2-0
Highgate U (Birmingham) v Boldmere St Michaels	0-3
Pershore United v Accles & Pollock (Oldbury)	2-5
8 Darlaston v Bournville Athletic	1-1
Jack Moulds Athletic v Sutton Coldfield Town	3-1
11 Berkhamsted Town v Stotfold	5-2
Buntingford Town v Baldock Town	1-1
Chesham United v Vauxhall Motors	2-1
Electrolux v Hemel Hempstead Town	1-4
Hertford Town v Shillington	10-0
Sandy Albions v Arlesey Town	2-2

12 Civil Service v Twickenham	6-0
Feltham v Willesden	3-0
Hampton v Edgware Town	5-2
Kingsbury Town v Wood Green Town	4-1
Polytechnic v Rayners Lane	0-2
Ruislip Manor v Wembley	1-4
13 Bexley v Beckenham	1-0
Brentstonians v Midland Bank	4-0
Cray Wanderers v Faversham Town	2-0
Crockenhill v Whitstable	2-1
Slade Green Athletic v Woolwich Polytechnic	3-2
14 Arundel v Eastbourne United	2-7
Seaford Town v Wigmore Athletic	5-1
15 Banstead Athletic v Godalming & Farncombe	3-1
Camberley v Whyteleafe	0-3
Dorking v Redhill	1-4
Frimley Green v Horsham	2-5
16 Cheshunt (2) v Ware	2-3
Crown & Manor v Kings Langley	0-1
Epping Town v Hoddesdon Town	1-3
Harpenden Town v Boreham Wood	2-3
17 Canvey Island v East Ham United	2-0
Eton Manor v Rainham Town	2-1
18 Addlestone v Molesey	0-3
Epsom & Ewell v Cobham	5-0
Malden Town v Westfield	1-1
ROF (SA) v Lion Sports	0-4
Ulysses v Petters Sports	1-4
West Wickham v Chobham	1-3
Whitehawk v BAC Weybridge	2-4
19 Bracknell Town v Wolverton Town & BR	2-8
Chalfont St Peter v Huntley & Palmers	6-1
Didcot Town v Hungerford Town	2-3
Hazells Aylesbury v Aylesbury United	3-2
20 Moreton Town v Chipping Norton Town	1-4
Morris Motors v Bicester Town	1-4
Witney Town v Abingdon Town	10-1
21 Gosport Borough Athletic v Winchester City	2-1
Hamworthy v Sholing Sports	1-2
Longfleet St Marys v Pirelli General Cable Works	2-8 N
Ryde Sports v Netley Sports	1-5
22 Bromham v Melksham Town	1-2
Calne Town v Ferndale Youth Centre	3-7
Devizes Town v Pinehurst Youth Centre	6-4
West Lavington v Westcott Youth Centre	4-3
23 Hanham Athletic v Forest Green Rovers	3-1
Ilminster Town v Clevedon	5-4
Wells City v Bristol St George	2-3
5r Doncaster United Amateurs v Harrogate Town	1-1
r Kingburn Athletic v Hull Amateurs	4-1
r Swallownest CW v Guiseley	5-2
8r Bournville Athletic v Darlaston	0-1
11r Arlesey Town v Sandy Albions	2-1
r Baldock Town v Buntingford Town	3-0
18r Westfield v Malden Town	3-4
5r2 Harrogate Town v Doncaster United Amateurs	6-3 N

Qualifying Round One

1 Hearts of Liddesdale v Marine Park	n/a
Heaton Stannington v Newcastle University	1-3
North Shields v Shankhouse	8-0
2 Billingham Synthonia v Stockton	0-2
Shildon v Consett	2-2
South Bank v Durham City	1-1
3 Chloride Recreation v Windscale Rovers	wo/s
Lytham St Annes & Fylde v Cleator Moor Celtic	2-1
Old Altrinchamians v Manchester YMCA	2-4e
Old Blackburnians v Chadderton	0-2
4 Ainsdale Hesketh Park v Linotype & Machinery	1-4
Northern Nomads v Marine	0-6
Stork v Guinness Exports	1-4
Warrington Town v Liverpool University	4-0
5 Harrogate Town v Leeds University	3-2
Kingburn Athletic v Leeds Ashley Road	2-0
Ossett Albion v Harrogate & District Railway	2-0
Thackley v Swallownest CW	4-1
6 Hallam v Nottingham University	6-1
7 Anstey Nomads v Paget Rangers	1-1
Coventry Amateur v Lutterworth Town	1-3
Staffordshire Casuals v Boldmere St Michaels	0-6
Stratford Town v Accles & Pollock (Oldbury)	3-5
8 Darlaston v Walsall Wood	0-1
Eastwood Hanley v Old Wulfrunians	4-1
Madeley College v Blakenall	4-2
Wrockwardine Wood v Jack Moulds Athletic	2-0
9 City of Norwich School OBU v Cromer	2-0
Soham United v Histon	3-0
St Ives Town v Ramsey Town	2-1
Wymondham Town v Gorleston	1-5
11 Arlesey Town v Baldock Town	2-2
Chesham United v Letchworth Town	2-0
Hemel Hempstead Town v Hertford Town	1-0
Tring Town v Berkhamsted Town	1-1
12 Hampton v Civil Service	3-0
Kingsbury Town v Staines Town	1-5
Rayners Lane v Wembley	1-4
Wingate v Feltham	2-3
13 Bexley v Callender Athletic	1-1
Crockenhill v Erith & Belvedere	0-2
Herne Bay v Cray Wanderers	2-0
Slade Green Athletic v Brentstonians	2-4

14 Bognor Regis Town v East Grinstead	2-2
Eastbourne United v Worthing	2-2
Lancing Athletic v Shoreham	3-0
Selsey v Seaford Town	1-2
15 Egham Town v Reigate Priory	2-0
Redhill v Banstead Athletic	3-1
Three Bridges United v Horsham	0-4
Whyteleafe v Sidley United	3-4
16 Harlow Town v Leavesden Hospital	3-1
Kings Langley v Boreham Wood	2-5
Saffron Walden Town v Hoddesdon Town	1-4
Ware v Rickmansworth Town	9-0
17 Canvey Island v Tilbury	0-2
Chingford v Barkingside	7-1
Edmonton (2) v Hornchurch	1-3
West Thurrock Athletic v Eton Manor	1-0
18 BAC Weybridge v Lion Sports	1-1
Chobham v Malden Town	4-1
Hermes v Petters Sports	3-4
Molesey v Epsom & Ewell	0-1
19 Chalfont St Peter v Hazells Aylesbury	2-2
Marlow v Newbury Town	1-3
Wokingham Town v Hungerford Town	1-0
Wolverton Town & BR v Slough Town	0-4
20 Chipping Norton Town v Wallingford Town	4-1
Kidlington v Witney Town	5-7
Pressed Steel v Thame United	3-5
Wantage Town v Bicester Town	2-4
21 Brockenhurst v Swaythling Athletic	4-0
Gosport Borough Athletic v Totton	2-1
Sholing Sports v Netley Sports	1-2
Waterlooville v Pirelli General Cable Works	2-0
22 Amesbury v Swindon Victoria	3-1
Melksham Town v Devizes Town	3-0
West Lavington v Warminster Town	0-1
Westbury United v Ferndale Youth Centre	1-2
23 Gloucester City YMCA v Bristol St George	1-5
Hanham Athletic v Sharpness	1-0
Keynsham Town v Lydbrook Athletic	0-1
Soundwell v Ilminster Town	8-1
24 EEM Dept (Devonport) v Falmouth Docks	3-0
2r Consett v Shildon	
r Durham City v South Bank	0-1e
7r Paget Rangers v Anstey Nomads	7-0
11r Baldock Town v Arlesey Town	5-1
r Berkhamsted Town v Tring Town	2-3
13r Callender Athletic v Bexley	4-1
14r Bognor Regis Town v East Grinstead	5-4
r Worthing v Eastbourne United	1-4
18r Lion Sports v BAC Weybridge	1-4
19r Hazells Aylesbury v Chalfont St Peter	0-1

Qualifying Round Two

1 Marine Park v Blyth Spartans	1-4
Newcastle University v North Shields	1-4
2 Consett v Acklam Steelworks	3-1
Stockton v South Bank	1-0
3 Lytham St Annes & Fylde v Chloride Recreation	0-2
Manchester YMCA v Chadderton	0-1
4 Guinness Exports v Warrington Town	1-0
Linotype & Machinery v Marine	0-2
5 Harrogate Town v Thackley	0-0
Kingburn Athletic v Ossett Albion	0-4
6 Bulwell Forest Villa v Hallam	3-2
Players Athletic v Sheffield	2-1
7 Accles & Pollock (Oldbury) v Lutterworth Town	8-0
Paget Rangers v Boldmere St Michaels	0-2
8 Eastwood Hanley v Madeley College	5-2
Walsall Wood v Wrockwardine Wood	2-1
9 Gorleston v City of Norwich School OBU	1-6
St Ives Town v Soham United	1-2
10 Brantham Athletic v Bungay Town	3-2
Whitton United v Waterside Works	4-1
11 Baldock Town v Hemel Hempstead Town	1-2
Tring Town v Chesham United	1-1
12 Feltham v Staines Town	1-0
Hampton v Wembley	1-1
13 Erith & Belvedere v Brentstonians	2-0
Herne Bay v Callender Athletic	3-1
14 Lancing Athletic v Bognor Regis Town	5-1
Seaford Town v Eastbourne United	0-4
15 Egham Town v Redhill	1-1
Horsham v Sidley United	5-0
16 Harlow Town v Boreham Wood	2-1
Hoddesdon Town v Ware	0-2
17 Hornchurch v Chingford	2-0
West Thurrock Athletic v Tilbury	0-3
18 Chobham v Epsom & Ewell	1-3
Petters Sports v BAC Weybridge	2-0
19 Newbury Town v Chalfont St Peter	1-2
Wokingham Town v Slough Town	0-3
20 Bicester Town v Chipping Norton Town	1-1
Thame United v Witney Town	0-4
21 Brockenhurst v Netley Sports	4-3
Waterlooville v Gosport Borough Athletic	1-1
22 Amesbury v Melksham Town	2-4
Ferndale Youth Centre v Warminster Town	5-2
23 Lydbrook Athletic v Bristol St George	1-1
Soundwell v Hanham Athletic	1-1
24 EEM Dept (Devonport) v Tiverton Town	4-1
St Lukes College v Nanpean Rovers	2-0

1965/66 to 1966/67

5r Thackley v Harrogate Town	4-4
11r Chesham United v Tring Town	4-2
12r Wembley v Hampton	2-1
15r Redhill v Egham Town	0-1
20r Chipping Norton Town v Bicester Town	3-1
21r Gosport Borough Athletic v Waterlooville	3-1
23r Bristol St George v Lydbrook Athletic	0-2
r Hanham Athletic v Soundwell	6-2
5r2 Thackley v Harrogate Town	5-1

Qualifying Round Three

1 North Shields v Blyth Spartans	3-1
2 Stockton v Consett	2-1
3 Chloride Recreation v Chadderton	0-2
4 Guinness Exports v Marine	0-0
5 Ossett Albion v Thackley	1-0
6 Bulwell Forest Villa v Players Athletic	4-1
7 Accles & Pollock (Oldbury) v Boldmere St Michaels	2-1
8 Eastwood Hanley v Walsall Wood	5-1
9 Soham United v City of Norwich School OBU	0-1
10 Brantham Athletic v Whitton United	4-2
11 Hemel Hempstead Town v Chesham United	3-1
12 Wembley v Feltham	2-0
13 Erith & Belvedere v Herne Bay	2-2
14 Lancing Athletic v Eastbourne United	3-1
15 Egham Town v Horsham	0-2
16 Harlow Town v Ware	3-2
17 Hornchurch v Tilbury	2-0
18 Epsom & Ewell v Petters Sports	4-1
19 Chalfont St Peter v Slough Town	0-1
20 Witney Town v Chipping Norton Town	6-1
21 Brockenhurst v Gosport Borough Athletic	1-2
22 Melksham Town v Ferndale Youth Centre	0-2
23 Lydbrook Athletic v Hanham Athletic	1-0
24 EEM Dept (Devonport) v St Lukes College	5-4
4r Marine v Guinness Exports	2-5
13r Herne Bay v Erith & Belvedere	3-2

Qualifying Round Four

Accles & Pollock (Oldbury) v Loughborough College	3-3
Aveley v Hornchurch	1-1
Barking v Harrow Town	6-0
Bulwell Forest Villa v Norton Woodseats	1-1
Chadderton v Prestwich Heys	1-3
City of Norwich School OBU v Stowmarket	4-6
Corinthian Casuals v Brantham Athletic	3-0
Croydon Amateur v Harlow Town	0-1
Dagenham v Southall	2-1
Eastwood Hanley v Moor Green	2-7
Epsom & Ewell v Leyton	1-4
Ferndale Youth Centre v Lydbrook Athletic	3-0
Gosport Borough Athletic v Alton Town	5-0
Guinness Exports v Skelmersdale United	2-3
Herne Bay v Ilford	3-0
Lancing Athletic v Horsham	2-1
Maidstone United v Ford United	3-1
North Shields v Stanley United	3-4
Slough Town v Hemel Hempstead Town	1-2
Stockton v Tow Law Town	1-3
Torpoint Athletic v EEM Dept (Devonport)	4-2
Uxbridge v Witney Town	3-5
Wembley v Leatherhead	1-5
Yorkshire Amateur v Ossett Albion	1-1
r Hornchurch v Aveley	0-0
r Loughborough College v Accles & Pollock (Oldbury)	0-3
r Norton Woodseats v Bulwell Forest Villa	7-0
r Ossett Albion v Yorkshire Amateur	0-2
r2 Aveley v Hornchurch	2-1

Round One

Bishops Stortford v Herne Bay	1-0
Bromley v Walthamstow Avenue	2-1
Corinthian Casuals v Torpoint Athletic	3-0 N
Dagenham v Harlow Town	1-0
Enfield v Walton & Hersham	5-1
Fareham Town v St Albans City	1-2
Ferndale Youth Centre v Carshalton Athletic	0-7 N
Ferryhill Athletic v Evenwood Town	4-2
Finchley v Dulwich Hamlet	2-0
Gosport Borough Athletic v Eastbourne	1-2
Hayes v Grays Athletic	3-3
Hendon v Harwich & Parkeston	3-1
Lancing Athletic v Kingstonian	0-3
Leyton v Hemel Hempstead Town	2-2
Leytonstone v Tooting & Mitcham United	4-2
Loughborough College v Norton Woodseats	3-0
Maidenhead United v Windsor & Eton	3-0
Maidstone United v Barking	1-2
Moor Green v Crook Town	1-2
Oxford City v Leatherhead	2-3
Skelmersdale United v Alvechurch	0-2
Spennymoor United v Eastwood Town	1-1
Stanley United v Penrith	0-2
Stowmarket v Woking	3-2
Sutton United v Clapton	7-0
Wealdstone v Hitchin Town	4-1
West Auckland Town v Prestwich Heys	4-2
Whitby Town v Bishop Auckland	1-3
Willington v Tow Law Town	1-3
Witney Town v Hounslow Town	2-1
Wycombe Wanderers v Aveley	2-1
Yorkshire Amateur v Whitley Bay	1-2
r Eastwood Town v Spennymoor United	2-3
r Grays Athletic v Hayes	1-2
r Hemel Hempstead Town v Leyton	0-1

Round Two

Barking v Ferryhill Athletic	1-0
Corinthian Casuals v Hayes	1-2
Crook Town v West Auckland Town	2-1
Eastbourne v Enfield	0-5
Finchley v Bishop Auckland	1-3
Hendon v Carshalton Athletic	4-0
Leytonstone v Bishops Stortford	3-1
Loughborough College v Bromley	4-1
Maidenhead United v Leatherhead	0-2
Spennymoor United v Leyton	1-3
Stowmarket v Alvechurch	2-2
Sutton United v Dagenham	5-0
Wealdstone v Tow Law Town	2-1
Whitley Bay v Kingstonian	3-0
Witney Town v St Albans City	2-2
Wycombe Wanderers v Penrith	1-0
r Alvechurch v Stowmarket	3-2
r St Albans City v Witney Town	4-1

Round Three

Barking v Wealdstone	1-3
Enfield v Alvechurch	2-3
Hendon v Leytonstone	2-1
Leatherhead v Hayes	2-2
Leyton v Whitley Bay	0-5
Loughborough College v Crook Town	1-2
Sutton United v Bishop Auckland	2-1
Wycombe Wanderers v St Albans City	1-1
r Hayes v Leatherhead	0-1
r St Albans City v Wycombe Wanderers	0-3

Round Four

Crook Town v Alvechurch	0-2
Hendon v Wycombe Wanderers	2-1 N
Wealdstone v Leatherhead	2-1 N
Whitley Bay v Sutton United	2-0 N

Semi Finals

Hendon v Whitley Bay	2-1 N
Wealdstone v Alvechurch	1-0 N

Final

Wealdstone v Hendon	3-1 N

1966/67

Preliminary Round

3 Lytham St Annes & Fylde v Manchester YMCA	2-4
4 Northern Nomads v Stork	3-1
Wembley v Newton	1-2
5 Doncaster United Amateurs v Thackley	1-0
Hall Road Rangers v Guiseley	1-4
Harrogate Railway Athletic v Brook Sports	0-3
Hull University v Ossett Albion	2-4
Keighley Central v Leeds Ashley Road	0-1
Kingburn Athletic v St Johns College (York)	1-4
Leeds University v North Ferriby United	1-1
Salts v Harrogate Town	0-4
7 Anstey Nomads v Accles & Pollock (Oldbury)	1-1
Lucas Sports v Coventry Amateur	3-1
Paget Rangers v Stratford Town	3-1
Pershore United v Boldmere St Michaels	3-1
Silhill v Smethwick Highfield	1-2
Staffordshire Casuals v Highgate U (Birmingham)	n/a
8 Birmingham City Police v Blakenall	5-2
Cross Castle United v Crescionians	3-2
Jack Moulds Athletic v Old Wulfrunians	3-1
Sutton Coldfield Town v Blackheath Town	7-1
Wrockwardine Wood v Bournville Athletic	5-0
9 Gorleston v City of Norwich School OBU	2-2
11 Arlesey Town v Shillington	0-0
Baldock Town v Letchworth Town	3-4
Electrolux v Ampthill Town	4-3
Hertford Town v Buntingford Town	6-3
Royston Town v Chesham United	0-3
Sandy Albions v Berkhamsted Town	5-1
Stotfold v Hemel Hempstead Town	0-2
Vauxhall Motors v Tring Town	2-2
12 Civil Service v Kingsbury Town	1-1
Edgware Town v Polytechnic	2-0
Hampton v Wembley	1-1
Highfield v Rayners Lane	2-3
Uxbridge v Staines Town	1-4
Wingate v Ruislip Manor	2-2
Wood Green Town v Willesden	2-6
13 Beckenham Town v Bexley	5-1
Crockenhill v Herne Bay	2-2
Faversham Town v Brentstonians	3-5
14 Bognor Regis Town v Shoreham	1-1
Haywards Heath v Lancing Athletic	4-1
Lewes v Selsey	4-3
Worthing v Chichester City	0-1
15 Egham Town v Croydon Amateur	1-0
Farnham Town v Dorking	4-3
Godalming & Farncombe v Camberley	4-2
Merstham v Reigate Priory	5-4
Merton Rushmore v Horsham	2-2
Redhill v Banstead Athletic	4-2
Sidley United v Frimley Green	0-0
Whyteleafe v Three Bridges United	1-1
16 Boreham Wood v Kings Langley	5-5
Cheshunt (2) v Ware	2-2
Epping Town v Leavesden Hospital	2-1
Saffron Walden Town v Shefford Town	1-2
17 Barkingside v Canvey Island	2-1
Eton Manor v Tilbury	0-1
Rainham Town v Chingford	1-0
18 Addlestone v Royal Arsenal Sports	6-1
BAC Weybridge v Lion Sports	1-2
Chobham v Malden Town	4-1
Epsom & Ewell v Ulysses	1-3
Hermes v Molesey	0-1
Petters Sports v West Wickham	0-1
Whitehawk v Westfield	5-2
19 Chalfont St Peter v Marlow	0-2
Didcot Town v Wolverton Town & BR	3-1
Hazells Aylesbury v Newbury Town	3-0
Wokingham Town v Aylesbury United	2-1
20 Morris Motors v Pressed Steel	6-0
21 Hamworthy v Longfleet St Marys	3-0
Netley Sports v Swaythling Athletic	n/a
22 Swindon Victoria v Warminster Town	5-2
23 Hanham Athletic v Keynsham Town	4-1
Lydbrook Athletic v Soundwell	1-0
5r North Ferriby United v Leeds University	0-2
7r Accles & Pollock (Oldbury) v Anstey Nomads	n/a
9r City of Norwich School OBU v Gorleston	1-3
11r Shillington v Arlesey Town	4-3
r Tring Town v Vauxhall Motors	0-2
12r Kingsbury Town v Civil Service	3-1
r Ruislip Manor v Wingate	2-1
r Wembley v Hampton	2-1
13r Herne Bay v Crockenhill	0-1
14r Shoreham v Bognor Regis Town	2-3
15r Frimley Green v Sidley United	0-2
r Horsham v Merton Rushmore	3-0
r Three Bridges United v Whyteleafe	2-3
16r Kings Langley v Boreham Wood	3-1
r Ware v Cheshunt (2)	2-4

Qualifying Round One

1 Blyth Spartans v North Shields	2-5
Hearts of Liddesdale v Egremont Town	9-0
Shankhouse v Heaton Stannington	3-4
2 Durham City v Stockton	3-0
Hylton CW v Acklam Steelworks	0-3
Shildon v Billingham Synthonia	3-4
South Bank v Consett	1-3
3 East Chorlton Amateur v Chadderton	1-1
Linotype & Machinery v Old Blackburnians	1-0
Manchester YMCA v Dukinfield Town	1-1
Old Altrinchamians v Chloride Recreation	2-2
4 Guinness Exports v Winnington Park	2-1
Marine v Formby	4-1
Newton v Northern Nomads	n/a
Port Sunlight v Ashville	2-2
5 Brook Sports v Leeds University	n/a
Harrogate Town v Doncaster United Amateurs	1-1
Leeds Ashley Road v Guiseley	1-6
St Johns College (York) v Ossett Albion	2-2
6 Chesterfield Tube Works v Heeley Amateur	4-0
Hallam v Sheffield	2-1
7 Accles & Pollock (Oldbury) v Lutterworth Town	4-2
Pershore United v Lucas Sports	1-0
Sankey of Wellington v Paget Rangers	0-3
Smethwick Highfield v Highgate U (Birmingham)	0-1
8 Cross Castle United v Birmingham City Police	2-1
Madeley College v Sutton Coldfield Town	0-1
Walsgrave Lodge v Jack Moulds Athletic	2-0
Wrockwardine Wood v Walsall Wood	2-2
9 Cromer v Gorleston	2-2
Ramsey Town v Histon	2-3
Soham United v Eynesbury Rovers	5-2
Warboys Town v Cambridge University	1-2
11 Electrolux v Sandy Albions	3-1
Hemel Hempstead Town v Vauxhall Motors	3-1
Hertford Town v Shillington	4-0
Letchworth Town v Chesham United	3-2
12 Edgware Town v Rayners Lane	0-0
Staines Town v Feltham	2-3
Wembley v Ruislip Manor	9-2
Willesden v Kingsbury Town	0-0
13 Callender Athletic v Woolwich Polytechnic	3-0
Cray Wanderers v Beckenham Town	6-0
Crockenhill v Brentstonians	5-0
Erith & Belvedere v Lloyds Bank	4-1
14 Bognor Regis Town v East Grinstead	2-3
Chichester City v Lewes	7-2
Eastbourne United v Haywards Heath	4-1
Ferring v Wigmore Athletic	1-0
15 Egham Town v Redhill	1-3
Godalming & Farncombe v Merstham	n/a
Horsham v Farnham Town	2-1
Sidley United v Whyteleafe	2-1

1966/67 to 1967/68

16 Harpenden Town v Kings Langley	0-4
Hoddesdon Town v Epping Town	1-1
Luton Skefco Athletic v Rickmansworth Town	1-0
Shefford Town v Cheshunt (2)	1-1
17 East Ham United v West Thurrock Athletic	2-2
Edmonton (2) v Barkingside	2-3
Hornchurch v Woodford Town	1-0
Tilbury v Rainham Town	2-2
18 Addlestone v Cobham	5-2
Molesey v Chobham	3-3
Ulysses v West Wickham	0-1
Whitehawk v Lion Sports	2-4
19 Bracknell Town v Slough Town	0-4
Hungerford Town v Marlow	1-2
Huntley & Palmers v Hazells Aylesbury	1-4
Wokingham Town v Didcot Town	1-2
20 Kidlington v Wallingford Town	1-2
Moreton Town v Bicester Town	1-3
Morris Motors v Abingdon Town	3-2
Thame United v Chipping Norton Town	1-0
21 Brockenhurst v Totton	4-3e
Gosport Borough Athletic v Hawker Siddeley	3-2
Hamworthy v Netley Sports	2-3
Ryde Sports v Portsmouth Royal Navy	1-2
Ferndale Youth Centre v West Lavington	2-1
Melksham Town v Caine Town	3-0
Swindon Victoria v Bromham	2-3
Westbury United v Devizes Town	3-3
23 Forest Green Rovers v Wells City	0-3
Gloucester City YMCA v Bristol St George	0-2
Hanham Athletic v Lydbrook Athletic	4-3
Sharpness v Clevedon	4-0
24 Wellington v Exmouth Town	0-2
3r Chloride Recreation v Old Altrinchamians	4-1
r Dukinfield Town v Manchester YMCA	2-1
r East Chorlton Amateur v Chadderton	2-1
4r Ashville v Port Sunlight	2-0
5r Doncaster United Amateurs v Harrogate Town	0-1
r Ossett Albion v St Johns College (York)	0-1
8r Walsall Wood v Wrockwardine Wood	0-3
9r Gorleston v Cromer	5-0
11r Vauxhall Motors v Hemel Hempstead Town	1-0
12r Edgware Town v Rayners Lane	6-0
r Kingsbury Town v Willesden	3-0
16r Cheshunt (2) v Shefford Town	7-0
r Epping Town v Hoddesdon Town	0-2
17r Rainham Town v Tilbury	1-4
r West Thurrock Athletic v East Ham United	3-1
18r Chobham v Molesey	1-2e
22r Devizes Town v Westbury United	4-2

Qualifying Round Two

1 Heaton Stannington v Hearts of Liddesdale	1-4
North Shields v Cleator Moor Celtic	7-1
2 Acklam Steelworks v Billingham Synthonia	0-3
Durham City v Consett	0-3
3 Dukinfield Town v East Chorlton Amateur	1-2
Linotype & Machinery v Chloride Recreation	2-0
4 Guinness Exports v Ashville	3-3
Newton v Marine	1-0
5 Brook Sports v Harrogate Town	4-0
Guiseley v St Johns College (York)	2-0
6 Chesterfield Tube Works v Swallownest CW	3-0
Hallam v Bulwell Forest Villa	1-1
7 Accles & Pollock (Oldbury) v Paget Rangers	2-0
Pershore United v Highgate United (Birmingham)	0-3
8 Cross Castle United v Walsgrave Lodge	10-2
Wrockwardine Wood v Sutton Coldfield Town	1-2
9 Histon v Gorleston	1-2
Soham United v Cambridge University	1-2
10 Brantham Athletic v Whitton United	6-1
Bungay Town v Achilles	3-2
11 Letchworth Town v Hertford Town	1-1
Vauxhall Motors v Electrolux	2-2
12 Edgware Town v Feltham	3-1
Kingsbury Town v Wembley	1-2
13 Crockenhill v Cray Wanderers	1-3
Erith & Belvedere v Callender Athletic	2-0
14 Chichester City v Eastbourne United	1-7
Ferring v East Grinstead	0-3
15 Horsham v Godalming & Farncombe	2-0
Sidley United v Redhill	4-5
16 Cheshunt (2) v Kings Langley	1-1
Hoddesdon Town v Luton Skefco Athletic	4-4
Hornchurch v West Thurrock Athletic	1-2
Tilbury v Barkingside	4-0
18 Lion Sports v West Wickham	1-1
Molesey v Addlestone	2-4
19 Didcot Town v Marlow	0-1
Hazells Aylesbury v Slough Town	2-2
20 Morris Motors v Bicester Town	4-1
Thame United v Wallingford Town	5-4
21 Gosport Borough Athletic v Netley Sports	2-0
Portsmouth Royal Navy v Brockenhurst	0-2
22 Bromham v Melksham Town	3-3
Devizes Town v Ferndale Youth Centre	1-0
23 Hanham Athletic v Bristol St George	3-4
Sharpness v Wells City	2-1
24 EEM Dept (Devonport) v St Lukes College	4-3
Falmouth Docks v Exmouth Town	1-4
4r Ashville v Guinness Exports	3-6
6r Bulwell Forest Villa v Hallam	1-2
11r Electrolux v Vauxhall Motors	2-4
r Hertford Town v Letchworth Town	0-2
16r Kings Langley v Cheshunt (2)	5-1
r Luton Skefco Athletic v Hoddesdon Town	1-3
18r West Wickham v Lion Sports	3-0
19r Slough Town v Hazells Aylesbury	7-0
22r Melksham Town v Bromham	1-3

Qualifying Round Three

1 Hearts of Liddesdale v North Shields	2-5
2 Billingham Synthonia v Consett	0-1
3 East Chorlton Amateur v Linotype & Machinery	2-5
4 Newton v Guinness Exports	2-3
5 Guiseley v Brook Sports	1-1
6 Chesterfield Tube Works v Hallam	1-2
7 Highgate U (Bir'ham) v Accles & Pollock (Oldbury)	4-1
8 Cross Castle United v Sutton Coldfield Town	4-1
9 Gorleston v Cambridge University	0-4
10 Bungay Town v Brantham Athletic	3-6
11 Letchworth Town v Vauxhall Motors	0-2
12 Wembley v Edgware Town	3-0
13 Cray Wanderers v Erith & Belvedere	2-4
14 Eastbourne United v East Grinstead	4-2
15 Horsham v Redhill	2-1
16 Kings Langley v Hoddesdon Town	1-1
17 Tilbury v West Thurrock Athletic	0-2
18 West Wickham v Addlestone	1-2
19 Marlow v Slough Town	1-2
20 Morris Motors v Thame United	0-2
21 Gosport Borough Athletic v Brockenhurst	4-3
22 Bromham v Devizes Town	0-1
23 Bristol St George v Sharpness	3-1
24 Exmouth Town v EEM Dept (Devonport)	5-0
5r Brook Sports v Guiseley	5-3
16r Hoddesdon Town v Kings Langley	4-2

Qualifying Round Four

Alton Town v Woking	3-5
Brantham Athletic v Cambridge University	1-1
Bristol St George v Devizes Town	5-0
Brook Sports v Norton Woodseats	2-2
Clapton v Aveley	3-1
Consett v Willington	2-0
Exmouth Town v Torpoint Athletic	3-3
Ford United v Hoddesdon Town	0-3
Gosport Borough Athletic v Eastbourne United	5-0
Grays Athletic v Harlow Town	3-1
Hallam v Cross Castle United	2-1
Harrow Borough v Windsor & Eton	1-4
Ilford v Horsham	3-0
Linotype & Machinery v Prestwich Heys	1-2
Maidstone United v Addlestone	0-3
Moor Green v Highgate United (Birmingham)	0-0
Skelmersdale United v Guinness Exports	2-0
Stanley United v North Shields	2-2
Thame United v Vauxhall Motors	1-2
Tooting & Mitcham United v Southall	1-2
Walton & Hersham v Wembley	0-2
West Thurrock Athletic v Erith & Belvedere	2-0
Witney Town v Slough Town	0-4
Yorkshire Amateur v Evenwood Town	0-2
r Cambridge University v Brantham Athletic	2-1
r Highgate United (Birmingham) v Moor Green	1-0
r North Shields v Stanley United	1-0
r Norton Woodseats v Brook Sports	0-1
r Torpoint Athletic v Exmouth Town	3-2

Round One

Addlestone v Windsor & Eton	2-2
Barking v Woking	1-2
Bristol St George v Dagenham	1-0
Bromley v Corinthian Casuals	2-1
Brook Sports v Whitby Town	1-0
Cambridge University v Wembley	1-1
Crook Town v Loughborough College	1-2
Eastbourne v Oxford City	0-3
Enfield v Sutton United	3-0
Evenwood Town v Highgate United (Birmingham)	0-2
Ferryhill Athletic v Prestwich Heys	1-1
Grays Athletic v Dulwich Hamlet	2-2
Hallam v Whitley Bay	0-3
Hayes v Gosport Borough Athletic	0-4
Hoddesdon Town v Clapton	0-0
Hounslow Town v Harwich & Parkeston	2-3
Ilford v Hendon	0-3
Kingstonian v Carshalton Athletic	2-0
Leatherhead v Bishops Stortford	1-1
Leyton v Torpoint Athletic	1-1
Leytonstone v Wycombe Wanderers	4-2
North Shields v Alvechurch	3-0
Penrith v Eastwood Town	1-3
Skelmersdale United v Bishop Auckland	3-0
Slough Town v Hitchin Town	1-1
Southall v Maidenhead United	6-1
Spennymoor United v Consett	1-1
Tow Law Town v West Auckland Town	1-0
Vauxhall Motors v Finchley	1-3
Walthamstow Avenue v St Albans City	2-0
Wealdstone v Stowmarket	1-1
West Thurrock Athletic v Fareham Town	1-4
r Bishops Stortford v Leatherhead	1-2
r Clapton v Hoddesdon Town	3-1
r Consett v Spennymoor United	2-0
r Dulwich Hamlet v Grays Athletic	0-2
r Hitchin Town v Slough Town	1-3
r Prestwich Heys v Ferryhill Athletic	4-0
r Stowmarket v Wealdstone	1-1
r Torpoint Athletic v Leyton	2-4
r Wembley v Cambridge University	5-2
r Windsor & Eton v Addlestone	3-2
r2 Wealdstone v Stowmarket	5-2 N

Round Two

Bristol St George v Hendon	0-0
Bromley v Kingstonian	1-4
Brook Sports v Wealdstone	0-3
Clapton v Fareham Town	2-0
Consett v Gosport Borough Athletic	1-5
Harwich & Parkeston v Slough Town	0-2
Highgate United (Birmingham) v Eastwood Town	2-1
Leytonstone v Grays Athletic	5-1
Oxford City v North Shields	0-0
Prestwich Heys v Finchley	3-1
Skelmersdale United v Leyton	3-0
Southall v Woking	2-1
Tow Law Town v Leatherhead	0-1
Wembley v Enfield	1-2
Whitley Bay v Loughborough College	4-1
Windsor & Eton v Walthamstow Avenue	3-3
r Hendon v Bristol St George	5-0
r North Shields v Oxford City	1-1
r Walthamstow Avenue v Windsor & Eton	5-0
r2 Oxford City v North Shields	4-3 N

Round Three

Clapton v Leatherhead	2-3
Hendon v Bristol St George	4-3
Kingstonian v Gosport Borough Athletic	4-0
Leytonstone v Enfield	1-1
Prestwich Heys v Highgate United (Birmingham)	1-2
Skelmersdale United v Wealdstone	1-0
Southall v Slough Town	0-1
Whitley Bay v Walthamstow Avenue	0-2
r Enfield v Leytonstone	1-0

Round Four

Leatherhead v Hendon	0-3
Slough Town v Skelmersdale United	2-2
Walthamstow Avenue v Kingstonian	5-0
r Highgate United (Birmingham) v Enfield	0-6 N
r Skelmersdale United v Slough Town	1-0

Semi Finals

Enfield v Walthamstow Avenue	1-0 N
Skelmersdale United v Hendon	0-0 N
r Skelmersdale United v Hendon	2-2 N
r2 Skelmersdale United v Hendon	3-1 N

Final

Enfield v Skelmersdale United	0-0 N
r Enfield v Skelmersdale United	3-0 N

1967/68

Preliminary Round

1 Billingham Synthonia v Shildon	5-1
Blyth Spartans v Heaton Stannington	5-2
Eldra United v South Bank	2-4
Haig Colliery v Cleator Moor Celtic	1-2
Hearts of Liddesdale v Egremont Town	4-1
Newcastle University v Durham City	0-3
Norton Cricket Club Trust v Acklam Steelworks	2-0
Willington v Stanley United	0-8
2 Old Altrinchamians v Curzon Amateur	4-0
Old Blackburnians v Chadderton	1-2
3 Ashville v Warrington Town	2-0
Formby v Middleton Amateurs	3-0
Hoylake Athletic v Port Sunlight	3-2
Linotype & Machinery v Keele University	5-1
Northern Nomads v Stork	3-0
Winnington Park v Guinness Exports	1-6
4 Kingburn Athletic v Hedon & Marfleet United	n/a
5 Altofts v Salts	1-1
Bradford Rovers v Ossett Albion	1-2
Harrogate Railway Athletic v Guiseley	0-1
Leeds University v Yorkshire Amateur	4-3
Thackley v Harrogate Town	7-0
6 Bulwell Forest Villa v Nottingham University	n/a
Chesterfield Tube Works v Sheffield	0-3
Frecheville Community v Norton Woodseats	0-1
Grantham St Johns v Lincoln Clayton	0-1
Heeley Amateur v Swallownest CW	0-5
Ransome & Marles v Players Athletic	0-2

1967/68

7	Anstey Nomads v Pershore United	4-1
	Lutterworth Town v Lucas Sports	2-1
	Oldbury United v Dunlop Sports	4-2
	Paget Rangers v Stratford Town	2-1
	Sankey of Wellington v Coventry Amateur	0-1
	Smethwick Highfield v Accles & Pollock (Oldbury)	6-3
	Staffordshire Casuals v Silhill	1-4
	Stoke Works v SDF Sports	n/a
8	Boldmere St Michaels v Cross Castle United	2-2
	Bournville Athletic v Blakenall	1-1
	City of Birmingham Ed College v Christ Church	1-3
	Jack Moulds Athletic v Birmingham City Police	1-3
	Old Wulfrunians v Moor Green	2-4
	Sutton Coldfield Town v Madeley College	0-2
	Tividale v Tipton Town	1-4
	Walsall Wood v Cresconians	2-1
9	Warboys Town v St Ives Town	1-1
10	Gorleston v Thetford Town	1-5
11	Arlesey Town v Ampthill Town	2-1
	Berkhamsted Town v Royston Town	4-1
	Hertford Town v Electrolux	3-0
	Letchworth Town v Vauxhall Motors	2-0
	Sandy Albions v Buntingford Town	3-2
	Stotfold v Baldock Town	0-4
	Tring Town v Shillington	2-0
	Wolverton Town & BR v Barton Rovers	4-3
12	Civil Service v Wood Green Town	0-0
	Feltham v Rayners Lane	1-3
	Hampton v Uxbridge	3-0
	Highfield v Wingate	4-0
	Polytechnic v Harrow Borough	0-2
	Ruislip Manor v Willesden	0-1
	Staines Town v Kingsbury Town	5-0
13	Cray Wanderers v Callender Athletic	4-1
	Faversham Town v Brentstonians	1-1
	Slade Green Athletic v Lloyds Bank	0-1
	Swanley v Herne Bay	1-1
	Woolwich Polytechnic v Crockenhill	1-1
14	Bexhill Town v Wigmore Athletic	4-0
	Chichester City v Bognor Regis Town	3-3
	East Grinstead v Lancing Athletic	1-1
	Ferring v Brighton Old Grammarians	1-4
	Selsey v Eastbourne United	0-0
	Worthing v Shoreham	6-0
15	Banstead Athletic v Chertsey Town	6-0
	Croydon Amateur v Camberley	3-0
	Dorking v Reigate Priory	6-0
	Egham Town v Merstham	2-2
	Godalming & Farncombe v Frimley Green	1-2
	Horsham v Whyteleafe	5-1
	Merton Rushmore v Farnham Town	2-0
	Three Bridges v Redhill	1-5
16	Crown & Manor v Luton Skefco Athletic	1-0
	Harpenden Town v Epping Town	2-1
	Leighton Town v Shefford Town	5-1
	Saffron Walden Town v Cheshunt (2)	1-3
	Ware v Kings Langley	3-1
17	Aveley v Tilbury	2-2
	Edmonton (2) v East Ham United	1-0
	Ford United v Rainham Town	0-0
	Maldon Town v Chingford	2-1
	Woodford Town v Eton Manor	1-1
18	BAC Weybridge v Whitehawk	4-2
	Cobham v Molesey	2-1
	Epsom & Ewell v Ulysses	1-1
	Hermes v West Wickham	2-3
	Malden Town v Addlestone	0-4
	Petters Sports v Westfield	0-5
	Royal Arsenal Sports v Lion Sports	1-3
19	Amersham Town v Marlow	1-1
	Bracknell Town v Hazells Aylesbury	3-3
	Chalfont St Peter v Stony Stratford Town	3-1
	Hemel Hempstead Town v Chesham United	0-2
	Huntley & Palmers v Newbury Town	1-1
	Wokingham Town v Aylesbury United	2-3
20	Abingdon Town v Pressed Steel	3-2
	Chipping Norton Town v Thame United	2-1
	Morris Motors v Moreton Town	2-0
21	Ryde Sports v Alton Town	3-3
	Waterlooville v Longfleet St Marys	8-0
22	Calne Town v Westbury United	0-1
	Melksham Town v Ferndale Youth Centre	1-0
	Wells City v Warminster Town	7-0
23	Forest Green Rovers v Lydbrook Athletic	3-1
	Malvern Town v Sharpness	4-5
5r	Ossett Albion v Bradford Rovers	4-3e
r	Salts v Altofts	0-1
7r	SDF Sports v Stoke Works	1-0
8r	Blakenall v Bournville Athletic	6-1
r	Cross Castle United v Boldmere St Michaels	2-1e
9r	St Ives Town v Warboys Town	4-4e
12r	Wood Green Town v Civil Service	0-6
13r	Brentstonians v Faversham Town	1-1
r	Crockenhill v Woolwich Polytechnic	1-0
r	Herne Bay v Swanley	4-3
14r	Bognor Regis Town v Chichester City	1-3
r	Eastbourne United v Selsey	6-2
r	Lancing Athletic v East Grinstead	2-2
15r	Merstham v Egham Town	0-5
17r	Eton Manor v Woodford Town	4-1
r	Rainham Town v Ford United	0-1
r	Tilbury v Aveley	3-0
18r	Ulysses v Epsom & Ewell	1-3
19r	Hazells Aylesbury v Bracknell Town	3-0
r	Marlow v Amersham Town	2-0
r	Newbury Town v Huntley & Palmers	2-3
21r	Alton Town v Ryde Sports	3-1
9r2	Warboys Town v St Ives Town	2-1 N
13r2	Faversham Town v Brentstonians	3-0
14r2	East Grinstead v Lancing Athletic	5-0 N

Qualifying Round One

1	Billingham Synthonia v Stanley United	2-4
	Blyth Spartans v Durham City	2-1
	Hearts of Liddesdale v Cleator Moor Celtic	3-0
	South Bank v Norton Cricket Club Trust	6-1
2	Chadderton v Dukinfield Town	5-3e
	Manchester University v Wythenshaw Amateurs	3-4
	Old Altrinchamians v Manchester YMCA	1-1
3	Ashville v Marine	1-1
	Guinness Exports v Formby	3-1
	Hoylake Athletic v Northern Nomads	2-1
	Linotype & Machinery v Newton	0-0
4	Ainthorpe OB v Hall Road Rangers	4-3
	Doncaster United Amateurs v North Ferriby United	2-0
	Kingburn Athletic v St Johns College (York)	2-5
	Westella & Willerby v Hull Amateurs	4-0
5	Altofts v Guiseley	1-4
	Leeds University v Manningham Mills	2-2
	Ossett Albion v Leeds Ashley Road	2-1
	Thackley v Eccleshill	4-0
6	Lincoln Clayton v Bulwell Forest Villa	3-0
	Norton Woodseats v Swallownest CW	3-1
	Players Athletic v Boston	3-3
	Sheffield v Chapel Town	6-1
7	Anstey Nomads v Smethwick Highfield	1-3
	Lutterworth Town v Oldbury United	2-0
	SDF Sports v Coventry Amateur	1-2
	Silhill v Paget Rangers	0-4
8	Blakenall v Christ Church	5-4
	Cross Castle United v Moor Green	0-1
	Madeley College v Walsall Wood	0-2
	Tipton Town v Birmingham City Police	n/a
9	Eynesbury Rovers v Ramsey Town	1-4
	Oundle Town v Histon	1-10
	Somersham Town v Cambridge University	4-1
	Warboys Town v Soham United	1-3
10	Achilles v Brantham Athletic	2-1
	Cromer v Bungay Town	5-5
	Ipswich Electricity Supply v Whitton United	1-2
	Thetford Town v City of Norwich School OBU	1-1
11	Arlesey Town v Sandy Albions	1-2
	Berkhamsted Town v Baldock Town	0-5
	Hertford Town v Wolverton Town & BR	5-2
	Tring Town v Letchworth Town	1-0
12	Hampton v Civil Service	6-0
	Harrow Borough v Staines Town	0-0
	Rayners Lane v Edgware Town	1-1
	Willesden v Highfield	2-0
13	Cray Wanderers v Lloyds Bank	4-1
	Crockenhill v Berkhamsted Town	3-3
	Faversham Town v Bexley	2-1
	Herne Bay v Erith & Belvedere	3-2
14	Bexhill Town v Worthing	2-1
	Chichester City v Haywards Heath	0-3
	Eastbourne United v East Grinstead	0-1
	Lewes v Brighton Old Grammarians	4-1
15	Croydon Amateur v Merton Rushmore	5-0
	Egham Town v Dorking	1-0
	Frimley Green v Banstead Athletic	0-3
	Redhill v Horsham	1-1
16	Cheshunt (2) v Boreham Wood	1-0
	Crown & Manor v Harpenden Town	0-2
	Leighton Town v Rickmansworth Town	6-1
	Ware v Harlow Town	5-0
17	Eton Manor v Barkingside	4-2
	Ford United v Hornchurch	0-2
	Maldon Town v Canvey Island	5-0
	Tilbury v Edmonton (2)	1-1
18	Addlestone v Lion Sports	2-2
	Cobham v Chobham	1-1
	Epsom & Ewell v BAC Weybridge	4-2
	Westfield v West Wickham	2-1
19	Aylesbury United v Hazells Aylesbury	2-0
	Chalfont St Peter v Hungerford Town	0-1
	Chesham United v Didcot Town	3-0
	Marlow v Huntley & Palmers	3-1
20	Abingdon Town v Wallingford Town	3-1
	Chipping Norton Town v Bicester Town	1-2
	Morris Motors v Princes Risborough Town	4-0
	Witney Town v Kidlington	5-0
21	Alton Town v Brockenhurst	1-1
	Hawker Siddeley v Totton	3-0
	Pirelli General Cable Wks v Portsmouth Royal Navy	1-0
	Waterlooville v Swaythling Athletic	5-0
22	Melksham Town v Amesbury	4-3
	Wells City v West Lavington	8-3
	Westbury United v Bromham	3-4
	Westcott Youth Centre v Devizes Town	4-3 N
23	Forest Green Rovers v Clevedon	0-0
	Hanham Athletic v Cirencester Town	1-2
	Pegasus Juniors v Gloucester City YMCA	2-3
	Sharpness v Soundwell	2-1
24	EEM Dept (Devonport) v Falmouth Docks	5-1
	Ilminster Town v Exmouth Town	5-4
	St Lukes College v Wellington	6-1
2r	Manchester YMCA v Old Altrinchamians	n/a
3r	Marine v Ashville	3-0
r	Newton v Linotype & Machinery	1-2e
5r	Manningham Mills v Leeds University	2-3
6r	Boston v Players Athletic	0-4
10r	Bungay Town v Cromer	2-3
r	City of Norwich School OBU v Thetford Town	2-1
12r	Edgware Town v Rayners Lane	2-1
r	Staines Town v Harrow Borough	1-3
13r	Berkhamsted Town v Crockenhill	1-2e
15r	Horsham v Redhill	0-1
17r	Edmonton (2) v Tilbury	0-2
18r	Chobham v Cobham	1-3
r	Lion Sports v Addlestone	2-0
21r	Brockenhurst v Alton Town	4-3
23r	Clevedon v Forest Green Rovers	2-3

Qualifying Round Two

1	Hearts of Liddesdale v Blyth Spartans	0-6
	Stanley United v South Bank	0-0
2	Chloride Recreation v Chadderton	3-3
	Wythenshaw Amateurs v Manchester YMCA	0-2
3	Guinness Exports v Linotype & Machinery	7-0
	Marine v Hoylake Athletic	3-1
4	Doncaster United Amateurs v Ainthorpe OB	0-1
	Westella & Willerby v St Johns College (York)	n/a
5	Guiseley v Ossett Albion	0-3
	Leeds University v Thackley	0-3
6	Norton Woodseats v Sheffield	2-2
	Players Athletic v Lincoln Clayton	n/a
7	Coventry Amateur v Paget Rangers	1-0
	Lutterworth Town v Smethwick Highfield	3-1
8	Birmingham City Police v Walsall Wood	0-2
	Blakenall v Moor Green	3-2
9	Soham United v Histon	2-0
	Somersham Town v Ramsey Town	1-3
10	City of Norwich School OBU v Whitton United	1-1
	Cromer v Achilles	1-1
11	Baldock Town v Tring Town	1-4
	Hertford Town v Sandy Albions	3-1
12	Edgware Town v Harrow Borough	1-2
	Hampton v Willesden	1-1
13	Cray Wanderers v Faversham Town	2-2
	Herne Bay v Crockenhill	6-1
14	East Grinstead v Haywards Heath	0-3
	Lewes v Bexhill Town	3-1
15	Banstead Athletic v Croydon Amateur	2-4
	Egham Town v Redhill	1-5
16	Harpenden Town v Cheshunt (2)	0-5
	Leighton Town v Ware	3-2
17	Hornchurch v Eton Manor	4-1
	Tilbury v Maldon Town	1-1
18	Cobham v Lion Sports	0-0
	Epsom & Ewell v Westfield	6-1
19	Hazells Aylesbury v Chesham United	0-1
	Hungerford Town v Marlow	0-3
20	Abingdon Town v Bicester Town	1-2
	Morris Motors v Witney Town	2-4
21	Hawker Siddeley v Pirelli General Cable Works	2-4
	Waterlooville v Brockenhurst	6-1
22	Melksham Town v Westcott Youth Centre	2-3
	Wells City v Bromham	2-3
23	Cirencester Town v Gloucester City YMCA	4-0
	Sharpness v Forest Green Rovers	4-2
24	Ilminster Town v St Lukes College	0-3
	Saltash United v EEM Dept (Devonport)	0-5
1r	South Bank v Stanley United	4-2
2r	Chloride Recreation v Chadderton	0-1
6r	Sheffield v Norton Woodseats	1-3
10r	Cromer v Achilles	4-3e
r	Whitton United v City of Norwich School OBU	3-4
12r	Willesden v Hampton	0-2
13r	Faversham Town v Cray Wanderers	0-3
17r	Maldon Town v Tilbury	0-4
18r	Lion Sports v Cobham	3-1

Qualifying Round Three

1	Blyth Spartans v South Bank	3-0
2	Chadderton v Manchester YMCA	3-1
3	Marine v Guinness Exports	2-0
4	Ainthorpe OB v St Johns College (York)	3-3
5	Thackley v Ossett Albion	2-3
6	Players Athletic v Norton Woodseats	3-4
7	Coventry Amateur v Lutterworth Town	2-0
8	Walsall Wood v Blakenall	0-2
9	Ramsey Town v Soham United	3-4
10	City of Norwich School OBU v Cromer	9-2
11	Hertford Town v Tring Town	3-2
12	Hampton v Harrow Borough	0-0
13	Cray Wanderers v Herne Bay	6-1
14	Haywards Heath v Lewes	2-2
15	Croydon Amateur v Redhill	1-2
16	Cheshunt (2) v Leighton Town	1-1
17	Tilbury v Hornchurch	1-0
18	Epsom & Ewell v Lion Sports	2-2
19	Chesham United v Marlow	3-1
20	Witney Town v Bicester Town	6-3
21	Pirelli General Cable Works v Waterlooville	1-3
22	Westcott Youth Centre v Bromham	1-5
23	Cirencester Town v Sharpness	4-5
24	EEM Dept (Devonport) v St Lukes College	1-7 N

1967/68 to 1968/69

4r St Johns College (York) v Ainthorpe OB 3-3e
12r Harrow Borough v Hampton 1-2
14r Lewes v Haywards Heath 4-0
16r Leighton Town v Cheshunt (2) 0-4
18r Lion Sports v Epsom & Ewell 1-0
4r2 St Johns College (York) v Ainthorpe OB 1-0 N

Qualifying Round Four

25 Bristol St George v St Lukes College 4-1
Bromham v Sharpness 1-2
Blyth Spartans v West Auckland Town 1-1
Chadderton v Marine 0-3
Coventry Amateur v Blakenall 3-2
Dulwich Hamlet v Wembley 2-1
Evenwood Town v Consett 1-1
Gosport Borough Athletic v Waterlooville 6-0
Hallam v Brook Sports 2-1
Hampton v Barking 1-0a
Hertford Town v Hounslow Town 0-0a
Hitchin Town v Cheshunt (2) 4-1
Lion Sports v Lewes 0-3
Norton Woodseats v Highgate United (Birmingham) 2-1
Redhill v Walton & Hersham 1-1
Slough Town v Hoddesdon Town 2-0a
Soham United v Chesham United 1-1
St Johns College (York) v Ossett Albion 1-2
Stowmarket v City of Norwich School OBU 1-1
Tilbury v Maidstone United 2-0a
Tooting & Mitcham United v Dagenham 1-3
West Thurrock Athletic v Cray Wanderers 1-4
Whitby Town v North Shields 2-2
Witney Town v Corinthian Casuals 1-1
r Chesham United v Soham United 1-0
r City of Norwich School OBU v Stowmarket 3-0
r Consett v Evenwood Town 2-2
r Corinthian Casuals v Witney Town 4-2
r Hampton v Barking 3-3
r Hertford Town v Hounslow Town 0-3
r North Shields v Whitby Town 1-0
r Slough Town v Hoddesdon Town 4-1
r Tilbury v Maidstone United 3-0
r Walton & Hersham v Redhill 2-1
r West Auckland Town v Blyth Spartans 4-0
r2 Barking v Hampton 4-2
r2 Evenwood Town v Consett 2-0

Round One

Alvechurch v Tow Law Town 1-2
Barking v Hendon 1-0
Bishops Stortford v Walthamstow Avenue 5-3
Bristol St George v Leyton 3-1
Bromley v Walton & Hersham 0-0
Carshalton Athletic v Kingstonian 2-2
Chesham United v Maidenhead United 2-2
City of Norwich School OBU v Wycombe Wanderers 1-0
Clapton v Leytonstone 0-2
Corinthian Casuals v Hounslow Town 4-1
Coventry Amateur v Hallam 2-1
Cray Wanderers v Eastbourne 4-1
Crook Town v Evenwood Town 1-2
Eastwood Town v Bishop Auckland 1-0
Harwich & Parkeston v Fareham Town 1-0
Hayes v Grays Athletic 3-0
Hitchin Town v Sutton United 1-2
Ilford v Lewes 1-2
Leatherhead v Dagenham 1-2
Marine v Ferryhill Athletic 3-1
North Shields v Ossett Albion 3-0
Norton Woodseats v Whitley Bay 0-2
Penrith v Prestwich Heys 1-2
Sharpness v Dulwich Hamlet 1-2
Skelmersdale United v Spennymoor United 0-1
Slough Town v Finchley 3-2
Southall v Woking 2-0
St Albans City v Oxford City 1-2
Tilbury v Gosport Borough Athletic 2-0
Torpoint Athletic v Wealdstone 2-4
West Auckland Town v Loughborough College 2-2
Windsor & Eton v Enfield 1-3
r Kingstonian v Carshalton Athletic 4-3
r Loughborough College v West Auckland Town 0-1
r Maidenhead United v Chesham United 2-2
r Walton & Hersham v Bromley 3-1
r2 Chesham United v Maidenhead United 2-1 N

Round Two

Barking v Coventry Amateur 3-0
Bishops Stortford v Bristol St George 3-1
Dulwich Hamlet v Chesham United 1-1
Eastwood Town v Whitley Bay 1-0
Evenwood Town v Sutton United 0-0
Harwich & Parkeston v Corinthian Casuals 0-1
Hayes v Cray Wanderers 0-0
Lewes v Tilbury 3-4
Leytonstone v Southall 1-0
Marine v City of Norwich School OBU 2-1
North Shields v Enfield 2-3
Oxford City v Tow Law Town 2-1
Spennymoor United v Prestwich Heys 1-1
Walton & Hersham v Dagenham 1-2
Wealdstone v Kingstonian 2-0
West Auckland Town v Slough Town 1-3

r Chesham United v Dulwich Hamlet 4-2
r Cray Wanderers v Hayes 1-0
r Prestwich Heys v Spennymoor United 2-1
r Sutton United v Evenwood Town 3-0

Round Three

Corinthian Casuals v Chesham United 0-0
Cray Wanderers v Barking 0-0
Dagenham v Marine 0-0
Eastwood Town v Wealdstone 1-1
Leytonstone v Bishops Stortford 7-2
Oxford City v Prestwich Heys 4-2
Slough Town v Sutton United 1-1
Tilbury v Enfield 0-2
r Barking v Cray Wanderers 2-0
r Chesham United v Corinthian Casuals 1-0
r Marine v Dagenham 3-4
r Sutton United v Slough Town 1-0
r Wealdstone v Eastwood Town 4-1

Round Four

Enfield v Leytonstone 0-0
Oxford City v Chesham United 0-0
Sutton United v Dagenham 2-1
Wealdstone v Barking 3-1
r Chesham United v Oxford City 2-0
r Leytonstone v Enfield 0-0
r2 Enfield v Leytonstone 0-1 N

Semi Finals

Chesham United v Wealdstone 2-0 N
Leytonstone v Sutton United 0-0 N
r Sutton United v Leytonstone 1-3 N

Final

Leytonstone v Chesham United 1-0 N

1968/69

Preliminary Round

1 Blyth Spartans v Newcastle University 5-0
Heaton Stannington v Alnwick Town 0-11
Kings Regiment (Catterick) v South Bank 0-3
Norton Cricket Club Trust v Willington 2-0
Penrith v Billingham Synthonia 0-2
Shildon v Wingate 2-0
Stanley United v Consett 1-3
Washington v Durham City 2-2
2 Cleator Moor Celtic v Alston 0-2
Hearts of Liddesdale v Spadeadam n/a
Manchester University v Blackpool Mechanics 0-2
Whitefield v Manchester YMCA n/a
3 Ashville v Winnington Park 2-3
Chloride Recreation v Formby 3-0
Earle v Guinness Exports 0-6
Keele University v Newton 0-6
Old Altrinchamians v Middleton Amateurs 4-0
Port Sunlight v Northern Nomads 4-2
Stork v Curzon Ashton 0-0
4 Leeds & Carnegie College v Hull Amateurs n/a
Leeds Ashley Road v Hedon & Marfleet United 9-5
5 Clayton v Guiseley 3-3
Firth Sports v Birkenshaw Rovers 5-1
Harrogate Town v Harrogate Railway Athletic 0-1
Keighley Central v Yorkshire Amateur n/a
Manningham Mills v Brook Sports 1-4
Thackley v Bradford Rovers n/a
6 Bulwell Forest Villa v Nottingham University n/a
Players Athletic v Harrowby United 4-3
Sheffield v Swallownest CW 1-5
Sheffield University v Chesterfield Tube Works n/a
Stocksbridge Works v Frecheville Community 2-1
7 Accles & Pollock (Oldbury) v Stratford Town 0-0
Highgate United (Birmingham) v Anstey Nomads 4-0
Ibstock Penistone Rovers v Dunlop Sports 0-2
Lutterworth Town v Whitmore OB 4-2
Pershore United v Paget Rangers 1-1
Sankey of Wellington v Bermuda WMC 1-2
Smethwick Highfield v Oldbury United 0-6
8 Boldmere St Michaels v Cross Castle United 1-1
Chelmsley Town v Mile Oak Rovers 2-3
Madeley College v Solihull Amateur 1-1
Moor Green v Blakenall 2-1
Sutton Coldfield Town v Cresconians 8-1
Walsall Wood v City of Birmingham Ed College wo/s
9 Eynesbury Rovers v St Ives Town 4-1
Rothwell Town v Soham United 4-4
10 Brantham Athletic v Whitton United 1-2
11 Ampthill Town v Hertford Town 1-5
Barton Rovers v Berkhamsted Town 2-0
Buntingford Town v Royston Town 3-1
Esavian Sports v Arlesey Town 1-5
Shillington v Letchworth Town 1-2
Tring Town v Sandy Albions 4-1
Vauxhall Motors v Stotfold 2-0
Wolverton Town & BR v Electrolux 4-1

12 Civil Service v Highfield 3-4
Edgware Town v Kingsbury Town 0-5
Harrow Borough v Wingate 1-5
Rayners Lane v Hampton 0-3
Staines Town v Polytechnic 7-1
Uxbridge v Wembley 0-5
Willesden v Ruislip Manor 1-1
13 Beckenham Town v Erith & Belvedere 0-8
Brentstonians v Maidstone United 0-5
Callender Athletic v Woolwich Polytechnic 1-0
Herne Bay v Faversham Town 6-2
Midland Bank v Lloyds Bank 0-1
Swanley v Crockenhill 4-3
14 Bognor Regis Town v Haywards Heath 0-3
Chichester City v Arundel 2-1
East Grinstead v Worthing 1-0
Selsey v Lancing Athletic 1-3
Shoreham v Seaford Town 2-5
Wigmore Athletic v Eastbourne United 1-5
15 Banstead Athletic v Frimley Green 1-1
Croydon Amateur v Dorking 1-0
Egham Town v Horsham 2-1
Merstham v Reigate Priory 2-1
Merton Rushmore v Godalming & Farncombe 3-2
Old Salesians v Camberley 0-1
Three Bridges v Farnham Town 1-4
Whyteleafe v Redhill 0-3
16 Boreham Wood v Harpenden Town 4-1
Crown & Manor v Hoddesdon Town 1-4
Edmonton (2) v Ware 5-1
Leighton Town v Kings Langley 2-1
Rickmansworth Town v Baldock Town 2-3
Shefford Town v Harlow Town 0-5
17 Aveley v Rainham Town 0-0a
Maldon Town v Ford United 3-1
Woodford Town v Epping Town 3-1
18 Addlestone v West Wickham 6-0
BAC Weybridge v Lion Sports 2-1
Chobham v Malden Town 1-2
Hermes v Whitehawk 3-7
Molesey v Epsom & Ewell 1-1
Ulysses v Tooting & Mitcham United 0-1
Westfield v Royal Arsenal Sports 2-0
19 Bracknell Town v Aylesbury United 1-5
Didcot Town v Newbury Town 1-1
Huntley & Palmers v Hungerford Town 3-0
Marlow v Hazells Aylesbury 2-1
Stony Stratford Town v Hemel Hempstead Town 2-2
20 Abingdon Town v Wallingford Town 4-1
Thame United v Pressed Steel 8-2
Witney Town v Moreton Town 3-1
21 Lymington v Totton 1-0
Swaythling Athletic v Ryde Sports 3-0
Waterlooville v Pirelli General Cable Works 3-1
22 Bromham v Westbury United 4-2
Melksham Town v Ferndale Youth Centre 4-2
Pinehurst Youth Centre v Dowty New Mendip 3-1
Warminster Town v Calne Town 6-3
Wells City v Devizes Town 2-1
23 Clevedon v Soundwell 1-3
Hereford Lads Club v Credenhill 1-3
Keynsham Town v Hanham Athletic 1-1
Lydbrook Athletic v Forest Green Rovers 4-0
Malvern Town v Gloucester City YMCA 4-1
1r Durham City v Washington 4-2
3r Curzon Ashton v Stork 3-3e
5r Bradford Rovers v Thackley 2-0
r Guiseley v Clayton 4-3
7r Paget Rangers v Pershore United 1-0
r Stratford Town v Accles & Pollock (Oldbury) 4-1
8r Cross Castle United v Boldmere St Michaels 0-1
r Solihull Amateur v Madeley College 1-1
9r Soham United v Rothwell Town wo/s
12r Ruislip Manor v Willesden 1-0
15r Frimley Green v Banstead Athletic 3-0
17r Rainham Town v Aveley 0-1
18r Epsom & Ewell v Molesey 1-0
19r Hemel Hempstead Town v Stony Stratford Town 2-0
r Newbury Town v Didcot Town 2-0
23r Hanham Athletic v Keynsham Town 3-5
3r2 Curzon Ashton v Stork 4-3 N
8r2 Solihull Amateur v Madeley College 1-0e

Qualifying Round One

1 Blyth Spartans v Consett 1-0
Durham City v Alnwick Town 2-1
Norton Cricket Club Trust v Billingham Synthonia 0-7
South Bank v Shildon 2-4
2 Chadderton v Blackpool Mechanics 1-1
East Chorlton Amateur v Old Blackburnians 5-0
Spadeadam v Alston 3-4
Wythenshaw Amateurs v unknown n/a
3 Chloride Recreation v Curzon Ashton n/a
Gatley Amateur v Old Altrinchamians 1-2
Guinness Exports v Port Sunlight 11-0
Winnington Park v Newton 0-1
4 Doncaster United Ams v Leeds & Carnegie College 2-2
Leeds Ashley Road v Hall Road Rangers 3-2
Middlefield Welfare v Kingburn Athletic 2-1
North Ferriby United v Leeds University 3-2
5 Brook Sports v Emley 0-0
Firth Sports v Keighley Central 2-3
Guiseley v Harrogate Railway Athletic 1-5
Salts v Bradford Rovers 0-2

1968/69

6 Linby CW v Lincoln United	2-7	
Players Athletic v Bulwell Forest Villa	n/a	
Stocksbridge Works v Chapel Town	n/a	
Swallownest CW v Chesterfield Tube Works	n/a	
7 Highgate United (Birmingham) v Bermuda WMC	4-2	
Paget Rangers v Dunlop Sports	0-1	
Solihull Borough v Lutterworth Town	2-1	
Stratford Town v Oldbury United	2-1	
8 Boldmere St Michaels v Solihull Amateur	1-1	
Mile Oak Rovers v Walsall Wood	2-1	
Moor Green v Bournville Athletic	3-2	
Old Wulfrunians v Sutton Coldfield Town	0-4	
9 Eynesbury Rovers v Ramsey Town	0-2	
Oundle Town v Somersham Town	1-2	
Parson Drove United v Soham United	wo/s	
Warboys Town v Histon	0-0	
10 Achilles v Leiston	2-3	
Bungay Town v Whitton United	0-3	
Stowmarket v Gorleston	2-1	
Thetford Town v Watton United	2-2	
11 Barton Rovers v Tring Town	3-1	
Buntingford Town v Arlesey Town	0-1	
Vauxhall Motors v Hertford Town	1-4	
Wolverton Town & BR v Letchworth Town	3-3	
12 Feltham v Hampton	0-2	
Kingsbury Town v Staines Town	0-2	
Wembley v Highfield	7-2	
Wingate v Ruislip Manor	0-1	
13 Bexley v Lloyds Bank	3-1	
Erith & Belvedere v Herne Bay	1-1	
Maidstone United v Callender Athletic	8-1	
Slade Green Athletic v Swanley	4-2	
14 Chichester City v East Grinstead	1-1	
Haywards Heath v Lancing Athletic	1-1	
Seaford Town v Brighton Old Grammarians	2-1	
Southwick v Eastbourne United	0-3	
15 Croydon Amateur v Merstham	4-1	
Egham Town v Camberley	4-2	
Farnham Town v Merton Rushmore	4-3	
Redhill v Frimley Green	1-2	
16 Baldock Town v Cheshunt (2)	0-3	
Boreham Wood v Leighton Town	1-2	
Hoddesdon Town v Edmonton (2)	3-1	
Saffron Walden Town v Harlow Town	0-1	
17 Barkingside v Eton Manor	1-1	
Canvey Island v Aveley	1-1	
Hornchurch v Woodford Town	2-1	
Maldon Town v East Ham United	1-1	
18 BAC Weybridge v Addlestone	3-1	
Cobham v Epsom & Ewell	0-1	
Malden Town v Tooting & Mitcham United	1-4	
Whitehawk v Westfield	2-0	
19 Aylesbury United v Amersham Town	2-1	
Huntley & Palmers v Marlow	0-3	
Newbury Town v Chalfont St Peter	1-3	
Wokingham Town v Hemel Hempstead Town	3-1	
20 Bicester Town v Morris Motors	5-2	
Chipping Norton Town v Abingdon Town	1-3	
Princes Risborough Town v Witney Town	2-2	
Thame United v Kidlington	10-0	
21 Alton Town v Portsmouth Royal Navy	2-1	
Hamworthy v Lymington	3-3	
Strongs Portsmouth v Waterlooville	0-2	
Swaythling Athletic v Longfleet St Marys	4-0	
22 Bromham v Amesbury	7-0	
Melksham Town v Warminster Town	6-1	
Pinehurst Youth Centre v Bemerton Athletic	3-2	
West Lavington v Wells City	3-4	
23 Cirencester Town v Soundwell	5-0	
Credenhill v Coleford United	4-0	
Keynsham Town v Lydbrook Athletic	2-1	
Pegasus Juniors v Malvern Town	2-3	
24 Exmouth Town v Saltash United	3-1	
2r Blackpool Mechanics v Chadderton	2-0	
4r Leeds & Carnegie College v Doncaster United Ams	4-1	
5r Emley v Brook Sports	3-2	
8r Solihull Amateur v Boldmere St Michaels	2-1	
9r Histon v Warboys Town	4-3	
10r Watton United v Thetford Town	0-2	
11r Letchworth Town v Wolverton Town & BR	2-1	
13r Herne Bay v Erith & Belvedere	7-3	
14r East Grinstead v Chichester City	0-2	
r Lancing Athletic v Haywards Heath	1-3	
17r Aveley v Canvey Island	3-1	
r East Ham United v Maldon Town	1-2	
r Eton Manor v Barkingside	2-0	
20r Witney Town v Princes Risborough Town	2-1	
21r Lymington v Hamworthy	1-0	

Qualifying Round Two

1 Billingham Synthonia v Blyth Spartans	4-3	
Durham City v Shildon	1-2	
2 Blackpool Mechanics v Wythenshaw Amateurs	4-0	
East Chorlton Amateur v Alston	2-1	
3 Chloride Recreation v Newton	4-4	
Guinness Exports v Old Altrinchamians	2-1	
4 Leeds Ashley Road v North Ferriby United	2-2	
Middlefield Welfare v Leeds & Carnegie College	n/a	
5 Emley v Keighley Central	4-2	
Harrogate Railway Athletic v Bradford Rovers	2-0	
6 Players Athletic v Swallownest CW	0-0	
Stocksbridge Works v Lincoln United	3-3	

7 Dunlop Sports v Solihull Borough	3-2	
Highgate United (Birmingham) v Stratford Town	1-1	
8 Moor Green v Mile Oak Rovers	7-3	
Solihull Amateur v Sutton Coldfield Town	1-2	
9 Parson Drove United v Ramsey Town	3-2	
Somersham Town v Histon	0-2	
10 Leiston v Thetford Town	2-7	
Whitton United v Stowmarket	0-3	
11 Hertford Town v Arlesey Town	5-0	
Letchworth Town v Barton Rovers	7-0	
12 Ruislip Manor v Staines Town	3-2	
Wembley v Hampton	2-1	
13 Bexley v Slade Green Athletic	4-5	
Maidstone United v Herne Bay	2-0	
14 Chichester City v Haywards Heath	3-0	
Seaford Town v Eastbourne United	0-3	
15 Farnham Town v Croydon Amateur	0-5	
Frimley Green v Egham Town	3-1	
16 Cheshunt (2) v Harlow Town	3-1	
Hoddesdon Town v Leighton Town	2-1	
17 Aveley v Maldon Town	4-2	
Hornchurch v Eton Manor	3-1	
18 BAC Weybridge v Epsom & Ewell	2-2	
Whitehawk v Tooting & Mitcham United	0-1	
19 Chalfont St Peter v Wokingham Town	2-9	
Marlow v Aylesbury United	1-0	
20 Abingdon Town v Thame United	0-0	
Bicester Town v Witney Town	0-5	
21 Alton Town v Waterlooville	3-0	
Lymington v Swaythling Athletic	2-1	
22 Bromham v Wells City	9-1	
Melksham Town v Pinehurst Youth Centre	3-1	
23 Cirencester Town v Malvern Town	1-1	
Keynsham Town v Credenhill	2-2	
24 Exmouth Town v Ilminster Town	0-0	
St Lukes College v Wellington	2-2	
3r Newton v Chloride Recreation	4-5	
4r North Ferriby United v Leeds Ashley Road	n/a	
6r Lincoln United v Stocksbridge Works	8-0	
r Swallownest CW v Players Athletic	2-1	
7r Stratford Town v Highgate United (Birmingham)	1-0	
18r Epsom & Ewell v BAC Weybridge	2-0	
20r Thame United v Abingdon Town	1-0	
23r Credenhill v Keynsham Town	1-4	
r Malvern Town v Cirencester Town	1-2	
24r Ilminster Town v Exmouth Town	2-3	
r Wellington v St Lukes College	0-3	

Qualifying Round Three

1 Billingham Synthonia v Shildon	2-2	
2 East Chorlton Amateur v Blackpool Mechanics	2-4e	
3 Chloride Recreation v Guinness Exports	2-3	
4 Leeds & Carnegie College v North Ferriby United	3-1	
5 Emley v Harrogate Railway Athletic	3-2	
6 Lincoln United v Swallownest CW	n/a	
7 Stratford Town v Dunlop Sports	4-1	
8 Moor Green v Sutton Coldfield Town	0-2	
9 Parson Drove United v Histon	0-1	
10 Stowmarket v Thetford Town	6-1	
11 Letchworth Town v Hertford Town	1-1	
12 Ruislip Manor v Wembley	0-0	
13 Maidstone United v Slade Green Athletic	1-1	
14 Chichester City v Eastbourne United	4-1	
15 Croydon Amateur v Frimley Green	2-2	
16 Hoddesdon Town v Cheshunt (2)	0-4	
17 Aveley v Hornchurch	0-1	
18 Tooting & Mitcham United v Epsom & Ewell	5-0	
19 Marlow v Wokingham Town	2-1	
20 Thame United v Witney Town	3-2	
21 Lymington v Alton Town	0-3	
22 Melksham Town v Bromham	6-4	
23 Keynsham Town v Cirencester Town	1-3	
24 Exmouth Town v St Lukes College	2-2	
1r Shildon v Billingham Synthonia	0-3	
6r Swallownest CW v Lincoln United	2-4	
11r Hertford Town v Letchworth Town	3-0	
12r Wembley v Ruislip Manor	3-1	
13r Slade Green Athletic v Maidstone United	2-4	
15r Frimley Green v Croydon Amateur	0-2	
24r St Lukes College v Exmouth Town	3-7	

Qualifying Round Four

Alvechurch v Stratford Town	4-0	
Bishop Auckland v Whitby Town	1-2	
Blackpool Mechanics v Guinness Exports	2-2	
Cheshunt (2) v Clapton	2-1	
Chichester City v Hornchurch	1-3	
City of Norwich School OBU v Hitchin Town	1-3	
Coventry Amateur v Sutton Coldfield Town	2-2	
Eastbourne v Carshalton Athletic	0-1	
Ferryhill Athletic v Billingham Synthonia	0-0	
Gosport Borough Athletic v Alton Town	0-0	
Hertford Town v Thame United	5-1	
Hounslow Town v Windsor & Eton	1-2	
Ilford v Tilbury	2-1	
Lewes v Cray Wanderers	1-1	
Loughborough College v Lincoln United	0-3	
Maidenhead United v St Albans City	0-1	
Maidstone United v Leyton	2-4	
Melksham Town v Exmouth Town	7-2	
Norton Woodseats v Leeds & Carnegie College	1-4	

Ossett Albion v Emley	0-2	
Sharpness v Cirencester Town	0-6	
Stowmarket v Histon	3-2	
Tooting & Mitcham United v Croydon Amateur	1-1	
Wembley v Marlow	5-1	
r Alton Town v Gosport Borough Athletic	5-1	
r Billingham Synthonia v Ferryhill Athletic	7-2	
r Cray Wanderers v Lewes	5-2	
r Croydon Amateur v Tooting & Mitcham United	2-0	
r Guinness Exports v Blackpool Mechanics	4-0	
r Sutton Coldfield Town v Coventry Amateur	0-1	

Round One

Alton Town v Croydon Amateur	3-0	
Carshalton Athletic v Finchley	2-1	
Chesham United v Walthamstow Avenue	0-2	
Coventry Amateur v Eastwood Town	1-1	
Dagenham v Windsor & Eton	4-0	
Dulwich Hamlet v Corinthian Casuals	1-1	
Emley v Evenwood Town	2-1	
Enfield v Leatherhead	0-0	
Fareham Town v Cirencester Town	1-1	
Grays Athletic v Barking	1-1	
Hayes v Bristol St George	2-1	
Hendon v Hornchurch	2-0	
Hertford Town v Wealdstone	0-0	
Hitchin Town v Stowmarket	2-0	
Ilford v Cheshunt (2)	0-1	
Kingstonian v Southall	1-1	
Leeds & Carnegie College v Billingham Synthonia	2-1	
Lincoln United v Crook Town	2-1	
Marine v West Auckland Town	2-2	
Melksham Town v Harwich & Parkeston	2-3	
North Shields v Spennymoor United	4-1	
Oxford City v Wycombe Wanderers	3-2	
Skelmersdale United v Hallam	3-0	
St Albans City v Bishops Stortford	3-0	
Sutton United v Bromley	9-0	
Torpoint Athletic v Cray Wanderers	1-3	
Tow Law Town v Alvechurch	3-1	
Walton & Hersham v Slough Town	2-2	
Wembley v Leyton	1-0	
Whitby Town v Guinness Exports	1-0	
Whitley Bay v Prestwich Heys	1-0	
Woking v Leytonstone	0-1	
r Barking v Grays Athletic	5-0	
r Cirencester Town v Fareham Town	3-1	
r Corinthian Casuals v Dulwich Hamlet	1-2	
r Eastwood Town v Coventry Amateur	1-3	
r Leatherhead v Enfield	1-1	
r Slough Town v Walton & Hersham	2-1	
r Southall v Kingstonian	0-4	
r Wealdstone v Hertford Town	3-3	
r West Auckland Town v Marine	0-2	
r2 Enfield v Leatherhead	1-0 N	
r2 Wealdstone v Hertford Town	1-1	
r3 Wealdstone v Hertford Town	1-1 N	
r4 Hertford Town v Wealdstone	0-1	

Round Two

Alton Town v Whitley Bay	0-2	
Barking v Wembley	4-1	
Carshalton Athletic v Whitby Town	2-2	
Cheshunt (2) v Enfield	0-0	
Cray Wanderers v Leytonstone	2-2	
Dagenham v Harwich & Parkeston	0-1	
Emley v Dulwich Hamlet	1-0	
Hayes v Tow Law Town	2-0	
Kingstonian v Lincoln United	2-0	
Leeds & Carnegie College v Sutton United	2-5	
Marine v Walthamstow Avenue	2-0	
North Shields v Coventry Amateur	3-0	
Skelmersdale United v Oxford City	1-1	
Slough Town v Hitchin Town	4-0	
St Albans City v Hendon	0-2	
Wealdstone v Cirencester Town	3-1	
r Enfield v Cheshunt (2)	2-1	
r Leytonstone v Cray Wanderers	2-0	
r Oxford City v Skelmersdale United	1-3	
r Whitby Town v Carshalton Athletic	1-0	

Round Three

Harwich & Parkeston v Enfield	1-1	
Leytonstone v Kingstonian	1-0	
North Shields v Hendon	1-1	
Skelmersdale United v Whitby Town	3-1	
Sutton United v Marine	2-0	
Wealdstone v Hayes	1-0	
Whitley Bay v Slough Town	3-2	
r Emley v Barking	0-1	
r Enfield v Harwich & Parkeston	4-0	
r Hendon v North Shields	0-2	

Round Four

Enfield v Skelmersdale United	1-2	
North Shields v Wealdstone	1-0	
Sutton United v Leytonstone	3-1	
Whitley Bay v Barking	5-1	

1968/69 to 1969/70

Semi Finals

	North Shields v Skelmersdale United	1-1 N
	Sutton United v Whitley Bay	4-2 N
r	Skelmersdale United v North Shields	1-2 N

Final

	North Shields v Sutton United	2-1 N

1969/70

Preliminary Round

1	Ashington v Winlaton Mill Athletic	5-2
	Billingham Synthonia v Ferryhill Athletic	3-1
	Blyth Spartans v Heaton Stannington	5-1
	Norton Cricket Club Trust v Alnwick Town	0-6
	Shildon v Stanley United	0-3
	Wallsend v Newcastle University	3-2
	Washington v Willington	1-2
	Wingate v South Bank	1-1
2	Annan Athletic v Hearts of Liddesdale	2-1
	Bishop Auckland v Consett	2-3
	Blackpool Rgrs v Lytham St Annes & Fylde YMCA	1-3
	Cleator Moor Celtic v Alston	0-1
	Manchester YMCA v Blackpool Mechanics	1-2
	North Withington v Little Lever	2-1
	Penrith v Durham City	2-5
	Wythenshaw Amateurs v Old Blackburnians	0-2
3	Curzon Ashton v Winnington Park	1-2
	East Chorlton Amateur v Stork	3-2e
	Irlam Town v Northern Nomads	1-0
	Middlewich Athletic v Middleton Amateurs	4-1
	Newton v Chadderton	0-2
	Old Altrinchamians v Chloride Recreation	1-3
	Port Sunlight v Formby	2-0
4	Brook Sports v Hull Amateurs	9-0
	Whitkirk Wanderers v Harrogate Railway Athletic	3-1
5	Keighley Central v Clayton	2-1
	Manningham Mills v Birkenshaw Rovers	3-2
	Yorkshire Amateur v Knaresborough	2-3
6	British Steel Co (Scunthorpe) v Clifton All Whites	wo/s
	Linby CW v Chesterfield Tube Works	n/a
	Players Athletic v Frecheville Community	n/a
	Roe Farm Athletic v Chapel Town	2-1
	Stocksbridge Works v Ollerton Colliery	3-3
	Swallownest CW v Nottingham University	0-0
7	Dunlop Sports v Anstey Nomads	2-3
	GKN Sankey v Bermuda WMC	n/a
	Highgate United (Birmingham) v Midland Athletic	2-3
	Oldbury United v Lutterworth Town	2-2e
	Paget Rangers v Stratford Town	1-0
	Pershore United v Newfoundpool WMC	0-3
	Smethwick Highfield v Solihull Amateur	0-3
	Solihull Borough v Whitmore OB	1-0
8	Boldmere St Michaels v Blakenall	2-0
	Chelmsley Town v Birmingham City Police	3-0
	Madeley College v Oldswinford	1-2
	Mile Oak Rovers v Walsall Wood	2-1
	Moor Green v Bournville Athletic	3-0
	Northfield Town v St Peters College Birmingham	4-1
	Westphilians v Sutton Coldfield Town	1-5
9	Histon v Parson Drove United	2-0
	Irthlingborough Diamonds v Ramsey Town	6-1
10	Thetford Town v Gorleston	1-4
11	Ampthill Town v Shillington	4-1
	Arlesey Town v Barton Rovers	1-1
	Buntingford Town v Tring Town	2-2
	Electrolux v Vauxhall Motors	0-5
	Kingston Rovers v Sandy Albions	0-0
	Letchworth Town v Wolverton Town & BR	6-1
	Royston Town v Berkhamsted Town	4-0
12	Civil Service v Willesden	2-1
	Edgware Town v Feltham	4-1
	Harrow Borough v Hampton	0-2
	Hounslow Town v Polytechnic	4-0
	Kingsbury Town v Highfield	2-0
	Rayners Lane v Uxbridge	3-3
	Ruislip Manor v Wingate	0-1
	Staines Town v Borough Road College	3-0
13	Brentstonians v Tunbridge Wells	0-2
	Callender Athletic v Maidstone United	1-8
	Faversham Town v Tunnel Sports	1-3
	Slade Green Athletic v Lloyds Bank	4-1
	Swanley v Woolwich Polytechnic	4-0
14	Bognor Regis Town v Chichester City	4-2
	Eastbourne United v East Grinstead	3-1
	Seaford Town v Eastbourne	5-0
	Selsey v Lancing Athletic	3-2
	Shoreham v Bexhill Town	2-2
	Southwick v Lewes	0-0
	Wigmore Athletic v Arundel	0-4
	Worthing v Ringmer	3-0
15	Camberley v Banstead Athletic	1-2
	Egham Town v Redhill	1-2
	Farnham Town v Three Bridges	2-1
	Frimley Green v Reigate Priory	3-0
	Godalming & Farncombe v Dorking	0-3
	Old Salesians v Merstham	1-2
	Whyteleafe v Horsham	0-4
16	Boreham Wood v Baldock Town	4-2
	Edmonton (2) v Rickmansworth Town	8-0
	Harlow Town v Ware	3-1
	Harpenden Town v Harefield United	0-2
	Hoddesdon Town v Saffron Walden Town	8-1
	Kings Langley v Norsemen	0-1
	Leighton Town v Crown & Manor	4-0
17	Canvey Island v Tilbury	2-1
	Ford United v East Ham United	4-1
	Maldon Town v Aveley	1-6
	Rainham Town v Clapton	2-2
18	BAC Weybridge v Whitehawk	2-3
	Chobham v Cobham	1-0
	Lion Sports v Epsom & Ewell	0-0
	Molesey v Malden Town	2-3
	Royal Arsenal Sports v Westfield	0-2
	Surbiton Byron v West Wickham	1-0
	Tooting & Mitcham United v Chertsey Town	6-4
	Ulysses v Addlestone	1-2
19	Bracknell Town v Maidstone United	2-0
	Chalfont St Peter v Aylesbury United	2-0
	Hemel Hempstead Town v Amersham Town	1-0
	Stony Stratford Town v Marlow	1-2
	Wokingham Town v Newbury Town	1-2
20	Thame United v Moreton Town	0-1
22	Amesbury v Calne Town	2-4
	Westbury United v Devizes Town	2-1
23	Clevedon v Keynsham Town	0-2
	Evesham United v Coleford United	3-0
	Forest Green Rovers v Mangotsfield United	1-2
	Malvern Town v Soundwell	4-0
	Pegasus Juniors v Lydbrook Athletic	1-0
	Sharpness v Hanham Athletic	0-0
24	Falmouth Docks v Taunton BR	3-0
	Newquay v Ilminster Town	4-0
	St Lukes College v Exmouth Town	2-1
1r	South Bank v Wingate	2-2e
6r	Ollerton Colliery v Stocksbridge Works	n/a
7r	Lutterworth Town v Oldbury United	1-3e
11r	Arlesey Town v Barton Rovers	3-1
r	Sandy Albions v Kingston Rovers	2-0
r	Tring Town v Buntingford Town	6-1
12r	Uxbridge v Rayners Lane	2-1
14r	Bexhill Town v Shoreham	1-0
r	Lewes v Southwick	1-0
17r	Clapton v Rainham Town	1-0
18r	Epsom & Ewell v Lion Sports	1-0
23r	Hanham Athletic v Sharpness	2-4
1r2	South Bank v Wingate	5-0 N

Qualifying Round One

1	Billingham Synthonia v Ashington	3-1
	Blyth Spartans v Stanley United	3-0
	South Bank v Alnwick Town	1-1
	Willington v Wallsend	3-1
2	Annan Athletic v Consett	0-3
	Durham City v Alston	1-1
	Lytham St Annes & Fylde v Blackpool Mechanics	1-3
	Old Blackburnians v North Withington	1-4
3	Chadderton v East Chorlton Amateur	0-0
	Hanley Town v Chloride Recreation	4-2
	Port Sunlight v Irlam Town	2-1
	Winnington Park v Middlewich Athletic	1-3e
4	Brook Sports v Whitkirk Wanderers	1-0
	Hall Road Rangers v Leeds Ashley Road	3-3
	North Ferriby United v Ossett Albion	3-2
	St Johns College (York) v Harrogate Town	2-0
5	Knaresborough v Sheffield	3-1
	Manningham Mills v Guiseley	2-3
	Norton Woodseats v Keighley Central	4-3
	Salts v Bradford Rovers	0-2
6	unknown v Harrowby United	n/a
	Bulwell Forest Villa v unknown	n/a
	Frecheville Community v British Steel Co (Sc'thorpe)	2-1
	Linby CW v Roe Farm Athletic	1-5
7	Midland Athletic v Anstey Nomads	1-1e
	Newfoundpool WMC v Oldbury United	1-3
	Paget Rangers v GKN Sankey	5-0
	Solihull Borough v Solihull Amateur	2-1
8	Astwood Bank Rovers v Boldmere St Michaels	2-2
	Mile Oak Rovers v Chelmsley Town	2-3
	Moor Green v Oldswinford	1-2
	Northfield Town v Sutton Coldfield Town	1-4
9	Histon v Irthlingborough Diamonds	4-2
	Oundle Town v Soham United	2-2
	Rothwell Town v Peterborough Rovers	0-0
	Warboys Town v St Ives Town	4-0
10	Brantham Athletic v Achilles	4-2
	Bungay Town v Whitton United	3-5
	City of Norwich School OBU v Leiston	4-0
	Watton United v Gorleston	1-1
11	Ampthill Town v Tring Town	2-2
	Royston Town v Letchworth Town	1-3
	Stotfold v Arlesey Town	3-3
	Vauxhall Motors v Sandy Albions	1-1
12	Edgware Town v Hounslow Town	2-2
	Hampton v Civil Service	3-0
	Uxbridge v Staines Town	3-0
	Wingate v Kingsbury Town	0-1
13	Erith & Belvedere v Tunnel Sports	2-0
	Herne Bay v Crockenhill	4-0
	Slade Green Athletic v Swanley	2-3
	Tunbridge Wells v Maidstone United	1-4
14	Bexhill Town v Arundel	5-1
	Bognor Regis Town v Worthing	1-1
	Lewes v Selsey	3-1
	Seaford Town v Eastbourne United	1-1
15	Dorking v Frimley Green	2-0
	Farnham Town v Horsham	0-2
	Merstham v Redhill	1-5
	Merton United v Banstead Athletic	1-1
16	Harefield United v Edmonton (2)	0-0
	Hoddesdon Town v Harlow Town	1-1
	Leighton Town v Norsemen	1-0
	Shefford Town v Boreham Wood	0-6
17	Barkingside v Chingford	1-2
	Canvey Island v Clapton	1-0
	Epping Town v Eton Manor	2-1
	Ford United v Aveley	1-2
18	Chobham v Surbiton Byron	0-2
	Tooting & Mitcham United v Malden Town	4-2
	Westfield v Addlestone	0-2
	Whitehawk v Epsom & Ewell	2-2
19	Bracknell Town v Chalfont St Peter	1-1
	Hemel Hempstead Town v Hazells Aylesbury	1-0
	Huntley & Palmers v Didcot Town	0-0
	Marlow v Newbury Town	3-1
20	Abingdon Town v Moreton Town	0-1
	Chipping Norton Town v Bicester Town	1-4
	Wallingford Town v Kidlington	1-6
	Witney Town v Morris Motors	5-2
21	Brockenhurst v Longfleet St Marys	3-0
	Pirelli General Cable Works v Moneyfield Sports	4-0
	Totton v Liphook	2-3
22	Bromham v Warminster Town	8-0
	Calne Town v Westbury United	1-1
	Pinehurst Youth Centre v Bemerton Athletic	7-2
	West Lavington v Melksham Town	0-0
23	Gloucester City YMCA v Mangotsfield United	0-3
	Keynsham Town v Sharpness	1-1
	Malvern Town v Credenhill	9-0
	Pegasus Juniors v Evesham United	0-4
24	Newquay v St Lukes College	5-3
	Saltash United v Falmouth Docks	1-0
	St Austell v John Conway (Plymouth)	8-2
	Wellington v Royal Naval Engineering College	2-1
1r	Alnwick Town v South Bank	0-1
2r	Alston v Durham City	1-3e
3r	East Chorlton Amateur v Chadderton	0-2
4r	Leeds Ashley Road v Hall Road Rangers	3-1
7r	Anstey Nomads v Midland Athletic	1-2
8r	Boldmere St Michaels v Astwood Bank Rovers	4-0
9r	Irthlingborough Diamonds v Histon	4-2
r	Peterborough Rovers v Rothwell Town	3-2 N
r	Soham United v Oundle Town	3-2
10r	Gorleston v Watton United	3-2e
11r	Arlesey Town v Stotfold	1-0
r	Sandy Albions v Vauxhall Motors	1-2
r	Tring Town v Ampthill Town	5-0
12r	Hounslow Town v Edgware Town	3-1
14r	Eastbourne United v Seaford Town	1-2e
r	Worthing v Bognor Regis Town	2-0
15r	Banstead Athletic v Merton United	2-0
16r	Edmonton (2) v Harefield United	2-0
r	Harlow Town v Hoddesdon Town	2-4
18r	Epsom & Ewell v Whitehawk	2-2
19r	Chalfont St Peter v Bracknell Town	1-3
r	Didcot Town v Huntley & Palmers	2-1
22r	Melksham Town v West Lavington	3-0
r	Westbury United v Calne Town	3-2
23r	Sharpness v Keynsham Town	3-2e
18r2	Epsom & Ewell v Whitehawk	1-1eN
18r3	Whitehawk v Epsom & Ewell	0-1

Qualifying Round Two

1	Billingham Synthonia v South Bank	1-1
	Blyth Spartans v Willington	2-1
2	Durham City v Consett	1-0
	North Withington v Blackpool Mechanics	1-3
3	Chadderton v Hanley Town	4-1
	Middlewich Athletic v Port Sunlight	3-4
4	Leeds Ashley Road v St Johns College (York)	2-2
	North Ferriby United v Brook Sports	1-0
5	Guiseley v Norton Woodseats	4-4
	Knaresborough v Bradford Rovers	2-3
6	Frecheville Community v Bulwell Forest Villa	4-2
	Harrowby United v Roe Farm Athletic	1-2
7	Oldbury United v Paget Rangers	2-4
	Solihull Borough v Midland Athletic	2-4e
8	Chelmsley Town v Oldswinford	0-4
	Sutton Coldfield Town v Boldmere St Michaels	3-2
9	Irthlingborough Diamonds v Peterborough Rovers	5-0
	Soham United v Warboys Town	0-5
10	Gorleston v Brantham Athletic	1-1
	Whitton United v City of Norwich School OBU	3-3
11	Letchworth Town v Vauxhall Motors	2-2
	Tring Town v Arlesey Town	0-0
12	Hampton v Kingsbury Town	0-0
	Hounslow Town v Uxbridge	1-2
13	Erith & Belvedere v Herne Bay	0-0
	Maidstone United v Swanley	3-3
14	Seaford Town v Lewes	0-1
	Worthing v Bexhill Town	0-1
15	Dorking v Horsham	2-0
	Redhill v Banstead Athletic	3-0

1969/70 to 1970/71

16	Hoddesdon Town v Boreham Wood	0-0
	Leighton Town v Edmonton (2)	2-1
17	Canvey Island v Aveley	1-1
	Chingford v Epping Town	2-1
18	Epsom & Ewell v Tooting & Mitcham United	1-2
	Surbiton Byron v Addlestone	0-3
19	Bracknell Town v Marlow	0-5
	Hemel Hempstead Town v Didcot Town	0-0
20	Moreton Town v Bicester Town	0-1
	Witney Town v Kidlington	6-5
21	Brockenhurst v Liphook	1-1
	Pirelli General Cable Wks v Portsmouth Royal Navy	1-1
22	Bromham v Melksham Town	0-1
	Westbury United v Pinehurst Youth Centre	0-2
23	Malvern Town v Mangotsfield United	7-0
	Sharpness v Evesham United	1-4
24	Newquay v Saltash United	5-2
	Wellington v St Austell	1-4
1r	South Bank v Billingham Synthonia	0-3
4r	St Johns College (York) v Leeds Ashley Road	1-0
5r	Norton Woodseats v Guiseley	4-1
10r	Brantham Athletic v Gorleston	2-4
r	City of Norwich School OBU v Whitton United	1-2
11r	Arlesey Town v Tring Town	1-0
r	Vauxhall Motors v Letchworth Town	3-2
12r	Kingsbury Town v Hampton	1-2
13r	Herne Bay v Erith & Belvedere	1-3
r	Swanley v Maidstone United	0-7
16r	Boreham Wood v Hoddesdon Town	1-2
17r	Aveley v Canvey Island	4-0
19r	Didcot Town v Hemel Hempstead Town	0-3
21r	Liphook v Brockenhurst	0-1
r	Portsmouth Royal Navy v Pirelli General Cable Wks	0-7

Qualifying Round Three

1	Billingham Synthonia v Blyth Spartans	2-0
2	Durham City v Blackpool Mechanics	1-0
3	Chadderton v Port Sunlight	5-1
4	North Ferriby United v St Johns College (York)	1-3
5	Bradford Rovers v Norton Woodseats	2-2
6	Frecheville Community v Roe Farm Athletic	6-2
7	Paget Rangers v Midland Athletic	4-0
8	Sutton Coldfield Town v Oldswinford	2-0 v
9	Warboys Town v Irthlingborough Diamonds	2-4
10	Whitton United v Gorleston	2-4
11	Arlesey Town v Vauxhall Motors	1-1
12	Uxbridge v Hampton	1-1
13	Erith & Belvedere v Maidstone United	0-3
14	Bexhill Town v Lewes	1-2
15	Redhill v Dorking	2-1
16	Hoddesdon Town v Leighton Town	4-1
17	Chingford v Aveley	2-2
18	Addlestone v Tooting & Mitcham United	0-5
19	Hemel Hempstead Town v Marlow	0-2
20	Witney Town v Bicester Town	1-1
21	Pirelli General Cable Works v Brockenhurst	0-1
22	Melksham Town v Pinehurst Youth Centre	1-0
23	Malvern Town v Evesham United	0-3
24	St Austell v Newquay	3-0
5r	Norton Woodseats v Bradford Rovers	n/a
8r	Oldswinford v Sutton Coldfield Town	0-0
11r	Vauxhall Motors v Arlesey Town	1-0
12r	Hampton v Uxbridge	1-2
17r	Aveley v Chingford	2-1
20r	Bicester Town v Witney Town	1-3
8r2	Sutton Coldfield Town v Oldswinford	3-1 N

Qualifying Round Four

	Chadderton v Guinness Exports	0-5
	Chesham United v Finchley	2-0
	Cheshunt (2) v Marlow	2-1
	Croydon Amateur v Maidstone United	2-1
	Durham City v Crook Town	0-0
	Emley v Frecheville Community	4-2
	Evenwood Town v Billingham Synthonia	3-1
	Evesham United v Melksham Town	2-1
	Fareham Town v Brockenhurst	6-0
	Gosport Borough v Alton Town	0-3
	Hornchurch v Hoddesdon Town	1-2
	Leeds & Carnegie College v Hallam	2-1
	Lewes v Tooting & Mitcham United	0-0
	Lincoln United v St Johns College (York)	1-2
	Loughborough College v Bradford Rovers	1-0
	Redhill v Corinthian Casuals	6-0
	Stowmarket v Gorleston	2-3
	Sutton Coldfield Town v Paget Rangers	0-2
	Torpoint Athletic v St Austell	1-1
	Uxbridge v Aveley	1-2
	Vauxhall Motors v Irthlingborough Diamonds	3-1
	Wembley v Grays Athletic	1-1
	Witney Town v Cirencester Town	3-3
	Wycombe Wanderers v Hertford Town	5-1
r	Cirencester Town v Witney Town	1-1
r	Crook Town v Durham City	1-6
r	Grays Athletic v Wembley	0-3
r	St Austell v Torpoint Athletic	2-0
r	Tooting & Mitcham United v Lewes	2-1
r2	Cirencester Town v Witney Town	2-3

Round One

	Alton Town v Walthamstow Avenue	5-0
	Aveley v Kingstonian	1-0
	Bishops Stortford v Dulwich Hamlet	5-2
	Bristol St George v Fareham Town	4-2
	Bromley v Oxford City	3-2
	Carshalton Athletic v Hitchin Town	0-0
	Chesham United v Slough Town	2-3
	Cheshunt (2) v Windsor & Eton	3-1
	Coventry Amateur v West Auckland Town	1-2
	Croydon Amateur v Wycombe Wanderers	0-1
	Durham City v Skelmersdale United	1-1
	Eastwood Town v Leeds & Carnegie College	0-2
	Enfield v Redhill	3-2
	Evesham United v Cray Wanderers	1-0
	Gorleston v Southall	1-4
	Guinness Exports v Emley	0-3
	Harwich & Parkeston v Leyton	9-0
	Hayes v Barking	0-2
	Hendon v St Austell	5-0
	Hoddesdon Town v Dagenham	1-2
	Ilford v Witney Town	1-0
	North Shields v Evenwood Town	0-0
	Paget Rangers v Alvechurch	1-1
	Prestwich Heys v Marine	1-0
	St Albans City v Wembley	0-0
	Sutton United v Leatherhead	2-0
	Tooting & Mitcham United v Leytonstone	0-0
	Tow Law Town v Spennymoor United	1-0
	Wealdstone v Vauxhall Motors	3-2
	Whitby Town v Loughborough College	1-1
	Whitley Bay v St Johns College (York)	1-0
	Woking v Walton & Hersham	0-0
r	Alvechurch v Paget Rangers	2-2
r	Evenwood Town v North Shields	0-0
r	Hitchin Town v Carshalton Athletic	3-0
r	Leytonstone v Tooting & Mitcham United	0-1
r	Skelmersdale United v Durham City	3-2
r	Walton & Hersham v Woking	2-1
r	Wembley v St Albans City	1-1
r	Whitby Town v Loughborough College	2-0
r2	Alvechurch v Paget Rangers	3-1 N
r2	Evenwood Town v North Shields	3-1 N
r2	St Albans City v Wembley	2-1

Round Two

	Alton Town v Hitchin Town	2-1
	Alvechurch v Whitby Town	3-0
	Bishops Stortford v Skelmersdale United	0-4
	Cheshunt (2) v Ilford	3-2
	Dagenham v Barking	1-1
	Evenwood Town v Hendon	1-2a
	Harwich & Parkeston v St Albans City	1-3
	Leeds & Carnegie College v Walton & Hersham	0-4
	Prestwich Heys v Sutton United	3-1
	Slough Town v Aveley	2-0
	Southall v Bristol St George	2-2
	Tow Law Town v Evesham United	1-0
	Wealdstone v Bromley	3-2
	West Auckland Town v Emley	0-1
	Whitley Bay v Enfield	0-0
	Wycombe Wanderers v Tooting & Mitcham United	0-0
r	Barking v Dagenham	1-3
r	Bristol St George v Southall	2-5
r	Enfield v Whitley Bay	4-1
r	Evenwood Town v Hendon	1-1
r	Tooting & Mitcham United v Wycombe Wanderers	1-2
r2	Hendon v Evenwood Town	4-2

Round Three

	Alton Town v Enfield	2-5
	Alvechurch v Slough Town	2-2
	Emley v Dagenham	0-0
	Hendon v Walton & Hersham	1-1
	Prestwich Heys v Southall	1-0
	Skelmersdale United v Cheshunt (2)	1-0
	St Albans City v Tow Law Town	4-0
	Wealdstone v Wycombe Wanderers	0-1
r	Dagenham v Emley	5-0
r	Slough Town v Alvechurch	2-0
r	Walton & Hersham v Hendon	1-0

Round Four

	Enfield v Prestwich Heys	2-0
	Slough Town v Skelmersdale United	0-0
	Walton & Hersham v Dagenham	0-1
	Wycombe Wanderers v St Albans City	0-2
r	Skelmersdale United v Slough Town	3-0

Semi Finals

	Dagenham v St Albans City	1-1 N
	Enfield v Skelmersdale United	1-0 N
r	Dagenham v St Albans City	1-0 N

Final

	Enfield v Dagenham	5-1 N

1970/71

Preliminary Round

1	Ashington v Consett	0-1
	Billingham Synthonia v Alnwick Town	2-2
	Bishop Auckland v Heaton Stannington	1-0
	Crook Town v Ferryhill Athletic	1-1
	Stanley United v Newcastle University	6-0
	Wallsend v Shildon	1-5
	Washington v Blyth Spartans	0-5
	Wingate v Willington	1-2
2	Alston v Ainsdale Hesketh Park	5-0
	Cleator Moor Celtic v Old Blackburnians	4-4
	Hearts of Liddesdale v Wigan Rovers	n/a
	Lytham St Annes & Fylde v Blackpool Mechanics	1-3
	Manchester YMCA v Whitefield Albion	2-0
	North Withington v Annan Athletic	2-2
	Wythenshaw Amateurs v Milnthorpe Corinthians	2-2
3	Chadderton v Hoylake Athletic	2-0
	Chester College v Lymm GS OB	2-1
	Chloride Recreation v Warrington Town	1-1
	Linotype & Machinery v Irlam Town	1-2
	Moreton v Middleton Amateurs	5-1
	Old Altrinchamians v Middlewich Athletic	5-4
	Port Sunlight v Curzon Ashton	0-3
	Winnington Park v East Chorlton Amateur	3-2
4	Brook Sports v Ainthorpe OB	5-0
	Leeds Ashley Road v Harrogate Railway Athletic	3-1
	Newton v Harrogate Town	3-2
	North Ferriby United v Darlington Railway Athletic	8-0
	Ossett Albion v Hall Road Rangers	2-0
	South Bank v Norton Cricket Club Trust	2-1
	Thackley v Northern Nomads	1-0
5	Birkenshaw Rovers v Salts	2-0
	Clayton v Bradford Rovers	2-0
	Keighley Central v Guiseley	0-2
	Knaresborough v Woolley MW	0-4
	Norton Woodseats v Firth Sports	4-2
	Sheffield v Manningham Mills	3-3
	Sheffield University v Worsborough Bridge MW	1-5
	Yorkshire Amateur v Bexley	2-0
6	Bulwell Forest Villa v Roe Farm Athletic	0-6
	Clifton All Whites v Stocksbridge Works	n/a
	Clipstone Welfare v Tipton Town	1-2e
	Frecheville Community v Players Athletic	0-4
	Harrowby United v Nottingham University	n/a
	Ollerton Colliery v Swallownest CW	0-1
7	Anstey Nomads v Bournville Athletic	6-2
	GKN Sankey v Highgate United (Birmingham)	5-1
	Midland Athletic v Great Wyrley Wednesday	2-1
	Oldbury United v Stratford Town	5-2
	Paget Rangers v Bermuda WMC	1-0
	Walsall Wood v Pershore United	2-3
	Whitmore OB v Solihull Borough	wo/s
8	Astwood Bank Rovers v Moor Green	1-1
	Birmingham City Police v Oldswinford	1-3
	Blakenall v Knowle	1-1
	Boldmere St Michaels v Chelmsley Town	3-0
	GEC Coventry v Northfield Town	1-4
9	Eynesbury Rovers v Peterborough Rovers	2-1
	Warboys Town v Histon	1-1
11	Arlesey Town v Buntingford Town	2-0
	Baldock Town v Ampthill Town	3-0
	Electrolux v Langford	0-0
	Letchworth Town v Barton Rovers	2-3
	Shillington v Royston Town	2-1
	Stotfold v Saffron Walden Town	3-1
	Tring Town v Berkhamsted Town	2-0
	Wolverton Town & BR v Vauxhall Motors	1-3
12	Civil Service v Hampton	0-3
	Crown & Manor v Borough Road College	1-2
	Edgware Town v Hounslow Town	2-2
	Harrow Borough v Highfield	2-2
	Ruislip Manor v Kingsbury Town	1-1
	Staines Town v Rayners Lane	8-0
	Uxbridge v Feltham	4-4
	Wingate v Willesden	4-3
13	Brentstonians v Bexley	1-2
	Erith & Belvedere v Woolwich Polytechnic	6-0
	Herne Bay v Crockenhill	4-0
	Maidstone United v Callender Athletic	3-0
	Royal Arsenal Sports v Slade Green Athletic	1-3
	Tunbridge Wells v West Wickham	3-0
14	Bexhill Town v Eastbourne Town	1-3
	Bognor Regis Town v Arundel	4-1
	Chichester City v Lewes	1-5
	Eastbourne United v Lancing Athletic	1-1
	Selsey v Ringmer	0-2
	Shoreham v Seaford Town	4-1
	Southwick v East Grinstead	3-1
	Worthing v Wigmore Athletic	3-1
15	Banstead Athletic v Merstham	5-0
	Camberley v Redhill	1-4
	Dorking v Reigate Priory	4-0
	Egham Town v Horsham	1-2
	Farnham Town v Frimley Green	3-1
	Old Salesians v Godalming & Farncombe	wo/s

1970/71

16	Boreham Wood v Byng Road OB	2-1
	Harpenden Town v Harefield United	2-3
	Hertford Town v Rickmansworth Town	4-0
	Hoddesdon Town v Edmonton (2)	3-1
	Kings Langley v Welwyn Garden United	2-0
	Shefford Town v Norsemen	0-1
	Ware v Harlow Town	5-1
17	Chingford v Ford United	1-3
	Eton Manor v Rainham Town	0-0
	Hornchurch v Maldon Town	2-1
18	Addlestone v Mascot Sports	2-0
	BAC Weybridge v Surbiton Byron	1-0
	Chertsey Town v Ulysses	3-3
	Chobham v Malden Town	1-0
	Cobham v Epsom & Ewell	1-3
	Lion Sports v Molesey	1-0
19	Aylesbury United v Huntley & Palmers	5-0
	Hemel Hempstead Town v Newbury Town	6-0
	Maidenhead United v Marlow	6-0
22	Calne Town v Mount Hill Enterprise	2-1
	Glenside Hospital v Paulton Rovers	0-0
23	Gloucester City YMCA v Soundwell	2-5
	Sharpness v Clevedon	3-1
1r	Alnwick Town v Billingham Synthonia	3-3
r	Ferryhill Athletic v Crook Town	0-0e
2r	Annan Athletic v North Withington	3-2
r	Milnthorpe Corinthians v Wythenshaw Amateurs	3-4
r	Old Blackburnians v Cleator Moor Celtic	n/a
3r	Warrington Town v Chloride Recreation	0-1
5r	Manningham Mills v Sheffield	1-3
8r	Knowle v Blakenall	n/a
r	Moor Green v Astwood Bank Rovers	3-1
9r	Histon v Warboys Town	2-0
11r	Langford v Electrolux	4-1
12r	Feltham v Uxbridge	1-1e
r	Harrow Borough v Highfield	0-1
r	Hounslow Town v Edgware Town	3-1
r	Kingsbury Town v Ruislip Manor	2-2
14r	Lancing Athletic v Eastbourne United	0-2
17r	Rainham Town v Eton Manor	0-1
18r	Ulysses v Chertsey Town	2-3e
22r	Paulton Rovers v Glenside Hospital	3-1
1r2	Alnwick Town v Billingham Synthonia	1-2
r2	Ferryhill Athletic v Crook Town	3-2
12r2	Feltham v Uxbridge	2-0eN
r2	Kingsbury Town v Ruislip Manor	5-0

Qualifying Round One

1	Bishop Auckland v Blyth Spartans	2-0
	Ferryhill Athletic v Billingham Synthonia	2-1
	Shildon v Willington	3-1
	Stanley United v Consett	3-3
2	Annan Athletic v Old Blackburnians	2-1
	Blackpool Mechanics v Penrith	1-0
	Manchester YMCA v Wythenshaw Amateurs	3-0
	Wigan Rovers v Alston	1-4
3	Chester College v Curzon Ashton	0-1
	Irlam Town v Chadderton	2-1
	Moreton v Winnington Park	2-1
	Old Altrinchamians v Chloride Recreation	1-0
4	Leeds Ashley Road v Whitkirk Wanderers	1-1
	North Ferriby United v Newton	4-0
	Ossett Albion v Thackley	0-1
	South Bank v Brook Sports	2-1
5	Guiseley v Sheffield	2-0
	Norton Woodseats v Birkenshaw Rovers	0-1
	Woolley MW v Yorkshire Amateur	2-2
	Worsborough Bridge MW v Clayton	4-0
6	Clifton All Whites v Alsager College	2-3
	Players Athletic v Hanley Town	1-6
	Swallownest CW v unknown	n/a
	Tipton Town v Roe Farm Athletic	1-1
7	Midland Athletic v Smethwick Highfield	1-0
	Oldbury United v GKN Sankey	0-0
	Paget Rangers v Pershore United	6-0
	Whitmore OB v Anstey Nomads	4-2
8	Moor Green v Birmingham University	1-1
	Northfield Town v Boldmere St Michaels	4-1
	Sutton Coldfield Town v Knowle	0-0
	Tividale v Oldswinford	3-1
9	Histon v Kempston Rovers	3-1
	Irthlingborough Diamonds v Sandy Albions	2-1
	Parson Drove United v Eynesbury Rovers	5-1
	Rothwell Town v Oundle Town	10-0
10	Bungay Town v Soham United	1-0
	City of Norwich School OBU v Achilles	4-1
	Gorleston v Whitton United	1-2
	Leiston v Brantham Athletic	1-0
11	Langford v Baldock Town	1-6
	Shillington v Arlesey Town	1-1
	Stotfold v Vauxhall Motors	0-1
	Tring Town v Barton Rovers	1-3
12	Highfield v Borough Road College	0-0
	Hounslow Town v Feltham	1-0
	Kingsbury Town v Hampton	1-1
	Staines Town v Wingate	1-1
13	Erith & Belvedere v Dartford Amateurs	3-0
	Herne Bay v Swanley	4-1
	Maidstone United v Slade Green Athletic	1-1
	Tunbridge Wells v Bexley	2-1
14	Eastbourne United v Bognor Regis Town	1-0
	Lewes v Southwick	6-0
	Ringmer v Eastbourne Town	4-2
	Worthing v Shoreham	2-0
15	Dorking v Banstead Athletic	3-0
	Old Salesians v Farnham Town	1-5
	Redhill v Whyteleafe	6-0
	Three Bridges v Horsham	0-3
16	Boreham Wood v Norsemen	7-0
	Harefield United v Leighton Town	0-6
	Hertford Town v Ware	3-3
	Hoddesdon Town v Kings Langley	4-3
17	East Ham United v Ford United	0-1
	Epping Town v Clapton	0-1
	Eton Manor v Canvey Island	0-1
	Hornchurch v Tilbury	1-2
18	BAC Weybridge v Whitehawk	1-2
	Chertsey Town v Addlestone	0-1
	Lion Sports v Epsom & Ewell	4-0
	Westfield v Chobham	0-1
19	Chalfont St Peter v Aylesbury United	0-1
	Hazells Aylesbury v Bracknell Town	0-3
	Hemel Hempstead Town v Amersham Town	3-0
	Maidenhead United v Wokingham Town	0-1
20	Abingdon Town v Thame United	5-0
	Didcot Town v Wallingford Town	1-0
	Moreton Town v Launton United	8-0
	Morris Motors v Bicester Town	3-2
21	Bemerton Athletic v Liphook	6-0
	Christchurch v Westbury United	4-0
	Swaythling Athletic v Brockenhurst	1-1
	Totton v Moneyfield Sports	0-1
22	Bromham v Shepton Mallet Town	4-0
	Mangotsfield United v Calne Town	2-3
	Melksham Town v Devizes Town	7-1
	Paulton Rovers v Clifton St Vincents	3-0
23	Cadbury Heath v Forest Green Rovers	1-0
	Malvern Town v Sharpness	2-3
	Pegasus Juniors v Frampton United	1-3
	Soundwell v Coleford United	2-3e
24	Elmore v Ottery St Mary	3-4
	Newquay v Wellington	5-0
	Saltash United v St Lukes College	2-0
	Torpoint Athletic v Exmouth Town	5-2
1r	Consett v Stanley United	6-2
4r	Whitkirk Wanderers v Leeds Ashley Road	0-2
5r	Yorkshire Amateur v Woolley MW	0-1
6r	Roe Farm Athletic v Tipton Town	5-2
7r	GKN Sankey v Oldbury United	1-3
8r	Knowle v Sutton Coldfield Town	2-4e
r	Moor Green v Birmingham University	3-0
11r	Arlesey Town v Shillington	1-4
12r	Borough Road College v Highfield	3-2
r	Hampton v Kingsbury Town	0-3
r	Wingate v Staines Town	1-2
13r	Slade Green Athletic v Maidstone United	0-1e
16r	Ware v Hertford Town	1-4
21r	Brockenhurst v Swaythling Athletic	0-1

Qualifying Round Two

1	Bishop Auckland v Shildon	1-0
	Ferryhill Athletic v Consett	0-2
2	Blackpool Mechanics v Annan Athletic	0-1
	Manchester YMCA v Alston	1-2
3	Curzon Ashton v Old Altrinchamians	1-2
	Irlam Town v Moreton	3-0
4	Leeds Ashley Road v Thackley	n/a
	North Ferriby United v South Bank	2-2
5	Guiseley v Birkenshaw Rovers	2-2
	Woolley MW v Worsborough Bridge MW	2-2
6	Alsager College v Swallownest CW	4-2
	Roe Farm Athletic v Hanley Town	2-1
7	Midland Athletic v Paget Rangers	0-0
	Oldbury United v Whitmore OB	1-0
8	Moor Green v Sutton Coldfield Town	1-2
	Tividale v Northfield Town	3-0
9	Irthlingborough Diamonds v Rothwell Town	1-0
	Parson Drove United v Histon	2-1
10	Bungay Town v Whitton United	4-1
	Leiston v City of Norwich School OBU	1-1
11	Baldock Town v Vauxhall Motors	1-5
	Shillington v Barton Rovers	0-8
12	Borough Road College v Staines Town	0-0
	Hounslow Town v Kingsbury Town	4-1
13	Erith & Belvedere v Maidstone United	2-0
	Herne Bay v Tunbridge Wells	4-0
14	Eastbourne United v Worthing	3-1
	Lewes v Ringmer	2-2
15	Dorking v Farnham Town	2-1
	Redhill v Horsham	4-1
16	Hertford Town v Hoddesdon Town	0-2
	Leighton Town v Boreham Wood	0-1
17	Ford United v Canvey Island	2-3
	Tilbury v Clapton	3-0
18	Addlestone v Lion Sports	2-0
	Whitehawk v Chobham	3-1
19	Aylesbury United v Hemel Hempstead Town	2-3
	Wokingham Town v Bracknell Town	1-2
20	Moreton Town v Didcot Town	2-1
	Morris Motors v Abingdon Town	2-2
21	Christchurch v Moneyfield Sports	3-1
	Swaythling Athletic v Bemerton Athletic	4-1
22	Bromham v Melksham Town	2-0
	Calne Town v Paulton Rovers	1-3
23	Cadbury Heath v Frampton United	1-0
	Sharpness v Coleford United	7-0
24	Newquay v Saltash United	2-0
	Torpoint Athletic v Ottery St Mary	5-1
4r	South Bank v North Ferriby United	2-1
5r	Birkenshaw Rovers v Guiseley	1-0
r	Worsborough Bridge MW v Woolley MW	6-1
7r	Paget Rangers v Midland Athletic	3-2
10r	City of Norwich School OBU v Leiston	4-1
12r	Staines Town v Borough Road College	2-1
14r	Ringmer v Lewes	1-2
20r	Abingdon Town v Morris Motors	2-1

Qualifying Round Three

1	Consett v Bishop Auckland	1-1
2	Annan Athletic v Alston	0-1a
3	Irlam Town v Old Altrinchamians	0-0
4	Thackley v South Bank	1-1
5	Birkenshaw Rovers v Worsborough Bridge MW	1-2
6	Alsager College v Roe Farm Athletic	1-1
7	Paget Rangers v Oldbury United	2-2
8	Tividale v Sutton Coldfield Town	1-2
9	Irthlingborough Diamonds v Parson Drove United	6-0
10	Bungay Town v City of Norwich School OBU	1-3
11	Vauxhall Motors v Barton Rovers	2-0
12	Staines Town v Hounslow Town	1-3
13	Herne Bay v Erith & Belvedere	1-0
14	Eastbourne United v Lewes	0-3
15	Redhill v Dorking	0-0
16	Boreham Wood v Hoddesdon Town	1-1
17	Tilbury v Canvey Island	1-0
18	Whitehawk v Addlestone	1-2
19	Bracknell Town v Hemel Hempstead Town	2-1
20	Moreton Town v Abingdon Town	1-3
21	Christchurch v Swaythling Athletic	0-1
22	Bromham v Paulton Rovers	2-2
23	Cadbury Heath v Sharpness	4-1
24	Newquay v Torpoint Athletic	7-0
1r	Bishop Auckland v Consett	2-1
2r	Annan Athletic v Alston	5-2
3r	Old Altrinchamians v Irlam Town	0-2
4r	South Bank v Thackley	3-2
6r	Roe Farm Athletic v Alsager College	2-1
7r	Oldbury United v Paget Rangers	2-0
15r	Dorking v Redhill	1-3
16r	Hoddesdon Town v Boreham Wood	2-3
22r	Paulton Rovers v Bromham	7-2

Qualifying Round Four

	Addlestone v Redhill	0-0
	Aveley v Grays Athletic	2-0
	Boreham Wood v Hounslow Town	2-0
	Cirencester Town v Witney Town	1-1
	Corinthian Casuals v Leyton	0-2
	Coventry Amateur v Loughborough College	1-2
	Croydon Amateur v Lewes	2-1
	Durham City v Annan Athletic	6-0
	Eastwood Town v Sutton Coldfield Town	0-0
	Fareham Town v Gosport Borough	2-0
	Finchley v Windsor & Eton	3-0
	Irlam Town v Roe Farm Athletic	4-0
	Newquay v Cadbury Heath	2-1
	Oldbury United v Evesham United	1-0
	Ormskirk v Hallam	3-1
	Paulton Rovers v Abingdon Town	1-0
	South Bank v Bishop Auckland	3-1
	Spennymoor United v Worsborough Bridge MW	5-0
	Stowmarket v Irthlingborough Diamonds	0-0
	Swaythling Athletic v Woking	0-0
	Tilbury v Herne Bay	2-0
	Tooting & Mitcham United v Chesham United	2-1
	Vauxhall Motors v City of Norwich School OBU	1-0
	Wembley v Bracknell Town	0-1
r	Irthlingborough Diamonds v Stowmarket	1-3
r	Redhill v Addlestone	3-1
r	Sutton Coldfield Town v Eastwood Town	2-0
r	Witney Town v Cirencester Town	2-0
r	Woking v Swaythling Athletic	2-1

Round One

	Alton Town v Hendon	1-1
	Alvechurch v Ormskirk	0-1
	Barking v Paulton Rovers	4-1
	Bracknell Town v Newquay	0-2
	Bristol St George v Boreham Wood	0-3
	Bromley v St Albans City	3-3
	Carshalton Athletic v Cheshunt (2)	2-1
	Cray Wanderers v Kingstonian	1-2
	Croydon Amateur v Harwich & Parkeston	1-4
	Dagenham v Leyton	5-0
	Durham City v Whitley Bay	2-3
	Fareham Town v Tooting & Mitcham United	1-3
	Finchley v Woking	2-1
	Irlam Town v Oldbury United	1-2
	Leeds & Carnegie College v Loughborough College	0-2
	Marine v Prestwich Heys	2-1
	Oxford City v Bishops Stortford	1-3
	Slough Town v Redhill	1-1
	South Bank v North Shields	1-3
	Southall v Dulwich Hamlet	2-3
	Spennymoor United v Skelmersdale United	1-1
	Stowmarket v Leatherhead	2-2
	Sutton Coldfield Town v Emley	4-0
	Sutton United v Leytonstone	0-0
	Tilbury v Aveley	0-1
	Tow Law Town v West Auckland Town	2-1

1970/71 to 1971/72

	Vauxhall Motors v Hayes	0-3
	Walthamstow Avenue v Ilford	2-0
	Walton & Hersham v Enfield	0-2
	Whitby Town v Evenwood Town	2-3
	Witney Town v Hitchin Town	2-1
	Wycombe Wanderers v Wealdstone	1-0
r	Hendon v Alton Town	6-0
r	Leatherhead v Stowmarket	2-2
r	Leytonstone v Sutton United	4-0
r	Redhill v Slough Town	1-3
r	Skelmersdale United v Spennymoor United	5-1
r	St Albans City v Bromley	4-0
r2	Leatherhead v Stowmarket	3-2 N

Round Two

	Bishops Stortford v Dagenham	0-1
	Boreham Wood v St Albans City	2-1
	Carshalton Athletic v Aveley	2-3
	Harwich & Parkeston v Slough Town	0-3
	Hayes v Witney Town	2-1
	Hendon v Barking	4-1
	Leatherhead v Dulwich Hamlet	0-0
	Leytonstone v Kingstonian	4-1
	Loughborough College v Evenwood Town	1-0
	Marine v Ormskirk	3-1
	Newquay v Oldbury United	1-7
	North Shields v Tow Law Town	0-0
	Skelmersdale United v Sutton Coldfield Town	3-0
	Tooting & Mitcham United v Walthamstow Avenue	3-1
	Whitley Bay v Finchley	2-0
	Wycombe Wanderers v Enfield	2-1
r	Dulwich Hamlet v Leatherhead	0-1
r	Tow Law Town v North Shields	6-0

Round Three

	Boreham Wood v Leatherhead	1-1
	Hendon v Slough Town	1-1
	Leytonstone v Dagenham	0-1
	Loughborough College v Hayes	0-3
	Marine v Aveley	0-1
	Tooting & Mitcham United v Whitley Bay	2-3
	Tow Law Town v Skelmersdale United	1-1
	Wycombe Wanderers v Oldbury United	4-0
r	Leatherhead v Boreham Wood	2-1
r	Skelmersdale United v Tow Law Town	1-0
r	Slough Town v Hendon	3-1

Round Four

	Aveley v Slough Town	0-2
	Dagenham v Whitley Bay	1-0
	Hayes v Leatherhead	1-1
	Wycombe Wanderers v Skelmersdale United	0-3
r	Leatherhead v Hayes	1-0

Semi Finals

	Dagenham v Slough Town	3-3 N
	Skelmersdale United v Leatherhead	2-0 N
r	Slough Town v Dagenham	1-2 N

Final

	Skelmersdale United v Dagenham	4-1 N

1971/72

Preliminary Round

1	Birkenshaw Rovers v Alnwick Town	1-4
	Blyth Spartans v Annan Athletic	6-1
	Brook Sports v Wingate	4-0
	East Chorlton Amateur v Blackpool Mechanics	0-1
	Harrogate Town v Crook Town	2-2
	Leeds Ashley Road v Alston	1-1
	Liversedge v Heaton Stannington	0-4
	North Withington v Thackley	1-3
	Old Blackburnians v Whitkirk Wanderers	1-1
	Penrith v Ferryhill Athletic	1-0
	Salts v Ainsdale Hesketh Park	1-4
	Washington v Chloride Recreation	2-0
	Willington v Woolley MW	3-1
2	Anstey Nomads v Middlewich Athletic	1-2
	Boldmere St Michaels v Highgate U (Birmingham)	0-3
	Frecheville Community v Prescot Town	2-2
	Healey v Walsall Wood	1-4
	Knowle v Warrington Town	2-0
	Lutterworth Town v Mile Oak Rovers	0-2
	Madeley College v Pershore United	2-1
	Messingham Trinity v Alcester Town	n/a
	Midland Athletic v Stork	2-1
	Newton v Moor Green	2-0
	Northfield Town v Evesham United	0-1
	Old Altrinchamians v Bermuda WMC	4-0
	Sheffield University v Stratford Town	3-4
	Solihull Amateur v Paget Rangers	1-2
	Tipton Town v Blakenall	0-1
3	Clacton Town v Maldon Town	4-0
4	Buckingham Athletic v Irthlingborough Diamonds	0-4
	Stony Stratford Town v Ampthill Town	1-1
5	Hemel Hempstead Town v Kings Langley	3-1
	Staines Town v Bracknell Town	1-2
6	East Barnet OG v Electrolux	1-3
	Royston Town v Baldock Town	2-3
7	Chingford v Hertford Town	0-4
	Epping Town v Clapton	0-3
	Grays Athletic v Hornchurch	0-2
	Hoddesdon Town v Rainham Town	0-2
	Ware v Edmonton (2)	2-0
8	Borough Road College v Civil Service	3-2
	Hounslow Town v Uxbridge	2-3
	Old Salesians v Edgware	1-2
9	Banstead Athletic v Slade Green Athletic	4-2
	Bexley v Faversham Town	0-5
	Herne Bay v Erith & Belvedere	1-2
	Mascot Sports v Whyteleafe	4-2
	Swanley v Thame United	3-0
10	Chertsey Town v Cobham	2-1
	Malden Town v Addlestone	0-3
11	Dorking v Farnham Town	1-2
	Ulysses v Camberley	3-0
12	Eastbourne Town v Eastbourne United	0-3
	Lewes v Bexhill Town	3-2
13	Abingdon Town v Thame United	2-1
	Amersham Town v Bicester Town	0-4
	Didcot Town v Aylesbury United	2-0
	Moreton Town v Wokingham Town	1-1
	Wallingford Town v Hazells Aylesbury	2-0
14	Arundel v Worthing	2-2
	Chichester City v Selsey	3-2
	Pagham v Bognor Regis Town	1-2
15	Calne Town v Melksham Town	1-3
16	Hanham Athletic v Clifton St Vincents	3-0
17	Forest Green Rovers v Frampton United	5-1
	Sharpness v Cirencester Town	4-0
1r	Alston v Leeds Ashley Road	4-1
r	Crook Town v Harrogate Town	2-1
r	Whitkirk Wanderers v Old Blackburnians	4-0
2r	Alcester Town v Messingham Trinity	2-1 v
r	Prescot Town v Frecheville Community	1-2
4r	Ampthill Town v Stony Stratford Town	0-2
13r	Wokingham Town v Moreton Town	4-0
14r	Worthing v Arundel	3-0
2r2	Messingham Trinity v Alcester Town	1-1
2r3	Messingham Trinity v Alcester Town	wo/s

Qualifying Round One

1	Ainsdale Hesketh Park v Norton Cricket Club Trust	1-1e
	Alston v Alnwick Town	2-3
	Ashington v Consett	0-1
	Billingham Synthonia v Thackley	2-0
	Bishop Auckland v Shildon	0-2
	Blackpool Mechanics v Yorkshire Amateur	0-0e
	Brook Sports v Stanley United	4-2
	Chadderton v Whitkirk Wanderers	3-0
	Curzon Ashton v Blyth Spartans	0-2 N
	Leeds University Union v Heaton Stannington	1-2
	North Ferriby United v Bradford Rovers	3-3e
	Ossett Albion v Guiseley	3-2
	Washington v Crook Town	0-1
	Wigan Rovers v Wythenshaw Amateurs	2-1
	Willington v Cleator Moor Celtic	2-2
	Worsborough Bridge MW v Penrith	6-1
2	Birmingham City Police v Hanley Town	3-2
	Blakenall v Old Altrinchamians	2-2
	Evesham United v Sheffield	3-1
	Frecheville Community v Paget Rangers	3-4
	Great Wyrley v Stratford Town	3-1
	Highgate United (Birmingham) v Clipstone Welfare	2-0
	Knowle v Linby CW	3-0
	Madeley College v Chester College	1-1
	Manchester YMCA v Middlewich Athletic	2-1
	Messingham Trinity v GEC Coventry	4-0
	Mile Oak Rovers v Walsall Wood	1-3
	Newton v Astwood Bank Rovers	4-0
	Northern Nomads v GKN Sankey	1-2 N
	Norton Woodseats v Hoylake Athletic	0-4
	Stocksbridge Works v Solihull Town	0-0
	Swallownest CW v Midland Athletic	n/a
3	Bungay Town v City of Norwich School OBU	0-1
	Eynesbury Rovers v Clacton Town	3-5
	Saffron Walden Town v Whitton United	4-4
	Warboys Town v Soham United	2-0
4	Irthlingborough Diamonds v Arlesey Town	4-0
	Rothwell Town v Stony Stratford Town	1-0
	Shefford Town v Stotfold	1-2
	Shillington v Wolverton Town & BR	3-3
5	Hemel Hempstead Town v Harrow Borough	1-1
	Maidenhead United v Bracknell Town	3-0
	Rayners Lane v Windsor & Eton	1-0
	Wingate v Rickmansworth Town	1-3
6	Electrolux v Berkhamsted Town	0-0
	Harpenden Town v Baldock Town	1-0
	Leighton Town v Tring Town	0-0
	Letchworth Town v Welwyn Garden United	3-3
7	Ford United v Eton Manor	2-0
	Hertford Town v Ware	1-2
	Hornchurch v Clapton	1-0
	Rainham Town v Harlow Town	2-3
8	Edgware v Borough Road College	2-0
	Harefield United v Uxbridge	1-2
	Kingsbury Town v Ruislip Manor	1-1
	Willesden v Norsemen	4-0
9	Banstead Athletic v Faversham Town	1-1
	Horley v Crockenhill	2-0
	Mascot Sports v Erith & Belvedere	0-2
	Swanley v Merstham	4-1
10	Chertsey Town v BAC Weybridge	1-2
	Egham Town v Addlestone	1-0
	Feltham v Molesey	3-0
	Hampton v Surbiton Byron	2-0
11	Farnham Town v Chobham	5-0
	Frimley Green v Ulysses	2-1
	Lion Sports v Virginia Water	1-1
	Reigate Priory v Westfield	0-1
12	East Grinstead v Lewes	1-3
	Eastbourne United v Burgess Hill Town	3-1
	Horsham v Ringmer	3-2
	Horsham YMCA v Three Bridges	2-1
13	Abingdon Town v Bicester Town	1-2
	Marlow v Chalfont St Peter	5-0
	Wallingford Town v Morris Motors	2-2
	Wokingham Town v Didcot Town	3-0
14	Bognor Regis Town v Worthing	1-0
	Brockenhurst v Chichester City	2-0
	Gosport Borough v Portsmouth Royal Navy	4-0
	Lancing Athletic v Wigmore Athletic	2-2
15	Bemerton Athletic v Bromham	2-1
	Hungerford Town v Melksham Town	1-0
	Sanford Youth Centre v Wantage Town	2-3
	Swaythling Athletic v Westbury United	0-1
16	Cadbury Heath v Clevedon	5-0
	Glenside Hospital v Hanham Athletic	2-1
	Mangotsfield United v Soundwell	2-1
17	Forest Green Rovers v Coleford United	4-3
	Gloucester City YMCA v Sharpness	1-0 v
	Malvern Town v Viney St Swithins	0-1
	Pegasus Juniors v Worrall Hill Athletic	0-2
18	Ottery St Mary v Paulton Rovers	0-1
	Radstock Town v Exmouth Town	3-2
	Saltash United v Torpoint Athletic	1-2
	Shepton Mallet Town v Wellington	6-0
1r	Bradford Rovers v North Ferriby United	0-5
r	Cleator Moor Celtic v Willington	1-5
r	Norton Cricket Club Trust v Ainsdale Hesketh Park	4-2
r	Yorkshire Amateur v Blackpool Mechanics	1-4
2r	Chester College v Madeley College	4-0
r	Old Altrinchamians v Blakenall	3-0
r	Solihull Town v Stocksbridge Works	2-0e
3r	Whitton United v Saffron Walden Town	0-2
4r	Wolverton Town & BR v Shillington	1-2
5r	Harrow Borough v Hemel Hempstead Town	1-2
6r	Berkhamsted Town v Electrolux	0-1
r	Tring Town v Leighton Town	1-2
r	Welwyn Garden United v Letchworth Town	0-1
8r	Ruislip Manor v Kingsbury Town	2-1
9r	Faversham Town v Banstead Athletic	5-2
11r	Virginia Water v Lion Sports	4-0
13r	Morris Motors v Wallingford Town	1-1e
14r	Wigmore Athletic v Lancing Athletic	4-3
17r	Sharpness v Gloucester City YMCA	wo/s
13r2	Morris Motors v Wallingford Town	1-1eN
13r3	Morris Motors v Wallingford Town	1-0 N

Qualifying Round Two

1	Alnwick Town v Brook Sports	5-2
	Blackpool Mechanics v Heaton Stannington	3-0
	Blyth Spartans v Norton Cricket Club Trust	5-0
	Chadderton v Consett	0-6
	Crook Town v Ossett Albion	0-1
	Shildon v North Ferriby United	7-1
	Willington v Billingham Synthonia	2-0
	Worsborough Bridge MW v Wigan Rovers	2-1
2	Birmingham City Police v Highgate U (Birmingham)	1-4
	Chester College v Old Altrinchamians	4-1
	GKN Sankey v Astwood Bank Rovers	0-0
	Great Wyrley v Knowle	1-0
	Messingham Trinity v Manchester YMCA	2-3
	Paget Rangers v Hoylake Athletic	1-0
	Swallownest CW v Solihull Town	0-1
	Walsall Wood v Evesham United	0-0
3	Saffron Walden Town v Clacton Town	1-2
	Warboys Town v City of Norwich School OBU	0-4
4	Shillington v Irthlingborough Diamonds	2-1
	Stotfold v Rothwell Town	2-0
5	Rayners Lane v Maidenhead United	0-3
	Rickmansworth Town v Hemel Hempstead Town	1-1
6	Leighton Town v Harpenden Town	1-3
	Letchworth Town v Electrolux	5-2
7	Ford United v Hornchurch	1-0
	Harlow Town v Ware	2-0
8	Ruislip Manor v Uxbridge	3-2
	Willesden v Edgware	1-3
9	Horley v Erith & Belvedere	0-2
	Swanley v Faversham Town	3-0
10	Feltham v Egham Town	0-3
	Hampton v BAC Weybridge	2-3
11	Virginia Water v Frimley Green	2-2
	Westfield v Farnham Town	1-3
12	Horsham v Lewes	1-0
	Horsham YMCA v Eastbourne United	2-0
13	Marlow v Wokingham Town	0-1
	Morris Motors v Bicester Town	0-1
14	Gosport Borough v Brockenhurst	2-1
	Wigmore Athletic v Bognor Regis Town	0-2

1971/72 to 1972/73

15	Wantage Town v Hungerford Town	3-0
	Westbury United v Bemerton Athletic	4-6
16	Mangotsfield United v Glenside Hospital	5-3
	Yate Town v Cadbury Heath	0-3
17	Viney St Swithins v Sharpness	0-4
	Worrall Hill Athletic v Forest Green Rovers	1-3
18	Shepton Mallet Town v Paulton Rovers	2-2
	Torpoint Athletic v Radstock Town	2-2
2r	Astwood Bank Rovers v GKN Sankey	2-0
r	Evesham United v Walsall Wood	4-1
5r	Hemel Hempstead Town v Rickmansworth Town	3-2
11r	Frimley Green v Virginia Water	1-0
18r	Paulton Rovers v Shepton Mallet Town	1-1
r	Radstock Town v Torpoint Athletic	3-0
18r2	Paulton Rovers v Shepton Mallet Town	3-2e

Qualifying Round Three

1	Alnwick Town v Ossett Albion	1-2
	Blackpool Mechanics v Shildon	1-1
	Consett v Willington	2-2
	Worsborough Bridge MW v Blyth Spartans	0-4
2	Evesham United v Paget Rangers	2-0
	Highgate United (Birmingham) v Chester College	1-0
	Manchester YMCA v Astwood Bank Rovers	2-0
	Solihull Town v Great Wyrley	1-7
3	Clacton Town v City of Norwich School OBU	0-3
4	Stotfold v Shillington	1-3
5	Maidenhead United v Hemel Hempstead Town	5-1
6	Letchworth Town v Harpenden Town	1-0
7	Harlow Town v Ford United	3-0
8	Ruislip Manor v Edgware	4-0
9	Swanley v Erith & Belvedere	2-3
10	Egham Town v BAC Weybridge	1-4
11	Frimley Green v Farnham Town	4-2
12	Horsham v Horsham YMCA	2-2
13	Bicester Town v Wokingham Town	0-2
14	Gosport Borough v Bognor Regis Town	1-3
15	Wantage Town v Bemerton Athletic	3-1
16	Mangotsfield United v Cadbury Heath	1-3
17	Sharpness v Forest Green Rovers	0-1
18	Radstock Town v Paulton Rovers	2-1
1r	Shildon v Blackpool Mechanics	5-1
r	Willington v Consett	3-0
12r	Horsham YMCA v Horsham	1-10

Qualifying Round Four

	BAC Weybridge v Corinthian Casuals	1-2
	Bristol St George v Radstock Town	1-1
	Cadbury Heath v Newquay	5-1
	Coventry Amateur v Highgate United (Birmingham)	1-1
	Cray Wanderers v Croydon Amateur	0-3
	Erith & Belvedere v Redhill	3-2
	Evesham United v Sutton Coldfield Town	2-1
	Fareham Town v Bognor Regis Town	1-3
	Forest Green Rovers v Wantage Town	0-3
	Great Wyrley v Oldbury United	2-5 N
	Horsham v Boreham Wood	1-1
	Leeds & Carnegie College v Manchester YMCA	4-0
	Leyton v Bromley	1-3
	Ruislip Manor v Frimley Green	0-0
	Shildon v Durham City	3-1
	Shillington v Letchworth Town	1-1
	South Bank v Hallam	2-2
	Spennymoor United v Ossett Albion	3-0
	Stowmarket v City of Norwich School OBU	1-2
	Tilbury v Chesham United	2-0
	Vauxhall Motors v Maidenhead United	0-3
	Wembley v Woking	0-2
	Willington v Blyth Spartans	0-3
	Wokingham Town v Harlow Town	5-2
r	Boreham Wood v Horsham	1-3
r	Frimley Green v Ruislip Manor	1-1
r	Hallam v South Bank	3-1
r	Highgate United (Birmingham) v Coventry Amateur	0-0
r	Letchworth Town v Shillington	3-0
r	Radstock Town v Bristol St George	0-2
r2	Frimley Green v Ruislip Manor	1-5
r2	Highgate United (Birmingham) v Coventry Amateur	5-0

Round One

	Alvechurch v Blyth Spartans	0-1
	Aveley v Wycombe Wanderers	2-2
	Bristol St George v Finchley	1-2
	Bromley v Oxford City	1-2
	Cheshunt (2) v Tilbury	1-1
	Corinthian Casuals v Maidenhead United	0-1
	Croydon Amateur v Wantage Town	4-0
	Evenwood Town v Oldbury United	3-3
	Evesham United v Prestwich Heys	2-1
	Hallam v North Shields	0-1
	Harwich & Parkeston v St Albans City	1-1
	Hayes v City of Norwich School OBU	5-1
	Hendon v Horsham	1-0
	Hitchin Town v Erith & Belvedere	0-0
	Ilford v Bognor Regis Town	4-0
	Leatherhead v Dagenham	2-1
	Letchworth Town v Cadbury Heath	1-1
	Leytonstone v Carshalton Athletic	1-0
	Loughborough College v Whitby Town	4-0
	Marine v Whitley Bay	4-1
	Ruislip Manor v Bishops Stortford	2-2
	Shildon v Ormskirk	1-1
	Slough Town v Kingstonian	2-0
	Spennymoor United v Emley	5-0
	Tooting & Mitcham United v Barking	1-2
	Tow Law Town v Leeds & Carnegie College	1-1
	Walthamstow Avenue v Enfield	1-3
	Walton & Hersham v Southall	1-1
	West Auckland Town v Highgate U (Birmingham)	1-4
	Witney Town v Dulwich Hamlet	2-1
	Wokingham Town v Sutton United	0-2
r	Bishops Stortford v Ruislip Manor	1-0
r	Cadbury Heath v Letchworth Town	2-1
r	Erith & Belvedere v Hitchin Town	1-3
r	Leeds & Carnegie College v Tow Law Town	0-3
r	Oldbury United v Evenwood Town	1-1
r	Ormskirk v Shildon	1-3
r	Southall v Walton & Hersham	0-1
r	St Albans City v Harwich & Parkeston	4-0
r	Tilbury v Cheshunt (2)	3-2
r	Wycombe Wanderers v Aveley	5-1
r2	Evenwood Town v Oldbury United	1-2 N

Round Two

	Barking v Hayes	1-2
	Cadbury Heath v Walton & Hersham	0-1
	Enfield v Evesham United	3-1
	Finchley v Bishops Stortford	0-0
	Highgate United (Birmingham) v Hendon	1-1
	Hitchin Town v Shildon	1-0
	Ilford v Maidenhead United	1-2
	Leytonstone v Loughborough College	1-1
	Oxford City v Leatherhead	0-3
	Slough Town v St Albans City	3-2
	Sutton United v Oldbury United	3-1
	Tilbury v Croydon Amateur	1-1
	Tow Law Town v Blyth Spartans	0-4
	Witney Town v Marine	2-2
	Woking v North Shields	1-0
	Wycombe Wanderers v Spennymoor United	2-1
r	Bishops Stortford v Finchley	2-0
r	Croydon Amateur v Tilbury	3-2
r	Hendon v Highgate United (Birmingham)	2-1
r	Loughborough College v Leytonstone	1-4
r	Marine v Witney Town	2-0

Round Three

	Bishops Stortford v Hitchin Town	1-1
	Hayes v Croydon Amateur	3-1
	Hendon v Maidenhead United	0-0
	Leytonstone v Leatherhead	2-2
	Marine v Enfield	0-3
	Slough Town v Sutton United	1-0
	Walton & Hersham v Wycombe Wanderers	1-2
	Woking v Blyth Spartans	0-3
r	Hitchin Town v Bishops Stortford	2-2
r	Leatherhead v Leytonstone	3-0
r	Maidenhead United v Hendon	0-1
r2	Bishops Stortford v Hitchin Town	2-2 N
r3	Hitchin Town v Bishops Stortford	1-0 N

Round Four

	Blyth Spartans v Leatherhead	1-1
	Enfield v Slough Town	5-1
	Hendon v Hitchin Town	2-0
	Wycombe Wanderers v Hayes	1-0
r	Leatherhead v Blyth Spartans	0-1

Semi Finals

	Enfield v Blyth Spartans	2-0 N
	Hendon v Wycombe Wanderers	2-1 N

Final

	Hendon v Enfield	2-0 N

1972/73

Preliminary Round

2	Willington v South Bank	2-1
3	Birkenshaw Rovers v Harrogate Town	0-2
	Brook Sports v Whitkirk Wanderers	0-2
	Liversedge v Guiseley	2-1
	Thackley v Bradford Rovers	1-1
4	Kirkby Town v Rylands Recreation	2-1
	Lostock Gralam v Warrington Town	1-0
	Middlewich Athletic v Blackpool Mechanics	1-3
	Prescot Town v Stork	1-0
5	Chloride Recreation v Anson Villa	1-1
	Hanley Town v Chadderton	4-1
	Kidsgrove Athletic v Irlam Town Amateur	0-1
	Old Altrinchamians v Northern Nomads	5-0
6	Heeley v Clipstone Welfare	2-3
	Swallownest CW v Sheffield	0-6
7	Coventry Amateur v Boldmere St Michaels	1-4
	GEC Coventry v Knowle	1-2
	Paget Rangers v Sutton Coldfield Town	0-0
	Racing Club Warwick v Players Athletic	3-0
8	Astwood Bank Rovers v Northfield Town	2-2
	Blakenall v Moor Green	1-3
	Rowley United v Walsall Wood	0-1
	Stratford Town v Madeley College	1-1
9	Coggeshall Town v Leiston	1-0
	Felixstowe Town v Clacton Town	0-1
	Stotfold v Shefford Town	0-1
10	Ampthill Town v Arlesey Town	5-1
11	Hazells Aylesbury v Rickmansworth Town	0-0
	Windsor & Eton v Tring Town	0-0
12	Harlow Town v Letchworth Town	4-1
	Welwyn Garden United v Hertford Town	0-0
13	Barkingside v Pegasus Athletic	15-2
	Clapton v Basildon United	0-0
	Ford United v Edmonton Haringey	0-2
14	Harefield United v Edgware	3-1
	Ruislip Manor v Rayners Lane	3-0
	Staines Town v Wembley	2-2
15	Crockenhill v Faversham Town	1-3
	Slade Green Athletic v Bexley	3-0
16	Egham Town v Ulysses	3-1
	Frimley Green v Chertsey Town	2-3
17	Civil Service v Old Salesians	3-2
	Hounslow Town v Cobham	5-1
	Westfield v Hampton	0-2
18	East Grinstead v Merstham	2-0
	Whyteleafe v Dorking	0-0
19	Chalfont St Peter v Morris Motors	0-0
	Didcot Town v Chesham United	1-1
	Wallingford Town v Bicester Town	0-0
20	Lancing Athletic v Eastbourne United	0-3
	Whitehawk v Eastbourne Town	1-0
	Wigmore Athletic v Arundel	1-7
21	Portsmouth Royal Navy v Newbury Town	4-1
22	Cirencester Town v Sanford Youth Centre	wo/s
	Melksham Town v Calne Town	3-1
	Yate Town v Forest Green Rovers	3-2
23	Malvern Town v Pegasus Juniors	4-1
	Soundwell v Hanham Athletic	3-2
3r	Bradford Rovers v Thackley	0-3
5r	Anson Villa v Chloride Recreation	1-2
7r	Sutton Coldfield Town v Paget Rangers	4-1
8r	Madeley College v Stratford Town	1-3
r	Northfield Town v Astwood Bank Rovers	2-1
11r	Rickmansworth Town v Hazells Aylesbury	2-1
r	Tring Town v Windsor & Eton	0-3
12r	Hertford Town v Welwyn Garden United	1-2
13r	Basildon United v Clapton	2-3
14r	Wembley v Staines Town	2-0
18r	Dorking v Whyteleafe	2-0
19r	Bicester Town v Wallingford Town	2-1
r	Chesham United v Didcot Town	3-1
r	Morris Motors v Chalfont St Peter	1-3

Qualifying Round One

1	Ashington v Annan Athletic	5-2
	Consett v Alston	3-2
	Penrith v Gretna	2-2
	Stanley United v Alnwick Town	2-2
2	Billingham Synthonia v Willington	0-0
	Durham City v Wingate	3-0
	Ferryhill Athletic v Crook Town	2-3
	Norton Cricket Club Trust v Bishop Auckland	1-3
3	Leeds Ashley Road v Whitkirk Wanderers	4-2
	Ossett Albion v Liversedge	2-0
	Thackley v Harrogate Town	0-2
	Yorkshire Amateur v Harrogate Railway Athletic	0-0
4	Ainsdale v Old Blackburnians	4-0
	Hoylake Athletic v Prescot Town	2-6
	Kirkby Town v Blackpool Mechanics	0-3
	Wigan Rovers v Lostock Gralam	1-1
5	Chloride Recreation v Hanley Town	0-2
	Curzon Ashton v Old Altrinchamians	1-2
	Manchester YMCA v Irlam Town Amateur	1-1
	Wythenshaw Amateurs v East Chorlton Amateur	4-1
6	Clipstone Welfare v North Ferriby United	1-1
	Frecheville Community v Sheffield	2-0
	Sheffield University v Norton Woodseats	3-2
	Worsborough Bridge MW v Lincoln United	3-1
7	Boldmere St Michaels v Racing Club Warwick	2-2
	Lutterworth Town v Anstey Nomads	1-2
	Midland Athletic v Sutton Coldfield Town	1-3
	Mile Oak Rovers v Knowle	3-2
8	Birmingham City Police v GKN Sankey	1-0
	Birmingham University v Northfield Town	2-3
	Moor Green v Stratford Town	4-0
	Solihull Borough v Walsall Wood	3-0
9	Coggeshall Town v Watton United	2-3
	Heybridge Swifts v Clacton Town	0-0
	Tiptree United v Whitton United	2-0
	Witham Town v Bungay Town	2-1
10	Ampthill Town v Saffron Walden Town	4-0
	Northampton Spencer v Royston Town	3-0
	Park Wanderers v Shillington	0-1
	Rothwell Town v Shefford Town	2-3
11	Berkhamsted Town v Windsor & Eton	3-0
	Boreham Wood v Hemel Hempstead Town	4-0
	Rickmansworth Town v Marlow	0-3
	Wolverton Town & BR v Aylesbury United	2-2
12	Harlow Town v Electrolux	5-0
	Hoddesdon Town v Harpenden Town	6-2
	Stansted v Welwyn Garden United	1-0
	Ware v Leighton Town	2-3

1972/73

13 Billericay Town v Clapton	2-0
Edmonton Haringey v Barkingside	6-3
Hornchurch v Chingford	0-2
Rainham Town v Epping Town	1-1
14 Harefield United v Ruislip Manor	3-2
Harrow Borough v Borough Road College	1-0
Kingsbury Town v Wingate	4-1
Uxbridge v Wembley	0-2
15 Cray Wanderers v Swanley	2-2
Faversham Town v Grays Athletic	0-1
Royal Arsenal Sports v Slade Green Athletic	3-1
Thames Polytechnic v Herne Bay	2-4
16 Camberley Town v BAC Weybridge	1-0
Chertsey Town v Addlestone	3-0
Chessington United v Egham Town	0-5
Farnham Town v Virginia Water	1-1
17 Hampton v Hounslow Town	1-1
Lion Sports v Malden Town	1-2
Molesey v Feltham	1-0
Willesden v Civil Service	2-2
18 Burgess Hill Town v Dorking	0-5
East Grinstead v Banstead Athletic	3-0
Horsham v Horley	5-0
Horsham YMCA v Reigate Priory	3-1
19 Bicester Town v Chalfont St Peter	0-2
Bracknell Town v Chesham United	2-3
Thame United v Abingdon Town	0-0
Wokingham Town v Pressed Steel	1-1
20 Lewes v Bexhill Town	2-0
Shoreham v Ringmer	1-5
Whitehawk v Eastbourne United	0-4
Worthing v Arundel	0-0
21 Bemerton Athletic v Portsmouth Royal Navy	3-0
Brockenhurst v Moneyfield Sports	0-1
Chichester City v Pagham	4-0
Gosport Borough v Selsey	3-0
22 Hungerford Town v Bromham	4-2
Melksham Town v Cirencester Town	6-2
Moreton Town v Devizes Town	0-3
Westbury United v Yate Town	1-1
23 Mangotsfield United v Sharpness	1-1
Pershore United v Malvern Town	2-2
Soundwell v Frampton United	2-3
Viney St Swithins v Glenside Hospital	0-5
24 Ottery St Mary v Radstock Town	0-2
Paulton Rovers v Clevedon	3-1
Topsham v Greenway Sports	1-1
Wellington v Saltash United	0-3
1r Alnwick Town v Stanley United	2-3
r Gretna v Penrith	2-4
2r Willington v Billingham Synthonia	3-2
3r Harrogate Railway Athletic v Yorkshire Amateur	0-2
4r Lostock Gralam v Wigan Rovers	0-1
5r Irlam Town Amateur v Manchester YMCA	1-0
6r North Ferriby United v Clipstone Welfare	6-2
7r Racing Club Warwick v Boldmere St Michaels	5-1
9r Clacton Town v Heybridge Swifts	1-0
11r Aylesbury United v Wolverton Town & BR	3-0
13r Epping Town v Rainham Town	1-2
15r Swanley v Cray Wanderers	5-1
16r Virginia Water v Farnham Town	0-1
17r Hounslow Town v Hampton	2-0
r Willesden v Civil Service	0-2
19r Abingdon Town v Thame United	2-0
r Pressed Steel v Wokingham Town	0-2
20r Arundel v Worthing	0-1
22r Yate Town v Westbury United	3-0
23r Malvern Town v Pershore United	2-1
r Sharpness v Mangotsfield United	1-2
24r Greenway Sports v Topsham	4-0 N

Qualifying Round Two

1 Ashington v Stanley United	1-0
Penrith v Consett	2-3
2 Crook Town v Bishop Auckland	1-2
Durham City v Willington	4-4
3 Harrogate Town v Ossett Albion	1-3
Leeds Ashley Road v Yorkshire Amateur	2-0
4 Blackpool Mechanics v Prescot Town	1-3
Wigan Rovers v Ainsdale	0-2
5 Hanley Town v Old Altrinchamians	1-4
Irlam Town Amateur v Wythenshaw Amateurs	2-2
6 North Ferriby United v Frecheville Community	4-0
Worsborough Bridge MW v Sheffield University	4-0
7 Racing Club Warwick v Mile Oak Rovers	0-1
Sutton Coldfield Town v Anstey Nomads	1-1
8 Moor Green v Solihull Borough	2-0
Northfield Town v Birmingham City Police	1-0
9 Watton United v Clacton Town	4-1
Witham Town v Tiptree United	2-1
10 Ampthill Town v Shefford Town	1-2
Northampton Spencer v Shillington	0-0
11 Boreham Wood v Aylesbury United	5-3
Marlow v Berkhamsted Town	2-1
12 Harlow Town v Stansted	4-0
Hoddesdon Town v Leighton Town	1-1
13 Chingford v Rainham Town	3-2
Edmonton Haringey v Billericay Town	1-0
14 Harefield United v Wembley	0-0
Harrow Borough v Kingsbury Town	2-1
15 Grays Athletic v Royal Arsenal Sports	5-0
Herne Bay v Swanley	2-4
16 Camberley Town v Farnham Town	0-0
Chertsey Town v Egham Town	1-4
17 Hounslow Town v Civil Service	2-1
Molesey v Malden Town	0-2
18 East Grinstead v Dorking	0-0
Horsham v Horsham YMCA	5-0
19 Abingdon Town v Wokingham Town	1-1
Chalfont St Peter v Chesham United	2-4
20 Eastbourne United v Worthing	2-1
Lewes v Ringmer	1-0
21 Chichester City v Bemerton Athletic	3-2
Gosport Borough v Moneyfield Sports	2-1
22 Hungerford Town v Devizes Town	0-5
Melksham Town v Yate Town	1-0
23 Frampton United v Malvern Town	2-5
Glenside Hospital v Mangotsfield United	0-3
24 Radstock Town v Paulton Rovers	1-1
Saltash United v Greenway Sports	0-0
2r Willington v Durham City	0-2
5r Wythenshaw Amateurs v Irlam Town Amateur	4-3
7r Anstey Nomads v Sutton Coldfield Town	0-1
10r Shillington v Northampton Spencer	4-4
12r Leighton Town v Hoddesdon Town	2-1
14r Wembley v Harefield United	3-0
16r Farnham Town v Camberley Town	3-2
18r Dorking v East Grinstead	1-0
19r Wokingham Town v Abingdon Town	2-1
24r Paulton Rovers v Radstock Town	1-0
r Saltash United v Greenway Sports	2-2
10r2 Shillington v Northampton Spencer	3-1
24r2 Saltash United v Greenway Sports	3-2

Qualifying Round Three

1 Ashington v Consett	4-1
2 Durham City v Bishop Auckland	0-0
3 Ossett Albion v Leeds Ashley Road	2-2
4 Prescot Town v Ainsdale	0-0
5 Old Altrinchamians v Wythenshaw Amateurs	5-1
6 North Ferriby United v Worsborough Bridge MW	1-1
7 Mile Oak Rovers v Sutton Coldfield Town	1-1
8 Moor Green v Northfield Town	1-0
9 Watton United v Witham Town	0-2
10 Shefford Town v Shillington	1-2
11 Marlow v Boreham Wood	0-0
12 Harlow Town v Leighton Town	2-0
13 Edmonton Haringey v Chingford	1-1
14 Wembley v Harrow Borough	2-1
15 Grays Athletic v Swanley	3-1
16 Egham Town v Farnham Town	4-0
17 Hounslow Town v Malden Town	3-0
18 Dorking v Horsham	2-1
19 Chesham United v Wokingham Town	2-0
20 Eastbourne United v Lewes	1-0
21 Chichester City v Gosport Borough	3-0
22 Melksham Town v Devizes Town	0-6
23 Malvern Town v Mangotsfield United	1-0
24 Paulton Rovers v Saltash United	4-2
2r Bishop Auckland v Durham City	4-0
3r Leeds Ashley Road v Ossett Albion	0-2
4r Ainsdale v Prescot Town	0-1
6r Worsborough Bridge MW v North Ferriby United	0-1
7r Sutton Coldfield Town v Mile Oak Rovers	4-0
11r Boreham Wood v Marlow	1-0
13r Chingford v Edmonton Haringey	1-2

Qualifying Round Four

Alton Town v Hounslow Town	1-4
Boreham Wood v Grays Athletic	3-2
Bristol St George v Cadbury Heath	1-1
Bromley v Harlow Town	0-1
Chesham United v Wembley	1-1
Cheshunt (2) v Southall	3-0
Chichester City v Redhill	2-1
City of Norwich School OBU v Stowmarket	1-1
Corinthian Casuals v Fareham Town	2-2
Devizes Town v Newquay	2-0
Dorking v Leyton	0-2
Emley v Bishop Auckland	2-2
Erith & Belvedere v Eastbourne United	0-1
Evesham United v Highgate United (Birmingham)	1-1
Hallam v Leeds & Carnegie College	1-2
Maidenhead United v Egham Town	5-0
Moor Green v Sutton Coldfield Town	2-2
North Ferriby United v Ashington	2-2
Old Altrinchamians v Prescot Town	1-2
Ossett Albion v Whitby Town	3-2
Paulton Rovers v Malvern Town	2-1
Shildon v West Auckland Town	2-1
Vauxhall Motors v Shillington	1-1
Witham Town v Edmonton Haringey	4-2
r Ashington v North Ferriby United	1-0
r Bishop Auckland v Emley	1-0
r Cadbury Heath v Bristol St George	3-0
r Fareham Town v Corinthian Casuals	3-2
r Highgate United (Birmingham) v Evesham United	2-0
r Shillington v Vauxhall Motors	1-0
r Stowmarket v City of Norwich School OBU	2-1
r Sutton Coldfield Town v Moor Green	3-0
r Wembley v Chesham United	1-0

Round One

Ashington v Alvechurch	0-1
Aveley v Wembley	3-1
Barking v Shillington	3-0
Bishop Auckland v Sutton Coldfield Town	0-0
Bishops Stortford v Boreham Wood	1-0
Carshalton Athletic v Harlow Town	0-2
Dagenham v Walthamstow Avenue	2-1
Devizes Town v Hitchin Town	1-4
Dulwich Hamlet v Tooting & Mitcham United	1-4
Enfield v Leytonstone	1-1
Evenwood Town v Tow Law Town	3-0
Harwich & Parkeston v Leatherhead	3-1
Hayes v Tilbury	2-0
Hendon v Chichester City	7-0
Highgate United (Birmingham) v Prescot Town	1-0
Hounslow Town v Eastbourne United	2-2
Ilford v Fareham Town	2-0
Maidenhead United v Leyton	1-1
Marine v Blyth Spartans	0-1
Ormskirk v Loughborough College	2-2
Ossett Albion v Oldbury United	1-1
Oxford City v Woking	2-1
Paulton Rovers v Croydon Amateur	0-1
Prestwich Heys v Leeds & Carnegie College	1-1
Shildon v Spennymoor United	0-1
Slough Town v Cadbury Heath	2-1
St Albans City v Finchley	0-0
Stowmarket v Kingstonian	0-2
Sutton United v Walton & Hersham	0-3
Whitley Bay v North Shields	1-2
Witney Town v Witham Town	5-0
Wycombe Wanderers v Cheshunt (2)	0-1
r Eastbourne United v Hounslow Town	4-2a
r Finchley v St Albans City	1-2
r Leeds & Carnegie College v Prestwich Heys	3-0
r Leyton v Maidenhead United	2-1
r Leytonstone v Enfield	3-2
r Loughborough College v Ormskirk	1-2
r Oldbury United v Ossett Albion	1-0
r Sutton Coldfield Town v Bishop Auckland	0-2
r2 Eastbourne United v Hounslow Town	1-0aN
r3 Eastbourne United v Hounslow Town	4-0 N

Round Two

Aveley v Witney Town	0-0
Barking v Evenwood Town	0-1
Bishops Stortford v Bishop Auckland	3-0
Blyth Spartans v Hendon	1-1
Cheshunt (2) v Ormskirk	0-1
Croydon Amateur v Alvechurch	1-4
Dagenham v Harwich & Parkeston	5-0
Eastbourne United v Slough Town	0-2
Highgate U (Birmingham) v Tooting & Mitcham U	3-0
Hitchin Town v Hayes	3-4
Ilford v Kingstonian	2-1
Leeds & Carnegie College v Walton & Hersham	0-3
Leyton v Spennymoor United	0-3
Leytonstone v Oldbury United	1-1
North Shields v Oxford City	1-0
St Albans City v Harlow Town	2-0
r Hendon v Blyth Spartans	0-1
r Oldbury United v Leytonstone	0-0
r Witney Town v Aveley	1-3
r2 Leytonstone v Oldbury United	1-0 N

Round Three

Bishops Stortford v Aveley	1-0
Evenwood Town v Alvechurch	3-1
Highgate United (Birmingham) v Ilford	3-0
North Shields v Blyth Spartans	0-1
Ormskirk v Dagenham	1-4
Slough Town v Leytonstone	2-1
Spennymoor United v Hayes	2-1
Walton & Hersham v St Albans City	5-0

Round Four

Dagenham v Bishops Stortford	1-1
Evenwood Town v Highgate United (Birmingham)	1-1
Slough Town v Blyth Spartans	2-1
Walton & Hersham v Spennymoor United	0-0
r Bishops Stortford v Dagenham	2-1
r Highgate United (Birmingham) v Evenwood Town	2-0
r Spennymoor United v Walton & Hersham	0-1

Semi Finals

Slough Town v Bishops Stortford	1-0 N
Walton & Hersham v Highgate United (Birmingham)	0-0 N
r Walton & Hersham v Highgate United (Birmingham)	4-0 N

Final

Walton & Hersham v Slough Town	1-0 N

1973/74

```
1973/74
```

Preliminary Round

1	Annan Athletic v South Bank	1-4
	Ashington v Wingate	2-1
	Billingham Synthonia v Wallsend	2-3
	Consett v Ferryhill Athletic	3-3
	Durham City v Penrith	4-1
	Norton Cricket Club Trust v Stanley United	0-4
	Willington v Heaton Stannington	3-0
2	Chadderton v Birkenshaw Rovers	5-0
	Harrogate Town v Brook Sports	0-2
3	Leeds Ashley Road v Frecheville Community	3-0
	Norton Woodseats v Hallam	0-5
4	Chloride Recreation v Anson Villa	1-2
	East Chorlton Amateur v Blackpool Mechanics	2-0
5	Kirkby Town v Ainsdale	0-1
	Middlewich Athletic v Hoylake Athletic	8-0
6	Clipstone Welfare v Paget Rangers	0-0
7	Malvern Town v Astwood Bank Rovers	4-2
	Pegasus Juniors v Knowle	1-3
8	Lutterworth Town v Racing Club Warwick	0-1
9	Letchworth Town v Arlesey Town	4-0
	Shefford Town v Baldock Town	2-3
10	Brightlingsea United v Braintree & Crittall Athletic	1-0
	Clacton Town v Brantham Athletic	4-0
11	Berkhamsted Town v Amersham Town	1-1
	Hazells Aylesbury v Aylesbury United	0-4
12	Hemel Hempstead Town v Ware	2-3
13	Harrow Borough v Rayners Lane	3-1 N
14	Civil Service v BAC Weybridge	3-1
	Feltham v Chessington United	1-2
15	Cray Wanderers v Bexley	1-0
	Ford United v Clapton	1-0
16	Billericay Town v Barkingside	4-0
	Dartford Amateurs v Basildon United	0-2
17	Egham Town v Borough Road College	2-0
	Marlow v Bracknell Town	0-0
18	Chertsey Town v Addlestone	0-1
	Cobham v Camberley Town	1-1
19	Horley v Reigate Priory	3-0
20	Eastbourne Town v Bexhill Town	1-2
	Lewes v Burgess Hill Town	6-1
21	Chichester City v Arundel	0-3
	Lancing Athletic v Brockenhurst	0-4
22	Calne Town v Abingdon Town	1-4
	Didcot Town v Bemerton Athletic	3-2
23	Forest Green Rovers v Avon	2-0
	Hanham Athletic v Cirencester Town	1-4
24	Ottery St Mary v St Lukes College	1-2
1r	Ferryhill Athletic v Consett	0-1
6r	Paget Rangers v Clipstone Welfare	6-0
11r	Amersham Town v Berkhamsted Town	1-4
17r	Bracknell Town v Marlow	1-1
18r	Camberley Town v Cobham	0-6
17r2	Marlow v Bracknell Town	1-0

Qualifying Round One

1	Ashington v Wallsend	5-2
	Consett v Crook Town	4-0
	Durham City v Willington	4-3
	Stanley United v South Bank	3-0
2	Chadderton v Brook Sports	2-1
	Guiseley v Thackley	1-2
	Old Blackburnians v Liversedge	1-1
	Whitkirk Wanderers v Yorkshire Amateur	1-5
3	Leeds Ashley Road v Hallam	0-2
	North Ferriby United v Sheffield University	1-0
	Swallownest CW v Worsborough Bridge MW	0-3
4	Anson Villa v East Chorlton Amateur	2-2
	Curzon Ashton v Northern Nomads	1-2
	Manchester YMCA v Irlam Town Amateur	1-4
5	Ainsdale v Middlewich Athletic	0-1
	Lostock Gralam v Prescot Town	1-1
	Old Altrinchamians v Moulton	4-0
	Stork v Wigan Rovers	0-1
6	Blakenall v Northfield Town	4-1
	Mile Oak Rovers & Youth v Boldmere St Michaels	1-1
	Paget Rangers v Anstey Nomads	3-3
	Players Athletic v Walsall Wood	1-5
7	Malvern Town v Knowle	2-1
	Moor Green v Solihull Borough	3-1
	Rowley United v Pershore United	1-4
	Stratford Town v Sutton Coldfield Town	0-0
8	Coventry Amateur v Northampton Spencer	9-2
	Midland Athletic v Friar Lane OB	1-3
	Racing Club Warwick v Burton Park Wanderers	3-0
	Rothwell Town v Valley Sports Rugby	3-0
9	Letchworth Town v Baldock Town	4-0
	Saffron Walden Town v Stotfold	4-2
	Stansted v Shillington	4-3
	Warboys Town v Peterborough Rovers	0-2
10	Brightlingsea United v Clacton Town	0-2
	Bungay Town v Tiptree United	2-4
	Heybridge Swifts v Coggeshall Town	0-4
	Watton United v Witham Town	1-0
11	Berkhamsted Town v Aylesbury United	1-2
	Chesham United v Tring Town	1-1
	Thame United v Leighton Town	2-0
	Wallingford Town v Wolverton Town & BR	2-3
12	Crown & Manor v Hoddesdon Town	1-0
	Hertford Town v Epping Town	2-1
	Ware v Chingford	4-3
	Welwyn Garden City v Wingate	0-1
13	Chalfont St Peter v Harrow Borough	1-4
	Edgware v Kingsbury Town	2-0
	Hounslow Town v Edmonton Haringey	2-0
	Ruislip Manor v Wembley	2-1
14	Civil Service v Chessington United	2-0
	Epsom & Ewell v Ulysses	0-1
	Malden Town v Hampton	1-2
	Virginia Water v Willesden	2-2
15	Cray Wanderers v Ford United	1-1
	Eton Manor v Rainham Town	0-2
	Hornchurch v Grays Athletic	1-0
	Royal Arsenal Sports v Thames Polytechnic	0-2
16	Billericay Town v Basildon United	2-1
	Crockenhill v Herne Bay	3-2
	Faversham Town v East Thurrock United	1-0
	Slade Green Athletic v Swanley	1-2
17	Egham Town v Marlow	1-1
	Harefield United v Uxbridge	0-2
	Staines Town v Molesey	0-0
	Windsor & Eton v Wokingham Town	1-2
18	Addlestone v Cobham	4-0
	Chobham v Frimley Green	0-3
	Farnham Town v Farnborough Town	0-4
	Lion Sports v Westfield	2-2
19	Dorking v Horsham YMCA	2-1
	Horley v Banstead Athletic	2-0
	Horsham v East Grinstead	5-0
	Tunbridge Wells v Whyteleafe	2-1
20	Bexhill Town v Lewes	0-3
	Eastbourne United v Whitehawk	1-0
	Shoreham v Ringmer	0-2
	Wigmore Athletic v Worthing	1-1
21	Arundel v Brockenhurst	0-3
	Gosport Borough v Portsmouth Royal Navy	2-1
	Pagham v Moneyfield Sports	0-3
	Portfield v Selsey	6-0
22	Abingdon Town v Didcot Town	3-1
	Devizes Town v Pressed Steel	0-0
	Newbury Town v Hungerford Town	1-3
	Swindon Victoria v Wantage Town	2-0
23	Forest Green Rovers v Cirencester Town	2-0
	Sharpness v Longlevens Star	3-0
	Westbury United v Yate Town	1-4
24	Exmouth Town v Radstock Town	2-1
	Paulton Rovers v Melksham Town	6-2
	Wellington v Wells City	3-2
2r	Liversedge v Old Blackburnians	4-1
3r	Sheffield v Ossett Albion	1-2
4r	East Chorlton Amateur v Anson Villa	1-3
5r	Prescot Town v Lostock Gralam	1-4
6r	Anstey Nomads v Paget Rangers	1-0
r	Boldmere St Michaels v Mile Oak Rovers & Youth	0-2
7r	Sutton Coldfield Town v Stratford Town	3-1
11r	Tring Town v Chesham United	1-2
14r	Willesden v Virginia Water	4-0
15r	Ford United v Cray Wanderers	3-2
17r	Marlow v Egham Town	5-1
r	Molesey v Staines Town	0-1
18r	Westfield v Lion Sports	1-1
20r	Worthing v Wigmore Athletic	2-1
22r	Pressed Steel v Devizes Town	0-3
24r	St Lukes College v Clevedon	2-0
18r2	Lion Sports v Westfield	2-1

Qualifying Round Two

1	Durham City v Ashington	0-1
	Stanley United v Consett	2-2
2	Chadderton v Yorkshire Amateur	1-2
	Thackley v Liversedge	1-3
3	Hallam v Worsborough Bridge MW	3-0
	North Ferriby United v Ossett Albion	3-1
4	Anson Villa v Warrington Town	4-2
	Northern Nomads v Irlam Town Amateur	1-0
5	Lostock Gralam v Old Altrinchamians	2-3
	Middlewich Athletic v Wigan Rovers	5-2
6	Anstey Nomads v Walsall Wood	2-2
	Blakenall v Mile Oak Rovers & Youth	4-1
7	Malvern Town v Sutton Coldfield Town	0-0
	Moor Green v Pershore United	2-0
8	Coventry Amateur v Friar Lane OB	1-3
	Racing Club Warwick v Rothwell Town	1-1
9	Letchworth Town v Peterborough Rovers	2-2
	Saffron Walden Town v Stansted	5-0
10	Clacton Town v Watton United	4-0
	Tiptree United v Coggeshall Town	1-1
11	Aylesbury United v Wolverton Town & BR	2-0
	Chesham United v Thame United	5-0
12	Crown & Manor v Hertford Town	0-3
	Ware v Wingate	2-0
13	Edgware v Hounslow Town	1-1
	Harrow Borough v Ruislip Manor	3-3 N
14	Civil Service v Willesden	0-3
	Ulysses v Hampton	0-4
15	Ford United v Thames Polytechnic	3-0
	Rainham Town v Hornchurch	0-3
16	Billericay Town v Swanley	2-0
	Crockenhill v Faversham Town	1-3
17	Marlow v Wokingham Town	1-2
	Uxbridge v Staines Town	2-1
18	Addlestone v Lion Sports	3-0
	Frimley Green v Farnborough Town	0-3
19	Dorking v Horsham	1-7
	Horley v Tunbridge Wells	1-1
20	Eastbourne United v Ringmer	1-2
	Lewes v Worthing	0-2
21	Brockenhurst v Portfield	3-2
	Gosport Borough v Moneyfield Sports	2-2
22	Abingdon Town v Swindon Victoria	1-0
	Devizes Town v Hungerford Town	2-0
23	Forest Green Rovers v Yate Town	0-1
	Viney St Swithins v Sharpness	1-2
24	Exmouth Town v Paulton Rovers	0-1
	St Lukes College v Wellington	3-2
1r	Consett v Stanley United	2-1
6r	Walsall Wood v Anstey Nomads	1-4
7r	Sutton Coldfield Town v Malvern Town	1-1
8r	Rothwell Town v Racing Club Warwick	3-0
9r	Peterborough Rovers v Letchworth Town	1-6
10r	Coggeshall Town v Tiptree United	3-1
13r	Hounslow Town v Edgware	2-1
19r	Tunbridge Wells v Horley	0-1
21r	Moneyfield Sports v Gosport Borough	2-1
7r2	Sutton Coldfield Town v Malvern Town	1-0
13r2	Ruislip Manor v Harrow Borough	1-1
13r3	Ruislip Manor v Harrow Borough	2-1 N

Qualifying Round Three

1	Consett v Ashington	0-1
2	Yorkshire Amateur v Liversedge	3-1
3	Hallam v North Ferriby United	0-0
4	Anson Villa v Northern Nomads	3-1
5	Middlewich Athletic v Old Altrinchamians	1-0
6	Anstey Nomads v Blakenall	2-1
7	Sutton Coldfield Town v Moor Green	2-1
8	Rothwell Town v Friar Lane OB	0-0
9	Letchworth Town v Saffron Walden Town	3-0
10	Clacton Town v Coggeshall Town	5-1
11	Aylesbury United v Chesham United	3-3
12	Ware v Hertford Town	0-1
13	Ruislip Manor v Hounslow Town	0-0
14	Willesden v Hampton	1-2
15	Ford United v Hornchurch	1-4
16	Billericay Town v Faversham Town	2-2
17	Wokingham Town v Uxbridge	2-0
18	Addlestone v Farnborough Town	0-0
19	Horley v Horsham	1-3
20	Worthing v Ringmer	4-1
21	Brockenhurst v Moneyfield Sports	3-0
22	Abingdon Town v Devizes Town	4-0
23	Yate Town v Sharpness	2-1
24	St Lukes College v Paulton Rovers	1-1
3r	North Ferriby United v Hallam	2-0
8r	Friar Lane OB v Rothwell Town	2-0
11r	Chesham United v Aylesbury United	2-1
13r	Hounslow Town v Ruislip Manor	1-2
16r	Faversham Town v Billericay Town	2-1
18r	Farnborough Town v Addlestone	1-0
24r	Paulton Rovers v St Lukes College	1-2

Qualifying Round Four

Abingdon Town v Hampton	1-1
Alton Town v Farnborough Town	2-1
Anson Villa v Middlewich Athletic	0-5
Ashington v Whitley Bay	2-0
Boreham Wood v Bromley	3-1
Bristol St George v Fareham Town	0-1
Brockenhurst v St Lukes College	2-0
Chesham United v Letchworth Town	1-0
City of Norwich School OBU v Clacton Town	2-3
Emley v Evesham United	2-0
Erith & Belvedere v Leyton	0-3
Faversham Town v Worthing	3-1
Harlow Town v Maidenhead United	0-0
Hornchurch v Vauxhall Motors	1-0
Horsham v Corinthian Casuals	3-0
North Ferriby United v Sutton Coldfield Town	1-2
Prestwich Heys v Anstey Nomads	0-0
Ruislip Manor v Carshalton Athletic	1-1
Southall v Redhill	2-1
West Auckland Town v Bishop Auckland	1-3
Whitby Town v Shildon	0-0
Wokingham Town v Hertford Town	1-3
Yate Town v Newquay	2-3
Yorkshire Amateur v Friar Lane OB	1-3
r Anstey Nomads v Prestwich Heys	1-3
r Carshalton Athletic v Ruislip Manor	1-0
r Hampton v Abingdon Town	1-0
r Maidenhead United v Harlow Town	2-0
r Shildon v Whitby Town	3-0

1973/74

Round One

Aveley v Alton Town	5-0
Bishop Auckland v Shildon	0-3
Bishops Stortford v Hayes	2-0
Blyth Spartans v Sutton Coldfield Town	3-0
Boreham Wood v Hitchin Town	1-1
Cadbury Heath v Tilbury	1-3
Chesham United v Maidenhead United	3-2
Croydon Amateur v Leyton	0-1
Dagenham v Walton & Hersham	1-3
Dulwich Hamlet v Newquay	3-0
Fareham Town v Cheshunt (2)	1-1
Faversham Town v Barking	1-6
Hampton v Leytonstone	2-4
Hendon v Harwich & Parkeston	0-0
Hertford Town v Finchley	2-0
Horsham v Clacton Town	2-1
Kingstonian v Ilford	0-0
Leatherhead v Enfield	4-0
Leeds & Carnegie College v Prestwich Heys	4-0
Loughborough College v Friar Lane OB	2-2
Marine v Ashington	1-2
Middlewich Athletic v Oldbury United	4-0
North Shields v Alvechurch	2-0
Ormskirk v Evenwood Town	1-2
Oxford City v Slough Town	1-1
Southall v Carshalton Athletic	2-2
Spennymoor United v Emley	4-0
St Albans City v Brockenhurst	1-1
Sutton United v Tooting & Mitcham United	3-1
Tow Law Town v Highgate United (Birmingham)	1-2
Walthamstow Avenue v Woking	1-2
Wycombe Wanderers v Hornchurch	5-0
r Brockenhurst v St Albans City	2-0
r Carshalton Athletic v Southall	1-2
r Cheshunt (2) v Fareham Town	1-1
r Friar Lane OB v Loughborough College	1-0
r Harwich & Parkeston v Hendon	1-1
r Hitchin Town v Boreham Wood	4-2
r Ilford v Kingstonian	2-1
r Slough Town v Oxford City	1-0
r2 Fareham Town v Cheshunt (2)	2-0 N
r2 Harwich & Parkeston v Hendon	2-2 N
r3 Hendon v Harwich & Parkeston	2-0

Round Two

Aveley v Leyton	0-0
Barking v Sutton United	1-3
Bishops Stortford v Hitchin Town	2-1
Blyth Spartans v Fareham Town	2-0
Evenwood Town v Wycombe Wanderers	0-3
Friar Lane OB v Chesham United	4-1
Highgate United (Birmingham) v Hertford Town	1-0
Horsham v Woking	2-2
Ilford v Brockenhurst	3-0
Leeds & Carnegie College v Dulwich Hamlet	0-2
Leytonstone v Walton & Hersham	0-1
Middlewich Athletic v Leatherhead	0-9
North Shields v Shildon	2-0
Slough Town v Ashington	1-1
Southall v Spennymoor United	1-1
Tilbury v Hendon	0-0
r Ashington v Slough Town	1-0
r Hendon v Tilbury	2-0
r Leyton v Aveley	0-1
r Spennymoor United v Southall	4-1
r Woking v Horsham	3-2

Round Three

Ashington v North Shields	1-1
Aveley v Woking	1-1
Blyth Spartans v Wycombe Wanderers	2-1
Dulwich Hamlet v Friar Lane OB	4-1
Hendon v Leatherhead	1-1
Ilford v Highgate United (Birmingham)	2-1
Spennymoor United v Sutton United	0-2
Walton & Hersham v Bishops Stortford	0-0
r Bishops Stortford v Walton & Hersham	1-0e
r Leatherhead v Hendon	1-1
r North Shields v Ashington	0-2
r Woking v Aveley	2-0
r2 Leatherhead v Hendon	2-0 N

Round Four

Ashington v Woking	2-0
Bishops Stortford v Blyth Spartans	3-1
Ilford v Dulwich Hamlet	1-1
Sutton United v Leatherhead	0-1
r Dulwich Hamlet v Ilford	0-1

Semi Finals

Bishops Stortford v Ashington	0-0 N
Ilford v Leatherhead	1-0 N
r Bishops Stortford v Ashington	3-0 N

Final

Bishops Stortford v Ilford	4-1 N

INDEX TO CLUB APPEARANCES

The following pages provide an index to the 2,655 clubs that have played in the tournament. The index shows the seasons they entered and the number of times they appear in the listings, including byes and games replayed after protest.

The seasons quoted are the final year of the season; for example, 1956 is season 1955/56. Two seasons on the same line are "from...to"; for example 1914 1953 is "from 1913/14 to 1952/53". The "war years" 1915/16 to 1918/19, and 1939/40 to 1944/45 are deemed "not to exist". Take this entry for example:

Dorking   1906 1914   135
                   1920 1936
                   1947 1974

This shows that Dorking appear 135 times in the listings. They played between seasons 1905/06 and 1913/14 inclusive, miss season 1914/15, appear between 1919/20 and 1935/36, miss a few seasons, then appear again between 1946/47 and 1973/74.

The club names in use at the time of the matches have been used as far as possible. The list of "other club names" in appendix one shows circumstances where the club is known to be the same club after a name change. Please note that this is an area where historical research is adding to our understanding of club development all the time.

Problems can arise when clubs change their names during the close season, after the draws for the early rounds have been published using their old name. If I have made a mistake in this regard (or anywhere else come to that) correspondence will be most welcome.

Abbreviations of club names have been avoided as far as possible, but some were inevitable. "T" is always "Town", "N" "North", "W" "West" and "S" "South". Others are:

Ath.	*Athletic*
Ams	*Amateurs*
Battn, Bn	*Battalion*
BL	*British Legion*
B.W.I	*British Workmen's Institute*
Ch	*Church*
Coms	*Comrades*
CW	*Colliery Welfare*
Engrs	*Engineers*
MW	*Miners Welfare*
OB	*Old Boys*
R	*Royal*
Regt, Rgmt	*Regiment*
RN	*Royal Naval*
Temp	*Temperance*
WM, WMC	*Working Men's Club*

Finally, some clubs were determined to exceed the space allowed for their names! Well done, Metal and Produce Recovery Depot Number One, Portland Prison Officers and Portland United, and Pirelli-General Cable Works Social and Sports.

1st Border Regiment to Beccles Town

Index of clubs

Club	From	To	Count
1st Border Regt	1931	1932	3
1st Cheshire Regiment	1908		2
1st Coldstream Guards	1897 1901	1899	9
1st Duke of Cornwall LI	1910 1912		2
1st Durham Light Infantry	1932	1935	12
1st Grenadier Guards	1906 1908 1922	1914 1923	14
1st Heavy Brigade RGA	1912	1914	7
1st Highland Light Infantry	1895 1900		4
1st Kings Dragoon Guards	1932		1
1st Kings Own Scots Borderers	1929	1930	7
1st Kings Own Yorkshire LI	1930	1931	4
1st Kings Royal Rifles	1911	1914	14
1st Leicestershire Regiment	1909	1910	5
1st Loyal North Lancs Regt	1913	1914	10
1st Middx Regt	1925	1926	6
1st North Staffs Regiment	1911		5
1st Queens Royal Regt	1926		1
1st Royal Scots Fusiliers	1899	1900	4
1st Royal Scots Guards	1908		11
1st Royal Warwickshire Regm	1921 1929		2
1st Royal Welsh Fusiliers	1913	1914	11
1st Scots Guards	1897 1900 1907	1898 1911	22
1st Sherwood Foresters	1931		2
1st South Lancs Regiment	1900		1
1st Welsh Guards	1924		1
1st Yorkshire Regiment	1900		1
2nd Argyll & Sutherland Highlanders	1924	1927	11
2nd Beds & Herts Regiment	1931	1933	4
2nd Black Watch	1931	1933	3
2nd Coldstream Guards	1896 1906 1909 1920	1899 1914	22
2nd Connaught Rangers	1921	1922	3
2nd Durham Light Infantry	1913		6
2nd East Lancs Regt (Aldershot)	1896	1897	9
2nd East Yorks Regt	1936	1937	3
2nd Gordon Highlanders	1897	1898	6
2nd Grenadier Guards	1897 1905	1898 1914	34
2nd Kings Royal Rifles	1912 1929 1931	1932	16
2nd Kings Shropshire LI	1934		4
2nd Lancs Fusiliers	1912	1913	7
2nd Leicestershire Regt	1926	1927	4
2nd Lincolnshire Regiment	1907	1908	13
2nd Loyal Regt	1933	1936	10
2nd Middlesex Regt	1935 1937	1938	4
2nd Northumberland Fusiliers	1912	1913	12
2nd Rifle Brigade	1926	1930	9
2nd Royal Dublin Fusiliers	1913		2
2nd Royal Fusiliers	1904		1
2nd Royal Scots	1925		4
2nd Royal Scots Fusiliers	1895 1898	1896	11
2nd Royal Warwicks Regiment	1907		5
2nd Scots Guards	1895 1913	1914	7
2nd Scottish Rifles	1909	1911	13
2nd Training Battn RAOC	1951		1
2nd Wiltshire Regiment (Gosport)	1912		4
37th Co. RGA	1910		1
3rd Coldstream Guards	1899 1914		6
3rd Grenadier Guards	1895 1909	1899 1914	17
3rd Kent RGA Volunteers	1905	1907	6
3rd Kent VA	1900 1904	1902	7
3rd Training Battn RASC	1948		5
4th Divisional Signals Regiment	1931	1934	13
4th Kings Royal Rifles	1907	1909	11
4th Middlesex Regiment	1911 1913	1914	6
4th Royal Fusiliers	1913		3
4th Royal Tank Corps	1935	1939	17
5th Co BB OB	1925		1
5th Northumberland Fusiliers	1911		3
5th Royal Tank Corps	1928 1936	1930	12
6th Durham Light Infantry	1926	1929	12
10th Royal Hussars	1926	1927	3
12th London Regt Rangers	1924		1
16th Co. RGA	1910		1
87th Royal Irish Fusiliers	1909	1910	5
AC Delco	1954	1960	11
AC Sphinx	1950	1953	9
APV Athletic	1956 1960	1958	8
Abbey United	1927 1929 1932	1930 1949	30
Abingdon	1908	1914	12
Abingdon Pavlova	1924	1928	11
Abingdon Town	1921 1947	1939 1974	92
Accles & Pollock (Oldbury)	1966	1969	14
Achilles	1948 1953 1967	1950 1965 1971	39
Acklam Steelworks	1966	1968	4
Acomb Working Men	1921	1922	4
Acton	1935		2
Acton Town	1947	1950	8
Adam Grimaldi	1920		1
Addlestone	1926 1955	1931 1974	66
Addlestone United	1925		1
Aero Engines	1939		2
Ainsdale	1973	1974	6
Ainsdale Hesketh Park	1956 1964 1971	1962 1966 1972	18
Ainthorpe OB	1968 1971		6
Alcan Industries	1962	1963	2
Alcester Town	1972		4
Alderley Edge Athletic	1925		1
Alderley Edge United	1927		1
Aldershot Albion	1925	1928	6
Aldershot Excelsior	1922		2
Aldershot Institute Albion	1922	1924	7
Aldershot Town	1922		1
Aldershot Traction Company	1923	1932	28
Alexandra Park	1929 1934 1955	1938	8
Alford	1908		1
Allen West	1924	1927	4
Allens Cross	1959	1960	2
Alleyn	1905	1906	4
Alnwick Alndale	1937	1938	3
Alnwick Town	1969	1973	14
Alsager College	1971		4
Alston	1969	1973	15
Altofts	1965 1968	1966	9
Alton	1907		2
Alton Town	1950 1973	1971 1974	77
Alvaston & Boulton	1923		1
Alvechurch	1958	1974	45
Amersham Town	1950 1968 1974	1963 1972	29
Amesbury	1959 1966 1968	1964 1970	13
Ampthill Town	1953 1967	1973	15
Andover	1938	1939	2
Anglo (Purfleet)	1936	1937	9
Annan Athletic	1970	1974	12
Annfield Plain	1959	1961	11
Annfield Plain Celtic	1899		2
Anson Villa	1973	1974	8
Anstey Nomads	1953 1961	1959 1974	58
Anston Reading Room	1928	1929	2
Apperley Bridge	1923	1928	17
Appleby	1948 1952	1949 1964	17
Appleby Frodingham Works	1960		1
Apsley	1898 1923 1938	1915 1936 1947	84
Aquarius	1920	1939	30
Arden	1912 1922	1913 1923	13
Arlecdon Red Rose	1949		1
Arlesey Town	1920 1922 1924 1931 1938 1947 1963	1928 1932 1939 1960 1974	77
Arlington	1922		1
Armley	1922		6
Armthorpe Welfare	1955	1960	18
Army Ordnance Corps	1910	1914	12
Army Ordnance Depot (Plumstead)	1913		2
Army Service Corps (Aldershot)	1911		1
Army Service Corps (Woolwich)	1903 1911	1914	21
Arnold St Marys	1958	1960	4
Arnold Town	1926	1928	3
Artillery College Sports	1923	1926	11
Arundel	1922 1928 1951 1969	1925 1966 1974	45
Asbury Richmond	1909	1910	2
Ash United	1914		1
Ashford (Middx)	1924	1927	5
Ashford United	1894	1895	3
Ashington	1894 1970	1974	25
Ashmore Benson Pease & Co.	1912	1913	6
Ashmore Recreation	1949 1953	1954	8
Ashville	1963	1969	13
Aspatria Spartans	1950		1
Aspley OB	1957	1961	13
Aston Old Edwardians	1895 1908	1896	6
Astwood Bank Rovers	1970	1974	11
Atherstone Town	1908	1911	22
Atherton Colliery	1953		1
Atlas & Norfolk (Sheffield)	1954	1958	9
Atlas Sports	1951	1954	10
Attercliffe United	1924	1928	15
Attercliffe Victory	1927		2
Avalon Rovers	1902		1
Aveley	1953 1955 1974	1974	79
Avon			1
Aylesbury United	1898 1906 1920	1903 1914 1974	182
Aylesford Paper Mills	1932 1937 1947 1963	1939 1954	40
BAC Weybridge	1965	1974	25
BL (Austin)	1952		1
Baddesley Colliery	1957	1961	10
Baddesley OB	1936		1
Badsey Rangers	1921 1929 1932 1948 1962	1926 1939 1953	60
Bakers Sports	1955	1957	3
Baldock Town	1923 1949 1974	1939 1972	91
Balham	1908		3
Banbury Central	1911	1914	6
Banbury Early Closers	1921		1
Banbury Harriers	1922	1939	23
Banbury Spencer	1935 1939	1937	17
Bank Head United	1956	1959	9
Banstead Athletic	1950	1974	69
Banstead Hospital	1939	1946	6
Banstead Mental Hospital	1935	1938	6
Barclays Bank	1935 1960	1939	8
Barkers Athletic	1949	1950	2
Barking	1906 1933	1915 1974	144
Barking Town	1920	1932	41
Barking Woodville	1896 1898		8
Barkingside	1955 1957 1973	1970 1974	24
Barnard Castle	1913 1947		4
Barnard Castle Athletic	1932	1939	13
Barnet	1920	1965	140
Barnet & Alston	1913	1915	9
Barnet (1)	1898		2
Barnet (2)	1912		1
Barnet Alston Athletic	1906	1912	23
Barnsley Corinthians	1910		1
Barnsley OG	1914		1
Barnstaple Town	1949		5
Barnt Green United	1926		2
Barnton Victoria	1939		1
Barton Hill (Bristol)	1898		1
Barton Rovers	1968	1971	10
Barwell Athletic	1955	1959	6
Basford United	1908 1929 1946	1927 1930 1965	74
Basildon Town	1956	1959	7
Basildon United	1973	1974	4
Basingstoke	1906 1912 1933	1910 1934	9
Basingstoke Town	1952		1
Bata Sports	1949 1954	1952 1961	20
Bath City	1907	1909	6
Battle Athletic	1949	1950	4
Bearpark CW	1950	1957	23
Beccles	1950	1962	34
Beccles Caxton	1899 1902 1959	1910	16
Beccles Town	1921 1924	1922 1932	25

Beckenham to Burgess Products

Team			
Beckenham	1926	1938	47
	1950	1966	
Beckenham Rovers	1910		2
Beckenham Town	1967		3
	1969		
Beddington Corner	1913	1914	13
	1929	1937	
Bedford Avenue	1946	1963	31
Bedford Corinthians	1950	1955	10
Bedford Lynton Works	1950	1951	2
Bedford Police	1950		1
Bedford Queens Works	1948	1952	5
Bedford St Cuthberts	1950	1951	2
Bedlington Mechanics	1954		1
Bedminster	1894	1898	8
Bedminster Down	1928		1
Bedminster Down Sports	1938		3
Bedminster St Francis	1901	1904	8
Bedminster St Pauls	1898		1
Beeston	1894	1895	5
Belmont Athletic Athletic	1915		5
Belvedere	1921	1922	2
Bemerton Athletic	1969	1974	10
Bentinck Welfare	1947		1
Bentinck Welfare Colts	1948		4
Bentley Engineering	1957		7
	1960		
Beresford Athletic	1914		5
Berkhamsted Sunnyside	1900		4
	1902	1903	
Berkhamsted Town	1922	1951	102
	1953	1974	
Bermuda WMC	1969	1972	5
Berridge Institute	1938		2
Berwick Rangers	1894	1896	5
	1898		
Bestwood Colliery	1950	1951	15
	1961	1964	
Betteshanger CW	1935	1939	8
Beverley Church Institute	1899		1
Beverley Town	1908	1909	3
Bexhill	1929	1939	20
Bexhill Town	1946	1965	56
	1968		
	1970	1974	
Bexley	1933	1939	51
	1947	1969	
	1971	1974	
Bexleyheath & Welling	1931	1932	9
	1952	1953	
Bexleyheath Labour	1921		1
Bexleyheath Town	1923	1930	18
Bicester Town	1923		92
	1925	1939	
	1947	1973	
Bigges Main Celtic	1938	1939	5
Biggleswade & District	1905		1
Biggleswade Town	1947	1951	8
Billericay Town	1973	1974	7
Billingham South	1938	1939	2
Billingham St Johns	1949		1
Billingham Synthonia	1937	1974	88
Bilsthorpe Colliery	1961	1963	3
Bilston Amateurs	1922	1923	4
Bilston Borough	1937	1938	4
Bingley	1906		2
Bingley Town	1923	1924	4
Birkenhead Amateurs	1924	1928	6
Birkenshaw Rovers	1969	1974	10
Birmingham City Police	1967	1968	11
	1970	1973	
Birmingham City Transport	1951	1957	12
Birmingham Gas Officials	1931	1933	8
Birmingham Tramways	1927	1931	16
Birmingham University	1921	1924	13
	1971		
	1973		
Birmingham University Assoc.	1907		2
Birmingham YMCA	1922		3
	1925	1926	
Birstall Parish Church	1923		1
Birtley	1896		2
Bishop Auckland	1894	1974	277
Bishops Stortford	1924	1974	126
Bitterne Nomads	1947	1949	11
	1963	1964	
Black Watch	1900		1
Blackburn Crosshill	1904	1910	16
Blackheath Town	1967		1
Blackhill	1934	1935	4
Blackpool Amateurs	1903		2
Blackpool Mechanics	1956	1963	36
	1969	1974	
Blackpool Metal Mechanics	1955		3
Blackpool Rangers	1953	1958	29
	1960	1965	
	1970		
Blackwall & TIW	1920	1922	4
Blairs	1923		1
Blakenall	1966	1974	19
Blandford	1921	1934	28
Blandford Institute	1924		2
Blandford United	1935	1938	32
	1948	1954	
	1956	1961	
Bletchley & Wipac Sports	1956	1958	6
Bletchley Town	1932	1934	20
	1951	1955	
	1959	1961	
Bletchley United	1961	1962	3
Blundellsands	1925	1927	10
	1929		
Blyth Spartans	1965	1974	42
Blyth YMCA	1964		1
Bodmin Town	1950	1953	7
Bognor	1904	1907	8
	1909		
Bognor Regis	1931	1939	14
Bognor Regis Town	1946	1972	59
Bognor Town	1922	1930	17
Bohemians	1908		1
Boldmere St Michaels	1924		96
	1931	1932	
	1935	1974	
Bolsover Colliery	1924		2
	1949		
Bolton SS OB	1922		1
Boothtown	1923		6
	1928	1929	
Boots Athletic	1920	1929	74
	1933	1937	
	1947	1964	
Boreham Wood	1924		55
	1955	1974	
Borough Road College	1970	1974	10
Boscombe	1907	1913	17
Bostall Heath	1922	1939	54
Boston	1900		3
	1968		
Boston Town	1920	1921	2
Boston Victoria	1899		1
Botley	1949		1
Bottom Boat	1938	1939	2
Botwell Mission	1920	1929	19
Boulton & Paul	1930	1935	26
	1950	1953	
Bourne Town	1936	1937	4
	1939		
Bournemouth	1895	1899	108
	1905	1914	
	1920	1939	
	1947	1959	
	1961	1964	
Bournemouth Gasworks Athletic	1920	1959	91
Bournemouth Tramways	1920	1931	40
Bournemouth Transport	1932	1936	9
Bournemouth Wanderers	1896		25
	1904	1914	
Bournville Athletic	1909		55
	1925	1929	
	1946	1971	
Bowater Lloyds	1950	1953	16
	1955	1957	
Bowes Park	1901	1907	11
Bowling Albion	1923	1924	4
Box Hill Sports	1965		1
Box Rovers	1961		2
Boxmoor	1926		1
Boxmoor St Johns	1934		1
Braby's	1913		3
Brackley Town	1932		1
Bracknell Town	1965	1974	21
Bradfield Waifs (Norbury Park)	1897	1900	6
Bradford	1897		3
Bradford Airedale	1907		2
Bradford Electricity	1955		2
Bradford Rovers	1935	1937	67
	1947	1966	
	1968	1973	
Bradford Town	1925	1927	5
Bradford-on-Avon	1900		5
	1909		
	1911		
Braintree	1896	1898	5
Braintree & Crittall Athletic	1974		1
Braithwaite	1951		2
Brandon CW	1946	1947	7
Brandon Rovers	1897		3
Brandon Social	1936	1937	8
Branksome Gasworks Athletic	1906	1914	23
Brantham Athletic	1922		69
	1926	1935	
	1937	1939	
	1948	1971	
	1974		
Braunston United	1926		2
Breaston	1933		1
Brentford	1898	1899	3
Brentstonians	1959	1963	21
	1966	1971	
Brentwood & Warley	1926	1934	62
	1947	1965	
Brentwood Mental Hospital	1925	1931	15
Brereton Social	1928		1
Bretforton OB	1951	1952	3
	1955		
Bridgetts United	1948		5
Bridgford Athletic	1904	1908	11
Bridgnorth Town	1939		2
Bridgwater	1902		1
Bridgwater Town	1949		1
Bridlington	1921		3
Bridlington Athletic	1910		1
Bridlington Central United	1949	1959	23
Bridlington Town	1960		1
Bridlington Trinity United	1949	1951	21
	1955	1960	
Bridport	1907		3
	1939		
	1949		
Brigade of Guards	1935	1938	11
Briggs Motor Bodies	1936	1939	6
Briggs Sports	1946	1959	44
Briggs Sports (Doncaster)	1955	1956	4
Brigham & Cowans	1946	1948	5
Brightlingsea United	1933	1939	18
	1949	1954	
	1974		
Brighton & Hove Amateurs	1920	1922	5
Brighton Amateurs	1904	1907	6
Brighton Mental Hospital	1933	1936	15
Brighton Old Corinthians	1953	1954	3
Brighton Old Grammarians	1951	1952	31
	1955	1965	
	1968	1969	
Brighton Railway Athletic	1924		1
Brighton St Margarets Athletic	1914		1
Brighton Tramways	1936	1939	4
Brighton West End (Newcastle)	1913	1922	8
Brimscombe	1924		28
	1926	1929	
	1956	1965	
Brislington	1904	1905	7
	1939		
Brislington St Annes	1906		2
Bristol Aeroplane Co	1947	1949	3
Bristol Amateurs	1900		1
Bristol Mental Hospital	1959	1960	3
Bristol South End	1895	1897	7
Bristol St George	1894	1897	101
	1902		
	1925	1930	
	1935		
	1939		
	1948	1974	
Bristol St Georges Sports	1922		10
	1924		
Bristol St Philips	1907	1908	7
British Insulators SC	1934	1935	5
British Ropes (Retford)	1950		8
	1952		
	1958	1959	
British Steel Corp (Scunthorpe)	1970		2
Broadwater	1923		15
	1925	1934	
Brockenhurst	1963	1964	32
	1966	1968	
	1970	1974	
Brodsworth Main	1957	1959	6
Bromborough Pool	1936	1938	5
Bromham	1925	1930	45
	1958	1973	
Bromley	1905	1974	186
Bronze Athletic	1912	1914	7
Brook Sports	1967	1974	24
Brooklands	1914		1
Brookwood Hospital	1939		4
	1947	1949	
Brookwood Mental Hospital	1937	1938	3
Broom Youth	1949	1950	4
Broomfield (1)	1936	1938	3
Broomfield (2)	1946		1
Broomhall Boys	1947		1
Brooms (Leadgate)	1913	1915	11
Brotton	1899		15
	1908		
	1913	1921	
	1923		
Broughton	1912	1914	7
Brunswick Avenue OB	1935	1938	4
Brunswick Institute	1906	1907	31
	1923		
	1938	1939	
	1947	1962	
Buckingham Athletic	1972		1
Buckingham Town	1950	1958	16
Bugle	1949	1956	21
	1959	1960	
Bulford United	1952	1960	27
Bulwell Forest Villa	1962	1971	23
Bulwell Town	1910		2
Bungay Town	1936	1939	76
	1947	1974	
Buntingford Town	1962	1971	15
Burberry	1915	1923	10
Burfield Park	1924	1925	2
Burgess Hill	1908		1
Burgess Hill Town	1972	1974	3
Burgess Products (Hinckley)	1954	1955	5

Burnham to Cotham Amateurs

Club	From	To	Count
Burnham	1898	1900	5
	1903		
Burnham United	1949	1953	5
Burnhope Institute	1929	1932	6
Burnley Belvedere	1903	1904	4
Burnside United	1954	1959	10
Burradon Welfare	1959		2
Burraton	1954	1960	8
Burton Casuals	1906	1907	2
Burton Lane Club & Institute	1922		3
Burton Park Wanderers	1974		1
Bury Alexandra	1905	1907	3
Bury Amateur	1964	1965	5
Bury Amateurs	1922		1
Bury Athenaeum	1902		5
Bury St Edmunds	1899	1901	17
	1906	1907	
	1913	1914	
	1921	1924	
Bury Town	1925	1926	51
	1928	1938	
	1947	1948	
	1956	1958	
Bush Hill Park	1924	1926	4
Bushey United	1933	1939	8
Butlers	1925		2
Butter Knowle WM	1926	1927	3
Buxton	1895	1896	12
	1906	1908	
Byng Road OB	1971		1
CSD (Hereford)	1921		1
CWS Silvertown	1937	1939	6
Cadbury Heath	1971	1974	15
Cadbury Heath YMCA	1931	1933	13
	1935	1939	
Cadbury's Athletic	1926	1928	6
Cadby Hall	1932		2
Caerleon Athletic	1913		1
Calgarth	1949		1
Callender Athletic	1929	1953	58
	1956	1971	
Calne & Harris United	1922	1939	64
	1947	1964	
Calne Town	1920	1921	18
	1965	1974	
Calverley	1921	1925	12
Camberley	1947	1972	39
Camberley & Yorktown	1913	1914	39
	1920	1939	
Camberley Town	1973	1974	5
Cambridge City	1952	1958	15
Cambridge House	1910		3
Cambridge St Marys	1907	1908	2
Cambridge Town	1915	1951	78
Cambridge United	1911		6
	1913	1914	
Cambridge University	1967	1968	8
Camelford	1950	1951	22
	1953	1958	
Camelford United	1959		2
Camerton	1908	1911	10
Cammell Laird	1926		1
Cannock	1897		1
Cannock Amateurs	1914		2
Canvey Island	1966	1971	13
Cardiff Albion	1921		2
Cardiff Amateurs	1922		1
Cardiff Bohemians	1922		2
Cardiff CS	1922		1
Cardiff Camerons	1922		2
Cardiff Corinthians	1912	1914	25
	1920	1922	
Cardiff Harlequins	1920	1921	2
Cargo Fleet & Cochranes	1933	1934	2
Cargo Fleet Ironworks	1915		11
	1921	1924	
Cargo Fleet Works	1935	1937	25
	1939		
	1947	1959	
Carlin How Athletic	1923	1927	17
	1936	1937	
Carlin How United	1921		3
Carlisle BR	1959	1960	4
Carlton United	1939		7
	1948		
	1958		
Carpathians	1948	1949	5
Carrow	1911	1915	8
Carrow Works	1909		21
	1923	1927	
	1929	1930	
	1949	1951	
Carshalton	1939		2
	1949		
Carshalton Athletic	1923	1939	126
	1947	1974	
Carter's Engineering Works	1902		3
Carter's Potteries Ath. (Poole)	1912	1914	3
Castle Hill	1925		8
	1927	1931	
Casuals	1894	1899	71
	1907		
	1923	1939	
Catford Southend	1910	1923	21
	1927		
Catford Wanderers	1931	1947	28
Catherine-de-Barnes	1949	1950	6
	1952		
Cavendish Amateurs (Barrow)	1906		1
Caversham Rovers	1908	1912	18
Caversham St Andrews	1925	1930	8
Celanese Amateurs	1931		1
Chadderton	1965	1974	30
Chadwell Heath	1950		1
Chalfont National	1962		2
Chalfont St Peter	1962	1974	31
Chalford	1926	1939	36
	1948	1952	
	1961	1963	
Chandos OB	1964		1
Chapel Town	1962	1965	10
	1968	1970	
Chard Town	1950	1960	22
Charlton Albion	1909	1910	3
Charlton Athletic	1915	1920	4
Charlton Kings	1949		9
	1951	1953	
Charlton Rovers	1908	1911	9
Chatham	1894	1895	10
	1937	1939	
	1947		
Chatham Amateurs	1901	1902	7
	1913	1914	
Chatham Institute	1910		1
Chatteris Engineering Works	1908	1910	9
Chatteris Engineers	1933	1937	13
Chatteris Town	1928	1937	31
	1939		
	1947	1949	
Chelmsford	1896	1897	80
	1902	1938	
Chelmsford Swifts	1908		1
Chelmsley Town	1969	1971	5
Chelston	1957	1964	12
Cheltenham Town	1906	1907	22
	1920		
	1924	1928	
	1930	1932	
Cherry Orchard	1939		1
Chertsey	1909		5
	1949	1950	
Chertsey Town	1951	1963	39
	1968		
	1970	1974	
Chesham	1894	1895	2
Chesham Generals	1894	1900	47
	1902	1914	
Chesham Town	1902	1914	28
Chesham United	1920	1974	157
Cheshire Magpies	1896		1
Cheshunt (1)	1896	1907	74
	1920	1931	
Cheshunt (2)	1948	1974	85
Chessington United	1973	1974	3
Chester College	1971	1972	6
Chesterfield Corinthians	1922	1923	4
	1926	1927	
Chesterfield Ramblers	1939		5
	1949	1950	
Chesterfield Tube Works	1967	1970	7
Chesterton Laurels	1909		1
Chichester	1911	1914	31
	1921	1927	
	1934	1939	
	1947	1948	
Chichester City	1949	1965	54
	1967	1974	
Chichester United	1956	1958	3
Chilton Athletic	1948	1958	16
Chilton Colliery Recreation	1923	1939	49
Chilton Street OB	1914		1
Chilton & Windlestone Senior Boys	1947		4
Chingford	1956	1968	28
	1970	1974	
Chippenham Rovers	1921	1928	25
	1930	1937	
Chippenham Town	1898	1899	84
	1901	1902	
	1907	1908	
	1914		
	1920	1948	
Chippenham United	1948		1
Chipperfield	1947	1951	8
Chipping Norton	1922		10
	1950	1952	
Chipping Norton CA	1935	1936	3
Chipping Norton Town	1953	1956	26
	1958		
	1963	1970	
Chirk	1894		3
Chiswick Town	1920	1922	5
Chloride Recreation	1964	1974	30
Chobham	1962	1972	23
	1974		
Christ Church	1968		2
Christ Church OB Harrogate	1957		1
Christchurch	1913	1914	14
	1922	1924	
	1949	1951	
	1971		
Churchmans Sports	1950	1953	4
Cinderford Town	1939		23
	1947	1955	
Cinderhill Colliery	1950	1956	11
Cirencester Town	1968	1974	21
City Ramblers	1895	1896	4
City of Birmingham Ed College	1968	1969	2
City of Norwich School OBU	1947	1950	72
	1952		
	1954	1963	
	1965	1974	
City of Westminster	1905	1906	13
	1909	1911	
	1914	1915	
Civil Service	1897	1907	119
	1921	1929	
	1931	1939	
	1947	1974	
Clacton Town	1914		55
	1921	1939	
	1947	1948	
	1972	1974	
Clandown	1920	1929	92
	1931	1961	
Clapham	1905	1910	6
Clapham Rovers	1894	1898	11
	1900		
Clapton	1894	1895	173
	1905	1974	
Claycross & Danesmoor	1958	1959	4
Clayton	1969	1971	5
Cleator Moor Celtic	1926		48
	1948	1958	
	1960	1963	
	1966	1972	
Cleckheaton	1923	1927	15
Cleethorpes Town	1929	1930	5
Clevedon	1908	1913	137
	1924	1929	
	1932	1974	
Cleveland Mines	1959		1
Cleveland Works	1937		2
Clifton	1895	1898	9
Clifton All Whites	1970	1971	3
Clifton Colliery	1922	1928	19
Clifton St Vincents	1971	1972	2
Cliftonville	1895		2
Clipstone Welfare	1964		8
	1971	1974	
Clove	1906	1911	9
Clowne Liberal	1927		1
Clulows United	1935		1
Clutton Wanderers	1921	1927	13
	1929		
Coalville Town	1903		2
Coalville Town Amateur	1938	1948	12
Cobham	1938	1939	46
	1948	1954	
	1956	1974	
Cochranes Sports	1949	1953	8
Cockermouth	1948	1949	3
Cockfield	1909		96
	1915	1937	
	1939		
	1949	1955	
	1957	1963	
Coggeshall Town	1973	1974	6
Colchester	1896	1897	4
Colchester Casuals	1948	1951	14
	1953	1956	
Colchester Crown	1903	1911	16
Colchester Town	1900	1902	74
	1904		
	1906	1912	
	1914		
	1920	1938	
Coleford Athletic	1923	1937	38
	1949	1953	
Coleford United	1969	1972	5
Collegiate OB	1924	1926	3
Consett	1964	1974	43
Consett Ironworks	1922	1924	4
Consett Swifts	1913	1915	5
Constable Street OB	1948		1
Coombs Wood	1923		2
Corby United	1954		4
	1958	1959	
Corinthian Casuals	1946	1974	69
Corinthians	1947	1948	2
Cornsay Park Albion	1955		2
	1960		
Corsham Town	1949	1959	15
Corton	1950	1951	3
Coryton	1926		1
Cosby United	1953		14
	1955	1957	
	1960	1964	
Cotham Amateurs	1902	1903	3

Cottingham to Exeter Argyle

Team	Year	Year	Num
Cottingham	1912	1914	9
	1921		
Coundon United	1921	1927	15
Courage & Co's Sports	1931	1937	10
Courtaulds	1932		1
Coventry Amateur	1947	1974	62
Coventry Magnet	1927		1
Coventry Strollers	1932		2
Cowans Sheldon	1956	1957	7
Cowes	1908	1910	4
Cowley	1922	1938	45
Craghead CW	1955	1957	8
Craghead Heroes	1920		1
Craghead United	1911	1914	16
Cranfield United	1953	1957	6
Cranleigh	1911	1913	13
	1934	1939	
Craven Arms	1948		1
Crawley	1929	1931	14
	1952	1953	
	1955	1959	
Crawley Town	1960	1962	7
Cray Wanderers	1894		109
	1908		
	1911	1912	
	1915		
	1923	1939	
	1947	1948	
	1953	1974	
Crayford	1908		1
Credenhill	1969	1970	5
Cresconians	1959		8
	1962	1964	
	1967	1969	
Crewe Alexandra	1895		3
Crittall Athletic	1926	1954	85
	1956	1963	
Crockenhill	1952	1974	51
Croft	1907	1909	5
Cromer	1905	1914	109
	1920	1921	
	1923	1938	
	1947	1968	
Crompton Parkinson	1938		1
Crook	1930		6
	1937	1939	
Crook Colliery Welfare	1946	1949	14
Crook Town	1897	1928	169
	1950	1974	
Crookhall CW	1931	1936	11
	1958	1959	
Crookhall Rovers	1939		1
Cross Castle United	1967	1969	10
Crouch End	1894	1897	8
Crouch End Vampires	1900	1907	22
Crown & Manor	1947	1950	36
	1955	1966	
	1968	1971	
	1974		
Crown Dynamos	1948		1
Croydon	1904	1907	31
	1909	1920	
	1922		
Croydon Amateur	1955	1958	57
	1960	1974	
Croydon Wanderers	1903	1907	5
Crumpsall	1937		1
Crusaders	1894	1896	7
Cuckfield	1954	1958	8
Curzon Amateur	1966		2
	1968		
Curzon Ashton	1969	1974	11
Custom House	1907	1936	68
Dagenham	1951	1974	83
Dagenham British Legion	1947	1954	15
Dagenham Cables	1937		23
	1950	1951	
	1953	1958	
	1960	1961	
Dagenham Park	1955		1
Dagenham Town	1930	1939	33
Dainite Sports	1958		1
Darlaston	1960	1962	9
	1966		
Darlington	1894	1908	37
Darlington &Simpson Rolling Mill	1957	1960	5
Darlington Amateurs	1937	1939	5
Darlington East End	1914	1915	2
Darlington Railway Athletic	1920	1928	17
	1971		
Darlington Rolling Mills	1939	1948	5
Darlington St Augustines	1894	1915	36
Darlington St Hildas	1894		9
	1902	1903	
Darlington Trinity	1908	1909	5
Dartford	1905	1908	7
Dartford Amateurs	1971		2
	1974		
Dartmouth United	1953	1961	25
Daventry	1925	1926	2
Daventry Town	1927		11
	1929	1934	
	1936		
	1939		

Team	Year	Year	Num
David Brown Athletic	1949		2
Dawley Amateurs	1922		2
Dawson Payne & Elliott Sports	1947		3
De Havilland Hatfield	1947	1950	4
De Havilland Vampires	1948	1950	3
Deal Town	1934	1946	10
Deanery Southampton	1921		1
Dearne Athletic	1948		1
Deerfield Athletic	1923		1
Deerness Sports	1956		2
Depot Middx Regt	1921	1922	2
Deptford Invicta	1908	1914	17
Derby Amateurs	1896	1897	2
Derby Constitutional	1897		1
Derby Hills Ivanhoe	1902	1906	11
Derby Nomads	1905		2
Dereham Town	1951	1954	9
	1961	1963	
Derwent Rangers	1948		2
Desborough Town	1959	1962	9
	1964		
Desford CW	1955	1956	5
Devas Institute	1951	1958	14
Devizes Town	1899	1900	144
	1903	1907	
	1910	1914	
	1920	1971	
	1973	1974	
Dick & Co's Sports	1922		1
Dickinsons Apsley	1949	1951	4
Didcot Town	1951	1953	55
	1955	1961	
	1963	1974	
Dilton Rovers	1947	1948	2
Dipton United	1913	1915	7
	1936	1937	
Diss Town	1927	1935	26
	1949	1950	
	1956	1958	
	1961	1963	
Distington	1947		1
Doddington United	1950		2
Doncaster United Amateurs	1960	1969	30
Donnington United	1949		1
Dorchester Town	1911	1914	41
	1922	1925	
	1927	1949	
Dorking	1906	1914	135
	1920	1936	
	1947	1974	
Dorman Long & Co. United	1910	1915	14
Douglas (Bristol)	1950	1952	5
Douglas (Kingswood)	1953		1
Dover	1894		4
	1936	1938	
Dover Marine Station	1926		2
Dover United	1922	1925	14
	1932	1933	
Downham Town	1954	1956	4
Downshall Athletic	1947	1951	8
	1953	1954	
Downton	1957	1958	4
Dowty New Mendip	1964		3
	1969		
Driffield North End	1928		1
Driffield Town	1910		1
Droitwich OB	1937	1938	4
Dronfield Woodhouse	1922		2
Dukinfield Town	1967	1968	4
Dulverton Town	1951	1952	2
Dulwich Hamlet	1905	1914	175
	1920	1974	
Dunlop Sports	1968	1970	6
Dunscroft Welfare	1953	1955	7
Dunstable Rangers	1906	1907	4
Dunstable Thursday	1900		2
Dunstable Town (1)	1897	1899	6
Dunstable Town (2)	1951	1954	8
Durham City	1952	1974	68
Durham County Constabulary	1956		1
Durham Light Infantry	1914		3
Durham University	1952	1956	8
Dursley Town	1924	1927	6
EEM Dept (Devonport)	1963	1968	14
Ealing	1895	1907	36
Ealing Association	1933	1939	9
Earl Shilton Institute	1951	1959	16
Earle	1923	1931	69
	1933	1961	
	1963	1964	
	1969		
Earlestown Bohemians	1936	1938	8
Earlsfield Town	1921	1922	4
Easington Sports	1962	1964	6
East Barnet OG	1972		1
East Bierley	1936	1946	7
East Chorlton Amateur	1957	1967	37
	1969	1974	
East Cowes	1926	1928	6
	1936		
East Cowes Victoria	1911		12
	1921		
	1953	1954	

Team	Year	Year	Num
East End Park	1923	1924	2
East End Park WMC	1957		4
East Grinstead	1909	1914	110
	1922		
	1924	1974	
East Ham	1906	1914	10
East Ham United	1956	1971	26
East Tanfield CW	1948		6
East Thurrock United	1974		1
Eastbourne	1896		153
	1898	1907	
	1920	1970	
Eastbourne Comrades	1931	1937	23
	1939		
	1947	1952	
Eastbourne Old Comrades	1925	1930	23
Eastbourne Old Town	1902	1906	8
Eastbourne RE Old Comrades	1922	1924	10
Eastbourne St Marys	1908		11
	1913	1915	
Eastbourne Swifts	1896	1902	10
Eastbourne Town	1971	1974	5
Eastbourne United	1953	1974	79
Eastern Coachworks (Lowestoft)	1938	1939	20
	1947	1955	
Eastern Counties United	1937		2
Eastham Athletic	1952	1955	6
Eastwood Hanley	1965	1966	5
Eastwood Town	1922		53
	1955	1971	
Eccleshill	1968		1
Eckington Works	1927		1
Eden CW	1931		1
Eden Colliery	1947		1
Eden Grove OB	1958	1960	4
Edgware	1972	1974	8
Edgware Town	1946	1971	74
Edlington Welfare	1929		2
Edmondsley Heroes	1913		1
Edmonton (1)	1922	1928	20
Edmonton (2)	1961	1972	22
Edmonton Borough	1948	1950	10
Edmonton Haringey	1973	1974	7
Egglescliffe & District	1930	1931	4
Egham	1923	1939	37
Egham Town	1966	1974	26
Egremont Town	1967	1968	2
Ekco	1947	1949	6
Eldon Albion	1904	1908	32
	1922	1926	
	1948	1954	
Eldra United	1968		1
Electric Supply & Transport	1956		1
Electrolux	1961	1973	21
Ellesmere Port Town	1930		2
	1932		
Elmore	1971		1
Ely City	1923	1936	46
	1947	1958	
Ely GE United	1924		2
Emley	1969	1974	19
Emsworth	1926		1
Enderby Town	1953	1958	11
Enfield	1897	1898	234
	1905	1974	
Enfield Cycle Co	1948	1949	2
English Electric (Stafford)	1963	1964	4
Epping Town	1937	1939	50
	1947	1951	
	1953	1974	
Epsom	1937	1961	57
Epsom & Ewell	1962	1971	37
	1974		
Epsom Town	1925	1936	42
	1946		
Equitation School	1924		2
Erdington	1913	1914	10
	1921	1923	
Erdington Celtic	1923		3
Ericsson Athletic	1959	1964	14
Erith	1894		1
Erith & Belvedere	1923	1974	153
Esavian Sports	1969		1
Esh Winning	1920	1935	49
Esh Winning Albion	1954	1959	16
Esh Winning Rangers	1909	1915	15
Esso	1938	1939	3
Eston United	1908	1929	58
Etherley	1947		1
Etherley United	1937	1938	2
Etherley Welfare	1927		3
Eton Manor	1935	1972	83
	1974		
Evenwood Crusaders	1937		2
Evenwood Town	1928	1974	118
Evergreen (Tunbridge Wells)	1895		1
Eversleigh (Balham)	1898		12
	1900	1907	
Evesham Town	1922	1926	25
Evesham United	1949	1952	24
	1970	1974	
Ewell & Stoneleigh	1937	1938	2
Excelsior Foundry	1932	1939	17
Exeter Argyle	1922		1

104

Exhall Colliery to Harrow Weald

Club	From	To	Count
Exhall Colliery	1927		1
Exmouth Town	1958	1959	20
	1967	1972	
	1974		
Exning United	1953	1955	4
Eynesbury Rovers	1933		18
	1935		
	1947	1949	
	1956		
	1961		
	1967	1969	
	1971	1972	
Fairfield (Buxton)	1907	1908	3
Fakenham	1910		3
Fakenham Town	1938	1939	11
	1951	1953	
Falmouth Docks	1965	1968	6
	1970		
Fareham	1922		29
	1925	1935	
	1937	1939	
Fareham Brotherhood	1933	1934	2
Fareham Casuals	1939		1
Fareham Town	1948	1974	83
Farnborough	1938		5
	1950	1953	
Farnborough Town	1974		5
Farncombe	1907	1912	27
	1954	1965	
Farnham	1908	1914	9
Farnham Town	1949	1951	56
	1953	1963	
	1965		
	1967	1974	
Farnham United Breweries	1922	1928	24
Farsley Celtic	1928	1933	29
	1935	1939	
	1949	1950	
	1959		
Faversham	1895	1898	11
	1912		
Faversham Town	1948	1970	70
	1972	1974	
Felixstowe Town	1929	1939	16
	1954	1955	
	1973		
Felixstowe United	1948	1953	8
Felpham	1924	1925	3
	1927		
Felstead (Silvertown)	1905		1
Feltham	1965	1974	20
Ferguson Pailin	1939	1946	8
Ferndale Road Working Mens	1922	1924	3
Ferndale Youth Centre	1965	1969	14
Fernhill Heath	1952	1961	19
Ferring	1967	1968	3
Ferrybridge Amateur	1955		1
Ferryhill Athletic	1922	1974	123
Ferryhill Station United	1937		2
Feversham Street	1923		3
Feversham United	1924	1927	7
Filey	1921		1
Filey Town	1928	1930	25
	1933	1938	
	1952	1954	
Filey United	1910		3
Finchley	1905	1915	165
	1922	1974	
Finedon Town	1955	1959	9
Finsbury	1957	1959	4
Firth Sports	1969		3
	1971		
Fleetwood Amateurs	1907		1
Folkestone	1894	1895	5
Folkestone Gas	1911	1913	8
Foots Cray	1909		29
	1927	1932	
	1953	1963	
Foots Cray Social	1947	1952	15
Ford Motors	1935		2
Ford Sports	1936	1959	41
Ford United	1960	1974	34
Forest Amateurs	1904		1
Forest Green Rovers	1963	1974	24
Formby	1926	1928	33
	1930		
	1933		
	1935	1939	
	1950	1951	
	1964		
	1967	1970	
Frampton United	1971	1973	5
Frecheville Community	1968	1974	14
Freemantle (Southampton)	1894		3
	1903		
Friar Lane OB	1974		9
Frickers Athletic	1921	1924	9
Frimley Green	1962	1974	32
Frizington United	1949	1951	6
Frome Town	1907	1910	83
	1914		
	1922	1953	
Frosts Athletic	1933	1934	11
	1936	1939	
Fry & Sons	1930	1932	3
Fryston CW	1960	1961	2
Fulford United	1928		2
	1950		
Fulham	1898	1899	5
Fulham Amateurs	1910	1913	4
Fulham St Andrews	1912	1913	6
Fulwood	1922	1923	12
	1925	1926	
	1937	1939	
	1947		
Fulwood Amateur	1950	1951	3
Furness Athletic	1923	1924	17
	1937	1939	
	1949	1954	
Furness Withy	1925	1928	11
GEC Coventry	1971	1973	3
GER Loco	1911		1
GER Loughton	1931	1932	2
GER Romford	1920	1930	38
GKN Sankey	1970	1973	9
Garforth	1923	1924	5
Garrard Athletic	1927	1933	14
Gaskill Chambers	1948	1949	2
Gatley Amateur	1969		1
Gedling CW	1960	1964	18
Gedling Colliery	1924	1926	40
	1928		
	1947	1949	
	1951	1959	
Gidea Park	1936	1938	3
Gillingham Old Collegians	1912		1
Gillingham Town	1925	1927	3
Glastonbury	1903	1904	26
	1906		
	1921	1933	
Gleadless	1922		3
Glendale Athletic	1924	1926	4
Glenside Hospital	1961	1962	8
	1971	1973	
Gloucester	1896		1
Gloucester City	1908	1910	29
	1927	1935	
Gloucester City YMCA	1964	1972	12
Gnome Athletic	1921	1923	7
Godalming	1904	1912	35
	1924	1939	
Godalming & Farncombe	1966	1971	8
Godalming United	1913	1914	2
Godmanchester Town	1924	1927	5
Golcar	1937		3
Golden Cross	1924	1925	10
	1927		
Golders Green	1934	1946	18
Goldsmith's Institute	1906		2
Goldstone	1955	1963	12
Goodyear Sports (Wolverhampton)	1957		1
Goole Amateurs	1905		2
Goole Town	1906		2
Gorleston	1909	1910	111
	1914		
	1920	1939	
	1947	1950	
	1961	1971	
Gorse Hill United	1960	1964	5
Gorsehill Workmen	1924	1925	4
Gosforth Amateurs	1937	1939	6
Gosport	1923	1925	25
	1929	1939	
Gosport Albion Sports	1924	1928	13
Gosport Athletic	1920	1922	22
	1924	1928	
Gosport Borough	1970	1974	11
Gosport Borough Athletic	1946	1969	70
Gosport United	1906	1908	18
	1911	1915	
Gothic	1947	1948	12
	1962	1963	
Gradwells Sports	1932	1934	10
Gramophone	1910	1911	2
Grange OB (Leeds)	1959		2
Grangetown Athletic	1899	1915	39
Grangetown St Marys	1913	1928	42
	1934	1939	
Grantham	1911		1
Grantham St Johns	1958	1961	7
	1968		
Grantham West End Albion	1907	1908	2
Gravesend Amateurs	1909		1
Gravesend Territorials	1932		1
Gravesend United	1935	1939	13
Grays Athletic	1909	1974	154
Grays United	1898		6
	1904		
Great Ayton Rovers	1913	1914	4
Great Ayton United	1939		1
Great Barford	1950		3
Great Western Railway Athletic	1905	1909	10
Great Wyrley	1972		4
Great Wyrley Wednesday	1971		1
Great Yarmouth	1898	1899	4
Great Yarmouth Town	1901	1938	111
	1947	1948	
	1959	1961	
Green & Silley Weir Athletic	1920	1921	6
	1951		
Green Waves	1950	1952	3
Greenfield Athletic	1923		1
Greenway Sports	1973		5
Gretna	1958		4
	1973		
Grimsby Albion	1926		1
Grimsby All Saints	1898	1901	14
Grimsby Haycroft Rovers	1922		6
	1929		
Grimsby Rovers	1923	1924	13
	1928	1929	
Grimsby Rovers Amateurs	1910		5
Grosmont	1922	1925	5
Grove Park	1905	1906	2
Guards Depot (Caterham)	1905	1910	27
	1912	1914	
	1920		
Guildford	1900		74
	1905	1953	
Guinness Exports	1960	1970	52
Guisborough	1948	1949	2
Guisborough Belmont Athletic	1920	1928	21
Guisborough Brigantes	1935		2
Guisborough Erimus	1912		1
Guisborough Red Rose	1908		2
Guisborough United	1913		1
Guiseley	1922	1923	104
	1925	1974	
Gwynne's Athletic	1923	1924	5
HMS Collingwood	1949		3
	1957		
HMS Daedalus	1953		8
HMS Dolphin	1937		1
HMS Excellent	1914		76
	1923	1954	
HMS Vernon	1936	1938	6
HMS Victory	1928	1932	29
	1934	1939	
Hadleigh United	1955	1961	10
Haig Colliery	1968		1
Haig United	1947	1948	5
Hailsham	1908	1909	3
	1911		
Halesworth	1900	1901	5
	1903		
	1907		
Halesworth Town	1925	1926	2
Hall Road Athletic	1938	1939	2
Hall Road Rangers	1967	1971	6
Hall's Engineers	1950		1
Hallam	1912		123
	1915	1922	
	1924	1931	
	1948	1974	
Halstead Town	1951	1955	17
	1961	1963	
Hammersmith Athletic	1897	1900	7
Hammersmith United	1950		2
Hampstead	1898	1907	18
Hampstead Town	1913	1933	44
Hampton	1961	1974	56
Hampton Sports	1952	1960	14
Hamsteels CW	1961		1
Hamworthy	1934	1939	55
	1948	1967	
	1969		
Handley Page	1920		1
Handsworth	1924	1925	3
Handsworth GS OB	1922		3
	1924		
Handsworth Oakhill	1905	1907	7
Handsworth United Sports	1929	1933	10
Handsworth Wood	1949	1951	5
Hanham Athletic	1924		105
	1926	1970	
	1972	1974	
Hanley Town	1970	1973	8
Hanwell	1905	1912	24
Hanwell Athletic	1922	1924	3
Hanwell Town	1925	1927	10
Harefield United	1970	1974	11
Harland & Wolff	1927		1
Harlow Town	1936	1939	75
	1947	1974	
Harpenden Town	1914	1915	41
	1950	1951	
	1958	1973	
Harpole Stars	1924		1
Harris Lebus	1956		4
Harrisons & Lewins	1936		1
Harrogate	1915		2
	1932		
Harrogate & District Railway	1952	1966	40
Harrogate Amateurs	1922	1923	2
Harrogate Railway Athletic	1967	1971	10
	1973		
Harrogate Town	1951	1959	46
	1965	1974	
Harrow Athletic	1899	1902	8
Harrow Borough	1967	1974	21
Harrow Town	1939	1966	61
Harrow Weald	1921	1926	10

Harrowby to Keele University

Club	From	To	No.
Harrowby	1915 1949 1959 1965	1939 1955 1962	59
Harrowby United	1969	1971	4
Hartlepool Railway Athletic	1951	1954	12
Harwich & Parkeston	1896 1921 1947	1914 1939 1974	189
Haslington	1908		1
Hastings & St Leonards	1902 1914 1922 1928 1957	1905 1926 1948 1960	87
Hastings Amateurs	1907		2
Hastings Athletic	1895		1
Hastings Rangers	1956 1964	1959	8
Hastings Rock-a-Nore	1905	1909	8
Hatcham Athletic	1907		2
Hatfield Town	1949	1964	31
Hatfield United	1939	1948	8
Hatford Main Welfare	1956		1
Hathersage	1909 1913 1929	1923 1930	28
Haverhill Rovers	1908		1
Haverton Hill	1921	1925	10
Hawker Athletic	1947 1951	1957	15
Hawker Siddeley	1967	1968	3
Hay Green	1947	1950	4
Haydon Street Workmen	1907	1909	3
Hayes	1930	1974	120
Hayesco Sports	1936	1937	10
Hays Wharf	1926	1927	2
Haywards Heath	1928 1967	1964 1969	73
Haywards Sports	1928	1931	8
Hazells Aylesbury	1935 1962	1939 1974	33
Head Wrightsons	1947 1949 1951	1956	20
Headingley	1914 1921 1925 1932	1923 1935	20
Headington United	1923 1932	1930 1949	36
Healey	1972		1
Heanor Town	1953		5
Hearts of Liddesdale	1950	1971	43
Heaton Chapel	1914		1
Heaton Chapel Amateurs	1922		1
Heaton Stannington	1921 1927 1935 1947 1955 1965 1974	1925 1929 1939 1953 1963 1972	74
Heavitree United	1924 1948	1964	44
Hebburn Old Boys	1912		3
Heckmondwike	1904		1
Hedon & Marfleet United	1968	1969	2
Heeley	1973		1
Heeley Amateur	1967	1968	2
Heighington Amateur	1956	1959	7
Helmston (Brighton)	1907 1910	1908	7
Helston Athletic	1949 1953	1951	5
Hemel Hempstead Town	1922 1948	1974	93
Hendon	1947	1974	121
Hendon Town	1926 1931	1929 1933	14
Henley	1897 1900 1905 1910 1914	1903 1911	9
Henley Comrades	1921	1926	10
Henley Town	1922	1964	52
Henley on Thames	1920	1921	5
Heptonstall	1938		1
Heptonstall Red Star	1933 1935		2
Hereford CSD	1922		1
Hereford City	1909 1924 1928 1935	1914 1926 1938	29
Hereford City Amateur	1939		3
Hereford Lads Club	1969		1
Hereford St Martins	1921	1924	5
Hereford Thistle	1895 1921	1925	17
Hermes	1963	1969	9
Herne Bay	1957	1974	62
Herrington Swifts	1913		3
Hersham	1930	1939	19
Hersham United	1910 1914 1921	1912 1924	13
Hertford Town	1910 1912 1920 1929 1950	1914 1927 1947 1974	137
Hesketh Park	1904 1910	1907 1911	7
Hessle	1904 1921	1906 1922	9
Heworth Parish Church	1910	1911	4
Hexham Hearts	1955	1956	4
Heybridge	1933	1935	3
Heybridge Swifts	1950 1973	1951 1974	8
Heys Old Boys	1962	1964	16
High Duty Alloys	1948	1950	5
High Littleton	1951	1953	3
Higham Ferrers Town	1952	1954	8
Higham Town	1955	1957	5
Highbridge Town	1950	1953	7
Highfield	1967	1971	10
Highgate	1906 1936	1907 1938	6
Highgate United (Birmingham)	1966	1974	40
Highgate United (Newcastle)	1957	1964	17
Highworth Town	1965		1
Hipperholme	1933	1934	2
Histon	1953	1971	53
Histon Institute	1932 1947 1949	1939 1952	32
Hitchin	1900 1910	1901	9
Hitchin Athletic	1923	1924	3
Hitchin Blue Cross	1922	1928	16
Hitchin Road OB	1951		3
Hitchin Town	1929	1974	125
Hobson Wanderers (Durham)	1899 1913	1900	6
Hoddesdon	1900 1905 1909	1907 1910	7
Hoddesdon Town	1924 1929	1927 1974	102
Hoffmann Athletic (Chelmsford)	1912 1925 1936 1949	1921 1927 1947 1951	32
Hoffmann Athletic (Stonehouse)	1947 1958 1961	1949 1959 1964	16
Holbeach United	1936	1937	2
Holborn	1907		1
Hollington United	1927 1938	1934 1939	14
Hollinwood	1922		2
Holme Head Works	1950	1954	9
Holt	1921	1923	3
Holt United	1937 1947 1952	1939 1949 1960	42
Holwell Works	1936	1949	19
Holy Guild (Sheffield)	1908		2
Home Park (Plymouth)	1894		3
Hoobrook Olympic	1909		1
Horbury	1937	1938	5
Horley	1953 1972	1955 1974	13
Horncastle Athletic	1921	1923	6
Horncastle Town	1921	1922	4
Horncastle United	1911	1912	3
Hornchurch	1962	1974	39
Hornchurch & Upminster	1953	1961	34
Hornsea	1911		4
Hornsea Town	1921	1923	7
Horsforth	1928	1933	12
Horsham	1899 1922	1915 1974	181
Horsham Trinity	1925	1928	4
Horsham YMCA	1972	1974	7
Houghton Rangers	1950	1952	5
Hounslow	1898 1907 1922	1899 1910 1931	29
Hounslow Town	1932	1974	128
Hove	1902 1905 1911 1914 1923	1903 1907 1915 1952	68
Hove Belmont	1912	1914	6
Hove Park	1907		2
Hove Town	1957	1959	5
Hove White Rovers	1953	1956	10
Howden BL	1928	1929	2
Howden Rangers	1895 1928		4
Howden-le-Wear	1896 1948 1952	1901 1950 1953	19
Hoxton Manor	1934	1939	13
Hoylake Athletic	1950 1954 1968 1971	1951 1962 1974	35
Hoylake Trinity	1923	1924	11
Hoylake United	1927		1
Hucknall Byron	1926	1927	2
Huddersfield	1897 1902		3
Hull	1898		1
Hull Albany	1896 1905		2
Hull Amateurs	1946 1961 1968	1947 1966 1970	18
Hull Central HG Old Boys	1905		3
Hull Dairycoates	1922		2
Hull Day Street OB	1910	1912	7
Hull Kingston Amateurs	1909	1910	2
Hull Nomads	1937 1949		3
Hull OB	1913 1920	1914 1931	22
Hull Old Grammarians	1953		1
Hull St Georges	1911	1912	4
Hull Technical College OB	1925		1
Hull University	1967		1
Hull Young Peoples Institute	1922 1924 1928	1926 1932	15
Humber Hillman Recreation	1933 1939		3
Humber Recreation	1925	1927	11
Humber United	1930	1937	20
Hungerford Town	1960 1972	1969 1974	22
Hunslet	1896	1902	21
Hunting Percival Athletic	1956	1958	4
Huntingdon Town	1913 1915 1929 1932	1923 1930	17
Huntingdon United	1914 1950 1954	1951 1955	7
Huntley & Palmers	1948 1958	1956 1971	52
Hunts County	1894		1
Huthwaite CWS	1947	1949	11
Hyde & Kingsbury	1921	1922	5
Hylton CW	1967		1
Hyson Green OB	1963		1
ICI Alkali	1936	1965	74
Ibstock Penistone Rovers	1934 1947 1953 1969	1939 1951 1960	46
Ibstock Swifts	1934	1936	7
Ilford	1894 1898 1902	1974	193
Ilfracombe Town	1923 1948	1925 1949	6
Ilkeston Town	1950		1
Ilkeston Town Reserves	1948		1
Ilkley	1926		1
Ilminster Town	1948 1964 1968	1962 1966 1970	43
Ings House	1923		1
Ipswich Electricity Supply	1948 1957 1960 1963 1965 1968	1954 1958	26
Ipswich Old Grammarians	1947	1949	3
Ipswich St John	1928		1
Ipswich Town	1894 1921	1907 1936	79
Ipswich Wanderers	1951 1954	1961	21
Ipswich Works	1921 1925	1922 1928	7
Irchester United Sports	1933	1934	4
Irlam Town	1970	1971	9
Irlam Town Amateur	1973	1974	7
Iron Acton	1963	1965	5
Irthlingborough	1903		1
Irthlingborough Diamonds	1970	1972	14
Islington Town	1920	1921	2
Iverston Villa	1911	1913	4
Jack Moulds Athletic	1935 1949	1939 1968	66
Jarrow	1896		1
Jesmond Villa	1926	1927	2
John Conway (Plymouth)	1970		1
Johnson & Barnes Athletic	1934 1937		4
Jurgens	1920 1931	1937	12
Keele University	1968	1969	2

Keighley Central to Maidstone Church Institute

Team	Year 1	Year 2	Count
Keighley Central	1967		7
	1969	1971	
Kellbank Rangers	1908	1910	6
Kelloe St Helens	1898		1
Kelloe United	1897		1
Kempston Rovers	1929	1934	21
	1953	1957	
	1971		
Kendal	1894		1
Kendal United	1963	1964	11
Kensington Town	1905		2
Kents Athletic	1953	1954	4
Kepax	1922	1923	6
	1925	1926	
Kettering United	1938	1939	2
Keynsham	1927	1939	35
Keynsham Town	1951	1967	60
	1969	1970	
Kidlington	1951	1963	25
	1965	1970	
Kidsgrove Athletic	1973		1
Kilburn	1911	1913	13
Kimberley St Johns	1903		4
King's Lynn	1898	1932	119
	1934	1938	
	1946	1948	
King's Lynn DS&S Federation	1920		1
King's Lynn Swifts	1923	1924	3
King's Lynn WM	1926	1927	2
Kingburn Athletic	1964	1969	12
Kings Heath	1922		3
Kings Langley	1938	1972	52
Kings Own Lancs Regt Portsmouth	1895		8
Kings Regiment (Catterick)	1969		1
Kingsbury Town	1948	1950	49
	1955	1974	
Kingsthorpe Church Institute	1928	1932	11
Kingston Rovers	1970		2
Kingston Wolves	1955	1956	15
	1958	1961	
Kingston upon Hull OG	1934	1936	3
Kingston-on-Thames	1900	1901	27
	1907	1914	
Kingstonian	1920	1974	133
Kingswood	1925	1935	37
	1938	1939	
Kington Town	1923	1927	6
Kirkby Stephen	1958		2
	1960		
Kirkby Town	1973	1974	3
Kirkley	1897	1914	75
	1924	1929	
	1933	1935	
Kirkley & Waveney	1930	1932	8
Kirtlington Sports	1955	1958	5
Kiveton Park Colliery	1947	1948	5
Knaresborough	1905		12
	1909		
	1970	1971	
Knaresborough Town	1930		2
Knebworth	1933	1935	4
Knowle	1953		12
	1971	1974	
L&NW Railway	1923		3
Lagonda Sports	1948		1
Lakenheath	1938	1948	20
	1951	1953	
Lamorbey	1924	1925	9
	1927	1929	
Lancashire Steel Recreation	1951	1953	3
Lanchester Rangers	1939		2
Lancing Athletic	1948	1974	68
Landseer	1955	1956	5
Landseer Youth	1957	1964	11
Langford	1929		4
	1971		
Langley Park	1909	1930	49
	1947		
Langley Park CW	1950	1965	28
Langley Park Villa	1939		2
Lathol Athletic	1953	1959	9
Latymer OB	1924	1925	2
Launton United	1971		1
Lawrence's Athletic	1903	1904	5
Lazenby Institute	1910	1912	13
	1922	1923	
Leadgate Exiles	1894	1898	9
Leadgate Park	1894	1915	56
Leadgate Villa	1910		1
Leagrave & District	1926	1931	19
Leagrave United	1910	1911	2
Leamington Southend	1948		1
Leasingthorne CW	1928	1929	12
	1931	1938	
Leasingthorne Eden Rovers	1922		1
Leasingthorne Village	1935	1937	8
Leatherhead	1908	1910	116
	1948	1974	
Leavesden Asylum	1910		14
	1912	1914	
Leavesden Hospital	1934	1939	58
	1947	1967	
Leavesden Mental Hospital	1920	1933	44
Leckhampton	1926		1
Leckhampton Sports	1924		1
Ledbury Town	1929		5
	1935	1936	
Lee	1900	1907	14
Leeds & Carnegie College	1969	1974	21
Leeds Amateurs	1908	1909	4
Leeds Ashley Road	1965	1974	26
Leeds City	1925		3
Leeds Harehills	1922	1924	11
Leeds Malvern	1922	1924	12
Leeds St Martins	1910		1
Leeds United	1912		1
Leeds University	1931		11
	1965	1969	
Leeds University Union	1972		1
Leeds University YMI	1950	1955	11
Leek	1895	1896	3
Leicester Amateurs	1954		5
	1957		
Leicester Belvoir	1920		1
Leicester Nomads	1908		4
	1912	1913	
Leicester YMCA	1895		1
Leicestershire Nomads	1928		15
	1933	1939	
Leigh Ramblers	1907	1908	3
Leighton Cee Springs	1900	1907	10
Leighton Town	1909	1911	32
	1964		
	1968	1974	
Leighton United	1923	1963	57
Leiston	1901	1902	56
	1904	1914	
	1946	1949	
	1952	1965	
	1969	1971	
	1973		
Leiston Works Athletic	1920	1935	28
Lenton	1924	1928	19
Lenton Gregory	1961		1
Leslies	1923		1
Letchworth Town	1926	1974	151
Lewes	1903	1904	72
	1912	1913	
	1921	1926	
	1928	1930	
	1950	1955	
	1957	1959	
	1961		
	1967	1974	
Lewisham Montrose	1905		1
Lewisham St Marys	1897		2
Leyland Motors	1921	1939	37
	1947		
Leyton	1914		177
	1920	1974	
Leytonstone	1897	1900	225
	1906	1974	
Liberty	1913		3
Lidgett Park	1921	1922	2
Limehouse Town	1907	1909	6
	1921		
Linby CW	1969	1970	4
	1972		
Linby Colliery	1958		1
Lincoln City School OBU	1953	1961	20
Lincoln Clayton	1957	1959	11
	1968		
Lincoln Lindum	1894		4
	1899	1901	
Lincoln United	1962		11
	1969	1970	
	1973		
Lingdale Institute	1920	1922	15
	1924	1931	
Lingdale Mines	1914	1915	2
Lingdale Mines WM	1950	1951	2
Linotype & Machinery	1964	1968	14
	1971		
Lion Sports	1966	1974	28
Liphook	1970	1971	4
Liskeard Athletic	1952	1953	18
	1956	1960	
	1962	1964	
Listers	1928	1934	9
Little Lever	1970		1
Littlehampton	1903	1910	61
	1912	1914	
	1921	1939	
	1946	1965	
Littlehampton Town	1931	1934	5
Littlemore	1906	1922	22
Liverpool Balmoral	1899	1900	9
Liverpool Casuals	1903	1904	
Liverpool Leek	1903		2
Liverpool Police	1950		1
Liverpool Ramblers	1895		4
	1904		
Liverpool Tramways	1923	1924	4
Liverpool University	1922	1923	4
	1966		
Liverpool West Derby Union	1934	1939	15
Liversedge	1923	1926	41
	1953	1960	
	1972	1974	
Liversey United	1923		1
Liverton Mines	1921		1
Lloyds	1934	1935	5
	1947		
Lloyds Bank	1967	1970	6
Lockheed Leamington	1949		1
Loftus	1894	1899	10
Loftus Albion	1914	1915	34
	1921	1930	
London Caledonians	1907	1939	81
London Hospital	1898	1899	4
London Labour	1934	1936	4
London Midland Athletic	1947		1
London Paper Mills	1935	1939	17
London Transport Central Buses	1946	1950	10
London University	1956	1958	6
London Welsh	1895	1896	17
	1898	1900	
	1936	1937	
Long Eaton Victoria	1905		4
Long Eaton Villa	1904	1905	3
Long Eaton Waverley	1908		3
Long Melford	1932	1934	8
	1936		
	1953		
Longfleet St Marys	1904	1915	51
	1948	1956	
	1965	1970	
Longlevens Star	1974		1
Looe	1952	1954	16
	1957		
	1959	1960	
Lostock Gralam	1973	1974	6
Loughborough College	1952	1974	71
Loughborough Corinthians	1901	1912	31
Lovells Athletic	1922		1
Low Moor	1924	1926	3
Lower Gornal Athletic	1956		12
	1960	1963	
Lowestoft Town	1899	1954	145
	1957		
Lowther United (York)	1915		3
	1921		
Lucas Great King Street	1957	1958	3
Lucas Sports	1967	1968	3
Luddendenfoot	1926	1933	9
	1937		
Luton (Chatham)	1956	1959	10
	1961	1963	
Luton Albion	1913	1915	10
Luton Amateur	1912	1933	59
	1939	1954	
Luton Amateur (Chatham)	1902	1906	8
Luton Celtic	1909	1910	2
Luton Clarence	1903		47
	1907	1926	
Luton Comrades	1920		1
Luton Crusaders	1911	1914	7
Luton Frickers	1925		1
Luton Reliance	1914	1915	3
Luton Skefco Athletic	1959		8
	1961		
	1967	1968	
Luton Trinity	1906		4
	1914	1915	
Lutterworth Town	1963	1970	19
	1972	1974	
Lydbrook Athletic	1959	1970	41
Lye Town	1947		1
Lymington	1928	1929	44
	1933	1934	
	1938	1939	
	1947	1957	
	1959	1960	
	1969		
Lymm GS OB	1971		1
Lynn North End	1902		1
Lynn St Nicholas	1915	1921	12
	1923	1929	
Lynn Swifts	1901	1902	5
	1921	1922	
Lynn United	1926	1929	4
Lyons	1931	1950	23
Lyrn & Lahy Sports	1939		1
Lysaght's Excelsior	1911	1913	6
Lytham St Annes	1964		3
Lytham St Annes & Fylde YMCA	1966	1967	6
	1970	1971	
Mackay's Sports	1937		1
Madeley College	1966	1970	14
	1972	1973	
Magdala Amateurs	1935		1
Maidenhead	1894	1914	51
Maidenhead Norfolkians	1900	1914	42
Maidenhead United	1920	1969	159
	1971	1974	
Maidstone	1894	1895	2
Maidstone Athletic	1909		2
Maidstone Church Institute	1904	1906	11
	1908		

Maidstone United to Nottingham Magdala Amateurs

Club	From	To	Count
Maidstone United	1929 / 1947	1939 / 1971	102
Malden Town	1952	1974	53
Maldon & Heybridge	1936	1939	7
Maldon Town	1968	1972	11
Malin Bridge OB	1921	1922	3
Malmesbury Town	1933	1936	6
Maltby MW	1965		1
Maltby Main	1947	1952	9
Malton Town	1922	1923	2
Malvern Holy Trinity	1927	1939	24
Malvern Town	1956 / 1968	1964 / 1974	47
Manchester Insurance	1922		2
Manchester Transport	1934	1938	7
Manchester University	1907 / 1914 / 1949 / 1955 / 1958 / 1968	1912 / 1953 / 1965 / 1969	38
Manchester YMCA	1922 / 1954 / 1958	1974	38
Manders Sports	1922		1
Mangotsfield United	1970	1973	11
Manningham Mills	1929 / 1962 / 1968	1933 / 1971	21
Manor Park Albion	1908		3
Mansfield Amateurs	1907	1908	2
Mapperley	1910 / 1962	1915 / 1964	16
Mapperley Park	1923		2
March GE United	1926 / 1933	1927 / 1937	13
March Town	1927 / 1948	1937 / 1949	21
Marcians	1906	1907	3
Marfleet	1921 / 1934		3
Margate	1907	1914	10
Margate Holy Trinity	1907	1908	2
Margate St Johns Guild	1907	1908	4
Marine	1922	1974	147
Marine Park	1966		2
Marlborough (Acton)	1907		1
Marlborough OB	1911	1914	5
Marlborough Town	1963	1965	5
Marlow	1894 / 1920 / 1966	1914 / 1964 / 1974	176
Marske	1923		1
Marske Parish Church	1909		1
Marske Rovers	1937	1938	5
Marske United	1922	1923	3
Marston Shelton Rovers	1949 / 1954	1952 / 1961	19
Marston United	1960	1963	5
Mascot Sports	1971	1972	3
Matlock Town	1931		2
McLaren Sports	1949	1956	13
Measham Imperial	1956	1958	9
Melksham	1898		2
Melksham & Avon United	1922	1923	3
Melksham Town	1911 / 1927	1912 / 1974	100
Melksham Town & Avon United	1923	1926	9
Melling	1902		2
Meltham Mills	1932	1933	6
Melton Town	1949 / 1951	1952	10
Merstham	1967	1973	11
Merton	1932 / 1946 / 1960	1938 / 1950 / 1961	17
Merton Rushmore	1967	1969	6
Merton Town	1923	1925	4
Merton United	1970		2
Messingham Trinity	1972		6
Metal & Produce Recovery Depot	1947	1949	3
Metal Box Company (Worcester)	1959	1960	3
Methley Perseverance	1930		3
Methley United	1957	1960	13
Metrogas	1907 / 1914 / 1924	1922	27
Metrogas Athletic	1909	1910	8
Metropolitan Police	1925	1965	91
Metropolitan Railway	1898	1899	6
Metropolitan Railway Athletic	1938		2
Mexborough SS OB	1934	1935	5
Michelin Athletic	1947 / 1950		4
Mickley	1898	1902	15
Mid Kent	1897	1898	2
Middlefield Welfare	1969		2
Middlesbrough	1894	1899	19
Middlesbrough Athletic	1923		1
Middlesbrough Cargo Athletic	1914		1
Middlesbrough OB	1911	1912	2
Middlesex Wanderers	1905		1
Middleton Amateurs	1956 / 1959 / 1968	1966 / 1971	15
Middleton Athletic	1920	1921	2
Middleton Wanderers	1947		1
Middlewich Athletic	1959 / 1970	1962 / 1974	22
Midhurst	1924	1925	3
Midland Athletic	1970	1974	13
Midland Bank	1962 / 1969	1966	8
Midland Woodworking	1958		5
Midland Woodworking Co Sports	1947		1
Mile Oak Rovers	1969 / 1972	1970 / 1973	11
Mile Oak Rovers & Youth	1974		3
Millbrook Rangers	1950	1952	4
Millwall United	1925	1929	11
Milnthorpe Corinthians	1971		2
Minehead	1921 / 1925 / 1929	1922 / 1938	19
Mitcham Wanderers	1924	1932	25
Molesey	1955	1974	46
Monarch United	1963		2
Moneyfield Sports	1970 / 1973	1971 / 1974	9
Monk Bretton Colliery	1956	1957	2
Monk Bridge Sports	1922	1923	3
Moor Green	1922 / 1925	1923 / 1974	133
Moresby Welfare Centre	1949		4
Moreton	1956 / 1961 / 1964 / 1971	1958 / 1962 / 1965	15
Moreton Town	1962 / 1965	1963 / 1973	18
Morley St Andrews	1923		1
Morris Motors	1922 / 1924 / 1936 / 1955 / 1958 / 1965	1934 / 1953 / 1956 / 1961 / 1973	84
Morris Motors (Coventry)	1933 / 1936 / 1947 / 1953	1939 / 1954	21
Morris Sports (Loughborough)	1952 / 1954 / 1960	1957	9
Morris United	1949		1
Morriston Busty CW	1961	1963	9
Morton's Athletic	1913 / 1920	1914 / 1924	15
Mottingham	1960		1
Moulsecoomb Rovers	1955	1964	12
Moulton	1974		1
Mount Hill Enterprise	1929 / 1948 / 1971	1939 / 1961	56
Mount Pleasant	1929	1939	24
Mount Pleasant (Tunbridge Wells)	1910	1911	2
Mousehole	1950 / 1953	1951 / 1956	11
Mullion	1951	1955	9
Muswell Hill	1900 / 1903		2
NAC Athletic	1949	1961	17
Nanpean Rovers	1950 / 1965	1962 / 1966	32
Napier	1920 / 1930		4
Napier/English Electric	1960 / 1963	1961	4
National Smelting Co	1935		1
Naval Yard (Walker)	1959 / 1965	1963	12
Nether Edge Amateurs	1909 / 1921 / 1930 / 1933	1914 / 1922 / 1935	27
Netherfield Albion	1937 / 1947 / 1950 / 1961	1939 / 1948 / 1956 / 1964	29
Netherfield Rangers	1909 / 1911	1923	21
Netherton Town	1962		3
Netley Sports	1960	1967	16
New Brancepeth CW	1957	1959	4
New Brighton Tower Amateurs	1907	1911	18
New Brompton	1894		3
New Brompton Amateurs	1902	1906	16
New Crusaders	1906 / 1914	1907	16
New Earswick	1948		1
New Houghton Villa	1947	1948	3
New Skelton Vulcan	1923		1
New York United	1926		2
Newark Athletic	1920 / 1922		4
Newbury	1895	1899	10
Newbury Town	1914 / 1920 / 1954 / 1973	1946 / 1971 / 1974	110
Newcastle Bohemians	1913 / 1920 / 1926 / 1930	1914 / 1923	10
Newcastle Derby PMG	1915		2
Newcastle University	1964 / 1968	1966 / 1971	10
Newcastle West End	1938	1939	2
Newcastle West End Amateurs	1931	1934	6
Newfoundpool WMC	1962 / 1970	1963	9
Newhaven	1905 / 1921 / 1928	1908 / 1926 / 1964	83
Newhaven Cement Works	1902	1904	8
Newmarket Town	1923 / 1952 / 1954	1949 / 1959	64
Newport I of W	1923 / 1927	1924 / 1928	6
Newportonians	1908	1922	13
Newquay	1951 / 1970	1952 / 1974	20
Newton	1954	1972	52
Newton Abbott Spurs	1957	1958	4
Newton Cap Bank	1936	1938	4
Newton Corinthians	1939		1
Newton Town	1924		1
Newton YMCA	1948		1
Newtown United	1951	1952	6
Norfolk Amateurs	1922 / 1926	1924 / 1927	16
Norley United	1960		2
Normanby Magnesite	1923 / 1936	1934 / 1939	40
Normanby Park Steels	1929		1
Norsemen	1903 / 1970	1972	8
North Derbyshire Ramblers	1936	1938	5
North Eastern Marine	1963	1965	6
North Ferriby United	1949 / 1967	1959 / 1974	46
North Hants Ironworks	1908	1909	4
North Ormesby	1936		1
North Shields	1964	1974	48
North Skelton	1908		2
North Skelton Athletic	1949	1958	23
North Skelton Rovers	1894		1
North Skelton Swifts	1914 / 1921	1915 / 1923	10
North Stafford Nomads	1908		1
North Staffordshire Casuals	1907		1
North Walsham Town	1921 / 1933 / 1936 / 1950 / 1955 / 1961	1923 / 1934 / 1939 / 1952 / 1959 / 1964	35
North Withington	1970	1972	6
North Woolwich	1909	1911	9
Northallerton	1906 / 1908		4
Northampton Amateurs	1947	1950	7
Northampton Nomads	1921 / 1937	1935 / 1939	56
Northampton Spencer	1973	1974	5
Northampton Wanderers	1924		1
Northern Nomads	1903 / 1924 / 1953	1921 / 1939 / 1974	143
Northfield Town	1970	1974	12
Northfleet United	1904	1905	4
Northmet	1937	1939	6
Northwich Victoria	1896		1
Norton	1911	1912	3
Norton Cricket Club Trust	1968	1974	11
Norton United	1922	1923	2
Norton Woodseats	1926	1974	110
Norwich Athletic	1922		1
Norwich B.L.	1922	1923	2
Norwich CEYMS	1895 / 1897	1938	91
Norwich City	1903	1905	10
Norwich City Wanderers	1924	1928	7
Norwich Civil Service	1930	1933	4
Norwich Electricity Works	1939		1
Norwich Federation	1921		2
Norwich Priory Athletic	1922	1930	13
Norwich St Barnabas	1931 / 1937	1933 / 1939	13
Norwich Thorpe	1894		2
Norwich VA	1898		1
Norwich YMCA	1925 / 1932	1930 / 1939	28
Norwood & Selhurst	1900	1902	5
Norwood Association	1907	1909	8
Nottingham Magdala Amateurs	1922 / 1930 / 1936	1926 / 1934 / 1938	18

Nottingham University to RMLI Gosport

Club	Year1	Year2	Num
Nottingham University	1960	1961	11
	1965	1966	
	1968	1971	
Nottinghamshire	1921	1923	5
Notts Jardines	1905	1913	27
Notts Magdala	1903	1908	16
Notts Magdala Amateurs	1903	1908	8
Notts Olympic	1909		1
Notts Rangers	1910	1914	9
Novocastrian	1898		5
Nunburnholme Liberal	1921		1
Nuneaton Borough	1938		4
Nunhead	1905	1939	83
Oadby Town	1954	1962	31
Oak Villa	1948	1953	9
Oakdale	1922		2
Oakengates Youth	1949	1950	3
Oakham Rovers	1948		1
Oaklands (Woolwich)	1905	1906	3
Odd Down	1947	1953	7
Ogden's Athletic	1914		4
Old Altrinchamians	1965	1974	30
Old Blackburnians	1950	1974	51
Old Boltonians	1922		4
	1964		
Old Brightonians	1894	1899	11
Old Carthusians	1894	1897	22
	1924		
Old Charlton	1924		1
Old Chorltonians	1922	1926	8
Old Cranleighans	1894	1898	7
Old Cravonians	1926		4
	1928	1929	
Old Danes	1900		1
Old Etonians	1894	1902	21
Old Felstedians	1898	1899	2
Old Finchleians	1934	1939	11
	1959	1961	
Old Foresters	1894		2
Old Harrovians	1894	1897	4
Old Hullensians	1937	1939	4
	1947		
Old Isleworthians	1929	1930	3
Old Johnians	1929	1939	14
Old Kingstonians	1909	1915	20
Old Latymerians	1923	1925	24
	1928	1939	
	1947		
Old Lyonians	1923	1939	29
Old Malvernians	1898	1902	24
Old Mexburians	1958		2
Old Owens	1935	1937	6
	1960	1961	
Old Plymouthians	1897		2
Old Salesians	1969	1973	6
Old Salfordians	1963	1965	3
Old St Marks	1894	1903	18
Old St Stephens	1894		5
Old Stationers	1936	1939	6
Old Swindon	1897		1
Old Tiffinian	1907		2
Old Varndonians	1957	1959	12
Old Westminster Citizens	1950		1
Old Westminsters	1894	1898	10
Old Weymouthians	1894	1900	22
Old Wilsonians	1895	1897	7
Old Wulfrunians	1897		56
	1907	1914	
	1920	1923	
	1926	1927	
	1929		
	1952	1969	
Old Wykehamists	1894		5
	1897	1898	
Old Xaverians	1902	1909	53
	1911	1939	
Oldbury Town	1927		3
Oldbury Town Recreation	1926		3
Oldbury United	1968	1974	29
Oldland	1904	1905	3
Oldswinford	1970	1971	8
Ollerton Colliery	1957	1958	13
	1970	1971	
Olympian	1898	1900	5
	1905	1906	
Olympic	1899	1903	12
	1905	1907	
Ordnance (Woolwich)	1920	1921	8
Ormskirk	1971	1974	10
Orpington	1911		9
	1922	1923	
Orpington Athletic	1965		3
Orrell	1913		30
	1922	1926	
	1933	1938	
	1947	1950	
Orrell Athletic	1925	1927	7
Orwell Works	1908	1911	48
	1920	1939	
	1960		
	1964		
Osberton Radiator	1932	1960	39
Osborn's Sports	1922		1
Osborne Athletic	1921	1939	21
Ossett Albion	1953	1959	74
	1961	1974	
Oswestry Town	1949		1
Oswestry Town Reserves	1948		1
Otley	1925	1927	5
Ottery St Mary	1971	1974	5
Oulton Roseville	1938	1939	3
Oundle Town	1968	1971	5
Oxford City	1895	1896	206
	1898	1974	
Oxford Cygnets	1898	1900	6
Oxford Gasworks Athletic	1923		2
Oxford University Press	1959	1963	9
Oxford YMCA	1955	1962	15
PO Engineers	1933	1939	20
PO Engineers (LTR)	1947		14
	1953	1959	
PO Telecomms	1948	1949	3
Padiham	1964		1
Page Green Old Boys	1906	1909	16
	1913	1920	
Paget Rangers	1950	1974	81
Pagham	1972	1974	3
Pandon Temperance	1912	1923	12
Park Royal	1932	1936	12
Park Wanderers	1973		1
Parkeston GER	1921		2
	1923		
Parkeston Railway	1924	1933	16
Parkgate Welfare	1953		1
Parkhill (Chingford)	1954	1955	3
Parliament Street Methodists	1947		28
	1950	1964	
Parson Drove United	1969	1971	7
Parthians (Clapham)	1906	1907	3
Parton United	1947	1949	3
Paulton Amateurs	1908		1
Paulton Rovers	1903	1911	134
	1920	1921	
	1927		
	1929	1963	
	1971	1974	
Paxman's Athletic	1912	1914	7
	1923	1924	
Pearl Assurance	1921		1
Peartree OB	1950	1953	10
Pease & Partners	1933	1937	10
Peasedown Athletic	1921		5
Peasedown Miners Welfare	1939	1962	43
Peasedown St Johns	1911		2
Peasedown St Johns Athletic	1922	1926	7
Peel Corner	1926		1
Pegasus	1949	1963	54
Pegasus Athletic	1973		1
Pegasus Juniors	1965		9
	1968	1974	
Pembroke Dock Town	1921		1
Penistone Church	1949	1964	30
Pennington St Marks	1938	1939	3
Penrith	1947	1974	86
Penzance	1948	1949	14
	1960	1962	
Percival Athletic	1950	1951	2
Percy Main Amateurs	1922	1933	36
	1947		
Pershore United	1960	1974	29
Peterborough	1895	1897	5
Peterborough GN Loco	1906	1907	3
Peterborough Rovers	1970	1971	7
	1974		
Peterborough Town	1904	1907	4
Peterborough Westwood Works	1948	1949	2
Petter & Bryce Sports	1957	1959	5
Petters Sports	1960	1968	19
Petters Westland Works	1930		2
Pewsey Vale	1921	1927	38
	1948	1962	
Pewsey Young Men	1938	1947	6
Philadelphia CW	1950		1
Phorpes Sports	1950	1951	2
Pickering Town	1953		1
Pilkington Recreation	1928	1932	17
	1957	1958	
Pinehurst Youth Centre	1956	1966	40
	1969	1970	
Pinner	1935	1961	28
Pirelli General Cable Works	1951	1954	40
	1957	1966	
	1968	1970	
Players Athletic	1914		98
	1923	1966	
	1968	1971	
	1973	1974	
Plumstead St Johns	1909	1911	5
Plumstead St Johns Institute	1906	1908	8
Plymouth	1896		1
Plymouth City Engineers Dept	1962		1
Plymouth United	1934		11
	1947	1952	
Pokesdown	1910	1914	8
Polytechnic	1895		70
	1908	1914	
	1921	1931	
	1933	1970	
Pont Institute	1947		7
	1949		
Poole	1903	1914	30
	1921	1924	
Poole & St Marys	1920		1
Poole Town	1931	1939	42
	1947	1952	
Poole Wednesday	1910		2
Port Clarence	1948		1
Port Clarence SS	1956		1
Port Sunlight	1933	1934	60
	1936		
	1947	1971	
Port Sunlight Amateurs	1927		2
Port of London Authority	1934		4
	1938	1939	
	1947		
Portfield	1974		2
Portland	1910	1913	7
Portland PO & Portland United	1907	1909	4
Portland United	1921	1939	60
	1947	1952	
Portrack Shamrocks	1932	1939	41
	1947	1953	
Portsea Island Gas Co	1922	1926	15
Portslade	1925	1927	3
Portsmouth Amateurs	1913	1924	18
Portsmouth Caledonions	1922		1
Portsmouth Corinthians	1923		1
Portsmouth Electricity	1948	1951	11
Portsmouth Gas Co	1927	1939	32
Portsmouth Royal Navy	1967	1970	10
	1972	1974	
Potternewton St Martins	1909		1
Potton United	1948		13
	1951	1957	
Prescot Town	1972	1974	11
Pressed Steel	1936	1969	57
	1973	1974	
Preston GS OB	1932	1936	7
Preston Winckley	1909	1911	7
Prestwich Heys	1965	1974	27
Princes Risborough Town	1968	1969	3
Prudhoe	1900		2
Pucklechurch	1958	1959	3
Pulborough	1926	1932	10
	1955		
Purton	1931	1959	53
Purton Workmen	1922	1923	2
Pye Radio	1933	1939	7
Quarry Nomads	1962		4
Queen's Park Rangers	1896	1897	7
Quorn	1955	1956	11
	1958	1964	
RA Shoeburyness	1931	1933	3
RA Woolwich	1922		2
RAE Farnborough	1920	1924	9
RAF Bicester	1937		2
RAF Cranwell	1921	1928	82
	1934	1939	
	1950	1964	
RAF Felixstowe	1932	1939	8
RAF Grantham	1929	1937	17
RAF Halton	1935	1939	9
RAF Henlow	1922		17
	1924		
	1931	1937	
RAF Locking	1955		1
RAF Martlesham Heath	1933	1939	14
RAF Uxbridge	1922	1931	19
RAMC Aldershot	1909	1914	83
	1920	1939	
	1949	1954	
RAOC Hereford	1923	1924	2
RAOC Hilsea	1927	1929	19
	1931	1937	
RAOC Portsmouth	1926		2
	1930		
RASC	1949	1950	2
RASC Aldershot	1924	1931	47
	1933	1939	
RE Civilian Staff	1927		2
RE Eastbourne	1921		1
RE Southampton	1922	1923	10
	1925	1926	
	1930		
RFA Farnborough	1908	1909	9
RGA Gosport	1922		3
RGA Inner Defence	1911		2
RGA Plymouth	1910		4
RGA Portsmouth	1914		1
RGA Weymouth	1907	1914	15
RM Artillery	1912		1
RM Chatham	1925	1933	41
	1935	1948	
RM Deal	1932	1939	12
RM Portsmouth	1925	1936	30
RMA Portsmouth	1914		20
	1920	1923	
RMLI Chatham	1911		9
	1922		
	1924		
RMLI Gosport	1909	1914	47
	1920	1924	

RN Barracks to Shirebrook

Name	Start	End	Count
RN Barracks	1950		2
RN Chatham	1947		1
RN Depot	1911	1914	63
	1920	1939	
	1955	1956	
RN Depot Portsmouth	1922	1927	13
RNVR Mitcham	1932		1
ROF (SA)	1957	1966	12
Racing Club Warwick	1973	1974	8
Radford & Wollaton	1961		1
Radipole	1907	1909	4
Radstock Town	1906	1909	128
	1922	1964	
	1972	1974	
Railway Clearing House	1923	1925	5
Rainham Town	1948	1974	62
Rainham WMC	1950		1
Raleigh Athletic	1936		57
	1939	1950	
	1952	1965	
Ramsey Town	1935	1938	43
	1949	1955	
	1958	1970	
Ramsgate Grenville	1938	1939	2
Ramsgate St Georges	1907		1
Ramsgate Town	1907	1914	19
Ransome & Marles	1925		13
	1928		
	1931		
	1934		
	1937		
	1968		
Raunds Town	1947	1948	11
	1953	1954	
	1956	1959	
Ravens Amateurs (Sheffield)	1925	1927	3
Ravenscourt Amateurs	1910	1912	3
Ravensthorpe	1936	1939	14
	1948	1952	
Rawdon	1921	1927	17
Rawdon OB	1952		1
Rawmarsh Athletic	1928	1929	8
Rawmarsh Welfare	1930	1935	62
	1938	1949	
	1951	1956	
	1961		
Rayners Lane	1960		23
	1962	1974	
Reading	1894	1895	10
Reading Amateurs	1896	1902	40
	1904	1911	
	1922	1923	
Reading B.W.I.	1922	1928	15
Reading Biscuit Factory	1900		3
	1924		
Reading Grovelands	1908	1914	14
Reading United	1920	1921	7
Reckitt & Sons	1959	1961	3
Reckitts	1928	1929	4
Red Cross	1925		3
Red Hill & Yardley Amateurs	1934		1
Red Hill Amateurs	1932	1933	7
Redcar	1914		15
	1920	1923	
Redcar Albion	1949	1960	39
	1963		
Redcar Crusaders	1897		6
	1905	1909	
Redcar Victoria	1910		1
Redcar Works	1934	1935	2
Redford Sports	1939		2
	1948		
Redhill	1901	1974	222
Reigate Priory	1905	1907	43
	1926	1939	
	1961	1974	
Revenue	1922		1
Rhos	1894		2
Rhyl Athletic	1903		1
Richard Thomas & Baldwin	1953	1954	3
Richmond Association	1899	1902	18
	1905	1907	
Richmond Hill Athletic	1922		1
Rickmansworth Town	1949	1973	38
Rifle Depot	1914		1
Riley Bros	1907		1
Rillington	1950	1951	4
Ringmer	1970	1974	11
Ringtons Welfare	1947	1948	6
	1950		
Ringwood Town	1934	1939	10
Ripon United	1904	1905	5
Rise Carr	1912		9
	1920	1923	
Rise Carr Primitive Methodists	1910	1911	4
Rise Carr Rangers	1898		3
	1910		
Rishton	1951		2
Roche	1953		2
Rochester	1908	1909	5
Rochester Argyll	1906		1
Rock-a-Nore	1921		16
	1923	1934	
Rocket Athletic	1937	1947	6
Roe Farm Athletic	1970	1971	11
Romanby (Northallerton)	1905	1907	6
Romford (1)	1895	1900	27
	1905	1906	
	1908	1911	
Romford (2)	1930	1959	75
Romford Town	1912	1915	9
Romford United	1910	1911	5
Romsey Town	1949		7
	1954	1956	
Roneo	1949	1950	2
Rootes Athletic	1953		7
	1955	1956	
Rootes Coventry	1947		2
Rose Amateurs	1914		3
Rose Green	1934	1935	3
Rosehill Athletic	1939		1
Rotherham Amateurs	1904	1905	49
	1907	1929	
Rothwell Athletic	1925	1927	13
	1947	1949	
	1957		
Rothwell OB	1920		1
Rothwell Town	1969	1974	14
Roundway Hospital	1950	1958	13
Rovers (Poplar)	1930	1931	2
Rowley	1922		3
Rowley Associates	1924	1925	6
Rowley United	1973	1974	2
Rowntrees	1902		2
	1904		
Roxonian	1938		1
Royal Arsenal Sports	1967	1971	8
	1973	1974	
Royal Artillery (Portsmouth)	1896	1897	15
	1899		
Royal Corps of Signals	1922	1923	10
	1925		
Royal Engineers	1899		12
	1902		
	1905	1907	
Royal Engineers (Aldershot)	1908	1915	38
	1922	1926	
Royal Engineers Depot Battn	1907	1911	28
	1921	1928	
Royal Engineers Service Battn	1904	1906	23
Royal Engineers Training Battn	1894	1895	6
	1897		
Royal Engineers United	1900		1
Royal Fusiliers	1894		1
Royal Naval Depot (Chatham)	1912		5
Royal Naval Engineering College	1970		1
Royal Ordnance	1950	1956	8
Royal Ordnance Factory	1894		3
Royal Signals	1948	1951	11
Royston Town	1948	1953	29
	1955	1963	
	1967	1973	
Rubery St Chads	1923	1924	2
Rufford Colliery	1952		7
	1961	1964	
Rugby Town Amateur	1947	1949	6
Rugeley Villa	1926	1928	7
Ruislip Manor	1949	1951	75
	1953	1974	
Ruislip Town	1950		1
Runcorn Athletic	1952	1962	25
Rushden	1894		4
Rushden OB BC	1925		2
Rushden Town	1921	1922	6
	1926		
Ruston & Hornsby	1897	1900	37
Rutherford College	1902	1920	
Ryde	1905	1912	16
Ryde Sports	1921	1926	73
	1929		
	1931	1935	
	1938	1964	
	1966	1969	
Rye	1906		5
	1909	1910	
Rylands Recreation	1973		1
SDF Sports	1968		3
Sacriston United	1913		4
	1939		
Saffron Walden Town	1936	1939	43
	1947	1974	
Salisbury	1948	1953	22
Salisbury City	1905		4
	1939		
Salisbury Corinthians	1922	1926	34
	1928	1930	
	1933	1946	
	1948	1949	
Salopian Amateurs	1911		1
Saltash United	1951	1959	61
	1961	1964	
	1968	1973	
Saltburn	1904	1914	30
Saltburn Swifts	1894	1897	8
Salterbeck	1952	1955	7
	1957		
	1959		
Salts	1948	1972	61
Sandbach Ramblers	1911	1912	10
	1952		
Sandown	1927		1
Sandown IofW	1947	1948	2
Sandy Albions	1965	1971	17
Sanford Youth Centre	1972	1973	2
Sankey of Wellington	1959	1960	7
	1967	1969	
Savoy Hotel	1924	1927	5
Sawbridgeworth	1947	1953	10
Sawston United	1949	1951	3
Scalegill	1947		5
	1950		
Scarborough	1894		61
	1898	1926	
Scarborough Juniors	1935	1939	7
Scarborough Penguins	1924	1926	5
Scarborough Rangers	1894		1
Scholes Athletic	1923		5
	1926		
Scunthorpe & Lindsey United	1912		1
Seaford	1910	1912	3
Seaford Town	1964	1966	19
	1969	1971	
Seaham White Star	1905		6
Seaton Delaval	1951	1956	16
	1960		
	1962		
	1964		
Seaton Holy Trinity	1952	1958	7
Seaton Sluice United	1956	1958	10
Sedgefield Town	1909	1910	2
Selby Olympic	1921		2
	1925		
Selsey	1965	1974	13
Seven Kings	1906		2
Severalls Athletic	1929	1939	18
Shaftesbury	1922	1925	21
	1927		
	1933	1935	
	1951	1955	
Shaftesbury Town	1938	1939	3
Shankhouse	1897	1898	20
	1960	1964	
	1966	1967	
Shanklin	1923	1924	2
Shap	1950		9
	1957	1959	
	1962		
Sharpness	1925	1928	73
	1955	1956	
	1958	1974	
Sheepbridge	1950		2
Sheffield	1894	1914	128
	1920	1939	
	1947	1974	
Sheffield Commercial Travellers	1910	1911	2
Sheffield Grasshoppers	1905	1914	23
Sheffield Municipal Officers	1925	1929	14
	1931	1933	
Sheffield Panthers	1923	1925	3
Sheffield University	1915		11
	1926		
	1930		
	1969		
	1971	1974	
Shefford Town	1951		43
	1954	1955	
	1957	1961	
	1963	1965	
	1967	1974	
Sheldon Town	1947	1955	14
Shelford Town	1952	1953	5
	1956		
	1962		
Shell	1957	1961	8
Shepherds Bush (1)	1904	1915	30
Shepherds Bush (2)	1933	1934	2
Sheppey United	1894	1895	68
	1935	1964	
Shepshed Albion	1948	1960	20
	1963		
Shepton Mallet Town	1908		59
	1911		
	1921	1922	
	1936	1937	
	1948	1962	
	1964	1965	
	1971	1972	
Sherborne	1947		1
Sherborne Town	1937	1939	7
Sheringham	1921	1939	64
	1947	1964	
Sherston	1955		1
Sherwood Foresters (Colchester)	1894		4
Sherwood Foresters (Plymouth)	1912	1914	9
Shildon	1933	1974	93
Shildon Athletic	1904	1907	12
Shildon Railway Athletic	1933	1935	4
Shildon United	1897	1899	7
	1947		
Shildon Wanderers	1913		1
Shillington	1961	1974	35
Shirebrook	1963		1

Shoeburyness Garrison to Sutton Bridge United

Club	From	To	Apps
Shoeburyness Garrison	1909	1914	29
	1920	1921	
	1924		
	1926		
	1928	1930	
Sholing Sports	1965	1966	3
Shoreham	1902	1912	97
	1921	1927	
	1933	1939	
	1947	1971	
	1973	1974	
Shredded Wheat	1932	1936	11
Shrewsbury Amateur	1936		1
Shrewsbury Town	1894	1896	11
Sidcup	1926	1929	5
Sidcup United	1950	1952	3
Siddal	1924	1926	3
Siddeley Deasy	1920		2
Sidley United	1930		20
	1960	1967	
Siemen's Sports	1926		1
Signal Service TC	1921		6
Sileby Town	1956	1960	10
Silhill	1921	1922	9
	1949	1951	
	1967	1968	
Silsden	1923	1926	5
Sittingbourne	1894	1897	10
	1932		
Skegness United	1921	1924	5
Skelmersdale United	1963	1971	51
Skelton Celtic	1911		13
	1914	1922	
Skelton Celtic & South Skelton U	1923		2
	1925		
Skinningrove & Carlin How United	1912		1
Skinningrove Ironworks	1901	1903	5
Skinningrove United	1904	1911	19
Skinningrove Works	1947	1957	15
Skyways	1951	1952	5
Slade Green	1956	1961	15
Slade Green Athletic	1962	1966	28
	1968	1974	
Slough	1895	1939	120
Slough Centre	1948	1956	31
Slough Town	1949	1974	105
Slough Trading Co	1921	1922	6
Slough United	1946	1948	8
Smethwick Highfield	1948	1952	27
	1964		
	1966	1971	
Smethwick Old Church	1922	1923	6
Smethwick Town	1953	1963	24
Smithills Amateurs	1922		3
Smiths Dock	1922		29
	1936	1949	
	1951	1954	
Smiths Dock Senior	1935		2
Sneinton	1906		47
	1908	1932	
Sneinton Church Institute	1933		1
Sneyd Park	1924	1931	14
	1933		
Snodland Town	1914		1
Soham Rangers	1929	1937	17
Soham United	1966	1972	18
Solihull Amateur	1969	1970	9
	1972		
Solihull Borough	1969	1971	9
	1973	1974	
Solihull Town	1972		4
Somersham Town	1955	1960	13
	1968	1969	
Somerton Amateur	1947	1949	5
Sonning	1934	1937	7
Soundwell	1946	1951	47
	1953	1962	
	1965	1973	
South Bank	1894	1974	192
South Bank Blue Star	1894		2
South Bank East End	1920	1928	57
	1932	1939	
	1947		
	1949	1951	
South Bank Gasworks	1925		1
South Bank St Peters	1927		34
	1934	1939	
	1947	1955	
South East Ham	1908	1909	2
South Hants Nomads	1932	1933	5
	1935	1936	
South Hetton CW	1934	1936	10
South Hetton Royal Rovers	1924		2
South Lynn	1949	1951	3
South Nottingham	1909	1914	24
	1922	1929	
South Oxford United	1959	1961	5
South Salford Amateurs	1930	1935	20
South Shields Ex Schoolboys	1949	1950	2
South Skelton	1921		2
South Tooting	1913	1915	3
South Weald	1904	1912	27
South West Ham (1)	1898		2
South West Ham (2)	1933	1934	4
Southall	1898		203
	1902	1904	
	1909	1974	
Southampton CS	1924	1925	5
Southampton Cambridge	1913		2
Southampton Post Office	1922		4
Southbroom (Devizes)	1897	1898	3
Southend Amateurs	1913	1914	3
Southend Athletic	1905	1907	13
Southend Corinthians	1921		6
	1939		
Southern Railway (1)	1925		1
Southern Railway (2)	1935	1936	7
Southfields	1908		2
Southport Leyland Road	1952	1958	10
Southport YMCA	1911	1913	6
Southsea Rovers	1921	1922	3
Southsea St Simons	1911	1914	6
Southwell Town	1909		1
Southwick	1898	1899	119
	1908	1914	
	1920	1965	
	1969	1971	
Sowerby United	1929		1
Spadeadam	1969		2
Spalding Town	1907		1
Spalding United	1922	1923	12
	1925		
	1927	1928	
Spencer Melksham	1923	1926	7
Spencer Moulton	1921	1939	62
	1947	1961	
Spennymoor Amateur	1954	1955	3
Spennymoor United	1906	1908	55
	1961	1974	
Spilsby United	1913		1
St Albans	1895	1897	5
St Albans Abbey	1907	1908	6
St Albans City	1909	1914	139
	1920	1974	
St Annes Athletic	1952	1958	17
St Annes Oldland	1928		2
St Austell	1947	1951	42
	1956	1958	
	1970		
St Blazey	1948	1951	8
St Clements United	1948		1
St Cuthberts Works	1930	1931	2
St Dennis	1951	1957	15
St Frideswides	1923	1927	29
	1947	1960	
St Helens United	1920		1
St Ives Town	1908		58
	1922	1937	
	1948	1950	
	1963	1966	
	1968	1970	
St Johns College (York)	1967	1968	16
	1970		
St Just	1953	1954	3
St Leonards	1901	1906	11
St Leonards Amateurs	1911	1913	12
St Lukes College	1956	1957	29
	1965	1971	
	1974		
St Neots	1908	1910	4
St Neots & District	1923		33
	1926	1927	
	1933	1936	
	1948	1949	
St Neots St Marys	1949	1959	14
St Pancras (Knowle)	1934	1939	24
	1947	1948	
St Peters Albion	1924		9
	1937		
	1939		
St Peters College Birmingham	1970		1
St Philips Athletic	1927	1931	21
	1933	1937	
St Philips Marsh Adult School	1929	1930	60
	1932	1935	
	1938	1939	
	1947	1965	
Stafford Old Edwardians	1935		6
	1937	1939	
Staffordshire Casuals	1948	1962	26
	1964	1968	
Staines	1906	1913	12
Staines Lagonda	1922	1925	16
Staines Town	1926	1935	70
	1949	1950	
	1956	1974	
Staithes United	1922	1923	5
Stamford Albion	1908	1909	5
Stamford Town	1907	1909	13
Stamshaw OB	1921	1923	6
Stand	1922		1
Standard Telephones	1930	1937	10
Stanhope	1932	1935	18
	1949	1951	
	1953		
Stanhope Rovers	1922		1
Stanhope Town	1956	1957	3
Stanley (Fulham)	1897	1898	3
Stanley United	1898	1974	183
Stansted	1949	1951	24
	1953	1957	
	1959	1962	
	1973	1974	
Stanton Ironworks	1950	1953	9
	1955		
Stantonbury St James	1902		1
Stapenhill	1955	1965	24
Staple Hill	1903	1904	3
Staple Hill Athletic	1926	1927	3
Stapleford Brookhill	1924		15
	1926		
	1931	1936	
Starbeck Athletic	1923	1925	3
Staveley Works	1954	1957	6
Stead & Simpson	1925		1
Sterling Athletic	1921	1924	5
Stevenage Town	1924	1925	68
	1927	1930	
	1932	1963	
Steyning	1905		2
	1911		
Stillington St Johns	1914	1922	6
	1924		
Stockbridge & District	1923		1
Stocksbridge Works	1969	1972	9
Stockton	1894	1939	179
	1957	1967	
Stockton Amateur	1953		2
	1955		
Stockton Enterprise Rangers	1921		2
Stockton Heath	1955	1961	20
Stockton Malleable Institute	1924	1928	16
Stockton Newtown	1924		1
Stockton OB	1908		1
Stockton Shamrock	1925	1926	16
	1928	1929	
Stockton St Johns	1900	1904	6
Stockton St Marys	1911	1912	7
Stockton Tilery	1926	1929	5
Stockton Victoria	1910		1
Stoke Institute	1931		1
Stoke Recreation (Guildford)	1946		1
Stoke United	1948	1950	6
Stoke Works	1968		2
Stokenchurch	1934		10
	1956	1963	
Stonehouse	1928	1930	7
	1933	1935	
Stones Athletic	1922	1930	18
	1932	1933	
Stoneycroft	1938		21
	1947	1951	
	1953	1957	
Stony Stratford Town	1907	1908	9
	1968	1970	
	1972		
Storey Athletic	1951		12
	1953	1955	
Stork	1938	1939	69
	1949	1970	
	1972	1974	
Stotfold	1954	1974	39
Stowmarket	1913	1914	91
	1921	1938	
	1950	1953	
	1962		
	1964	1973	
Stowmarket Corinthians	1949		1
Stowuplands Corinthians	1947	1948	4
Stratford Town	1957	1974	50
Stratford on Avon Rangers	1949		1
Streatham Town	1934	1937	5
Street	1898	1904	30
	1909	1911	
	1922	1931	
Strongs Portsmouth	1969		1
Strood	1915		2
Stroud	1910		1
Sudbury	1898		3
Sudbury Town	1913		9
	1923		
	1933	1935	
	1948		
	1950		
Summerstown	1907	1928	45
Sunderland Nomads	1897		5
Sunningend	1927		1
Sunningend Works	1920		1
Sunnybrow CW	1947	1948	3
Sunnybrow Olympic	1924	1929	9
	1931		
Sunnybrow United	1936		2
Sunnyside United	1924		1
Surbiton Byron	1970	1972	5
Surbiton Hill	1894	1896	15
	1899		
	1901	1902	
Surbiton Town	1950	1961	22
Surrey Wanderers	1912	1913	3
Sutton	1921		1
Sutton Bridge United	1957	1960	8

Sutton Coldfield Athletic to Washington Glebe Welfare

Club	From	To	Count
Sutton Coldfield Athletic	1952		1
Sutton Coldfield Town	1954		51
	1963	1974	
Sutton Court	1907	1914	28
	1920	1922	
	1926	1927	
Sutton Junction	1927	1928	13
	1930	1931	
Sutton Town	1924		13
	1936	1939	
Sutton United	1911	1914	174
	1920	1974	
Sutton-on-Hull	1912	1913	2
Suttons	1931		1
Swallownest CW	1960	1974	31
Swanage	1925		10
	1927		
	1929		
	1934	1938	
Swanage Town	1950	1958	13
Swanley	1968	1974	19
Swanley Athletic	1927		12
	1929		
	1932	1937	
Swanscombe	1904		1
Swansea Amateurs	1921	1922	7
Swaythling Athletic	1959	1969	21
	1971	1972	
Swifts	1894		1
Swillington MW	1958	1961	13
Swindon Amateurs	1898		10
	1907		
	1909	1912	
Swindon BR Corinthians	1949	1963	20
Swindon Casuals	1922		10
	1925	1930	
Swindon Corinthians	1921	1923	47
	1925	1939	
Swindon GWR Corinthians	1946	1948	4
Swindon Social Union	1910		1
Swindon St Pauls Athletic	1913		1
Swindon Town	1894	1895	2
Swindon Victoria	1911	1959	106
	1961	1967	
	1974		
Syston St Peters	1953	1956	12
Tamerton	1950		12
	1952		
	1954		
	1956	1958	
Tangyes Recreation	1949	1950	8
Tarmac	1923		1
Tate Institute	1927	1930	7
	1932	1933	
Taunton	1950	1953	9
Taunton Amateurs	1939		1
Taunton BR	1951	1954	10
	1970		
Taunton Castle	1906		1
Taunton Town	1949		2
Tavistock	1949	1953	7
	1956		
Tavistock Battery RFA	1909		1
Temple Mills	1920	1923	8
Terrington	1921		1
Terrys	1934	1935	3
Teversall & Silverhill Collieries	1937		2
Tewkesbury Town	1927	1928	3
Thackley	1950		58
	1955	1969	
	1971	1974	
Thame	1899		14
	1908	1911	
	1913		
Thame United	1924		64
	1929	1939	
	1947	1954	
	1956	1974	
Thames Mills	1950		1
Thames Polytechnic	1973	1974	3
Thameside Amateurs	1947	1964	34
Thatcham	1929	1930	7
	1937	1939	
	1961		
The Hook (Northaw) Sports	1936		2
Thetford Recreation	1922	1923	12
	1925	1926	
Thetford Town	1928	1939	76
	1947	1964	
	1968	1970	
Thorley Works	1926	1927	3
Thornaby	1897	1900	20
	1935	1937	
	1939		
Thornaby St Patricks	1909	1913	15
	1935	1937	
Thornaby Utopians	1897	1901	15
Thorncliffe Recreational	1956	1962	15
	1964		
Thorndale	1927	1929	5
Thorneycroft	1956	1958	5
Thorneycroft Athletic	1920		18
	1926		
	1929	1930	
	1936	1939	
	1949	1953	
Thornhill Edge	1946	1947	21
	1951	1959	
Thornley Albion	1926	1927	4
Thornley CW	1932		1
Thornton United	1923	1924	4
Three Bridges	1968	1972	5
Three Bridges United	1958	1967	13
Threlkeld	1951	1952	2
Throston Wanderers	1959		1
Thurcroft Main	1952	1953	4
	1958		
Thurcroft Welfare	1959	1964	11
Thynnes Athletic	1936		3
	1938		
Tilbury	1928	1939	131
	1947	1974	
Timsbury Athletic	1922	1923	24
	1935	1939	
	1949	1952	
	1957		
	1961		
Tipton Town	1968		6
	1971	1972	
Tiptree United	1973	1974	5
Tiverton Town	1934		6
	1936	1938	
	1966		
Tividale	1968		4
	1971		
TocH	1935		1
Tooting	1912	1915	10
Tooting & Mitcham United	1933	1974	105
Tooting Graveney	1910	1911	5
Tooting Town	1920	1932	28
Topsham	1973		2
Torpoint Athletic	1963	1972	32
Tottenham Hotspur	1894	1896	11
Tottenhoe	1964		2
Tottington	1908	1910	6
Totton	1933	1950	70
	1952	1971	
Tow Law	1896	1905	12
Tow Law Town	1910	1914	140
	1921	1974	
Townley Park	1904	1907	9
Treeton Reading Room	1929		3
Trimdon Colliery United	1934	1935	4
Trimdon Grange	1923		10
	1949	1950	
	1952		
Trimdon Grange Colliery	1931	1937	14
Tring Town	1950	1953	61
	1955	1974	
Trowbridge Town	1896	1897	73
	1901		
	1910	1914	
	1922	1936	
Truro City	1948	1952	12
Tufnell Park	1908	1950	101
Tufnell Park Edmonton	1951	1960	21
Tufnell Spartan	1912	1914	7
	1920		
Tunbridge Wells	1898		63
	1901	1908	
	1912	1914	
	1948		
	1950	1951	
	1970	1971	
	1974		
Tunnel Sports	1970		2
Tushingham Brick Works	1937	1939	7
Twerton St Michaels	1937	1939	4
Twickenham	1947	1950	27
	1952	1953	
	1955	1966	
Twizell United	1922		3
UGB Charlton	1939		7
	1948	1949	
UGB St Helens	1949	1951	5
UGBM Sports	1930	1932	11
	1934	1938	
Ulverston Town	1927		1
Ulysses	1960	1974	25
Union Jack	1926	1927	2
Unit Construction (Liverpool)	1957	1958	5
	1964		
United Cantabs	1936	1937	2
United Services Officers	1908		1
Upminster	1947	1952	9
Uppingham	1908		1
Upton Park	1897	1911	24
Upwey & Broadway	1956	1960	7
Urmston	1938	1939	10
Uxbridge	1898	1900	142
	1904	1914	
	1937	1974	
Uxbridge Town	1920	1936	41
Vale Orton United	1926		2
Valley Sports Rugby	1974		1
Valley United	1939		2
Vampires	1894	1895	2
Vauxhall Motors	1920	1921	94
	1927		
	1932	1933	
	1935		
	1939	1974	
Venner Sports	1938	1939	8
Vernon Athletic	1912	1914	38
	1920	1939	
Vickers	1928		2
Vickers (Weybridge)	1954	1964	18
Vickers Armstrong	1947	1953	14
Vickers Armstrong (Newcastle)	1952		1
Vickers Aviation	1938	1946	5
Viking Sports	1962	1963	4
Viney St Swithins	1972	1974	4
Virginia Water	1972	1974	8
Vulcan (Acton)	1902	1903	2
Wadebridge Town	1949	1952	15
Walgrave Amber	1926	1932	14
Walker Church Institute	1910	1913	7
Walker Church Lads Brigade	1911		1
Walker Park	1922	1925	7
	1927	1928	
Walker St Christophers	1912		1
Walker Wellbeck	1912		1
Wallingford	1903		2
Wallingford Town	1938	1939	58
	1948	1974	
Wallington	1929	1931	4
Wallsend	1965		6
	1970	1971	
	1974		
Wallsend Corinthians	1963	1964	10
Wallsend Gordon	1939		2
Wallsend Park Villa	1897		2
Wallsend Rising Sun	1959	1960	10
	1962		
Wallsend St Lukes	1939	1959	27
Wallsend St Lukes Institute	1961		1
Walsall Jolly Club	1939		1
Walsall LMS Engineering	1928		3
Walsall Phoenix	1913		12
	1921	1922	
	1924	1925	
	1927	1928	
Walsall Trinity	1952	1959	19
Walsall Wood	1947	1974	82
Walsgrave Lodge	1967		2
Waltham	1912	1913	4
Waltham Comrades	1928	1932	6
Waltham Glendale	1908	1911	5
Waltham Town	1929		1
Walthamstow Avenue	1922	1974	143
Walthamstow Grange	1912	1931	36
Walthamstow Town	1924	1925	6
Walton & Hersham	1946	1974	104
Walton United	1922		24
	1926	1939	
Walton-on-Thames	1908	1931	57
	1933	1939	
Wandsworth	1897	1900	15
	1902		
Wandsworth United	1938		3
Wanstead	1904	1911	15
Wantage Town	1907	1914	35
	1922	1923	
	1959	1966	
	1972		
	1974		
War Office	1904	1905	4
Warboys Town	1931	1936	30
	1938	1939	
	1967	1972	
	1974		
Ward Street OB	1949	1951	7
Ware	1899	1914	128
	1924	1925	
	1927	1939	
	1947	1974	
Wareham	1922		1
Wareham Town	1914		1
Warminster Town	1913	1915	82
	1921	1927	
	1929	1931	
	1934	1937	
	1939	1970	
Warmley	1894	1895	4
	1932	1933	
Warmley Amateurs	1904	1908	7
	1932		
	1934		
Warmsworth	1927	1928	8
Warrington St Elphins	1894		2
Warrington Town	1962	1966	16
	1968		
	1971	1974	
Warwick Saltisford Rovers	1952		3
Warwick Town	1932		7
	1949	1950	
Washington	1969	1972	6
Washington CW	1951		21
	1955	1962	
Washington Glebe Welfare	1961		3

112

Washington Welfare to Youlgrave

Club	Year1	Year2	Num
Washington Welfare	1938	1950	21
	1952	1954	
Watchet	1931		2
	1947		
Watchet Town	1951	1953	7
	1959		
Waterlooville	1959	1961	33
	1963	1966	
	1968	1969	
Waterlows Amateur	1920		2
Waterlows Dunstable	1921	1923	46
	1931	1939	
	1948	1952	
	1954	1960	
	1962		
Waterlows Walthamstow	1921		1
Waterside Works	1951	1960	27
	1966		
Watford BL	1933	1937	7
	1939		
Watford Corinthians	1925		1
Watford OB	1921	1922	17
	1925	1930	
Watford Orient	1913	1914	2
Watford Spartans	1931	1932	3
Watford St Marys	1896	1897	4
Watford Victoria Works	1908		1
Watton United	1969	1970	9
	1973	1974	
Wealdstone	1914		150
	1920	1971	
Wearmouth CW	1947	1949	6
	1951	1952	
Wellingborough Nomads	1925	1927	3
Wellingborough Town	1894		1
Wellington	1967	1974	11
Wellington Victoria	1956	1963	18
Wellington Works	1922	1923	21
	1925	1935	
Wells City	1904		86
	1907	1910	
	1922	1939	
	1960	1969	
	1974		
Welton Rovers	1905		133
	1907	1910	
	1912		
	1925	1963	
Welwyn	1910		13
	1922	1926	
Welwyn Garden City	1927	1935	57
	1939	1965	
	1974		
Welwyn Garden United	1971	1973	6
Wembley	1948	1974	85
Wensleydale Wanderers	1960		1
Wesley Castle	1939		1
Wesley Rangers	1932	1934	4
West Auckland	1901		27
	1904	1913	
	1915		
West Auckland Town	1921		143
	1923	1924	
	1926	1974	
West Brixton	1904	1905	4
West Bromwich Amateurs	1923		4
	1925		
	1938	1939	
West Bromwich Baptists	1921		1
West Croydon	1900	1903	11
West End Rovers	1949		1
West Ham Garfield	1901	1903	4
West Hampstead	1899	1900	22
	1904	1906	
	1908	1911	
West Hartlepool	1900	1910	31
West Hartlepool Expansion	1909	1910	26
	1914		
	1920	1922	
West Hartlepool Grays	1921		2
West Hartlepool NER	1896	1898	5
West Hartlepool Perseverance	1928	1932	8
West Hartlepool St Josephs	1913	1914	36
	1920	1923	
	1954	1957	
	1960	1965	
West Herts	1894	1897	9
West Hull Albion	1915		1
West Kirby	1926	1927	4
West Lavington	1964		8
	1966	1970	
West London OB	1912	1914	5
	1921		
West Norwood	1900		58
	1904	1923	
	1925	1939	
West Thurrock Athletic	1947	1968	52
West View Albion	1960		3
West Wickham	1963	1971	16
Westbury United	1922	1974	110
Westcott Youth Centre	1959	1966	11
	1968		
Westella & Willerby	1968		2
Western Road House	1927		2
Westfield	1965	1974	19
Westham	1922	1924	7
Weston-super-Mare	1924	1939	38
Weston-super-Mare St Johns	1949	1956	9
Weston-super-Mare UDC Employees	1937	1939	7
Westphilians	1970		1
Weybridge	1898	1901	17
	1907		
	1924	1927	
	1929	1930	
Weymouth	1896	1910	28
Whalley Range	1922	1929	11
Whalley Range Amateur	1961	1965	14
Whiston Parish	1922		1
Whitby	1894	1897	26
	1899	1900	
	1902	1907	
	1924		
	1946	1948	
Whitby Albion Rangers	1929	1937	30
	1947	1957	
Whitby Shamrock	1909	1911	4
Whitby Town	1925	1926	85
	1949	1974	
Whitby United	1927	1939	38
Whitby Whitehall Swifts	1922	1926	11
Whitchurch Alport	1952		4
	1958		
White City	1938		6
Whitefield	1969		1
Whitefield Albion	1971		1
Whitehall Printeries	1924	1939	50
Whitehaven Athletic	1935		3
Whitehawk	1958	1971	36
	1973	1974	
Whitehawk & Manor Farm OB	1953	1957	14
Whitehead Sports	1949	1950	3
Whiteheads	1946		3
Whiteheads (Weymouth)	1902	1910	35
Whitkirk	1938	1939	4
Whitkirk Wanderers	1970	1974	10
Whitley Bay	1951	1974	78
Whitmore OB	1969	1971	5
Whitstable	1912	1914	24
	1934		
	1936	1938	
	1947		
	1953		
	1960	1966	
Whitton United	1948	1973	72
Whitwick Colliery	1947	1949	7
Whitwick PCC	1946		1
Whitwick White Cross	1901		11
	1936	1939	
	1947	1948	
Whitwick White Star	1900		2
Whyteleafe	1960	1962	23
	1964	1974	
Whyteleafe Albion	1930	1931	5
Wibsey	1923	1925	9
Wick	1922	1937	19
Wigan Rovers	1971	1974	9
Wigmore Athletic	1953	1974	48
Willesden	1948	1974	54
Willesden Town	1901	1902	6
	1904		
	1921	1922	
William Colliery	1948		5
Willington	1912	1974	131
Willington Athletic	1894	1896	8
Willington Rovers	1899	1901	6
Willington Temperance	1910	1911	9
Wills Sports	1933	1936	8
Wilmorton & Alvaston	1957		1
Wilton ICI	1956		3
Wilts County Mental Hospital	1938	1939	7
	1947	1949	
Wimbledon	1906	1910	149
	1914	1964	
Wimblington OB	1950		4
Wimborne	1923	1927	30
	1938	1939	
	1949	1953	
	1955	1959	
Winchester	1906		1
Winchester City	1935	1939	64
	1948		
	1950	1966	
Wincombe	1965		1
Windscale Rovers	1966		1
Windsor & Eton	1894	1897	161
	1899		
	1902		
	1905	1914	
	1920	1974	
Wingate	1948	1950	61
	1953		
	1955	1974	
Wingate Albion Comrades	1928		3
Wingate Celtic	1937		1
Wingate St Marys	1936		1
Wingate Welfare	1957	1959	8
Winlaton Mill Athletic	1970		1
Winnington Park	1966	1971	9
Winsford United	1902		1
Winterton Hospital	1951	1958	9
Wisbech	1898		2
	1900		
Wisbech St Augustines	1912	1915	5
Wisbech Town	1921	1935	40
Witham Town	1973	1974	6
Withernsea	1909	1911	6
	1913	1914	
	1921		
Withernsea OB	1936		2
Witney Town	1924	1939	108
	1950	1973	
Witton Park	1957	1959	3
Witton Park Institute	1927	1929	29
	1934	1939	
	1952	1956	
Woking	1904	1914	152
	1920	1974	
Wokingham Athletic	1910	1911	5
Wokingham Town	1955	1974	74
Wolseley (Crayford)	1909		1
Wolseley Athletic	1927	1928	4
Wolsingham	1897		1
Wolsingham Welfare	1951	1959	25
Wolvercote	1958	1963	6
Wolverhampton Amateurs	1921	1939	33
Wolverhampton Gas Co	1923		1
Wolverhampton Old Church	1913	1915	4
Wolverhampton Town	1920		2
Wolverton LNWR Works	1896		1
Wolverton Town	1907		41
	1914		
	1923		
	1925		
	1930	1937	
	1947	1951	
Wolverton Town & BR	1952	1974	51
Wood Green	1921	1930	21
Wood Green Town	1910	1914	75
	1931	1968	
Woodbridge Athletic	1953	1957	5
Woodbridge Town	1928	1933	8
Woodford	1902	1910	16
Woodford Albion	1913	1914	2
Woodford Crusaders	1914	1920	9
Woodford Town	1947	1964	46
	1967	1969	
Woodhorn CW	1948	1950	3
Woodland Celtic	1935		1
Woodlands	1962		2
Woodseat Reform	1909		1
Woodstock Town	1950	1959	16
Woodthorpe	1922	1924	7
Woodville	1895		2
Wooley Legion	1924		2
Woolley MW	1971	1972	6
Woolwich	1922	1923	9
	1926	1928	
Woolwich Borough Council Ath.	1932	1937	7
Woolwich Polytechnic	1904	1907	101
	1909	1911	
	1915	1971	
Wootton Bassett Town	1937	1939	42
	1947	1961	
	1965		
Wootton Blue Cross	1931		36
	1948	1957	
Worcester Park	1948	1963	24
Workington	1898	1899	2
Worle OB	1953	1964	22
Worrall Hill Athletic	1972		2
Worsborough Bridge MW	1971	1974	15
Worthing	1900	1914	193
	1920	1974	
Worthing Rovers	1905		1
Worthington Simpson	1955	1957	11
	1961	1964	
Wrockwardine Wood	1959	1962	26
	1964	1967	
Wycombe Redfords	1947		1
Wycombe Wanderers	1895	1914	215
	1920	1974	
Wyke OB	1935		1
Wymondham	1934	1939	9
Wymondham Town	1947	1966	42
Wythenshaw Amateurs	1968	1973	13
Yate Town	1972	1974	9
Yeadon Celtic	1922		6
	1936		
	1950	1952	
Yeovil Casuals	1897	1898	12
	1900	1902	
Yiewsley	1909	1910	72
	1920	1927	
	1935	1958	
York City	1909	1911	11
York City St Clements	1904		4
York NER United	1907		1
York Railway Institute	1936		5
	1947	1949	
York St Clements	1902	1903	2
York St Pauls	1909	1914	8
York YMCA	1921		1
Yorkshire Amateur	1920	1974	115
Youlgrave	1923	1927	14

APPENDICES

ONE

    Changes of club name
        Please consult both club names when using the club index

TWO

.   Dates of rounds
        The scheduled dates for the rounds, which are not necessarily the date on which a match took place

THREE

.   Details of seasons for which a draw has not been found

FOUR

.   Draw for the 1939/40 competition
        The competition was cancelled on the outbreak of WWII. No games had been played at the time of the cancellation

FIVE

.   Top 20s
        The clubs who played most games, and those with the best percentage of games won

SIX

    Final Line-ups
        Players and goal scorers in all the finals, including replays

SEVEN

    Some high scoring games
        More than 12 goals scored at home, more than 11 scored away, and other games with an aggregate of more than 14

APPENDIX ONE: CHANGES OF CLUB NAMES

Name	See Also	Name	See Also
Acton	Shepherds Bush (2)	Hornchurch & Upminster	Upminster
Adam Grimaldi	Earlsfield Town	Hoxton Manor	Crown & Manor
Aero Engines	Douglas	Huntley & Palmers	Reading Biscuit Factory
Allens Cross	Northfield Town	Hyde & Kingsbury	Deerfield Athletic
Apsley	Hemel Hempstead Town	ICI Alkali	Winnington Park
Belvedere	Erith & Belvedere	Jack Moulds Athletic	Solihull Amateur
Botwell Mission	Hayes	Leagrave & District	Luton Frickers
Bournemouth Gasworks Athletic	Branksome Gasworks Athletic	Leeds City	Leeds Harehills
Bowater Lloyds	Lloyds	Leeds Harehills	Leeds City
Braintree & Crittall Athletic	Crittall Athletic	Liversey United	Metrogas
Branksome Gasworks Athletic	Bournemouth Gasworks Athletic	Lloyds	Bowater Lloyds
Bridgwater Town	Crown Dynamos	Luton Frickers	Leagrave & District
Briggs Sports	Ford United	Maldon & Heybridge	Heybridge
Brighton Railway Athletic	Southern Railway (1)	McLaren Sports	Petters & Bryce Sports
Catherine-de-Barnes	Solihull Town	Metrogas	Liversey United
Chesterfield Ramblers	North Derbyshire Ramblers	Milnthorpe	Corinthians
Corinthians	Milnthorpe	Mitcham Wanderers	Tooting & Mitcham United
Crittall Athletic	Braintree & Crittall Athletic	Moneyfield Sports	Strongs Portsmouth
Cross Castle United	Northfield Town	North Derbyshire Ramblers	Chesterfield Ramblers
Crouch End Vampires	Vampires	Northfield Town	Allens Cross
Crown & Manor	Hoxton Manor	Northfield Town	Cross Castle United
Crown Dynamos	Bridgwater Town	Old Latymerians	Sutton Court
Dagenham British Legion	Dagenham Park	Old St Stephens	Shepherds Bush (1)
Dagenham Park	Dagenham British Legion	Ordnance (Woolwich)	Woolwich
Deerfield Athletic	Hyde & Kingsbury	Ormskirk	Guinness Exports
Devizes Town	Southbroom (Devizes)	Petters & Bryce Sports	McLaren Sports
Distington	High Duty Alloys	PO Engineers (LTR)	Hermes
Douglas	Aero Engines	Portsea Island Gas Co	Portsmouth Gas Co
Earlsfield Town	Gwynne's Athletic	Portsmouth Gas Co	Portsea Island Gas Co
Earlsfield Town	Adam Grimaldi	Prestwich Heys	Heys Old Boys
East Ham United	Storey Athletic	Reading Biscuit Factory	Huntley & Palmers
Eastern Coachworks (Lowestoft)	Eastern Counties United	Rock-a-Nore	Hastings Rock-a-Nore
Eastern Counties United	Eastern Coachworks (Lowestoft)	ROF (SA)	Royal Arsenal Sports
Epsom & Ewell	Ewell & Stoneleigh	Royal Arsenal Sports	ROF (SA)
Erith & Belvedere	Belvedere	Shepherds Bush (1)	Old St Stephens
Ewell & Stoneleigh	Epsom & Ewell	Shepherds Bush (2)	Acton
Finsbury	Harris Lebus	Solihull Amateur	Jack Moulds Athletic
Ford United	Briggs Sports	Solihull Town	Catherine-de-Barnes
Gnome Athletic	Walthamstow Town	Southbroom (Devizes)	Devizes Town
Golders Green	Hendon	Southern Railway (1)	Brighton Railway Athletic
Golders Green	Hampstead Town	Storey Athletic	East Ham United
Guinness Exports	Ormskirk	Streatham Town	Wandsworth United
Gwynne's Athletic	Earlsfield Town	Strongs Portsmouth	Moneyfield Sports
Hampstead Town	Golders Green	Strongs Portsmouth	Hawker Siddeley
Harris Lebus	Finsbury	Sutton Court	Old Latymerians
Hastings Rock-a-Nore	Rock-a-Nore	The Hook (Northaw) Sports	White City
Hawker Siddeley	Strongs Portsmouth	Tooting & Mitcham United	Mitcham Wanderers
Hayes	Botwell Mission	Upminster	Hornchurch & Upminster
Hemel Hempstead Town	Apsley	Vampires	Crouch End Vampires
Hendon	Golders Green	Walthamstow Town	Gnome Athletic
Hermes	PO Engineers (LTR)	Walton & Hersham	Hersham
Hersham	Walton & Hersham	Wandsworth United	Streatham Town
Heybridge	Maldon & Heybridge	White City	The Hook (Northaw) Sports
Heys Old Boys	Prestwich Heys	Winnington Park	ICI Alkali
High Duty Alloys	Distington	Woolwich	Ordnance (Woolwich)

APPENDIX TWO: SCHEDULED DATES OF ROUNDS

	EP	PR	Q1	Q2	Q3	Q4	R1	R2	R3	R4	SF	F	Fr
1893/94	-	-	21.10	11.11	2.12	-	3.2	17.2	3.3	-	17.3	7.4	-
1894/95	-	-	20.10	10.11	1.12	22.12	2.2	16.2	2.3	-	13.4	27.4	-
1895/96	-	-	12.10	2.11	23.11	14.12	1.2	15.2	29.2	-	21.3	28.3	-
1896/97	-	-	10.10	31.10	21.11	12.12	30.1	13.2	27.2	-	13.3	27.3	17.4
1897/98	-	-	16.10	30.10	20.11	11.12	29.1	12.2	26.2	-	12.3	23.4	-
1898/99	-	-	15.10	29.10	19.11	10.12	28.1	11.2	25.2	-	11.3	25.3	-
1899/00	-	30.9	14.10	28.10	18.11	9.12	20.1	3.2	17.2	-	10.3	31.3	-
1900/01	-	-	20.10	3.11	17.11	8.12	19.1	2.2	16.2	-	9.3	6.4	13.4
1901/02	-	5.10	19.10	2.11	16.11	7.12	18.1	1.2	15.2	-	8.3	12.4	-
1902/03	-	-	11.10	1.11	22.11	13.12	24.1	14.2	28.2	-	14.3	28.3	4.4
1903/04	-	-	10.10	31.10	21.11	12.12	23.1	13.2	27.2	-	12.3	4.4	-
1904/05	-	1.10	8.10	29.10	19.11	10.12	7.1	28.1	18.2	-	11.3	8.4	-
1905/06	-	23.9	7.10	28.10	18.11	9.12	20.1	10.2	24.2	-	10.3	24.3	-
1906/07	15.9	22.9	6.10	27.10	17.11	8.12	12.1	26.1	16.2	-	9.3	30.3	-
1907/08	-	-	12.10	26.10	9.11	30.11	11.1	25.1	15.2	7.3	21.3	11.4	-
1908/09	-	26.9	10.10	24.10	7.11	28.11	9.1	23.1	13.2	6.3	20.3	17.4	-
1909/10	-	-	9.10	23.10	6.11	27.11	8.1	22.1	12.2	5.3	19.3	16.4	-
1910/11	-	-	8.10	22.10	5.11	26.11	7.1	21.1	11.2	4.3	18.3	8.4	-
1911/12	-	-	7.10	21.10	4.11	25.11	6.1	20.1	10.2	2.3	16.3	13.4	18.4
1912/13	-	-	5.10	19.10	2.11	23.11	4.1	18.1	15.2	1.3	15.3	12.4	19.4
1913/14	-	20.9	4.10	18.10	1.11	22.11	3.1	17.1	14.2	28.2	13.3	4.4	-
1914/15	-	-	21.11	5.12	-	-	2.1	16.1	13.2	27.2	13.3	17.4	-
1919/20	-	-	4.10	18.10	1.11	22.11	3.1	17.1	14.2	28.2	13.3	17.4	-
1920/21	-	-	2.10	1610	30.10	20.11	1.1	15.1	12.2	26.2	12.3	16.4	-
1921/22	-	17.9	1.10	15.10	29.10	19.11	10.12	14.1	11.2	25.2	11.2	1.4	-
1922/23	-	16.9	30.9	14.10	28.10	18.11	9.12	20.1	17.2	3.3	17.3	21.4	-
1923/24	-	15.9	29.9	13.10	27.10	17.11	8.12	19.1	16.2	1.3	15.3	5.4	-
1924/25	-	27.9	11.10	25.10	15.11	6.12	3.1	17.1	14.2	28.2	14.3	18.4	-
1925/26	-	26.9	10.10	24.10	14.11	5.12	2.1	16.1	13.2	27.2	13.3	17.4	-
1926/27	-	25.9	9.10	23.10	13.11	4.12	1.1	15.1	12.2	26.2	12.2	9.4	-
1927/28	-	24.9	8.10	22.10	12.11	3.12	31.12	14.1	11.2	25.2	10.3	14.4	-
1928/29	-	22.9	6.10	20.10	.10.11	1.12	15.12	19.1	9.2	23.2	9.3	20.4	-
1929/30	-	28.9	12.10	26.10	9.11	23.11	14.12	18.1	8.2	22.2	8.3	12.4	-
1930/31	-	27.9	11.10	25.10	8.11	22.11	13.12	17.1	7.2	21.2	7.3	11.4	-
1931/32	-	26.9	10.10	24.10	7.11	21.11	12.12	16.1	6.2	20.2	5.3	16.4	-
1932/33	-	24.9	8.10	22.10	5.11	19.11	10.12	14.1	4.2	25.2	11.3	22.4	-
1933/34	-	23.9	7.10	21.10	4.11	18.11	9.12	13.1	3.2	24.2	10.3	21.4	-
1934/35	-	22.9	6.10	20.10	3.11	17.11	12.1	2.2	23.2	9.3	30.3	13.4	20.4
1935/36	-	28.9	12.10	26.10	9.11	23.11	4.1	1.2	22.2	7.3	28.3	18.4	2.5
1936/37	12.9	26.9	10.10	24.10	7.11	21.11	9.1	6.2	27.2	20.3	3.4	17.4	-
1937/38	11.9	25.9	9.10	23.10	6.11	20.11	15.1	5.2	26.2	19.3	2.4	23.4	-
1938/39	10.9	24.9	8.10	22.10	5.11	19.11	14.1	4.2	25.2	18.3	1.4	22.4	-
1945/46	-	15.9	29.9	13.10	27.10	10.11	19.1	2.2	16.2	9.3	23.3	20.4	-
1946/47	14.9	28.9	12.10	26.10	9.11	23.11	18.1	1.2	15.2	8.3	22.3	19.4	-
1947/48	13.9	27.9	11.10	25.10	8.11	22.11	17.1	31.1	14.2	28.2	13.3	17.4	-
1948/49	11.9	25.9	9.10	23.10	6.11	20.11	15.1	29.1	12.2	26.2	19.3	23.4	-
1949/50	10.9	24.9	8.10	22.10	5.11	19.11	14.1	28.1	11.2	25.2	18.3	22.4	-
1950/51	9.9	23.9	7.10	21.10	411	18.11	13.1	27.1	10.2	24.2	10.3	21.4	-
1951/52	8.9	22.9	6.10	20.10	3.11	17.11	15.12	12.2	9.2	23.2	22.2	26.4	-
1952/53	6.9	20.9	4.10	18.10	1.11	15.11	13.12	24.1	7.2	21.2	14.3	11.4	-
1953/54	5.9	19.9	3.10	17.10	31.10	14.11	19.12	23.1	6.2	20.2	13.3	10.4	19.4, 22.4
1954/55	4.9	18.9	2,10	16.10	30.10	13.11	18.12	22.1	5.2	26.2	12.3	16.4	-
1955/56	2.9	16.9	30.9	14.10	28.10	11.11	21.1	4.2	18.2	3.3	17.3	7.4	14.4
1956/57	1.9	15.9	29.9	13.10	27.10	10.11	12.1	26.1	9.2	23.2	16.3	13.4	-
1957/58	14.9	28.9	12.10	26.10	9.11	23.11	11.1	25.1	8.2	22.2	15.3	12.4	-
1958/59	13.9	27.9	11.10	25.10	8.11	22.11	10.1	24.1	7.2	21.2	21.3	18.4	-
1959/60	12.0	26.9	10.10	24.10	7.11	21.11	9.1	23.1	6.2	20.2	12.3	23.4	-
1960/61	17.9	1.10	15.10	29.10	12.11	26.11	21.1	4.2	18.2	4.3	25.3	22.4	-
1961/62	-	30.9	14.10	28.10	11.11	2.12	20.1	3.2	17.2	3.3	24.3	14.4	21.4
1962/63	-	29.9	13.10	27.10	10.11	8.12	12.1	2.2	16.2	2.3	23.3	4.5	-
1963/64	14.9	28.9	12.10	26.10	9.11	30.11	11.1	1.2	22.2	7.3	21.3	18.4	-
1964/65	-	26.9	10.10	24.10	7.11	28.11	2.1	23.1	13.2	6.3	27.2	24.4	-
1965/66	-	25.9	9.10	23.10	6.11	27.11	1.1	22.1	12.2	26.2	19.3	16.4	-
1966/67	-	24.9	8.10	22.10	5.11	10.12	14.1	28.1	11.2	25.2	18.3	22.4	29.4
1967/68	-	23.9	7.10	21.10	4.11	9.12	13.1	27.1	10.2	24.2	16.3	20.4	-
1968/69	-	14.9	28.9	12.10	26.10	23.11	14.12	11.1	1.2	22.2	15.3	12.4	-
1969/70	-	13.9	27.9	11.10	25.10	22.11	13.12	10.1	31.1	21.2	14.3	4.4	-
1970/71	-	12.9	26.9	17.10	31.10	28.11	9.1	30.1	13.2	27.2	20.3	24.4	-
1971/72	-	11.9	25.9	16.10	30.10	20.11	8.1	29.1	19.2	4.3	18.3	22.4	-
1972/73	-	9.9	23.9	14.10	28.10	18.11	9.12	6.1	27.1	17.2	10.3	14.4	-
1973/74	-	8.9	29.9	27.10	17.11	8.12	5.1	26.1	9.2	2.3	23.3	20.4	-

APPENDIX THREE: RECONSTRUCTED DRAWS

Draws for some rounds were not available and have been reconstructed from the results.

BOTH DIVISIONS						
	Extra Preliminary	Preliminary	First	Second	Third	Fourth
1895/96			*			
1903/04				*	*	*
1904/05						*
1906/07	*	*				
Nothing available: 1893/94 1894/95 1945/46 1947/48						

NORTHERN DIVISION ONLY			
	Second	Third	Fourth
1897/98		*	*
1898/99	*	*	*
1899/1900		*	*
1904/05		*	*
1905/06	*	*	*
1907-1910		*	*
1910-1914		*	
1919-1939	*	*	
1946/47	*	*	*
1948/49	*	*	

APPENDIX FOUR: DRAW FOR THE 1939/40 COMPETITION

EXEMPTED TO THE FOURTH QUALIFYING ROUND		
Billingham	Chesham United	Oxford City
Boldmere St Michaels	Eton Manor	Slough
Evenwood Town	Finchley	Southall
Ferguson Pailin	Gorleston	Southwick
Ferryhill Athletic	Hitchin Town	Tooting & Mitcham United
Guiseley	Leavesden	Tufnell Park
Rawmarsh Welfare	Lowestoft Town	Uxbridge
Whitehall Printeries	Maidenhead United	Worthing
EXEMPT TO THE FIRST ROUND		
Badsey Rangers	Barking	Ilford
Bishop Auckland	Barnet	Kingstonian
Farsley Celtic	Bournemouth Gasworks	Leyton
Heaton Stannington	Bromley	Leytonstone
ICI Alkali	Cambridge Town	Metropolitan Pol ice
Marine	Corinthian Casuals	Portland United
Moor Green	Clapton	Romford
Norton Woodseats	Dulwich Hamlet	St Albans City
Shildon	Enfield	Sutton United
South Bank	Erith & Belvedere	Walthamstow Avenue
Willington	Golders Green	Wealdstone
Yorkshire Amateur	Harwich & Parkeston	Wimbledon
	Hastings & St Leonards	Woking
	Hayes	Wycombe Wanderers

QUALIFYING COMPETITION

NORTHERN DIVISION

DISTRICT 1
PRELIMINARY ROUND
Wallsend Corinthians v Royal Tank Regt (Newcastle)
FIRST ROUND
Bigges Main Celtic v Wallsend St Lukes
Central Amateurs (Gateshead) v Vickers Armstrong (Newcastle)
Willington Athletic v Parsons Athletic (Newcastle)
Wallsend Corinthians or Royal Tank Regt v South Shields Ex Schoolboys
DISTRICT 2
EXTRA PRELIMINARY ROUND
Brandon Social v Durham St Giles
Mackays Sports (Durham) v Witton Park Institute
PRELIMINARY ROUND
Brandon Social or Durham St Giles v Chilton Colliery Recreation
Sacriston United v Stanley United
Tow Law Town v Crookhall Rovers
Darlington Amateurs v Cockfield
Mackays Sports or Witton Park Institute v Crook
Washington Welfare Rovers v Darlington Rolling Mills
Barnard Castle Alliance v Lanchester Rangers
Rocket Athletic (Darlington) v West Auckland Town
FIRST ROUND
Darlington Amateurs or Cockfield v Washington Welfare Rovers or Darlington Rolling Mills
Barnard Castle Alliance or Lanchester Rangers v Sacriston United or Stanley United
Tow Law Town or Crookhall Rovers v Mackays Sports or Witton Park Institute or Crook
Rocket Athletic or West Auckland Town v Brandon Social or Durham St Giles or Chilton Colliery Recreation
DISTRICT 3
PRELIMINARY ROUND
Whitby Albion Rangers v North Skelton Mine
Grangetown St Marys v Normanby Magnesite
Thornaby v South Bank St Peters
Portrack Shamrocks v Smith Dock (Eston)
Great Ayton United v Whitby United
Scarborough Amateurs v South Bank East End
FIRST ROUND
Grangetown St Marys or Normanby Magnesite v Whitby Albion Rangers or North Skelton Mine
Cargo Fleet Steel Works v Portrack Shamrocks or Smith Dock
Thornaby or South Bank St Peters v Billingham Synthonia Recreation
Great Ayton United or Whitby United v Scarborough Amateurs or South Bank East End

DISTRICT 4
FIRST ROUND
Liverpool W D U v Old Xaverians
Tushington Brick Works (Prescot) v Earle (Liverpool)
Barnton Victoria v Formby (Liverpool)
Northern Nomads v Harrowby
DISTRICT 5
PRELIMINARY ROUND
East End Park W M C (Leeds) v Ravensthorpe
Bradford Rovers v York Railway Institute
FIRST ROUND
East End Park W M C or Ravensthorpe v Old Hullensians
East Bierley (Bradford) v Brunswick Institute (Hull)
Bradford Rovers or York Railway Institute v Whitkirk (Leeds)
Oulton Roseville (Leeds) v Carlton United (Wakefield)

MIDLAND DIVISION

DISTRICT 6
FIRST ROUND
Stapleford Brookhill v Excelsior Foundry (Sandiacre)
Fulwood (Sheffield) v Raleigh Athletic
Boots Athletic (Nottingham) v Players Athletic (Nottingham)
Sutton Town (Nottinghamshire) v Bourne Town
DISTRICT 7
FIRST ROUND
Ibstock Penistone Rovers v Kettering United
Leicestershire Nomads v Chesterfield Ramblers
Ho!well Works (Melton Mowbray) v Coalville Town Amateur
Derbyshire Amateurs v Whitwick White Cross
DISTRICT 8
PRELIMINARY ROUND
Enfield Cycles (Redditch) v Morris Motors (Coventry)
FIRST ROUND
Daventry Town v Enfield Cycles (Redditch) or Morris Motors (Coventry)
Jack Moulds (Birmingham) v Wolverhampton Amateur
Northampton Nomads v Cherry Orchard (Worcester)
West Bromwich Amateur v Humber Hillman Recreation

SOUTHERN DIVISION—(Central Area)

DISTRICT 9
FIRST ROUND
St Neots & District v Newmarket Town
Abbey United (Cambridgeshire) v Eynesbury Rovers
Ramsey Town v RAF (Mildenhall)
Pye Radio (Cambridge) v Warboys Town
DISTRICT 10
PRELIMINARY ROUND
Kings Lynn v Wymondham Town
Norwich C E Y M S v Gt Yarmouth Town
Holt United v Norwich St Barnabas
Fakenham Town v Lakenheath
Norwich Electricity Works v Sheringham
FIRST ROUND
North Walsham v Fakenham Town or Lakenheath
Kings Lynn or Wymondham Town v Norwich C E Y M S or Gt Yarmouth Town
Thetford Town v Holt United or Norwich St Barnabas
Frosts Athletic (Norwich) v Norwich Electricity Works or Sheringham
DISTRICT 11
PRELIMINARY ROUND
Old Grammarians (Ipswich) v Leiston
Bungay Town v RAF (Felixstowe)
FIRST ROUND 7th October 1939
Brantham Athletic v Felixstowe Town
Orwell Works (Ipswich) v Old Grammarians (Ipswich) or Leiston
Bungay Town or RAF (Felixstowe) v Eastern Coach Works (Lowestoft)
RAF (Martlesham) v Walton United (Felixstowe)
DISTRICT 12
PRELIMINARY ROUND
Leighton United v Apsley
Wendover v Berkhamsted Town
Aylesbury United v RAF (Halton)
Bushey United v Vauxhall Motors (Luton)

FIRST ROUND
Aylesbury United or RAF (Halton) v Hazell's (Aylesbury)
Wendover or Berkhamsted Town v Bushey United or Vauxhall Motors (Luton)
Kings Langley v Leighton United or Apsley
Luton Amateur v Waterlows (Dunstable)
DISTRICT 13
PRELIMINARY ROUND
Hoddesdon Town v Harlow Town
Welwyn Garden City v Bishops Stortford
Arlesey Town v Epping Town
Baldock Town v Ware
Letchworth Town v Murphy Radio (Welwyn)
FIRST ROUND
Letchworth Town or Murphy Radio (Welwyn) v Baldock Town or Ware
Stevenage Town v Welwyn Garden City or Bishops Stortford
Hatfield United v Hertford Town
Hoddesdon Town or Harlow Town v Arlesey Town or Epping Town
SOUTHERN DIVISION—(Eastern Area)
DISTRICT 14
PRELIMINARY ROUND
Tilbury v Esso (Purfleet)
Highgate v Port of London Authority
FIRST ROUND
Highgate or Port of London Authority v Grays Athletic
Ford Sports (Dagenham) v Briggs Motor Bodies
Stork (Purfleet) v Tilbury or Esso (Purfleet)
Southend Corinthians v Dagenham Town
DISTRICT 15
FIRST ROUND
Crittall Athletic v Clacton Town
Severalls Athletic v Brentwood & Warley
Brightlingsea United v Saffron Walden Town
Bye : Hoffman Athletic
DISTRICT 16
EXTRA PRELIMINARY ROUND
Darenth Park (Dartford) v Royal Ordnance Factories (Plumstead)
White Horse (Belvedere) v Sidcup & Footscray
RAF (Manston) v RN Depot (Chatham)
RM (Chatham) v Maidstone United
Grenville (Ramsgate) v Deal Town
Training Battalion R E v Sheppey United
Dover v RM (Deal)
PRELIMINARY ROUND
Woolwich Polytechnic v Callender Athletic
U G B (Charlton) Sports v Darenth Park or Royal Ordnance Factories (Plumstead)
White Horse (Belvedere) or Sidcup & Footscray v London Paper Mills (Dartford)
Bexley v Catford Wanderers
Aylesford Paper Mills v Gravesend United
Grenville (Ramsgate) or Deal Town v RAF (Manston) or RN Depot (Chatham)
Chatham v Dover or RM (Deal)
Training Bn R E or Sheppey United v RM (Chatham) or Maidstone United
FIRST ROUND
Woolwich Polytechnic or Callender Athletic v Training Bn R E or Sheppey United or RM (Chatham) or Maidstone United
White Horse (Belvedere) or Sidcup & Footscray or London Paper Mills (Dartford) v Aylesford Paper Mills or Gravesend United
Chatham or Dover or RM (Deal) v Grenville (Ramsgate) or Deal Town or RAF (Manston) or RN Depot (Chatham)
U G B (Charlton) Sports or Darenth Park or Royal Ordnance Factories (Plumstead) v Bexley or Catford Wanderers
DISTRICT 17
PRELIMINARY ROUND
Redhill v West Norwood
Epsom v Reigate Priory
Leyland Motors (Kingston) v Aquarius
Carshalton v Carshalton Athletic
Merton v Nunhead
Epsom Town v Banstead Hospital
Venner Sports v Cobham
FIRST ROUND -
Epsom or Reigate Priory v Venner Sports or Cobham
P O Engineers (Wallington) v Merton or Nunhead
Epsom Town or Banstead Hospital v Redhill or West Norwood
Carshalton or Carshalton Athletic v Leyland Motors or Aquarius
DISTRICT 18
EXTRA PRELIMINARY ROUND
London Welsh (Hendon) v Old Latymerians
Wood Green Town v Northmet
Lensbury & Britannic House v Norsemen (Edmonton)

PRELIMINARY ROUND
London Welsh (Hendon) or Old Latymerians v Wood Green Town or Northmet
Lyons(Greenford) v Hounslow Town
Polytechnic v Old Lyonians
Harrow Town v Pinner
Old Stationers (Barnet) v Ealing Association
Yiewsley v Old Finchleians
Lensbury & Britannic House or Norsemen (Edmonton) v Civil Service
Old Johnians v Hoxton Manor
FIRST ROUND
Harrow Town or Pinner v Lyons (Greenford) or Hounslow Town
Yiewsley or Old Finchleians v Old Johnians or Hoxton Manor
London Welsh (Hendon) or Old Latymerians or Wood Green Town or Northmet v
       Lensbury & Britannic House or Norsemen(Edmonton) or Civil Service
Old Stationers (Barnet) or Ealing Association v Polytechnic or Old Lyonians

DISTRICT 19
PRELIMINARY ROUND
Abingdon Town v Thatcham
Osberton Radiator (Oxford) v Bicester Town
Newbury Town v Pressed Steel (Cowley)
Witney Town v Wallingford Town
Morris Motors (Cowley) v Cowley
Henley Town v Redford Sports (Wycombe)
Headington United v Windsor & Eton
FIRST ROUND 7th October 1989
Marlow v Witney Town or Wallingford Town
Henley Town or Redford Sports (Wycombe) v Abingdon Town or Thatcham
Headington United or Windsor & Eton v Osberton Radiator (Oxford) or Bicester Town
Morris Motors (Cowley) or Cowley v Newbury Town or Pressed Steel (Cowley)

DISTRICT 20
PRELIMINARY ROUND
Egham v Brookwood Hospital
Binfield v Guildford
4th Bn Royal Tank Regt (Farnborough) v Vickers Armstrong (Byfleet)
Walton-on-Thames v Godalming
Camberley & Yorktown v Andover
FIRST ROUND
Egham or Brookwood Hospital v R A S C
Camberley & Yorktown or Andover v Hersham
Binfield or Guildford v Thornycroft (Basingstoke)
Walton-on-Thames or Godalming v 4th Bn Royal Tank Regt or Vickers Armstrong (Byfieet)

DISTRICT 21
PRELIMINARY ROUND
Bexhill v Eastbourne Comrades
Eastbourne v Bognor Regis Town
Haywards Heath v Horsham
East Grinstead v Littlehampton
Shoreham v Chichester
FIRST ROUND -
Shoreham or Chichester v Haywards Heath or Horsham
Hove v East Grinstead or Littlehampton
Bexhill or Eastbourne Comrades v Eastbourne or Bognor Regis Town
Brighton Transport v Newhaven

SOUTHERN DIVISION--(Western Area)

DISTRICT 22
EXTRA PRELIMINARY ROUND
Fareham Casuals v Totton (Southampton)
PRELIMINARY ROUND
Bournemouth v Ringwood Town
Ryde Sports v Fareham Casuals or Totton (Southampton)
Hamworthy (Poole) v Gosport
Bridport v Fareham
H M S Victory(Portsmouth) v Osborne Athletic
Poole Town v Portsmouth Gas Company
Dorchester Town v Wimborne
Winchester City v H M S Excellent (Portsmouth)
FIRST ROUND
Hamworthy or Gosport v Poole Town or Portsmouth Gas Company
Winchester City or H M S Excellent (Portsmouth) v Dorchester Town or Wimborne
H M S Victory (Portsmouth) or Osborne Athletic v Bridport or Fareham
Hyde Sports or Fareham Casuals or Totton (Southampton) v Bournemouth or Ringwood Town

DISTRICT 23
EXTRA PRELIMINARY ROUND
Bristol Aeroplane Co v Bristol St George
Chalford v Mount Hill Enterprise (Bristol)
Welton Rovers v Hanham Athletic
St Pancras (Knowle) v Soundwell (Bristol)
PRELIMINARY ROUND
Clevedon v St Pancras (Knowle) or Soundwell (Bristol)
Brislington v Taunton Amateurs
Shell Mex (Avonmouth) v Minehead
Radstock Town v Watchet Town
Eastville United v Bristol Aeroplane Co or Bristol St George
Twerton St Michaels v Welton Rovers or Hanham Athletic
Chalford or Mount Hill Enterprise (Bristol) v Peasedown Miners Welfare
Paulton Rovers v Clandown (Bath)
FIRST ROUND
Eastville United or Bristol Aeroplane Co or Bristol St George v Radstock Town or Watchet Town
Twerton St Michaels or Welton Rovers or Hanham Athletic v Shell Mex (Avonmouth) or Minehead
Clevedon or St Pancras (Knowle) or Soundwell (Bristol) v Chalford or Mount Hill Enterprise (Bristol) or Peasedown Miners Welfare
Brislington or Taunton Amateurs v Paulton Rovers or Clandown (Bath)
DISTRICT 24
PRELIMINARY ROUND
Purton v Wootton Bassett Town
Pewsey Y M v Melksham
Swindon Victoria v Swindon Corinthians
Wiltshire County M H v Devizes Town
Calne & Harris United v Spencer Moulton (Bradford-on-Avon)
Salisbury Corinthians v Frome Town
Salisbury City v Westbury United
Warminster Town v Chippenham Town
FIRST ROUND
Salisbury City or Westbury United v Warminster Town or Chippenham Town
Swindon Victoria or Swindon Corinthians v Salisbury Corinthians or Frome Town
Purton or Wootton Bassett Town v Pewsey Y M or Melksham
Calne & Harris United or Spencer Moulton v Wiltshire County M H or Devizes Town

APPENDIX FIVE

TOP TWENTY CLUBS ON GAMES PLAYED

	p	w	d	l	f	a	w	d	l	f	a	% won
Bishop Auckland	274	95	11	13	367	129	83	24	48	325	222	64.96
Enfield	232	77	17	20	355	134	59	20	39	233	198	58.62
Leytonstone	224	66	17	18	245	127	52	27	44	204	186	52.68
Redhill	221	72	18	21	328	157	54	12	44	229	206	57.01
Wycombe Wanderers	215	85	12	24	353	177	32	17	45	167	190	54.42
Oxford City	202	64	10	24	340	136	41	20	43	203	194	51.98
Southall	201	63	13	21	257	109	39	25	40	216	210	50.75
Ilford	191	59	15	23	253	130	42	13	39	204	173	52.88
Worthing	191	63	8	29	290	157	37	18	36	218	214	52.36
South Bank	190	53	14	27	218	149	36	17	43	173	191	46.84
Bromley	186	62	12	13	264	105	43	12	44	170	182	56.45
Harwich & Parkeston	183	48	14	28	242	152	45	11	37	160	164	50.82
Aylesbury United	181	78	10	28	350	177	22	8	35	117	161	55.25
Horsham	180	58	12	20	289	154	33	14	43	191	220	50.56
Stanley United	177	51	18	22	226	132	32	11	43	158	175	46.89
Stockton	177	64	11	13	264	107	41	12	36	158	152	59.32
Dulwich Hamlet	175	56	9	13	233	81	42	13	42	156	172	56.00
Leyton	175	44	11	19	189	108	55	16	30	180	157	56.57
Marlow	175	53	14	26	255	149	27	11	44	167	214	45.71
Sutton United	173	49	12	19	204	113	44	15	34	170	158	53.76

TOP TWENTY CLUBS ON PERCENTAGE OF GAMES WON (MINIMUM OF 50 GAMES)

	p	w	d	l	f	a	w	d	l	f	a	% won
Bishop Auckland	274	95	11	13	367	129	83	24	48	325	222	64.96
Skelmersdale United	51	21	2	2	68	20	11	9	6	51	27	62.75
Bostall Heath	52	19	3	12	90	55	13	0	5	52	28	61.54
Guinness Exports	52	15	4	6	57	22	17	5	5	73	39	61.54
Barnet	140	52	6	14	222	91	34	9	25	158	116	61.43
Trowbridge Town	72	29	2	8	112	44	15	3	15	68	74	61.11
Marine	146	62	3	16	244	99	25	9	31	135	126	59.59
Eastbourne United	79	23	4	8	89	47	24	6	14	109	61	59.49
Stockton	177	64	11	13	264	107	41	12	36	158	152	59.32
King's Lynn	117	47	5	5	186	65	22	4	34	113	162	58.97
Wokingham Town	73	24	3	13	94	56	19	7	7	94	48	58.90
Enfield	232	77	17	20	355	134	59	20	39	233	198	58.62
Gosport Borough Athletic	70	29	2	7	118	40	12	3	17	59	82	58.57
Ossett Albion	74	23	6	9	83	53	20	4	12	79	53	58.11
Slough Town	105	35	10	8	156	58	26	8	18	97	71	58.10
Epsom	57	21	3	9	110	57	12	2	10	68	47	57.89
Letchworth Town	151	59	11	17	275	135	28	10	26	158	132	57.62
Northampton Nomads	56	19	2	5	121	49	13	5	12	74	67	57.14
Redhill	221	72	18	21	328	157	54	12	44	229	206	57.01
Leyton	175	44	11	19	189	108	55	16	30	180	157	56.57

Games played may not be the same as the figure shown in the index of clubs, since the latter includes byes and void games

APPENDIX SIX: FINAL LINE-UPS

Season	Date	Team			1	2	3	4	5	6	7	8	9	10	11
1893/94	Apr 7	Old Carthusians	2	3500	Wilkinson	Walters AM	Bray	Bliss	Streatfield	Wreford-Brown	Hewitt	Richardson	Buzzard 1	Wilson	Stanbrough 1
1894/95		Casuals	1		Harrison	Lodge	Hatton	Barker	Topham A	Grierson	Topham R 1	Carlton	Perkins	Rhodes TB	Rhodes HA
1894/95	Apr 27	Middlesbrough	2	4000	Cooper	Piercey	Wilson D	Allport	Morren	Bach	Johnson	Gettings	Mullen 1	Nelmes 1	Murphy
1895/96	Mar 28	Old Carthusians	1		Wilkinson	Walters AM	Walters PM	Buzzard	Kite	Streatfield	Hewitt	Broadbent	Smith GO 1	Wilson GS	Stanbrough
1895/96		Bishop Auckland	1	3000	Ward	Pennington	Tuson	Marshall	Lunson	Adams	Lewins	Lodge 1	Foster	Wilson	Manners
1896/97	Mar 27	Royal Artillery (Portsmouth)	0		Reilly	Phillips	Harms	Patterson	Hill	Kinnan	Jardine	Hanna	Cook	Walsh	Meggs
1896/97		Old Carthusians	1	9000	Wilkinson	Bray	Timmis	Bliss	Wreford-Brown	Darvell	Wilson G	Buzzard	Smith 1	Stanborough	Hewitt
Replay	Apr 17	Old Carthusians	4		Hamilton	Brannan	Wilson C	Shaw	Murray	Monteith	Robson	Daniel	Addison	Sanderson 1	Lakey
1897/98		Stockton	1	10000	Wilkinson	Bray	Timmis	Bliss	Wreford-Brown	Darvell	Hewitt 1	Jameson	Smith GO 1	Buzzard 2	Stanbrough
1897/98	Apr 23	Middlesbrough	2		Hamilton	Brannan	Wilson C	Shaw	Murray	Monteith	Robson	Lee	Halfpenny 1	Sanderson	Lakey
1897/98		Uxbridge	0	1500	Smith	Moore	Piercey	Allport	Jackson	Nelmes	Frost 1	Bishop	Kempley 1	Longstaff	Wanless
1898/99	Mar 25	Stockton	2		Gumbrell	Gayland	Skinner	Brown	Bensted	Jacobs	Woodbridge A	Hickman	Browning	Knight	Woodbridge E
1898/99		Harwich & Parkeston	1	7000	Fall	Shaw W	Wilson	Brannan	Baker	Monteith	Shaw R	Chatt	Byron	Fairbairn 1	Lakey
1899/00	Mar 31	Bishop Auckland	5		Kettle	Bacon	Howard	Ingham	Garton	Whitehead	Garland	Eley	Harwood	Taylor	Snodgrass
1899/00		Lowestoft Town	1	1000	Proud	Bousfield	Condon	Ord 1	Thomas	Pennington	Marshall Joe	Allan 1	Marshall T 2	Marshall Jim 1	Crawford
1900/01	Apr 6	Crook Town	1	4000	Ayres	Simoney	Mewse	Beaton	Royal	Marr	Crews	Cole	Allen	Baker	Wilkins 1
1900/01		King's Lynn	1		Nattress	Ward	Rule	Law	Rippon	Hammill	Lear	Creesor	Iley 1	Dargue	Harwood
Replay	Apr 13	Crook Town	3	1500	Gay	Haylock	Gifton	Reed	Stevens	Sporne	Orviss	Holroyd	MacDonald 1	Horsley	Smith
Replay		King's Lynn	0		Nattress	Ward	Rule	Law	Rippon 1	Hammill 1	Lear	Creesor	Iley	Dargue	Harwood 1
1901/02	Apr 2	Old Malvernians	5	1000	Gay	Sporne	Gifton	Reed	Stevens	Haylock	Orvis	Holroyd	MacDonald	Horsley	Smith
1901/02		Bishop Auckland	1		Tuff	Simpson-Hayward	Ransome	Todd	Canny	Simpson	Day 1	Foster B	Graeme 1	Foster RE 2	Corbett 1
1902/03	Mar 28	Stockton	0	4000	Proud	Harwood	Condon	Marshall Jim	Thomas	Marshall T	Marshall Joe	Allan	Newton	Wood 1	Crawford
1902/03		Oxford City	0		Lowe	Starling	King	Rutter	Bell	Hassett	Dunn	Payne	Morgan	Freeland	Blake
Replay	Apr 4	Stockton	0	7000	Selby	Witherington	Smith H	Craddock	Ashworth	Dickinson	Draper	Foster	Blackburn	Smith W	Arnett
Replay		Oxford City	0		Lowe	Starling	King	Rutter	Bell	Hassett	Dunn	Payne	Morgan 1	Freeland	Blake
1903/04	Apr 4	Sheffield	3	6000	Selby	Witherington	Smith H	Craddock	Ashworth	Egley	Draper	Foster	Blackburn	Smith W	Arnett
1903/04		Ealing	1		Bolsover	Chambers	Milnes 1(p)	Green	Potts	Frost	Silvester	Bedford 1	Hoyland G	Hoyland J 1	Forsdyke
1904/05	Apr 8	West Hartlepool	3	4000	Findlay	Blackburn	Fox	Wood	Mitchell	Pryce	Grice	Hebden 1	Doll	Powell	Rogers
1904/05		Clapton	3		Bainbridge	Hegarty T 1	Hegarty D	Black	Hyslop	Stokes	Larkin	Farweather	Robinson	Trechmann 2	Hodgson
Replay	Mar 24	Clapton	3	5000	Wilding	Bayley	Langhorne	Milton	Farnfield P	Hollis	Folks	Brown	Purnell 2	Farnfield H	Farnfield A
1905/06		Oxford City	1		Keates	Scothern	Blackburn	Organ	Smith W	Bumpus	Draper	Dickinson	Tabernacle 2	Hodges 1	Davis
1906/07	Mar 30	Bishop Auckland	0	6000	Proud	Ord	Campbell	Kirby	Robinson	Parker	Crawford	Douglas	Hopper	Charnock	Blaylock
1906/07		Clapton	2		Wilding	Bayley	Ewan	Parkinson	Randall	Olley	Eastwood	Russell 1	Rance 1	Purnell	Harvey
1907/08	Apr 11	Royal Engineers Depot Battn	1	8000	Gary	Chariton	Chapman	Prosser	Bell	Hassett	Williamson	Featherstone	Chambers 1	Freeland	Marwood
1907/08		Stockton	1		Aston	Stanton	May	Shallcross	Webber	Daffern	Lowe	Keir 1	Pearson 1	Shepherd	Hawthorne
1908/09	Apr 17	Clapton	6	5000	Jackson	Bell	Chapman	Prosser	Chariton	Hassett	Williamson	Chambers	Henderson	Freehand	Lowther 1
1908/09		Eston United	0		Harrison	Bayley	Duce	Parkinson	Rist	Olley	Atwood 1	Purnell 2	Rance 3	Tull	Harvey
1909/10	Apr 16	RMLI Gosport	2	8000	Turner	Vintner	Bell	Callaghan	Housham	Bunn	Smith W	Cail	Best	Ellis	Hollis
1909/10		South Bank	1		Howling	Wilkinson	Hirst	Revill	Yates	Wiseman	Exford	White	Holmes 1	Jack 1	Smith
1910/11	Apr 8	Bromley	1	3000	Wood	Rand	Oakley	Biggs 1	Prest	Carr W	Thompson	Carr J	Carr H	Cartwright	Jones
1910/11		Bishop Auckland	0		Walton	Peacock	Watson	McWhirter	Smith P	Smith P	Dilley 1	Noble	Kennard	Landrey	Grayer
1911/12	Apr 13	Stockton	1	20000	Callaghan	Rudd	Ansell	Kirby	Hedley	Robinson	Waniess	Healey	Hopper	Kent	Sowerby
1911/12		Eston United	1		Hill	Loney	Chapman	Evans	Stamper	Veitch A	Bradford	Dobinson	Sutherland 1	Davis	Callender
Replay	Apr 18	Stockton	1	12000	Callaghan	Roddam	Davidson	Smith J	Howsam	O'Hara	Allan	Parsons 1	Smith W	Morris	Hollis
Replay		Eston United	0		Hill	Loney	Chapman	Evans	Stamper	Veitch A	Bradford	Dobinson	Sutherland 1	Davis	Hollis
1912/13	Apr 12	South Bank	1	6000	Howling	Roddam	Davidson	Smith J	Howsam	O'Hara	Allan	Parsons	Smith W	Morris	Evans
1912/13		Oxford City	1		Harley	Unwin	Oakley	Henry	Prest	Anderson	Carr	Clarke	Barrie 1	Heron	Honeysett
Replay	Apr 19	South Bank	1	7000	Howling	Caldwell	Ansell	Radnage	Hunt	Slatter	Carr 1	MacKinnon	Barrie	Vernon	Evans
Replay		Oxford City	0		Harley	Urwin	Oakley	Henry	Prest	Anderson	Carr 1	Clarke	Buckingham 1	Jakeman	Smith HG
1913/14	Apr 4	Bishop Auckland	1	5000	North	Caldwell	Ansell	Radnage	Hunt	Slatter	Draper	Berry	Buckingham	Spence	Lunson
1913/14		Northern Nomads	0		Peever	Roe	Rudd	Hopper	Spence	Maddison	Appleby	Douglas A	Kirby 1	Boardman	Salt
1914/15	Apr 17	Clapton	1	6000	North	Barlow	Cunliffe	Gotobed	Porter	McKinnon	Davies	Douglass H	Cruse	Sherwood 1	Cordell
1919/20		Bishop Auckland	0		Wood	Sharpley	Bartlemeh	Ward	Prescott	Mellows	Walden	Cox	Lloyd	Fleming	Lunson
1919/20	Apr 17	Dulwich Hamlet	1	25000	Coleman	Pilkington	Rudd	Kasher	Green	Maddison	Brown	Gardner	Hopper	Nicol	Fuller
		Tufnell Park	0		Leese	Butcher	Evans	Goodman	Read	Swayne	Fricker	Kail 1	Lloyd	Williams	Elkington

Season	Date	Opponent			1	2	3	4	5	6	7	8	9	10	11
1920/21	Apr 16	Bishop Auckland	4	25000	North	Wilson	Garbutt	Nattrass	Atkinson	Kasher	Brown	Cook 1	Binks 1	Ward 2	Wensley
1921/22	Apr 1	Swindon Victoria	2		Weston	Saunders	Poole 1(p)	Roberts 1	Cooper	Summers	Rees	Blumsden	Eggleton	Dawson	Chivers
1922/23	Apr 1	Bishop Auckland	5	20000	Potts	Wilson	Taylor	Nattrass 1	Atkinson	Maddison	Burrows	Cook 1	Binks 2	Mullen 1	Goldsborough
	Apr 21	South Bank	2		Burns	Thompson	Thomas	Lloyd	Brighton	Tubb	Spencer	Peacock 2	Towse	Hepworth	Robinson
1922/23	Apr 21	London Caledonians	2	14132	Dawson	Gates B	Bridges	Blyth	Barr	Finn	McCubbin 1	Noble	Sloan	May 1	Hamilton
	Apr 5	Evesham Town	1		Jones R	Stokes	Gates E	Gould	Ratcliff	Pennell	Hampton	Busby	Meaking	Jones S 1	Osborne
1923/24	Apr 5	Clapton	3	32000	Moore	Penstone	Blake	Williams	Bryant	Cable	Riley A	Earle	Gibbins	Potter 2	Barnard 1
	Apr 18	Erith & Belvedere	0		Evans R	Evans C	Wilson	Marks	Dudley	Swayne	Gooch	McKee	Yates	Hillier	Beckford
1924/25	Apr 18	Clapton	2	25000	Moore	Penstone	Blake	Williams	Bryant	Cable	Ryley AN	Potter	Gibbins 2	Miller	Barnard 1
	Apr 17	Southall	1		Holding	Buttery	Gower	Johnson	Harvey-Wenham	Waker	Jackson	Clark	Corben	Hillier	Howell
1925/26	Apr 17	Northern Nomads	7	13300	Menham	Blair	Abbott	Jones	Fairweather	Vance	Loxham	Robertson 1	Beswick 3	Hawkins 1	Fairclough
		Stockton	1		Murray	Longstaff	Shanks	Lowther	Pritchard	Waker	Evans	Clare	Thompson 1	Randle 3	McGiffin
1926/27	Apr 9	Leyton	3	12864	Grainger	Preston	Terris	Graves	Scarfe	Goldsmith	Salmons 1	Hall	Bowyer	Pass	Hawkins T
	Apr 14	Barking Town	3		Carmen	Preston	Norrington	Kemp	Cable 2	Young	Evans	Hawkins J 1	Scarborough	Smith G	Lucas
1927/28	Apr 14	Leyton	3	12200	Burr	Carmen	Goldsmith	Graves	Vango	Margetts	McKinlay 1	Hall	Avery	Guyton	Hawkins
	Apr 20	Cockfield	2		Wedge	Dixon	Coates	Barker	Cable 1	Oldfield	Longstaffe	Pearson	Rutter 2	Smith G 1	Kirby
1928/29	Apr 20	Ilford	3	35000	Norman	Banks	Wade	Gilderson	Harrison	Barrett	Potter 1	Welsh	Dellow	Thompson	Peploe 1
	Apr 12	Ilford	5	21800	Jones	Preston	Goldsmith	Graves	Craymer	Margetts	Collins	Hall	Ives	Drane 1	Hawkings
1929/30	Apr 12	Ilford	5	21800	Watson	Triesman	Winterburn	Sheppard	Wright	Webb	Potter 1	Welsh 1	Dellow 1	Smith G 1	Peploe 2
		Bournemouth Gasworks Ath.	1		Joyce	Saunders	Cobb	Turner	Phillips	Gillingham	Smith B	Petty 1	Lovell	Drane	Tapper
1930/31	Apr 11	Wycombe Wanderers	1	32000	Kipping	Crump	Cox	Rance	Badrick	Greenwell	Simmons	Brown	Vernon	Cornibeer	Britnell 1
		Hayes	0		Holding	Maskell	Gower	Caesar E	Wainwright	Caesar W	Knight	Rowe	Morgan	Braisher	Lloyd
1931/32	Apr 16	Dulwich Hamlet	7	22000	Miles	Hugo	Osmond	Murray	Hamer	Aitken	Morrish	Kall 2	Goodliffe 1	Welsh	Robbins HS
		Marine	1		Drury	Jackson	Rankin	Crilley	Kelly	Halsall	Keir	Garvey	O'Donnell	Moseley 4	Bamford
1932/33	Apr 8	Kingstonian	1	20448	Brodrick	Rassell	Urpeth	Lee	Daley	Edwards	McCarthy	Gibson	Whitehead 1	King	Okin
		Stockton	1		Newton	Thompson	Little	Foster	Butler	Keene	Stephenson	Smith RA	Coulthard	Prest	Anderson 1
Replay	Apr 22	Kingstonian	4	16492	Brodrick	Rassell	Urpeth 1(p)	Lee	Daley	Keene	McCarthy	Gibson 1	Whitehead 2	Macey	Okin
		Stockton	1		Newton	Thompson	Little	Foster	Pass	Edwards	Stephenson	Smith RA	Coulthard 1	Prest	Henderson
1933/34	Apr 21	Dulwich Hamlet	2	33000	Cummings	Hugo	Gregory	Murray	Harner	Toser	Morrish	Miller	Goodliffe	Benka	Court 1
		Leyton	1		Holding	Loveday	Scott	Caesar E	Richardson	Mercer	Collins	Brown	Skeels	Coates	Davis 1
1934/35	Apr 13	Bishop Auckland	0	20000	Hopps	Minton	Balkwill	Birbeck	Straughton	Shield	Dodds	Bryan	Wilson	Stephenson	Hogg
		Wimbledon	0		Irish	Goodchild	Scott	Wright	Bridge	Reeves	Batchelor	Barnes	Dowden	Turner	Smith
Replay	Apr 20	Bishop Auckland	2	20000	Hopps	Minton	Balkwill	Birbeck	Straughan	Shield	Dodds	Bryan 1	Wilson 1	Stephenson	Hogg
		Wimbledon	1		Irish	Goodchild	Scott	Wright	Bridge	Reeves	Smith L	Barnes	Dowden 1	Turner	Zenthon
1935/36	Apr 18	Casuals	1	25064	Huddle	Whewell	Evans	Allen	Joy B	Couchman	Shearer	Fabian	Clements	Webster	Riley 1
		Ilford	2		Tietjen	Holmes	Hayes	Male	Myers	Craymer	Gilderson	Manley	Watts	Bunce	Braund 1
Replay	May 2	Casuals	0	27000	Huddle	Whewell	Evans	Allen	Joy	Couchman	Shearer 1	Fabian	Clements	Webster 1	Riley
		Ilford	0		Tietjen	Holmes	Hayes	Male	Myers	Craymer	Gilderson	Manley	Watts	Halcrow	Braund
1936/37	Apr 7	Dulwich Hamlet	2	33516	Hill	Weymouth	Robbins HS	Murray	Hugo	Toser	Morrish 2	Anderson	Wright	Ingleton	Ball
		Leyton	0		Self	Gentry	Clark	Hunt	Preston	Burns	Smith F	Leek	Avery	Boatwright	Cameron
1937/38	Apr 23	Bromley	1	33000	Bartaby	Gray	Clark	Wade	Weeks	Barnes	Thomas	Stroud 1	Brown	Holbrook	Reece
		Erith & Belvedere	0		Gibbs	Little	O'Hara	Smee	Fuller	Bennett	Young	Scott	Southcombe	Beal	Saunders
1938/39	Apr 22	Bishop Auckland	3 e	20000	Washington	Kirtley	Humble	Wanless	Straughan	Paisley	Twigg	Wensley 3	Slee	Evans	Young
		Willington	0		Coe	Cooper	Etheridge	Hardy	Lumby	Hindmarsh	Mitchell	Pratt	McLean	Davidson	Elliot
1945/46	Apr 20	Barnet	3	53832	Powell	Wheeler	Bunker	Gerrans	Pullen	Weightman	Jordan	Kelleher 1	Phipps 1	Finch	Reilly 1
		Bishop Auckland	2		Washington	Humble	Farrer	Longstaff	Hadfield	Fairs	Shergold	Richardson	Teasdale 2	Tait	Anderson
1946/47	Apr 19	Leytonstone	2	47000	Jarvis	Nicholls	Childs	Banham	Lister	Lemmer	Smith E 1	Noble 1	Groves	Bunce	Crowe
		Wimbledon	1		Haydock	Wallis	Cousins	Magill	Clark	Kavanagh	Nash	Stannard 1	Edelston	Head	Laker
1947/48	Apr 17	Leytonstone	1	59605	Powell	Nicholls	Childs	Wilson	Paviour	Kavanagh	Smith FW	Noble	Groves 1	Bunce	Joseph
		Barnet	0		Haydock	Wheeler	Hawkins	Leek	Fuller C	Hawkes	Haskow	Kelleher	Phipps	Mott	Finch
1948/49	Apr 23	Bromley	1	93000	Cornthwaite	Cameron	Yenson	Fuller T	Barton	Fright	Martin	Hopper 1	Brown	Dunmall	Ruddy
		Romford (2)	0		Ivey	Collier	Fryatt	Mackenzie	Yeardley	Regan	Brooks	Maddick	Bridge	Jennings	Patterson
1949/50	Apr 22	Willington	4	88000	Snowden	Craggs	Howe	Leuthwaite	Davison	Dodd	Robinson	Taylor 1	Larmouth	Armstrong 1	Rutherford 1
		Bishop Auckland	0		Washington	Coxon	Farrer	Taylor	Yeardley	Nimmins	Major	Hardisty	McIlvenny	Gilholme	Palmer
1950/51	Apr 21	Pegasus	2	100000	Brown	Cowan	Maughan	Platt	Shearwood	Saunders	Pawson	Dutchman	Tanner 1	Carr DB	Potts 1
		Bishop Auckland	1		White	Marshall	Farrer	Hardisty	Davison	Nimmins 1	Taylor	Anderson	McIlvenny	Williamson	Edwards
1951/52	Apr 26	Walthamstow Avenue	2	100000	Gerula	Young	Stratton	Lucas	Brahan	Saunders	Rossiter	Bailey TE	Lewis 1	Hall 1	Camis
		Leyton	1		Sullivan	Dixon	Pullinger	Gardiner	Yenson	Casey	Fitch	Facey	McIntree	Goddard	Skipp 1

Season	Date	Opponent		Attendance	1	2	3	4	5	6	7	8	9	10	11	Substitutes
1952/53		Pegasus	6	100000	Brown	Alexander	McKenna	Vowels	Shearwood	Saunders 1	Pawson	Car DB 2	Laybourne 1	Lunn	Sutcliffe 2	
1953/54	Apr 11	Harwich & Parkeston	0		King	Nightingale	Tyrell	Christie	Bloss	Haugh	Stremp	Pearson	Davies	Cooper	Jennings	
	Apr 10	Crook Town	2 e	100000	Jarrie	Riley	Steward	Jeffs	Davison	Taylor	Appleby 1	Thompson 1	Harrison	Williamson	McMillan	
Replay	Apr 19	Bishop Auckland	2		Sharratt	Marshall	Frye	Hardisty	Cresswell	Nimmins	Major	Dixon 1	Oliver 1	O'Connell	Watson	
	Apr 22	Bishop Auckland	2	56008	Jarrie	Riley	Steward	Jeffs	Davison	Taylor	Appleby	Thompson	Harrison 2	Coxon	McMillan	
Replay 2		Bishop Auckland	2	36727	Sharratt	Marshall	Steward	Hardisty	Cresswell	Wilkinson	Major	Dixon	Oliver 2	O'Connell	Watson	
1954/55	Apr 16	Bishop Auckland	0	100000	Jarrie	Marshall	Steward	Jefts	Davison	Taylor	Appleby	Thompson	Harrison 1	Coxon	McMillan	
		Bishop Auckland	2		Sharratt	Marshall	Stewart	Hardisty	Cresswell	Nimmins	Major	Dixon	Oliver	O'Connell	Watson	
		Hendon	0		Ivey	Fisher	Beardsley	Topp	Adams	Nimmins	Saffery	Lewin 2	Bahler	O'Connell	Edwards	
1955/56	Apr 7	Bishop Auckland	1	80000	Sharratt	Fryer	Stewart	Hardisty	Cresswell	Nimmins	McKenna 1	Lewin	Oliver	Cunningham	Parker	
		Corinthian Casuals	1		Ahm	Alexander	Stewart	Hardisty	Cowan	Vowels	Insole DJ	Sanders	Laybourne	Citron	Edwards	
Replay	Apr 14	Bishop Auckland	4	30000	Sharratt	Marshall	Stewart 1	Hardisty 1	Cresswell	O'Connell	McKenna	Lewin 2	Oliver	Bradley	Kerruish 1	
		Corinthian Casuals	1		Ahm	Alexander	Newton	Shuttleworth	Cowan	Vowels	Insole DJ	Sanders	Laybourne	Citron 1	Edwards	
1956/57	Apr 13	Bishop Auckland	3	90000	Sharratt	Marshall	Childs	Thursby	Cresswell	Nimmins	Bradley 1	Lewin 1	Russell 1	Hardisty	Kerruish	
		Wycombe Wanderers	1		Syrett	Lawson	Westley	Truett G	Wicks	Truett J	Worley	Trott	Bates	Tomlin	Smith F 1	
1957/58	Apr 12	Woking	3	71000	Burley	Ellerby	Parsons	Collingwood	Turner	Clacey	Littlejohn	Hebdon 2	Mortimore	Hamm	Stratton 1	
		Ilford	1		Gibbins	Simmons	Cross	Sharod	Whittall	Dodkins	Durston	Taylor	Winch	Butler	Castle	
1958/59	Apr 18	Crook Town	3	60000	Snowball	Gardiner	Steward	Carr	Bainbridge	Wilkie	Coates	O'Connell	Keating 1	Tracey 2	McMillan	
		Barnet	2		Goymer	Duncan	Cooper	Sleap	D'Arcy A	Cantwell R	Welch	D'Arcy D	Brown 2	Harding	Drake	
1959/60	Apr 23	Hendon	2	60000	Shearing	Widdowfield	Harris	Topp 1	Fisher	Murphy	Candey	Figg	Spector	Quail	Howard 1	
		Kingstonian	2		Groves	Davies	Bird	Richards	Ashworth	Gibson	Harris K	Coates	Whing 1	Lindsay	Oakes	
1960/61	Apr 22	Walthamstow Avenue	2	45000	McGuire	Edwards	Bambridge	Andrews	Prince	Keenes	Groves 1	Minall	Lewis 1	Saggers	Harvey	
		West Auckland Town	1		Bowmaker	Siddle	Stafford	Mendum	Summerson	Carter	Briggs	Broomfield	Curtis	Skelton	Douglas 1	
1961/62	Apr 14	Crook Town	1	43000	Snowball	Gardener	Clark	Storey	Heatherington	Brown	Sparks	Garbutt	Coates	Pearcy	McMillan 1	
		Hounslow Town	1		Rhodes	MacDonald	Creasey	Evans	Taylor	Digweed	Somers	Fennell	McHattie	McHattie	Patterson 1	
Replay	Apr 21	Crook Town	4	43000	Snowball	Gardener	Clark	Storey	Heatherington	Brown	Sparks 1	Garbutt	Coates 2	Pearcy	McMillan 1	
		Hounslow Town	0		Rhodes	MacDonald	Creasey	Evans	Taylor	Digweed	Alder	Somers	McHattie	Dipper	Patterson	
1962/63	May 4	Wimbledon	4	45000	Kelly	Martin J	Willis	Ardrey	Law	Murphy	Brown	Martin B	Reynolds 4	Hamm	Williams	
		Sutton United	2		Roffey	Gamblin	Shears	Shepherd	Price	Clack	Bladon 1	Osborne	Bates	Hermitage	Goodall 1	
1963/64	Apr 18	Crook Town	2	37000	Snowball	McCourt	Reid	Storey	Garbutt	Brown 1	Weir	Goodfellow 1	Lumsden	Roughley	McMillan	
		Enfield	1		Mitchell	Neale	Harris	D'Arcy A	Kingsland	Cantwell R	Thomas	Broomfield	Edwards	Day 1	Howard	
1964/65	Apr 24	Hendon	3	45000	Swannell	Hogwood	Sleap	Evans	Riddy	Moody	Drake	Slade	Hyde 2	Quail 1	Lakey	
		Whitby Town	1		Pybus	Durnall	Hobbs	Kennerley	Barker	Dillsworth	Geldart	McHale	Mulvaney 1	Edwards	Crosthwaite	
1965/66	Apr 16	Wealdstone	3	45000	Goymer	Doyle	Sedgley	Townsend	Ashworth	Cantwell R	Allen	Childs 2	Cooley	Lindsay	Bremer 1	
		Hendon	1		Swannell	Hogwood	Cooper	Shacklock	Riddy 1	Cantwell R	Churchill L	Evans	Swain	Sleap	Hyde	
1966/67	Apr 22	Enfield	0	75000	Wolstenholme	Sedgley	Reid	Payne	D'Arcy A	Moxon	Churchill L	Connell	Hill	Day	Howard	Adams
		Skelmersdale United	0		Crosbie	Bermingham	Bridge	Unsworth	Wade	Moorcroft	Whitehead	Worswick	Bennett	Burns	Mansley	McDermott
Replay	Apr 29	Enfield	3	55388	Wolstenholme	Sedgley	Reid	Payne	D'Arcy A	Moxon	Churchill L	Connell 1	Hill 2	Day	Adams	Howard
		Skelmersdale United	0		Crosbie	Bermingham	McDermott	Unsworth	Wade	Moorcroft	Whitehead	Worswick	Bennett	Burns	Mansley	Felmingham
1967/68	Apr 20	Leytonstone	1	52000	Hadlow	Tilley	Harnes	Andrews	Thomson	Walker	Charles	Gray 1	Diwell	Minall	Harvey	Albon
		Chesham United	0		Wells	Thackeray	Smith D	Caterer	Burgess	McCaffrey	Ellis	Black	Fruen	Harper	Kent	Frost
1968/69	Apr 12	North Shields	2	47500	Morgan	Driver	Twaddle	Hall 1	Tatum	Thompson	Wrightson	Lister	Joicey 1	Cassidy	Rutherford	Orrick
		Sutton United	1		Roffey	Garfield	Grose	Brookes	Clarke	Gradi D	Bladon	Mellows 1	Drabwell	Pritchard	Howard	Gane
1969/70	Apr 4	Enfield	5	33000	Wolstenholme	Clayton	Fry	Payne	Betson	Day	Adams 1	Connell 2	Feely 1	Gray	Hill	D'Arcy A (9)
		Dagenham	1		Huttley	Robertson	Dudley	Daniels	Still	Moore	Leakey	Drake	Smith M	Smith B	Brooks 1	Scarfe (2)
1970/71	Apr 24	Skelmersdale United	4	45000	Frankish	Allan	Poole 1(p)	Turner	Bennett	McDermott	Swift	Wolfe	Dickin 3	Hardcastle	Clements	Windsor (7) 1
		Dagenham	2		Huttley	Ford	Dudley	Davidson	Still	Moore	Leakey	Fry	Bass A 1	Dear	Dear	Smith M (11)
1971/72	Apr 22	Hendon	2	38000	Swannell	Jennings	Hand	Deadman	Phillips	Haider	Childs	Connell	Bass A 1	Baker D	Jameson	Albon
		Enfield	0		Williams	Gibson	Hill	Payne	Betson	Smith M	Albon	Adams	Butterfield	Baker J	Gray	Frost
1972/73	Apr 14	Walton & Hersham	1	41000	Teale	Thomas	Edwards	Bassett	Donaldson	Lambert	Wolfinden	Connell R 1	Smith	Morris	Turley	Brooks (7)
		Slough Town	0		Wolstenholme	Reid	Eaton	Mead	D'Arcy A	Reardon	Chatterton	Day	O'Sullivan	Gaine	Somers	Foskett
1973/74	Apr 20	Bishops Stortford	4	30500	Moore	Gibson	Coombes	Lawrence 1	Still	Payne	Leakey 1	Dear	Bass A	Smith M 1 (p)	Anthony	Jamieson (5)
		Ilford	1		James	Bowhill	Bennett	Betson	Anderson	Day	Bookman	Butterfield	Drabwell 1	McDermid	Turfey	Scott

Own goals were credited to Daniels (1969/70) and Smith (1971/72)

Substitutes named in italics were not used

APPENDIX SEVEN: SOME HIGH SCORING GAMES

The year is the final year of the season

1924 Q1	Wealdstone	22	12th London Regt Rangers	0	
1928 Q2	Enfield	18	Stevenage Town	0	
1962 PR	Windsor & Eton	17	Henley Town	0	
1908 Q3	Scarborough	16	Leeds Amateurs	1	
1947 PR	St Frideswides	16	Thame United	0	
1921 Q2	Summerstown	15	Pearl Assurance	0	
1933 Q2	Tufnell Park	15	Baldock Town	2	
1935 Q1	Hastings & St Leonards	15	Wick	0	
1935 Q2	Stowmarket	15	Brantham Athletic	2	
1963 PR	Oxford City	15	Alcan Industries	1	
1973 PR	Barkingside	15	Pegasus Athletic	2	
1933 Q2	Leavesden Mental Hospital	14	Luton Amateur	0	
1953 EP	Maidenhead United	14	Buckingham Town	1	
1953 PR	Vauxhall Motors	14	Bedford Corinthians	2	
1962 PR	Eastbourne	14	Moulsecoomb Rovers	1	
1962 Q1 r	Saltash United	14	Liskeard Athletic	3	
1965 PR	Slough Town	14	Hungerford Town	1	
1898 Q2	Faversham	13	Mid Kent	1	
1912 Q1	Craghead United	13	Iverston Villa	0	
1922 Q1	Gnome Athletic	13	Dick & Co's Sports	1	
1926 PR	Gorleston	13	Halesworth Town	1	
1929 Q1	Maidenhead United	13	Abingdon Town	0	
1929 Q2	Yorkshire Amateur	13	Horsforth	0	
1930 R1	Ilford	13	Eastbourne	1	
1934 Q2	RAF Cranwell	13	Stapleford Brookhill	0	
1935 PR	Park Royal	13	Old Latymerians	0	
1935 Q1	Bradford Rovers	13	Heptonstall Red Star	0	
1936 Q1	Epsom Town	13	Reigate Priory	1	
1939 Q1	Orwell Works	13	RAF Felixstowe	1	
1950 PR	Sheldon Town	13	Evesham United	0	
1937 PR	Watford BL	0	Leighton United	15	
1930 Q1	Leyland Motors	2	Whyteleafe Albion	13	
1932 Q2	Abingdon Town	2	Slough	13	
1955 R3	Kingstonian	3	Bishop Auckland	12	
1903 Q2	York St Clements	2	Grangetown Athletic	12	
1933 Q2 r	Red Hill Amateurs	0	Birmingham Gas Officials	12	
1931 PR	Crittall Athletic	11	2nd Black Watch	4	
1933 Q2	Wisbech Town	11	Abbey United	4	
1959 PR	Beccles	11	Brantham Athletic	4	
1963 PR	Hoddesdon Town	11	Rickmansworth Town	4	
1946 PR	Littlehampton Town	10	Bognor Regis Town	5	
1961 Q4	Loughborough College	10	Moor Green	5	
1963 PR	Shoreham	8	Haywards Heath	7	
1951 Q1	Cargo Fleet Works	5	Bridlington Central United	10	e
1954 PR	Chichester City	4	Worthing	11	

from 3-2 Books   PO Box 115 Upminster Essex RM14 3AQ

The success of Clapton, Arsenal, Spurs. and more recently Chelsea, alongside Wasps, Harlequins and Saracens is the national face of football and rugby in Middlesex. A county thought to have disappeared more than forty years ago.

This is the story of football and rugby in Middlesex. It looks beyond this national perspective to a rich history including the battle between amateur and professional.

Between the wars soccer's senior amateur clubs grew apart from junior soccer. In recent years the loss of their grounds has seen other clubs develop within the National League System. For rugby, the Middlesex Sevens, lead to 15-a-side knock-out cups, merit tables and leagues. Old boys clubs, now mostly open, continue in both codes.

Kick-abouts in the park may be rarer, but today both codes reach well beyond their Premierships to a recreational base that is flourishing, directed by its county bodies. The book's title reflects this width from the landmarks of Hackney Marshes and the now gone Twin Towers of 'old' Wembley

FROM MARSHES TO TWIN TOWERS

Ronald Price

£12 post paid

THE SOULLESS STADIUM
FRED HAWTHORN AND RONALD PRICE

The illustrated story of London's White City, complete with statistics and unusual facts for the many sports it hosted. While best known for athletics and greyhound racing, baseball, cricket, lacrosse, rugby and hockey also played a part. By far the largest stadium of its type, built for the 1908 Olympic Games, discarded in favour of Wembley, it could never overcome the soulnessness of its original design.

FOOTBALL'S SECRET HISTORY
JOHN GOULSTONE

Association football derives from the public school codes of the 19th century? The differences between soccer and rugby arose from the dispute about hacking at the early meetings of the FA in 1863? True? - This book provides an alternative view from medieval times to the 19th century which links commerce, Sheffield and London to the early laws. Herein are answers for the unexplainable gaps in the game's history.

A PLEASING AND UNOBJECTIONABLE RECREATION
JOHN BAILEY

The Thames Valley was the first area to whole-heartedly endorse the new Association laws, in preference to local or the Rugby School rules—pure or amended. This book specifically investigates six towns —Henley-on-Thames, Marlow, Maidenhead. Reading, Windsor and Wycombe within a three-season window (1870-1873)

NOT JUST ON CHRISTMAS DAY
JOHN BAILEY

The Football League, and acting independently the London-based professional clubs continued to play soccer during the First World War. This story which takes its title from the well known 'football matches' staged at the front on Christmas Day 1914 provides the first fuller picture of soccer between 1914 and 1919 mainly in the British Isles, with some mention of Western Europe. Fully indexed by club and league

£5 each—All Four for £18

www.3-2books.com

from 3-2 Books PO Box 115 Upminster Essex RM14 3AQ

The support of the 'Essex' public schools such as Bancroft, Chigwell, Forest and Felsted for the 'London-based' FA code....

The public school missions and university settlements using football and cricket to deliver their message to the East End urban poor...

Elementary school teachers enthusing their pupils' with their love of games and their battles to provide open space for recreation...

The short-lived East End FA and the early days of the South Essex League...

The emerging senior amateur clubs—Barking, Custom House, Clapton, Ilford, Leyton and Leytonstone and the leagues they played in...

The Southern League rivalry of Millwall (The Dockers) and West Ham (The Irons)...

IS THE FASCINATING STORY OF
EAST LONDON: A Hotbed of Football 1867-1918
Colm Kerrigan
£12 post paid

Now in its 14th Year—Non League Retrospect is published four times per year covering the history of the game below the Football League.

ANNUAL SUBSCRIPTION -£15

INTRODUCTORY OFFER
Two editions of Volume 13
for £4

www.3-2books.com

SoccerData Publications

Extracts from the current catalogue. For more details, please write the publisher or visit the web site at www.soccerdata.com.

THE EARLY FA CUP FINALS

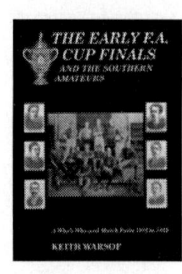

By Keith Warsop. A detailed account of the F.A. Cup finals 1872 to 1883 with short biographies of all the men that took part. Includes an account of the development of the rules of the game and the tactics adopted by the teams. Price £15, hardback.

THE FA CUP COMPLETE RESULTS

The definitive guide to football's oldest competition. All FA Challenge Cup results to the end of season 2005-06. An index to all the clubs that have taken part. Results of meetings between the leading clubs. Tables of statistics. Price £24, large format paperback.

THE FA TROPHY COMPLETE RESULTS

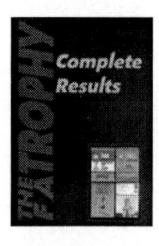

All Trophy results to the end of season 2004-05. An index to all the clubs that have taken part. Results of meetings between the leading clubs. Price £10, large format paperback.

THE FA VASE COMPLETE RESULTS

All Vase results to the end of season 2004-05. An index to all the clubs that have taken part. Results of meetings between the leading clubs. Price £10, large format paperback.

PREMIERSHIP & FOOTBALL LEAGUE REFEREES 1888 TO 2005

The first complete list of referees to be published. Includes season-by-season listings and identifies the referees of the major cup finals in England. Price £9, paperback.

FOOTBALL LEAGUE PLAYERS' RECORDS

Career details of every player to appear in the Football League from 1888 to 1939. Includes date and place of birth and appearances and goals at each club. Price £25, large format paperback.

SCOTTISH LEAGUE PLAYERS' RECORDS

Details of every player that has appeared in the top division of Scottish football. Volumes cover the periods 1890/91 to 1938/39 (£20), 1946/47 to 1974/75 (£15) and 1975/76 to 1999/2000 (£12). Buy all three together for £40.

IRON IN THE BLOOD

The story of Thames Ironworks FC, the forerunners of today's West Ham United. Includes full statistics of friendly matches and Southern League games. Price £10, paperback.

ALL ABOUT AVENUE

The story of Bradford Park Avenue. Includes an A-Z section on players and events and full statistics for the old club and the re-formed one. Price £14, paperback.

THE DEFINITIVE NEWTON HEATH

An account of the early years of Manchester United, to 1902. Includes match reports and full statistics. Price £8.99, paperback.

Postage and packing

UK customers please add £2 per order towards postage and packing costs and those in Mainland Europe £5. Rest of the World postage is 'at cost' – please ask for a quote.